INTERCULTURAL MANAGEMENT

Dirk Holtbrügge

INTERCULTURAL MANAGEMENT

Concepts, Practice, Critical Reflection

Los Angeles | London | New Delhi
Singapore | Washington DC | Melbourne

SAGE Publications Ltd
1 Oliver's Yard
55 City Road
London EC1Y 1SP

SAGE Publications Inc.
2455 Teller Road
Thousand Oaks, California 91320

SAGE Publications India Pvt Ltd
B 1/I 1 Mohan Cooperative Industrial Area
Mathura Road

New Delhi 110 044
SAGE Publications Asia-Pacific Pte Ltd
3 Church Street
#10-04 Samsung Hub
Singapore 049483

Library of Congress Control Number: 2021946918

British Library Cataloguing in Publication data

A catalogue record for this book is available from the British Library

Editor: Matthew Waters
Assistant editor: Jessica Moran
Assistant editor, digital: Mandy Gao
Production editor: Sarah Cooke
Copyeditor: Christobel Colleen Hopman
Proofreader: Benny Willy Stephen
Indexer: TNQ Technologies
Marketing manager: Lucia Sweet
Cover design: Francis Kenney
Typeset by: TNQ Technologies

ISBN 978-1-5297-8975-1
ISBN 978-1-5297-8974-4 (pbk)

TABLE OF CONTENTS

Preface   xi

Acknowledgments   xiii

About the Author   xiv

Online Resources for Instructors   xv

Praise for this Book   xvi

1   Relevance of Intercultural Management   1

    Learning Objectives   1

    1.1   Cultural Diversity—A Blessing or a Curse?   1

    1.2   Intercultural Management Challenges in Different Areas   3

    1.3   Reasons for Studying Intercultural Management   7

    Summary   9

2   Definitions, Manifestations, Delineations, and Functions of Culture   11

    Learning Objectives   11

    2.1   Definitions of Culture   12

    2.2   Manifestations of Culture   17

    2.3   Delineations of National Culture   20

    2.4   Origins of Culture   28

          2.4.1   Physical Environment   29

          2.4.2   Legal–Political System   30

          2.4.3   Economy   31

          2.4.4   Religion   32

          2.4.5   Biology   35

    2.5   Functions of Culture   37

    Summary   40

3   Intercultural Management Research: Conceptual and Methodological Issues 42

    Learning Objectives   42

    3.1   Historical Roots and Interdisciplinary References   42

    3.2   Current Research Streams and Theoretical Foundations   46

          3.2.1   Epistemological Perspectives   46

          3.2.2   Comparative Management Research   49

          3.2.3   Cross-Cultural Management Research   50

          3.2.4   Indigenous Management Research   51

          3.2.5   Postcolonial Management Research   53

3.3 Methodological Challenges of Intercultural Management Research   56
   3.3.1 Conceptualization of Research Projects   57
   3.3.2 Data Collection   58
      3.3.2.1 Sample   58
      3.3.2.2 Methods   59
   3.3.3 Data Analysis   62
   3.3.4 Interpretation of Results   64
Summary   66

4 Concepts of Culture   69
Learning Objectives   69
  4.1 The Concept of Kluckhohn and Strodtbeck   70
   4.1.1 Overview   70
   4.1.2 Basic Cultural Orientations   71
      4.1.2.1 Human–Nature Orientation   71
      4.1.2.2 Man–Nature Orientation   73
      4.1.2.3 Relational Orientation   73
      4.1.2.4 Activity Orientation   74
      4.1.2.5 Time Orientation   75
   4.1.3 Critical Evaluation   75
  4.2 The Concept of Hall   76
   4.2.1 Overview   76
   4.2.2 Dimensions of Culture   77
      4.2.2.1 Context Orientation   77
      4.2.2.2 Time Orientation   79
      4.2.2.3 Space Orientation   81
   4.2.3 Critical Evaluation   83
  4.3 The Concept of Hofstede   84
   4.3.1 Overview   84
   4.3.2 Dimensions of Culture   89
      4.3.2.1 Power Distance   89
      4.3.2.2 Uncertainty Avoidance   90
      4.3.2.3 Individualism vs. Collectivism   91
      4.3.2.4 Masculinity vs. Femininity   93
      4.3.2.5 Long-term Orientation   94
      4.3.2.6 Indulgence vs. Restraint   96
   4.3.3 Critical Evaluation   97
  4.4 The Concept of Trompenaars and Hampden-Turner   99
   4.4.1 Overview   99
   4.4.2 Dimensions of Culture   100
      4.4.2.1 Universalism vs. Particularism   100
      4.4.2.2 Individualism vs. Communitarianism   101

		4.4.2.3 Neutral vs. Emotional	101
		4.4.2.4 Specificity vs. Diffuseness	101
		4.4.2.5 Achieved Status vs. Ascribed Status	102
		4.4.2.6 Inner Direction vs. Outer Direction	102
		4.4.2.7 Sequential Time vs. Synchronous Time	103
	4.4.3	Critical Evaluation	103
4.5	Schwartz's Concept of Cultural Value Orientations		104
	4.5.1	Overview	104
	4.5.2	Dimensions of Culture	106
		4.5.2.1 Autonomy vs. Embeddedness	106
		4.5.2.2 Egalitarianism vs. Hierarchy	106
		4.5.2.3 Harmony vs. Mastery	107
	4.5.3	Critical Evaluation	107
4.6	The GLOBE Study		108
	4.6.1	Overview	108
	4.6.2	GLOBE's Cultural Dimensions: Cultural Practices vs. Cultural Values	116
	4.6.3	Critical Evaluation	117
4.7	Thomas' Concept of Cultural Standards		119
	4.7.1	Overview	119
	4.7.2	Examples of Cultural Standards	119
	4.7.3	Critical Evaluation	123
4.8	The Constructivist Concept of Culture		124
	4.8.1	Overview	124
	4.8.2	Application in Intercultural Management	125
	4.8.3	Critical Evaluation	129
4.9	Concepts of Culture: A Critical Evaluation		130
	Summary		132
5	**Cultural Differences and Cultural Similarities**		**135**
	Learning Objectives		135
5.1	Cultural Clusters		135
	5.1.1	The Typology of Galtung	136
	5.1.2	Huntington's Classification of Civilizations	138
	5.1.3	Cattell's Concept of Syntality Patterns	140
	5.1.4	Taxonomy of Cultures Based on Hofstede	141
	5.1.5	Schwartz's Spatial Map of Cultural Regions	143
	5.1.6	The GLOBE Cultural Clusters	145
	5.1.7	Cultural Clusters of Ronen and Shenkar	147
	5.1.8	Critical Evaluation	150
5.2	Cultural Distance and Cultural Attractiveness		153
	5.2.1	The Kogut and Singh Index of Cultural Distance	153
	5.2.2	The Cultural Attractiveness Concept of Li et al.	157

5.2.3 Shenkar's Concept of Cultural Frictions   159
5.2.4 Bilateral Trade in Cultural Goods as a Proxy for Cultural Attractiveness   160
5.2.5 Critical Evaluation   163
5.3 Cultural Diversity   165
5.3.1 Level-Based Concepts of Cultural Diversity   166
5.3.2 Variance-Based Concepts of Cultural Diversity   170
5.3.2.1 Gelfand's Concept of Cultural Tightness and Looseness   171
5.3.2.2 The Concept of Ethnolinguistic Fractionalization   173
5.3.3 Pattern-Based Concepts of Cultural Diversity   178
5.3.4 Critical Evaluation   184
Summary   186

6 Intercultural Communication and Negotiation   189
Learning Objectives   189
6.1 Process Model of Intercultural Communication   190
6.2 Elements of Intercultural Communication   192
6.2.1 Verbal Communication   194
6.2.1.1 Phonology   194
6.2.1.2 Morphology   196
6.2.1.3 Syntax   197
6.2.1.4 Semantics   198
6.2.1.5 Pragmatics   202
6.2.2 Para-Verbal Communication   204
6.2.2.1 Oral Communication   204
6.2.2.2 Written Communication   206
6.2.3 Non-Verbal Communication   208
6.2.3.1 Oral Communication   208
6.2.3.2 Written Communication   214
6.2.4 Extra-verbal Communication   217
6.2.4.1 Oral Communication   217
6.2.4.2 Written Communication   221
6.3 Language and Cognition   222
6.4 Language and Translation   225
6.5 Intercultural Negotiation   233
6.6 Instrumental Forms of Intercultural Communication   239
6.6.1 Tactics of Instrumental Communication   240
6.6.1.1 Fake News   240
6.6.1.2 Doublespeak   243
6.6.1.3 Non-Linguistic Tactics of Instrumental Communication   246
6.6.2 Responses to Instrumental Communication   247
6.6.2.1 Disputing about Facts   247
6.6.2.2 Redirecting the Discourse   249

	6.6.2.3	Impeaching the Person's Credibility	250
	6.6.2.4	Irony	251
	6.6.2.5	Ending the Conversation	251
Summary			252

7 Intercultural Management of Individuals, Teams, and Organizations — 254

Learning Objectives — 254

7.1 Individual Level: Career Patterns, Motivation, and Leadership in Different Cultures — 254

   7.1.1 Culture and Career Patterns — 254

      7.1.1.1 Recruitment and Selection — 255

      7.1.1.2 Training and Development — 257

      7.1.1.3 Promotion — 257

      7.1.1.4 Typology of Career Models by Evans, Lank and Farquhar — 260

   7.1.2 Culture and Work Motivation — 262

   7.1.3 Culture and Leadership — 264

   7.1.4 Critical Evaluation — 269

7.2 Group Level: Multicultural Teams — 271

   7.2.1 Cultural Diversity and Multicultural Team Performance — 271

   7.2.2 Moderators of Multicultural Team Performance — 273

   7.2.3 Critical Evaluation — 274

7.3 Corporate Level: Organization in Different Cultures — 275

   7.3.1 Culture and Organizational Design — 275

   7.3.2 Culture and Interorganizational Collaboration — 278

   7.3.3 Cross-Cultural Transfer of Organizational Practices — 280

   7.3.4 Critical Evaluation — 282

Summary — 282

8 Intercultural Competence — 285

Learning Objectives — 285

8.1 Relevance and Definition — 285

8.2 Dimensions of Intercultural Competence — 286

8.3 Stage Model of Intercultural Competence — 290

   8.3.1 Ethnocentric Stages — 291

   8.3.2 Ethnorelative Stages — 292

8.4 Developing Intercultural Competence as Learning Cycle — 292

8.5 Antecedents of Intercultural Competence — 294

   8.5.1 Psychographic Factors — 294

   8.5.2 Demographic Factors — 296

8.6 Outcomes of Intercultural Competence — 297

   8.6.1 Cultural Adjustment — 297

   8.6.2 Cultural Boundary Spanning — 299

8.7   Measuring Intercultural Competence   300

    8.7.1   Self-Reported Evaluations   300

    8.7.2   Informant-Based Evaluations   302

    8.7.3   Observer-Based Evaluations   302

8.8   Critical Outlook and Future Directions   303

Summary   304

9   Intercultural Training   307

Learning Objectives   307

9.1   Relevance and Definition   307

9.2   Typology of Intercultural Training Methods   308

9.3   Culture-Specific Training   310

    9.3.1   Intellectual Culture-Specific Training   310

    9.3.2   Experiential Culture-Specific Training   313

9.4   Culture-General Training   316

    9.4.1   Intellectual Culture-General Training   316

    9.4.2   Experiential Culture-General Training   316

9.5   Effectiveness of Intercultural Training   320

9.6   Critical Outlook and Future Directions   323

Summary   325

References   329

Index   384

PREFACE

AIMS AND SCOPE

Intercultural encounters are omnipresent. In business, politics, education, and sports, collaborations between people with different cultural backgrounds have become part of our everyday lives. Cultural diversity offers many opportunities, such as increased creativity, innovation, and adaptability, but there are also challenges that can range from misunderstandings and financial losses to violent clashes. Intercultural competence is, therefore, becoming an essential capability of individuals and organizations to grow in a globalized world.

This book is aimed at readers who want to learn about intercultural management beyond the notion that Chinese value harmony, Germans are punctual, and Americans are easy-going. Intercultural relationships rarely fail due to the ignorance of local greeting rituals, eating habits, or dress codes. It is, therefore, not sufficient to learn the do's and don'ts of other cultures, but to understand the reasons for intercultural differences and their effects on the behavior of individuals and organizations.

This book takes a critical perspective. Instead of a naïve appraisal of multiculturalism, intercultural management is analyzed from a multitude of perspectives. Whenever individuals of diverse cultural backgrounds interact, stereotypes, prejudices, and supposedly simple solutions often exacerbate the challenges of intercultural encounters. Instead, cognitive complexity that goes beyond factual knowledge is required and includes the tolerance of ambiguity and critical thinking.

This book takes an interdisciplinary approach. It integrates findings from management research, psychology, and sociology, including those from art, pop culture, history, geography, and political science. Intercultural management is understood as a phenomenon that transcends disciplinary boundaries. It concerns questions of efficacy and performance, as well as identity constructions, power relations, and ethics.

This book has a strong research focus. While statements on intercultural management appear plausible, they are often lacking validity and analytical rigor. Intercultural management research is fragmented, often inconclusive and faced with several methodological challenges. Intercultural understanding, therefore, requires comprehending the assumptions, methods, and inferences of intercultural research.

Focusing on academic rigor, however, does not imply that the book is dry. Examples from different contexts and cultures should make the book accessible and relatable to the readers' own experiences. Particular care was taken to avoid an ethnocentric perspective and to feature as many different voices as possible.

STRUCTURE OF THE BOOK

This book is divided into *nine chapters*:

Chapter 1	**Relevance of Intercultural Management**
Chapter 2	**Definitions, Manifestations, Delineations, and Functions of Culture**
Chapter 3	**Intercultural Management Research: Conceptual and Methodological Issues**
Chapter 4	**Concepts of Culture**
Chapter 5	**Cultural Differences and Cultural Similarities**
Chapter 6	**Intercultural Communication and Negotiation**
Chapter 7	**Intercultural Management of Individuals, Teams, and Organizations**
Chapter 8	**Intercultural Competence**
Chapter 9	**Intercultural Training**

All chapters begin with the introduction of the *learning objectives* and a short *overview of the chapter contents*. The chapters end with a brief *summary* and provide *further reading*. A number of *reflection questions* are designed to encourage readers to relate important concepts of intercultural management to their own intercultural experiences. *End-of-chapter exercises* help readers apply important concepts to real-world problems and, thus, further improve their intercultural competence.

ACKNOWLEDGMENTS

This book is based on over 30 years of intercultural experience. Certain parts were written during various research stays in Austria, Belarus, China, France, Germany, India, Japan, Russia, South Africa, Thailand, the United Arab Emirates, the United Kingdom, the United States, and Vietnam. I would like to thank my hosts for their hospitality and invaluable intercultural insights.

This book benefited enormously from valuable contributions from colleagues and friends. While it would be impossible to name all of them, I am especially grateful to Tatjana Nikitina, Raju Ravitej, Lena Sambuk, and Sascha Sambuk. The conversations with you are always inspiring experiences of intercultural learning. Nicola Berg accompanied the writing of this book from the first ideas to its completion. Her contributions deserve particular mention. I would also like to thank three anonymous reviewers for the valuable comments and suggestions for improvement. Special thanks go to Theresa Bernhard, Marcus Conrad, Franziska Engelhard, Ritam Garg, Helmut Haussmann, Christina Heidemann, Amanda Hooper, Laura Kirste, Marc Oberhauser, Nikhila Raghavan, Tassilo Schuster, Marion Wehner, and Luisa Wicht at the Department of International Management for their continuous support and enthusiasm.

ABOUT THE AUTHOR

Dirk Holtbrügge is Professor of International Management at the School of Business, Economics and Society, Friedrich-Alexander-University Erlangen-Nürnberg, Germany. He is a regular visiting professor at universities in China, India, France, Russia, and the United Kingdom. His research focuses on international management, human resource management, and management in emerging markets. He has published seven books, nine edited volumes, and more than 80 articles in leading journals, such as *Academy of Management Learning & Education, European Journal of International Management, International Business Review, International Journal of Cross Cultural Management, International Journal of Human Resource Management, Journal of Business Ethics, Journal of International Business Studies, Journal of International Management,* and *Management International Review.* Professor Holtbrügge is regularly listed in research-related rankings as one of the top 5% professors of business administration in Germany, Austria, and German-speaking Switzerland. The Stanford University's "Top 2 percent scientists list" lists him as one of the 2 percent most frequently cited scientists worldwide in 2020. He has extensive experience in executive education and works as a consultant for firms in Germany and abroad.

ONLINE RESOURCES
FOR INSTRUCTORS

Lecturers can visit **https://study.sagepub.com/holtbrugge** to access a range of online resources that are designed to support teaching and assessment. *Intercultural Management* is accompanied by:

FOR INSTRUCTORS

- A **teaching guide** providing summaries of chapter content, further reading, and video links to **support wider reading and students' understanding of the text.**

- **PowerPoints** prepared by the author that will allow you to seamlessly **incorporate the chapters into your weekly teaching.**

PRAISE FOR THIS BOOK

'*Intercultural Management* is a detailed, up-to-date contribution to management literature. Through illustrative cases from a wide variety of cultures, the book provides a captivating angle on the most recent research in the field. It makes the reader reflect and demonstrates the importance of cultural understanding in intercultural management. Through systematic composition and comprehensive figures, the book shines a light on aspects such as communication, psychology, and history. *Intercultural Management* is well suited to give students increased cultural understanding and knowledge of international business.'

Ilan Alon, Professor of Strategy and International Marketing, School of Business and Law, University of Agder, Norway

'This book is very timely and well written. There is a coherent golden thread in the book, and the chapters build on each other consistently and logically. It contains the most extensive collection of relevant theories and concepts I have ever seen in one place. The examples provided are carefully selected and very helpful to add currency to the theoretical claims. They offer opportunity for students to better understand what the content means for the real world and organizations. I also very much appreciate that the book is informed by the state-of-the-art literature in international business and management and that (bold) statements are backed up with substantial academic reference and evidence.'

Benjamin Bader, Deputy Head of Leadership, Work and Organisation and Senior Lecturer (Associate Professor) in International HRM, Newcastle University Business School, UK

'*Intercultural Management* is the textbook I have been waiting on for a long time. It starts where many other textbooks about this topic end. Instead of mainly repeating the obvious, the book contains many interesting and relevant aspects that are new even to experts in the field. The well-founded text mixes perfectly with sound practical examples, exercises, and references to videos and online resources. Students and managers alike will enjoy reading the book as it opens up new perspectives and stimulates critical reflection.'

Nicola Berg, Professor of Strategic Management, University of Hamburg, Germany

'Digitalization has increased the possibilities and necessities to establish and maintain productive collaboration between people of different race, cultural backgrounds, and ethical attitudes. In addition, companies active on global markets have to adjust their value proposition to customers from different cultures. *Intercultural Management* by Dirk Holtbrügge is an easy-to-master, step-by-step guide on how to develop intercultural competencies at the individual, group, and organizational levels, and how to use these competencies in intraorganizational and interorganizational collaboration. I also must stress that unlike many 'do-it-yourself' guides, this book is deeply rooted in academic research.'

Igor Gurkov, Research Professor, Graduate School of Business, National Research University Higher School of Economics, Moscow, Russia

'This book provides an excellent overview of intercultural management. It not only covers the major frameworks one would expect but also broadens the discussion to less-commonly covered disciplines, such as geography, economic and political systems, and biology. In addition, it has a strong research focus, providing research-based critiques of frameworks and describing challenges of conducting intercultural research. The historical lens is unusual and insightful, and the inclusion of recent research and concepts in intercultural management makes the text timely. Finally, there are several practical examples drawing from many cultures and countries across the world, which are interesting and successfully illustrate concepts from the text. With *Intercultural Management*, students will gain an understanding of intercultural management concepts, recognize their complexity, and find themselves reflecting on ideas. In brief, the broad interdisciplinary approach, strong research orientation, historical perspective, inclusion of recent topics, and use of several diverse examples make this a well-rounded, thoughtful, and relevant intercultural management text that will spur student learning.'

Davina Vora, Professor of International Business, State University of New York at New Paltz, USA

1

RELEVANCE OF INTERCULTURAL MANAGEMENT

LEARNING OBJECTIVES

By the end of this chapter, you will be able to

- name potential positive and negative effects of cultural diversity,
- comprehend the basis for studying intercultural management research,
- analyze the opportunities and challenges of cultural diversity,
- evaluate the intercultural management challenges in different areas.

Since the concept of culture found attention in the management literature, a key question has been whether cultural diversity is more a challenge and reason for serious management problems or an opportunity that companies can leverage to achieve competitive advantage. The first section discusses this question and provides arguments for both positions. Afterwards, the impact of culture in different areas, such as business, politics, society, education and sports is outlined. In the final section, important reasons for studying intercultural management are presented.

1.1 CULTURAL DIVERSITY–A BLESSING OR A CURSE?

Intercultural encounters are omnipresent. In many areas, such as business, politics, education and sports, collaborations of people with different cultural backgrounds are common. However, there is a very controversial debate about whether cultural diversity in societies and organizations has predominantly positive or negative effects and how it can be managed successfully (Figure 1.1).

In international management literature, cultural diversity has traditionally been regarded as a **challenge and reason for serious management problems** (Stahl & Tung 2015). The famous management scholar *Peter Drucker* is credited with the statement "Culture eats strategy for breakfast," meaning that promising strategies of firms are often undermined by cultural influences. Also *Geert Hofstede*, one of the most prominent and influential intercultural management scholars, states: "Culture is more often a source of conflict than of synergy. Cultural differences are a nuisance at best and often a disaster" (Hofstede & Hofstede 2005, p. 37).

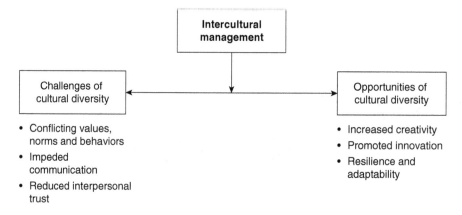

Figure 1.1 Challenges and opportunities of cultural diversity

The potential negative effects of cultural diversity reach from misunderstandings to massive financial losses and can occur on the individual, organizational, and societal level. Intercultural management challenges at the *individual level* often arise from varying norms, values, and behaviors. This may include, among others, religious beliefs, relations between sexes, time perspectives, and ways of working. Moreover, different communication styles and lack of language skills reduce interpersonal trust and impede intercultural collaboration.

On the *firm level*, many international collaborations fail due to insufficient consideration of cultural differences. Firms often focus on strategic and structural integration and neglect the persistence of different national and organizational cultures. Examples of intercultural management and marketing failures are frequent and include, among others, inadequate product decisions, communication styles, and leadership practices.

Cultural diversity also poses a great challenge to the identity and legitimacy of *societies*. The very idea of nation states is based on the acceptance and enforcement of common values, norms, and behaviors. This is questioned by both, massive immigration of people with fundamentally different cultural backgrounds and the transfer of powers to supranational organizations with blurred identity. As a reaction, nationalist and fundamentalist movements are gaining power in many parts of the world, attempting to protect cultural identity that they perceive as threatened.

While the many challenges of cultural diversity are obvious, it offers also several **opportunities**. In the most general sense, these are formulated in the UNESCO Universal Declaration of Cultural Diversity (2001): "As a source of exchange, innovation and creativity, cultural diversity is as necessary for humankind as bio-diversity is for nature" (Art. 1). Like monocultures in agriculture are susceptible to disruption and crises, monoculturalism in organizations and societies reduces resilience and adaptability. Cultural diversity, on the contrary, promotes *innovation and creativity* through a wider range of perspectives. Multicultural organizations and societies are therefore better equipped for *comprehensive perception and to discover new opportunities*.

Leveraging the strengths of different cultures also leads to better problem solutions. Historically, cultures often emerged under specific geographic and natural conditions to solve their specific problems. The more that physical boundaries are becoming permeable through modern means of transportation and communication, the more important the *tolerance of ambiguity and transboundary thinking* become. These capabilities are more common in culturally diverse societies than homogeneous societies.

The benefits of cultural diversity are increasingly confirmed by empirical research. In a McKinsey study of 589 companies in 12 countries, companies in the top-quartile for ethnic and cultural diversity were 33% more likely to *outperform on profitability* (measured in EBIT margin) than companies in the fourth quartile. The authors conclude that companies which address the challenge of building an inclusive corporate culture across cultural differences could significantly strengthen organizational effectiveness (Hunt et al. 2018).

1.2 INTERCULTURAL MANAGEMENT CHALLENGES IN DIFFERENT AREAS

Intercultural relations are relevant in different areas. In the **business context**, culture has affected import and export activities for ages. Already in the year 1300, the Italian merchant, explorer and writer Marco Polo recorded the commercial practices of China, Persia and Constantinople in his *Book of the Marvels of the World* and proposed guidelines for culturally adequate behavior. More recently, the impact of culture on internationalization strategies of firms has become a key topic in international management and marketing literature (e.g., Barkema, Bell & Pennings 1996; Kogut & Singh 1988; Brouthers & Brouthers 2001).

The relevance of culture is even higher in more enduring forms of international cooperation, such as joint ventures, mergers & acquisitions, and strategic alliances (Holtbrügge 2004). The management of cultural differences can be a major success factor, such as in the cases of Airbus (Barmeyer & Mayrhofer 2008) and Renault-Nissan (Barmeyer & Mayrhofer 2009). However, if neglected or mismanaged, cultural differences can also be a primary reason for massive failures, such as at DaimlerChrylser (Vlasic & Stertz 2000) or after the acquisition of Rover by BMW (Woodman 2003; Fuller-Love 2008).

A vivid example of the management challenges and opportunities of cultural differences is **Star Alliance**. Founded in 1997, this multipartner alliance consists of 27 member airlines that employ more than 440,000 people across the globe. As many partner airlines have been state-owned companies and regarded as national symbols, they possess a strong national identity. They are also characterized by a large diversity in corporate cultures and languages. This distinct cultural identity is appreciated by many customers and was maintained even after they became Star Alliance members.

At the same time, an alliance culture was created that is shared by all partners and promotes a common identity. The harmonization of systems and processes is aimed to ensure worldwide security and quality standards. Moreover, it should stimulate the feeling of seamless travel and coordinated customer service. The challenge of Star Alliance is therefore to balance the tension between the cultural diversity of the individual members and the homogenization of values and behaviors of the entire organization (Holtbrügge, Wilson & Berg 2006).

Cultural differences are particularly challenging in areas with intense and frequent personal interactions, such as **human resource management**. Several studies have analyzed the *impact of culture on the motivation to work*. A main conclusion of these studies is that Maslow's (1954) hierarchy of needs is culture-bound. For example, the need for self-realization that is regarded as the most important work motive in Western cultures has a much lower relevance in many Asian countries where social motives predominate (Gambrel & Cianci 2003).

Another cultural difference is the *relationship between work and private life*. In specific cultures, like Germany and the United States, these two spheres are clearly separated. Private issues do not interfere with work-related matters. Diffuse cultures, such as Argentina and Spain, regard their personal and work life as interconnected. For example, social activities with work colleagues outside the work context are common (Hampden-Turner & Trompenaars 2012).

Leadership styles and leadership preferences are another area where cultural differences are visible. While the Scandinavian countries and the Netherlands, for example, are characterized by cooperative and democratic leadership styles, authoritarian leadership is prevalent in countries like China, India, and Russia (House et al. 2004). Intercultural management challenges arise when managers with cooperative leadership styles work together with employees who have authoritarian leadership preferences and vice versa.

Cultural differences in work-related values and behaviors are particularly pertinent in *multicultural teams*. Different time perspectives, ways of working and communication styles make collaboration often difficult. At the same time, they can promote creativity and innovation. It is therefore often not the cultural differences per se, but the way they are managed that decides the success or failure of multicultural teams. Moreover, the relationship between cultural diversity and team success is moderated by several other factors, such as task complexity, time pressure, and intensity of interaction between the team members (Ely & Thomas 2001; Earley & Gibson 2002; Stahl et al. 2010).

Another field where intercultural differences are relevant is **marketing**. Culture affects, for example, product policies, choices of distribution channels, pricing decisions, and promotion strategies (Czinkota & Ronkainen 2012; Ghauri & Cateora 2014; de Mooij 2019). The unawareness or misinterpretation of cultural influences can lead to serious intercultural marketing blunders (Table 1.1).

Table 1.1 Examples of intercultural marketing blunders

Reasons	Examples
Misleading brand name	Puffs marketed its tissues under that brand name in Germany even though "puff" is German slang for "brothel."
Translation error	Pepsi Cola's slogan "Come alive with Pepsi" was translated in China as "Pepsi brings your ancestors out of the grave."
Inadequate product design	Nike had to recall thousands of products when a decoration intended to illustrate fire on the back of the shoes resembled the Arabic word for Allah.
Lack of religious empathy	In 2015 during Ramadan, Pringles displayed an aisle in London featuring "Smokey Bacon Flavor" chips with the message "Ramadan Mubarak" ('Have a blessed Ramadan').

Sources: Adapted from Ricks (2006) and White (2009).

Many examples of apparent **intercultural marketing blunders** are in fact urban legends. For example, several textbooks and articles refer to the case of General Motors' Chevrolet Nova which arguably sold poor in Latin America because "nova" translates as "doesn't go" in

Spanish (Wilton 2004). "This anecdote is frequently used to illustrate the perils of failing to do adequate preparation and research before introducing a product into the international marketplace. It's a wicked irony, then, that the people who use this example are engaging in the very thing they're decrying, because a little preparation and research would have informed them that it isn't true (…). This is another one of those tales that makes its point so well (…) that nobody wants to ruin it with a bunch of facts" (Mikkelson 1999).

The word "nova" (from the Latin "novus" or "new") has the accent on the first syllable while the phrase "no va" is pronounced with the accent on the second word. Thus, the English word "nova" and the Spanish phrase "no va" are two distinct entities with different pronunciations. "Assuming that Spanish speakers would naturally see the word 'nova' as equivalent to the phrase 'no va' and think 'Hey, this car doesn't go!' is akin to assuming that English speakers would spurn a dinette set sold under the name *Notable* because nobody wants a dinette set that doesn't include a table" (Mikkelson 1999). Sometimes the influence of culture seems to be so plausible that alternative explanations, misinterpretations, or factual errors are ruled out.

The influence of culture is not restricted to business activities, but prevalent in many other areas like politics, society, military, education, and sports. An important example of intercultural interactions in **politics** is supranational organizations, such as the UNO, EU, WTO, and IMF. Different values, time perspectives, languages, etc. make agreements and coordinated activities often difficult (Reeves 2004; Lawson 2006; Persaud & Sajed 2018). For example, all official documents and speeches in the EU are translated into all 24 official languages, which bear the risk of misunderstandings and deviant interpretations (Fidrmuc & Ginsburgh 2007; Phillipson 2015). Also, political negotiations between countries are often affected by cultural differences. A vivid example is the UK-EU Brexit negotiations where diverse parliamentary rituals, democratic practices, legal cultures, and negotiations styles collieded (Ott & Ghauri 2019).

A major intercultural challenge in **society** is the cultural integration of migrants and refugees. Unlike in business, politics and sports, intercultural encounters in this context are characterized by extreme power asymmetries between citizens of the host country and foreign immigrants (Triandafyllidou 2016). The latter come predominantly from economically underdeveloped and politically unstable countries that have poor reputations in the host country (Jubany 2017). Their cultural adjustment and integration into the host country's society is therefore especially important and challenging (Ager & Strang 2008).

Germany is the second most popular migration destination in the world after the United States (UNDESA 2017). As of 2017, more than 12 mn. immigrants live in Germany, which is close to 15% of the entire German population. Since 2015, particularly the number of refugees, asylum seekers, and illegal immigrants has dramatically increased. Major countries of origin are Syria, Iraq, Afghanistan, Nigeria, and Pakistan, all countries affected by massive conflicts or civil war.

The fact that most refugees and asylum seekers are Muslim has caused a very controversial debate in Germany. While former Federal President Christian Wulff spoke against growing anti-Islam sentiment in Germany, saying "Islam belongs to Germany," and many

(Continued)

Germans welcoming migrants and offering help, the right-wing Alternative for Germany Party and many right-wing populists warn against the "Islamization of Germany." Xenophobic attitudes are mainly fueled by alleged and actual involvement of refugees in social security fraud, sexual assaults, and terrorist attacks. In response, violent right-wing mobs repeatedly set fire to migrant hostels and centers.

In the **military**, intercultural encounters occur particularly in multilateral peace missions, such as the UN peacekeeping forces in the former Yugoslavia, Rwanda and Darfur. As of 2018, 124 countries were contributing nearly 90,000 military observers, police and troops (UN 2019). Similarly, NATO operations are often confronted with intercultural challenges. For example, photos showing German soldiers playing with a skull in Afghanistan shocked the German public in 2006 and cast shadows over their image of social workers engaged primarily in humanitarian missions (Kucera 2012). The revelations led to a call for better intercultural training for soldiers, i.e., an area where it has originally been developed to prepare military personnel on international missions (Pusch 2004).

Another area where intercultural encounters are becoming increasingly relevant is **education**. In many countries, the number of foreign students enrolled at university has increased over the last decade. The United States is the most popular destination for international students, hosting about 1.1 mn. of the 4.6 mn. enrolled worldwide in 2017 (Institute of International Education 2017). Other countries with high shares of foreign students are the United Kingdom, China, Australia, and Canada. In 2018, the share of foreign students at German universities reached 13.2% (DAAD & DZHW 2018). This internationalization of higher education services has become an important financial pillar for many of these countries (Altbach & Knight 2007; Deardorff et al. 2012). The worldwide recruiting of students leads to culturally diverse student cohorts in which individuals may differ significantly with regard to their preferred learning styles, study expectations, and study behaviors (Holtbrügge & Mohr 2010).

Intercultural diversity is also common in many **team sports**, such as soccer, hockey, and handball (Maderer, Holtbrügge & Schuster 2014). For example, almost 70% of the players in the English Premier League are foreigners, representing 65 different nationalities (UEFA 2015). In the National Hockey League, 27% of the players come from 15 countries other than Canada and the United States (http://www.nhl.com/stats/). The share of foreign players in the German Handball-Bundesliga is close to 50% (Handball Time 2013).

The European Champions League Final on May 28, 2016 between Real Madrid Club de Fútbol and Club Atlético Madrid at the San Siro stadium in Milan, Italy, was a multicultural event. Although both teams were from the same Spanish city, Spanish players on both sides were in the minority. In all, 11 of the 18 players of Real Madrid and 12 of the 18 players of Atlético Madrid were born outside the home country of these two clubs. Altogether, players from 14 countries and three continents participated in the match, including Costa Rica, Portugal, Brazil, Croatia, Germany, Wales, France, Colombia, Slovenia, Montenegro, Uruguay, Argentina, Belgium, and Ghana. Not only the teams but also the coaches of the two teams were multicultural. Real Madrid coach Zinedine Zidane is French (of Algerian Kabyle descent), who played for clubs in France, Italy, and Spain. His Atlético counterpart Diego Pablo Simeone is Argentinian, but spent a considerable part of his career in Italy, France, and Spain. Notably,

Atlético Madrid has two minority owners from Israel and China (Maderer, Holtbrügge & Schuster 2014; Mandis 2016).

Even national teams may consist of players with different cultural backgrounds. For example, the success of France in the 2018 Football World Cup was largely attributed to the integration of players with different ethnic identities. Of the 23 players on the French squad, two-thirds are of Arab or African descent. Nine of the 14 French players who appeared in the Final Match were born in Africa or the French Caribbean or to parents who emigrated from those places. Raphaël Varane's father is from Martinique; Samuel Umtiti was born in Cameroon; Paul Pogba's parents are from Guinea; Corentin Tolisso's father is from Togo; N'Golo Kanté's parents are from Mali; Kylian Mbappé's father is from Cameroon; Ousmane Dembélé's parents are from Mauritania; Blaise Matuidi's father is from Angola; Nabil Fekir's parents are from Algeria; and Steven Nzonzi's parents are from the Democratic Republic of Congo (Smith 2018).

In contrast, one reason for the resignation of the German national team in the group phase was said to be its disintegration into small groups. One group consisted of players with ethnic heritage, such as Jérôme Boateng, Mesut Özil, İlkay Gündoğan, and Antonio Rüdiger. The other group formed players like Thomas Müller, Mats Hummels, Manuel Neuer, Timo Werner, etc. The two groups, understood to have differing tastes in areas such as music, cars, and lifestyle, then engaged in a derogatory banter, in which one side called the other "Kanake"—a pejorative term taken to mean "wog" or a non-white immigrant. In response, the other group then fired back with "Kartoffel" (potato)—a derogatory term for Germans used by the ethnic immigrant population, originating from the prominence of the ingredient in German cuisine. Between the two groups stood Julian Draxler who felt drawn to Jérôme Boateng. Both spend their holidays in Los Angeles, celebrated parties in clubs, heard hip-hop and hung out by the pool (Buschmann, Hujer & Pfeil 2018).

1.3 REASONS FOR STUDYING INTERCULTURAL MANAGEMENT

Studying intercultural management is important for a number of reasons (Table 1.2). First, the internationalization of population and family structures bring about a **demographic imperative**. In 2016, approximately 10% of people living in the EU had been born outside of their current country of residence. Marriages involving at least one foreigner accounted for 10.5 % of all marriages in the EU in 2015 (Eurostat 2015). In the United States, the number of interracial marriages has increased five times to approximately 17% in the last 50 years. In 2015, 14% of infants were biracial, which is nearly three times higher than in 1980 (Livingston & Brown 2017). As a result, the cultural diversity of firms, workforces, customers, etc. is continuously increasing.

In a globalized world, the proficiency to interact with other cultures is a major **economic imperative**. It helps identifying new business opportunities in foreign markets and marketing products in culturally appropriate and effective ways. Intercultural competence is particularly important in countries with high levels of foreign trade and foreign direct investment. For example, in small and open economies, such as Luxembourg, Hong Kong, Singapore, Malta, and Ireland, the volume of exports exceeds gross domestic product (The World Bank 2019). Under these conditions, the understanding of commercial practices and consumer behavior in other cultures becomes vital.

Table 1.2   Imperatives for studying intercultural management

Demographic imperative	Cultural diversity is a fact of life (e.g., travel, media, intercultural marriages, labor migration, workforce, etc.).
Economic imperative	In a globalized world, the understanding of and ability to interact with other cultures enhances business opportunities.
Technological imperative	New technologies are creating complex relationships between an increasing diversity of previously separated people.
Self-awareness imperative	The better we understand other cultures, the better we understand ourselves as individuals.
Ethical imperative	Intercultural encounters force people to reflect about the consequences (good vs. bad) of their words and behavior.
Peace imperative	The ability to interact with other cultures brings peace and stimulates respectful relationships.

Source: Adapted from Martin & Nakayama (2017).

The **technological imperative** to study intercultural management is reinforced through innovations in mobility and communication that intensify the relationships between different cultures. Mobile devices, the internet and global media link an increasing diversity of people by minimizing the effects of spatial and temporal separation. While traveling to other countries in previous centuries was time-consuming and allowed for a gradual cultural adjustment, modern means of transportation make it possible to reach any point on earth within a few hours and at an affordable price (Urry 2002). As a consequence, intercultural encounters are becoming more frequent, more immediate, and more diverse.

Studying intercultural management also has a **self-awareness imperative**. Individuals who are socialized in a culturally homogeneous society often believe that their values and behaviors are universal. Encounters with other cultures allow them to reflect on the idiosyncratic nature of their beliefs and practices (Fei 2015). As Swiss psychologist *C.G. Jung* remarks: "Everything that irritates us about others can lead us to an understanding of ourselves" (Jung 1961, p. 246).

Intercultural collaborations have an **ethical imperative** as they force people to reflect about the consequences and judgment of their behavior by others. Practices that are common and accepted in one country may be regarded as unethical and not tolerable in others. The popular recommendation "When in Rome, do as the Romans do" may therefore raise severe ethical concerns in many countries. A key dispute is whether there exist universal values and guidelines for behavior or whether the evaluation of human behavior must be context-dependent. Intercultural management is therefore challenged by the tension between ethical imperialism and ethical relativism (Jackson 2011; Scherer & Patzer 2011).

In March 2019, US-American film star George Clooney called for a boycott of nine hotels because of their links to Brunei, where homosexual acts have been declared punishable by death. Days before, the Sultan of Brunei who owns these hotels had announced that the country will stone or whip to death citizens caught committing adultery or participating in homosexual relations. Theft will be punished by amputation of arms and legs under the new laws. "Let that sink in. In the onslaught of news where we see the world backsliding into authoritarianism this stands alone," Clooney said. He called for the public to join him in immediately boycotting nine hotels–three in the United Kingdom, two in the United States, two in France and two in Italy. "Every single time we stay at, or take meetings at or dine at any of these nine hotels we are putting money directly into the pockets of men who choose to stone and whip to death their own citizens for being gay or accused of adultery. Are we really going to help pay for these human rights violations? Are we really going to help fund the murder of innocent citizens?" (Clooney 2019).

Ethical judgment about other cultures is particularly challenging when the stake is high. While the consequences of the boycott are marginal for George Clooney and those who follow his call–they refrain from staying in a small number of luxury hotels–only few individuals and firms have stopped significant business relations with Brunei. A rare example is STA Travel, the world's largest student and youth travel company. The London-based company wrote on Twitter that it would no longer sell flights on Brunei's national carrier, Royal Brunei Airlines, "to add our voice to the calls on Brunei to reverse this change in the law and in support of LGBTQI people everywhere." On the contrary, the German company ThyssenKrupp that has received an order from the state-owned Brunei Fertilizer Industries in 2017 to build a new fertilizer production facility sees no reason for withdrawal from the country. A company spokesman told the German press: "We do not believe in foreclosure, but in dialogue. However, we welcome the efforts of the German Government to influence the political leadership of Brunei" (cited in Hennersdorf 2019).

Finally, studying intercultural management has a **peace imperative**. Cultural differences have been a major reason of conflicts and wars in and between societies for ages. From the Christian Crusaders and the American Civil War to the Holocaust, genocides in Bosnia and Rwanda, and the jihadist terror regimes of al-Qaeda and ISIS, cultural and religious fanaticism and fundamentalism have justified violence and massive killings of people across the world. The fight for cultural and religious beliefs has not only been a major reason for "many millions of people (…) to kill, (but also) willingly to die for" (Anderson 2006, p. 7). Intercultural competence is therefore an important prerequisite for peace and respectful relationships and helps individuals, organizations, and societies to prevent that disputes do not escalate into violence and war.

SUMMARY

Cultural diversity offers great opportunities for organizations and societies, such as increased creativity, innovation, and adaptability. However, it also poses considerable management challenges, including conflicting values, norms and behavior, impeded communication, as well as reduced interpersonal trust.

Intercultural relations are gaining importance in the business context, but also in politics, society, military, and education. Consequently, becoming aware of and learning about intercultural management is important, particularly due to the increasing cultural diversity of societies and organizations.

Intercultural understanding allows for economic gains, enables individuals to obtain a better understanding of their own culture, helps people judge the morality of their behavior, and stimulates peace.

Reflection Questions

1. What are the general reasons for studying intercultural management and why are you interested in it?
2. From your point of view: What are the most important positive and negative outcomes of cultural diversity?
3. Do you think that cultural diversity will become more challenging or more advantageous in the future?
4. Based on your own experience: Do you feel that intercultural teams are more or less effective to achieve good outcomes for a specific task?
5. In the context of cultural diversity, would you say that human rights are universal?
6. How do you evaluate the statement that cultural segregation eliminates problems related to diversity and leads to more prosperity and peace?

 End of Chapter Exercise

Managing Cultural Diversity

Imagine you are the newly appointed Chief Diversity Officer (CDO) at a large multinational corporation. Your aim is to develop a strategy that helps your company leverage the advantages of cultural diversity.

1. Do you regard cultural diversity more as an opportunity or a challenge?
2. In which areas do you believe cultural diversity serves as an advantage or a disadvantage?
3. How can your company leverage the advantages and mitigate the disadvantages you have identified?
4. How would you position the relevance of cultural diversity in comparison to other aspects of diversity (gender, age, etc.)?

 Further Reading

The textbooks by Holden (2002), Thomas and Peterson (2018), Browaeys and Price (2019), Steers and Osland (2020) and Barmeyer, Bausch and Mayrhofer (2021) provide concise introductions to intercultural management.

The handbooks of Holden, Michailova and Tietze (2015) and Szkudlarek et al. (2020) discuss recent developments in intercultural management research.

2

DEFINITIONS, MANIFESTATIONS, DELINEATIONS, AND FUNCTIONS OF CULTURE

LEARNING OBJECTIVES

By the end of this chapter, you will be able to

- differentiate between culture, biology, and personality,
- define culture from a multidisciplinary perspective,
- understand the advantages and disadvantages of different delineations of culture,
- recognize the manifestation of stereotypes,
- comprehend the role of the physical environment, legal-political system, economy, religion, and biology for the formation in different cultures,
- interpret and compare different definitions of culture,
- assess your personal cultural background from different points of view.

Before discussing the impact of culture on management, it is important to define what the term culture actually means. Culture can be described by a number of attributes that are outlined in the following section. Afterwards, manifestations of culture in various areas, such as corporate cultures, industry cultures, professional cultures, etc., are outlined, before different delineations of national culture are discussed. In particular, the advantages and disadvantages of legal-political, geographic, ethnical, linguistic and intellectual-historical delineations are analyzed.

A variety of approaches to the factors and mechanisms that influence the formation of different cultures, such as the physical environment, legal-political system, economy, religion, and biology, exist. These factors are outlined in the next section. The final section focuses on the various functions of culture for individuals, organizations, and societies.

2.1 DEFINITIONS OF CULTURE

Although culture is the key concept in intercultural management research, its attributes, delineations, and origins are largely disputed. Already in the early 1950s, Kroeber and Kluckhohn (1952) identified 164 different concepts and definitions of culture. Since then, existing definitions have been modified and new definitions have been proposed. This variety not only reflects the **multitude of perspectives** but also limits the comparability of existing research on culture and its relevance for management. So what is culture?

The basis of many definitions of culture is—at least implicitly—the **demarcation of culture, biology, and personality** which is reflected, for example, in the fundamental statement of Kluckhohn and Murray (1965, p. 53): "Every man is in certain respects like all other men, like some other men, like no other man." According to this statement, human behavior is a product of universal biology ("all"), collectively-shared culture ("some"), and individual personality ("no") (Figure 2.1). All humans have common physiological and psychological properties (e.g., the need to eat, drink, and sleep, logical reasoning, reflectivity, etc.) which distinguish them from other species. The underlying principles of behavior are therefore determined by biological human nature and the universalities of human life. The specific formulation of these inherited predispositions, however, is a product of socialization and social interaction. Thus, the ways in which these biological properties express themselves within a social group are characterized by some sense of coherence and unity in affective, cognitive, and behavioral dimensions, while they differ between various social groups. At the same time, each individual is of unique biological heredity (e.g., fingerprint, iris, physiognomy) and owns unique characteristics (e.g., personality, life experience), which gives an idiosyncratic coloring to social values, norms, and behaviors (Kluckhohn & Strodtbeck 1961). A fundamental prerequisite of any study of culture is therefore to distinguish behaviors that are shared collectively among the members of a particular social group from those that have universal or individual reasons. In the first case, the **unit of analysis** is the society, while in the latter two, it is all of mankind and the individual, respectively.

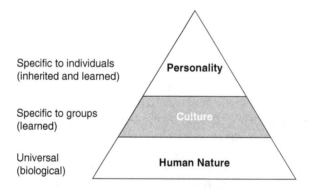

Figure 2.1 Demarcation of culture, biology, and personality

When people strive to find reasons for behaviors, their perceptions of causality are often distorted by cognitive biases. According to Heider (1958), the **fundamental attribution error** describes the tendency to attribute the behavior of individuals to their personality instead considering external factors. In intercultural encounters, people may underestimate or overestimate the role of culture for the explanation of human behavior compared to personality-based and environmental factors. This **cultural attribution bias** may lead to inappropriate perceptions and interpretations of and inadequate behavior in intercultural encounters. For example, the perceived reserved and taciturn reception of an Italian guest in a hotel in Finland may be ascribed to the restrained Finish culture. However, it may also have personal reasons (e.g., the Finish receptionist may be exceptionally shy) or be caused by situational factors (e.g., the receptionist may be tired or in a bad mood).

Extant definitions typically propose a number of attributes that distinguish culture from other social phenomena (von Keller 1982; Hofstede 2001; Minkov 2011; Schein 2017). While these definitions often emphasize different aspects, the following **attributes of culture** are commonly recognized (Figure 2.2):

- Culture is *man-made.* It is the result of human thinking and acting, and is comprised of visible and invisible elements. Visible elements are cultural products (works of art, music, literature, etc.), forms of behavior (customs, traditions, rituals, etc.), and institutions (matrimony, organizations, etc.). Invisible elements are, for example, norms and values, as well as basic assumptions about time, space, and human nature (Schein 1984).

- Culture is *collectively-shared.* It is a social phenomenon that is common to a larger group of people. This commonality distinguishes culture from personality: "If it ain't shared, it ain't culture" (Dickson et al. 2012, p. 484). Cultural traits are not necessarily shared by all members of a society, but characterize it as a whole. They are typical for a society and can be found among its members with a certain probability (Minkov 2011).

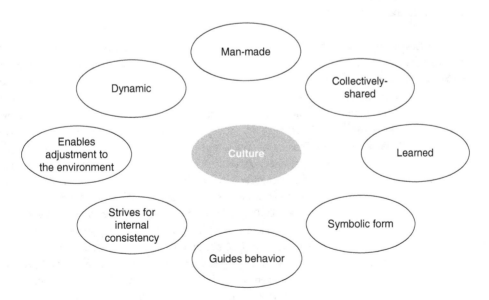

Figure 2.2 Attributes of culture

- Culture is *learned*. It is the social heritage of a society in contrast to the innate genetic predispositions of an individual. Culture is transferred from generation to generation through socialization and education. This process of social learning ensures that each generation inherits the knowledge, attitudes, and behaviors of its predecessors, even if these are not transmitted genetically (Richerson & Boyd 2005).
- Culture has a *symbolic form*. It is largely invisible and expresses itself in language, rituals, and institutions that impose meaning on the world and make it understandable (Geertz 1973). The meaning of the inherited conceptions of culture has to be revealed through the interpretation of its symbolic expressions. Thus, from a methodological perspective, culture is a latent, hypothetical construct that can only be inferred from its manifestations (Schwartz 2014).
- Culture *guides behavior*. It represents ideal patterns of behavior that are accepted and familiar within a certain social community. In contrast to explicit laws and regulations, culture directs the actions of individuals in an implicit way, thus allowing them a certain discretionary space.
- Culture *strives for internal consistency*. The elements of a culture tend to form a consistent and integrated whole. Internal consistency facilitates the identification with a culture among its members and reinforces the demarcation from other cultures.
- Culture *enables adjustment to the environment*. It consists of proven instruments that allow individuals to solve basic human problems and satisfy human needs. Different environments therefore typically evoke different cultural patterns. Values and behaviors that are useful in one context may be useless or even dysfunctional in other contexts.
- Culture is *dynamic*. It tends to adapt itself to changes in the environment in which people live and to their changing biological and psychological demands. The process of cultural change is mostly uncontrollable and unpredictable. The visible symbols of a culture tend to change faster than norms, values, and basic assumptions, which are often more persistent and enduring.

For a closer look at the dimensions of culture, it is suitable to distinguish between an actor's and an observer's perspective. From an **actor's perspective**, cultures can be understood as **glasses with different optical lenses** that lead to different views of the world. Like how lenses with different focal distances and colors are useful for different purposes (e.g. reading, foresight, sun protection), cultures are generally not superior or inferior, but are more or less appropriate under certain conditions. Their "cultural glasses" allow people to see only part of the "reality." Different cultural norms and values direct the attention of individuals to different aspects of their environment. Thus, perception is always affected by cultural bias. And like people who have been accustomed to wearing glasses, socialization in a homogeneous society has made individuals unaware, to a certain degree, of their cultural imprints. It is therefore necessary to take off or change one's "cultural glasses" to understand that other cultures may have different views of the world.

An **observer's perspective** is prevalent in **Osgood's epistemological concept of culture**. This concept distinguishes between descriptive aspects (cultural percepta) and explicative aspects (cultural concepta) (Figure 2.3). *Cultural percepta* consist of all observable results of behavior which express themselves in the form of *material culture* (tools, dress-code, architecture, works of art, etc.). A second element is *social culture* which includes, for example, language, habits, social structures, and codes of conduct. These attributes of behavior are observable, but partly unconscious.

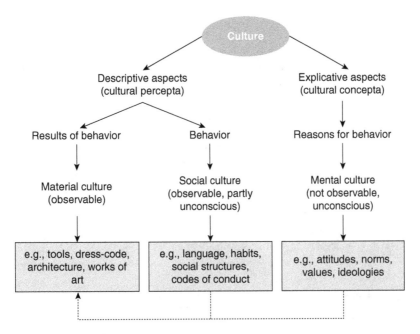

Figure 2.3 Epistemological categories of culture (Osgood)
Source: Adapted from Osgood (1951).

Cultural concepta consist of a society's attitudes, norms, values, and ideologies. While these attributes of *mental culture* are not observable and unconscious, they represent the ideas in the minds of human beings and the reasons for their behavior. "The student of culture is clearly not only interested in the activities and productions of mankind but in man's ideas as well. We are concerned with his religion and his philosophy, his mythology and his ideas of beauty, his mental attitudes, and his ideals. It is in this that anthropology strikingly differs from the natural sciences in what is to be considered as fundamental objective data. It is here, however, that we face complexities in the classification of our data on the basis of truth values" (Osgood 1951, p. 212).

A similar differentiation is made in **Schein's iceberg model of culture**. It distinguishes between three layers of culture with different characteristics and assumes that most parts of culture—like an iceberg—are not visible (Figure 2.4):

- The top layer consists of *symbols and artifacts,* such as language, architecture, manner of dress, gestures, etc. Symbols are visible and can easily be observed, but need interpretation to be fully understood. "We can describe 'how' a group constructs its environment and 'what' behavior patterns are discernible among the members, but we often cannot understand the underlying logic—'why' a group behaves the way it does" (Schein 1984, p. 3).
- *Norms and values* represent the second layer of the model. They are only partly visible (e.g., in the form of written rules) and partly unconscious, even to the members of the culture. Norms and values indicate what is

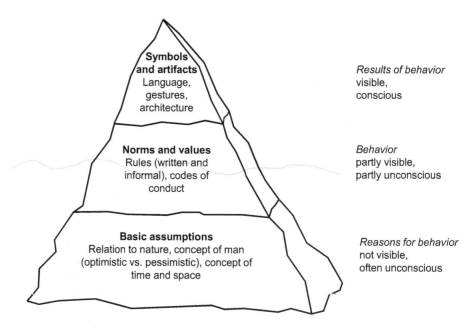

Figure 2.4 Schein's iceberg model of culture
Source: Adapted from Schein (1984, p. 4).

regarded as right and wrong in a society, and provide the legitimacy for social behavior. As abstract guidelines, they coordinate the activities of the members of a society in an implicit way.

- The foundation of the iceberg constitutes the *basic assumptions*, such as the relation to nature, concept of man, and concept of time and space. Basic assumptions are invisible, tacit, and often unconscious. "Taken-for-granted assumptions are so powerful because they are less debatable and confrontable than espoused values. We know we are dealing with an assumption when we encounter in our informants a refusal to discuss something, or when they consider us 'insane' or 'ignorant' for bringing something up" (Schein 1984, p. 4).

Intercultural management guidebooks often focus on the top layer of visible symbols and artifacts and give recommendations for appropriate behavior. Their impact on intercultural relations, however, is often low. For example, the adaption of common greeting rituals (handshake, bow, kiss on the cheek, etc.) is usually appreciated as an act of courtesy, but hardly affects intercultural relationships in a substantial way. It is rather necessary to understand the underlying norms and values as well as the basic assumptions of a culture to manage intercultural relations successfully. For example, different time orientations may impede decisions about a firm's strategic objective (e.g., short-term profits vs. market share), product development (e.g., quality vs. time to market), or compensation policy (bonus payments vs. ownership plans). The knowledge of a culture's values and basic assumptions is also needed for the appropriate interpretation of behaviors. Similar symbols and artifacts can have different meanings in different cultures. For example, the swastika is regarded as symbolic expression of Nazism in Germany, while it symbolizes peace and harmony in Buddhism, Jainism, and Hinduism (Nakagaki 2018). Therefore, the attribution of familiar signs and behavior to one's own cultural values and basic assumptions neglects that their reasons and meaning may be fundamentally different. This **cultural perception error** can lead to serious intercultural management problems. Like with icebergs, the main challenges are caused by the invisible parts of culture that are situated below the waterline.

The implications of the three different layers of culture become visible, for example, in international tourism. Many people enjoy visiting touristic sites and are curious to taste local food. They read about tip-customs and other etiquette, make the acquaintance of the hotel staff, and bring souvenirs and ethnic clothing back home. However, many tourists avoid confrontation with the deeper layers of other cultures' norms and values, and are frustrated when they learn that the things below the waterline are different than they expected. The relaxed attitude of service representatives and tour guides in, for example, Africa and Southeast Asia, is mostly appreciated by tourists from Europe and North America. The underlying polychronic time orientation, however, becomes problematic if it affects more fundamental aspects, such as delays of administrative procedures or flight schedules. Without the understanding of the lower layers of norms, values, and basic assumptions, every attempt to access other cultures lacks adequate cognitive complexity and remains superficial.

2.2 MANIFESTATIONS OF CULTURE

Intercultural management research focuses primarily on **national cultures**, such as the German culture, the American culture, the Indian culture, etc., and shows that citizens of a particular country share common values, beliefs, and behaviors. At the same time, individuals are members of various social groups and exposed to several manifestations of culture, such as corporate cultures, industry cultures, professional cultures, department cultures, generation cultures, class cultures, and gender cultures, which often overlap and interdepend, but may also contradict each other. While national cultures shape the values and behaviors of individuals, their impact may thus be amplified, mitigated, or modified by other manifestations of culture. For example, while the German national culture is typically regarded as linear-active (i.e., task-oriented, focused on planning, and direct on speaking) and the Italian national culture as multiactive (i.e., relationship-oriented, impulsive, and talkative), a German salesperson may have a more multiactive time orientation than an Italian engineer (Lewis 2012).

Corporate cultures express the values and beliefs that companies develop over time (Schein 2017). The corporate culture defines the way in which a firm conducts its business and interacts with its key stakeholders. It stems from the company's history, founders, and corporate heroes, and is manifested in symbolic forms, such as myths, rituals, stories, legends, and unique language (Smircich 1983; Hofstede et al. 1990). The corporate culture often originates in the respective national culture, but advances during the firm's history and transcends national borders once the firm internationalizes. Research on corporate culture was strongly influenced by Peters and Waterman (1982) who found that firms with a distinct set of core managerial values often show superior financial performance. However, several firms that they had regarded as excellent during the time of their study faced serious difficulties in the following decades. Recent research therefore expresses that an unreasonably strong corporate culture bears the risk of overemphasizing internal aspects, makes firms blind to disruptive innovations, and increases their resistance to change (Alvesson & Sveningsson 2015).

Differences in **industry cultures** result from different task environments, such as the nature of the products or services, technological innovations, degree of state intervention, and market structures. Deal and Kennedy (1982) argue that industry cultures are mainly a function of the degree of risk and the speed of feedback in the respective industry, and distinguish between four types of industry cultures:

- Heavy industries, such as automotive, steel, and mechanical engineering, are dominated by *process cultures* with clear organizational roles and standardized procedures. As risk is low and feedback slow, the core value is technical perfection.
- Low risk and quick feedback are typical for consulting firms and start-ups. Informal language, casual dress code, and flexible working hours are common and stand for a *work hard/play hard culture*.

- *Macho/tough guy cultures* are characterized by high risks, intense pressure, and quick feedback. They can be found in such industries as construction, advertising, and entertainment.
- *Bet-your-company cultures* imply high risk, slow feedback, and large fixed investments. They are prevalent in, for example, extracting, aerospace, chemical, and energy sectors.

Professional cultures have often evolved over centuries of practice, norming, and education. Already medieval guilds established strict codes of conduct and rituals that sometimes persist until today (Kieser 1989). Dress codes of several professions are universal (e.g., doctors wear white coats, judges black robes, and cooks toques and checked trousers), as are many emblems and insignia (e.g., Aesculapian staff, scales of justice, compass, pharmacy cross). The continuation of professional ethics and rituals is often passed on by professional associations and artisan guilds (Greenwood, Suddaby & Hinings 2002).

The impact of professional cultures goes beyond symbol systems and also involves thinking and behavior. "Doctors may learn to be cautious and not too aggressive in their bedside manner or in surgery. However, for lawyers aggressiveness, at least in court, may be encouraged. Law assumes adversarial relationships between conflicting parties while in medicine it is a joint effort to defeat a common enemy, the disease. For a lawyer, being convincing (establishing truth) may be more related to displaying and evoking emotions rather than remaining cool, calm, and collected (...). In terms of method, scientists may be more excited by abstract theory, while engineers are impatient to work out the practical application. Medical doctors and lawyers have been trained to look for evidence in previous cases, while scientists have been taught to look for truth in large samples and statistical significance. For engineers, the proof is in making it work" (Schneider & Barsoux 2003, p. 63).

Department cultures are mainly shaped by their institutional logic. For example, research and development is mostly focused on technical excellence and directed toward product characteristics and functionalities. Production managers are more action-oriented and characterized by a short-term time orientation. Employees in financial departments work in quiet offices, interact primarily with other staff, and are concerned with numbers rather than products and technologies. On the contrary, marketing specialists care about customer needs, competitiveness, and corporate image. Responsiveness and flexibility are more important than operational effectiveness and technical perfection. Given the significant cultural differences between departments, the management of cross-departmental interfaces is often regarded as a firm's key success factor (Song & Thieme 2006; Fain & Wagner 2014; Homburg et al. 2017).

Strong commonalities also exist between individuals of similar age. **Generation cultures** (e.g., post-war generation, baby boomers, generation Y, millennials, digital natives) stem from important historical events (e.g., wars and revolutions) or breakthrough technologies (e.g., automobiles, the Internet). As major trends spread quickly around the world, generation cultures have often a global scope (Howe & Strauss 2000; Tulgan & Martin 2001; Gibson, Greenwood & Murphy 2009).

Class cultures also share similar values, norms, and behaviors. According to Marx (1867), class consciousness is based on individuals' relationship to means of production. Traditionally, differences existed between capitalists (owners of land, firms, etc.) and people who generated their income from manual labor, such as between the aristocracy and the working class in England or between the bourgeoisie and the prolétariat in France. In modern societies, the access to education and cultural goods have become important markers of class cultures (Bourdieu 1973).

Gender cultures manifest themselves in common values among members of the same sex. That involves, for example, preferences for certain school subjects, hobbies, or occupations (male vs. female professions). Management studies also identified distinct patters of male vs. female leadership styles (Joshi et al. 2015). While early studies attributed gender differences to inherited biological factors, recent research stresses that gender cultures—like most other manifestations of culture—are to a high degree socially constructed (Ely 1995; Nicolson 2015).

The complex interplay between different manifestations of culture can be illustrated using the examples of the sporting goods company Adidas and the automotive supplier Schaeffler (Holtbrügge & Haussmann 2017). Both companies are headquartered in the same Franconian town (Herzogenaurach), were founded in the same period shortly after World War II, and are similar in size. While the German national culture shaped the two companies in the initial years, their corporate cultures developed in fundamentally different directions afterwards.

Georg Schaeffler, the founder and long-standing CEO of Schaeffler, was a mechanical engineer who emphasized on innovation and technical perfection. Despite its fast internationalization, the main activities of the Schaeffler Group remained in Middle Franconia ever since. Most employees were born in this region and have worked for the company for generations. The staff is male-dominated and calls themselves—with ironic reference to the company's products—as "old iron." Even after the initial public offering in 2015, the majority of shares is still owned by the Schaeffler family. The organizational culture can be described as process culture with clear organizational roles and standardized procedures. Thus, the norms and values at Schaeffler are similar to the German national culture.

In contrast, Adidas is a marketing-driven company characterized by a work hard/play hard culture. The staff is young and multicultural with a high percentage of female employees. Adidas regards itself as a "truly global company" that employs people from about 100 nations at its headquarters in Herzogenaurach. The six members of the management board come from five different countries. Dress code is sporty and language informal. Even the Danish CEO is addressed with the informal "Du." Despite its strong German roots, the culture at Adidas is strongly influenced by US-American characteristics.

2.3 DELINEATIONS OF NATIONAL CULTURE

While national cultures are in the focus of intercultural management research, the important question of how they can be defined and demarcated is discussed controversially. The affiliation of an individual to a certain national culture may be delineated in different ways which all have specific advantages and disadvantages (Table 2.1).

Existing research most often defines national culture in legal–political terms. According to the **legal–political delineation** of culture, all citizens of a country irrespective of their current residence are regarded as members of that specific culture. This "passport approach" (Taras, Steel & Kirkman 2016, p. 460) is closely related to the *concept of nation states* (Section 3.1). From a legal perspective, a nation is typically characterized by a larger group of citizens governed by institutions that set and enforce binding

Table 2.1 Delineations of national culture

Delineation	Criteria	Advantages	Disadvantages	Examples
Legal-political	Nation/citizenship	Most common approach that facilitates comparisons of various studies	Does not consider inward and outward migration; citizenship laws vary	Nation states; Japan, Korea, African countries
Geographic	Territory/ residency	Considers national identification of diaspora and regional subcultures	Geographic borders are increasingly perforated by global media, travel, education, and careers	Chinese (domestic, overseas), Nonresident Indians; East Coast vs. California vs. "Bible Belt", Crimea, Alsace
Ethnic	Origin/biology	Considers multiethnic societies	Concept of ethnicity as social construct rather arbitrary; often misused to justify racism and xenophobia	Jews, Russian (russkie/ русские vs. rossijane/ россияне)
Linguistic	Language	Appropriate for studies about intercultural communication	Decreasing relevance with growing popularity of English as global business language	German Language Area, Hispanophone, Francophonie
Intellectual-historical	History of thought	Appropriate to identify larger cultural clusters and civilizations	Risk of problematic simplifications and inaccurate stereotyping	Western, Islamic World, British

rules (Smith 1991). These rules are based on common values derived from a shared history. The unifying function of nation states results from the preference of people to be governed and politically represented by institutions consistent with their values (Spruyt 2002; Peterson & Søndergaard 2014). "Nation states can thus be the result of shared values and national institutions that, in turn, further perpetuate shared values" (Taras, Steel & Kirkman 2016, p. 461).

The legal–political delineation is particularly useful for ethnically homogeneous countries with little inward migration (e.g., Japan, Korea), while it is less appropriate in immigrant countries (e.g., Canada, Israel), multiethnic countries (e.g., India), and countries at the intersection of two or more language areas (e.g., Belgium, Switzerland). It is also problematic in most African countries that have only a short history as independent nation states and whose national borders were defined after the end of colonization with little regard for cultural specificities. According to Rubenstein & Crocker (1994), at most 15 out of the approximately 180 states that compose the current world system can be called nations in the sense that a vast majority of people believe that they share a common ancestry and cultural identity. Moreover, the criteria as to who is entitled citizenship differ between countries (Carens 2000). While in some countries (e.g., China, Germany, India, United Kingdom), citizenship is predominantly determined by having one or both parents who are citizens of the state (*jus sanguinis*), it is based on place of birth (*jus soli*) in others (e.g., Mexico, Pakistan, United States). Since many developed countries (e.g., Australia, France, Germany, Switzerland, the United Kingdom, and the United States) allow dual and multiple citizenship, this delineation can also be ambiguous (Faist & Kivisto 2007).

The **geographic delineation** of national cultures includes residents who are not citizens, and excludes citizens who are not residents of the particular country. It is also used in various other fields, such as the calculation of the gross domestic product, the most common indicator of a country's economic wealth. The geographic delineation is based on the anthropological argument that physical barriers, like mountains and oceans, separate social groups from each other, foster the formation of unique ways of thinking, feeling, and behavior and defend social groups from unwelcome incursions by outside groups (Peterson & Søndergaard 2014). While the geographic conditions (topography, size, distances, etc.) may have been relevant in the past, modern means of transportation and communication weaken their separating effect. Media, travel, education, and careers are becoming increasingly international and perforating geographic boundaries (Kraidy 2006; Pieterse 2015).

The geographic delineation leads to a similar classification as the legal–political delineation in countries that have been largely isolated from other countries throughout their history, such as Japan (Weiner 2004), while it differs in cases of large inward migration. One example is the large community of *Overseas Chinese* who have migrated to other Asian countries, such as Thailand, Malaysia, Indonesia, Singapore, etc., since the nineteenth century. Great Chinese minorities outside Greater China live also in Australia, Canada, and the United States (Barabantseva 2011). *Non-resident Indians* constitute the largest diaspora population in the world with over 15.6 mn. people. Major recipient countries are Saudi Arabia, Nepal, the UAE, South Africa, the United Kingdom, the United States, and Canada (Lall 2001). Members of cultural diaspora often identify themselves strongly with their culture of origin even after living in another country for a long time (Cohen 2008).

A challenge to both the legal-political and geographical delineations of culture is the **change of national borders**. Poland, for example, ceased to exist as a nation state after three partitions in 1772, 1793, and 1795. While the north-western provinces around Gdansk and Poznan

(Continued)

fell to Prussia, the south-western provinces around Lvov were occupied by Austria-Hungary. The rest of the country came into possession of Russia. Poland was only reconstituted as a state in smaller size and with quite different borders in the Treaty of Versailles in 1919, before it was divided again between Germany and the Soviet Union pursuant to the Molotov-Ribbentrop Pact in 1939. After World War II, the borders were changed again and Poland was formed into its current territory (Batt & Wolczuk 2002).

Another example of a region that has been part of different countries throughout its history is the Crimean peninsula. After being a khanate of the Ottoman Empire since 1449, it was conquered by the Russian Empire in 1783. After the Russian Revolution, Crimea became part of the Russian Soviet Federative Socialist Republic in 1921. In 1954, it was transferred to the Ukrainian SSR. After the dissolution of the Soviet Union in 1991, the Autonomous Republic of Crimea was formed as a constituent entity of independent Ukraine. In 2014, the Crimean peninsula was annexed from Ukraine by the Russian Federation and has been administered since then as two Russian federal subjects (Figes 2010; Teper 2016).

In countries with large regional diversity, it may be appropriate to apply the geographic delineation also on the *subnational level*. Regional cultures can be the results of topographic conditions, foreign influences, as well as political and economic reasons. Significant cultural differences exist, for example, in the United States between the liberal East Coast (Boston, New York), the laid-back culture in California, and the conservative "Bible Belt" in the South and Midwest (Chinni & Gimpel 2011). In Germany, cultural differences prevail between East and West (as consequence of the German partition between 1949 and 1990) as well as between the predominantly Protestant North and the mostly Catholic South (Nees 2000; Bernstein 2004). In France, north-western Brittany has retained part of the Celtic heritage, while in the Southern Provence, traces of Roman history are still visible. Alsace and Lorraine, which have been part of the Frankish Kingdom and the German Empire for centuries, share many cultural similarities with adjacent Germany (Dunlop 2015).

The **ethnic delineation** of culture was originally based on *racial and biological categories* and regarded ethnicity as determinant of the human gene pool (skin color, hair, size, physiognomy, etc.). Since *Max Weber*, ethnicity is predominantly regarded as a *social construct* (Banton 2007). In this sense, membership of an ethnic group is defined by shared ancestry, origin myth, history, homeland, language or dialect, symbolic systems such as religion, mythology and ritual, cuisine, style of dress, art, and physical appearance (Gellner 1983; Smith 1986). The relevance of these characteristics may vary, and not all characteristics may be applied in all cases. "For example, 'Jews' are often described as an ethnic group despite lacking a common language, universally shared customs, or even common religious practice (since non-believers are typically included in the group, and it is contested whether conversion can make one ethnically Jewish)" (Fearon 2003, p. 200).

The question of the ethnic groups in a country is often not easy to answer. "Constructivist or instrumentalist arguments about the contingent, fuzzy, and situational character of ethnicity seem amply supported. Take, for example, the United States. What are its ethnic (or racial) groups? Let us make things much easier by restricting attention to groups with at least 1% of country population. If we consult official census categories, we get three 'races'–white,

African American, and Asian—and an additional group, Hispanic, which the government emphatically declares is 'not a race'. Is this the right list for the United States? Why not disaggregate Hispanic into Puerto Rican Americans, Cuban Americans, Mexican Americans, and so on, or likewise for Asian? Why not distinguish between Arab Americans, Irish Americans, Italian Americans, German Americans, and so on? And why should we use the current census categories, when earlier censuses formulated the categories quite differently?" (Fearon 2003, p. 197).

Until 1930, Mexicans were categorized as "white" according to the US Census Bureau. Since then, Mexicans were given their own "racial" category. After protests of the Mexican government, Mexicans were again labeled as "white" in the three subsequent censuses. From 1970 on, the term "race" in association with skin color was omitted and substituted by the "cultural" category "Hispanics," meaning "a person of Cuban, Mexican, Puerto Rican, South or Central American or other Spanish culture or origin regardless of race." Thus, the ethnic demarcation of cultures is highly contingent on volatile political circumstances and negotiations (Mateo et al. 2012).

The ethnic delineation leads to a similar classification as the legal–political delineation in ethnically homogeneous countries. For example, Han Chinese make up about 92% of the total population of Mainland China and about 95% of the population of Taiwan (Li & Shan 2015). With 1.3 bn. people, they constitute the world's largest ethnic group, making up about 18% of the global population.

The ethnic delineation is more appropriate than the legal–political and geographic delineation for multiethnic countries, such as Brazil, Canada, India, Mexico, South Africa, Spain, the United States, the former Yugoslavia, and most African countries (Fearon 2003; Patsiurko, Campbell & Hall 2012). In Russia, the difference between Russian citizens and ethnic Russians is also reflected linguistically. While ethnic Russians are called "russkie" (русские), the term "rossijane" (россияне) labels Russians citizens irrespective of their ethnic origin. The term was coined by *Michail Lomonosov* to denote that Russia became a multiethnic empire after the occupation of the Khanate of Kazan in the 1550s (Kolstø & Blakkisrud 2004; Kappeler 2014).

Figure 2.5 presents a map of countries classified by their ethnic fractionalization. It is based on the study of Fearon (2003) that covers 822 ethnic groups (mainly based on the criteria of descent basis, self-consciousness as a group, and common language, religion, and customs) in 160 countries that made up at least 1% of the country population in the early 1990s. On average, countries have five ethnic groups with half of the world's countries having between three and six such groups. About 70% of the countries in the world have an ethnic group that forms an absolute majority of the population and 21% of the countries are homogenous in the sense of having a group that claims 9 out of 10 residents.

The **linguistic delineation** presumes that people who speak the same language share similar cultural characteristics. This is based on the assumption that linguistic similarities facilitate interaction and cooperation among people. Linguistic differences, on the other hand, increase the risk of mis-understandings. The linguistic delineation is therefore particularly useful in intercultural communication research.

An example is the *German Language Area* which consists of three countries where German is the sole nationwide official language (Germany, Austria, and Liechtenstein) and three countries where it is the coofficial nationwide or regional language (German community in Belgium, German-speaking part of

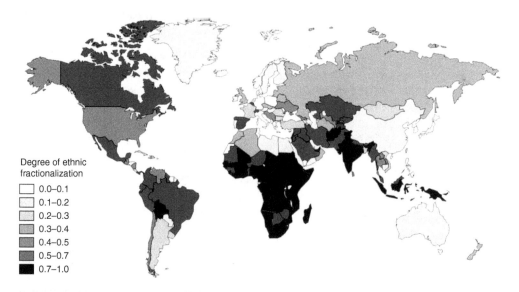

Figure 2.5 Map of countries classified by their ethnic fractionalization
Source: Based on Fearon (2003).

Switzerland, Luxembourg) (Ammon 2003). Despite their linguistic communalities, however, these countries are separated by large historic differences. For example, Germany consists of several former principalities which had their own dialects, habits, and traditions. Austria has long been a multinational great power with strong Hungarian and Slavic influences, while the German-speaking Switzerland has developed its own Swiss German dialect with distinct phonology, grammar and vocabulary (Cline 1984; Rash 1998).

The differences are even larger in other language areas, such as the *Hispanophone*. It consists of around 500–550 mn. residents of Spain and Latin America where Spanish is the majority language. Their communality is the heritage as being former Spanish colonies which made Spanish their official language. However, the Spanish-speaking countries are characterized by large differences in terms of geography, history, ethnicity, as well as traditions and habits. Hispanics or Latinos in the United States, for example, may descent from any of more than 20 Hispanic countries (often faced with national rivalries), be of any race, and not speak Spanish any more (Fraga & Garcia 2010; Arreola 2004). Even the "motherland" Spain is highly fractionalized in terms of ethnic composition and language (e.g., Castilian, Andalusian, Aragonese, Asturian, Basque, Catalan, Galician, and Valencian) (Mar-Molinero 2000).

The *Francophonie* involves a similar degree of diversity. French is an official language in 29 countries across five different continents. It was introduced to new territories in the Americas, Africa, and Asia as result of French and Belgian colonialism from the sixteenth century onward. Despite the active promotion of the French language, there are huge differences in lifestyle and worldview not only between France and other Francophone countries but also within France (e.g., between Paris and the provinces). Moreover, the cohesive role of the French language is decreasing as a result of the growing dominance of English as *lingua franca* (Albert 1999; Avanzi & Mettra 2017).

The **intellectual–historical delineation** of culture considers the attribution (in terms of self-perception and ascription by others) of a person to a particular worldview. Not affiliation to a nation state, but the state of mind is decisive. A uniform mindset can either emerge from the confrontation with specific physical conditions or be enforced by the state and other powerful institutions (e.g., religion, media). This perspective is useful to cluster larger cultural spheres of influence, cultural clusters, and civilizations (Huntington 1997). It is based on the observation that the cultural legacies of old empires often continue long after their formal institutions have disappeared (Toynbee 1946; Kennedy 1987). The intellectual–historical delineation, however, is based on very broad criteria and may cover highly diverse values, norms, and behaviors. It may thus lead to problematic simplifications and inaccurate stereotyping. Moreover, conflicts within civilizations are more common than conflicts between civilizations (Henderson & Tucker 2001).

The term "Western," for example, is mostly referred to European and North American countries on the Western hemisphere which share a common history of thought and understanding of reason as the primary source of authority and legitimacy. However, it is sometimes used in a broader sense of democratic and economically developed countries and may then also include countries on the Eastern hemisphere, such as Japan, Australia, and New Zealand. The "Islamic World" may include secular countries where the majority of the population is Muslims (e.g., Burkina Faso, Nigeria, Syria, Turkey), neutral Muslim majority countries (Bosnia and Herzegovina, Indonesia, Niger), countries with Islam as state religion (e.g., Egypt, Iraq, Morocco), and Islamic States that use Shariʿa Law as basis for the government, laws, and social norms (Afghanistan, Iran, Mauritania, Pakistan, Saudi Arabia, and Yemen) (Rippin 2008). "British" applies, in the narrow sense, to the member states of Great Britain which have been a part of a political union since 1801 with a common political and legal system and a common language (although with local variations). In a wider sense, the term may be used for the Commonwealth of Nations, i.e., the territories of the former British Empire. While sharing English as main administrative language, important values of democracy, freedom of speech, human rights, and the rule of law as well as some habits (e.g., tea ceremonies, cricket), the specific manifestations of these values and habits differ considerably. Moreover, the attitude toward the colonial heritage differs from positive and neutral (e.g., Australia) to predominantly negative (e.g., India) which strongly affects the dissemination and acceptance of British values in the respective society (Ferguson 2003; Tharoor 2018).

The intellectual-historical delineation of culture may be useful in cases where other commonalities are rare. A good example is India where the "Idea of India" (Khilnani 1999) unites 1.3 bn. people with different languages, ethnical backgrounds, religions, and partly even countries of residence. The identity of India is based on "the idea of an ever-ever land–emerging from an ancient civilization, united by a shared history, sustained by pluralist democracy (…). The Indian idea is the opposite of what Freudians call 'the narcissism of minor differences'; in India we celebrate the commonality of major differences. If America is a melting-pot, then to me India is a thali, a selection of sumptuous dishes in different bowls. Each tastes different, and does not necessarily mix with the next, but they belong together on the same plate, and they complement each other in making the meal a satisfying repast (…). So the idea of India is of one land embracing many. It is the idea that a nation may endure differences of caste, creed, color, conviction, culture, cuisine, costume and custom, and still rally around a consensus" (Tharoor 1997, p. 76).

The **evaluation of common delineations of national culture** shows that no single approach is able to cover all relevant aspects and that different demarcations are appropriate for different purposes. The various approaches are not clear-cut, but overlap and are even partly tautological (McSweeney 2009). For example, the ethnic and intellectual–historical delineations often refer to common cultural values and thus merge *explanandum* and *explanans*. Despite an increasing number of sophisticated approaches (e.g., Peterson & Søndergaard 2014; Venaik & Midgley 2015; Taras, Steel & Kirkman 2016), a certain degree of uncertainty about the assignment of individuals to a particular culture and its boundaries to other cultures remains. Studies about intercultural management should therefore specify their underlying delineation of culture to allow for assessments of their validity and limitations.

One approach to cope with the advantages and disadvantages of the different delineations is not to consider them as mutually exclusive alternatives, but integrate them into a **cultural pentagon model** (Figure 2.5). It consists of the five dimensions citizenship, residentship, language, ethnicity, and history of thought. The degree of intracultural diversity with regard to the five dimensions is noted on the five axes of the pentagon (with 0 = minimal diversity and 100 = maximal diversity). Based on a *configuration approach*, the five delineations are considered as interdependent and interrelated. The resulting area of the pentagon therefore reflects the overall intracultural homogeneity vs. diversity of the particular country:

- *Citizenship*: This axis indicates the percentage of inhabitants who were not born in and are not citizens of the particular country. Two extreme examples are North Korea with virtually no foreign inhabitants and Luxembourg where around 50% of the inhabitants have no Luxembourg citizenship. Data for inward migration as measure of citizenship can be obtained from UNDESA (2017).
- *Residentship*: This measure of outward migration reflects the number of citizens who live outside their country of birth. In absolute numbers, this is the highest for India, Mexico, Russia, and China. The number of outward migrants as percentage of total population is the highest for Syria, Libya, and Georgia (UNDESA 2017).
- *Language*: A value of 0 means that all inhabitants speak the same mother tongue and other languages are not common. A value of 100 indicates that the country is characterized by a maximum level of linguistic diversity.

According to UNESCO (2009), linguistic diversity is particularly high in many Sub-Saharan African countries and low in many Latin American and Caribbean countries.
- *Ethnicity*: A value of 0 means that the country is ethnically homogeneous, while a value of 100 is assigned to a country with maximum ethnic diversity. A measure of ethnic fractionalization can be found in Fearon (2003).
- *History of Thought*: This axis indicates whether a country is characterized by a pluralistic or rather uniform mindset. Examples for the latter are strong state ideologies (e.g., Israel, Russia), one-party states (e.g., China, Vietnam), and theocracies (e.g., Iran, Saudi Arabia). Pluralist countries are often located at the crossroads of different intellectual–historical directions. They typically emphasize the freedom of information and right to privacy (e.g., Sweden, Netherlands). An indicator of this dimension is the World Press Freedom Index (https://rsf.org/en/ranking).

Figure 2.6 illustrates the cultural pentagons of Germany, India, Russia, and the United States. India is characterized by a very large linguistic and ethnic diversity. There are 22 officially recognized languages, 30 languages spoken by more than a million native speakers and 122 spoken by more than 10,000 people, according to the 2001 Census (Benedikter 2009). Similarly, India's ethnic fractionalization is among the

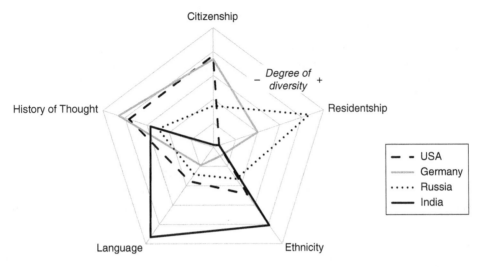

Figure 2.6 Cultural pentagon model

highest in the world (Fearon 2003). The country has a pluralistic mindset with different ideologies that are articulated rather openly. Despite the—compared to other countries—absolute high number of nonresident Indians, the ratio of outward migrants to the entire population is very small. The share of foreigners living in India is insignificant.

The *United States* is also a pluralist and multiethnic country with Whites, African Americans, Asians, and Hispanics constituting the largest ethnic groups. English as the national language is increasingly being supplemented by Spanish and—at least in some regions—Chinese (Lippi-Green 2012). Being the largest immigration country in the world for centuries, the ratio of foreign citizens living in the United States is the highest of the four exemplary countries. On the contrary, outward migration is very low.

While *Russia* is also a multiethnic country, the degree of ethnic diversity is considerably smaller (Kappeler 2014). Russians represent around 80% of the population, with Tatars and Ukrainians as the two largest of 185 officially recognized ethnic minorities. Russian is by far the most important language with a number of other languages, such as Tatar, Chuvash, Bashkir, Chechen, and Ukrainian spoken in various regions of the country. As a consequence of the breakup of the former Soviet Union, outward migration is among the highest in the world. While the absolute number of foreigners living in Russia is also high, their share of the entire population is lower than in India and the United States. The intellectual–historical diversity is the lowest among the exemplary countries. After a brief period of pluralism in the late 1980s and 1990s, the Russian government is enforcing an increasingly uniform state ideology (David-Fox 2015).

Germany scores the highest among the four exemplary countries on the intellectual–historical axis. Freedom of expression is one of the most protected rights, which excludes mainly only the glorification of the Nazi regime (Payandeh 2010). Around 15% of the residents migrated to Germany from other countries, making Germany host to the second-highest number of international migrants after the United States. On the contrary, outward migration is much lower. The largest ethnic groups of non-German origin are the Turkish, Polish, and immigrants from the successor states of the Soviet Union and Yugoslavia (Mushaben 2008). Over 95% of the population speak standard German or German dialects as their first language.

Recognized minority languages are Danish, Frisian, Romani, and Sorbian—a West Slavic language spoken by an ethnic minority in the Lusatia region of eastern Germany.

The cultural pentagon model is not only useful to illustrate the homogeneity and heterogeneity of a country on various dimensions but allows also to derive important management implications. These will be discussed in Chapter 7.

2.4 ORIGINS OF CULTURE

A variety of approaches to the factors and mechanisms that influence the formation of different cultures exist. In particular, the role of the physical environment, legal–political system, economy, religion, and biology is frequently mentioned in intercultural management literature and adjacent fields, such as anthropology, psychology, and sociology (Minkov 2011). The integration and systematization of these factors leads to three theories of the emergence of culture (Figure 2.7).

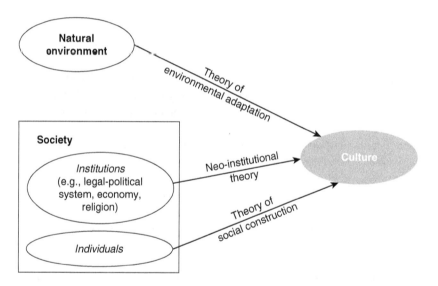

Figure 2.7 Theories of the emergence of cultures

The **theory of environmental adaptation** assumes that people who live in a particular environment face similar problems and are equipped with similar resources. To deal with their specific problems, they develop a unique set of cultural traits in a trial-and-error process that are functional in this specific environment, but may be useless or even dysfunctional under different conditions. The emergence of culture is thus regarded as a process of environmental adaptation that is evaluated in terms of *functionality*.

Neo-institutional theory assumes that societies develop specific institutions (e.g., legal–political system, economy, religion) which gain legitimacy through the acceptance of its members. Strong institutions facilitate the development of particular values, norms, and behaviors that are commonly followed by the society (Kara & Peterson 2012). The emergence of culture is therefore regarded as a process of institution building and institutional governance that is evaluated in terms of *acceptance*.

The **theory of social construction** assumes that any cultural traits are socially situated. Reality is not objectively given, but individuals perceive and construct reality through interaction with others. Frequent and complex interactions facilitate the development of particular values, norms, and behaviors that are commonly shared and accepted by the society. The emergence of culture is thus regarded as process of social construction that is evaluated in terms of *collective sense-making*.

The relationship between the environment, society, and culture is not unidirectional. Culture also shapes individuals and institutions and facilitates or impedes them to cope with their environment. However, in the following, the focus will be on the origins and not on the consequences of culture. These will be discussed in Chapter 4.

2.4.1 Physical Environment

There is general consensus in the intercultural management literature that a society's values, norms, and behaviors are shaped by the physical environment in which it lives. According to the theory of environmental adaptation, the natural conditions (e.g., latitude, elevation, climate, water and soil resources, flora and fauna, mineral resources, and the strategic importance of the society's physical location) offer specific opportunities and cause specific challenges that favor the emergence of particular cultural traits (van de Vliert 2009).

For many centuries, the geographic and topographic characteristics largely influenced the development of particular traditional occupations, such as agriculture, trade, hunting, and seafaring. Some natural environments facilitated settledness and others nomadism. Different occupations and forms of life produced different values as well as social relationships and ties. For example, nomadic cultures characterized by small groups developed strong in-group collectivism, while the permanent cohabitation in larger communities required the emergence of abstract rules. The institutionalization of specific legal and political norms was therefore to great extent the result of different natural conditions as well as the technologies and social structures people developed to cope with the challenges of nature (Berry 1976; Triandis 1995a).

Empirical research in this context refers particularly to the **role of climate**. For example, van de Vliert et al. (2000) observe a link between temperature and *citizen competitiveness*. Individuals in warmer countries appear to try harder when they are in competition with others and find winning more important in both work and games. This observation is explained by the fact that life in the past was more arduous for individuals in cold than in hot climates, requiring more cooperation to survive.

Similarly, Hofstede (2001) shows that decreases in geographic latitude as indicator of a country's warmer climate correlate with greater *power distance*. In the relatively cold climates of, for example, North America and Scandinavia, survival and population growth are more dependent on domain knowledge and collaboration than in the relatively hot climates of, for example, Central America and South-East Asia. Because warmer environments are less challenging and easier to cope with, authorities are obeyed rather than questioned—even if their policies are regarded as improvable.

A 53-nation study of van de Vliert et al. (1999) provides evidence for more inequality of *gender roles* in temperate climates than in colder and hotter climates. In countries with temperate climates (e.g., Italy and

Japan) where adaptation is less critical, men are supposed to be more assertive, tough, and focused on material success, whereas women are supposed to be more modest, tender, and concerned with the quality of life. In contrast, the greater joint investments of men and women in adapting to more extreme climates favor the development of cultural customs characterized by sacrifice, delay of gratification, and cooperation by both genders. As a consequence, in countries with relatively low temperatures (e.g., Norway and Sweden) or relatively high temperatures (e.g., Indonesia and Thailand), gender roles are more similar.

More recent research argues that the influence of climate on culture is not linear, but **moderated by the level of economic development**. "A more accurate understanding of culture may unfold when we think of (the environment) as an integrated climato-economic habitat requiring integrated cultural responses" (van de Vliert 2009, p. 25). According to this view, the impact of the demandingness of thermal climate on culture depends on the level of collective wealth. The availability of financial resources allows individuals to protect themselves against very cold and very hot temperatures and makes harsher climates less threatening. Thus, extreme climate particularly influences the culture of poorer societies.

2.4.2 Legal-Political System

The role of the legal–political system for the formation of different culture is particularly discussed from the perspective of neo-institutional theory. A nation's constitution and laws set the general framework that **regulates the coexistence of all members of a society**. The state has the monopoly on the legitimated use of physical force and can direct the behavior of individuals through coercion. It can also formulate expectations and create or limit scope for action in the form of education and health policy, social policy, foreign policy, etc. For example, investments into education are likely to promote progressive values, while public health care and social welfare reduce the role of the family as social safety net, thus stimulating individualism. Also, governments can erect legal and economic boundaries that impede exchange with other countries, thus promoting conservativism and ethnocentrism.

Empirical studies in this context focus particularly on the cultural **implications of democratic vs. authoritarian systems** and compare, for example, Western societies with the former socialist countries in Eastern Europe. Since a major characteristic of these regimes was the attempt to indoctrinate their people in the form of massive socialist propaganda, it could be expected that this also affected their culture. However, existing research is indecisive.

For example, Kaasa, Vadi, and Varblane (2014) analyze cultural differences within Germany and reveal higher levels of power distance for the eastern German states than for western Germany. Moreover, two of the five eastern German states show the lowest level of individualism. However, the level of individualism in the other three eastern German states is above the German average and significant differences for power distance are also found among the western German states. It is therefore questionable whether the observed differences were caused by the former division of the country or have different reasons, such as different levels of economic development or religious affiliations (protestant vs. catholic vs. atheist).

Similar results are also revealed by studies in other countries. Ardichvili and Kuchinke (2002) compare cultural values of over 4,000 managerial and nonmanagerial employees in Russia, Georgia, Kazakhstan, Kyrgyzstan, Germany, and the United States. The study finds that the four former USSR countries differ primarily by much lower levels of power distance and femininity as compared to the two Western countries. However, significant differences are found not only between the two groups of countries but also between individual countries within these groups.

While existing research shows that the legal–political system of a country impacts its culture, this effect cannot be described in terms of simplified dichotomies between democratic and authoritarian systems. Authoritarian regimes are obviously able to impose certain symbols and rituals, but have only low influence on the deeper value systems of their people. Many Eastern Europeans dissociated themselves mentally from the socialist propaganda and followed it mainly ritualistically. The "Homo Sovieticus" (Zinoviev 1986) publically obeyed to everything that government imposed, but at the same time developed an inner opposition to the socialist ideology which became apparent in private life. Given the **inertia of cultural change**, it is also plausible to argue that the authoritarian rule in Eastern Europe did not last long enough to displace deeply embedded beliefs with socialist values. Minkov (2011, p. 33) therefore concludes: "It is conceivable that people who lived for centuries under oppressive regimes nowadays have cultures that distinguish them from those who lived under more liberal conditions. But the totalitarian governments that ruled Eastern Europe for half a century did not have enough time to produce a massive cultural change."

2.4.3 Economy

Economic historians have frequently demonstrated a strong link between the type of economy prevalent in a society and its culture. Many societies today still carry a cultural imprint in them that was left by the type of economy they practiced for centuries. *Nomad hunters and gatherers* are typically characterized by a high degree of individualism because it is more effective to gather food in a dispersed rather than in a collective manner. Hunting and gathering societies therefore encourage independent decision-making, assertiveness, and risk taking. On the contrary, *sedentary farmers* are characterized by a more interdependent social orientation and obedience to group norms. Moreover, they tend to foster compliance, conscientiousness, and conservatism (Berry 1976; Triandis 1995). Recent research in East Asian countries further revealed that variations in farming practices could result in cultural differences. For example, *rice farming* requires farmers to coordinate water usage with their neighbors and to establish irrigation systems. *Wheat farming*, on the other hand, can rely on rainfall and requires less social coordination (Talhelm et al. 2014).

The **transition from agrarian to industrial and later service societies**, however, reduced the need for environmental adaptation and subsequently affected cultural values. Industrial and service societies are characterized by a high degree of anonymity and decreasing social ties which foster individualism. This shift from cohesive groups of family members and friends (collectivism) to looser ties between individuals (individualism) is further amplified through increased regional and sectional mobility of labor.

Inglehart (1997) also points to the important **role of growing national wealth**. The members of richer nations are more tolerant, less religious, and less concerned about survival, while placing a greater emphasis on the quality of life. This postmodernization of societies is also reflected in growing individualism and negatively associated with power distance (Hofstede 2001).

While the strong relationship between economic development and cultural values is demonstrated by several empirical studies, there is less consensus about its **causality**. Some authors argue that economic wealth fosters self-enhancing values (Inglehart 1997, 2018), while others postulate that the individualization of societies and the dissolution of traditional ties promote economic development (Hayek 1949; Lewis 2003).

As mentioned earlier, the level of economic development can also **moderate the impact of other factors** on culture. For example, economic prosperity diminishes the role of climate (van de Vliert 2009).

Similar effects on the relationship between religion and culture can be expected. Religious beliefs tend to be stronger in poorer than in richer countries with secular legal–political systems (Inglehart 2018).

2.4.4 Religion

The role of religion as major source of cultural differences is frequently discussed in intercultural management literature (Peltonen 2020). World religions, such as Christianity, Judaism, Islam, Buddhism, and Hinduism, were created many centuries ago and are therefore likely to have a significant impact on culture (Table 2.2). One of the oldest and most prominent advocates of this view was *Max Weber* (1930) who argued that the *Protestant Ethics* of thrift and hard work favored the development of a particular capitalist culture. In a similar vein, authors speak of an *Islamic work ethic* (Yousef 2000; Ali & Al-Owaihan 2008), a *Buddhist work ethic* (Gould 1995), or a *Confucian work ethic* (Yeh & Xu 2010).

The role of religion for the emergence of culture has been analyzed in various empirical studies—with inconclusive results. Huntington (1993) argues that religion not only shapes human values but that **religion is a major differentiator of people**. "Even more than ethnicity, religion discriminates sharply and exclusively among people. A person can be half French and half-Arab and simultaneously even a citizen of two countries. It is more difficult to be half-Catholic and half-Muslim" (Huntington 1993, p. 27). In line with neo-institutional theory, Inglehart and Baker (2000, p. 49) find that the historically dominant religion of a nation impacts on both survival versus self-expression and traditional versus secular rational values. They conclude that "a history of Protestant or Orthodox or Islamic or Confucian traditions give rise to cultural zones with distinct value systems that persist after controlling for the effects of economic development."

At the same time, however, the authors state that "the differences between the values held by members of different religions within given societies are much smaller than are cross-national differences" (Inglehart & Baker 2000, p. 19). This applies particularly to people from different **religious denominations that have cohabited in one in the same society for a long time**. For example, Schwartz (1994) finds only moderate differences between Israeli Muslim Arabs and Israeli Christian Arabs on most of his seven value dimensions. In fact, the two groups are closer together than any two nations or even some large Chinese cities. Schwartz concludes that Christianity and Islam have virtually no divisive effect on the values of their followers. Similarly, Esmer (2002) finds only small value differences between Muslims and non-Muslims within a number of countries where these communities had cohabited for centuries.

Historically powerful religious institutions that operate across national borders, such as the Roman Catholic Church, are also likely to have a powerful influence on culture. This applies particularly to the **level of symbols and artifacts**. Indeed, there are several mainly ritualistic elements of culture that have been shaped by global religions. Examples are bans on certain foods (e.g., pork consumption in Islam, beef consumption in Hinduism) and the celebration of religious holidays (e.g., Easter, Ramadan, Diwali, Hanukah). Moreover, some religions were able to create symbols that are used and recognized across national borders, such as signs (Christian cross, Islamic crescent, Jewish star, Buddhist lotus flower) and the design of sacral architecture (churches, mosques, synagogues, temples, etc.).

However, it is doubtful whether any religion is able to make significant impacts on the deeper levels of cultural norms and values across countries. According to Minkov and Hofstede (2014), even world

Table 2.2 Characteristics of major religious groups

	Buddhism	Christianity	Hinduism	Islam	Judaism	Shintoism	Sikhism
Name of deity	The Buddha (did not teach a personal deity)	God	Three main gods: Brahma, Vishnu, Shiva	Allāh	Yahweh	Gods stretch from ancestors, people who died a tragic death or made a great achievement, ancient gods from old texts, nature itself, the weather, terrain, etc.	Waheguru
Founder	Siddhārtha Gautama aka The Buddha	Jesus Christ	No one founder	Muhammad	Abraham	No prophet or founder	Guru Nanak
Holy book	No one book–sacred texts, including Pāli Canon, Taishō Tripitaka, Kangyur	Bible	No one book–sacred texts, including Vedas, Upanishads, Puranas	Qur'an	Torah	No one book–sacred texts including Kojiki, Nihon Shoki, Kogo Shūi, Senmyou	Guru Granth Sahib
Leadership	Dalai Lama, monks and nuns	Pope (for Catholics), priests, ministers, monks, and nuns	Guru, holy man, Brahmin priest	No clergy, but a scholar class called the ulama and the imam, who may lead prayers	Rabbis	Priests (shinshoku, kannushi)	No clergy
Important festivals	Dalai Lama Week, Dharma Day	Christmas, Easter	Diwali, Holi, many local festivals	End of Ramadan	Hanukkah, Passover (Pesach)	Many local festivals (matsuri)	Vaisakhi
Afterlife	Nirvana	Heaven–Hell	Reincarnation	Heaven–Hell	Eden-Gehenna	No belief in life after death	Reincarnation, unless the soul is liberated

(Continued)

Table 2.2 Characteristics of major religious groups (Continued)

	Buddhism	Christianity	Hinduism	Islam	Judaism	Shintoism	Sikhism
Main beliefs	People achieve complete peace and happiness (nirvana) by eliminating their attachment to worldly things.	There is only one God, who watches over and cares for his people. Jesus Christ was his only son. He died to save humanity from sin. People shall observe the Ten Commandments.	The soul never dies, but is continually reborn. Persons achieve happiness and enlightenment after they free themselves from their earthly desires. This comes from a lifetime of worship knowledge and virtuous acts.	People achieve salvation by following the Five Pillars of Islam: Faith, prayer, charity, fasting, pilgrimage to Mecca	There is only one God, who watches over and cares for his people. God loves and protects his people, but also holds them accountable for their sins and shortcomings. Persons serve God by studying the Torah and living by his teachings.	Four Affirmations: Tradition and family, physical cleanliness, love of nature, festivals (matsuri)	People should live according to the Three Pillars: Wake up early in the morning to mediate and worship God, work hard with honesty to earn their living, share their wealth with the deprived and needy.
Followers worldwide (estimated 2001 figures)	362 mn.	2 bn.	820 mn.	1.2 bn.	14.5 mn.	100 mn.	25 mn.
Location	China, Thailand, other Asian countries	Worldwide	India, Pakistan, United States	North Africa, Middle East, Indonesia, United States	Israel, small populations in Europe, Russia, United States	Japan	North India (Punjab)
Main sects (estimated 2001 figures)	56% Mahayana 39% Hinayana 6% Tantrayana	36% Catholic 29% Protestant 22% Orthodox	70% Vaishnavites 25% Shaivites 2% neo-Hindu	83% Sunni 16% Shiite	Orthodox, Conservative, Reformed		Khalsa, Udasi, Nirmala, Nanakpanthi, Sahajdhari, Namdhari Kuka, Nirankari, Sarvaria

Sources: Boyett (2006), Bowker (2006), and Smith (2009).

religions that are present on different continents cannot generate sufficiently complex and frequent interactions among their members across the globe. Their comprehensive study about the role of religion shows that there are far **greater differences in values between nations than between religions**. A hierarchical cluster analysis reveals that—with very few exceptions—most nations have all of their in-country religious groups in a single cluster, without any religious groups from other nations. This means that the nominally different religious groups within a given nation are actually similar in terms of values while being different from the religious groups of other nations, even if they bear the same name and supposedly teach the same tenets. In particular, the authors could not find a single global religion cluster that consists of at least two nominally identical religious groups from two different nations. Minkov & Hofstede (2014, p. 819) conclude: "Global religions do not pull together their subsidiaries in different nations into value-sharing supra-national cultural conglomerates. There is no such thing as worldwide Islamic culture, or Protestant culture, or any worldwide religious culture, that consists of shared basic values."

One reason for the inconsistent results of empirical studies about the role of religion for the emergence of culture is that **religion and ethnic affiliation are often theoretically and empirically confounded**. "When one compares Americans and Japanese, one is often comparing Christians with members of Eastern religions. Thus, cultural differences (e.g., Easterners are collectivist, Westerners are individualist) might be interpreted as religious differences (e.g., Buddhists are collectivist, Protestants are individualist" (Saroglou & Cohen 2013, p. 331). Moreover, future research should not only consider a person's nominal affiliation to a religion but also their degree of **religiousness**. Fundamentalist and orthodox Christians, Muslims, Hindus, and Jews often show similar values and behaviors that differ significantly from moderate followers of these religions (Hood, Hill & Spilka 2018). Thus, the strength of affiliation to a particular religion may have a stronger effect on culture than the differences between the attributes of various religions.

2.4.5 Biology

The role of biology as a source of cultural differences is discussed very controversially. For a long time, the debate was dominated by *Charles Darwin's* (1859) concept of **natural selection**. This is based on the observation of random mutations in the genomes of individual organisms. Throughout the lives of individuals, their genomes interact with their environments to cause variations in traits. Because individuals with certain variants of the trait tend to survive and reproduce more than individuals with other, less successful variants, the population evolves (Boas 1901). On the collective level, this process is argued to bring forth certain genetic compositions which allow societies to cope with their environmental conditions better than others (Mesoudi 2011).

The division of people into races was and is first and foremost a social and political classification, followed and supported by an anthropological construct based on arbitrarily chosen characteristics such as hair and skin color (…). The linking of features such as skin color with characteristics or even supposedly genetically fixed personality traits and behaviors, as was done in the heyday of anthropological racism, has now been soundly refuted. To use such arguments today as seemingly scientific is both wrong and malicious. There is also no scientifically proven connection between

(Continued)

intelligence and geographical origin, but there is a clear connection with social background. Here too, racism in the form of exclusion and discrimination creates supposed races.

(Fischer et al. 2019)

In the twentieth century, the Darwinian concept of natural selection was often **misused by racist regimes** to justify the practice of classifying humans based on biological markers and ascribing particular cultural characteristics to them (Bethencourt 2013; Cazenave 2016). Socially constructed categories were biologized based on pseudo-scientific theories and intentional studies. The cruelest consequences of the various ideologies of racial supremacy and attempts to restore the "purity of the blood" were the criminal ethnic cleansings in Nazi Germany, apartheid-South Africa, Rwanda, former Yugoslavia, and other countries (Najmark 2002; Mann 2005).

While racist ideologies and practices have long discredited research about the relationship between biology and culture, academic studies in this field have regained relevance at the turn of this century. In particular, recent advances in genetics (e.g., the sequence of the human genome) and molecular evolution allow reexamination of the complex relations between genes and culture with more sophisticated methods that are often adopted from natural sciences (Chen & Moyzis 2018) Most of these studies question the Darwinian concept of environmental adaptation and natural selection, and postulate a **complex interaction of genetic disposition and social construction**.

An emerging interdisciplinary research field that integrates theories and methods from cultural psychology, brain sciences, and population genetics is **cultural neuroscience**. It examines whether genes affecting human brain function are likely to influence the adaptation and formation of certain cultural traits (Kim & Sasaki 2014; Warnick & Landis 2015; Chiao et al. 2016). Genes are the fundamental physical and functional unit of heredity. They substantially influence every level of human biology, including regulating neurotransmission within the brain. Research focuses mostly on the serotonin transporter polymorphism 5-HTTLPR which shows robust allelic variation across countries and is therefore regarded suitable for cross-cultural comparisons.

The 5-HTTLPR consists of a 44-base pair insertion or deletion, generating either a long (l) or a short (s) allele. Evidence from behavioral genetics indicates that the s allele of this serotonin transporter gene is associated with increased negative emotion, including heightened anxiety harm avoidance, fear conditioning, attentional bias to negative information, as well as increased risk for depression in the presence of environmental risk factors (Chiao 2009). The prevalence of the s allele of the 5-HTTLPR is the highest in East and Southeast Asian countries (70–80% s carriers), followed by some other Asian countries (India, Turkey), high in Latin America and Southern Europe (around 50% s carriers), low in Europe and North America (50% or less s carriers), and lowest in sub-Saharan Africa (around 20% s carriers) (Chiao & Blizinsky 2010; Murdoch et al. 2013).

Based on this observation, Chiao & Blizinsky (2010) demonstrate in a study across 29 countries that there exists a robust association between allelic frequency of the serotonin transporter gene and cultural values of individualism-collectivism according to Hofstede (2001), controlling for associated economic and disease factors. Geographical regions characterized by cultural collectivism exhibit a greater prevalence of the short allele of the 5-HTTLPR serotonin transporter gene. Being part of a dense and dependable social network appears to particularly benefit those with the putative social sensitivity forms of this gene in the sense that intense social relationships can buffer these individuals from the adverse consequences of stress and improve life satisfaction (Way & Lieberman 2010).

Summarizing the results of existent research in the field of cultural neurogenetics it is plausible to assume that genetic differences account for a certain degree of cultural differences among societies (Nguyen-Phuong-Mai 2020). However, empirical studies are rare, come to different conclusions, focus only on a small number of cultural dimensions, and are often unrepresentative (Mateo et al. 2012). In particular, African and Latin American cultures are hardly studied. Another shortcoming is the focus on single genes, such as 5-HTTLPR, which neglects that genes most likely do not produce societal effects single-handedly, but work synergistically with other genes and enhance or diminish each other's effect (Minkov, Blagoev & Bond 2015).

Moreover, there is strong evidence that the relationship between biology and culture is not unidirectional (Shaules 2015). Genetic predispositions are not only likely to influence the adaptation and formation of cultural norms, but culture can also shape the expression and selection of genes. Thus, the relationship of biology and culture is that of a **gene–culture coevolution** (Kim & Sasaki 2014).

2.5 FUNCTIONS OF CULTURE

Culture has important functions for individuals, organizations, and societies. At the individual level, culture is important for **identity establishment** (Markus & Kitayama 1998). According to social identity theory (Tajfel 1981, 1982), an individual's personal identity is based in part on membership in significant social groups as well as the value and emotional significance attached to that membership. Strong *cognitive and affective identification* with a social group reduces uncertainty in self-concept and bolsters self-identity and self-enhancement. Moreover, it fosters a sense of belonging and inward unity (integration) while it creates outward borders toward other social groups (segregation) at the same time. "That is, culture allows us to feel as though we are a part of something larger than ourselves—from a national organization to an organizational group" (Faulkner et al. 2006, p. 39).

We should be careful meanwhile not to overstate the role culture plays in behavior. What we have called culture—people's values, beliefs, and assumptions—is indeed a major influence on the things they say and do, but it is almost never the whole story, nor even always the most important part of the story. What happens in any given interaction between two or more individuals is the result of numerous causes, from the sublime (such as values) to the very mundane (whether the person slept well the night before) to everything in between (how well the people know each other, how they're getting along today, who else is present, whether either of them is in a hurry, age differences, gender differences, the weather, time of day, and so on) (…). Culture *is* a piece of the puzzle, and it's certainly better to have that piece than not to have it, but it's not the whole picture.

(Storti 2007, p. 12)

Culture also facilitates the orientation of individuals in a social context. Societies establish distinctive norms, values, symbols, and behavioral scripts that convey what is considered right or wrong in a given context. They receive consensual validity through the belief that they are appropriate to resolve a society's specific problems (Chao & Chiu 2011). This **orientation function** of culture as a *normative guideline for appropriate behavior* is particularly strong for individuals with pronounced need for *cognitive closure*, i.e., persons who desire certain and definite answers and rely on established knowledge and tools to make judgments and responses in given circumstances (Kruglanski et al. 2006).

The strength of identification and orientation depends largely on the ability of culture to allocate deeper meaning to the actions of individuals and organizations. Culture can be regarded as a *sensemaking system* that allows to systematically scan, evaluate, and interpret information from the environment. The process of **sensemaking** is triggered by cues, such as issues, events, or situations for which the meaning is ambiguous and outcomes are uncertain (Weick et al. 2005). Moments of ambiguity or uncertainty interrupt people's ongoing flow, disrupting their understanding of the world and creating uncertainty about how to act. When such occurrences are perceived, individuals seek to clarify what is going on by extracting and interpreting cues from their environment and use these as the basis for a plausible account that provides order and makes sense of what has occurred (Weick 1995). A fundamental feature of sensemaking is the cultural context, i.e., individuals perceive situations and human behavior through their cultural lenses and interpret them based on the background of the underlying cultural codes. The episteme of a given culture therefore gives sense to the actions of individuals. Without a cultural backbone, the process of sense-making cannot succeed (O'Leary & Chia 2007).

Another important function of culture is **complexity reduction**. Culture simplifies and canalizes impressions of other people through generalization and classification. Individuals are permanently over-loaded with information from their social environment. For the purpose of complexity reduction, they develop *stereotypes*, i.e., shared beliefs about other people based on social distinctions such as race, language, and origin (Schneider 2004; Wright & Taylor 2007). The process of stereotyping begins with the perception of similarities and differences among people (Figure 2.8). "These various observations are then subjected to an act of categorization, whereby the complexity of the stimuli is reduced to a smaller number of sets. The observed similarities then become attributed to members of the category; and the observed differences then become the basis for differentiating the categories. Finally, generalizations are made, so that all members of a category are believed to share in the same basic attributes of the group, resulting in loss of individuality" (Berry et al. 2011, p. 351).

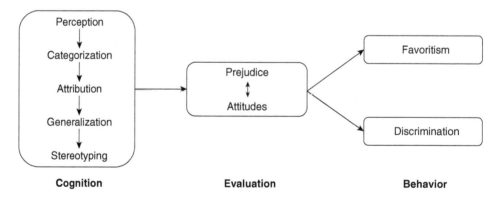

Figure 2.8 Stereotypes, prejudice, favoritism, and discrimination
Source: Adapted from Berry et al. (2011, p. 350).

Stereotypes as cognitive categories are necessary and useful psychological tools to reduce informa-tion-processing complexity and bring order to diversity. They can become malignant, however, when they result in unreflective ethnic, racial, or religious *prejudices*. Prejudices are evaluations toward a culture based on little or no experience (Fiske 1998; Dovidio et al. 2010). While stereotypes are cognitive classifications of other people, prejudices involve positive or—in many cases—negative attitudes and judgments. These may result in *discrimination* (or—in the positive case—favoritism). Discrimination is a behavior that excludes or distances others from resources, institutions, positions, etc., without legitimate reasons. Treating people more or less favorable based on the (perceived) category they belong to is often caused by *cultural attribution error*, i.e., the exaggeration of cultural explanations of human behavior compared to personality-based and environmental factors. Discrimination also involves power and knowledge asymmetries that give people the *ability* to exclude or distance others (Foucault 1977).

In a madly complex world, it takes rules of thumb, cognitive shortcuts and judgment heuristics (...) just to save mental energy and to quickly orientate. So it would be somewhat unrealistic just to celebrate the individual and to always praise the difference everywhere. Generalizations are a useful sorting instrument, mental tools that allow clarifying confrontation as well as the progress of abstraction.

The total individualization of perceptions has its own dangers. At some point, you would no longer be able to deliver descriptions of society, and you would no longer be able to diagnose class and group affiliations (...). If you just want to observe infinite fine grain, you become the ideologue of social microscopy who sees the smallest differences and the finest ramifications everywhere, but loses sight for the big picture.

(Pörksen 2018)

At the organizational and societal level, culture has an important **coordination function**. Culture conveys abstract representations of meaning among people within a collective that can be generalized across contexts. By restricting the permissible diversity of activities in social interactions, culture leads the cognitions and behaviors of individuals in a similar direction. This implicit form of coordination is particularly effective in novel situations of high complexity and uncertainty (Kashima 2000) and more pronounced in tight than in loose cultures (Gelfand et al. 2011). Tight cultures have strong social norms with little tolerance for deviance, whereas loose cultures have relatively weak social norms and higher tolerance for deviant behaviors. Thus, individuals in tight cultures will behave in a more coordinated way than those in loose cultures.

Finally, culture serves **social control function**. It transcends self-interest and promotes common good within a society (Chao & Chiu 2011). Cultural norms and values legitimize societies to sanction behaviors of their members that are deemed disruptive and malignant to the society. Similar to the coordination function, this propensity is more pronounced in tight cultures (e.g., India, Malaysia, Singapore) than in loose cultures (e.g., Estonia, Hungary, Israel) that are more inclined to reinforce adherence to moral conventions and facilitate social order (Gelfand 2018). In this sense, culture provides an ideology that people within a single society could use for control over resources and meanings and create patterns of superordination and subordination (Faulkner et al. 2006). "Culture is manipulated by the more powerful to sustain their privilege and to mask the underlying conflicts of interest between those who have and those who do not have wealth, power, and other valued resources" (Turner 1985, p. 74).

SUMMARY

Culture is a multidimensional and multifaceted concept that can be defined by eight different attributes which describe its evolution (man-made; collectively-shared; learned), purpose (guides behavior; enables adjustment to the environment), and enactment (dynamic; guides behavior; symbolic form).

A well-known concept is Schein's iceberg model that distinguishes three layers of culture, namely visible and conscious symbols and artifacts, partly visible norms and values, as well as invisible and mainly unconscious basic assumptions.

Culture manifests itself in different forms, such as national cultures, industry cultures, and organizational cultures. Intercultural management focuses particularly on national cultures which can be delineated according to five criteria: nation/citizenship, territory/residency, origin/biology, language, and history of thought.

Culture has important functions for individuals, organizations, and societies. It constitutes an essential source of identification, serves as a normative guideline for appropriate behavior, enables individuals to interpret their environment, and reduces complexity.

 Reflection Questions

1. Name an example for each layer of Schein's iceberg model for your national culture based on your experience.
2. Find information about Brazil, China, the Netherlands, Norway, and the United Kingdom and position them in the cultural pentagon model. Which implications can you derive from your positioning?
3. Have you ever experienced that someone wrongly attributed your behavior to your culture instead of your personality? If so, what was the situation like?
4. Explain how religion has impacted the formation of your national culture.
5. From your point of view: To what extent and how does the economic system prevalent in your home country align with your home country's national culture?
6. From your point of view: What is the most commonly believed stereotype about your culture? Do you think that this stereotype is a correct assumption that is helpful in understanding your culture?
7. What are the differences between cultural stereotypes, cultural prejudices, and cultural discrimination? What can individuals and companies do to prevent cultural stereotypes from leading to cultural discrimination?
8. Do you think some layers of Schein's iceberg model are more or less relevant to the formation of stereotypes? If so, which one(s)?

End of Chapter Exercise

Stereotypes about the Germans

Germans are often described as perfectionists, rule-oriented, and obedient to authority. They arrive on time, value planning, and procedures seem to exist for almost all matters of life. Moreover, Germans are often perceived as direct, humorless, and unapproachable.

1. According to your own experience, do you think that these stereotypes about the German culture are true? Are there any differences with regard to regions, professions, industries, and generations?
2. How would you classify these stereotypes according to Schein's iceberg model of culture? How relevant do you regard these stereotypes for intercultural collaboration with Germans?
3. Do you think that Austrians would mention the same stereotypes as North Americans and Japanese when asked about typical characteristics of Germans?

 Further Reading

Extant definitions of culture are discussed by von Keller (1982), Hofstede (2001), and Minkov (2011).

Sackmann (1997) and Schein (2017) exemplify different manifestations of culture.

Common delineations of culture are critically discussed by Taras, Steel & Kirkman (2016).

Warnick & Landis (2015), Chiao et al. (2016), and Nguyen-Phuong-Mai (2020) offer interesting insights into the emerging field of cultural neuroscience.

3

INTERCULTURAL MANAGEMENT RESEARCH: CONCEPTUAL AND METHODOLOGICAL ISSUES

LEARNING OBJECTIVES

By the end of this chapter, you will be able to

- know the historical development of intercultural management research,
- know and compare the main assumptions and implications of comparative management research, cross-cultural management research, indigenous management research, and postcolonial management research,
- understand the differences between emic and etic approaches of intercultural management research,
- evaluate the validity and reliability of intercultural management studies,
- choose an appropriate methodology for an intercultural management study.

Before the concept of culture found attention in management research, it had long been discussed in various other areas, such as military, politics, and cultural studies. In the following, these historical roots and interdisciplinary references are outlined. Afterward, current streams of intercultural management research and their theoretical foundations are discussed. The final section focuses on methodological challenges of intercultural management research. While management research in general must cope with a number of conceptual and methodological issues, these are multiplied when studies in an intercultural context are conducted.

3.1 HISTORICAL ROOTS AND INTERDISCIPLINARY REFERENCES

Research on culture originated in the military context and dates back to **ancient times** (Kennedy, Roy & Goldman 2013). Whenever countries fought war, they were interested in exploring the values and behavior of their enemies to predict their warfare and military strategies (Lee 2011). Several early treatises on warfare have found their way into intercultural management literature since then. The most notable example is Sun Tzu's *The Art of War* (fifth century BC), which became a key source of understanding Chinese strategic thinking and negotiation styles (Liu 2015; Ma & Tsui 2015; Garg & Berning 2017). Julius Caesar's *Gallic War* (58–49 BC) shaped the cultural image of France, Germany, Italy, and Switzerland for many centuries (Wells 1999). Around two millennia later, Carl von Clausewitz's *On War* (1832) became a major source for understanding Prussian military thought and leadership style (von Ghyczy, von Oetinger & Bassford 2001).

The **colonization** of large parts of Africa, Asia, and Latin America extended the interest in foreign cultures to the civil context. For example, after the colonial conquest of India in the seventeenth century, the British became interested in discovering local traditions and languages. The study of culture, however, was less motivated by curiosity than by the attempt to substantiate the presumption of Western superiority (Singh 1996). According to Said (1978), clichéd analytical models were applied which fictionally depicted the Orient as an irrational, psychologically weak, and feminized, non-European Other and negatively contrasted it with the rational, psychologically strong, and masculine West. The study of culture therefore served mainly as implicit justification for the colonial ambitions and the imperial endeavors of the Western powers (Said 1993).

An important historic event that inspired studies of national cultures was the **emergence of nation states** in Europe in the eighteenth and nineteenth centuries. The resolution of empires composed of many countries under a single monarch or ruling state government went along with cultural unification and replacement of various regional dialects and languages by a centralized language with common grammar and vocabulary (Hobsbawm 1992). The struggle for independence and redefinition of national borders required the establishment of common cultural identity and demarcation from other cultures (Inkeles 1997).

The idea that the members of a people possess common cultural characteristics which confer upon them identity and distinguish them from others inspired several **typologies of national characters**. In most cases, the own national character was regarded as the norm and others were portrayed as inferior. This is obvious, for example, in the typology of Darton (1790), which describes Englishmen in a very positive manner and Frenchmen in a rather negative manner (Figure 3.1). Opposite stereotypes were presented by French authors, such as d'Argens (1738) and de Laborde (1743) (Kra 2002).

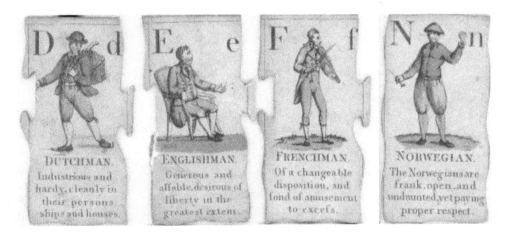

Figure 3.1 National characters according to Darton
Source: Darton (1790).

The valorization of national characters often depended on the political circumstances. Political or economic rivals were usually described in negative terms, while countries which did not pose any threat were represented politely, giving rise to exoticism. Thus country images could shift along with changing political circumstances. For example, "Spain as a world power in the seventeenth century provoked, throughout Europe, fear and disgust, and a strongly marked discourse began to focus on matters like the Inquisition, the ruthless control of Crown and Church over the individual, and the genocidal policies in the Americas. The specific allegations of cruelty featured in this 'leyenda negra' (Juderías 1914) could by the late seventeenth century be transferred wholesale to similar allegations concerning France, while the Spanish decline from world power and its occupation by Napoleonic France made it possible for a more romanticized image to emerge: the Spain of castanets, bullfights, balmy evenings, and colorful passions schematized in Washington Irving's *Sketches from the Alhambra* or Prosper Mérimée's *Carmen*" (Leerssen 2000, p. 277).

In the early twentieth century, **fascist regimes** in Germany, Italy, Japan, and other countries developed typologies of national characters and supplemented them with pseudo-academic arguments. Their purpose was less to describe and explain cultural differences and similarities, as to justify discrimination, nationalism, and racism (Reisigl & Wodak 2001). Foreigners and ethnic minorities were often titled as "animals" or "barbarians" who should be "transformed" or even "extinguished" (Dikötter 2015).

The most horrible form of racism was practiced in Nazi Germany between 1933 and 1945. The Nazis believed that the Aryans had the "purest blood" of all the people on earth and that the Aryan race was superior to all others. A league table of "races" was created with the Aryans as "master race" at the top. Centuries-long residents in German territory who were not ethnic Germans, such as Jews, Romani, along with the vast majority of Slavs and all other persons of color, were labeled as inferior non-Aryan sub-humans and placed at the bottom. They were excluded from Reich citizenship and prohibited from marrying or having sexual relations with persons of "German or related blood."

The Nazis were obsessed by the belief that Aryan superiority was being threatened, particularly by the Jews. According to the Nürnberg Race Laws introduced in 1935, Jews were not regarded as people with particular religious beliefs. Instead, anyone who had three or four Jewish grandparents was defined as a Jew, regardless of whether that individual identified themself as Jewish or belonged to the Jewish religious community. Even people with Jewish grandparents who had converted to Christianity were treated as Jews. This ethnic classification as Jew regularly decided one's life and death, as millions of Jews were killed in concentration camps or died from starvation and diseases during the time of the Holocaust (Burleigh & Wippermann 1991; Wildt 2012).

As early research on culture was less interested in objective analysis than in justifying existing power relations, it was characterized by the **lack of solid methodological and theoretical foundations** (Inkeles 1997). Descriptions of national characters were often based on secondary sources (e.g., fiction literature, diaries, travelogues) instead of rigorous empirical methods, such as participant observation and representative surveys. Moreover, national characters were derived from individual behavior without considering the psychological coherence of the culture as a whole and its various institutions. The result was stereotypical portraits with low explanatory value and of little practical use (Benedict 1934).

This changed after the US intervention in World War II, when a group of anthropologists (notably Gregory Bateson, Ruth Benedict, Geoffrey Gorer, Clyde Kluckhohn, and Margaret Mead) became involved with the US Office of War Information. The primary intention of their **cultural studies** was to produce a statement about the American national character which would help maintain the high morale of Americans during the conflict. Later, its activities turned toward attempts at understanding allied and enemy nations (Neiburg & Goldman 1998). This was accompanied by the application of rigorous methods adapted from ethnography, history, anthropology, and psychology (Malinowski 1948; Lévi-Strauss 1958).

A seminal study conducted at the invitation of the US Office of War Information during World War II is Ruth Benedict's (1946) book, *The Chrysanthemum and the Sword: Patterns of Japanese Culture*, which became very influential for US foreign policy in Japan. After Japan's surrender, the American government decided to maintain the Tenno (Japanese emperor) in power, as had been recommended by Benedict. This helped to ensure stability in postwar Japan and to guarantee that, despite the dropping of the atom bombs on Hiroshima and Nagasaki, a new state of equilibrium between the two countries could be established. This concurrence between US foreign policy and the anthropological analysis of the place of the Emperor in Japanese culture has been cited ever since as convincing evidence of the efficacy of cultural studies (Neiburg & Goldman 1998).

In the 1960s and 1970s, the experience of totalitarian regimes in Nazi Germany, the Stalinist Soviet Union, and Maoist China evoked fundamental skepticism toward the understanding of people's identities as intrinsic properties and state-defined cultural norms and values. **Postmodern and poststructuralist approaches** reject the "grand narrative" (Lyotard 1984) of uniform cultural ideologies and proclaim a pluralist and differentiated concept of culture. Massive migration makes the idea of nation states obsolete and promotes the *emergence of multicultural societies* (Benhabib 2002). Instead of boundaries and the search for commonalities, postmodern and poststructuralist cultural studies refer to the juxtaposition and incommensurability of diverse values, norms, and behavior within societies (Welsch 2008; Barker & Jane 2016).

The **Fall of the Iron Curtain** marked another important turning point in cultural studies. While the main sources of conflict in the world after World War II were ideological and political, more and more they started being replaced by religious and cultural fault lines (Huntington 1997). Globalization and economic modernization began separating people from longstanding local identities and weakening the nation state as a source of identity. This gap is becoming increasingly filled by *nationalist movements* that define belongingness and identity in ethnic and religious terms (Malešević 2006). Examples are the *Hinduization* of India, the *Russianization* of Russia, and the *re-Islamization* of the Middle East. In Europe and North America, the *Identitarian Movement* is gaining support. A common ideology of these movements is the concept of *ethnopluralism*. Different from fascist ideologies, particular cultures are superficially not classified as generally superior or inferior. Instead, it is propagated that different peoples and cultures shall be kept separate from each other to ensure their inner homogeneity and protect them from supposedly negative foreign influences (Zúquete 2018).

The confrontation with nationalist movements in North America and Europe has recently led to a **general questioning of the concept of cultural identity**. From a *political perspective*, the essentialization of culture is criticized for exaggerating putative similarities within particular social groups and differences with others (Appiah 2018). These delineations are not innate and predetermined, but often constructed for political and economic reasons. "There is no natural identity capable of imposing itself on man by the very nature of things" (Bayart 2005, p. ix). In this sense, the perception of being dismissed and marginalized has become a pretext for identity politics and cultural demarcation (Fukuyama 2018). From an *ontological perspective*, the concept of cultural identity is criticized for its understanding of cultures as sets of immutable beliefs instead of mutable practices and communities. By classifying cultures and reducing them to banalities that make up their most distinct differences, the relationships between them inevitably end up in a clash (Jullien 2016). Instead of essentializing and isomorphizing cultural identity, the focus should therefore be placed on commonalities as citizens (Lilla 2018), on culture as activity (verb) and not a thing (noun) (Appiah 2018), and on the "inter" between cultures (Jullien 2016).

The problem of the idea of identity can be illustrated using the example of Europe. "When it came to drafting a preamble to the European Constitution, we wanted to define what constitutes Europe and to agree about its identity. However, this endeavor proved hopeless—we ended up in a dead end. Some claimed that Europe was Christian (thereby referring to its Christian roots). The others insisted that Europe was primarily secular (and thought of the momentous enlightenment and the rise of rationalism). Since one could not agree on a European identity, one finally did not write a preamble (…). What *makes* Europe is, of course, the fact that it is at the same time Christian *and* secular (and more). It has developed *in the distance between* the two: in the great distance of reason and religion, of faith and enlightenment. 'Between' the two is not a compromise, a simple in-between, but a tension between the two, brightening both" (Jullien 2016, p. 49).

3.2 CURRENT RESEARCH STREAMS AND THEORETICAL FOUNDATIONS

3.2.1 Epistemological Perspectives

Research on the **impact of culture on management** was inspired by growing international trade and foreign economic relations in the 1950s and 1960s. Initially, studies from other disciplines, such as anthropology, ethnography, and psychology, were adapted to the business and management context. Notable examples are Florence Kluckhohn & Fred Strodtbeck's (1961) *Variations in Value Orientations* and Edward Hall's (1959) *The Silent Language* which soon became widely cited in intercultural management literature. One of the first publications of management scholars was Geert Hofstede's (1980) *Culture's Consequences* which decisively shaped the emerging discipline of intercultural management research in the following decades. In contrast to previous research on national characters that aimed to explore the unique features of a specific culture (emic approach), the aim of these studies was to develop universal dimensions that allow for identification of similarities and differences between cultures with standardized methodologies (etic approach).

The terms emic and etic originated in *linguistics* and relate to two different **epistemological perspectives** (Pike 1954). *Phonemics* deals with sounds which are specific to a particular language and distinguish one word from another in that language. *Phonetics* is the branch of linguistics that studies the sounds of human speech which are similar in all languages. It is concerned with the physical properties of speech in the areas of speech production, transmission, and perception.

Pike (1954) adapted this concept to intercultural management and distinguishes between emic and etic research approaches (Table 3.1). The **emic approach** attempts "to discover and to describe the pattern of (a) particular (…) culture in reference to the way in which the various elements of that culture are related to each other in the functioning of that particular culture" (Pike 1954, p. 8). It follows in the tradition of *interpretative anthropology and ethnography* and is based on the ontological position that cultures are socially constructed. Hence, it strives to understand culture from "the native's point of view" (Malinowski 1948). The emic approach assumes that culture is best understood as an interconnected, holistic system and aims to explore the idiographic terms and concepts that resonate with the members' self-understanding. Common research methodologies are in-depth field research and participative observation in a single culture (Morris et al. 1999).

Table 3.1 Emic vs. etic approaches of intercultural management research

	Emic approach	Etic approach
Number of cultures studied	One	Several
Reference point of researcher	Within the culture	Outside the culture(s)
Ontological concept	Interpretative	Positivist
Epistemological concept	Exploration (structure discovered by the researcher)	Construction (structure created by the researcher)
Analytical focus	Idiographic	Nomothetic
Constructs to describe cultures	Specific (intracultural)	Absolute or universal (cross-cultural)
Methods of data collection and analysis	Differentiated (qualitative)	Standardized (quantitative)

Source: Adapted from Berry (1969, p. 123).

In the **etic approach**, a researcher "(a) classifies systematically all comparable data, of all cultures in the world, into a single system; (b) provides a set of criteria to classify any bit of such data; (c) organizes (such data) into types the elements so classified; (d) studies, identifies, and describes any new found data in reference to this system which has been created by the analyst before studying the particular culture within which the new data have been found" (Pike 1954, p. 8). The etic perspective is based on a *positivist research paradigm* and the ontological position that cultures are objectively given. It follows in the tradition of comparative and cross-cultural psychology and aims to discover the nomothetic principles of coexistence in social groups. The terms and constructs used for this comparison are created ex-ante by the researcher. Methods in etic research are likely to involve structured observations and standardized surveys across several cultures (Morris et al. 1999).

The differences between emic and etic perspectives of cultural behavior are illustrated by Buckley et al. (2014) using the example of German-Polish acquisitions. One issue that German and Polish managers raise in this study concerns alcohol consumption. For the Germans, any alcohol in the workplace is a problem. The presence of one half-empty bottle of vodka in a locker or hidden behind a crate, for example, is evidence for them that the entire Polish staff occupied the space unacceptably. From a Polish perspective, the presence of only one half-empty bottle of vodka means that the problem of heavy alcohol consumption that was tolerable and normal in many state-owned companies during socialist times is mostly solved, and that the German standards of sobriety are being achieved. "The half-empty bottle does not change, but the conclusions drawn from it, according to the 'emic' categories surrounding it, are dramatically different" (Buckley et al. 2014, p. 319).

The distinction between emic and etic epistemologies is also useful to classify the different directions in intercultural management research. Combining the epistemological perspective with the main research objective, four **major research streams** can be distinguished (Figure 3.2). Their classification and delineation is not clear-cut but partly overlapping, and the terminology is often used inconsistently. Within the four research streams, a broad spectrum of approaches exists that have been labeled more often metaphorically as a chaotic "jungle" than a well-ordered "zoo" (Schollhammer 1969; Redding 1994). There is also a striking imbalance between emic and etic approaches. While the etic perspective is dominant in scholarly research, the emic perspective has only recently gained attention. Accordingly, positivist research methodologies are elaborated and frequently applied, while subjectivist and interpretative methodologies are less common and less accepted (D'Iribarne et al. 2020).

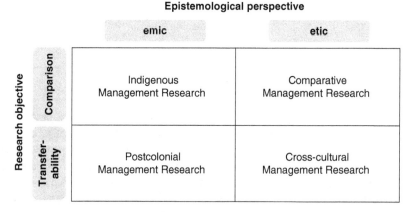

Figure 3.2 Major streams in intercultural management research

3.2.2 Comparative Management Research

Comparative management research aims to explore similarities and differences between values and management styles across cultures. It originates in **contingency theory** and assumes that management practices are influenced by the situational conditions under which they are implemented. In the 1970s, researchers from the *Aston Group* conducted several large-scale research projects in which the impact of factors such as size, technology, and environment on organizational structures is explored (Pugh & Hickson 1976). Early research concluded that "these relationships (…) hold for work organizations in all societies" (Hickson et al. 1974, p. 74) and that management principles are valid all over the world. The key argument for this **culture-free approach** is that the process of industrialization does not leave any scope for cultural differences to influence management. "The industrial process has its own set of imperatives: things which all societies must do if they hope to conduct a successful march to industrialism" (Harbison & Myers 1959, p. 117).

Later studies criticized the dominant logic of industrialization and argued for a **culture-bound approach**. In particular, institutional theory (Meyer & Scott 1983) and economic systems theory (Maurice et al. 1980; Child 1981) emphasize the role of culture in determining management styles. Moreover, the relevance of culture is stressed in anthropological and sociopsychological studies (Triandis 1980; Berry et al. 2011; Sorge, Noorderhaven & Koen 2015). The culturalist perspective culminated in the conclusion of Hofstede (1980, p. 372) in his landmark study of work-related cultural differences and their management implications: "The main finding is that organizations are culture-bound."

The opposition between the universalist and the culturalist approach can be resolved by considering different **moderators of cultural influence on management**, such as management functions, hierarchical levels, and industries (Miller 1987). Existing research shows that the impact of culture on management varies between *management functions*, and that technical functions of management are less affected by cultural differences than behavioral functions. Technical functions (e.g., auditing, controlling, strategy) are dominated by an economic logic and rely mostly on technocratic instruments, such as standardized procedures and IT systems. On the contrary, behavioral functions (e.g., marketing, human resource management) deal with and depend on human behavior. Accordingly, the influence of culture is usually stronger (Aycan et al. 2000; Gelfand et al. 2007).

Moreover, culture has a stronger impact at lower *hierarchical levels* than at the top of organizations. Higher ranking individuals were often educated at institutions with similar curricula and have more intercultural experience and a more cosmopolitan mindset (Levy et al. 2007; Osland et al. 2012). Thus, they are likely to be less influenced by their native culture. On the contrary, individuals at lower hierarchical levels are more deeply embedded in their local communities and have often more ethnocentric attitudes. Their behavior is therefore more culture-bound.

The influence of culture on management also differs between *industries*. Large intercultural differences can be observed in service industries that require frequent customer interaction, such as tourism, banking, and consulting. For example, service expectations, brand evaluations, and customer behavior vary largely across cultures (Furrer et al. 2000; Soares et al. 2007). The impact of culture is lower in industries with strong technological imperatives or where natural laws are relevant, such as in the steel industry and chemical industry. As Braun and Warner (2002, p. 13) emphasize in this context: "An oil refinery is an oil refinery."

Comparative management research has been the **dominant paradigm** in culture-related management studies. For example, the seminal works of Hofstede (1980, 2001), Hampden-Turner & Trompenaars (2012), Schwartz (1992, 1994), and GLOBE (House et al. 2004) are based on this paradigm (Chapter 4). Despite their great impact, however, the underlying emic and positivist epistemology has been frequently criticized (e.g., Søndergaard 1994; McSweeney 2002; Tung & Verbeke 2010). This critique has particularly inspired indigenous (Section 3.2.4) and postcolonial (Section 3.2.5) approaches which are based on an emic and subjectivist epistemology. So far, however, these approaches have received less attention in intercultural management literature and practice.

3.2.3 Cross-Cultural Management Research

While the main aim of comparative management research is to compare different cultures, the focus of cross-cultural management research is on the **transferability of management practices across cultures**. The rise of multinational corporations stimulated interest in the question of whether management concepts developed in one culture can be successfully applied in other contexts as well. Thus, in contrast to comparative research, the unit of analysis is not single culture, but their interactions on an individual and organizational level. Despite this main difference, the epistemological concepts and research methodologies are similar and several studies mix comparative and transformative research aims (Usunier, van Herk & Lee 2017). As in comparative management research, two opposite positions exist.

The **standardization approach** proposes that successful management principles can be transferred to other countries without major adaptations. The universal validity and transferability of management concepts is reflected in many US-American management classics. For example, the seminal works on corporate strategy by Porter (1980), organizational learning by Senge (1991), and innovation management by Christensen (1997) contain almost no reference to culture. Instead, it is implicitly assumed that these concepts are universal and unchangeable. This view is supported by several examples of US-American firms, such as Apple, Coca-Cola, and McDonald's, which successfully standardize their management and marketing practices globally.

In contrast, many European—and recently also Asian—scholars argue that different cultures require different management styles. The **differentiation approach** stresses the great impact of cultural differences and recommends individuals and organizations that operate in other cultures localize their behavior accordingly: "When in Rome, do as the Romans do." A prominent concept on the *individual level* is Black et al.'s model of cultural adjustment, which assumes that expatriate managers need to adapt to the local culture to achieve high job performance and job satisfaction (Black, Mendenhall & Oddou 1991). On the *corporate level*, the need for local adaptation is often stressed, for example, in the international market entry literature (e.g., Brouthers 2002; Tihanyi, Griffith & Russell 2005).

Like comparative management research, cross-cultural studies have identified several **moderators** that facilitate or impede the transferability of management concepts across cultural borders. An important finding is that the transfer of *behavioral functions* is more difficult than of technical functions. Particularly, marketing and human resource management require a high degree of local responsiveness (Schmid & Kotulla 2011; Edwards et al. 2016).

Moreover, the transfer of management concepts is easier at higher than at lower *hierarchical levels*. International human resource management research reveals that people at the top level have often similar educational backgrounds and share similar professional values (e.g., Levy et al. 2007; Osland et al. 2012). They are typically more fluent in other languages, which allows them to communicate with their counterparts in other cultures more easily. At lower hierarchical levels, transferability is often impeded by less cultural open-mindedness. While in industrialized countries, the influx of management practices from other cultures tends to be associated with the fear of job losses, it is often perceived as neocolonial behavior in developing countries. In both cases, resistance of employees is likely.

A vivid example of how the transferability of management practices differs between hierarchical levels is the failed merger of Daimler and Chrysler (Vlasic & Stertz 2000; Hammerich & Lewis 2013). Shortly after this "merger of equals, merger of growth, and merger of unprecedented strength" (former Daimler-Benz CEO Jürgen Schrempp) was announced, a post-merger integration team was installed to manage the expected intercultural challenges. The team was led by Andreas Renschler, a Daimler-Benz senior executive who had worked several years in the United States and was well-versed in the German and American cultures. Initially, everything seemed to work well. As Robert Lutz, former Vice-Chairman of Chrysler, realized: "There was a remarkable meeting of the minds at the senior management level. They look like us, they talk like us, they're focused on the same things, and their command of English is impeccable. There was definitely no culture clash there."

At the lower hierarchical levels, however, severe cultural clashes occurred. While the American managers preferred an informal communication style, their German colleagues relied on formal guidelines and procedures. They emphasized on uncompromised quality, while Chrysler was known for its flexibility and cost-controlled working style. Integration was also impeded by language barriers. While few Chrysler managers spoke German, their colleagues at Daimler-Benz were often reluctant to turn to English. Intercultural communication for people living in a part of Germany that advertises itself with the slogan "We can do everything—except speaking proper German" is obviously particularly challenging.

The interest of cross-cultural management research in intercultural interactions has inspired the development of several **measures of cultural distance**. While early approaches, such as the *Kogut-Singh Index*, conceptualize cultural distance based on etic dimensions of culture (Kogut & Singh 1988), more recent research argues for the integration of emic approaches. One example is the *concept of cultural frictions* (Shenkar 2012) which considers the historic and political relations between two cultures. These and other concepts of cultural distance will be discussed in Chapter 5.

3.2.4 Indigenous Management Research

The basis of indigenous management research is the observation that the canon of management knowledge almost entirely originated in Western countries. Although the impact of cultural differences has been increasingly recognized since the 1960s, the conceptualization, measurement, and interpretation of management studies is often strongly affected by a Western bias. However, management research that is based on European and North American epistemological traditions is likely to "ignore the rich resources, both practical and intellectual, which exist in non-Western societies" (Marsden 1991, p. 32). Indigenous management research addresses this limitation and seeks to explore management knowledge developed in non-Western countries for two main reasons, namely to better understand management concepts and techniques developed and applied in these countries and to contribute to global management knowledge in a broader sense (Holtbrügge 2013).

The attempt to **better understand management concepts and techniques developed in non-Western countries** relates to the fact that seemingly universal paradigms can often not sufficiently explain phenomena discovered in studies based on etic research methodologies. For example, Xu and

Yang (2009) reveal in a study of the indigenous conceptual dimensions of corporate social responsibility (CSR) in China that several widely accepted CSR dimensions in the Western world have no embodiments in China. Das (2010) shows how the Indian view of good management practices is deeply rooted in ancient Indian epics, such as the Mahabharata and the Ramayana. Also Holtbrügge and Garg (2016) illustrate that Indian management concepts often originate from ancient local philosophies and practices (Table 3.2). Jackson et al. (2008) demonstrate how the success of firms in Africa is affected by the use of local management techniques that have evolved over several centuries. In a similar vein, Ledeneva (1998) and Puffer et al. (2010) argue that the use of informal agreements and connections in Russia should not always be misinterpreted as corrupt and inefficient. Thus, to understand the success of firms from non-Western countries, it becomes essential to analyze indigenous management concepts such as, for example, *ubuntu* (South Africa), *jugaad* (India), *guanxi* (China), or *blat* (Russia) and their impacts on management behavior and outcomes in these countries (Holtbrügge 2013).

Table 3.2 Ancient Indian philosophies and modern management equivalents

Ancient Indian philosophy	Modern management practice	Examples
Sattwa (knowledge, wisdom, ethical and moral conduct)	Leadership: Managing "self" by conducting honest, ethical, and morally valuable business, for the betterment of the society	N.R. Narayana Murthy, Ratan Tata
Rajarshi (Arthashastra)	Good of the people, nation, and the community	Tata Group, Infosys
Rajas (passion, action, and perseverance)	Empowering and engagement of employees: support, knowledge, recognition, and transformation	HCL, Bank of Baroda
Karma Yoga	Vision, passion, hands-on, and direct involvement	HDFC, ICICI, Baggit
Dharma (duty)	Corporate social responsibility	Tata, Infosys
Simple living high thinking	Being Indian in everything	Future Group
Nishkam karma	Shakti (rural self-help), enabling people to rise	Hindustan Unilever
Periodic change of management (Arthashastra)	Succession Planning/Mentorship	Tata Group, Infosys

Source: Holtbrügge & Garg (2016, p. 71).

There are many examples of famous Indian managers relying on ancient Indian wisdom to solve problems in modern India. "One example is the appointment of Devdutt Pattanaik as India's first chief belief officer by the Future Group of India (…). Pattanaik is a leadership consultant, mythologist, and author whose works focus largely on the areas of myth, mythology, and management. In his books he uses stories, rituals, and symbols drawn from Hindu, Jain, and Buddhist mythology to provide a more subjective way of approaching management. He argues that the Indian way of doing business accommodates subjectivity and diversity, and offers an inclusive, more emphatic way of achieving success. By stressing the relevance of indigenous management concepts in daily business operations, he seeks to leverage the power of myth in business, management, and life" (Holtbrügge & Garg 2016, p. 66).

Studying indigenous management concepts can also be useful for understanding the implicit assumptions of Western theories of management and thus **contribute to global management knowledge** (Welge & Holtbrügge 1999; Tsui 2004). "'Local', 'traditional' or 'folk' knowledge is no longer the irrelevant vestige of 'backward' people who have not yet made the transition to modernity, but the vital well-spring and resource bank from which alternative futures might be built" (Marsden 1991, p. 32). Consequently, the analysis of management concepts originating from non-Western countries may improve seemingly universal theories of corporate strategy, innovation management, or leadership (Cappelli et al. 2010; Leung 2012). "As countries such as India and China aspire to play an increasingly important role in the world economy and indigenous managers attempt to build and lead world-class companies, possibilities of the emergence of a richer model for managers need to be explored (…). The choice is clearly for not only the indigenous management to tap into its deep-routed ethos, but also to contribute the contemporary concepts and practices of governance in developing a true globally relevant cross-verging managerial frame to emerge" (Chatterjee 2009, p. 138).

A major challenge of indigenous management research is the **lack of generally accepted research methods**. Established criteria of intercultural management research, such as representativeness, cross-cultural validity, etc., may not apply because indigenous research is often interested in analyzing unique, exceptional, and context-specific phenomena. While this leaves much room for innovative research approaches, indigenous studies often receive less attention in intercultural management literature (Holtbrügge 2013).

3.2.5 Postcolonial Management Research

Like indigenous management research, postcolonial management research is based on the observation that the canon of management knowledge is largely dominated by theories and practices developed in Europe and the United States. This is criticized not only for its epistemological and methodological bias but also for its **political and ideological hegemony**. "The economics-based positivist paradigm is (not only) seriously inadequate (…), but dangerously imperialist" (Redding 1994, p. 323).

While military power was used to colonize large parts of Africa, Asia, and Latin America in previous centuries, colonization is argued to continue through the **domination of knowledge** (Young 2003). Postcolonial management research seeks to disrupt the hegemonic posture of Western management knowledge, demonstrating that it is not a superior form of knowledge, but a particular form among many others, and revealing its historical, political, cultural, and ideological limitations. It questions the presumption that Western knowledge can speak on behalf of the world through its categories and argues that the "West" is an ideological construction (Westwood & Jack 2007).

One of the main foundations of postcolonialism is the **concept of binarism**, most prominently developed by Edward Said in his seminal work *Orientalism* (1978). Said argues that the West created a structure of hierarchical binaries in which the Occident was coupled with privileged terms like "civilized," "modern," and "scientific," while the Orient was linked with terms like "savage," "archaic," or "superstitious." This binary thinking considered the entire non-Western world as something logically inferior to the West and legitimized Western supervision, guidance, and assistance for non-Western countries in becoming fully civilized and developed (Banerjee & Prasad 2008).

Just as colonialism classified between the "modern West" and "backward rest," management research is argued to create a seemingly coherent canon organized around rational management where non-Western concepts are represented as exotic and inferior (Frenkel & Shenhav 2006; Fougère & Moulettes 2007). The result of this form of dichotomist thinking is not only a strongly biased view of non-Western cultures but also a reductionist self-perception of the West. "Even though it is usually 'the non-West' that is stereotyped most obviously and crudely, the depiction of the West can also become, through a mirror effect, a highly stereotypical one" (Fougère & Moulettes 2011, p. 14).

An example of neocolonialism through measurement is the corruption perception index (https://www.transparency.org/research/cpi). As argued by de Maria (2008), the conceptualization of this measure is not objective and universal, but strongly affected by Western bias. For example, it does not distinguish between unproductive and productive forms of corruption that are particularly relevant in countries with weak institutional regimes. Moreover, de Maria argues with regard to African countries that the Western conception of corruption interiorizes African problems rather than looking at external factors such as debt, dumping, poor commodity prices, and globalization lockout. The corruption perception index is also likely to tolerate Western-initiated corruption in Africa, for example, in big project bribery, but not host country corruption. Finally, corruption is not so much targeted for the injustices it extracts from ordinary people, but for the structural problems it causes for private investment. De Maria (2008, p. 189) concludes: "Clearly one cannot evaporate such a powerful construct as 'corruption' from any modern analysis; social, organizational, historical or economic. Nor can one ignore that very bad things happen in the chemistry between power, money, and violence in Sub-Saharan Africa. There is a real phenomenon here (…). (However, the analysis should not be based on) transplanted, culturally desensitized explanations about wrongdoing."

Instead of binary thinking prevalent in positivist epistemology, postcolonial management research proposes the **concept of hybridization**. Based on the idea of "*cultural third spaces*" (Bhabha 1994), cultures are not regarded as pure, given, and fixed, but historic constructs that are shaped and reshaped through interactions with other cultures ("*creolization*"). The transfer of management practices to other cultures can therefore not be adequately conceptualized in terms of standardization and differentiation, but produces hybrid configurations between the original and the new (Frenkel 2008). While positivist approaches of intercultural management research are concerned with cultural comparisons and cultural multiplicity, postcolonialism therefore focuses on the interactions, negotiations, translations, and mutual enrichments among these cultures (Shimoni 2006; Westwood 2006; Özkazanç-Pan 2008).

The relevance of epistemological third spaces can be illustrated with the example of the African management concept *Ubuntu*. *Ubuntu* is a worldview prevalent in sub-Saharan Africa that is rooted and anchored in people's daily life (Karsten & Illa 2005). It can be literally translated as "man is a man because of man" or "man is man through others" and is based on the fundamental principles of unconditional African collective contribution, solidarity, acceptance, dignity, stewardship, compassion and care, hospitality, and legitimacy (Mbigi 2005). From an *Ubuntu* perspective, the individual cannot be understood without taking into consideration the group of which he or she is a part.

As Seremani and Clegg (2016, p. 177) emphasize, "such an approach is a departure from Descartes who focused solely on the individual with the existence of the individual being based on their ability to think, captured in his famous proposition, 'I think, therefore I am.' In *Ubuntu*, the individual cannot exist if the group does not exist (…). The understanding of the organization changes from an *Ubuntu* perspective because the organization is no longer primarily viewed as a group of individuals who represent their own interest but a group of individuals representing group interests. The organization is hence conceived as a circumscribed space or arena in which group interests converge or collide from an *Ubuntu* standpoint (…)."

Colonial hegemony and "parochial" North American intellectual protectionism cannot only be observed in management practice, but also in **management research** (Boyacigiller & Adler 1991). The vast majority of management journals are published in Western countries, edited by Western scholars, and dominated by Western and Western-based authors. On the contrary, contributions from Africa and Latin America are almost completely absent and those from Asia substantially underrepresented (Murphy & Zhu 2012). Researchers from these countries who want to publish their work in "elite" journals are requested to conform to dominant Western research paradigms and methodologies and to the English language. The pressure is so strong that it is extremely difficult for alternative approaches to find recognition and publication (Jack & Westwood 2010).

Most striking is the significant disparity between the fast growing economic power of many Asian countries and the **underrepresentation of Asia in management journals**. "If practical business and management in Asia is apparently in the process of overtaking its Western counterparts, then either management scholarship is utterly irrelevant to and disconnected from this process, or if not (as management scholars would like to assume), then the processes by which management scholarship is translated into management practice in emerging economies is being completely missed by the 'world-elite' management journals" (Murphy & Zhu 2012, p. 919).

Even more than the other three research streams, postcolonial management research is marked by **intense debates and extraordinary heterogeneity** (Prasad 2003). It comprises diverse approaches such as critical theory, postmodernism, poststructuralism, feminism, and neo-Marxism. Consequently, postcolonial management research provides more often a critical re-reading and deconstruction of existing research (e.g., Frenkel & Shenhav 2006; Fougère & Moulettes 2011) than a coherent and comprehensive research agenda. Only few empirical studies exist in this context and they are often inspired by Michel Foucault's concepts of genealogy and discourse analytics (e.g., Prasad 2009; Boussebaa et al. 2014).

3.3 METHODOLOGICAL CHALLENGES OF INTERCULTURAL MANAGEMENT RESEARCH

Intercultural management research is faced with several methodological challenges. While management research in general must cope with a number of conceptual and methodological issues, these are multiplied when studies in an intercultural context are conducted. Without adequate research methodologies, valid and reliable intercultural management research is impossible (Minkov 2013; Usunier, van Herk & Lee 2017; Ghauri, Grønhaug & Strange 2020).

The key methodological challenge is to *avoid systematic errors and biases of data collected and analyzed in different cultural contexts*. Potential errors and biases depend, among others, on the epistemological perspective (emic vs. etic) and research approach (quantitative vs. qualitative). They may occur at all stages in the research process, i.e., the conceptualization of the research project, data collection, data analysis, and interpretation of results (Table 3.3). If systematic errors and biases—for reasons explained in the next sections—cannot be completely evaded, the results of intercultural management studies need to be interpreted under consideration of their limitations.

Table 3.3 Methodological challenges of intercultural management research

Stages in the research process	Steps	Potential sources of errors and biases
Conceptualization of research project	Identifying relevant and interesting research question	Ethnocentrism, cultural perception bias
	Specifying constructs and relevant variables	Neglecting contextual variations
Data collection	Definition of study population	Sampling bias
	Selection of adequate sampling method	Coverage bias (noncontact bias, nonresponse bias)
	Selection of adequate data collection methods	Measurement bias (calibration, metric, and translation bias), social desirability bias
Data analysis	Aligning theoretical framework and methods of data analysis	Misspecification of culture and its causal effects
	Determining appropriate level of analysis	Ecological fallacy
Interpretation of findings	Explanation of causal inferences	Factual errors and discretionary interpretations
	Derivation of theoretical and practical implications	Causal inference error
	Disclosure of limitations and boundary conditions	Cultural attribution error
		Affirmation bias
		Overgeneralization of findings

3.3.1 Conceptualization of Research Projects

Most research projects start with the **identification of interesting and relevant research questions**. In intercultural management research, this task bears the risk of *ethnocentric bias*. Researchers don't live in a cultural vacuum, but were socialized in a particular culture that is likely to affect their perception of other cultures. This *cultural perception bias* can affect the choice of topics and identification of research questions. What may be interesting and relevant in one country can be irrelevant or nonexisting in other countries.

According to a study by Wong-MingJi and Mir (1997), intercultural management research is strongly dominated by US-based researchers. More than one-third of all articles in international and intercultural management journals between 1954 and 1994 were published by authors affiliated with US-American universities. An additional 15% work in Canada and the United Kingdom, respectively. Around 90 countries were not covered by intercultural management research in this period. Although the number of contributions by authors from countries like China and India has likely increased since then, a strong Anglo-American bias is still prevalent.

One way to cope with the culturally bound focus on particular themes is a multicultural composition of the research team. The *involvement of local researchers* with sound substantial knowledge and relevant local expertise (languages, customs, etc.) can reduce ethnocentrism in study design and ensure the identification of research projects that are relevant and interesting in all considered cultures (Cavusgil & Das 1997). However, local knowledge is not *per se* superior and more valuable. As Briggs (2005, p. 107) argues, "there exists a real danger of over-valorizing and over-romanticizing indigenous knowledge (…). The difficulty then is that indigenous knowledge tends not to be problematized, but is seen as a 'given', almost a benign and consensual knowledge, simply waiting to be tapped into."

The second step in the conceptualization of a research project typically involves the appropriate **specification of constructs and relevant variables**. When the key constructs of a research framework are not identical across different contexts, the study is affected by *construct bias*. Comparative and cross-cultural management studies must therefore ensure construct equivalence across countries. Moreover, potential differences with regard to control and moderating variables must be considered. For example, in some countries, work attitudes are significantly influenced by the economic conditions (e.g., the wage level), while in other countries climate or religiosity may be more relevant. Thus, research models must account for the variety of contextual factors to ensure cross-cultural validity.

Indigenous and postcolonial studies generally question that seemingly universal theories and methodologies appropriately reflect management concepts in diverse cultural contexts. Instead of striving for construct equivalence, they apply research methods where the context is explicitly modeled in the study, either as an independent variable or as a moderator variable. "(This) involves scientific studies of local phenomena using local language, local subjects, and locally meaningful constructs" (Tsui 2004, p. 501). Beyond the **application of context-sensitive research methods** (Denzin et al. 2008; Chilisa 2011), the critical re-reading and deconstruction of "Western" stereotypes and ethnocentrism is pursued (Nkomo 2011; Smith 2012).

3.3.2 Data Collection

3.3.2.1 Sample

Data collection as the second phase of the typical research process starts with the **definition of the study population**. When—like in most research projects—it is not possible to carry out a full survey, a meaningful selection of participants is required (Hult et al. 2008). *Probability sampling* includes different methods of random selection which ensure that each member of the population has a known and equal chance of being selected. This requires full information about the entire population and the characteristics which may influence the results of the study and their interpretation.

In intercultural management studies, relevant characteristics of the population, such as age, education level, income, socioeconomic status, etc., are often not completely known. In this case, *nonprobability sampling* (for example, in the form of convenience or snowball sampling) is used. It is less costly, but bears the risk of not accurately reflecting the general population. While this is generally suited for in-depth explorations of new and unknown phenomena that do not strive for sample representativeness, non-probability sampling entails considerable **selection bias**, precluding robust statistical inferences (Agadjanian & Zotova 2012).

The impact of excluding specific segments of the population from sampling frames differs across countries (Braun 2003). For example, if the rural population is excluded, this will have little effects on findings in highly urbanized societies, such as Monaco, the Netherlands, or Singapore. However, in countries such as Brazil, India, or Russia, the rural population makes up an important segment of the entire population that is likely to differ significantly from the urban population in terms of values and behavior.

Comparative studies in cultures with heterogeneous population structures are also affected by the **trade-off between intracultural and cross-cultural representativeness**. Intracultural representativeness ensures that the selected sample represents the structure of the entire study population in the respective countries. Cross-cultural representativeness means that the structures of the matched country samples are comparable with regard to relevant characteristics and "that apples are not compared with oranges." The more the population structures of the involved countries differ, the less compatible are these two criteria of representativeness.

The **incommensurability of study populations** can be illustrated using the examples of Germany and India. A remarkable difference between these two countries is their share of urban and rural population and their distinct cultural values. In Germany, around 80% of the population lives in urban areas, while in India, the rural population amounts to nearly 70%. Moreover, the definition and delineation of "urban" and "rural" is likely to differ between the two countries.

A comparative study that is based on cross-cultural representativeness would therefore underestimate either the impact of the urban population in Germany or the rural population in India. On the contrary, two country samples based on intracultural representativeness would reflect more the cultural differences between people living in urban and rural areas than cultural differences between the two countries.

Even if researchers manage to select a sample that meets the criteria of representativeness, data collection in intercultural management research may be affected by **coverage bias** (Braun 2003). This can be induced by either the researchers or the respondents and is likely to vary across cultures:

- *Noncontact bias* may be caused by the inability of the researcher to reach potential respondents. Reasons can be, for example, unknown contact persons, limited access to contact information like email or postal address, or insufficient internet connection.

- *Nonresponse bias* refers to the decision on the part of selected respondents not to participate in a study. This may be caused by time constraints, general unwillingness, or unwillingness to provide information about matters that are regarded as sensitive.

Reluctance to participate in empirical studies is particularly high among *marginalized population segments*. These groups may include moonlighters, illegal immigrants, drug users, and sex workers, but—depending on the cultural context—also employees in the LGBTQ community, temporary workers, and employees in low-prestige jobs. Marginalized population segments are not only difficult to reach, but often unwilling to share information that involves sensitive matters that define their marginality. "The same social characteristics and constraints that hinder access to these individuals may also impair their willingness or ability to answer survey questions" (Agadjanian & Zotova 2012, p. 132).

Generally, the willingness to participate in empirical studies differs across countries (Harzing 2000; Stoop et al. 2010). It is the highest in highly urbanized open societies with low crime rates, such as Switzerland, Norway, Finland, and Belgium, and the lowest in former communist and socialist countries, such as Bulgaria, Hungary, and Russia. Large countries with high export share, such as Germany, France, Japan, the United Kingdom and the United States, take a middle position. The refusal rate is further affected by the *geographical and cultural distance* between the researchers' and the respondents' home countries. Collectivist cultures, such as China, are more reluctant to cooperate with foreign researchers than individualistic cultures. Respondents may also be unable or unwilling to participate in studies administered in languages that are not their mother tongue. This form of *language-induced nonresponse bias* is likely to be high in multilingual countries, such as Belgium, Canada, and India, and in many Africa countries where multiple languages are spoken within small geographical areas (Harkness 2003).

3.3.2.2 Methods

Decisions about adequate **methods of data collection** as the second step in this stage of the research process depend largely on the research aims and research epistemology. In comparative management studies, attention must be given particularly to **measurement equivalence** (Hult et al. 2008; van de Vijver & Leung 1997). This ensures that the results are caused by cultural variables and not measurement and scaling artifacts. Three overlapping areas of measurement equivalence can be distinguished: calibration, metric, and translation equivalence (Mullen 1995).

Calibration equivalence requires correct conversions of measures to different contexts. This includes, for example, the country-specific use of units of length (e.g., miles vs. km), weight (e.g., lb vs. kg), volume (e.g., liter vs. gallon), temperature (e.g., °C vs. °F), currencies (e.g., ₹ vs. ¥), etc. Another potential source of error is the different use of points and commas to divide numbers (e.g., 100,000 vs. 100.000 vs. 1,00,000).

Metric equivalence exists when the psychometric properties of data from different cultures exhibit the same coherence, i.e., individuals must perceive and respond to measurement scales in the same way across cultures. There are particularly two threads to metric equivalence in comparative research: inconsistent scoring across populations and scalar inequivalence (Mullen 1995):

- *Inconsistent scoring* refers to the *reliability of measurements across countries*. Individuals in countries that are rarely covered in intercultural management studies may be less familiar with various scaling and scoring formats or research methodologies than those in other countries. Moreover, question-order effects vary across cultures. For example, people from collectivist cultures are more likely to disregard information they had provided earlier when answering a subsequent question (Schwartz 2003).
- *Scalar inequivalence* relates to cultural differences with regard to response styles. It refers to the tendency of respondents to provide a systematic response to questionnaire items regardless of the content of the question and affects the *validity of cross-national comparisons* (Baumgartner & Steenkamp 2001). For

example, Harzing (2006) found in a study across 26 countries strong correlations between response set bias and some of Hofstede's (2001) cultural dimensions. Respondents in countries with high power distance values prefer positive extreme response styles to middle response styles and negative extreme response styles. Collectivism appears to lead to a preference for acquiescence and middle response styles. Uncertainty avoidance is associated with a higher level of acquiescence and extreme positive answers. In order to reduce this form of response set bias across countries, the use of 7-point Likert scales instead of 5-point scales is recommended. Moreover, ranking rather than rating leads to more consistent response patterns (Harzing et al. 2009).

Translation equivalence as the third aspect of measurement equivalence is one of the most frequently mentioned issues in intercultural management research (Harkness 2003). Equivalence of meaning in each language is essential to ensure that the researchers and respondents understand the questionnaire and instructions in the same way (Douglas & Craig 2007). This is particularly relevant in the case of large linguistic differences between the involved countries, such as between China and the United States (Farh, Cannella & Lee 2006).

The most common method to ensure translation equivalence is *back translation* (Brislin 1970). First, the research instrument is translated into another language by a bilingual native of the target country. Afterward, the translated document is translated back into the source language by a bilingual native speaker of the source language. Then the two versions in the source language are compared for differences and comparability. The validity of this procedure can be increased by involving two or more independent translators (*parallel translation*).

Back translation aims to ensure that the target language wording is as close as possible to the source language. This mechanical translation procedure, however, ignores the emic meaning in the target context by forcing source meaning into that context (Usunier 2011). It "assumes an etic approach to linguistic translation or, in other words, that there is always an equivalent word or construct in the target language (...). Consequently, back translation is likely to be most useful when a literal or direct translation is required, but it is less helpful when idioms need to be translated or when the equivalence of a term or construct in another language needs to be established" (Douglas & Craig 2007, p. 33).

In such cases, *collaborative approaches to instrument translation* are more appropriate. They involve a number of translators from the involved countries and languages who work together in a group (Douglas &

Craig 2007). This decenters the development of research instruments for comparative research and emphasizes the experiential and semantic equivalence instead of a merely lexical and mechanical translation. "The non-technical use of translation makes it possible to identify *faux amis* (deceptive cognates) and hidden 'emicity' in seemingly *etic* concepts" (Usunier 2011, p. 317).

The emic character of languages can be illustrated by using the example of accounting terms. *"Einzahlungen-Auszahlungen, Einnahmen-Ausgaben, Ertrag-Aufwand*, and *Leistungen-Kosten"* are key terms of cost accounting in Germany. They are precisely defined and refer to different forms and timings of financial inflows and outflows. While these terms can be lexically translated into "deposits-withdrawals, revenues-expenses, earnings-losses, benefits-costs," this translation hides important semantic elements that are understood only in the original context. Due to the idiosyncratic character of the German system of cost accounting, semantic equivalence of translation is impossible.

Another example is the translation of the German term *"Aufsichtsrat."* The widely accepted English lexical equivalent of *"supervisory board"* loses the emic meaning of the German concept. First, the German two-tier system of "Vorstand" (management board) and "Aufsichtsrat" (supervisory board) may not be easily compared to the one-tier board system consisting of executive and nonexecutive directors that is common, for example, in the United Kingdom and United States. Secondly, unlike in these two countries, employees in large German companies have the statutory right to equal representation in the supervisory board. Thus, respondents who are not accustomed to employees being stakeholders in corporate governance are likely to miss out this crucial facet of the *Aufsichtsrat* concept and misunderstand the English lexical equivalent of *supervisory board* (Usunier 2011).

A more general way to reduce translation errors on the side of the researcher is the use of a *lingua franca* (most likely English) across all countries. This requires that all participants are equally fluent in this language. Otherwise, language-related response bias is likely. For example, Harzing (2005) found in a study in 24 countries that responses across countries differ considerably less when an English-language instead of a local-language questionnaire is applied.

While calibration, metric, and translation errors are generally viewed as unintentional forms of measurement error, **social desirability bias** consists of deliberate distortions of answers. Social desirability is the "tendency of individuals to 'manage' social interactions by projecting favorable images of themselves, thereby maximizing conformity to others and minimizing the danger of receiving negative evaluations from them" (Johnson & van de Vijver 2003, p. 194).

Dispositions for social desirability differ across countries. It is higher, for example, in collectivistic cultures and countries with a high degree of uncertainty avoidance (Bernardi 2006). Individuals in these countries are more accustomed to observe the behavior of others and have a more pronounced ability to perceive what is desired in societies or social encounters. On the contrary, persons coming from more influential groups in society or from more affluent countries tend to show lower scores on social desirability (Johnson & van de Vijver 2003).

> In countries where sexual activities of women are subject to normative restrictions, questions on the frequency of sexual intercourse in general, and on extramarital intercourse in particular, will not only be regarded as sensitive and potentially embarrassing. People will also have a clear understanding of what is regarded as desirable in their society and if such questions are answered at all, the actual frequency is likely to be underreported.
>
> (Braun 2003, p. 142)

Cultural norms do not only activate perceptions of desirability or undesirability, but will also influence a person's propensity to give either accurate responses or distort answers. Within collectivistic cultures, the restrictions against providing distort answers to members of external groups are generally weaker than within individualistic cultures (Triandis 1995a). This effect is likely to increase with growing cultural distance between researcher and respondent.

While surveys and experiments are dominant methods of data collection in comparative and cross-cultural management research, *indigenous and postcolonial studies* often apply qualitative methods, such as **observation** and the use of **storytelling** (Gabriel 2000; Boje 2008). Stories enable participants to share knowledge with rich tacit dimensions and are therefore a very powerful way to represent and convey complex ideas and phenomena (Nkomo 2011). Since stories are contextually embedded, story-telling allows for consideration of the local context under which management practices are applied. Storytelling is not reduced to naïve sequences of quotations, but adheres to the "thick description" (Geertz 1973) of local phenomena. This inevitably implies the inclusion of local voices and their idiosyncratic perspectives.

For some research projects, **non-verbal methods**, such as visual ethnography, may be useful (Pink 2007). *Visual ethnography* engages with pictures, videos, and other audio-visual media throughout the process of research, analysis, and representation. It is essentially collaborative and participatory and strongly emphasizes the context of research. Visual ethnography decenters the written word as the primary source of knowledge and understanding and proceeds from the belief that culture is also manifested through visible symbols embedded in gestures, ceremonies, rituals, and artifacts. It is particularly useful for representing phenomena that are otherwise challenging to articulate, such as feelings, emotions, and unconscious expressions (Stanczak 2007). Moreover, visual media may be applied in high-context cultures where large parts of the information are likely to be lost in the process of translation (Hall 1959).

3.3.3 Data Analysis

The study of intercultural management phenomena not only adds an additional layer of influences to the relationships that exist in a national context, but can also modify the strengths, directions, and interactions of these relationships as new mechanisms emerge that alter existing arguments (Cuervo-Cazurra et al. 2016). An important prerequisite to identify such mechanisms is the **conceptualization of culture** and its adequate reflection in the applied methods of data analysis. Intercultural management studies often suffer from a misspecification of the main constructs which Anant Negandhi criticized starting in the 1970s: "It seems that culture, although being used as an independent variable in most cross-cultural management studies, has a most obscure identity. Under such circumstances, it is difficult to know what is being linked with what. This suggests that culture has been used as a residual variable rather than an independent or explanatory variable. Hence, the real identity of culture as a variable is left to the imagination of the reader" (Negandhi 1974, p. 62).

While recent studies are increasingly encountering this criticism and adapt substantial conceptualizations of culture, such as those developed by Hofstede and GLOBE (Chapter 4), a **careful explanation of the proposed effects of culture** is often missing. Intercultural management research often seems to assume "that describing the set of constructs or variables studied is sufficient theoretical development and that the relationships among concepts will appear—as if by magic" (Thomas, Cuervo-Cazurra & Brannen 2011, p. 1074). Instead, the assumed causal effects of culture need to be reflected not only in the theoretical framework but also in the selected methods of data analysis. This includes the specification of relevant variables, the direction of cultural effects, and the conditions under which these effects are predicted to exist.

The specification of culture and its causal relationships with other variables includes the **determination of the appropriate level of analysis**. Intercultural management research is often affected by *ecological fallacy*, i.e., the error of assuming that statistical relationships at the country level (ecological level) also hold for individuals (Nasif et al. 1991). Although it is frequently mentioned that cultural dimensions constructed at the national level "are meaningless as descriptors of individuals or as predictors of individual differences because the variables that define them do not correlate meaningfully across individuals" (Minkov & Hofstede 2011, p. 12), ecological correlations are often employed for the purpose of discovering something about individuals and used on occasions when individual correlations are not available (Brewer & Venaik 2014). A notable exception is the GLOBE study that applies varying measurements for cultural constructs at different levels of analysis (House et al. 2004). An example is the measurement of "national participative systems" and "corporate participative leaders": "Although the same term 'participative' is used to refer to both national systems and corporate leaders, the underlying measures and characteristics are completely different at the two levels. It would therefore be erroneous to simply assume that nations with 'participative systems' also have 'participative corporate leaders'" (Brewer & Venaik 2014, p. 1067).

The phenomenon of ecological fallacy is illustrated in Figure 3.3. On the individual level, data of 11 respondents (x_1–x_{11}) for two cultural dimensions (a, b) were collected, measured on Likert scales with 1 = low and 5 = high. The mean values are $\emptyset$ a = 2.91 and $\emptyset$ b = 3.82. On the organizational/regional level, the individuals are assigned to three entities (y_1–y_3). The mean values of the two dimensions range from $\emptyset$ a = 1.75-4.00 and $\emptyset$ b = 1.67-4.75. The correlation between the cultural dimensions a and b is positive and highly significant for y_1 (r = 0.90***) and y_3 (r = 0.87***). When aggregated on the societal/national level, the correlation between the two cultural dimensions becomes negative (r = -0.25*).

A method of data analysis that allows for the **consideration of various influences of culture on different levels of analysis** (country, region, organization, individual, etc.) is *multi-level analysis*. Hierarchical linear modeling (HLM) is an ordinary least square (OLS) regression-based analysis that takes the hierarchical structure of the data into account (Raudenbush et al. 2011). Hierarchically structured data is

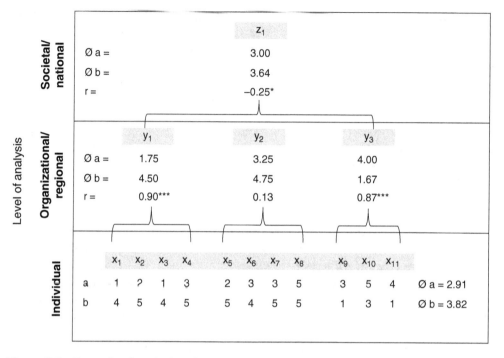

Figure 3.3 Example of ecological fallacy

nested data where groups of units are clustered together in a systematic way, such as individuals within organizations within countries. The nested structure of the data violates the independence assumption of OLS regression, because the clusters of observations are not independent of each other.

HLM assesses the predictability of the dependent variable across different levels of analysis. This can be illustrated by a Venn diagram where the different circles represent the dependent variable's variance at various levels (Hanges, Dickson & Sipe 2004). In the example illustrated in Figure 3.4, the variance of cultural practices cuts across three levels of analyses. Approximately 30% of the dependent variable's variance is at the individual level, 50% is at the organizational level, and 20% is at the societal level.

3.3.4 Interpretation of Results

The final stage of the research process consists of the interpretation of results. In intercultural management research, the explanation of causal inferences is often affected by interpretation bias. **Factual errors and discretionary interpretations** are likely if researchers lack sound substantial knowledge and relevant local expertise. Researchers may attribute observations in other cultures to norms and values common in their own culture. However, similar behaviors, symbols, and artifacts can have different meanings in different cultures. For example, nepotism is considered corruption in most Western countries, but responsibility in large parts of Africa and Asia (de Maria 2008). At the same time, different behaviors, symbols, and artifacts can be used for similar purposes across cultures, such as greeting customs like handshakes, hugs, kissing, bowing, waving, etc. Therefore, interpretations of findings always need to be contextualized.

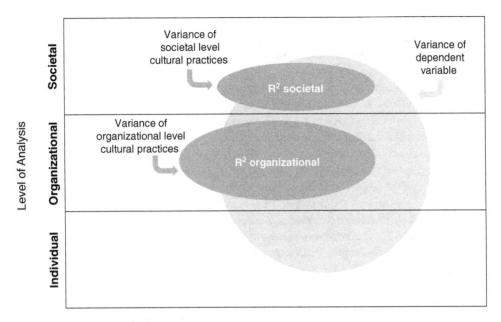

Figure 3.4 Venn diagram illustrating R^2 in hierarchical linear modeling analysis
Source: Adapted from Hanges, Dickson & Sipe (2004, p. 227).

Statements on culture often suffer from factual errors and discretionary interpretations. For example, Tipton (2008) refers to a statement made by Deresky (2006, p. 105): "Christianity underlies much of German culture—more than 96% of Germans are Catholics or Protestants. This may be why Germans tend to like rule and order in their lives, and why there is clear public expectation of acceptable and unacceptable ways to act." This statement neglects that, according to official statistics, only 57% of the population in Germany is Christians (in fact, 96% of Christians in Germany are Catholics or Protestants). Moreover, it ignores a number of other countries with a similarly high percentage of Christians (e.g., Spain, the Philippines, Latin America) where the clichés run in the opposite direction.

Another example of a misconceived causal relationships is the statement of Daniels, Radebaugh & Sullivan (2004, p. 73) that "Japan's island status makes it less prone to cultural borrowing." This interpretation ignores that Japan has intensively borrowed cultural traditions from China in earlier centuries and that, before the railway, communication by water was far easier and cheaper than movement over land. Moreover, the statement raises the question why other islands, such as Australia, are prone to cultural borrowing (Tipton 2008).

Before making far-reaching statements about the effects of culture it is necessary to **rule out alternative explanations**. In particular, the legal-political and geographic delineations of culture may lead to **causal inference errors** caused by confounding culture with geographical, political and economic factors. Robustness checks should therefore *consider alternative influences* on the dependent variable and how they affect it (Cuervo-Cazurra et al. 2016). For example, the impact of personality traits and contextual factors may be examined instead of or in combination with cultural variables. Moreover, a *control group* may be included in the research design against which the relation of interest can be contrasted and compared.

Another important aspect at the final stage of research is to disclose its **limitations and boundary conditions**. Research is always situated in a specific context and shall not be generalized to other countries, industries, organizations, individuals, etc. A specific limitation of intercultural management research is that it frequently discriminates cultures from each other on the basis of their *typical members*. For example, the country scores in most empirical studies, such as those of Hofstede, Trompenaars, GLOBE, etc., represent the "central tendencies in the answers from each country" (Hofstede 1991, p. 253). Mathematically, a typical member is represented by the country mean. While the comparison of country means may be relevant in some contexts (e.g., when analyzing similarities between countries), other studies may be more interested in the extreme members of a culture (e.g., studies of cultural extremism or culturally distant countries). Merely studying the means does not completely reveal the distribution of cultural values within a country (Au 1999). While the number of individuals whose values are close to the country mean is higher in countries with low variance of cultural values, it is lower in countries with high variance and more individuals have values that are different from the typical member represented by the country mean.

Intercultural management research is also likely to be affected by **cultural attribution error** and **affirmation bias**. Researchers in this field are often characterized by a high degree of *cultural empathy*. While this is advantageous for the identification of relevant and interesting research topics, it may lead to systematically overemphasizing cultural and underestimating other explanations. Moreover, management research in general and intercultural management research in particular is characterized by a liberal, rational and enlightened worldview. Findings that contradict these fundamental beliefs are difficult to publish in leading academic journals. Researchers may thus be affected by *social desirability and political correctness bias* and unconsciously advocate interpretations that are consistent with this view (MacCoun 1998).

An appropriate measure to avoid oversimplified, erroneous, and biased interpretations is the **inclusion of the participants** in empirical studies not only in the process of data collection, i.e., as survey respondents, but also in framing research questions, interpreting results and deriving theoretical and practical conclusions. This kind of participatory research requires that "researcher and participants co-create *what* is said and *how* things are said" (Jackson 2013, p. 18) and assigns the participants a high degree of control over the collected data and their interpretation.

Finally, it may be useful to conduct **replica studies** of previous research or to allow other researchers to **reanalyze existing data sets**. However, in contrast to studies in economics, there is a very limited tradition of replicability that can help uncover researchers' biases in data analysis and interpretation (Cuervo-Cazurra et al. 2016).

SUMMARY

Research on culture originated in the military context was driven by the increasing interest in cultures during colonization and was further inspired by the emergence of nation states in Europe in the eighteenth and nineteenth centuries.

Early research on culture strongly focused on typologies of national characters and lacked solid methodological and theoretical foundations. The internationalization of firms has shaped the emergence of intercultural management research as an academic discipline and inspired a multitude of theoretical concepts and empirical studies.

Approaches in intercultural management research can be categorized based on their epistemological perspective (etic vs. emic) and research objective (comparison vs. transferability).

Intercultural management research is faced with various methodological challenges related to systematic errors and biases of data collected and analyzed in different cultural contexts. To minimize these biases, intercultural equivalence of research methods must be achieved.

 Reflection Questions

1. Do you agree with Jullien's (2016) statement that Europe has failed to establish a common identity? Why (not)? Would you say a common understanding of cultural identity is necessary for political unions of states, such as the EU?
2. "In our normal lives, we see ourselves as members of a variety of groups," as Sen (2006) states. Think about your own identity–how would you define your cultural identity and how important is it to your personal identity?
3. What are the main advantages and disadvantages of emic and etic management research methods? When would you chose an emic and when an etic research approach?
4. Comparative management research and cross-cultural management research have been the prevalent streams in intercultural management research in the past. What are potential reasons and consequences of this dominance? Do you think that indigenous and postcolonial management research may become more relevant in the future?
5. Statements on culture often suffer from factual errors and discretionary interpretations. Are you aware of any misleading or false statements about your own culture or a culture you know well?
6. Two of the major challenges of intercultural management research are ethnocentric bias and lack of translation equivalence. What can researchers do to minimize these risks?
7. What are the main advantages and challenges of conducting intercultural management research in teams that consist of members with different cultural backgrounds?

 End of Chapter Exercise

Conducting Intercultural Research

Imagine you work in the human resource department of a large multinational corporation. Your task is to analyze if and how culture impacts the use of LinkedIn as a recruitment tool.

1. How would you investigate this question? Which methodology would you find as most appropriate to assess the question?
2. Which challenges are you likely to face in data collection and analysis and how would you address them?
3. How would you establish a high reliability and validity of your study?

—— **Further Reading** ———————————————————

Seminal introductions to comparative and cross-cultural management research are the studies of Hofstede (2001), Trompenaars and Hampden-Turner (2012), Schwartz (1992, 1994), and House et al. (2004).

Holtbrügge (2013) gives a short overview of indigenous management research.

Key aspects of postcolonial management research are discussed in the book by Jack and Westwood (2010).

A concise comparison between current streams and epistemological perspectives in intercultural management research is provided by Romani et al. (2018).

The methodologies of intercultural management research are elaborated upon in the books by van de Vijver and Leung (1997), Minkov (2013), and Usunier, van Herk and Lee (2017). The field guide to intercultural research by Guttormsen, Lauring and Chapman (2021) focuses especially on qualitative research.

4

CONCEPTS OF CULTURE

LEARNING OBJECTIVES

By the end of this chapter, you will be able to

- name and describe the most important concepts of culture,
- describe cultural differences in neutral and objective terms,
- understand reasons for differences and commonalities of cultures,
- assess the advantages and disadvantages of etic and emic concepts,
- explain the behavior of a typical member in a number of different cultures,
- measure and compare cultural attributes.

Since the interest of management studies in culture began to grow in the 1950s and 1960s, several concepts of culture were developed. While the early approaches of Kluckhohn and Strodtbeck and Hall originated in other disciplines, such as anthropology, ethnography, and psychology, and were later adapted to the business and management context, the study of Hofstede was one of the first publications by management scholars. It decisively shaped the emerging discipline of intercultural management research in the following decades and inspired many subsequent concepts, such as those of Trompenaars, Schwartz and GLOBE. All these etic approaches are based on the assumption that cultures can be "meaningfully measured and ordered along a discrete set of dimensions, representing different answers to universal problems of human societies" (Hofstede 2006, p. 883).

This central tenet of intercultural management research has been recently challenged by the interpretative and constructivist concepts of Thomas and Geertz. They are based on an emic research epistemology and propose the exploration of idiographic and specific constructs to describe cultures.

In the following sections, eight of the most prominent concepts of culture are explained. First, the context in which the concepts were developed is outlined. Afterward, the main lines of argumentation are discussed. The sections close with a critical evaluation of the concepts.

4.1 THE CONCEPT OF KLUCKHOHN AND STRODTBECK

4.1.1 Overview

One of the first concepts of culture that aimed to describe and analyze the cultural orientation of people was developed by Clyde Kluckhohn and Fred Strodtbeck. Both were American anthropologists and social psychologists and based their concept on a *long-term study of Native American cultures*, such as Zuni, Navahos, and Mormon in the 1940s and 1950s. After Clyde Kluckhohn's death, his widow Florence Kluckhohn and Fred Strodtbeck operationalized the observations made in this study and developed a set of cultural orientations. Although the concept was initially not directed at understanding the values and behavior of managers and employees in different countries, it has been *frequently revisited, adapted and extended in the intercultural management literature* since the 1960s.

Kluckhohn and Strodtbeck (1961) argue that **human behavior is a product of universal biology, individual personality, and collectively-shared culture**. This is reflected in the fundamental statement: "Every man is in certain respects like all other men, like some other men, like no other man" (Kluckhohn & Murray 1965, p. 53). According to this view, all humans share common biological traits and characteristics which form the basis for the development of culture.

Kluckhohn and Strodtbeck (1961) distinguish five **basic cultural orientations** that pose questions about common human problems and present a range of variations in responses to each (Table 4.1). These cultural variations are regarded "as definite and as essential as the (..) systematic variation in physical and biological phenomena" (p. 3).

Table 4.1 Kluckhohn and Strodtbeck's five basic cultural orientations

Question	Orientation	Description
Human nature orientation What is the nature of people?	Good (mutable/ unmutable)	People can be trusted and strive to rise as human beings.
	Evil (mutable/ unmutable)	People have to be controlled. Basic human nature is unchangeable.
Man-nature orientation What is the person's relationship to nature?	Mastery	We can and should control and change the environment around us.
	Harmonious	We should strive to maintain a balance with the natural environment.
	Subjugation	We cannot and should not exercise control over natural forces but accept to be influenced by these forces.
Relational orientation What is the person's relationship to other people?	Individualist	Emphasis on the individual who make decisions independently from others.
	Hierarchical	Emphasis on hierarchical principles and deferring to higher authority.
	Collectivist	Emphasis on consensus within the extended group of equals.

Table 4.1 Kluckhohn and Strodtbeck's five basic cultural orientations (Continued)

Question	Orientation	Description
Activity orientation What is the modality of human activity?	Doing	Our motivation is external to us, emphasizing activity that is both valued by ourselves and approved by others.
	Being	Our motivation is internal, emphasizing activity valued by ourselves but not necessarily by others.
Time orientation What is the temporal focus of human activity?	Past	We focus on the past and on preserving traditional teachings and beliefs.
	Present	We focus on the immediate needs and circumstances.
	Future	We focus on the future, planning ahead, and seeking new ways to replace the old.

Source: Adapted from Kluckhohn & Strodtbeck (1961, p. 10).

4.1.2 Basic Cultural Orientations

4.1.2.1 Human-Nature Orientation

According to Kluckhohn and Strodtbeck, individuals may have different assumptions of other people. In some cultures, people are believed to be principally good and in others as principally evil (Figure 4.1). Cultures with an **optimistic image of man** believe that others can be trusted. They are therefore more likely to give them greater autonomy and to allow them to take initiative. On the contrary, cultures with a **pessimistic image of man** feel a greater need for control and supervision. This encourages a greater emphasis on rules and regulations and other disciplinary measures.

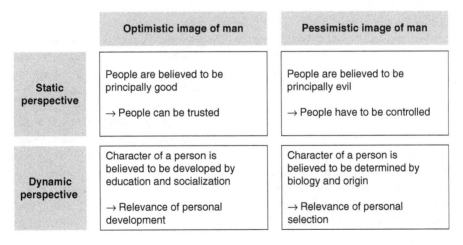

Figure 4.1 Optimistic and pessimistic image of man in static and dynamic perspective

Beliefs about human nature often originate in religion (Ward 1998). Fundamental to the **Christian understanding of human nature** is the belief that the first humans were created in the image of God and thus to be principally good. However, after Adam and Eve have eaten from the tree of knowledge of good and evil and were expelled from the Garden of Eden, every human being is believed to be born with a *tendency toward sin*. "The Christian estimate of human evil is so serious precisely because it places evil at the very center of human personality: in the will" (Niebuhr 1941, p. 16). This view begins in the new testament with the Apostle Paul who declared that "all have sinned and fallen short of the glory of God" (Romans 3:23). Christians are therefore expected to confess, to ask forgiveness, and to repent.

The concept of human nature also plays an important role in **Chinese moral philosophy**. While Confucius did not explicitly comment on this subject, it became central to the work of his successor Mencius (Mengzi). Basically, Mencius assumes that human nature has an innate tendency toward goodness, but that bad environments tend to corrupt the human will. Therefore, education is necessary to awaken the positive abilities of the human mind (Chan 2002).

This understanding is in contrast, for example, to the **Buddhist concept of human nature**. Buddhists believe that humanity has no inherent nature and that good and evil are innate, inseparable aspects of living. This antagonistic duality shall be overcome by avoiding sinful acts and maintaining the harmony of present circumstances. The ultimate goal of life is to avoid doing evil, to cultivate the good, and to purify one's mind (Harvey 2000).

McGregor (1964) adapted the distinction between good and evil to the **management context** and distinguished between two contrasting views that explain how managers' beliefs about what motivates their employees can affect their management style. *Theory X* assumes that people dislike work and are not motivated to do a good job. Managers with such a pessimistic image of man tend to think that employees need to be controlled, supervised and punished constantly to make sure that they complete their tasks. In *Theory Y*, managers have an optimistic image of man. They are likely to use a participative management style, encourage their team members to take initiative, and suggest improvements.

According to Kluckhohn and Strodtbeck, human nature is not static, but has also a **dynamic aspect** (Figure 4.1). Again, an optimistic and a pessimistic perspective can be distinguished. The **optimistic perspective** assumes that the character of a person can be developed through *education and socialization*. This view is expressed, for example, in the *achievement orientation* of the American culture, where the belief that people can rise "from dishwasher to millionaire" is proverbial. It can be attributed to Max Weber's (1930) *Protestant Ethics*, which regards human nature as independent and self-reliant. Protestants believe that they can raise their position in life through thrift, hard work, and competitive struggle. The focus of management should therefore be on personal development, training, and appropriate incentives.

The **pessimistic perspective** emphasizes the *role of biology and origin* and assumes that people hardly change their character. This belief is central, for example, to the *Hinduist caste system*. According to Hinduism, every human being is born into a certain caste and cannot move out of it, but shall perform the duties that arise from their caste affiliation (Perrett 2016). Consequently, the focus of management should be on recruiting and selecting the right person for a particular job instead of investing in training and personal development.

4.1.2.2 Man-Nature Orientation

The second cultural orientation proposed by Kluckhohn and Strodtbeck relates to a person's relationship with nature. Generally, a mastery, subjugation, and harmony orientation can be distinguished.

Western cultures are characterized by the profound belief that people can exercise control over nature. This **mastery orientation** is based on the assumption that nothing is predetermined and that it is man's duty to overcome obstacles. Human is regarded as separate from nature and destined to dominate it. Particularly, many Western countries place great emphasis on technology and management which allow humans to use nature for their purposes. Cultures with a mastery orientation therefore often strive for technological innovations that overcome the limits of natural laws.

In contrast, Arab cultures are characterized by a **subjugation orientation** and the belief that people cannot and should not exercise control over nature (Nydell 2012). Life is predetermined by fate and should be accepted as immutable and inevitable. In Islamic countries, this fatalistic orientation is exemplified in the phrase *Insh'allah* (if Good wills), underlying the belief that nothing happens unless God wills it and that only what God wills will happen. Any attempts to change destiny is considered insane or irreligious.

The **harmony orientation** is prevalent in many Asian countries. Human and nature are regarded as inseparable and maintaining a balance between the two is a key value. The harmony orientation is reflected in several Asian architectural concepts, such as *zenshūyō* (Japan), *feng shui* (China), and *vastu shastra* (India).

Vastu shastra is a traditional Hindu science of architecture that intends to integrate architecture with nature. Central to the concept is the idea that the various energy flows (solar energy, lunar energy, thermal energy, magnetic energy, wind energy, etc.) in a building should be directed in a positive way to achieve peace, prosperity, and happiness (Chakrabarti 1998).

The relevance of *vastu shastra* in modern India is illustrated by the example of Antilla, the world's most expensive house in Mumbai finished in 2011. Because the building's eastern side did not have enough windows or other openings to let residents receive sufficient morning light, the owners feared that it will curse them with bad luck. The Ambani family has, therefore, reportedly moved in only after the building was reconstructed accordingly (Bajaj 2011).

4.1.2.3 Relational Orientation

The relational orientation describes the relationship of individuals to other people. Most Western countries are characterized by a strong **individualistic orientation**. The focus is on the unique personality who makes decisions independently from others. This is most prominently addressed in Abraham Maslow's (1954) *hierarchy of needs* which regards self-actualization, i.e., the process of growing and developing as a person to reach his or her full potential, as the highest level of human motivation. At the same time, individualistic cultures emphasize the relevance of equal rights and opportunities. This is reflected in the dictum that "*All men are created equal*" which has become a key value in the United States and most Western countries since the US Declaration of Independence (Greene 1976). Equality also relates to the moral obligation for others regardless of their social status, as underlined, for example, in the principle of Christian charity.

The **hierarchical orientation** is prevalent in countries with distinct social stratification. This may be caused by historic class membership, such as in England and France (Saunders 1990), or by belonging to a powerful political or economic class, such as the *nomenklatura* and the *oligarchs* in Russia (Iastrebov 2013). Another example is the caste system in India, where all aspects of social status are ascribed and the social position of a person at birth holds for a lifetime (Perrett 2016). In hierarchical cultures, people accept that certain laws do not apply to everyone, but that more powerful people can exercise more rights than others. This belief is illustrated, for example, in George Orwell's famous quote: "All men are equal, but some are more equal than others."

Many Asian countries, such as China and Japan, are characterized by a **collectivistic orientation**. Collectivist cultures make a clear distinction between "us" and "them." Their members think of themselves as highly interconnected with others (Triandis 1995a). They feel primarily obliged to their family and close friends and strive to maintain harmony within their group (Li 2016). Responsibility for outsiders is much lower. In business, people are hired often on connections and less on merit (ability and past accomplishments). Moreover, collective cultures believe that relationship with others must be established before business can be conducted. Thus, while trust in individualistic cultures is rule-based, it is relationship-based in collectivistic cultures.

The collectivistic orientation of the Chinese culture is best reflected in the concept of *guanxi* (e.g., Luo 1997; Lovett et al. 1999; Park & Luo 2001; Fan 2002). *Guanxi* originates in Confucianism and has been pervasive for centuries in every aspect of the Chinese society and economy. It consists of a web of personal relations to secure favors in personal and organizational relations. The network of connections with members of the extended family and individuals of the same birthplace, educational institution, or workplace contains implicit mutual obligations, assurances, and understanding and governs attitudes toward long-term social and personal relationships.

4.1.2.4 Activity Orientation

With regard to activity orientation, Kluckhohn and Strodtbeck distinguish between the concepts of doing and being. Cultures with a **doing orientation** are motivated by external incentives. People strive for "accomplishments that are measurable by standards conceived to be external to the acting individual" (Kluckhohn & Strodtbeck 1961, p. 17). They have a strong readiness to take action and willingness to take risks. This is reflected, for example, in the American proverb "*It is better to make the wrong decision than no decision*" and the belief that failure in business is not a stigma, but expected to increase the likelihood of future success.

On the contrary, cultures with a **being orientation** regard quick decisions as sign of actionism and insufficient reflection. For example, a Russian proverb says that one should measure seven times before one cuts once ('Семь раз отмерь—один раз отрежь'). This belief is mainly caused by the attempt to avoid the negative consequences of failure. The being orientation may also be based on the belief that many problems solve themselves. The attitude of "waiting to let things happen" is reflected, for example, in the famous aphorism of the former French Prime Minister Henri Queuille: "Any problem, however complex, can be solved by failing to take a decision" ("Il n'est pas de problème dont une absence de solution ne finisse par venir à bout").

4.1.2.5 Time Orientation

Finally, cultures may be distinguished with regard to their time orientation. Here, Kluckhohn and Strodbeck (1961) distinguish between past, present, and future orientation.

In cultures with strong **past orientation**, people focus on preserving traditional teachings and beliefs. Past orientation can be found particularly in Asian countries where ancestor worship and family traditions are strong. Older people are highly respected and often influential in politics and business even after their official retirement. Also in England, century-long traditions are still practiced today. People are proud of their history and historical facts are widely known. In Russia, this is visible in numerous monuments and frequent historical references. In the management context, past orientation is often reflected by the idealization of company founders, risk aversion, and conservative business models.

In cultures with strong **present orientation**, people pay little attention to what has happened in the past and regard the future as both vague and unpredictable. Individuals live in the moment, enjoy high-intensity activities, seek sensation, and act with minimal concern for the consequences of their behavior. Tasks are often done at the last moment. Present orientation is particularly strong in South American cultures.

Future orientation is dominant in the United States. Americans believe that the future can be planned and controlled, and thus optimistically view it as an improvement on the past. The proverb "Don't cry over spilt milk" expresses the belief that it is often not worth to worry about something that has already happened. Instead, change and innovation are highly valued.

4.1.3 Critical Evaluation

Since the concept of Kluckhohn and Strodtbeck was not developed in the management context, the authors did not refer to studies in this field and did not derive any managerial implications. Moreover, while Kluckhohn and Strodtbeck carried out extensive field research in Native American cultures, they did not collect any empirical data on the manifestations of the five cultural dimensions in different countries.

Despite these weaknesses, the concept has largely impacted intercultural management literature. It is regularly referred to in intercultural management textbooks and has inspired several **subsequent studies**. For example, Maznevski et al. (2002) developed a Cultural Perspectives Questionnaire based on Kluckhohn and Strodtbeck's cultural dimensions and tested it in Canada, Mexico, the Netherlands, Taiwan, and the United States. Their results are mostly consistent with the assumptions of Kluckhohn and Strodtbeck. For example, the average respondents of the United States and Canadian samples are among the most individualistic in the study, while the average respondents from the Netherlands, Mexico, and Taiwan are among the least individualistic. Mastery relation is strongest in the United States and Canada, and weakest in the Netherlands and Taiwan where a harmony orientation prevails. The study of Woldu et al. (2006) on

Indian, Polish, Russian, and American employees comes to similar results. Both studies show, however, that Kluckhohn and Strodtbeck's cultural dimensions shall not be understood as principal categories in the sense that a country belongs exclusively to one or another category. Instead, *different manifestations of a cultural dimension can be prevalent with different strengths*. For example, while Maznevski et al. (2002) and Woldu et al. (2006) found a strong individualistic orientation for the United States, the collectivistic orientation is also moderately high. Similarly, the mastery orientation is dominant in this country, while there also exists a strong sense of harmony with nature.

Several **adaptions of Kluckhohn and Strodtbeck's cultural dimensions** exist. For example, Zimbardo and Boyd (1999) extended Kluckhohn and Strodtbeck's spectrum of time perspectives and argue that two different manifestations of past orientation can be distinguished. The *past-positive* manifestation represents pleasurable, usually sentimental and nostalgic views of one's past while emphasizing the maintenance of relationships with family and friends. In contrast, the *past-negative* manifestation reflects a focus on personal experiences that were aversive, noxious, traumatic, or filled with regret. Moreover, a hedonistic and a fatalistic manifestation of present orientation are distinguished. *Present-hedonistic* cultures live in the moment, enjoy high-intensity activities, sensation seeking, and act with minimal concern for the consequences of their behavior. The *present-fatalistic* manifestation reflects a helpless and hopeless attitude toward the future and one's life that seems fated and not under personal control.

Sircova et al. (2015) tested the classification of Zimbardo and Boyd (1999) and found, for example, that the past negative orientation and future orientation are negatively associated with the Human Development Index, i.e., these time orientations are the highest in countries associated with a lower income, educational level, and life expectancy. The present hedonistic orientation is particularly high in Mediterranean and Latin American countries, while the present fatalistic orientation prevails, for example, in China.

4.2 THE CONCEPT OF HALL

4.2.1 Overview

Edward T. Hall was an American anthropologist and cross-cultural researcher. From 1933 through 1937, he lived on Native American reservations in northeastern Arizona and studied the cultural characteristics of the Navajo and Hopi. After he had served in the US Army in Europe and the Philippines during World War II, he extended his research to countries such as Germany, France, and Japan. In the later stages of his career, Hall also worked as management consultant and advised many companies on their intercultural collaborations. Since the 1970s, Hall's concept of culture has become influential in intercultural management literature and inspired many subsequent studies.

While Kluckhohn and Strodtbeck base their concept on the analysis of major human problems and their solutions in different social groups, Hall examines the communication of individuals with different cultural backgrounds. This **focus on communication** is reflected in the fundament statement: "Culture is communication and communication is culture" (Hall 1959, p. 217).

Hall's considerations about culture were not formulated as a coherent concept, but exhibited in a number of books with different foci (Hall 1959, 1966, 1976, 1983). Essentially, **three dimensions of culture** are distinguished: context orientation, time orientation, and space orientation (Table 4.2).

Table 4.2 Hall's cultural dimensions

Cultural dimension	Manifestations	
Context orientation	Low: Focus is on *what* is said.	High: Focus is on *who* says *what, when, where* and *how*.
Time orientation (chronemics)	Monochronic: Do one thing at a time.	Polychronic: Do many things at once.
Space orientation (proxemics)	Private: Protection of private sphere important.	Public: Relaxed attitude with regard to private matters.

4.2.2 Dimensions of Culture

4.2.2.1 Context Orientation

Given the centrality of communication in his concept, Hall (1966, 1990) classifies cultures into high-context and low-context cultures, depending on the degree to which communication is explicit or rather implicit (Table 4.3). Figure 4.2 summarizes exemplary countries according to their context orientation.

Table 4.3 Low-context vs. high-context cultures

Low-context cultures	High-context cultures
• Focus is on *what* is said; everything is said explicitly.	• Focus is on *who* says *what, when, where, and how.*
• Large part of the information is included in the content of the message.	• Information is largely embedded in the relations between the participants (age, location, time).
• Good communication is precise, simple, and clear.	• Good communication is nuanced, sophisticated, and layered.
• Are at loss when high-context people do not provide enough background information.	• Become impatient and irritated when low-context people provide information they do not need.
• Agreements are written, final, and binding.	• Agreements are spoken, flexible, and changeable.

In **low-context cultures**, such as Germany, Scandinavia, and the United States, communication is direct, clear, and explicit. Members of low-context cultures are relatively unconditioned in non-verbal communication codes. Senders are expected to "come to the point" as they cannot expect the receiver to infer the message from the context. Relationships between individuals tend to be more surface level and deep personal involvement with others is valued less. The transmitted message is significant and the explicit code requires little prior knowledge of the situation. Events are usually accompanied by

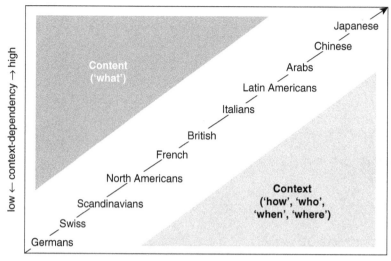

Figure 4.2 Context orientation in different cultures
Source: Adapted and extended from Hall (1976, pp. 91 and 102).

explanations and extensive supporting material. Agreements tend to be written rather than spoken, and contracts are regarded as final and legally binding. Communication is more detailed, yet redundancies lead to slower transmission. Since insiders and outsiders are less easily distinguished, foreigners find it relatively easy to adjust.

On the contrary, Asian and Latin American countries are **high-context cultures**. People in these countries usually have extensive information networks among family members, friends, colleagues, and clients and keep themselves informed about everything that has to do with the people who are important in their lives. Relationships between individuals are relatively long-lasting, and individuals feel deep personal involvement with each other. High-context communication contains little explicit information and requires the recipient of the message to refer to the context in which the communication takes place (participants, location, time, etc.) to make sense of it. The understanding of the external conditions and non-verbal behavior is crucial in creating and interpreting communication. Agreements tend to be spoken rather than written. Communication is fast and efficient, but requires extensive prior knowledge. Like twins who have known each other since birth, individuals in high-context cultures can communicate more economically if they share the same background. Because high-context cultures tend to be ethnically and linguistically homogeneous, foreigners often find it difficult to adjust (Rösch & Segler 1987).

Galtung (1981) analyzed **scientific communication styles** across cultures and found significant differences between the context orientation in the United States and United Kingdom, Germany, Japan, and France.

The *saxonic style* is characterized through politeness and supporting others. "The US professor at a graduate seminar would do his very best to find even in the most dismal performance that little nugget which, when polished, might produce a credible shine. He will tend to brush aside all the other things, go straight for it and bring it forth: 'I really think you had a point there!'" Only after emphasizing the strengths of a presentation, critique will be raised: "I greatly enjoyed listening to Mr. X's presentation, admiring his mastery of the facts of the case as well as his way of marshalling the facts together, but ..." The "but" clause may then become quite extensive, with lots of cutting edges and biting points, but more likely than not there will be a complimentary, congratulatory point at the end.

In contrast, the *teutonic approach* to scientific communication is less polite and often even ironic or sarcastic. A German discussant "will go straight for the weakest point. That weakest point will be fished out of the pond of words, brought into the clearest sunlight for display, so as to leave no doubt, and for dissection, which is done with considerable agility and talent. Probably most of the debate will be devoted to such aspects, and there will be few if any soothing comments towards the end to put the defendant together as a human being; no attempt will be made to mop up the blood and put wounded egos together: 'You have not mentioned that ...'"

According to the *nipponic approach*, an academic discourse is more as a social than intellectual debate. "It is not so much a question of exploring paradigms, questioning data bases and scrutinizing the adequacy of the inferences made in the theory formation. It is much more a question of classification." Typical questions of Japanese discussants are: "Which school do you belong to? Where did you get it from? Who said it first?"

Finally, "the *gallic approach* is certainly a stringing-together-of-words, but not necessarily deductively. The words connote something, they carry conviction (...). Persuasion is carried, perhaps, less by implication than by *élégance*. Behind the *élégance* is not only the mastery of good style as opposed to the dryness of German social-science prose, often bordering on drabness, but also the use of bons mots, double entenders, alliterations and various types of semantic and even typographical tricks." An academic discourse in France will often start with the statement: "Je ne suis pas d'accord ..."

4.2.2.2 Time Orientation

Like Kluckhohn and Strodtbeck, Hall conceptualizes time orientation (*chronemics*) as the second dimension of his concept of culture. He distinguishes between cultures with a predominantly monochronic and polychronic orientation (Table 4.4).

Monochronic time orientation is prevalent in North America as well as in Northern and Western Europe. Monochronic time is experienced and used in a linear way. It is scheduled and compartmentalized into small fractions, making it possible to concentrate on one thing at a time. Plans, time schedules, and agendas are followed rigorously. People are concerned about not disturbing others and strictly follow rules of privacy and consideration. Monochronic time is tangible and regarded as something that can be "saved, spent, wasted, lost, made up, crawling, killed and running out" (Hall 1983, p. 45). Consequently, punctuality is very important. Monochronic time orientation originated in the industrial revolution where factory life required the labor force to be on hand and in place at an appointed hour.

Table 4.4 Monochronic and polychronic time orientations

Monochronic orientation	Polychronic orientation
• Do one thing at a time ("linear thinking").	• Do many things at once ("cyclic thinking," "multitasking").
• Take time commitments (deadlines, schedules) seriously.	• Consider time commitments as provisional and not binding.
• Adhere religiously to plans.	• Change plans often and easily.
• Be concerned about privacy and not disturbing others.	• Be committed to people and human relationships.
• Give importance to punctuality and fixed agendas ("time is money").	• Value loose scheduling and flexible agendas ("relationships matter").
• Strive for order, reliability, and uncertainty reduction.	• Regard chaos as normality and source of creativity.

Source: Adapted from Hall & Hall (1990, p. 15).

Polychronic time orientation grew out of the natural rhythms associated with daily, monthly, and annual cycles, such as growing seasons. It is characterized by the occurrence of many things at once. There is more emphasis on the relationship with people and completion of transactions than the adherence to schedules and tasks. Appointments are not taken very seriously and are frequently missed. Time is seldom experienced as wasted. Business meetings are likely to be more fragmented with many interruptions from phone calls and visitors, and agendas are seen as nonbinding orientation that could be changed at any time. "Polychronic people, such as the Arabs and Turks, who are almost never alone, even in the home, make very different uses of 'screening' than Europeans do. They interact with several people at once and are continually involved with each other. Tight scheduling is therefore difficult, if not impossible" (Hall 1983, p. 46).

The encounter of monochronic and polychronic time orientations can lead to intercultural misunderstandings and management problems. Storti (1999, p. 58) illustrates this in a short episode between an Australian and a peace corps volunteer on Fiji: "An Australian man once visited the island and asked me when the stores were open, since it was afternoon and he hadn't seen a store open yet. Taken aback at what seems a stupid question, I told him the obvious truth, 'They're open when their doors are open.' When I walked away I realized it was a question I would have asked myself when I first arrived on Fiji."

Since time can be seen as either limited or expandable, monochronic and polychronic cultures attach different importance on **punctuality**. Levine (1997) found in a large cross-cultural study that punctuality is most valued in Switzerland, Ireland, Germany, and Japan. Like money, time is regarded as scare resource that should be used in the most economical way. This observation is based on three measures: the accuracy of public clocks, the average time it takes a postal clerk to complete a stamp-purchase transaction, and the average speed of pedestrians in big cities. According to these indicators, punctuality is not regarded very important in countries like Brazil, Indonesia, and Mexico. Here people are strolling rather than hurrying from one place to another. A good illustration of this attitude toward time is the Ethiopian proverb: "If you wait long enough, even an egg will walk."

Cultures may not only differ in their views of punctuality, but what is signaled by being "on time." In polychronic cultures, time may be used as an **indication of hierarchy**. The more important a person is, the more permissible it is to keep others waiting. In monochronic cultures, punctuality signals reliability. The lateness of a superior is no more tolerable than that of a subordinate, in fact quite the opposite.

4.2.2.3 Space Orientation

The third dimension of Hall's concept of culture is space orientation (*proxemics*) which can be understood in a literal and a figurative sense. **Space orientation in a literal sense** refers to *Kurt Lewin's* concept of space (1936) and assumes that individuals not only scan their environment for spatial cues, such as the location and movement of objects and people, but develop a sense of space based on "a synthesis of many sensory inputs: visual, auditory, kinesthetic, olfactory and thermal" (Hall 1966, p. 181). This demarcation of private sphere—an invisible bubble of space which other persons are not allowed to enter without permission—varies between cultures.

In Japan and Northern Europe, the distance between two persons in a conversation is usually around an arm's length. If people need to stand closer to each other, they tend to feel uncomfortable. Even a brushing of the overcoat sleeve elicits an apology. In Southern Europe and Arab countries, people (of the same sex) stay much close together and frequently touch each other. Keeping large spatial distance between another person is regarded as unkind and repellent.

According to Schneider & Barsoux (2003), space orientation can be linked to the geographic conditions and population density of a country. In a small country with large population, such as Japan, personal space is carefully managed. The lack of physical space leads to a high degree of formality and personal distance. For example, Japanese do not appreciate touching or being touched and prefer bowing to handshakes. In the United States—a large and sparsely populated country—there is less constraint with regard to physical space. As a result, there is less emphasis on living in harmony or respecting privacy. Abundance of space means that disputes can always be settled by moving on or "heading west." American mobility, both geographic and professional, is a manifestation of this "frontier spirit." Sorokowska et al. (2017) found in a comparative study across 42 countries that space orientation is also related to climate. The higher the annual temperature of a country, the smaller the preferred distance to strangers.

Space orientation in a figurative sense refers to aspects of life that a person does not share openly with other people. Private sphere contains central personal matters, such as emotions, attitudes, and personal problems. General personal matters constitute the public space. People are likely to share these even with people they don't know very well. Based on Lewin (1936), the concept of personal space is often described with the metaphors of a coconut and a peach. The outer layer of the fruit represents the public space and the inner layer the private space. Figure 4.3 illustrates the perception of private vs. public space in selected countries.

- Russia, Switzerland, and Germany are examples of *coconut cultures*. They are hard and hairy at the outside, but have a soft core. They rarely smile at strangers, do not easily engage in conversations, and may look unfriendly first. Members of coconut cultures give others access to their private space only if they are interested in and have time for a more intimate

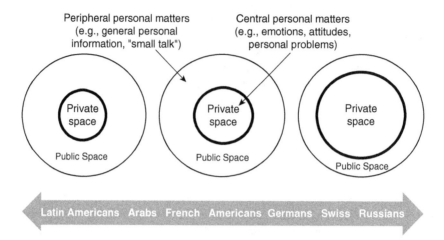

Figure 4.3 Space orientation in different cultures
Source: Adapted from Hall & Hall (1990, p. 131).

relationship with them. However, if another person manages to break through their hard outer shell, they tend to open up and become close loyal friends. This is indicated, for example, by the use of first names instead of surnames and informal second-person pronouns.

- *Peach cultures* are soft on the outside, but have a hard core. They talk more openly about topics that coconut cultures regard as private and tend to make less difference between friends and people they know less well. Members of peach cultures are talkative and perceived as approachable and relaxed. However, their inner world and intimacy is protected by a hard stone. Everyday relationships are therefore less solid and nondurable.

Space orientation is not only relevant in personal interactions, but also in **electronic communication**. Holtbrügge, Weldon and Rogers (2012) analyzed the cultural determinants of email communication styles and revealed that high-space cultures are more task-oriented and maintain social distance. They distinguish clearly between work life and private life, and limit office communication to work-related aspects. Thus, they show a higher preference for task-relatedness in email communication to maintain the symbolic space. In contrast, low-space cultures put more emphasis on social interaction and relationships in email communication, even in a work context. They stress the importance of interpersonal exchange and tend to build longer-term relationships. Therefore, low-space cultures show in emails a tendency to have smaller private spheres and are more concerned with cultivating their interpersonal relationships than high-space cultures.

Differences in privacy orientation are also evident in the context of social media. Individuals in contact cultures, like China, India, the Middle East, and Latin America, are more willing to share personal information, such as private photos, date of birth, names of friends, etc. on social media, such as Facebook and Instagram. On the contrary, individuals in noncontact cultures, like Germany and Switzerland, regard **online privacy** as more relevant. They are more concerned about the risks and potential negative consequences associated with sharing information on social media and more likely to apply privacy-enhancing technologies (Cho, Rivera-Sánchez & Sun 2009; Reed, Sprio & Butts 2016).

Like with context and time orientation, **different space orientations** may lead to serious intercultural management challenges. Peach cultures often perceive coconut cultures as reserved, impolite, and humorless. On the contrary, coconut cultures find peach cultures superficial, infantile, and unreliable. Particularly problematic is the **asymmetric overlap of private and public spheres**. During a longer relationship, the members of coconut cultures tend to open up and allow others access to their private sphere. This shall signal increased trust and intimacy. Members of peach cultures, however, will perceive this as normal form of relaxed interaction and not attach any special relevance to it. For them, the status of the relationship has not changed significantly.

4.2.3 Critical Evaluation

Hall's concept of culture has been frequently cited and applied in various areas, such as leadership, marketing, and communication research. Despite its popularity, however, it is criticized for **methodological shortcomings**. In particular, the qualitative methodology *lacks analytical rigor and intersubjective verifiability* (Cardon 2008). While several comments suggest that his conceptualizations are based on interviews, observations, and personal experiences, Hall does not explain how these were developed and measured. He provides numerous anecdotal examples for his country classifications, but fails to validate and triangulate them with independent sources.

Several subsequent studies developed measures of Hall's three dimensions of culture and tested them empirically. Existing research focuses primarily on context orientation and reveals **inconsistent country classifications**. While the experimental study of Holtbrügge and Kittler (2007) supports Halls's classification of China as high-context and Germany as low-context cultures, Richardson and Smith (2007) show only slight differences between Japan (considered a prototypical high-context culture) and the United States (considered a prototypical low-context culture). Other countries, such as Britain, France, Israel, and Russia, are sometimes classified as high-context and sometimes as low-context cultures (Kittler, Rygl & Mackinnon 2011). Generally, the range of countries in extant research is low. Most studies include the United States as low-context country and compare it with Asian countries as examples of high-context countries, while other countries are rarely considered. Kittler, Rygl, and Mackinnon (2011, p. 77) therefore conclude in their literature review that most studies "do not provide convincing empirical support for the extant country classifications. None of these studies analyses variation in the use of context for more than four national cultures or ethnic groups within a national culture and they do not employ a comprehensive set of countries. In addition, the geographic focus of our sample shows an imbalance, as the studies analyzed mainly employ the classic dichotomous US–Asian comparison."

Another shortcoming of existing research on Hall's cultural dimensions is the **lack of intercultural studies**. In most cases, the prevalence of specific cultural patterns *within* a culture are analyzed, while there are only few studies which focus on interactions *between* individuals with different cultural backgrounds. Again, this can be illustrated with the example of context orientation. While there is extensive literature about communication in high-context cultures as well as in low-context cultures, little is known about communication between high- and low-context cultures, and even less about communication between different high-context cultures, such as, for example, Japan and India (Zaidman 2001).

4.3 THE CONCEPT OF HOFSTEDE

4.3.1 Overview

The Dutch organizational psychologist Geert Hofstede was one of the first management scholars who empirically studied the work-related values of individuals in different cultures and their impact on management. His landmark study *Culture's Consequences* (1980, 2001) is based on a survey among 116,000 employees (at a range of managerial and nonmanagerial levels) at branches and affiliates of the IBM group in 72 countries between 1968 and 1972. According to Hofstede (2001, p. 48), this was "probably the largest body of survey data ever collected with one survey instrument up to that time." Initially, data were analyzed for the 40 largest subsidiaries, each of which had at least 50 employees. The number of countries was later extended to 50, while 14 other countries were grouped into the three multicountry regions East Africa, West Africa, and Arabic countries, so that data were available for 53 countries and regions of the world. Later, replications and extensions of the original IBM study using the Values Survey Module (Hofstede 2013) with data from other populations enlarged the number of countries, multicountry regions, and subcountry regions to currently 111. Table 4.6 shows the data for Hofstede's six cultural values (with 1 being the theoretical minimum and 100 the theoretical maximum).

In contrast to earlier concepts, the etic dimensions along which cultural differences are analyzed were not predefined, but derived empirically from the collected data. Based on factor analysis, four **universal dimensions of culture** were identified which explain 49% of the variance in work-related values: power distance, uncertainty avoidance, individualism vs. collectivism, and masculinity vs. femininity. After recognizing that these four dimensions do not adequately reflect Asian perspectives on culture (Hofstede & Bond 1988), a fifth dimension was introduced: long-term orientation (originally called Confucian dynamism). Based on the World Values Survey, Hofstede, Hofstede, and Minkov (2010) added a sixth dimension: indulgence vs. restraint. Table 4.5 presents an overview of Hofstede's six dimensions of culture and their definitions.

Table 4.5 Hofstede's six cultural dimensions

Dimension	Definition
Power distance	Extent to which the less powerful members of institutions and organizations expect and accept that power is distributed unequally.
Uncertainty avoidance	Extent to which the members of a culture feel threatened by ambiguous or unknown situations and the degree to which they try to avoid such situations by formal rules and regulations.
Individualism vs. collectivism	Degree to which individuals are supposed to look after themselves or remain integrated into basic groups, usually around the family.
Masculinity vs. femininity	Distribution of emotional roles between the genders and relevance of status vs. personal relationships.
Long-term orientation	Extent to which a culture programs its members to accept delayed gratification of their material, social, and emotional needs.
Indulgence vs. restraint	Degree to which a society allows relatively free gratification of basic and natural human drives related to enjoying life and having fun.

Source: Compiled from Hofstede (2001).

Table 4.6 Hofstede's cultural values

	Power distance	Uncertainty avoidance	Individualism vs. Collectivism	Masculinity vs. femininity	Long-term orientation	Indulgence vs. restraint
Africa East	64	52	27	41	32	40
Africa West	77	54	20	46	9	78
Albania	-	-	-	-	61	15
Algeria	-	-	-	-	26	32
Andorra	-	-	-	-	-	65
Arab countries	80	68	38	53	23	34
Argentina	49	86	46	56	20	62
Armenia	-	-	-	-	61	-
Australia	38	51	90	61	21	71
Austria	11	70	55	79	60	63
Azerbaijan	-	-	-	-	61	22
Bangladesh	80	60	20	55	47	20
Belarus	-	-	-	-	81	15
Belgium	65	94	75	54	82	57
Belgium (French)	67	93	72	60	-	-
Belgium (Netherland)	61	97	78	43	-	-
Bosnia	-	-			70	44
Brazil	69	76	38	49	44	59
Bulgaria	70	85	30	40	69	16
Burkina Faso	-	-	-	-	27	18
Canada	39	48	80	52	36	68
Canada (French)	54	60	73	45	-	-
Chile	63	86	23	28	31	68
China	80	30	20	66	87	24
Colombia	67	80	13	64	13	83
Costa Rica	35	86	15	21	-	-
Croatia	73	80	33	40	58	33
Cyprus	-	-	-	-	-	70
Czechia	57	74	58	57	70	29

(Continued)

Table 4.6 Hofstede's cultural values (Continued)

	Power distance	Uncertainty avoidance	Individualism vs. Collectivism	Masculinity vs. femininity	Long-term orientation	Indulgence vs. restraint
Denmark	18	23	74	16	35	70
Dominican Republic	-	-	-	-	13	54
Ecuador	78	67	8	63	-	-
Egypt	-	-	-	-	7	4
Ethiopia	-	-	-	-	-	46
El Salvador	66	94	19	40	20	89
Estonia	40	60	60	30	82	16
Finland	33	59	63	26	38	57
France	68	86	71	43	63	48
Georgia	-	-	-	-	38	32
Germany	35	65	67	66	83	40
Germany (East)	-	-	-	-	78	34
Ghana	-	-	-	-	4	72
Great Britain	35	35	89	66	51	69
Greece	60	112	35	57	45	50
Guatemala	95	101	6	37	-	-
Hong Kong	68	29	25	57	61	17
Hungary	46	82	80	88	58	31
Iceland	-	-	-	-	28	67
India	77	40	48	56	51	26
Indonesia	78	48	14	46	62	38
Iran	58	59	41	43	14	40
Iraq	-	-	-	-	25	17
Ireland	28	35	70	68	24	65
Israel	13	81	54	47	38	-
Italy	50	75	76	70	61	30
Jamaica	45	13	39	68	-	-
Japan	54	92	46	95	88	42
Jordan	-	-	-	-	16	43
Korea South	60	85	18	39	100	29
Kyrgyzstan	-	-	-	-	66	39

Table 4.6 Hofstede's cultural values (Continued)

	Power distance	Uncertainty avoidance	Individualism vs. Collectivism	Masculinity vs. femininity	Long-term orientation	Indulgence vs. restraint
Latvia	44	63	70	9	69	13
Lithuania	42	65	60	19	82	16
Luxembourg	40	70	60	50	64	56
Macedonia	-	-	-	-	62	35
Malaysia	104	36	26	50	41	57
Mali	-	-	-	-	20	43
Malta	56	96	59	47	47	66
Mexico	81	82	30	69	24	97
Moldova	-	-	-	-	71	19
Montenegro	-	-	-	-	75	20
Morocco	70	68	46	53	14	25
Netherlands	38	53	80	14	67	68
New Zealand	22	49	79	58	33	75
Nigeria	-	-	-	-	13	84
Norway	31	50	69	8	35	55
Pakistan	55	70	14	50	50	0
Panama	95	86	11	44	-	-
Peru	64	87	16	42	25	46
Philippines	94	44	32	64	27	42
Poland	68	93	60	64	38	29
Portugal	63	104	27	31	28	33
Puerto Rico	-	-	-	-	0	90
Romania	90	90	30	42	52	20
Russia	93	95	39	36	81	20
Rwanda	-	-	-	-	18	37
Saudi Arabia	-	-	-	-	36	52
Serbia	86	92	25	43	52	28
Singapore	74	8	20	48	72	46
Slovakia	104	51	52	110	77	28
Slovenia	71	88	27	19	49	48
South Africa	-	-	-	-	34	63

(Continued)

Table 4.6 Hofstede's cultural values (Continued)

	Power distance	Uncertainty avoidance	Individualism vs. Collectivism	Masculinity vs. femininity	Long-term orientation	Indulgence vs. restraint
South Africa (White)	49	49	65	63	-	-
Spain	57	86	51	42	48	44
Suriname	85	92	47	37	-	-
Sweden	31	29	71	5	53	78
Switzerland	34	58	68	70	74	66
Switzerland (French)	70	70	64	58	-	-
Switzerland (German)	26	56	69	72	-	-
Taiwan	58	69	17	45	93	49
Tanzania	-	-	-	-	34	38
Thailand	64	64	20	34	32	45
Trinidad and Tobago	47	55	16	58	13	80
Turkey	66	85	37	45	46	49
United States	40	46	91	62	26	68
Uganda	-	-	-	-	24	52
Ukraine	-	-	-	-	86	14
Uruguay	61	100	36	38	26	53
Venezuela	81	76	12	73	16	100
Vietnam	70	30	20	40	57	35
Zambia	-	-	-	-	30	42
Zimbabwe	-	-	-	-	15	28

Source: https://geerthofstede.com/research-and-vsm/dimension-data-matrix/

Hofstede (1980, p. 13) defines culture as "the **collective programming of the mind** which distinguishes one category of people from another." Culture is understood as "software of the mind" (Hofstede 1991) that programs the values and behaviors of people in one way or another. Although Hofstede recognizes that culture has a profound impact on each individual member of society, he continuously stresses that any comparison between cultures needs to be conducted at a country or nation level rather than an individual or group level. "We do not compare individuals, but we compare what is called central tendencies in the answers from each country. There is hardly an individual who answers each question exactly by the mean score of his or her group: the 'average person' from a country does not exist" (Hofstede 1991, p. 253).

4.3.2 Dimensions of Culture

4.3.2.1 Power Distance

Power distance indicates the extent to which the less powerful members of institutions and organizations expect and accept that power is distributed unequally. Thus, not the actual equal or unequal distribution of power is relevant, but whether this is expected and accepted in the particular culture. Power distance is the highest in many Asian countries, Africa, Latin America, and Eastern Europe. It is the smallest in Scandinavia, Israel, and the German-speaking countries Austria, Germany, and German-speaking Switzerland.

Russia is among the countries with the largest power distance in the world. This is reflected, for example, in the accentuated position of political leaders. Since tsarism, the Russian people have expected and accepted that high-ranking politicians enjoy extensive privileges. Accordingly, Russian President Vladimir Putin presents himself not only in a very powerful way, but defies all attempts of effective control by law. The constitution gives the president unrestricted power and allows him to operate above the system of legislative, judicial, and executive separation of powers. The vast majority of Russians does not only accept this enormous concentration of power, but welcomes it as sign of strength and assertiveness (Zimmerman 2014).

The opposite attitude can be found in Norway. Along with the other Scandinavian countries, Norway is a very egalitarian society where everybody is treated equally and nobody is accepted to be above the law. This ideology was famously captured in a photo in 1973 when the King of Norway hopped on to a train during the OPEC oil crisis in solidarity and support for his fellow Norwegians who were asked to leave their cars at home and use public transport instead. The ticket collector offered him a free ride, but Olav V insisted to pay the ticket fare. Norwegian satirist Odd Børretsen (2003) captured the spirit of this important sense of absolute equality amongst Norwegian people: "A Norwegian's attitude to God is about the same as his attitude to the king: he thinks that God—and the King—er OK kind of guys, as long he behaves like a proper Norwegian and doesn't believe he is anything special."

At the workplace, **large power distance** is associated with adherence to hierarchies, respect for superiors, and a general acceptance of the presence of inequalities on the part of the subordinate (Table 4.7). Organizations tend to have more hierarchical levels (vertical differentiation), a higher proportion of supervisory personnel (narrow span of control), and more centralized decision-making. A paternalistic and autocratic leadership style is favored over a participative approach. Coercive and referent power is stressed over reward, expert, and legitimate power. Employees follow the instructions of their superiors unconditionally and will typically not initiate interactions with them, even if orders are not understood or regarded as unreasonable.

Small power distance reflects an egalitarian perspective according to which social class and status are of little relevance. Participation in decision-making is not determined by an employee's position or rank in the organization. Status symbols and privileges restricted to managers are avoided. Both superiors and subordinates can seek communication and contribute suggestions and recommendations. Employees value independence rather than conformity. Hierarchical relationships are perceived as convenience

Table 4.7 Key differences between small- and large-power distance societies at the workplace

Small-power distance	Large-power distance
• Hierarchy in organizations means an inequality of roles, established for convenience.	• Hierarchy in organizations reflects existential inequality between higher and lower levels.
• Decentralization is popular.	• Centralization is popular.
• There are fewer supervisory personnel.	• There are more supervisory personnel.
• There is a narrow salary range between the top and the bottom of the organization.	• There is a wide salary range between the top and the bottom of the organization.
• Managers rely on their own experience and on subordinates.	• Managers rely on superiors and on formal rules.
• Subordinates expect to be consulted.	• Subordinates expect to be told what to do.
• The ideal boss is a resourceful democrat.	• The ideal boss is a benevolent autocrat, or "good father."
• Subordinate-superior relations are pragmatic.	• Subordinate-superior relations are emotional.
• Privileges and status symbols are frowned upon.	• Privileges and status symbols are normal and popular.
• Manual work has the same status as office work.	• White-collar jobs are valued more than blue-collar jobs.

Source: Hofstede, Hofstede & Minkov (2010, p. 76).

arrangements rather than as having existential justification. Managers like to see themselves as practical and systematic, and they admit a need for support. They are more likely to make decisions only after consulting with subordinates. Subordinates dislike close supervision and prefer a participative leadership style.

4.3.2.2 Uncertainty Avoidance

Uncertainty avoidance is defined as the extent to which the members of a culture feel threatened in ambiguous or unknown situations and the degree to which they try to avoid such situations by formal rules and regulations. Cultures with **strong uncertainty avoidance** are characterized by rigid beliefs and behavior guidelines and a strong emotional need for formal rules: "Everything is forbidden which is not explicitly allowed." Uncertainty avoidance is particularly strong in Japan, Eastern Europe, Latin America, and Mediterranean countries, and correlated across countries with measures of anxiety symptoms, neuroticism, and lower subjective well-being.

At the workplace, rules and regulations are valued (Table 4.8). They are regarded as means to increase the reliability of expectations and thus to reduce uncertainty. Managers are expected to issue clear instructions, and subordinates' initiatives are more tightly controlled. Employees typically have a strong preference for job security and long-term career planning and will change their employer less often. Organizations show a high degree of formalization and specialization that becomes evident in the importance attached to technical competence in the tale of staff and in defining jobs and functions. Managers avoid taking risks and focus on approved procedures and tools. The classical leadership functions of planning, organizing, coordinating, and controlling dominate.

Table 4.8 Key differences between weak and strong uncertainty-avoidance societies at the workplace

Weak uncertainty avoidance	Strong uncertainty avoidance
• More changes of employer, shorter service.	• Fewer changes of employer, longer service, more difficult work–life balance.
• There should be no more rules than strictly necessary.	• There is an emotional need for rules, even if they will not work.
• Work hard only when needed.	• There is an emotional need to be busy and an inner urge to work hard.
• Time is a framework for orientation.	• Time is money.
• Tolerance for ambiguity and chaos.	• Need for precision and formalization.
• Belief in generalists and common sense.	• Belief in experts and technical solutions.
• Top managers are concerned with strategy.	• Top managers are concerned with daily operations.
• More new trademarks.	• Fewer new trademarks.
• Focus on decision process.	• Focus on decision content.
• Intrapreneurs are relatively free from rules.	• Intrapreneurs are constrained by existing rules.
• There are fewer self-employed people.	• There are more self-employed people.
• Better at invention, worse at implementation.	• Worse at invention, better at implementation.
• Motivation by achievement and esteem or belonging.	• Motivation by security and esteem or belonging.

Source: Hofstede, Hofstede & Minkov (2010, p. 217).

Cultures with **weak uncertainty avoidance** have a higher tolerance for deviations. Dealing with problems is characterized by serenity and convenience and low stress inclination: "Everything is allowed which is not explicitly forbidden." Uncertainty avoidance is weak in many Asian countries as well as in Scandinavia. In contrast to people in high uncertainty cultures who tend to believe that "what is different is dangerous," people in low uncertainty cultures believe that "what is different is curious" (Hofstede 2001, p. 155). Countries lower in uncertainty avoidance tend to be Protestant, Hindu, or Buddhist, i.e., characterized by religions that are less absolute than Catholicism.

At the workplace, individuals have a greater willingness to change. Firms are typically very innovative, but may find it more difficult to implement new concepts and to achieve operational efficiency. Management careers are preferred over specialist careers, and professional managers do not feel constrained to develop technical expertise in the field they manage. Interorganizational conflict is considered natural, and compromise is an accepted route for reconciliation. Managers are prepared to break formal rules and bypass hierarchical structures to communicate with a superior or peer if necessary. Foreigners are accepted as managers with relatively little suspicion.

4.3.2.3 Individualism vs. Collectivism

Individualism describes the degree to which people are supposed to look after themselves or remain integrated into basic groups. This conceptualization of individualism vs. collectivism is very similar to the Kluckhon and Strodtbeck's (1961) dimension of relational orientation. Hofstede also frequently refers to

Triandis (1995a) who has conducted extensive research on individualism and collectivism and regards this as the most important dimension to understand cultural differences. According to the meta-analysis of Field et al. (2021), individualism explains the highest proportion of variance among Hofstede's six dimensions of culture in intercultural management studies.

People in **individualistic cultures** view themselves as independent of others. The interests of the individual prevail over those of the group. Self-interest and the need for self-realization are emphasized. Ties between individuals are loose and often goal oriented. Based on the ideal of equality, other people are all treated in the same way. In Christianity, this is most prominently reflected in the "commandment of charity." Accordingly, individualism prevails especially in North America and Western Europe, where Christian influence is strong.

In the workplace, individualistic cultures stress individual achievements and rights, and expect individuals to focus on satisfying their own needs (Table 4.9). Individual decisions are generally preferred over group decisions, and the individual has a right to thoughts and opinions which differ from those held by the majority. Managers lack emotional attachment to the company, and their involvement is essentially calculative. They aim for variety rather than conformity at work. Recruitment and promotion are primarily merit based.

Table 4.9 Key differences between collectivist and individualist societies at the workplace

Collectivist	Individualist
• Occupational mobility is lower.	• Occupational mobility is higher.
• Employees are members of in-groups who will pursue the in-group's interest.	• Employees are "economic persons" who will pursue the employer's interest if it coincides with their self-interest.
• Hiring and promotion decisions take employee's in-group into account.	• Hiring and promotion decisions are supposed to be based on skills and rules only.
• The employer–employee relationship is basically moral, like a family link.	• The employer–employee relationship is a contract between parties in a labor market.
• Management is management of groups.	• Management is management of individuals.
• Direct appraisal of subordinates spoils harmony.	• Management training teaches the honest sharing of feelings.
• In-group customers get better treatment (particularism).	• Every customer should get the same treatment (universalism).
• Relationship prevails over task.	• Task prevails over relationship.

Source: Hofstede, Hofstede & Minkov (2010, p. 124).

In **collectivistic cultures**, people have a pronounced "we-consciousness" and think of themselves as part of a "we group" or "in-group"—first and foremost the (extended) family and then coworkers, tribe, nation, etc. According to Hsu (1963), the primary allegiance of an individual in China is the *clan* and in India the *caste*, which is in sharp contrast to the United States where the social structure is perceived as a number of individuals who come together in various *clubs* that they can voluntarily join or leave. In collectivist cultures, the overall benefit of the group prevails over the interest of the individual. Group members and outsiders are treated differently. This is often reflected in different linguistic codes for in-group and out-group members (Yum 1988). Interpersonal relationships and caring for members of the group are more important than rational valuations of their advantages and disadvantages. Violations of social rules are sanctioned morally (shame) and less legally (guilt). Collectivism is most prevalent in Asia, Africa, and Latin America.

Collectivistic cultures prefer group decisions as opposed to individual decision-making. Consensus and cooperation are more valued than individual initiative and effort. Motivation derives from a sense of belonging, and rewards are based on loyalty and tenure. The role of leadership in collectivist cultures is to facilitate team effort and integration, to foster a supportive atmosphere, and to increase group cohesion. This is also reflected in recruitment decisions which usually pay more attention to group fit than individual achievements.

In collectivist cultures, the responsibilities of leaders regularly go far beyond work-related matters and involve also private issues. In Asian countries, like China, Japan, and Korea, superiors are often perceived as fathers who are obliged to care for the subordinates like family members. A study of Kim (1994) in Korea, for example, found that firms regularly congratulate employees on the birth of a child. 79% congratulate employees when their children marry. Even school admission of an employee's child is cause for congratulation in 15% of the participating firms. Another characteristic of the collectivistic orientation and paternalistic leadership style is that 47% of Korean firms send condolences to employees whose grandparents died and 40% for the death of a parent-in-law. 31% congratulate employees for the birthday of one of their parents-in-law.

4.3.2.4 Masculinity vs. Femininity

Masculinity vs. femininity refers to the distribution of emotional roles between the genders and relevance of status vs. personal relationships. In **masculine cultures**, emotional gender roles are sharply differentiated. Men are supposed to be assertive, tough, and focused on material success, whereas women are supposed to be more modest, tender, and concerned with the quality of life. Material values and meritocracy are emphasized. Conflicts are openly addressed and discharged. Masculinity is the highest in Japan, China, Latin America, the Anglo-Saxon countries, and the German-speaking countries.

In the workplace, masculinity is reflected in a decisive and aggressive leadership style (Table 4.10). Managers see their main role in achieving bottom-line profits to satisfy shareholders. Challenging work tasks and the opportunity for advancement to higher-level jobs are more valued. Task accomplishment is more important than taking care of oneself. Individuals are primarily motivated by monetary incentives. Labor relations are often marked by hostility and frequently result in fierce and extended fights with labor unions.

In **feminine cultures**, emotional gender roles overlap, and little differentiation is made between men and women in the same job. Both men and women are supposed to be modest, tender, and concerned with the quality of life. Interpersonal relationships, cooperation, and solidarity are more important than power and property. Femininity is the highest in Scandinavia and the Baltics, and to a lesser extent in some Eastern European countries and diverse countries like Angola, Costa Rica, and Thailand.

Table 4.10 Key differences between feminine and masculine societies at the workplace

Feminine	Masculine
• Management as ménage: intuition and consensus.	• Management as manège: decisive and aggressive.
• Resolution of conflicts by compromise and negotiation.	• Resolution of conflicts by letting the strongest win.
• Rewards are based on equality.	• Rewards are based on equity.
• Preference for smaller organizations.	• Preference for larger organizations.
• People work in order to live.	• People live in order to work.
• More leisure time is preferred over more money.	• More money is preferred over more leisure time.
• Careers are optional for both genders.	• Careers are compulsory for men, optional for women.
• There is a higher share of working women in professional jobs.	• There is a lower share of working women in professional jobs.
• Humanization of work by contact and cooperation.	• Humanization of work by job content enrichment.
• Competitive agriculture and service industries.	• Competitive manufacturing and bulk chemistry.

Source: Hofstede, Hofstede & Minkov (2010, p. 170).

Feminine cultures value atmosphere at the worksite and caring for the environment more than interesting job tasks. The role of leaders is to safeguard employee well-being and demonstrate concern for social responsibility. Great emphasis is placed on consensus building. Competition and career advancement are less important than work–life balance: People "work in order to live" and not "live in order to work." Work and private spheres are separated. Men are accepted to work in professions that may elsewhere be associated with the feminine role—primary-school teaching, nursing, and homemaking. Feminine cultures show a high degree of part-time employment in higher positions.

4.3.2.5 Long-term Orientation

Long-term orientation is defined as the extent to which a culture programs its members to accept delayed gratification of their material, social, and emotional needs. It is similar to Kluckhohn and Strodtbeck's (1961) dimension of time orientation. Since it has been introduced much later than the initial four dimensions and is not based on the original IBM study, it has received less attention in the intercultural management literature and been adapted less often in subsequent empirical studies (Fang 2003).

Long-term-oriented cultures are characterized by persistence and perseverance in the pursuit of goals (Table 4.11). Saving and investment have higher value than spending. Employer loyalty is high and job changes are less frequent. Education is regarded as most important means to progress in life. Employees value long-term career plans and accept deferred compensation. There are no absolute, universal guidelines. Instead, people show high tolerance of ambiguity. Long-term orientation is prevalent in Asia and many Eastern European cultures. In East Asia, this is significantly caused by the philosophy of Confucius. One of its main features is to initiate, develop, and maintain social relationships which are enduring and often last for life (Hofstede & Bond 1988).

In contrast, **short-term-oriented cultures** strive for quick profits. Accordingly, the propensity to consume is high and the savings rate low. Reward systems focus on bonus payments rather than long-term development. Analytical thinking and rational decision-making are prevalent and based on abstract and universal guidelines. Personal loyalties are weak and vary with business needs. On the labor market, job changes are frequent and regional as well as hierarchical mobility are high. Consumer decisions are often made based on more immediate desires with less contemplation of future consequences. Short-term orientation is prevalent in Africa, many Latin American countries, and the United States.

Table 4.11 Key differences between short- and long-term orientation societies at the workplace and ways of thinking

Short-term orientation	Long-term orientation
• Main work values include freedom, rights, achievement, and thinking for oneself.	• Main work values include learning, honesty, adaptiveness, accountability, and self-discipline.
• Leisure time is important.	• Leisure time is not important.
• Focus is on the "bottom line."	• Focus is on market position.
• Importance of this year's profits.	• Importance of profits 10 years from now.
• Managers and workers are psychologically in two camps.	• Owner-managers and workers share the same aspirations.
• Meritocracy, reward by abilities.	• Wide social and economic differences are undesirable.
• Personal loyalties vary with business needs.	• Investment in lifelong personal networks, *guanxi*.
• Concern with possessing the Truth.	• Concern with respecting the demands of Virtue.
• There are universal guidelines about what is good and evil.	• What is good and evil depends on the circumstances.
• Dissatisfaction with one's own contributions to daily human relations and to correcting injustice.	• Satisfaction with one's own contributions to daily human relations and to correcting injustice.
• Matter and spirit are separated.	• Matter and spirit are integrated.
• If A is true, its opposite B must be false.	• If A is true, its opposite B can also be true.
• Priority is given to abstract rationality.	• Priority is given to common sense.
• There is a need for cognitive consistency.	• Disagreement does not hurt.
• Analytical thinking.	• Synthetic thinking.

Source: Hofstede, Hofstede & Minkov (2010, p. 251).

An indicator of long-term orientation is a country's savings rate. China and Germany, two countries that score particularly high on this dimension, have among the highest saving rates in the world. The counterexample is the United States where the savings rate is low and large purchases are predominantly financed by loans. The share of equity in the purchase of real estate is very low and the average debt level of consumers high.

While the correlation between long-term orientation and savings rate is consistently found in empirical studies, the explanations of this relationship vary. While Galor and Özak (2016) trace variation in long-term orientation across countries back to preindustrial agroclimatic

(Continued)

characteristics, Chen (2013) relates future orientation attitudes of individuals to the grammatical structure of the language spoken by them. Languages that disassociate future from the present make the future more distant and therefore provide less incentives to save.

4.3.2.6 Indulgence vs. Restraint

Indulgence is the degree to which a society allows relatively free gratification of basic and natural human drives related to enjoying life and having fun. Individuals in **indulgent cultures** believe themselves to be in control of their own life and emotions (Table 4.12). Leisure and having friends are regarded as important. People tend to be optimistic and remember more positive emotions. Countries and regions that rank high on indulgence are North America, South America, West Africa, and Oceania.

Table 4.12 Key differences between indulgent and restrained societies

Indulgent	Restrained
• Higher percentages of very happy people.	• Lower percentage of very happy people.
• A perception of personal life control.	• A perception of helplessness: what happens to me is not my own doing.
• Higher importance of leisure.	• Lower importance of leisure.
• Higher importance of having friends.	• Lower importance of having friends.
• Thrift is not very important.	• Thrift is important.
• Loose society.	• Tight society.
• More likely to remember positive emotions.	• Less likely to remember positive emotions.
• Less moral discipline.	• Moral discipline.
• Positive attitude.	• Cynicism.
• More extroverted personalities.	• More neurotic personalities.
• Higher percentages of people who feel healthy.	• Lower percentages of people who feel healthy.
• Higher optimism.	• More pessimism.

Source: Hofstede, Hofstede & Minkov (2010, p. 291).

In the workplace, this is likely to impact the willingness of employees to voice opinions and give feedback. Employees are more likely to leave their employer when they are not satisfied with their job. Interaction with coworkers and customers are typically more emotional.

Restrained cultures control the gratification of needs and regulate it by means of strict social norms. They place high value on control and moral discipline. Individuals believe that their life is dictated by others. Emotions are typically not shown in public and people tend to be more pessimistic. Most countries in Asia, the Middle East, Eastern Europe, and the Baltics rank high on this dimension.

Organizations in restrained cultures are characterized by a high degree of professionalism. Technical features (quality, functionality, precision, etc.) are more important than emotional aspects (design, aesthetics, image, etc.). Emotions in the workplace are considered inappropriate and inefficient.

4.3.3 Critical Evaluation

Hofstede's concept of culture has received outstanding attention in management literature. With more than 200,000 quotations on Google Scholar as of December 2021, Hofstede is one of the most influential management scholars worldwide. Reviewers emphasize the rigorous research design, systematic data collection, and large sample size (Søndergaard 1994; Taras, Kirkman & Steel 2010). A major advantage compared to previous concepts of culture is the fact that Hofstede provides numerical data for the proposed dimensions of culture which has greatly facilitated the concept's application in managerial practice and empirical research (Bing 2004). After his initial study, Hofstede published numerous subsequent academic works and supporting materials (such as books for practitioners, case studies, intercultural trainings, etc.) that further popularized his concept. According to Kirkman, Lowe, and Gibson (2006), Hofstede's framework accounts for more than half of the scholarly articles published between 1980 and 2002 that at least mention cultural dimensions, making it by far the most often cited concept of culture in intercultural management literature, far ahead of Trompenaars, Schwartz, and GLOBE. Peterson (2003, p. 128) summarizes **Hofstede's Consequences** as follows: "Perhaps the first edition of *Culture's Consequences* did not create the field of comparative cross-cultural studies but it certainly has shaped the field's basic themes, structure and controversies for over 20 years."

Hofstede's concept of culture received much attention beyond the business context. A recent example is research on **societies' responses to COVID-19**. The study of Lu, Jin, and English (2021) provides evidence that collectivism (vs. individualism) is positively associated with the willingness to wear protective masks. Collectivism is also supportive of utilizing digital technologies to curb the spread of the pandemic. According to Huynh (2020), uncertainty avoidance increases the preparedness of social distancing in the public. For example, while social distancing is largely accepted in Germany (i.e., a country that scores high on uncertainty avoidance), northern European countries Denmark and Sweden are less prone to social distancing since these countries have lower uncertainty avoidance indices. Other studies found positive effects of power distance and restraint on compliance with governmental social restriction policies (Dheer, Egri & Treviño 2021; Gokmen, Baskici & Ercil 2021).

Despite these achievements, Hofstede's concept has been frequently criticized. While some **criticism** is not limited to Hofstede but apply to etic concepts of culture in general (and will therefore be discussed in Chapter 4.9), some specific considerations with regard to the theoretical conceptualization and research methodology of his study need further discussion.

A major criticism relates to the **construction and labeling of the cultural dimensions**. While Hofstede conceptualizes them as universal, some reviewers argue that they are culture bound and affected by Western cultural bias (McSweeney 2002; Baskerville 2003; Ailon 2008). This is reflected, for example, in the dimension of individualism vs. collectivism. While in the United States, individualism is mostly understood as preference for competition over cooperation, it represents the struggle against the impersonal state in authoritarian countries (Triandis 1995a). And while the United States is regarded as the most individualistic country in Hofstede's study, it shows remarkable signs of collectivism at the same time. For example, Americans form more voluntary associations than any other country in the world and have a high preference for teamwork (Hampden-Turner & Trompenaars 1997). Similarly, collectivist behavior in one context might have other connotations elsewhere. For example, Yeh (1988) points out that the Japanese are mostly loyal to their organizations and the Chinese to their families. Thus, a Chinese employee who places his collectivist family interests over the interests of the organization is regarded disloyal by Japanese and vice versa. Hofstede has partially responded to this criticism by extending the original concept with the fifth dimension of long-term orientation that was aimed to better reflect the specific features of Asian cultures. Moreover, he emphasizes in later studies that "adding locally defined items would have made the studies more meaningful" (Hofstede et al. 2010, p. 336).

Hofstede's concept is **restricted to the level of work-related values**. The conflation of culture with values is problematic because it focuses on just a subset of psychological constructs, while the possible roles of others (desires, goals, motives, needs, traits, aversions, tastes, interests, likes, attractions, dispositions, valences, attitudes, preferences, cathexes, sentiments, etc.) are neglected (McSweeney 2013). According to Schein's (2017) iceberg model of culture, for example, values represent only one layer of culture next to basic assumptions and symbol systems. Thus, values are an important aspect of culture, but they cannot be equated with culture (Baskerville 2003; Ailon 2008).

The **validity of the items** in Hofstede's questionnaire is also frequently criticized (e.g., McSweeney 2002; Schmitz & Weber 2014). As the original four dimensions of culture were empirically derived from the results of explorative factor analyses, the items that load on the four factors often lack of theoretical consistency. For example, the uncertainty avoidance dimension was compiled based on the following items. "How often do you feel nervous or tense at work?," "How long do you think you will continue working for this company?," and "Company rules should not be broken—even when the employee thinks it is in the company's best interests." It is hard to see how stress, employment stability, and rule orientation lead to the dimension of uncertainty avoidance. This is also acknowledged by Hofstede (2001, p. 148) when he states: "It is possible that other and perhaps better survey indicators of national levels of uncertainty avoidance can be developed, but I had to use the data available in the IBM archives, and uncertainty avoidance was not a familiar concept to us when we composed the IBM questionnaire in 1967." In other cases, theoretically similar items that sometimes even paraphrase each other are used to measure different cultural dimensions. For instance, "high value put on independence" is regarded as indicator of low power distance, while "belief in the independent decision maker" is interpreted as sign of high masculinity.

Even more problematic is that the items which are applied to measure the cultural dimensions are often not reflected in their explanations, while the pairs of opposites used to describe the cultural dimensions include a great variety of facets and were not part of their measurement (see, for example, Tables 4.7–4.12). Most components of Hofstede's cultural dimensions were neither explored nor confirmed empirically, but written in them based on secondary sources. This causes a significant **lack of analytical clarity**.

Another methodological concern relates to the **generalizability of the findings**. The survey respondents are from a single large multinational corporation (IBM), occupied mainly in marketing and servicing, and male-dominated. While some reviewers regard this as restriction (e.g., Søndergaard 1994; McSweeney 2002; Moulettes 2007), Hofstede (2001) argues that the focus on one single company and similar occupations is more of an advantage as the results are not biased by potential influences of different industry, corporate, and occupational cultures.

The **age of the study** is another point of criticism. Data were collected between 1968 and 1973, and it is doubtful whether the study is valid still today. Particularly, the "westernization" of many emerging markets leads to significant changes of cultural values. For example, the longitudinal meta-analysis of the development of Hofstede's dimensions between 1970 and 2000 conducted by Taras, Steel, and Kirkman (2012) finds an overall gradual increase in individualism and a decrease in power distance, masculinity, and uncertainty avoidance. The pace and direction of these changes, however, vary greatly among the countries. The biggest shifts toward values of developed capitalist societies are observed for the countries that experienced changes in their political and economic systems, such as China, the former member states of the USSR (e.g., Russia, Ukraine) as well as the emerging economies of Latin America (e.g., Brazil, Argentina). For example, while power distance was much higher in Latin America than the United States in the 1970s, both regions show similar values in 2000. During the same period, Latin American countries became significantly more individualistic, while a light shift toward collectivism is observed in the United States. Despite this frequently observed "cultural crossvergence" (Ralston 2008), however, results of Hofstede's original study are **confirmed by a large number of replica studies** (the results of those published until the year 2000 are summarized in the annex of Hofstede 2001). This applies both to the corroboration of the cultural dimensions as well as the ranking of countries along these dimensions (Beugelsdijk, Maseland & van Hoorn 2015).

Finally, reviewers discuss the **unit of analysis** and question whether Hofstede has really studied cultures and not countries (Baskerville 2003). In particular, it is criticized that Hofstede did not consider *country-spanning cultures* (e.g., Armenians, Chinese, Kurds) and *multicultural countries* (e.g., Brazil, Belgium, India, Russia, South Africa, Switzerland, United States). The latter criticism has led Hofstede to collect data for some countries (Belgium, Canada, Germany, South Africa, and Switzerland) based on linguistic differences (e.g., French-speaking and Dutch-speaking Belgium, French-speaking and German-speaking Switzerland) (Table 4.6).

Summarizing the concerns of several reviewers and considering the various extensions and amendments of Hofstede's original study, it is less the study itself, but the "stampede toward Hofstede's framework" (Sivakumar & Nakata 2001) and "on-going unquestioning acceptance of Hofstede's national culture research by his evangelized entourage" (McSweeney 2002, p. 112) that causes critique. Intercultural management scholars therefore increasingly demand to overcome the "Hofstedian Hegemony" (Javidan et al. 2006, p. 910) and to go "beyond Hofstede" (Nakata 2009).

4.4 THE CONCEPT OF TROMPENAARS AND HAMPDEN-TURNER

4.4.1 Overview

Fons Trompenaars is a Dutch-French management consultant and intercultural trainer. His concept of culture originates in his doctoral dissertation at the University of Pennsylvania's Wharton School of Business in 1983 (Trompenaars 1994). It was later refined together with the British management philosopher Charles Hampden-Turner, who became the coauthor of *Riding the Waves of Culture* from the second edition on. Their model of cultural diversity consists of seven bipolar dimensions (Figure 4.4). The first five dimensions describe relationships with other people. They are based on the relational orientations of Parsons and Shils (1951). The remaining two dimensions are orientation in time and attitude toward the environment, taken from Kluckhohn and Strodtbeck (1961).

To explore cultural differences with regard to these seven dimensions, data from approximately 80,000 managers working for multinational companies in more than 60 countries were collected (Hampden-Turner & Trompenaars 2012). Some of the respondents were participants in the authors' intercultural training programs, while others were contacted in questionnaire surveys. The respondents were confronted with a series of briefly described imaginary dilemma situations (several of these were taken from

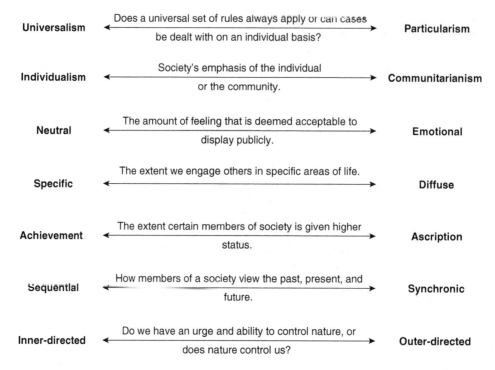

Figure 4.4 Hampden-Turner and Trompenaars's cultural dimensions
Source: Compiled from Hampden-Turner & Trompenaars (2012).

Stouffer & Toby 1951) and asked how they would react. Other questionnaire items provide a forced choice between two value statements referring to aspects of organizational behavior or more general issues. The national averages of the responses to the dilemma situations are summarized in a number of bar charts.

4.4.2 Dimensions of Culture

4.4.2.1 Universalism vs. Particularism

The dimension universalism vs. particularism concerns the standards by which relationships are measured. **Universalism** is the belief that ideas and practices can be applied everywhere without modification. Universalist cultures see one reality and focus on formal rules. They are inclined to follow the rules and try to treat all cases the same, even when friends are involved. Firms operating in universalist cultures typically excel in exploration, scientific management, and mass production.

Particularism is the belief that circumstances dictate how ideas and practices should be applied. Particularist cultures find personal relationships more important than abstract rules. Rules can be suspended or bended for family members, close friends, or important persons. Cultures with particularist values see reality as more subjective and find it important to get to know the people one is doing business with. Firms in particularist cultures favor strong personal ties and custom-tailored solutions.

To measure the preference for more universalist or particularist values, Hampden-Turner and Trompenaars (2012, p. 45) present the members of different cultures the following dilemma situation (from Stouffer & Toby 1951): *"You are riding in a car driven by a close friend. He hits a pedestrian. You know he was going driving at least 35 miles per hour in an area of the city where the maximum allowed speed is 20 miles per hour. There are no witnesses. His lawyer says that if you testify under oath in court that he was only driving 20 miles per hour it may save him from serious consequences. What do you think you would do in view of the obligations of a sworn witness and the obligation to your friend?"* The results show that Western industrialized countries are generally more universalist, while Asian and Latin American countries are more particularist.

4.4.2.2 Individualism vs. Communitarianism

The second dimension proposed by Hampden-Turner and Trompenaars is associated with the needs and rights of individuals in comparison to the well-being of the community. This dimension is closely related to the respective concepts of individualism vs. collectivism of Kluckhohn and Strodtbeck and Hofstede.

Individualist cultures are characterized by a strong sense of self-expression, self-reliance, and self-interest. Individualism leads to a search for talents and an emergence of strong competition among people and firms. Individuals are expected to make their own decisions and to take care mainly of themselves. The quality of life results from personal freedom and individual development. Decisions are often made on the spot and without consultation.

Communitarian cultures place greater emphasis on common goals, collective efforts, and concern for others. People believe that quality of life greatly depends on relationships with other people. They are firmly integrated into groups which provide help and protection in exchange for loyalty. Decision-making is slower as many people are involved. Group rewards are more common than individual incentives. This makes stronger cooperation in business and long-term partnerships between companies and their various stakeholders more likely.

Similar to universalism vs. particularism, individualism is particularly strong in Western Europe and North America. Communitarianism prevails in Asia, Africa, and Latin America.

4.4.2.3 Neutral vs. Emotional

This dimension focuses on the degree to which people express emotions, and the interplay between reason and emotion in human relationships. It is similar to Hofstede's dimension of indulgence vs. restraint.

In **neutral cultures**, individuals carefully control emotions and are reluctant to show feelings. Reason dominates interactions with others. Individuals often appear cool and rational. Neutral cultures include Germany, Japan, the Netherlands, and the United Kingdom.

In **emotional cultures**, feelings are expressed openly and naturally. People often smile, talk loudly when excited, and greet each other with enthusiasm. Examples of emotional or affective cultures include Italy, Spain, and Latin America.

4.4.2.4 Specificity vs. Diffuseness

This dimension relates to the distinction between a system and its various parts. It becomes visible, for example, in the separation or diffusion of personal and professional life.

In **specific cultures**, each element of a situation is analyzed separately, viewing the whole as the sum of its parts. Personal and work life are kept separate and overlaps between the two spheres are avoided. Specifically oriented individuals concentrate on hard facts. Others are engaged in specific areas of life, affecting single levels of personality. For example, a manager separates the task relationship with a subordinate from the private sphere.

Diffusive cultures acknowledge complexities and accept irregularities in relationships, value systems, and organizations. All elements of a situation are related to each other and seen in the perspective of the complete picture. Consequently, people tend to regard their personal and work life as interconnected. For example, social activities with work colleagues outside the work context are common.

To measure the preference for more specific or diffuse values, Hampden-Turner & Trompenaars (2012, p. 108) present the members of different cultures the following dilemma situation: *"If you were asked by your supervisor to help him paint his house, would you do it?"*. Individuals in Western industrialized countries perceive no obligation to assist their superiors in their free time. On the contrary, work life and private life are regarded more interwoven in Asia, Africa, and Latin America.

4.4.2.5 Achieved Status vs. Ascribed Status

The dimension achievement vs. ascription focuses on how personal status is assigned and treated (Linton 1936). **Achieved status** is about gaining status through knowledge, skills, and performance. Individuals earn and lose their status through what they do. Anyone can challenge a decision if they have a convincing argument. Cultures where status is achieved are characterized by a high social mobility and emphasize personal development. Examples of achievement cultures include Scandinavia, North America, the United Kingdom, Australia, and New Zealand.

Ascribed status is attributed to a person by virtue of age, class, gender, education, etc. It is not based on what individuals do, but who they are. The focus of human resource management is on personal selection. A decision will only be challenged by someone with higher authority. Examples are the British monarchy and the Indian caste system.

Firms from an achievement culture doing business in an ascription culture are recommended to select older and experienced managers with formal titles as expatriates. On the other hand, for firms from an ascription culture doing business in an achievement culture, it is more important to send knowledgeable specialists with strong performance orientation abroad (Trompenaars & Woolliams 2003).

4.4.2.6 Inner Direction vs. Outer Direction

Similar to Kluckhohn and Strodtbeck (1961), the beliefs about an individual's ability and power to control nature and to influence the environment constitute another dimension of Hampden-Turner and Trompenaars' concept of culture.

Members of **innerdirected cultures** are driven by the belief that they can control their environment to achieve their goals. Winning is important and aggressive personalities are thus prevalent. The role of managers is seen in making decisions and imposing them on their subordinates. Examples of internal direction cultures include the United States, the United Kingdom, and Australia.

Societies where an **outerdirected perspective** prevails emphasize the role of chance and fate. People believe that they must work with their environment to achieve their goals. Winning isn't as important as maintaining a strong relationship with the outer world. Examples of outerdirected cultures include China, Russia, and Saudi Arabia.

4.4.2.7 Sequential Time vs. Synchronous Time

In line with the concepts of Kluckhohn and Strodtbeck (1961) and Hall (1983), Hampden-Turner and Trompenaars lastly regard time perception as important dimension of culture. Time orientation has two aspects: the relative importance cultures give to the past, present, and future and their approach to structuring time.

If a culture is predominantly oriented toward the *past*, the future is often seen as a repetition of previous experiences. In a culture predominantly oriented toward the *present*, day-by-day experiences tend to direct people's lives. In a *future-oriented* culture, most human activities are directed toward future prospects. In this case, the past is not considered to be vitally significant to the future.

Sequentialism and synchronism form the different approaches to structuring time. People with a **sequential time orientation** view time as a series of passing events. They tend to do one thing at a time and prefer planning and keeping to plans once they have been made. Time commitments are taken seriously and staying on schedule is important. Examples of sequential time cultures include the United States, the United Kingdom, and Germany.

Synchronous time orientation relates to reoccurring opportunities and possibilities that ought to be considered and seized when they arise. Past, present, and future are seen as interwoven. Time commitments are desirable but are not absolute. Plans and deadlines are regarded as flexible and punctuality is less important. Examples of synchronous time cultures include Greece, India, and Mexico.

4.4.3 Critical Evaluation

While the concept of Hofstede has found large attention in academic literature, Trompenaars and Hampden-Turner's concept is more popular among intercultural management practitioners. Trompenaars has been frequently named one of the most influential management thinkers worldwide. Hampden-Turner and Trompenaars' (2012) major book *Riding the Waves of Culture* is explicitly addressed to managers. It is easy to read, avoiding academic language and statistical formulas. The practical applicability is supported by training materials, case studies, and illustrations (Hampden-Turner & Trompenaars 2000).

Reviewers criticize that the popularity of the concept among practitioners comes at the expense of academic rigor. A major **criticism** is that the seven cultural dimensions were neither empirically derived nor tested, but predefined by the authors. Thus, they are affected by an **ethnocentric bias** and **lack of content validity**. "Trompenaars did not start his research with an open-ended inventory of issues that were on the minds of his future respondents around the world; he took his concepts, as well as most of his questions, from the American literature of the middle of the century, which was unavoidably ethnocentric" (Hofstede 1996, p. 197).

Hofstede (1996) also criticizes that the answers of the respondents to the dilemma situations are not aggregated. Since **no country scores are calculated**, it is not clear where exactly a country is supposed to be positioned on the seven dimensions. Hampden-Turner and Trompenaars (1997) respond that research on cultural differences needs to acknowledge the complexities and the context of cultural phenomena rather than to rely on mutually exclusive categories and linear models. "Since cultures consist of interdependent, self-organizing values by definition, no truly independent variable exists. Cultures have meanings which depend upon the entire context. No one element in that context dictates meaning to the whole" (Hampden-Turner & Trompenaars 1997, p. 151).

Moreover, the recalculation of Hampden-Turner & Trompenaars' data provided only **limited empirical support for the proposed seven-dimensional model** (Smith, Dugan & Trompenaars 1996). For example, Hofstede (1996) performs an ecological factor analysis based on their data and identifies three instead of seven factors. The first factor is highly correlated with Hofstede's dimension of individualism and accounts for 40% of the total variance. Hofstede (1996, p. 198) concludes: "Trompenaars does (..) ride the waves of commerce: he tunes his messages to what he thinks the customer likes to hear (..). The result is a fast food approach to intercultural diversity and communication."

4.5 SCHWARTZ'S CONCEPT OF CULTURAL VALUE ORIENTATIONS

4.5.1 Overview

While the concepts of Hofstede and Trompenaars and Hampden-Turner were developed in a management context, the theory of cultural values of the American-Israeli social psychologist Shalom Schwartz has its origins in intercultural psychology. And unlike the former, the concept of Schwartz was not expressed in a seminal monograph, but developed in a number of journal articles published over a timeframe of more than 25 years.

The focus of Schwartz's concept is on values, defined as concepts or beliefs about desirable end states or behaviors that transcend specific situations, guide selection or evaluation of behavior and events, and are ordered by relative importance (Schwartz & Bilsky 1987). Based on this general definition, **cultural values** represent the implicitly or explicitly shared abstract ideas about what is good, right, and desirable in a society (Schwartz 1999). By considering three basic issues that confront all societies and the polar value preferences that might evolve to deal with these issues, three dimensions of values for comparing cultures that lead to **seven value orientations** were derived (Table 4.13).

Table 4.13 Schwartz' cultural value orientations

Dimension	Value orientation	Goal
Nature of the relations and boundaries between the person and the group	Embeddedness	Sharing collective goals
	Affective Autonomy	Protection of the individual's affective rights
	Intellectual Autonomy	Protection of the individual's intellectual rights
Behavior that preserves the social fabric	Egalitarianism	Negotiating interests between an individual and the group
	Hierarchy	Allocation of fixed roles and distribution of resources
Treatment of human and natural resources	Mastery	Gaining control over the social and natural environment
	Harmony	Pursuit of a harmonious fit between groups and individuals

Source: Based on Schwartz (2006).

Figure 4.5 illustrates the seven value orientations and the relations among them in a circular structure. The **circular model** reflects the cultural orientations that are compatible (adjacent in the circle) or incompatible (distant around the circle). This view of cultural dimensions as forming an integrated, non-orthogonal system distinguishes Schwartz's theory of cultural values from the concept of Hofstede which conceptualizes the cultural dimensions as independent, orthogonal factors.

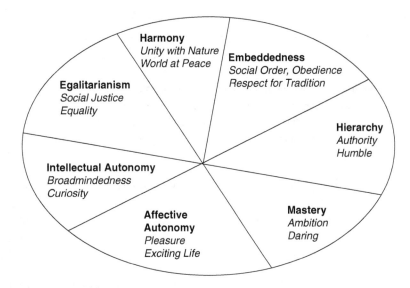

Figure 4.5 Circular model of value orientations
Source: Schwartz (2006, p. 142).

Based on this theoretical conceptualization of cultural values, the **Schwartz Value Survey** (SVS) was developed to measure their manifestations across different countries (Schwartz 1992). It contains 56 abstract items (e.g., social justice, humility, creativity, social order, pleasure, ambition), each followed in parenthesis by a phrase that further specifies their meaning. Respondents are asked to rate the importance of each "as a guiding principle in my life." The importance of each value item is measured on a nonsymmetrical scale to encourage the respondents to think about each of the questions. Schwartz (1994) claims that the items were close to an exhaustive set of etic cultural dimensions and that Hofstede's initial four cultural dimensions are included within these dimensions.

Between 1988 and 2007 **data for 80 countries and sub-national regions** were collected. Respondents are college students of varied majors and school teachers of varied topics (K–12) who teach in the majority type school in an urban area of the country. In countries where either a student or teacher sample was missing, scores for the missing sample were estimated by regression based on the first 59 countries in which both types of samples were available. The means for observed and estimated samples were then averaged. Over the years, the theorizing, conceptualization, and labeling of some cultural values have been updated and modified (https://www.researchgate.net/publication/304715744_The_7_Schwartz_cultural_value_orientation_scores_for_80_countries).

4.5.2 Dimensions of Culture

As explained above, the concept of Schwartz focuses on three universal problems and the ways how different cultures deal with them. He proposes seven culture-level value types which are summarized into three dimensions, namely autonomy vs. embeddedness, egalitarianism vs. hierarchy, and harmony vs. mastery.

4.5.2.1 Autonomy vs. Embeddedness

The first issue is the nature of the relation or the boundaries between the person and the group. The two polar value preferences represent the extent to which people are autonomous vs. embedded in their groups.

In **autonomy cultures**, people are viewed as autonomous, bounded entities. Individuals have control over their choices and are reluctant to consider others and shared rules. In practice, autonomy is about freedom as opposed to the policed control of embeddedness culture. Individuals cultivate and express their own preferences, feelings, ideas, and abilities, and find meaning in their own uniqueness. There are two types of autonomy:

- **Intellectual autonomy** encourages individuals to pursue their own ideas and intellectual directions independently. Examples of important values in such cultures include broadmindedness, curiosity, and creativity.

- **Affective autonomy** encourages individuals to pursue affectively stimulation and hedonism interests and desires for themselves. Important values include pleasure, exciting life, and varied life.

In cultures with an emphasis on **embeddedness**, people are viewed as entities embedded in the collectivity. Meaning in life comes largely through social relationships, through identifying with the group, participating in its shared way of life, and striving toward its shared goals. Embedded cultures emphasize maintaining the status quo and restraining actions that might disrupt in-group solidarity or the traditional order. Important values in such cultures are social order, respect for tradition, security, obedience, and wisdom.

4.5.2.2 Egalitarianism vs. Hierarchy

The second societal problem is to guarantee that people behave in a responsible manner that preserves the social fabric. That is, people must engage in the productive work necessary to maintain society rather than compete destructively or withhold their efforts. People must be induced to consider the welfare of others, to coordinate with them, and thereby manage their unavoidable interdependencies.

Egalitarian cultures seek to induce people to recognize one another as moral equals who share basic interests as human beings. People are socialized to internalize a commitment to cooperate and to feel concern for everyone's welfare. They are expected to act for the benefit of others as a matter of choice and transcendent selfless interests. Important values in such cultures include equality, social justice, responsibility, help, and honesty.

Hierarchy cultures rely on hierarchical systems of ascribed roles to insure responsible, productive behavior. They define the unequal distribution of power, roles, and resources as legitimate and even desirable. There is a clear social order, with some people in superior positions while others are in inferior positions. People are socialized to take the hierarchical distribution of roles for granted and to comply with the obligations and rules attached to their roles. Values like social power, authority, humility, and wealth are highly important in hierarchical cultures.

4.5.2.3 Harmony vs. Mastery

The third societal problem is to regulate people's treatment of human and natural resources. Similar to Kluckhohn and Strodtbeck (1961), cultures with a harmony orientation and those with a mastery orientation are distinguished.

Harmony cultures emphasize fitting into the social and natural world as it is, trying to appreciate and accept rather than to change, direct, or exploit. People do not seek self-improvement, but are happy to accept their place in the world. Important values in harmony cultures include world at peace, unity with nature, and protecting the environment.

Mastery cultures encourage active self-assertion to master, direct, and change the natural and social environment to attain personal goals and get ahead of others. Individuals seek success through personal action, sometimes at the expense of others. Values such as ambition, success, bravery, and competence are especially important in mastery cultures.

4.5.3 Critical Evaluation

Schwartz's concept of culture offers several **advantages compared to Hofstede's concept**. First, while Hofstede's cultural dimensions were empirically derived, Schwartz's values are conceptualized theoretically (Schwartz 1994). This leads to higher construct validity. Moreover, the comprehensive sets of multiitem constructs allow capturing more aspects of culture than Hofstede's concept (Steenkamp 2001; Ng, Lee & Soutar 2007). For instance, Schwartz & Ros (1995) found that Western European countries and the United States, categorized as individualistic cultures according to Hofstede (1980), are significantly different on six of Schwartz's (1994) seven cultural values. Thus, Schwartz's values may have the potential to explain greater cultural variation than Hofstede's values.

The two approaches are based on **different sample compositions**. While Hofstede's sample consists of employees of a multinational corporation, Schwartz collected data with matched samples of students and teachers. Thus, the applicability of the results in the business context is doubtful. Moreover, in some countries either a student or teacher sample is missing. In these cases, scores for the missing sample were estimated by regression based on the first 59 countries in which both types of samples were available. The means for observed and estimated samples were then averaged. This imputation of scores entails some measurement error (Ng, Lee & Soutar 2007).

Another difference between the two approaches is the **methods of data collection**. Rather than to collect data on an individual's desired outcome in a particular situation, Schwartz asks the study participants to indicate their preferences regarding a range of principles and values. While such an approach could reduce the possibility for situational variables to have an impact on the choices made by respondents, there is also an increased likelihood that individuals select those values which they perceive to be socially desirable (Schwartz et al. 1997).

Reviewers also criticize the **complexity of Schwartz's methodology**. The SVS is difficult to answer because respondents have to first read the entire set of value items and give one value the highest as well as the lowest ranking depending on whether an item is in accordance with or opposed to their values. Hence, completing one questionnaire is time-consuming, resulting in a significant amount of incomplete forms (Lindeman & Verkasalo 2005). Furthermore, many respondents have a tendency to give the majority of the values a high score, resulting in skewed responses to the upper end (Hood 2003). Another methodological limitation is the resulting ordinal, ipsatized scores that limit the type of useful analyses researchers can perform (Lee, Soutar & Louviere 2005).

Despite these differences, there are also several **similarities between Schwartz's and Hofstede's concepts** which cause strong correlations between the two datasets. Schwartz (1994) reports that Hofstede's individualism score is highly positively correlated (on a p <0.05-level) with his affective autonomy, intellectual autonomy and egalitarian dimensions, and negatively correlated with embeddedness and hierarchy. Hofstede's power distance score is positively correlated with embeddedness and negatively correlated with affective autonomy. Further, Hofstede's uncertainty avoidance score is positively correlated with harmony and Hofstede's masculinity score is positively correlated with mastery. Smith et al. (2002) also find significant correlations (on a p <0.05-level) between Schwartz's three higher-order dimensions and Hofstede's dimensions. Hofstede's individualism is positively correlated with Schwartz's autonomy-embeddedness and egalitarianism-hierarchy dimensions. Hofstede's power distance is negatively correlated with Schwartz's three dimensions autonomy vs. embeddedness, egalitarianism vs. hierarchy, and harmony vs. mastery. Finally, Hofstede's uncertainty avoidance is positively correlated with Schwartz's egalitarianism vs. hierarchy dimension.

Summarizing the differences and similarities between Schwartz's and Hofstede's concepts, Drogendijk & Slangen (2006, p. 376) conclude: "We found that (…) the Hofstede and Schwartz-based measures is comparable (…). It may thus be premature to dismiss Hofstede's work as outdated or as misrepresenting national cultures and to consider Schwartz's framework to be superior, even though the latter's research design was purposefully chosen for the goal of the research."

4.6 THE GLOBE STUDY

4.6.1 Overview

The GLOBE (Global Leadership and Organizational Behavior Effectiveness) research program was founded by Robert House (Wharton School of Business) in 1991. It is inspired by Hofstede's work and seeks to examine the interrelationships between national culture, societal effectiveness, and leadership attributes. The **multiphase, multimethod, and multisample research project** involves around 170 investigators from 62 countries and resulted in "a very adequate data set to replicate Hofstede's (1980) landmark study" (House 2004, p. XXV).

Since 1991, the GLOBE research program has continued in three interrelated phases. In the first phase, existing measures of societal culture were reviewed and tested in a number of qualitative and quantitative pilot studies. Their assessment led to the development of **nine dimensions of societal culture** that were mostly adapted from previous research (Table 4.14). In the third phase, an empirical study among 17,370 middle managers working for 951 companies in the financial services, food processing, and telecommunication sector in 62 countries was conducted to explore differences along the nine culture dimensions. For each culture dimension, country scores were calculated as to the present *practices* and the *values* as to what the country aspires to be.

The results of the GLOBE study are presented in a large number of journal articles and two comprehensive edited volumes. The book of House et al. (2004) is structured around the nine cultural dimensions and includes extensive descriptions and analyses of the quantitative findings of the GLOBE

Table 4.14 GLOBE's nine cultural dimensions

Dimension	Definition	Source
Uncertainty avoidance	The extent to which members of an organization or society strive to avoid uncertainty by relying on established social norms, rituals, and bureaucratic practices. People in high uncertainty avoidance cultures actively seek to decrease the probability of unpredictable future events that could adversely affect the operation of an organization or society and remedy the success of such adverse effects.	Hofstede (2001)
Power distance	The degree to which members of an organization or society expect and agree that power should be stratified and concentrated at higher levels of an organization or government.	Hofstede (2001)
Collectivism I (Institutional collectivism)	The degree to which organizational and societal institutional practices encourage and reward collective distribution of resources and collective action.	Hofstede (2001); Triandis (1995a)
Collectivism II (In-Group collectivism)	The degree to which individuals express pride, loyalty, and cohesiveness in their organizations or families.	Hofstede (2001)
Gender egalitarianism	The degree to which an organization or a society minimizes gender role differences while promoting gender equality.	Hofstede (2001)
Assertiveness	The degree to which individuals in organizations or societies are assertive, confrontational, and aggressive in social relationships.	Hofstede (2001)
Future orientation	The degree to which individuals in organizations or societies engage in future-oriented behaviors such as planning, investing in the future, and delaying individual or collective gratification.	Kluckhohn & Strodtbeck (1961); Hofstede (2001)
Performance orientation	The degree to which an organization or society encourages and rewards group members for performance improvement and excellence.	McClelland (1961)
Humane orientation	The degree to which individuals in organizations or societies encourage and reward individuals for being fair, altruistic, friendly, generous, caring, and kind to others.	Kluckhohn & Strodtbeck (1961)

Source: Compiled from House & Javidan (2004, p. 11).

project. The book of Chhodkar, Brodbeck and House (2007) provides in-depth country-specific analyses of cultural values, practices, and leadership expectations. It also includes the findings from a variety of qualitative studies that are based on an emic research design.

Tables 4.15 and 4.16 present the scores for the nine culture dimensions (practices and values) for the 62 countries in the GLOBE study (with 1 being the theoretical minimum and 7 the theoretical maximum).

Table 4.15 GLOBE scores for societal cultural practices scales

	Uncertainty avoidance	Power distance	Collectivism I	Collectivism II	Gender egalitarianism	Assertiveness	Future orientation	Performance orientation	Humane orientation
Albania	4.57	4.62	4.54	5.74	3.71	4.89	3.86	4.81	4.64
Argentina	3.65	5.64	3.66	5.51	3.49	4.22	3.08	3.65	3.99
Australia	4.39	4.74	4.29	4.17	3.40	4.28	4.09	4.36	4.28
Austria	5.16	4.95	4.30	4.85	3.09	4.62	4.46	4.44	3.72
Bolivia	3.35	4.51	4.04	5.47	3.55	3.79	3.61	3.61	4.05
Brazil	3.60	5.33	3.83	5.18	3.31	4.20	3.81	4.04	3.66
Canada (English-speaking)	4.58	4.82	4.38	4.26	3.70	4.05	4.44	4.49	4.49
China	4.94	5.04	4.77	5.80	3.05	3.76	3.75	4.45	4.36
Colombia	3.57	5.56	3.81	5.73	3.67	4.20	3.27	3.94	3.72
Costa Rica	3.82	4.74	3.93	5.32	3.56	3.75	3.60	4.12	4.39
Czech Republic	4.44	3.59	3.60	3.18	3.79	3.69	3.63	4.11	4.17
Denmark	5.22	3.89	4.80	3.53	3.93	3.80	4.44	4.22	4.44
Ecuador	3.68	5.60	3.90	5.81	3.07	4.09	3.74	4.20	4.65
Egypt	4.06	4.92	4.50	5.64	2.81	3.91	3.86	4.27	4.73
El Salvador	3.62	5.68	3.71	5.35	3.16	4.62	3.80	3.72	3.71
England	4.65	5.15	4.27	4.08	3.67	4.15	4.28	4.08	3.72
Finland	5.02	4.89	4.63	4.07	3.35	3.81	4.24	3.81	3.96
France	4.43	5.28	3.93	4.37	3.64	4.13	3.48	4.11	3.40
French Switzerland	4.98	4.86	4.22	3.85	3.42	3.47	4.27	4.25	3.93
Georgia	3.50	5.22	4.03	6.19	3.55	4.18	3.41	3.88	4.18

Germany (East)	5.16	5.54	3.56	4.52	3.06	4.73	3.95	4.09	3.40
Germany (West)	5.22	5.25	3.79	4.02	3.10	4.55	4.27	4.25	3.18
Greece	3.39	5.40	3.25	5.27	3.48	4.58	3.40	3.20	3.34
Guatemala	3.30	5.60	3.70	5.53	3.02	3.89	3.24	3.81	3.89
Hong Kong	4.32	4.96	4.13	5.32	3.47	4.67	4.03	4.80	3.90
Hungary	3.12	5.56	3.53	5.25	4.08	4.79	3.21	3.43	3.35
India	4.15	5.47	4.38	5.92	2.90	3.73	4.19	4.25	4.57
Indonesia	4.17	5.18	4.54	5.68	3.26	3.86	3.86	4.41	4.69
Iran	3.67	5.43	3.88	6.03	2.99	4.04	3.70	4.58	4.23
Ireland	4.30	5.15	4.63	5.14	3.21	3.92	3.98	4.36	4.96
Israel	4.01	4.73	4.46	4.70	3.19	4.23	3.85	4.08	4.10
Italy	3.79	5.43	3.68	4.54	3.24	4.07	3.25	3.58	3.63
Japan	4.07	5.11	5.19	4.63	3.19	3.59	4.29	4.22	4.30
Kazakhstan	3.66	5.31	4.29	5.26	3.84	4.46	3.57	3.57	3.99
Kuwait	4.21	5.12	4.49	5.80	2.58	3.63	3.26	3.95	4.52
Malaysia	4.78	5.17	4.61	5.51	3.51	3.87	4.58	4.34	4.87
Mexico	4.18	5.22	4.06	5.7	3.64	4.45	3.87	4.10	3.98
Morocco	3.65	5.80	3.87	5.87	2.84	4.52	3.26	3.99	4.19
Namibia	4.20	5.29	4.13	4.52	3.88	3.91	3.49	3.67	3.96
Netherlands	4.70	4.11	4.46	3.70	3.50	4.32	4.61	4.32	3.86
New Zealand	4.75	4.89	4.81	3.67	3.22	3.42	3.47	4.72	4.32
Nigeria	4.29	5.80	4.14	5.55	3.01	4.79	4.09	3.92	4.10
Philippines	3.89	5.44	4.65	6.36	3.64	4.01	4.15	4.47	5.12
Poland	3.62	5.10	4.53	5.52	4.02	4.06	3.11	3.89	3.61

(Continued)

Table 4.15 GLOBE scores for societal cultural practices scales (Continued)

	Uncertainty avoidance	Power distance	Collectivism I	Collectivism II	Gender egalitarianism	Assertiveness	Future orientation	Performance orientation	Humane orientation
Portugal	3.91	5.44	3.92	5.51	3.66	3.65	3.71	3.60	3.91
Qatar	3.99	4.73	4.50	4.71	3.63	4.11	3.78	3.45	4.42
Russia	2.88	5.52	4.50	5.63	4.07	3.68	2.88	3.39	3.94
Singapore	5.31	4.99	4.90	5.64	3.70	4.17	5.07	4.90	3.49
Slovenia	3.78	5.33	4.13	5.43	3.96	4.00	3.59	3.66	3.79
South Africa (Black Sample)	4.59	4.11	4.39	5.09	3.66	4.36	4.64	4.66	4.34
South Africa (White Sample)	4.09	5.16	4.62	4.50	3.27	4.60	4.13	4.11	3.49
South Korea	3.55	5.61	5.20	5.54	2.50	4.40	3.97	4.55	3.81
Spain	3.97	5.52	3.85	5.45	3.01	4.42	3.51	4.01	3.32
Sweden	5.32	4.85	5.22	3.66	3.84	3.38	4.39	3.72	4.10
Switzerland	5.37	4.90	4.06	3.97	2.97	4.51	4.73	4.94	3.60
Taiwan	4.34	5.18	4.59	5.59	3.18	3.92	3.96	4.56	4.11
Thailand	3.93	5.63	4.03	5.70	3.35	3.64	3.43	3.93	4.81
Turkey	3.63	5.57	4.03	5.88	2.89	4.53	3.74	3.83	3.94
United States	4.15	4.88	4.20	4.25	3.34	4.55	4.15	4.49	4.17
Venezuela	3.44	5.40	3.96	5.53	3.62	4.33	3.35	3.32	4.25
Zambia	4.10	5.31	4.61	5.84	2.86	4.07	3.62	4.16	5.23
Zimbabwe	4.15	5.67	4.12	5.57	3.04	4.06	3.77	4.24	4.45

Source: https://globeproject.com/study_2004_2007#findings

Table 4.16 GLOBE scores for societal cultural values scales

	Uncertainty avoidance	Power distance	Collectivism I	Collectivism II	Gender egalitarianism	Assertiveness	Future orientation	Performance orientation	Humane orientation
Albania	5.37	3.52	4.44	5.22	4.19	4.41	5.42	5.63	5.34
Argentina	4.66	2.33	5.32	6.15	4.98	3.25	5.78	6.35	5.58
Australia	3.98	2.78	4.40	5.75	5.02	3.81	5.15	5.89	5.58
Austria	3.66	2.44	4.73	5.27	4.83	2.81	5.11	6.10	5.76
Bolivia	4.70	3.41	5.10	6.00	4.75	3.73	5.63	6.05	5.07
Brazil	4.99	2.35	5.62	5.15	4.99	2.91	5.69	6.13	5.68
Canada (English-speaking)	3.75	2.70	4.17	5.97	5.11	4.15	5.35	6.15	5.64
China	5.28	3.10	4.56	5.09	3.68	5.44	4.73	5.67	5.32
Colombia	4.98	2.04	5.38	6.25	5.00	3.43	5.68	6.42	5.61
Costa Rica	4.58	2.58	5.18	6.08	4.64	4.05	5.20	5.90	4.99
Czech Republic	3.64	4.35	3.85	4.06	3.78	4.14	2.95	2.35	3.39
Denmark	3.82	2.76	4.19	5.50	5.08	3.39	4.33	5.61	5.45
Ecuador	5.16	2.30	5.41	6.17	4.59	3.65	5.94	6.32	5.26
Egypt	5.36	3.24	4.85	5.56	3.18	3.28	5.80	5.90	5.17
El Salvador	5.32	2.68	5.65	6.52	4.66	3.62	5.98	6.58	5.46
England	4.11	2.80	4.31	5.55	5.17	3.70	5.06	5.90	5.43
Finland	3.85	2.19	4.11	5.42	4.24	3.68	5.07	6.11	5.81
France	4.26	2.76	4.86	5.42	4.40	3.38	4.96	5.65	5.67
French Switzerland	3.83	2.80	4.31	5.35	4.69	3.78	4.80	5.98	5.62
Georgia	5.24	2.84	3.83	5.66	3.73	4.35	5.55	5.69	5.60

(Continued)

Table 4.16 GLOBE scores for societal cultural values scales (Continued)

	Uncertainty avoidance	Power distance	Collectivism I	Collectivism II	Gender egalitarianism	Assertiveness	Future orientation	Performance orientation	Humane orientation
Germany (East)	3.94	2.69	4.68	5.22	4.90	3.23	5.23	6.09	5.44
Germany (West)	3.32	2.54	4.82	5.18	4.89	3.09	4.85	6.01	5.46
Greece	5.09	2.39	5.40	5.46	4.89	2.96	5.19	5.81	5.23
Guatemala	4.88	2.35	5.23	6.14	4.53	3.64	5.91	6.14	5.26
Hong Kong	4.63	3.24	4.43	5.11	4.35	4.81	5.50	5.64	5.32
Hungary	4.66	2.49	4.50	5.54	4.63	3.35	5.70	5.96	5.48
India	4.73	2.64	4.71	5.32	4.51	4.76	5.60	6.05	5.28
Indonesia	5.23	2.69	5.18	5.67	3.89	4.72	5.70	5.73	5.16
Iran	5.36	2.80	5.54	5.86	3.75	4.99	5.84	6.08	5.61
Ireland	4.02	2.71	4.59	5.74	5.14	3.99	5.22	5.98	5.47
Israel	4.38	2.72	4.27	5.75	4.71	3.76	5.25	5.75	5.62
Italy	4.47	2.47	5.13	5.72	4.88	3.82	5.91	6.07	5.58
Japan	4.33	2.86	3.99	5.26	4.33	5.56	5.25	5.17	5.41
Kazakhstan	4.42	3.15	4.04	5.44	4.75	3.84	5.05	5.41	5.62
Kuwait	4.77	3.17	5.15	5.43	3.45	3.76	5.74	6.03	5.06
Malaysia	4.88	2.97	4.87	5.85	3.78	4.81	5.89	6.04	5.51
Mexico	5.26	2.85	4.92	5.95	4.73	3.79	5.86	6.16	5.10
Morocco	5.32	3.11	5.00	5.68	3.74	3.44	5.85	5.76	5.51
Namibia	5.13	2.86	4.38	6.07	4.25	3.91	6.12	6.40	5.40
Netherlands	3.24	2.45	4.55	5.17	4.99	3.02	5.07	5.49	5.20
New Zealand	4.10	3.53	4.20	6.21	4.23	3.54	5.54	5.90	4.49
Nigeria	5.60	2.69	5.03	5.48	4.24	3.23	6.04	6.27	6.09

Philippines	5.14	2.72	4.78	6.18	4.58	5.14	5.93	6.31	5.36
Poland	4.71	3.12	4.22	5.74	4.52	3.90	5.20	6.12	5.30
Portugal	4.43	2.38	5.30	5.94	5.13	3.58	5.43	6.40	5.31
Qatar	4.82	3.23	5.13	5.60	3.38	3.80	5.92	5.96	5.30
Russia	5.07	2.62	3.89	5.79	4.18	2.83	5.48	5.54	5.59
Singapore	4.22	3.04	4.55	5.50	4.51	4.41	5.51	5.72	5.79
Slovenia	4.99	2.57	4.38	5.71	4.83	4.59	5.42	6.41	5.25
South Africa (Black Sample)	4.79	3.65	4.30	4.99	4.26	3.82	5.20	4.92	5.07
South Africa (White Sample)	4.67	2.64	4.38	5.91	4.60	3.69	5.66	6.23	5.65
South Korea	4.67	2.55	3.90	5.41	4.22	3.75	5.69	5.25	5.60
Spain	4.76	2.26	5.20	5.79	4.82	4.00	5.63	5.80	5.69
Sweden	3.60	2.70	3.94	6.04	5.15	3.61	4.89	5.80	5.65
Switzerland	3.16	2.44	4.69	4.94	4.92	3.21	4.79	5.82	5.54
Taiwan	5.31	3.09	5.15	5.45	4.06	3.28	5.20	5.74	5.26
Thailand	5.61	2.86	5.10	5.76	4.16	3.48	6.20	5.74	5.01
Turkey	4.67	2.41	5.26	5.77	4.50	2.66	5.83	5.39	5.52
United States	4.00	2.85	4.17	5.77	5.06	4.32	5.31	6.14	5.53
Venezuela	5.26	2.29	5.39	6.17	4.82	3.33	5.79	6.35	5.31
Zambia	4.67	2.43	4.74	5.77	4.31	4.38	5.90	6.24	5.53
Zimbabwe	4.73	2.67	4.87	5.35	4.46	4.60	6.07	6.45	5.19

Source: https://globeproject.com/study_2004_2007#findings

4.6.2 GLOBE's Cultural Dimensions: Cultural Practices vs. Cultural Values

While the nine cultural dimensions proposed by the GLOBE project were mostly adapted from existing research (in particular from the concepts of Kluckhohn and Strodtbeck and Hofstede) and therefore do not require detailed explanation, a remarkable difference to previous concepts is the distinction between two manifestation of culture, namely cultural *practices* ("as is" scores) and *values* ("should be" scores).

Cultural practices refer to current perceptions of each culture. They were measured with survey items assessing "what is" or "what are" common behaviors and institutional practices in society. Cultural practices represent the way things are currently done.

Cultural values were expressed in response to the same questionnaire items in the form of judgments of "what should be." They reflect the respondents' desires and aspirations in terms of how people should behave and how the society should develop in the future.

Figure 4.6 visualizes the scores for the nine cultural dimensions taking the example of Germany. It shows large differences between the cultural practices and the cultural values for most of the nine dimensions. The largest differences can be observed for power distance. While the respondents state that power distance should be small, it is actually perceived to be one of the highest among all countries in the study. For performance orientation, the opposite relation between values and practices is found.

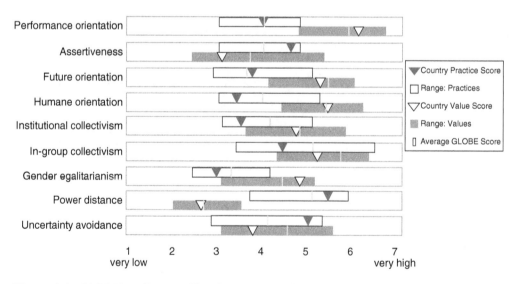

Figure 4.6 GLOBE's culture profile of Germany (West)

Source: Compiled from House et al. (2004).

An analysis of all 62 countries in the GLOBE study reveals significant **negative correlations between cultural practices and values** for seven out of nine dimensions. The seven dimensions showing a negative correlation on a $p < 0.05$-level are assertiveness ($r = -0.26$), institutional collectivism ($r = -0.61$), future orientation ($r = -0.41$), humane orientation ($r = -0.32$), performance orientation ($r = -0.28$), power distance ($r = -0.43$), and uncertainty avoidance ($r = -0.62$). The only dimension showing a significantly positive correlation is gender egalitarianism ($r = 0.32$). In-group collectivism shows a positive but insignificant correlation (House et al. 2004, p. 736).

The authors of GLOBE call this result "both counterintuitive and counter to conventional wisdom" (Javidan et al. 2006, p. 901) and find it basically "unclear why the relationship should be negative rather than positive" (House et al. 2004, p. 729) because values have been usually considered as predispositions of practices. They conclude that the relationship between values and practices must be much more complex than previous research suggests and provide a **deprivation hypothesis** to explain this finding. Cultures that have more of a practice become more satiated while cultures that have less of a practice feel more deprived whereby creating a gap between values and practices (Javidan et al. 2006).

Maseland and van Hoorn (2009) explain the negative correlation between practices and values with the **law of diminishing marginal utility**. The more an objective is satiated, the less the further realization of that objective is valued. "If an objective, say consuming bread, is satiated, the value one attaches to the realization of that objective falls. By contrast, that which is scarce—be it bread, butter, law and order, or equality—is generally valued highly. There is nothing counterintuitive about this" (Maseland & van Hoorn 2009, p. 529).

GLOBE's distinction between practices and values has inspired interesting subsequent studies. For example, Li et al. (2017) develop a **cultural attractiveness index** that conceptualizes whether the members of a focal culture view another culture as desirable. It is calculated by matching a culture's values with another culture's practices. A major advantage of this concept of cultural attractiveness as compared to measures of cultural distance that are based on the Hofstede scores, such as the Kogut-Singh-Index (Kogut & Singh 1988), is the consideration of asymmetric relationships between cultures, i.e., the calculation of country A's perceived cultural attractiveness of country B differs from the calculation of country B's perceived cultural attractiveness of country A. For example, Germany perceives countries like France, Italy, and the United States as culturally more attractive than these countries perceive the German culture. Contrary relations are observed between Germany and China, Indonesia and Korea (Chapter 5.2.2).

4.6.3 Critical Evaluation

The GLOBE program is one of the most comprehensive, detailed, and up-to-date studies in the field of intercultural management. One of the main advantages when compared to the study of Hofstede (1980, 2001) is the **conceptualization of the country scores**. Hofstede does not report the national average scores on items used to measure his national culture dimensions. Instead, he transformed the raw scores on the measures of each national culture dimension into an index ranging from 0 to 100 which does not accurately represent their relativities. Moreover, the index formula artificially inflates differences between countries even when there is a general tendency toward high or low values (Venaik & Brewer 2013). In contrast, House et al. (2004) present the average scores (rather than a formula-based index on a 0–100 scale) for each country on each of the eighteen national culture dimensions (practices and values). They found that some cultural values are generally desired and others generally undesired across all countries. For example, power distance is a universally undesired value (mean = 2.77, min = 2.04, max = 3.65 on a 7-point scale), while performance orientation is a universally desired value (mean = 5.88, min = 2.35, max = 6.58).

While several reviewers praise the GLOBE program for its sophisticated methodology and comprehensive data base, it has also received frequent **criticism**. Not surprisingly, one of the harshest reviewers is Hofstede. He criticizes, among others, the **high complexity** of the concept which makes it difficult to use for practitioners. "With nine dimensions of culture times two, the GLOBE researchers' psychologic has surpassed the limits of our capacity for processing information" (Hofstede 2006, p. 895). This reduces both the practical applicability of the concept as well as its use for intercultural training (Hofstede 2010).

Another criticism is the **multicollinearity between several culture scores**. As House et al. (2004) admit, there are substantial correlations between future orientation, uncertainty avoidance, performance orientation, and low power distance among the practices measures. On the values measures, future orientation and uncertainty avoidance are particularly strongly linked, and there are also strong associations between some of the values measures and some of the practices measures. Hofstede (2006) conducted a principal components factor analysis of the 18 dimension scores. This reveals five factors that account for 75.7% of the variance in the data. "As my re-analysis of GLOBE's data showed, their respondents' eco-logic allows reducing the GLOBE dimensions to five, and these show a family likeness with the Hofstede model" (Hofstede 2006, p. 895).

Despite these criticisms, the GLOBE scores are being increasingly used by researchers in ways similar to the ways the Hofstede scores have been used over many years. One reason for its **popularity in the intercultural management literature** is the fact that the GLOBE program is a team effort. Around 170 country coinvestigators from 62 countries who were either natives of the country studied or had extensive knowledge and experience in that country took a direct role in designing the study, collecting and analyzing the data, and publishing the results. Although most of the main authors hold management or psychology degrees from US universities (Hofstede 2006), this allows for the integration of emic research epistemologies in the etic-dominated research field. Moreover, the sheer number of participants who published a large number of journal articles contributed to the popularity of the concept (Javidan et al. 2006).

Smith (2006, p. 919) summarizes the **achievements of the GLOBE study compared to Hofstede's concept** as follows: "Hofstede's (1980) pioneering study provided the impetus for our endeavors in understanding psychological aspects of national cultures. The methodological problems that he faced remain salient to all cross-cultural researchers. There are no simple solutions. The methods employed by the GLOBE researchers address these problems in somewhat different ways and draw upon the greater power of recently developed procedures for statistical analysis. Nonetheless, the methods employed by the GLOBE researchers also entail contingent risks and ambiguities. We should continue to survey cultural differences by using a broad range of methodologies, and can hope to achieve confidence in the results obtained when findings are found to converge, as they quite often do."

In 2020, the first GLOBE study way replicated and extended. GLOBE 2020 covers more than 160 countries that represent around 95% of the world population. First results shall be published in 2022 (https://globeproject.com/about?page_id=intro#globe2020_intro).

4.7 THOMAS' CONCEPT OF CULTURAL STANDARDS

4.7.1 Overview

While the concepts described in the previous sections are based on an etic epistemology, the concept of cultural standards developed by the German intercultural psychologist Alexander Thomas follows an **emic approach**. The main assumption is that culture is not a reified phenomenon that exists within a person, but **expresses itself in interactions with others**. Thomas' interactionist concept of culture focuses therefore on intercultural encounters and aims to identify cultural standards that influence the interactions of individuals from two different countries (Thomas 1993).

Cultural standards are forms of perception, thought patterns, judgment, and interaction that are shared by a majority of the members of a society and regarded as normal, typical, and binding (Thomas 2010). They are distinct systems of orientation that are specific to each society and universal for its members. Individuals use cultural standards as benchmarks for the assessment of their own behavior, the behavior of others, and for behavioral adjustment. Behavior that exceeds the tolerated range is sanctioned by the respective society. Individuals are often not completely aware of their cultural standards, but their existence and effects become manifest only through contact with foreign cultures.

From an epistemological perspective, cultural standards differ from universal cultural dimensions as proposed by the etic concepts of Kluckhohn and Strodtbeck, Hofstede, GLOBE, etc. as they are culture-specific. They are not predefined by the researcher, but **empirically discovered** through researching **culturally overlapping situations**. Thus, the unit of analysis is not the individual or the country, but the interaction between members from two different countries.

The exploration of cultural standards follows a standardized **research methodology** (Figure 4.7). The process starts with the *identification of persons with experience in encounters with members of the target culture*, for example, within the context of student and youth exchange programs, field experts assigned overseas or international experts working on foreign assignments. These persons are then interviewed about *critical incidents* in interactions with members of the target culture that were perceived as unpleasant, annoying, or depressing to the persons involved. Afterward, the interviewed persons are asked about their *subjective interpretation* of the others' behavior. The next step includes the *historical and philosophical explanation* of the critical incidents. The analysis is conducted by experts in the field of comparative culture studies, who are indigenous to and well versed in both cultures. In the ideal case, these experts are biculturals with strong roots in both the culture of origin and the target culture. The synthesis of recurring critical incidents leads then to the *derivation of idiographic cultural standards*. In the last step, these are *validated through comparison with other academic research* about the target culture (Romani, Primecz & Topçu 2010). "Cultural standards identified in this manner, say eight to twelve core cultural standards, are in no way indicative of an entire culture. Nor does a network of such cultural standards provide insight into what makes up the respective culture as a whole. They are, however, helpful in navigating and accumulating knowledge about the other-culture system of orientation and serve to explain unexpected and unfamiliar behavior on the part of the interaction partner" (Thomas 2010, p. 26).

4.7.2 Examples of Cultural Standards

Thomas and his colleagues conducted a large number of empirical studies in which the interactions of Germans with members of a variety of target cultures are analyzed. The results are published in a series of

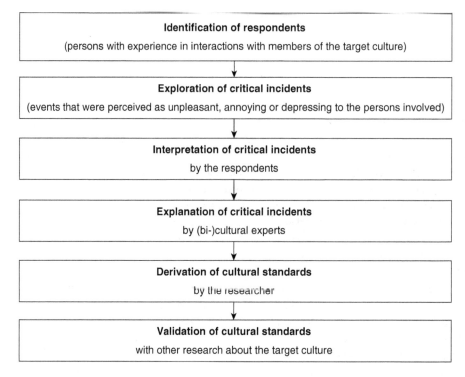

Figure 4.7 Exploration of cultural standards

around 50 booklets (in German language) entitled *Doing Business in …* ("Beruflich in …"). The target cultures include, for example, Argentina, Australia, Brazil, Canada, China, Czech Republic, Hungary, India, Indonesia, Ireland, Italy, Japan, Kenya, Malaysia, Mexico, Poland, Russia, Slovakia, South Africa, South Korea, Tanzania, Thailand, United States, and Vietnam. Moreover, a study of German cultural standards as perceived by foreigners was published by Schroll-Machl (2016).

Table 4.17 displays in an exemplary way the cultural standards of Germany and the United States, the only two countries that are explored as both culture of origin and target culture by Thomas and colleagues. They were identified in two studies of American exchange students in Germany and German exchange students in the United States (Markowski & Thomas 1995; Müller & Thomas 1995). The order of entries reflects the perceived relevance of the respective cultural standard by the respondents.

The identified cultural standards have some **similarities with the cultural dimensions ascribed to the two countries in etic studies**, such as those of Hofstede and GLOBE. For example, individualism is named the most relevant cultural standard of the United States in the study of Müller & Thomas (1995), while the country scores highest on the individualism dimension in Hofstede's study. The cultural standard of interpersonal distance orientation ascribed to both cultures is very similar to Hall's concept of space orientation. While Americans seek to minimize interpersonal distance and strive for openness in personal matters (e.g., general personal information, helpfulness, and hospitality), Germans hardly talk about personal matters during first social contacts and prefer a much larger interpersonal distance. Similarities also exist between the cultural standards of traditional role expectations (Germany) and relation between sexes (United States), and Hofstede's cultural dimension of masculinity vs. femininity.

Table 4.17 Central cultural standards of Germany and the United States

Cultural standards of Germany	Cultural standards of the United States
Formalism	Individualism
Power orientation	Egalitarian orientation
Performance of one's duty	Action orientation
Family orientation	Achievement/competition orientation
Interpersonal distance regulation	Interpersonal distance regulation
Physical distance regulation	Social acceptance
Frankness/outspokenness	Calmness/"easy-going"
Personal property	Patriotism
Traditional role expectations	Relation between sexes
	Future orientation

Source: Adapted from Markowski & Thomas (1995) and Müller & Thomas (1995).

In other cases, similar terms are used, but they involve **different interpretations**. For example, the finding of Markowski and Thomas (1995) that Americans regard Germans to have strong power orientation contradicts Hofstede's finding that the power distance in Germany is slightly lower than in the United States. Remarkable is not only the asymmetry between the two studies, but that the respondents in Markowski and Thomas' study regard this difference between the two countries a major reason for critical incidents in intercultural encounters.

Beyond these similarities, the identified cultural standards show several **principal differences** when compared to the concepts that are based on universal cultural dimensions. For example, the American cultural standard of patriotism can hardly be explained by etic concepts of culture. Similarly, the German cultural standard of performance of one's duty has no equivalence in etic concepts.

The cultural standard of **performance of one's duty** (*Pflichterfüllung*) dates back to the German protestant reformer *Martin Luther*. According to Luther, work is not a hardship, but a duty to God. A god-pleasing life is not achieved through monastic asceticism, but through hard work. *Max Weber* (1930) regards performance of one's duty as a key principle of Protestant Ethics.

In the eighteenth century, the performance of one's duty became one of the *Prussian Virtues* (among others, such as courage, discipline, diligence, obedience, and sense of order) promoted by King Frederick William I of Prussia and his son King Frederick the Great. Initially developed for the military, it has later also significantly influenced wider German culture (Haffner 1998). According to Kant's (1788) morale philosophy, performance of one's duty and obedience to the laws of the state always presupposed that these laws are reasonable, based on moral judgment and do not deny human dignity.

(Continued)

This fundamental principle was suspended by the Nazis. From 1934 on, the German military oath contained a clause that promised "unconditional obedience" (Kane 2002). A value which in the Reformation and the German Empire has been used in a positive sense came to be used derogatorily in reference to fanatical loyalty that is characteristic of fascism. Thus, the value of performance of one's duty has not only contributed to Germany's economic and political strength, but is also "perfectly suited to run a concentration camp," as German leftist politician Oskar Lafontaine once said (cited in Hammelehle 2018).

The **emic character of cultural standards** becomes particularly visible when analyzing intercultural encounters between Western and non-Western countries (Table 4.18). For example, the cultural standards of South Africa as identified by Mayer, Boness, and Thomas (2004) relate to several indigenous concepts, such as ubuntu, NDaba, and spirituality that cannot be captured adequately by universal dimensions (Jackson 2013). The cultural standard of ethnic diversity even contradicts the key principle of etic concepts of culture to assign exactly one value to each cultural dimension.

Similarly, most cultural standards of China are incommensurable with universal dimensions of culture. The *danwei* was the smallest social and political unit in Maoist China. It cocured welfare through education, medical care, retirement pension, etc. At the same time, it involved a loss of anonymity and allowed for extensive social control (Bray 2005). Although it is related to the cultural dimension of collectivism as proposed by Kluckhohn and Strodtbeck, Hofstede, and GLOBE, its specific indigenous character is only partially reflected by this universal concept.

The cultural standard of hierarchy is deeply rooted in Confucian philosophy. It consists of the asymmetrical order of *five key relationships* between ruler to ruled, father to son, husband to wife, elder brother to younger brother, and friend to friend. While Hofstede & Bond (1988) refer to Confucian philosophy and tried to incorporate it into Hofstede's fifth dimension of long-term vs. short-term orientation, reviewers criticize this attempt as a "philosophical flaw" (Fang 2003, p. 355) because the bipolar conceptualization of this dimension violates the Chinese Yin Yang principle according to which each Confucian value has its

Table 4.18 Central cultural standards of South Africa and China from a German perspective

Cultural standards of South Africa	Cultural standards of China
Communicative variance	Unit system (*danwei*)
Rule and hierarchy orientation	Hierarchy
Social network management (*ubuntu*)	Trickery
Ethnic diversity	Social harmony
Kinship funding	Keeping face
Consensus-oriented decision-making (*NDaba*)	*Guanxi*
African concept of time	Bureaucracy
Religion and spirituality (in bantu-speaking ethnic groups)	Etiquette

Source: Adapted from Mayer, Boness & Thomas (2004) and Thomas & Schenk (2015).

bright and dark sides and involves constructive and destructive qualities. "Given the distorted research methodology, the fifth dimension cannot lay claim to (have captured the essence) of Confucianism" (Fang 2003, p. 362).

Trickery, another cultural standard identified by Thomas and Schenk (2015), relates to Sun Tzu's *The Art of War* (fifth century BC). The 36 stratagems described in this book became extremely influential not only in military, but later also in the business context and are still a key source of understanding Chinese strategic thinking and negotiation styles (Liu 2015; Ma & Tsui 2015; Garg & Berning 2017).

Another important Chinese cultural standard is the concept of face (*mianzi*) (Hwang 1987). The need for face is intrinsic to various aspects of personal and interpersonal relationship development and an essential element of Chinese politeness (Fang 2003). Maintaining face contains, for example, carefully controlling emotions, avoiding conflicts, and not criticizing superiors in public. However, this applies mainly to relationships among Chinese, while interactions with foreigners can be more confrontational and direct (Bond 1991). Thus, while the concept of face has some similarities with Hall's high-context communication style and Hofstede's dimension of indulgence vs. restraint, its complexity is not adequately addressed by universal cultural dimensions.

The **differences between emic and etic conceptualizations of cultural values** are vividly illustrated in the study of Pan et al. (2011). Based on the review of five major schools of ancient Chinese philosophy that implicitly influence current management thought (i.e., Confucianism, Taoism, Buddhism, Legalism, and The Art of War), the authors develop a four-factor structure of Chinese cultural traditions model (SCCT). In an empirical study based on a nation-wide sample of 718 business employees, the emic SCCT model is then compared with the etic Schwartz Value Survey (SVS). The results show that the ten SVS domains explain no more than 16% of the variance in any of the four SCCT factors. The authors conclude that "the SVS value domains are plausibly related to the SCCT dimensions, but the relationships are not strong enough to suggest that the two are the same" (Pan et al. 2011, p. 88).

4.7.3 Critical Evaluation

The concept of cultural standards has received large attention among practitioners working in an intercultural environment. A main advantage of its emic research philosophy is that the characteristics of a particular culture are not only described with universal dimensions, but also explained within their historical and philosophical context. The terminology of cultural standards is rooted in the particular culture and based on the language of its members. Thus, from a linguistic perspective, they are **closer to real life** than abstract cultural dimensions.

Another advantage is the qualitative research methodology that allows for collection of a **large number of exemplary situational descriptions** that are common in encounters between the members of the two involved countries. These critical incidents provide more culture-specific knowledge than etic cultural dimensions as they are likely to vary across cultures (Romani, Primecz & Topçu 2010). They are therefore useful starting points for the development of intercultural training programs (Chapter 9). **Cultural assimilator trainings** are based on the idea of learning through examples and that individuals are likely to behave more adequately in intercultural encounters if they are aware of the respective cultural standards and understand their relevance in practice (Fiedler, Mitchell & Triandis 1971). Thus, cultural standards facilitate the transfer of cultural knowledge from exemplary to concrete situations.

However, the concept of cultural standards is also frequently criticized. A main criticism relates to the **lack of analytical rigor** of the underlying research methodology. The interviews are based on convenience samples of respondents with doubtful representativeness. It is also unclear which measures have been taken to reduce construct bias, interviewer bias, and interpretation bias, and how the cultural standards were derived from the exemplary descriptions of critical incidents (Fink, Neyer & Kölling 2006). Thus, the validity of the identified cultural standards is questionable.

Another criticism is the **lack of replica studies** that test the cultural standards identified by Thomas and colleagues. The few existing studies often come to different results. For example, Faust (2018) argues with regard to the cultural standards of China as identified by Thomas & Schenk (2015) that some standards need to be modified and others left out. The latter relates to etiquette, which, according to Faust, is not discussed in Chinese literature. Moreover, bureaucracy should not be understood as a cultural standard of its own, but as a consequence of following hierarchical principles.

The concept of cultural standards has also **limits with regard to generalization**. There is no evidence of whether cultural standards identified in a specific context (e.g., in a student exchange program) are applicable across different environments and equally valid, for example, in the business context. Finally, the bicultural focus of cultural standards limits their **practical applicability**. As cultural standards can only be determined by comparing one's home culture to a target culture, individuals who frequently interact with members from several different countries may find it arduous to read a large number of country-specific guides and derive conclusions from a variety of etic concepts (Holzmüller & Stöttinger 2001).

4.8 THE CONSTRUCTIVIST CONCEPT OF CULTURE

4.8.1 Overview

The constructivist concept of culture associated with American anthropologist Clifford Geertz regards culture as a medium to impose meaning on the world and make it understandable. It is defined as "a system of inherited conceptions expressed in symbolic forms by means of which people communicate, perpetuate, and develop their knowledge about and attitudes toward life" (Geertz 1973, p. 89). The concept originates in extensive ethnographical research in Southeast Asia and North Africa from the 1960s to the 1980s, which included the analysis of such cultural practices and institutions as Balinese cockfighting, and bazaars, mosques, olive growing and oral poetry in Morocco. Based on an **emic epistemology**, Geertz applied a qualitative research methodology named *thick description* that reflected his belief that the analysis of culture is "not an experimental science in search of law but an interpretive one in search of meaning" (Geertz 1973, p. 5). A key feature of this research methodology is the *contextualization* of the analyzed cultural phenomena through incorporating essential local symbols, institutions, and practices that are not obvious to outsiders, but necessary to fully understand and cogently interpret them (Geertz 1983).

The basic assumption of the constructivist concept is that culture is not an objectively given and preexisting reification, but constructed in a process of social interaction. While Hofstede regards culture as "collective programming" and "software of the mind," the constructivist concept replaces the computer metaphor with the view of culture as "webs of significance that man himself has spun" (Geertz 1973, p. 5). Referring to Berger and Luckmann's (1966) understanding of **social construction of reality**, Geertz argues that cultural practices become institutionalized through mutual observation and agreement among the members of a society. Individuals negotiate the norms which will guide their actions and behaviors and the individual roles and places they will hold within that society. Cultural norms, values, and behaviors make sense only in a particular local context and are not fully understood in other contexts. The *process of* *sense-making* can therefore be analyzed only with idiographic, interpretative, and explorative research methodologies.

The perspective of culture as social construct is reflected, for example, in the **cricket test** proposed by former British cabinet minister Norman Tebbit. Post-war Britain experienced mass immigration from the West Indies and Southeast Asia. According to Tebbit, many of these immigrants identified themselves strongly with their country of origin even after living in Britain for a long time. He argues that this cultural affiliation can be observed in their loyalty to the national cricket team—a popular sport in both Britain and the immigrants' home countries. "A large proportion of Britain's Asian population fail to pass the cricket test. Which side do they cheer for? It's an interesting test. Are you still harking back to where you came from or where you are?" (Tebbit 1990, cited in Carvel 2004).

4.8.2 Application in Intercultural Management

While Geertz' concept has become very influential in anthropology and sociology—Geertz was considered the single most influential cultural anthropologist for three decades (Shweder & Good 2005)—it has found much less attention in intercultural management literature. The main reason is that, in contrast to the more popular etic concepts of, for example, Hofstede, Trompenaars, and GLOBE, it was not developed in the management context and offers less tangible practical implications. Only recently has the constructivist concept of culture been gradually adapted in indigenous and postcolonial management studies and applied to phenomena such as ethnic consumer behavior, migration and expatriation, and bicultural managers—often without giving reference to Geertz' work.

An early example is the study of Stayman and Deshpande (1989) about the impact of social surroundings on **consumer behavior of immigrants**. The study shows that Chinese-Americans and Mexican-Americans emphasize their ethnic origin (measured in terms of food choices) more strongly in a family context when they are together with their Chinese and Mexican relatives than in a more formal business context where the majority has an Anglo-American background. Subsequent studies in other contexts support the notion of *situational ethnicity* (Okamura 1981) by showing that one's felt ethnic identity depends upon the social situation and the individual's perception of the situation (Cox, Lobel & McLeod 1991; Xu et al. 2004; Askegaard, Arnould & Kjeldgaard 2005). Ethnicity is "not only a stable sociological trait of individuals that is manifested in the same way at all times, but also a transitory psychological state manifested in different ways in different situations" (Stayman & Deshpande 1989, p. 361).

An example of social construction of culture in the field of brand management is the spread of **German fake brands in Russia**. Several Russian firms market their products with German-sounding brand names, such as "Thomas Münz" "Kaiser," "Erich Krause," "Danke Anke," "Bork," and "Meine Liebe." Like in many other countries, German products are perceived by Russian consumers as durable, reliable, and of high quality. German-sounding brand names are therefore used to signal these positive brand associations to Russian consumers although the products are not produced in Germany and the firms have no relation to this country (Lokshin 2014).

Situational ethnicity is also a central concept in **intercultural psychology**. An important tenet is the conceptualization of the individual as a multifaceted and transitory *dialogical self* (Hermans & Hermans-Konopka 2010) who "fluctuates among different and even opposed positions, and has the capacity imaginatively to endow each position with a voice so that dialogical relations between positions can be established" (Hermans 2001, p. 248). In an intercultural context, these voices represent different cultural patterns that enter into a polyphonic discourse. As a result of globalization, individuals are increasingly exposed to multiple and sometimes conflicting cultural voices which they can blend, combine, mix, and shift depending on the context and the volume of each voice.

The constructivist concept of culture has recently also been adapted in research on **biculturals**, i.e., individuals who identify with two distinct cultures (Brannen & Thomas 2010; Hong et al., 2000). Born biculturals are individuals with parents coming from two different cultural backgrounds. Typical examples of these "hyphenated identities" (Bhatia 2002) are French-Algerians, German-Turks, and Mexican-Americans. Another group of biculturals is people who migrated to another country during childhood or adolescence. They are often bilingual and have internalized two different sets of cultural schemas (Fitz-simmons 2013; Hong 2010).

Brannen, Garcia, and Thomas (2009) developed a **typology of biculturals** that distinguishes between four different forms of identity construction (Figure 4.8):

- *One-Home biculturals* identify mostly with one of their two cultures. An American-Chinese, for example, may feel and behave first and foremost as American, although the person is aware of the Chinese origin and outer appearance, may speak mandarin, participate in Chinese customs at home, or celebrate Chinese holidays. Outside the family context, however, the Chinese part of the personality is suppressed.
- *Neither/Nor biculturals* feel marginalized and not a part of either of their cultures. For example, individuals may grow up in a country that is so distant (geographically or culturally) from their home country that they are not accepted into their host country culture. At the same time, connections to the home country that might have been left long time ago are minimal. Examples are some second-generation German-Turks who speak neither German nor Turkish fluently and are treated as foreigners in both countries.
- *Either/Or (or Two-homes) biculturals* identify with both of their cultural identities but change their orientation and behavior based on context. This frame-switching capability of biculturals depends mainly on their equal identification with the two cultures and the perceived conflict or harmony between the two (Benet-Martínez et al. 2002; Fitzsimmons 2013). Biculturals with pronounced frame-switching capabilities act often as cultural boundary-spanners in multicultural teams (Engelhard & Holtbrügge 2017).
- *Both/And biculturals* blend and merge both of their cultures and combine them into a new one. The hybridization and creolization of cultures create "cultural third spaces" (Gutiérrez, Baquedano-López & Tejeda 1999) with unique norms, values, and behaviors that facilitate the identity formation of otherwise marginalized individuals. Examples of this type of biculturals are the Nuyoricans (persons from Puerto Rican descent living in New York) and Tejanos (descendants of Mexican settlers living in Texas).

Postcolonial studies argue that the cultural identity of individuals does not emerge from *consensual and dominance-free discourse* (Habermas 1984), but is constructed through historically negotiated processes

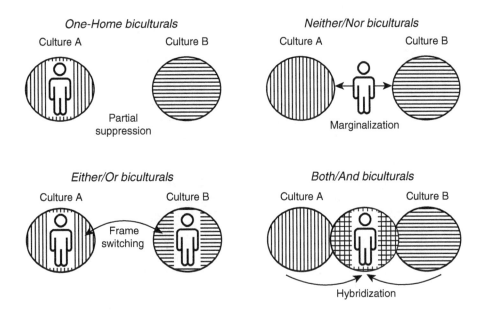

Figure 4.8 Typology of biculturals

Source: Adapted from Brannen, Garcia & Thomas (2009).

that are inherently and in multiple ways unequal (Bhatia 2002). The affection to a particular culture is not regarded as a choice between different functionally equivalent sets of options, but a reflection of *power and reputation asymmetries*. This means that the imitation of and adaptation to the practices of persons with higher economic and social status is regarded as more attractive than of those with lower status, and these practices are more likely to become the norm. For example, migrant workers and inpatriates, i.e., managers and specialists delegated from a peripheral foreign subsidiary to the corporate headquarters, often try to hide their cultural origin and adjust—at least superficially and ritualistically—to the behavior of the more powerful members of the host organization (Schuster, Holtbrügge & Engelhard 2019).

The complexity of cultural identity construction can be illustrated using the example of the football player **Mesut Özil**. Özil was born in the German town of Gelsenkirchen in 1988 as son of Turkish parents. His grandparents migrated with his then 2-year-old father to Germany in the 1970s. Because of his Turkish descent, he was eligible to play for both Germany and Turkey. "Whilst I grew up in Germany, my family background has its roots firmly based in Turkey. I have two hearts, one German and one Turkish" (Özil 2018). "My technique and feeling for the ball is the Turkish side to my game. The discipline, attitude and always-give-your-all is the German part" (cited in Smith 2010).

Mesut Özil is one of several talented third-generation Turkish immigrant football players who was born and grew up in Germany. While he together with İlkay Gündoğan and Emre Can chose German citizenship and to play for the German national team, others, such as Hamit Altıntop,

(Continued)

Hakan Çalhanoğlu, and Nuri Şahin, chose Turkey. Özil played in the German Bundesliga for FC Schalke 04 and Werder Bremen before he was transferred to Real Madrid in 2010. Since 2013 he has played for Arsenal London and resided in England before he moved to Fenerbahçe Istanbul in 2021.

Özil is a practicing Muslim and performed Umrah pilgrimage to Mecca in 2016. He observes fasting during the Islamic month of Ramadan, but admitted: "Because of my job I cannot follow Ramadan properly. I do it only the few days I can, only when I have a free day. But other than that it's impossible, because you have to drink and eat a lot to stay at peak fitness" (cited in Singh 2011).

In 2010, he received the Bambi award for being a prime example of successful integration within the German society. Despite this, his Turkish origin and Muslim religion has been a frequent topic in the German media and right-wing politicians often criticized him for not singing the German national anthem before matches. Özil explained in his autobiography: "While the anthem is being played, I pray, and I am sure that this will give us strength and confidence to drive the victory home" (Özil 2018).

Big tension among the German public caused a photo showing Özil and international teammate İlkay Gündoğan together with the hardline Turkish President Recep Tayyip Erdoğan in May 2018 shortly before the World Cup. The photo was interpreted as a form of political support for Erdoğan and criticized by the head of the German Football Federation (DFB) Reinhard Grindel: "The DFB of course respects the special situation for our players with migrant backgrounds, but football and the DFB stands for values that Mr. Erdoğan does not sufficiently respect. Therefore, it is not a good thing that our internationals have let them-selves be exploited for his election campaign stunt. It certainly hasn't helped the DFB's integration efforts" (https://www.dfb.de/en/news/detail/statement-on-meeting-with-erdo-gan-186745/?no_cache=1).

After remaining silent in this controversy for several months, Özil announced in an English Tweet in July 2018 that he will no longer play international football for Germany. "I feel unwanted and think that what I have achieved since my international debut in 2009 has been forgotten (…). Despite paying taxes in Germany, donating facilities to German schools and winning the World Cup with Germany in 2014, I am still not accepted into society. I am treated as being 'different' (…). In the eyes of Grindel and his supporters, I am German when we win, but I am an immigrant when we lose (…). Are there criteria for being fully German that I do not fit? My friends Lukas Podolski and Miroslav Klose [two recently retired former Germany internationals] are never referred to as German-Polish, so why am I German-Turkish? Is it because it is Turkey? Is it because I'm a Muslim? (…) I was born and educated in Germany, so why don't people accept that I am German?" (https://twitter.com/MesutOzil1088/status/1021093637411700741).

Özil's Twitter statement received mixed reactions in the German public. While some commentators raised concern over the country's attitude toward Germans with foreign roots, the DFB denied Özil's claims of racism. Former Justice Minister Katarina Barley tweeted: "It is an alarm signal when a great German footballer such as Mesut Özil feels unwanted in his country because of racism and not represented by the DFB" (https://twitter.com/katar-inabarley/status/1021123693534117888?lang=de). Former German Foreign Minister Heiko Maas responded: "I don't think the case of a multimillionaire living and working in England tells you much about Germany's capacity for integration" (https://twitter.com/heikomaas/status/1021399309529616385?lang=de).

Intercultural management research reveals that the *process of cultural adjustment* is not only influenced by the involved individuals and institutions, but differs also between various elements and levels of culture. People living in a foreign country often adopt some appealing aspects of the host culture while simultaneously retaining strong affiliations, identifications, and loyalties to the deeper-rooted values of their home country. For example, many immigrants easily appropriate some of the goods and practices (dress code, language, festivals, etc.) that are common in the host country–often endowing them with meanings related to the cultural norms and values of their home country–but resist its religious, moral, and sexual practices (Bhatia 2002; Khan, Lindridge & Pusaksrikit 2018). Referring to Schein's (2017) iceberg model of culture, this behavior can be interpreted as adaptation of visible and symbolic elements on the surface level, while the more fundamental norms and values as well as basic assumptions remain largely unaffected.

The notion of deconstructing the different representations and expressions of culture is particularly salient in **postmodern management research** (Welge & Holtbrügge 1999). *Deconstruction* refers to the relationship between language and meaning (Derrida 1976) and strives for the critical and reflective analysis of the language of concepts of culture. Culture is not conceptualized as a fixed and reified entity, but as a semantic and cognitive program. Instead of searching for anthropological roots of individual behaviors, postmodern approaches question the seemingly objective status of cultural differences and seek to deconstruct the veil of rationality that hides the underlying normative statements. Thus, deconstruction seeks to expose the mechanisms of construction, historical contexts, and power relations that create the various linguistic categories and classifications of culture (Wagener 2012).

4.8.3 Critical Evaluation

The constructivist concept of culture addresses several limitations of the etic concepts of Hofstede, Trompenaars, Schwartz, GLOBE, etc. While the latter conceptualize cultures in terms of dichotomous dimensions (such as, for example, individualism vs. collectivism, sequential vs. synchronous time, egalitarianism vs. hierarchy, etc.), constructivism challenges this approach of cultural categorizations. Instead of viewing cultures as internally homogeneous, externally distinctive, and temporarily stable, it emphasizes the **relevance of diversity, variations, and transformations**. Individuals, organizations, and societies are regarded as multifaceted and contingent. They can internalize distinct cultural schemas and activate them depending on different situational cues. Constructivist approaches are therefore less interested in classification and measurement, but in contextualization and contestation.

An important consequence of this understanding is the rejection of determinist conceptualizations of cultural values and behaviors. While cultural dimensions approaches analyze cultural values and assume that these determine cognition and behavior, it emphasizes the varied **interactions between the levels of symbols, norms and values, and basic assumptions**. Instead of assuming a "seamless superorganic unit within whose collective embrace the individual simply disappears into a cloud of mystic harmony" (Geertz 1965, p. 145), it is interested in exploring the psychological, social, and political negotiation processes in individuals and organizations. Cultures are not captured with a set of independent dimensions, but attention is given to the ambiguities, contradictions, and mutual interferences of cultural positions. As McSweeney (2013, p. 496) notes: "Life is made in impurity and intermingling."

Another difference between cultural dimensions and constructivist concepts is the focus of analysis. Cultural dimensions approaches consider the core aspects of culture and its representative members. The aim is to identify cultural values which are shared by the majority of the population. From a constructivist point of view, the periphery becomes salient as the meeting point between different cultures (Holmes 2015). It decentralizes the notion of culture and postulates that the study of "central tendencies" (Hofstede 1991, p. 253) becomes less pertinent. As borders between cultures are getting permeable and porous, interesting, relevant, and challenging "cultural action and the construction of identities takes place not in the 'middle' of the dwelling but in the contact zones between nations, peoples and locales" (Hermans 2001, p. 269). These **intercultural contact zones** involve, for example, international trade and investment, foreign assignments, and multicultural teamwork. Constructivist approaches are therefore less interested in comparisons between different cultures, but more their connections, overlaps, clashes, and amalgamations.

Despite their achievements, constructivist approaches have gained less attention in intercultural management literature thus far. While the concepts of Hofstede, Trompenaars, GLOBE, etc. provide appealing models and vivid illustrations, constructivist concepts appear bulky and less accessible. Their **interpretative ontology** contradicts the predominant positivist paradigm as it questions the possibility of objective measurement (D'Iribarne et al. 2020). As constructivist approaches do not provide quantitative data, they are not applicable in quantitative research. Moreover, the emphasis on localization and contextualization impedes the derivation of universal managerial implications.

4.9 CONCEPTS OF CULTURE: A CRITICAL EVALUATION

In the previous sections, eight seminal concepts of culture that found attention in intercultural management literature were discussed. Figure 4.9 distinguishes these concepts along two dimensions: the epistemological perspective (etic vs. emic) and the exploration of constructs (theoretical vs. empirical).

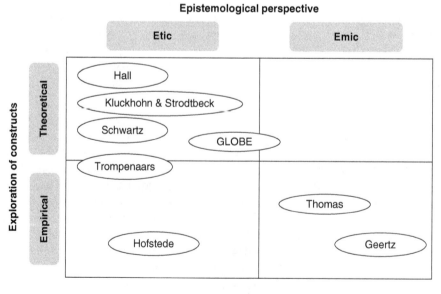

Figure 4.9 Classification of concepts of culture

The etic approaches of Hall, Kluckhohn and Strodtbeck, Schwartz, GLOBE, Trompenaars, and Hofstede propose a discrete set of cultural dimensions that are used to measure and classify the ways in which societies respond to universal human problems. According to Hofstede (2002, p. 2), "this idea of dimensions of national cultures has become part of (…) 'normal science' (..) since the later 1980s." With the exception of Hofstede, who derived the cultural dimensions predominantly from empirical data, the cultural dimensions were based on theoretical considerations. The main advantage of etic approaches is the facilitation of intercultural comparisons and classifications. However, they foster stereotypes because cultural characteristics are only described, but not explained.

The concepts of Thomas and Geertz are based on an emic epistemology. Their main assumption is that cultures can only be grasped through idiographic and specific constructs. Consequently, an explorative and empirical research approach is applied. Emic concepts make comparisons between cultures more difficult as indigenous terms and constructs are used. However, they provide a more authentic and differentiated picture. Cultural norms and behaviors are not only described, but contextualized and interpreted. Despite these advantages, the vast majority of publications in intercultural management research has adopted an etic approach. Of the 136 empirical papers on culture published in the *Journal of International Business Studies* over 24 years, only two adopted an emic approach (Tung & Stahl 2018).

Regardless of their widespread use, the existent concepts of culture are often criticized for insufficiently contributing to the analysis and solution of intercultural management problems. Four **major limitations** are particularly salient.

First, the level of analysis is the country, while intercultural management typically deals with individuals, teams, and organizations. Cultural dimensions constructed at the national level "are meaningless as descriptors of individuals or as predictors of individual differences because the variables that define them do not correlate meaningfully across individuals" (Minkov & Hofstede 2011, p. 12). The projection of national-level culture characteristics onto individuals or organizations therefore commits an **ecological fallacy**. Presuming isomorphism in national to individual culture characteristics creates "false stereotypes and, to the extent that such ideas are accepted and adopted by international business managers, they may well be misleading and counterproductive" (Brewer & Venaik 2014, p. 1079).

Another limitation is the—often implicit—legal-political delineation of cultures. With the exception of constructivist approaches, cultures are equated with countries. As discussed in Chapter 2.3, this **neglects the intracultural diversity of many countries**, such as Belgium, Canada, India, South Africa, and the United States. For example, what does the score on a particular cultural dimension, such as individualism or time orientation, tell for a country like India that unites 1.3 bn. people with dozens of different languages, ethnical backgrounds, religions, and partly even countries of residence?

Moreover, the increasing exposure of individuals and organizations to a variety of cultures has only recently found attention in constructivist concepts. **Polyculturalism** involves the *multitude of different national cultures* (e.g., in the form of biculturals) as well as the *interferences between different manifestations of culture*, such as professional cultures, age cultures, gender cultures, etc. The cultural mosaic of a person is composed of demographic (age, gender, ethnicity, and race), geographic (climate, coastal/inland, urban/rural, region/country), and associative characteristics (family, religion, profession, politics, and avocations) (Chao & Moon 2005). An interesting phenomenon in this context is the emergence of *global subcultures*. For example, a banker in New York may have more in common with a banker in New Delhi than a banker in New York with a punk in New York.

A person can be a German (born in Westphalia, living in Hamburg, and working in a Franconian city in the state of Bavaria), who married in Mauritius, regularly spends around a quarter of the year in various countries abroad, whose grandparents were born in a region that today belongs to Poland, a Friend of India, who studied Russian language and history, speaks English as main working language, admires a former South African apartheid fighter and president, likes French films, British rock music, and Dutch novels, enjoys Italian food, wears clothes mostly produced in Turkey and Vietnam, uses a smartphone designed in California and assembled in China, goes skiing in Austria, drives a Swedish car, and has been a long-time board member of a joint-venture in Belarus.

Finally, the concepts of culture bear the risk of causing the problems they seek to solve. In particular, the categorization of people along cultural dimensions and the **overemphasis of culture as criterion of distinction between individuals** may direct our perceptions toward differences that would otherwise not be noticed: "A major source of potential conflict in the contemporary world is the presumption that people can be uniquely categorized based on religion or culture. The implicit belief in the overarching power of a singular classification can make the world thoroughly inflammable (…). Indeed, the question 'do civilizations clash?' is founded on the presumption that humanity can be preeminently classified into distinct and discrete civilizations, and that the relations between different human beings can somehow be seen, without serious loss of understanding, in terms of relations between different civilizations (…). In our normal lives, we see ourselves as members of a variety of groups—we belong to all of them. The same person can be, without any contradiction, an American citizen, of Caribbean origin, with African ancestry, a Christian, a liberal, a woman, a vegetarian, a long-distance runner, a historian, a schoolteacher, a novelist, a heterosexual, a believer in gay and lesbian rights, a theater lover, an environmental activist, a tennis fan, and a jazz musician" (Sen 2006, p. vii).

SUMMARY

Intercultural management research has long been dominated by etic research concepts, such as those of Kluckhohn and Strodtbeck, Hall, Hofstede, and GLOBE, which measure cultures based on a universally applicable set of dimensions.

Only more recently, emic research concepts, such as the interpretive concepts of Thomas and Geertz, have gained importance, which propose the exploration of specific, idiographic constructs to describe cultures.

While both etic and emic concepts are useful for intercultural comparisons, they are less suitable for analyzing encounters between members of different cultures. Another limitation is the ecological fallacy problem that occurs when national-level characteristics are projected onto individuals and organizations. Concepts of culture bear the risk of overemphasizing culture as an underlying motive for behavior compared to individual and situational factors.

Reflection Questions

1. Find your home country and the related values for Hofstede's cultural dimensions in Table 4.6. Do you think that these values represent your culture appropriately or do you perceive your culture differently?

2. Would you talk about private issues, e.g., conflicts with your romantic partner, with your work colleagues? Do you think that people in different cultures would answer this question differently?

3. Would you lie to protect a close friend in court? Do you think that people in different cultures would answer this question differently?

4. Imagine your supervisor asks you to play a tennis match with him/her. Assuming that you are a better tennis player: Would you be willing to let him/her win? Which cultures might have different views on this?

5. Around 30 years after the initial GLOBE study, new data were collected in the GLOBE 2020 study. For which countries and for which dimensions of culture would you expect the greatest changes?

6. Think about Mesut Özil's case. Do you agree or disagree with the former German Foreign Minister Heiko Maas: "I don't think the case of a multi-millionaire living and working in England tells you much about Germany's capacity for integration"? Why?

7. The social construction of cultures can often be observed in the field of brand management. Do you know any examples of "foreign" brands from your country? Try to find photos!

 End of Chapter Exercise

British Expatriates in India

Imagine you are an expatriate of a British multinational corporation working as a team leader in India for three years.

1. According to your opinion: Which concept(s) of culture could best predict potential intercultural management challenges you are likely to face?

2. Do you think you could also face *intra*cultural management challenges in your job?

3. Do you think your Indian colleagues and subordinates would expect the same intercultural management challenges as you?

4. How could the ecological fallacy problem affect the relevance of the predicted intercultural management challenges?

Further Reading

The seminal studies of Kluckhohn and Strodtbeck (1961), Hofstede (2001), and House et al. (2004) explicate the development, validation, and empirical test of etic concepts of culture.

Hall (1976) and Hofstede, Hofstede, and Minkov (2010) provide a more practitioner-oriented overview.

The edited volume of Nakata (2009) discusses approaches seeking to overcome the dominance of Hofstede's concept.

The concept of cultural standards is elaborated upon in the handbook of Thomas, Kinast, and Schroll-Machl (2010).

D'Iribane et al. (2020) provide a fresh look at interpretative concepts of culture.

5

CULTURAL DIFFERENCES AND CULTURAL SIMILARITIES

LEARNING OBJECTIVES

By the end of this chapter, you will be able to

- know different approaches of cultural clusters,
- critically discuss the concept of cultural distance,
- evaluate various approaches of cultural diversity.

Comparative and intercultural management research has long been interested in exploring similarities and differences between cultures. This is based on the assumption that similar cultural norms and values facilitate the standardization of management practices across countries. Cultural distance, on the contrary, requires a differentiated approach that is often associated with higher costs and increased management efforts. In recent years, the discussion about cultural similarities and differences has surpassed the national level and inspired research on cultural variations within countries.

In the following, common approaches that cluster countries along cultural dimensions are discussed. The second section is devoted to concepts of cultural distance and attractiveness. Finally, the focus is directed to intracultural diversity and its impact on management practices and outcomes.

5.1 CULTURAL CLUSTERS

Classifications of cultural clusters seek to explore supranational similarities between cultures. Depending on the underlying concept of culture, etic and emic approaches can be distinguished. While emic approaches aim to explore the unique features of a specific culture and are more common in political science and sociology, etic approaches employ standardized methodologies and prevail in intercultural psychology and management research.

5.1.1 The Typology of Galtung

An early attempt to explore similarities between cultures was proposed by the Norwegian sociologist and peace researcher *Johan Galtung* (1992). Galtung primarily focuses on **intellectual styles**, i.e., the way how knowledge is produced and communicated in academic discourse, which he regards as important elements of the subcivilizational or macrocultural level and frequently refers to cultural influences.

Galtung's approach to develop "a world map of intellectual styles" (Galtung 1981, p. 819) is based on a **center-periphery scheme** of the world. He argues that there exist four centers with distinct intellectual styles: the United Kingdom/United States, Germany, France, and Japan (China, India, and the Arab world are explicitly excluded from the study). These four centers are surrounded by various peripheral cultures (Figure 5.1):

- *Periphery under the influence of zero centers*: These are intellectually marginalized countries, free to develop in any way. Given that they do not feel any obligation to imitate others, they often develop novel intellectual styles. While Galtung does not give any examples for these types of countries, one may think of Israel.

- *Periphery under the influence of one center*: These countries are determined on using identification. Examples are the French-speaking parts of Belgium and Switzerland,

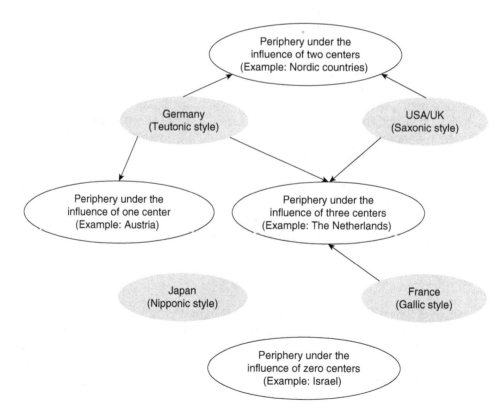

Figure 5.1 Galtung's center-periphery scheme of cultures

Austria as periphery of Germany, and Ireland as periphery of England.

- *Periphery under the influence of two centers*: Countries falling into this category are potentially benefiting from the cross-beaming influence. That is, they are picking up the strong points of both. An example is the Nordic countries, which have been under both saxonic and teutonic influence. People in Denmark, Norway, and Sweden often speak German and English fluently and share elements of both cultures.

- *Periphery under the influence of three centers or more*: In these countries, the cultural influence of different centers is possibly too overwhelming to elaborate on anything new. An example is the Netherlands, which is exposed not only to saxonic and teutonic influences but also to gallic. While the Dutch culture has absorbed elements of several other cultures, it has not been very innovative in creating a novel intellectual style.

The influence of two or more centers on a periphery does not necessarily happen simultaneously, but can occur sequentially. A notable example is **Belarus**. Situated between Poland and Russia both geographically and linguistically, the Belarussian culture has been shaped over centuries through a number of pendulum effects.

The history of the Belarusian ethnicity begins with the migration and expansion of the Slavic peoples throughout Eastern Europe between the sixth and eighth centuries. East Slavs settled on the territory of present-day Belarus, Russia, and Ukraine, assimilating local Baltic, Finno-Ugric, and steppe nomads already living there. The common cultural bonds were Eastern Orthodox Christianity and written Church Slavonic.

From the thirteenth century onwards, the West Ruthenian (Belarusian) principalities became part of the Grand Duchy of Lithuania and later the Polish–Lithuanian Commonwealth. Several larger cities including Brest, Grodno, and Minsk were granted municipal self-government which facilitated contacts with Western Europe and nurtured self-reliance, entrepreneurship, and a sense of civic responsibility. An East Slavic variety gradually influenced by Polish became the language of administration until the late seventeenth century when it was eventually replaced by Polish language. Most residents belonged to the Uniate Church, i.e., they were Greco Catholics who abided by Orthodox rites but recognized the supremacy of the Pope. Ruthenians formed in most cases rural population, with the power held by people of Lithuanian, Polish, or Russian descent. As in the rest of Central and Eastern Europe, the trade and commerce was mostly monopolized by Jews, who formed a significant part of the urban population.

After the Partition of Poland, all its lands annexed by the Russian Empire in 1795. A policy of de-Polonization and Russification began, which included the return to Orthodoxy. In the 1840s, Nicholas I forbade the use of the term Belarusia and renamed the region the North-Western Territory. He also prohibited the use of Belarusian language in public schools, campaigned against Belarusian publications, and tried to pressure those who had converted to Catholicism under the Poles to reconvert to the Orthodox faith. In 1864, the Russian government reintroduced the use of Cyrillic to Belarusian and banned the use of the Latin alphabet.

After the Russian Revolution and the foundation of the Soviet Union, Belarus became the Belarusian Soviet Republic. In 1991, Belarus declared independence and became the Republic

(Continued)

of Belarus. This went along with the resurrection of the Belarussian language and national symbols, like the white-red-white flag and the Pahonia coat of arms. With Alexander Luka-shenko becoming president in 1994, Belarussian language and emblems were again banned as symbols of the pro-European opposition and Russian became de facto the official language in administration, business, and other sections of Belarusian society (Holtbrügge 2002; Ioffe 2003; Snyder 2004; Wilson 2021).

Galtung provides a novel approach of cultural similarities and influences that differ significantly from other taxonomies of cultural clusters. However, despite the concept being frequently cited in political science, it has failed to receive much attention in intercultural management literature. Major **limitations** are due to the lack of methodological rigor (country assignments are based on personal judgments rather than systematic analysis) and the minimal number of included countries.

5.1.2 Huntington's Classification of Civilizations

Political scientist *Samuel Huntington* argues in his seminal book *Clash of Cultures* (1996) that the primary axis of conflict in the future will be along cultural lines. As an extension, he posits that the lines of conflict will not be between individual countries, but larger civilizations. "A civilization is (…) the highest cultural grouping of people and the broadest level of cultural identity people have" (Huntington 1996, p. 43). Huntington proposes a classification of **eight major civilizations** (Table 5.1; Figure 5.2):

- The *Western civilization* comprises the United States and Canada, Western and Central Europe, Australia, Oceania, and most of the Philippines. Common characteristics of these countries are the Christian religion and tradition of enlightenment.

Table 5.1 Classification of civilizations according to Huntington

Civilization	Historical origin	Population (1992, in thousands)	Estimated Shares of World Population (2025, in %)	Shares of World GDP (1992, in %)
Western	700–800 BC	805,400	10.1	48.9
Latin American		507,500	9.2	8.3
Orthodox	1054 AD	261,300	4.9	6.2
Confucian	1500 BC	1,340,900	21.0	10.0
Hindu	1500 BC	915,800	16.9	3.5
Japanese	100–400 AD	124,700	1.5	8.0
Islamic	650 AD	927,600	19.2	11.0
African		392,100	14.4	2.1
Others			2.8	2.0

Source: Huntington (1997, p. 85).

Figure 5.2 Classification of major civilizations according to Huntington
Source: Based on Huntington (1996, p. 26).

- *Latin America* is composed of Central America, South America (excluding Guyana, Suriname, and French Guiana), Cuba, the Dominican Republic, and Mexico. These countries share the heritage of being part of the Spanish Empire from the sixteenth to the nineteenth century, which had a major influence on their culture and language.
- The *Orthodox world* consists of the successor states of the former Soviet Union (excluding the Protestant and Catholic Baltic states Estonia, Latvia and Lithuania, Muslim Azerbaijan, most of Central Asia, and a majority of Muslim regions in the Caucasus and central Russia, such as Tatarstan and Bashkortostan), Bulgaria, Cyprus, Greece, Romania, and Serbia. They developed as a distinct civilization after the East-West Schism of 1054.
- The *Confucian civilization* includes China, the Koreas, Singapore, Taiwan, and Vietnam. It also includes the Chinese diaspora in Southeast Asia.
- The *Hindu civilization* is mainly located in India, Bhutan, and Nepal and culturally adhered to by the global Indian diaspora.
- *Japan* is considered a hybrid of Chinese civilization and older Altaic patterns.
- The *Muslim world* include the Greater Middle East (excluding Armenia, Cyprus, Ethiopia, Georgia, Israel, Malta, and South Sudan), northern West Africa, Albania, Bangladesh, parts of Bosnia and Herzegovina, Brunei, Comoros, Indonesia, Malaysia, Maldives, and southern Philippines.
- The *civilization of sub-Saharan Africa* is located in southern Africa, Middle Africa (excluding Chad), East Africa (excluding Ethiopia, the Comoros, Mauritius, and the Swahili coast of Kenya and Tanzania), Cape Verde, Ghana, the Ivory Coast, Liberia, and Sierra Leone.

The *Buddhist areas* of Bhutan, Cambodia, Laos, Mongolia, Myanmar, Sri Lanka, and Thailand are identified as separate from other civilizations. However, Huntington believes that they do not constitute a major civilization in the sense of international affairs.

Instead of belonging to one of the major civilizations, Ethiopia and Haiti are labeled as *lone countries*. Israel is considered a unique state with its own civilization that is, however, extremely similar to the West. According to Huntington, the former British colonies in the Caribbean also constitute a distinct entity.

Cleft countries contain very large groups of people identifying with separate civilizations. Examples include Ukraine (cleft between its Eastern Rite Catholic-dominated Western section and its Orthodox-dominated east), French Guiana (cleft between Latin America and the West), and Benin, Chad, Kenya, Nigeria, Tanzania, and Togo (all cleft between Islam and sub-Saharan Africa).

Finally, *torn countries* are those seeking to affiliate with another civilization. The most prominent example is Turkey, whose political leadership has systematically tried to Westernize the country since the 1920s. While Turkey's history, culture, and traditions are derived from Islamic civilization, over the years, the country has imposed Western institutions and dress, embraced the Latin alphabet, acquired NATO membership, and subsequently sought to join the European Union. According to Huntington, other torn countries include Mexico, Russia, and Australia which oscillates between its Western civilizational heritage and its growing economic engagement with Asia.

Huntington's classification of civilizations garnered a lot of attention; however, it also received harsh **critique**. For example, Huntington posits that religious identity is a civilization's defining cultural characteristic and that that cultural differences are based primarily on religion, thus neglecting other important elements of culture. Moreover, Huntington discusses the influence of religion in a very general sense and neglects the various and often conflicting forms of Christianity, Hinduism, Islam, and especially the very diverse natural religions in large parts of Africa, Asia, and South America. In contrast to Huntington, Berman (2003) argues that distinct cultural boundaries do not presently exist and that there is neither "Islamic civilization" nor "Western civilization." According to Said (2001), Huntington's categorization of the fixed civilizations omits the dynamic interdependencies and interactions of cultures. "In fact, Huntington is an ideologist, someone who wants to make 'civilizations' and 'identities' into what they are not: shut-down, sealed-off entities that have been purged of the myriad currents and countercurrents that animate human history, and that over centuries have made it possible for that history not only to contain wars of religion and imperial conquest but also to be one of exchange, cross-fertilization and sharing" (Said 2001). Apart from this, empirical studies also refute Huntington's key assumption of a clash *between* civilizations and point to the many clashes that occur *within* civilizations (Senghaas 2002). "Many of the interethnic and inter-religious conflicts that occur in the post-Cold War era are clashes within rather than between civilizations (…). In fact, in the post-Cold War era (…), their number has actually declined, if only marginally" (Henderson 2005, p. 458).

5.1.3 Cattell's Concept of Syntality Patterns

One of the first etic approaches to cluster countries along cultural dimensions was proposed by Cattell (1950). Analogous to individual personality, Cattel analyzed about 80 variables to construct 12 factor dimensions of *national syntality* that measures various psychological, sociological, demographic, and economic characteristics of 69 countries. He identified **ten cultural patterns** using average Euclidean distances between the factor scores for each pair of countries (Table 5.2).

The larger developed nations, such as France, Germany, the United Kingdom, the United States, the former Soviet Union, and Japan, could not be clustered with any of these patterns and emerged as independent units in the analysis.

Table 5.2 Cultural patterns according to Cattell

Cultural patterns	Characteristics
Catholic (Catholic Homeland, Catholic Colonial, and Catholic Fringe pattern)	Shows a relatively high level of peaceful progressiveness and patriarchal conservatism and a low level of cultural integration. This is most emphasized in the Catholic Homeland pattern.
Older Catholic Colonial	Differs from the catholic pattern as being high in bourgeois carefulness and low in pace and patriarchal stability.
Eastern European	Low on bourgeois carefulness and high on peaceful progressiveness and fastidiousness.
Mohammedan	Conspicuous by being low in the factors of enlightened affluence, pace, fastidiousness, and peaceful progressiveness.
East Baltic	No marked characters except low enlightenment affluence.
Scandinavian	Uniformly high in scientific industriousness, order, pace, and enlightened affluence.
Commonwealth	Somewhat similar to the Scandinavian pattern. High in order and enlightened affluence, but lower in scientific industriousness.
Oriental (China and India)	Low in order and peaceful progressiveness and high in the Buddhism-Mongolism factor.
Infused Catholic Colonial	Relatively low in integration and high in conservative patriarchalism.
Infused Hamitic	Combines low enlightenment affluence with low progressiveness and low pace (high unsophisticated stability).

Source: Compiled from Cattell (1950).

The examination of the 10 clusters suggests that common historical diffusions from a center, collectively-shared historical trauma, common root language, similar geography, similarity of religion, and ethnic similarity are important factors in determining within-cluster similarity. In comparison, geography and history are less relevant than the last two factors.

While the concept of Cattell is based on—for the time of the study—sophisticated methods of multivariate data analysis (factor analysis and cluster analysis), it is faced with **limitations** regarding input data. Since no direct measures of culture were available, variables such as expenditure on education, restrictions on divorce, and frequency of population in trade unions were used as proxies. Despite these shortcomings, the taxonomy has influenced many subsequent studies in this field.

5.1.4 Taxonomy of Cultures Based on Hofstede

Hofstede's taxonomy of cultural clusters is based on his original four dimensions of culture (i.e., power distance, uncertainty avoidance, individualism vs. collectivism, and masculinity vs. femininity). He conducted a hierarchical cluster analysis, resulting in a dendrogram of the 53 countries and regions covered in his IBM study that was "somewhat arbitrarily" (Hofstede 2001, p. 62) split into 12 **regional clusters**:

- Korea, Peru, El Salvador, Chile, Portugal, and Uruguay (in which Korea is historically/linguistically the odd one out)
- (Former) Yugoslavia, Turkey, Arabic-speaking countries, and Greece, plus Argentina, Spain, and Brazil (two different historical subclusters intermingled)
- Ecuador, Venezuela, Colombia, and Mexico
- Pakistan and Iran, Indonesia, Thailand, Taiwan, and East and West Africa (three or four subclusters intermingled)
- Guatemala, Panama, and Costa Rica

- Malaysia, Philippines, India, Hong Kong, Singapore, and Jamaica (all former British or American colonies)
- Denmark, Sweden, the Netherlands, Norway, and Finland
- Australia, the United States, Canada, the United Kingdom, Ireland, and New Zealand
- Germany, Switzerland, South Africa, and Italy (two or three subclusters intermingled)
- Austria and Israel
- Belgium and France
- Japan

Hofstede (2001) provides no further information on the underlying statistical methodology and no discussion of the identified clusters. Therefore, it remains unclear which cultural characteristics the countries assigned to the 12 clusters have in common and how strongly they discriminate from each other.

Several **subsequent studies** re-examined the data collected by Hofstede and provided individual taxonomies. For example, Müller and Gelbrich (2004) conducted an agglomerative hierarchical cluster analysis of Hofstede's original four cultural dimensions that are available for 84 countries (excluding Japan as singleton) and identified **seven cultural clusters** (Table 5.3):

Table 5.3 Cultural clusters according to Hofstede

Denomination	Associated Countries	Cultural dimensions			
		PDI	IDV	MAS	UAI
Collectivists	Caucasus, China, Fiji, Ghana, Indonesia, Iraq, Malawi, Namibia, Nepal, Pakistan, Sierra Leone, Taiwan, Tanzania, Thailand, Zambia	69	<u>23</u>	43	54
Uncertainty tolerators	Bhutan, Dominican Republic, Ethiopia, Hong Kong, India, Jamaica, Kenya, Lebanon, Malaysia, Nigeria, Philippines, Singapore	76	32	58	<u>38</u>
Power distant collectivists	Albania, Colombia, Ecuador, Guatemala, Mexico, Panama, Romania, Saudi Arabia, Serbia, Venezuela	**86**	<u>17</u>	57	83
Collectivist uncertainty avoiders	Chile, Costa Rica, El Salvador, Peru, Portugal, Slovenia, South Korea, Uruguay	60	<u>23</u>	32	**91**
Uncertainty avoiders	Argentina, Belgium, Brazil, Bulgaria, Croatia, Egypt, France, Greece, Russia, Spain, Surinam, Ukraine, Turkey	68	46	46	**85**
Feminine individualists	Czech Republic, Denmark, Estonia, Finland, Latvia, Lithuania, Netherlands, Norway, Sri Lanka, Sweden	36	**65**	<u>19</u>	47

Table 5.3 Cultural clusters according to Hofstede (Continued)

Denomination	Associated Countries	Cultural dimensions			
		PDI	IDV	MAS	UAI
Masculine individualists	Australia, Austria, Canada, Germany, Hungary, Ireland, Israel, Italy, Luxembourg, New Zealand, Poland, South Africa, Switzerland, United Kingdom, United States	34	**71**	**65**	58
	Overall mean	*61*	*40*	*48*	*64*

Note: **Bold** values mean significantly above average; underlined values mean significantly below average
Source: Adapted from Müller & Gelbrich (2004, p. 522).

- Three clusters—collectivists, uncertainty tolerators, and uncertainty avoiders—show significantly below- or above-average values for one of the four cultural dimensions. The values for the other three dimensions do not significantly vary from the mean values.

- Four clusters—power distant collectivists, collectivist uncertainty avoiders, feminine individualists, and masculine individualists—show significantly higher or lower values for two of the four dimensions.

A major advantage of taxonomies based on the values of the Hofstede study compared to previous classifications is their underlying theoretical concept and direct measure of culture. Instead of using proxies that only partially reflect cultural norms and values, theoretically grounded and empirically validated measures are applied. At the same time, however, these taxonomies are characterized by the same **limitations** as the underlying study of Hofstede (Chapter 4.3.3). Due to these limitations taxonomies based on Hofstede have received considerably less attention in the intercultural management literature than his cultural dimensions on the national level.

5.1.5 Schwartz's Spatial Map of Cultural Regions

Like Hofstede, Schwartz's theory of cultural values has been applied to analyze cultural groupings on the supranational level. Based on his study of cultural orientations, Schwartz (2006) generated a worldwide empirical mapping of 76 national cultures (73 countries, with Israel split into Arabs and Jews, Germany into East and West, and Canada into Anglo and French-speaking national groups).

For this purpose, he first standardized the mean importance of all seven cultural orientations within each group. Each group profile reflects the relative importance of each cultural orientation within a national group. Based on the *co-plot multidimensional scaling technique*, a matrix of profile differences between all pairs of groups was calculated by summing the absolute differences between the groups on each of the seven value orientations. From this matrix, a **two-dimensional spatial representation** of the similarities and differences among cultural groups was generated. Then vectors (optimal regression lines) that show the direction of increasing scores for each of the seven cultural orientations were calculated.

Figure 5.3 shows the full vector for embeddedness from lower left to upper right. The farther a country is positioned toward the upper right, the greater the cultural emphasis on embeddedness relative to other nations. Conversely, the farther a country is positioned toward the lower left, the less cultural emphasis there is on embeddedness. Short arrows indicate the angles of the vectors for the other six cultural orientations. These other vectors also extend through the center of gravity of the figure. The locations of countries along these vectors relative to one another illustrate graphically the specific ways in which national cultures resemble or differ from one another. The correlation between the actual scores of the cultural groups on an orientation and their locations along the vector that represents the orientation appear in parentheses. High correlation coefficients (.75 < r < .98) indicate pronounced cultural similarities within the country groupings.

Seven **supranational cultural groupings** that showcase striking parallels with the main civilizations of Huntington (1993) and the taxonomy of cultures proposed by Hofstede (2001) are revealed:

- The *West European region* emphasizes intellectual autonomy, egalitarianism, and harmony more than any other region. It is classified as the lowest region on hierarchy and embeddedness. This profile remains consistent even after controlling for national wealth. Although West Europe's high economic level may influence its culture, other factors are apparently relevant. In comparison to other regions, West European countries share a broad culture, while also possessing a substantial cultural variation within the region. For example, intellectual autonomy is high in France and Germany, while egalitarianism is more pronounced in Scandinavia and Switzerland.

- The culture of the *English-speaking region* is particularly high in affective autonomy and mastery and relatively low in harmony and embeddedness, in comparison to the rest of

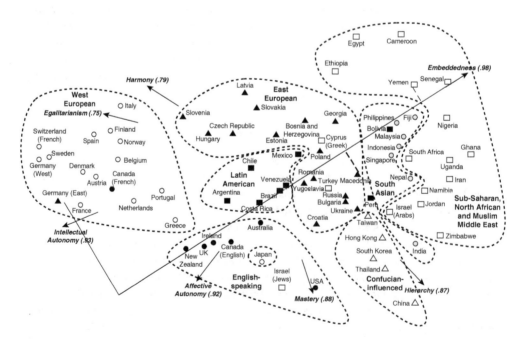

Figure 5.3 Co-plot map of 76 national groups on Schwartz's seven cultural orientations
Source: Based on Schwartz (2006, p. 156).

the world. It is average in intellectual autonomy, hierarchy, and egalitarianism. The culture in the United States differs from that in other English-speaking countries because it emphasizes mastery and hierarchy more and intellectual autonomy, harmony, and egalitarianism less. With the exception of the United States, this region is particularly homogeneous.

- The *Confucian-influenced region* exhibits a pragmatic, entrepreneurial orientation. However, this orientation places a heavy emphasis on hierarchy and mastery with a rejection of egalitarianism and harmony as compared with other regions. This region emphasizes embeddedness more than any other European or English-speaking cultures. Within-region differences are small except for Japan, which presents a striking exception. The country strongly emphasizes hierarchy and harmony but not embeddedness, which is adjacent to them, and it strongly emphasizes intellectual autonomy but not the adjacent egalitarianism. The location of Japan in the co-plot is therefore necessarily misleading.

- The *cultural groups from sub-Saharan, North Africa, and the Muslim Middle East* are especially high in embeddedness and low in affective and intellectual autonomy. There are great variations within the region on all but embeddedness, egalitarianism, and intellectual autonomy.

- The culture in the *South Asian region* is particularly high in hierarchy and embeddedness and low in autonomy and egalitarianism. With the exception of India's exceptionally high rating in mastery, the region is culturally

quite homogeneous. The variety of dominant religions (Hinduism, Roman Catholicism, Islam, Buddhism, Methodist Protestantism) in this region does not produce cultural heterogeneity on the basic orientations.

- The *East European cultures* are low in embeddedness and hierarchy compared with Africa, Asia, and the Middle East, but higher in these cultural orientations than Western Europe and the English-speaking countries. Although the East European cultures do form a region in the spatial projection, they vary substantially on hierarchy, mastery, and harmony. The Baltic and Central European states form a subregion toward the top center and the Balkan and more Eastern states form a subregion to their right and below. The former are higher in harmony, intellectual autonomy, and egalitarianism and lower in mastery and hierarchy than the Balkan and more Eastern states.

- Finally, the culture of the *Latin American region* is close to the worldwide average in all seven orientations. With the exception of Bolivia and Peru whose populations have been least exposed to European culture, this region is particularly homogeneous culturally. Latin America is higher in hierarchy and embeddedness, presumably the main components of collectivism, and lower in intellectual autonomy, presumably the main component of individualism. The opposite is the case, however, when compared to Africa, the Middle East, and South Asia and Confucian-influenced cultures.

5.1.6 The GLOBE Cultural Clusters

While the taxonomies of Hofstede and Schwartz—like most previous classifications—apply an explorative approach, the authors of the GLOBE study proposed *a priori* that the 61 countries included in this study can be grouped into 10 distinct clusters (Figure 5.4). Discriminant analysis was used to statistically test the empirical validity of the proposed typology.

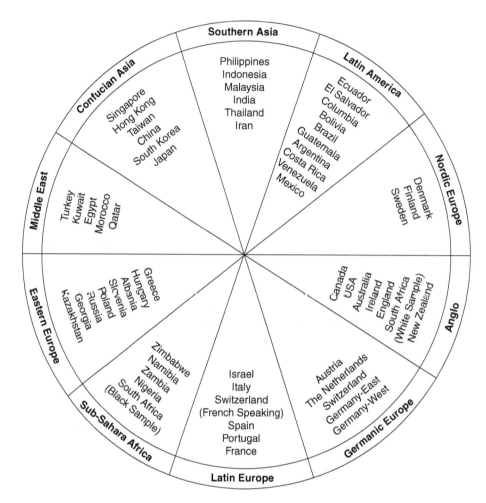

Figure 5.4 Societal cluster classification according to GLOBE

Source: Gupta & Hanges (2004, p. 190).

The authors randomly split each societal sample into two halves and computed societal practice and societal values scores based on the nine GLOBE cultural scales. A discriminant linear function for predicting the classification of societies into the GLOBE hypothesized clusters was constructed for one-half of each societal cluster sample. For the development sample (i.e., the sample used to develop the linear discriminant function), five discriminant functions captured 92.8% of the variation among the GLOBE societal clusters. For the base sample, 59 of the 61 societies were classified accurately into the hypothesized clusters, yielding 96.7% classification reliability of the discriminant functions. Two countries not accurately classified were Costa Rica and Guatemala, both of which had greater probability of classification into the Latin European cluster than into the hypothesized Latin American cluster. A cross-validation largely confirmed these results. Gupta, Hanges & Dorfman (2002, p. 14) therefore concluded that "the cluster classification of GLOBE societies finds very good support."

The authors also examined the extent to which individuals' values and practices in their societal culture are influenced by societal clusters as distinguished from the independent society (i.e., nation). The results indicate that societal cluster effects account for more than two-thirds of the intersociety differences in values as well as practices of uncertainty avoidance, future orientation, and institutional collectivism. "This suggests that the societal cluster is an appropriate and relevant unit of analysis, and that the GLOBE cluster classifications are reliable indicators of worldwide cultural attributes" (Gupta, Hanges & Dorfman 2002, p. 15).

While some classifications of GLOBE are intuitive (e.g., the Nordic Europe, Germanic Europe, and Anglo clusters), others are disputable. For example, the eight countries assigned to the Eastern Europe cluster exhibit great diversity with regard to a number of criteria.

Kazakhstan is not a European country, but belongs *geographically* to Asia. More than three quarters of Russian territory is located in Asia, causing Russia's identity to be significantly shaped by the spread of the country over two continents.

In terms of *linguistics*, Russian belongs to the East Slavic, Polish to the West Slavic, and Slovenian to the South Slavic language branch. Kazakh is a Turkic language of the Kipchak branch and Hungarian belongs to the Uralic language family. Georgian is a Kartvelian language and has no relationship with other language families. Greek and Albanian are their own language branches.

There are also vast *religious* differences between the countries. In Russia, Russian Orthodoxy is the most widely professed faith, but with significant minorities of nonreligious people and adherents of other faiths. Orthodox Christianity is also the major religion in Georgia and Greece. The majority of religious people in Hungary, Slovenia, and Poland are Roman Catholics, with Poland being one of the most religious countries in Europe. The majority of Kazakhstan's citizens identify as nondenominational Muslims. Islam (mainly Sunni) is also the most commonly practiced religion in Albania.

Given these vast geographic, linguistic, and religious differences, there is hardly any emic dimension that unites the eight countries assigned to the Eastern Europe cluster.

5.1.7 Cultural Clusters of Ronen and Shenkar

One of the first meta-taxonomies of cultural clusters in the field of intercultural management was published by Ronen and Shenkar (1985). Based on a review of eight previous empirical studies that cluster countries according to attitudinal data, such as work goals, values, needs, and job attitudes (including Haire, Ghiselli & Porter 1966 and Hofstede 1980), a map that integrates and synthesizes the available data was created. It contains 46 countries, of which 42 countries are assigned to eight cultural clusters and four countries that are labeled as independent. The **cluster formation** is based on geographic, linguistic, and religious criteria:

- The names of the clusters describe *geographic areas*. This is based on the assumption that "geography casually precedes other variables, such as language and religion, because a culture spreads first to those areas nearest its 'birthplace' (Ronen & Shenkar 1985, p. 444). The only exception is the Anglo cluster that contains countries from all five continents. In this case, the spread of culture is attributed to colonization and immigration.

- *Language* is the second dimension underlying the clusters. For the most part, the countries in each cluster share a language or a language group. For example, people in the Anglo countries speak English and people in the Germanic countries speak German. The most notable exception is the Far Eastern cluster that comprises a large variety of languages and scripts, such as Chinese, Filipino, Malay, Thai, Vietnamese, etc.
- The third dimension is *religion*. Most groupings of this cluster share a common religion. For example, the Anglo, Germanic, and Nordic clusters are predominantly Protestant, while the Latin American and Latin European clusters are mainly Catholic. A special exception is the Near Eastern cluster that includes one Orthodox country (Greece) and two Islamic countries, Turkey and Iran. Turkey is a secular country with a predominantly Sunnite population, and Iran has an overwhelmingly Shiite population and uses Sharia Law as basis for the government, laws, and social norms.

Ronen and Shenkar (1985, p. 446) point to the fact that the three dimensions geography, language, and religion are not independent. "In fact, it is likely (though not certain) that countries with one of these elements in common will share all three." This statement reveals one of the major **shortcomings** of the taxonomy. The application of correlated, but substantially different criteria leads to *blurred delineations of clusters*. While geography, language, and religion are interrelated with culture, they are mostly regarded as distinct concepts (Saroglou & Cohen 2013). The proposed clusters therefore only reflect partial and coincidental cultural similarities.

Another shortcoming is the *limited geographical scope* of the considered countries. According to Ronan & Shenkar (1985, p. 452), the clusters include "much of the non-Communist world" of that time, while many regions, such as Eastern Europe, China, and Africa, are excluded. Other regions, such as the Middle East and the Far East, had not been studied sufficiently until that time, which makes it difficult to draw well-grounded conclusions about their cluster membership. As Blunt (1986) argues, the typology is therefore affected by *ethnocentric and technocentric bias* and predominantly reflects a North-American view of the world.

The *methodology of cluster formation* is also frequently criticized due to its lack of rigor and validity as it is primarily based on plausibility and not on statistical analysis. As Ronan & Shenkar (2013, p. 868) admit, in retrospect: "Statistical techniques available at the time did not permit rigorous investigation of topics of theoretical and practical significance, such as nested cluster formation, cohesiveness, and adjacency—leaving them open to intuitive if not speculative or tautological interpretation."

Around 30 years after their initial study, Ronan and Shenkar (2013; 2017) published an **extended and revised taxonomy** based on an updated dataset and extended to world areas that were nonaccessible in the mid-1980s. While the cluster boundaries in the original study were drawn intuitively, they are now derived empirically. Based on a review of 11 empirical studies that cluster countries according to cultural dimensions (including the original study of Ronen & Shenkar 1985; Trompenaars 1994; Schwartz 1999; Inglehart & Baker 2000; Hofstede 2001; and House et al. 2004), a hierarchical cluster analysis was conducted that—like in the original study—examines the combined role of geography, language, and religion.

Based on a **nesting procedure**, 70 countries that appeared in at least two input studies and are still in existence were clustered hierarchically, resulting in a tree-like dendrogram showing hierarchical relations among all countries. The dendrogram tree was cut at three heights, indicating three levels of similarity across given country pairs. Afterward, 26 countries were reassigned to the clusters based on the single study in which they appeared, leading to a final sample of 96 countries that are illustrated in an oval diagram with three concentric circles (Figure 5.5):

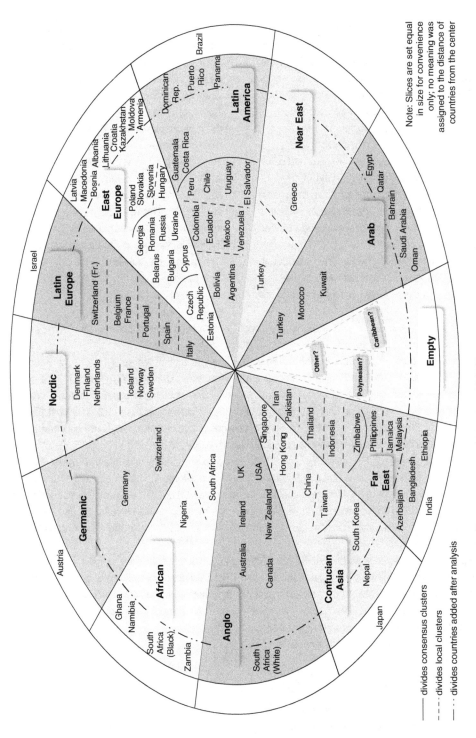

Note: Slices are set equal in size for convenience only; no meaning was assigned to the distance of countries from the center

Figure 5.5 Cultural clusters according to Ronen & Shenkar (2013)

Source: Ronen & Shenkar (2013, p. 884).

— divides consensus clusters

--- divides local clusters

—·· divides countries added after analysis

- First, the tree was cut at the point representing clusters of countries that, on average, appeared together in a single cluster in the input studies at least half the time ($p = 0.5$). Through this procedure and after including countries that appeared only in one study, a total of 16 *consensus clusters* and five singletons were identified, with each of the 16 nonsingleton clusters showing a cohesive level of work-related attitudes and behaviors differing from other clusters. Similarly, attitudes and behaviors manifested in singleton countries differ from those exhibited in other consensus clusters.

- At the higher end, the dendrogram was cut at $p = 0.75$, obtaining 11 *global clusters*. Ten out of 11 global clusters are similar to the clusters in the original study, but occasionally named differently and containing different countries. For example, Iran was assigned to the Near Eastern cluster in Ronen and Shenkar (1985), while it now appears in the Far East cluster. The level of global clusters is consistent with the consensus clusters. Excluding singletons, nine consensus clusters collapse into four, and seven clusters remain unchanged.

- At the lower end of the dendrogram where country congruence is higher, the tree was cut at $p = 0.25$. This resulted in 38 *local clusters*, many of which consist of a single country, such as in the case of the Latin European and Confucian Asia clusters. Eight local clusters have three to seven members each, such as in the case of East Europe.

Five *independents* (Austria, Israel, Brazil, India, and Japan) were moved to an appended zone outside each cluster, but positioned in relation to their originating global cluster.

Cluster adjacency (p) and **cluster cohesiveness** (p_w) vary to a high degree. The Arab (three members, $p = 0.00$, $p_w = 0.00$) and Anglo clusters (six members, $p = 0.10$, $p_w = 0.07$) exhibit the highest cohesiveness and are identical as local, consensus, and global clusters. The least cohesive are the Confucian Asia ($p_w = 0.55$), Far East ($p_w = 0.55$), and African clusters ($p_w = 0.50$). The East Europe Global cluster (13 members, $p = 0.68$, $p_w = 0.48$) also has a low cohesiveness, but has three highly cohesive, geographically adjacent consensus clusters ($p_w = 0.00–0.22$).

While the taxonomy of Ronan & Shenkar (2013) seeks to synthesize and integrate most existing supranational classifications of cultures, it has a number of **limitations**. First, Africa is largely underrepresented with only five out of 55 African countries included. In total, 96 out of the 193 member states of the United Nations (49.7%) are considered. While this makes it the most comprehensive taxonomy of cultures available, it must be taken into consideration that the assignment of 26 out of the 96 countries is only based on a single study.

More fundamentally, Ronan and Shenkar (2013) did not analyze or re-examine country-level data, but conducted a meta-analysis of 11 original studies with diverse theoretical concepts, country samples, methodologies, sample sizes, etc. While cluster analysis is generally a powerful methodology, here it is applied with a maximum number of only 11 observations per country (often even less). Thus, the sophisticated methodology and provision of statistical coefficients gives the illusion of rigor and robustness that is not reflected in the very small sample size.

5.1.8 Critical Evaluation

The concepts of cultural clusters discussed in the previous sections posit that **cultural differences are more region-specific than country-specific** and that the cultural context mostly changes between

Table 5.4 Synopsis of concepts of cultural clusters

	Galtung	Huntington	Cattell	Hofstede	Schwartz	GLOBE	Ronen and Shenkar
Theoretical foundations	Center-periphery scheme	Political sciences	Not specified	Hofstede's concept of culture	Schwartz's theory of cultural values	GLOBE study	Not specified
Dimensions of culture	Intellectual styles	Civilizations	Various psychological, sociological, demographic, and economic characteristics	Power distance, uncertainty avoidance, individualism vs. collectivism, masculinity vs. femininity	Embeddedness, affective autonomy, intellectual autonomy, egalitarianism, hierarchy, mastery, harmony	Uncertainty avoidance, power distance, institutional collectivism, in-group collectivism, gender egalitarianism, assertiveness, future orientation, performance orientation, humane orientation	Language, religion, geography
Periods of data collection	Not specified	Not specified	1940s	1968-1972	Since the 1980s	1990s	Not specified (meta-analysis of previous studies)
Number of countries	Not specified	Entire world	69	53	76	61	96
Methods of data analysis	Personal judgments	Not specified	Factor analysis	Cluster analysis	Co-plot multidimensional scaling	Discriminant analysis	Meta-analysis, cluster analysis
Number of resulting clusters	4	8 (plus "others" "lone," "cleft," and "torn" countries)	10	12	7	10	38 "local" clusters, 16 "consensus" clusters, 11 "global" clusters (plus 5 independents)

regions and less between countries. While this argumentation is widely accepted in the intercultural management literature (Beugelsdijk, Kostova & Roth 2017; Taras et al. 2016), there is less consensus about the adequate conceptualization and measurement of cultural clusters. The existing concepts differ in their theoretical foundations, cultural constructs and dimensions, methods of measurement, periods of data collection, included countries, and number and composition of resulting clusters (Table 5.4).

Despite these differences in conceptualization and methodology, the existing concepts show many **similarities**. For example, most approaches agree upon the following supranational cultural regions: Western (often further differentiated), East-Central Europe, Africa, Islamic/Arabic/Middle East, Latin America, Confucian-influenced countries, and South-East Asia. Another commonality is the treatment of *Japan* as singleton or independent unit.

Differences are apparent for countries at the periphery or intersection of two or more supranational clusters. For example, *Israel* is considered as a unique state or independent (Huntington and Ronen and Shenkar), belonging to the masculine individualistic cluster (Müller and Gelbrich), or assigned to the English-speaking cluster (GLOBE). Schwartz splits the country into a Jewish and an Arab part, assigning the former to English-speaking and the latter to the sub-Saharan, North African, and Muslim Middle East cluster. Similarly, *India* is regarded as part of the Hindu civilization (Huntington) or Oriental pattern (Cattell), member of the British colonies cluster (Hofstede), belonging to the South East Asian region (Schwartz, GLOBE), independent or singleton (Ronen and Shenkar), or belonging to the uncertainty avoiders cluster (Müller and Gelbrich).

A vivid example of a disputable country classification is Taiwan. Huntington, Schwartz, GLOBE, and Ronen and Shenkar assign Taiwan (officially "Republic of China") together with China (officially "People's Republic of China") to the Confucian cluster. Indeed, the two countries share a long *history* and have been largely influenced by Confucianism for centuries. Taiwan was a part of China until 1949 and is still considered by China as a renegade province. The *geographic distance* is small, with the island of Taiwan lying 180 km across the Taiwan Strait from the southeastern coast of mainland China. Both countries are also extremely similar *linguistically*. Standard Taiwanese Mandarin parallels Standard Chinese—the official language of Mainland China—with only minor differences in their writing systems (Taiwanese Mandarin uses traditional Chinese characters rather than the simplified Chinese characters used in Mainland China), some pronunciations and vocabulary (Schubert 2016).

However, when comparing the two countries along the *cultural dimensions* of Hofstede, significant differences become visible. These differences are particularly large for uncertainty avoidance (China: 30; Taiwan 69), indulgence vs. restraint (China: 24; Taiwan 49), power distance (China: 80; Taiwan: 58), and masculinity vs. femininity (China: 66; Taiwan: 45). Similarities can only be observed for long-term orientation (China: 87; Taiwan: 93) and individualism vs. collectivism (China: 20; Taiwan: 17). The latter leads Müller and Gelbrich to assign both countries to the cluster of collectivists. Also, in Schwartz's study, large differences with regard to hierarchy (China: 3.49; Taiwan: 2.69), mastery (China: 4.41; Taiwan: 4.00), and harmony (China: 3.78; Taiwan: 4.12) are revealed. On the co-plot map of countries on Schwartz's cultural orientations, Taiwan is therefore graphically closer to countries such as Russia, Israel (Arabs), India and the United States as opposed to China.

One of the major shortcomings of existing taxonomies and typologies is their **lack of solid theoretical foundations**. The classifications are often based on arbitrary mixtures of cultural, political, linguistic, religious, and geographic criteria. This applies particularly to the taxonomies of Galtung, Huntington, and Ronen and Shenkar. Although the classifications of Schwartz and GLOBE are based on an explicit theoretical concept of culture, the resulting cultural clusters are named after geographical and not cultural terms. An exception is the taxonomy of Müller and Gelbrich that uses Hofstede's cultural dimensions to denote cultural groupings on the supranational level.

Even if one agrees that cultural values tend to be shared in supranational cultural clusters, they only have a **weak impact on people's identification**. For example, US-Americans predominantly identify themselves with their country and do not regard themselves as members of an Anglo-American or Western cultural cluster (Huddy & Khatib 2007). According to the World Values Survey and the European Values Survey, between 22% and 55% of the respondents assigned to the 11 supranational cultural clusters as defined by Ronen & Shenkar (2013) regard the country as their main source of identification, while only between 2% and 8% identify themselves primarily with the particular supranational region. Even the local (22–46%) and subnational regions (12–39%) are more important sources of identification than the supranational region (Beugelsdijk, Kostova & Roth 2017).

As a consequence of these theoretical and methodological flaws, the supranational classifications of culture have **little impact on intercultural management research**. While the concepts of cultural dimensions of Hofstede, Schwartz, GLOBE, etc., have been applied in a very large number of subsequent empirical studies in various areas of research, taxonomies and typologies of cultural clusters are rarely cited in the intercultural management literature (Flores et al. 2013).

5.2 CULTURAL DISTANCE AND CULTURAL ATTRACTIVENESS

While research on cultural clusters seeks to explore similarities between cultures on the supranational level, concepts of cultural distance and attractiveness are focused on the measurement of cultural differences between country dyads. Analogous to the concepts of cultural clusters discussed in the previous section, etic and emic approaches can be distinguished.

5.2.1 The Kogut and Singh Index of Cultural Distance

One of the first concepts of cultural distance is the index developed by Kogut and Singh (1988). It aggregates cultural differences along the initial four cultural dimensions of Hofstede (1980) (i.e., power distance, uncertainty avoidance, masculinity vs. femininity, and individualism vs. collectivism). Hofstede's dimensions of culture are treated as bases in a Cartesian space, in which the distances between interior points are measured as Euclidean distances. The deviations between two countries are corrected for differences in the variances of each cultural dimension and then arithmetically averaged. Algebraically, the index is calculated with the following formula:

$$CD_{jk} = \sum_{n=1}^{4} \frac{(D_{ij} - D_{ik})^2 / V_i}{4}$$

where CD_{jk} stands for the cultural distance between countries j and k, D_{ij} for the value of dimension i for country j, D_{ik} for the value of dimension i for country k, and V_i for the variance of dimension i for all countries in Hofstede's study.

Table 5.5 presents the values for cultural distance between 20 selected countries.

Table 5.5 Cultural distance indices according to Kogut and Singh

Target country

Observing country		BRA	CHN	EGY	FRA	GER	IND	IDN	ITA	JPN	MEX	NGA	PHL	RUS	ZAF	KOR	ESP	THA	TUR	UK	USA
Brazil	BRA																				
China	CHN	2.30																			
Egypt	EGY		0.65	1.87																	
France	FRA		1.45	3.40	1.73																
Germany	GER		2.23	3.21	2.53	2.17															
India	IND		1.64	1.34	1.25	2.28	2.42														
Indonesia	IDN		1.59	1.33	1.34	2.86	3.23	1.53													
Italy	ITA		2.12	3.29	2.31	1.74	0.92	2.36	3.33												
Japan	JPN		2.66	3.41	2.76	3.04	2.28	3.19	3.63	1.96											
Mexico	MEX		1.27	2.2	1.08	2.27	2.74	2.02	1.99	2.40	2.03										
Nigeria	NGA		1.78	1.64	1.64	3.16	3.51	2.05	0.55	3.64	3.71	2.05									
Philippines	PHL		1.96	1.01	1.35	2.89	3.24	1.13	1.43	3.05	3.25	1.71	1.80								

Russia	RUS	1.54	3.29	1.56	1.84	3.58	2.55	2.37	3.22	3.65	1.96	2.46	2.60							
South Africa	ZAF	1.98	2.49	2.06	2.08	0.95	1.58	2.66	1.23	2.60	2.51	3.05	2.52	3.33					
South Korea	KOR	1.13	2.86	1.62	2.22	2.86	2.54	1.80	2.97	3.23	1.95	1.69	2.75	1.83	2.80				
Spain	ESP	0.96	3.13	1.53	0.97	1.97	2.26	2.41	1.90	2.85	2.03	2.59	2.83	1.83	2.02	1.37			
Thailand	THA	1.22	2.34	1.47	2.34	2.91	2.01	1.16	3.10	3.65	2.20	1.22	2.34	2.03	2.59	0.93	1.66		
Turkey	TUR	0.45	2.71	1.05	1.40	2.36	2.07	1.89	2.25	2.77	1.49	2.00	2.38	1.42	2.26	0.89	0.73	1.26	
United Kingdom	UK	3.26	3.54	3.35	2.99	1.54	2.65	3.87	1.89	3.45	3.79	4.29	3.65	4.51	1.33	4.03	3.10	3.77	3.50
United States	USA	2.93	3.54	3.05	2.49	1.30	2.51	3.73	1.49	3.25	3.51	4.15	3.51	4.10	1.16	3.74	2.69	3.54	3.14	0.56

Source: Compiled from Hofstede data.

The Kogut and Singh Index has become one of the most frequently used instruments in intercultural management research and in other fields for measuring cultural distance with more than 6,000 citations to date (Beugelsdijk et al. 2018). It has been applied, among others, in international market entry, international human resource management, international marketing, and intercultural communication research (Håkanson & Ambos 2010; Beugelsdijk et al. 2018; Cuypers et al. 2018).

Despite its popularity, the Kogut and Singh Index has faced frequent criticism. From a conceptual perspective, it has been criticized for its **oversimplification** of the complex phenomenon of culture (Shenkar 2001; Maseland, Dow & Steel 2018). The index is a rather simplistic aggregate of Hofstede's cultural dimensions and is hence liable to the same criticism leveled against Hofstede (see Chapter 4.3.3). It even amplifies the problems associated with the Hofstede framework by further reducing the original four dimensions into one. The index measures cultural distance as a nation-to-nation comparison of country means on cultural values, thereby neglecting the cultural variation that exists within countries (Beugelsdijk et al. 2015). Moreover, by considering the *magnitude* rather than the *nature* of difference, the essence of the underlying concept of culture gets blurred and it becomes unclear what the index actually measures. However, the reduction of complexity has contributed to the great popularity of the index. The Kogut and Singh Index provides a seemingly simple, standardized, convenient, and extremely user-friendly measure "that scholars who are not primarily interested in institutions or cultures can throw into a regression equation to deal with what they have an uncomfortable feeling is an important unobserved feature of interaction between societies" (Zaheer, Schomaker & Nachum 2012, p. 20).

Indeed, the separate inclusion of all four of Hofstede's constituent dimensions in regression analyses often shows significant effects for several dimensions, although with different signs, canceling out their impact in the aggregate Kogut and Singh Index. This shows that not all cultural differences have the same effect in all situations, but that some dimensions can be complementary and conducive while others are disruptive and dysfunctional, and further dimensions may have no effect at all (Reus & Lamont 2009; Shenkar 2012). Zaheer, Schomaker, and Nachum (2012, p. 22) therefore conclude: "If the goal of reducing dimensionality is to simplify a complex web of relations by transforming it into a one-dimensional representation, perhaps the best way to remedy the problems occasioned by this 'flatness' is to focus on one or two well-chosen dimensions rather than compress many dimensions into one."

From a methodological perspective, the index has been criticized for its **mathematical misspecification**. Konara and Mohr (2019) exemplify that the index does not measure the Euclidean distance—as argued by Kogut and Singh (1988) and several reviews, such as Beugelsdijk et al. (2018) and Cuypers et al. (2018)—but rather the *squared Euclidean distance* between two countries. Instead of taking the square root of the sum of the squared differences for the four cultural dimensions—as per the Euclidean distance—Kogut and Singh (1988) divide this sum by four (i.e., they take the arithmetic average of the squared differences). The creation of a quadratic function leads to an exaggeration of large over small cultural distances.

A related critique argues that Euclidean distance is an inappropriate measure to estimate cultural distance between two countries if—like in the case of the Hofstede data—the underlying constructs are correlated and not independent (Berry, Guillen & Zhou 2010). Under these conditions, the *Mahalanobis method* is a more appropriate measure of distance. Compared to the Kogut and Singh Index of cultural distance, the Mahalanobis formula takes into consideration the covariance matrix of Hofstede's cultural dimensions, thereby adjusting for the interrelationship between the dimensions (Yeganeh 2014). However, while this may be more suitable mathematically, the results are very similar to those calculated using the

Kogut and Singh Index and their interpretation is more difficult (Beugelsdijk, Ambos & Nell 2018; Cuypers et al. 2018).

Finally, a fundamental critique is related to the **assumption of symmetry** (Shenkar 2001). The Kogut and Singh Index considers the differences between two countries along Hofstede's cultural dimensions as absolute values (i.e., irrespective of the direction of these differences). The cultural difference between country A and country B is therefore regarded as equal to the cultural difference between country B and country A. This assumption of symmetry is not realistic. While the distance between the bottom and the top of a hill is the same in either direction, the way downwards may be much faster and less exhausting. Similarly, the perception of cultural distance may depend on the direction (i.e., the cultural distance from country A to country B may be perceived smaller than from country B to country A). Reasons for this asymmetry of perceived cultural distance can be gravitational effects caused by different sizes of countries, asymmetric migration, and the impact of "large" vs. "small" languages, among others.

The asymmetry of perceived cultural distance can be illustrated by using the examples of **Germany** and **Hungary**. First, the two countries differ significantly in *size*. With a population of 83.7 mn., Germany is the largest country in Europe and attracts considerable international attention. Hungary, on the contrary, is a small country with 9.7 mn. inhabitants that receives little media coverage abroad. The twentieth century observed significant *migration* from Hungary to Germany. Particularly during socialist times (1949-1989), many intellectuals (such as the writers Imre Kertész and George Tabori) moved to Germany. Today, around 120,000 Hungarians live in Germany. In contrast, while migration from Germany to Hungary played an important role until the nineteenth century, it has been negligible since then. With 185 mn. native and non-native speakers, German is the 10th largest *language* in the world. In contrast, the Hungarian language has about 13 mn. native and very few non-native speakers. Unlike Germany, only few Hungarian publications are translated into other languages. While German is the most popular second foreign language in Hungary with 46% of students learning the language in upper secondary general education, the number of non-native Hungarian speakers in Germany is insignificant (Eurostat 2015). Thus, it is reasonable to assume that Germany is perceived culturally closer to Hungary from the viewpoint of most Hungarian citizens than Hungary is to a German citizen.

5.2.2 The Cultural Attractiveness Concept of Li et al.

While the Kogut and Singh Index is based on the assumption of symmetry between two cultures, the concept of Li et al. (2017) takes into consideration that the perceived cultural attractiveness of culture A by culture B may differ from the perceived cultural attractiveness of culture B by culture A. Cultural attractiveness is defined "as the desirability of a culture for members of another culture, based on the extent to which the former culture's practices reflect the latter culture's values" (Li et al. 2017, p. 952).

In order to take into account such asymmetric perceptions of two cultures, Li et al. refer to the GLOBE study that has developed parallel items to assess both the *practices* ("as is" scores) and *values* ("should be" scores) of each cultural dimension (House et al. 2004). The parallel structure of the items allows for the calculation of cultural attractiveness by matching a target culture's values with an observer culture's practices.

Algebraically, cultural attractiveness is calculated with the following formula

$$CA_{(O,T)} = \sqrt{\sum_{d=1}^{9} (6 - |P_{T,d} - V_{O,d}|)^2}$$

where $CA_{(O,T)}$ stands for the cultural attractiveness of the target country T perceived by the observer country O. Each has its own cultural values V and practices P for cultural dimension d. The observer country O possesses certain values $V_{O,d}$ ("should be") for dimension d. Target culture T is assessed by the observer on its attractiveness based on its cultural practices $P_{(T,d)}$ ("as is") for dimension d. The value 6 is included in the formula because it is the largest possible difference between practices and values of any dimension (GLOBE items' scale is 1–7). Thus, cultural attractiveness for dimension d is 6 when the congruence between host country practices and home country values is largest and zero when it is smallest. Like the Kogut and Singh Index, the absolute differences rather than real differences between cultural values and practices are calculated. This is based on the assumption that the deviation from an ideal value in either direction renders a culture and its cultural dimension less attractive.

The calculation of all 61 countries in the GLOBE study shows that—unlike the Kogut and Singh Index of cultural distance—no country dyad has symmetric cultural attractiveness scores (i.e., the cultural attractiveness of country A viewed by an observer country B never equals with the cultural attractiveness of country B viewed by an observer country A). For the 20 largest countries, a correlation coefficient of $r = 0.4$ ($p < 0.01$) is revealed.

The notion of asymmetric cultural attractiveness scores is supported by several empirical studies. For example, Selmer, Chiu and Shenkar (2007) found that German expatriates are better adjusted in the United States than American expatriates are in Germany. The cultural attractiveness scores show that the American culture is more attractive to Germans than the other way around by 0.6 standard deviations, making it easier for Germans to adjust to the American culture. Similar asymmetries were observed for the cultural attractiveness of China vs. Sweden (Yildiz & Fey 2016) and France vs. Russia (Muratbekova-Touron 2011), among others.

A closer look at the country dyads reveals some disputable results. An interesting example is **Germany**. With the exception of South Korea, China, and (to a very low degree) India, the cultural attractiveness of Germany in the view of all other countries is lower than the cultural attractiveness of these countries perceived by Germany. From the perspective of the United States, Germany is regarded as the least culturally attractive country behind countries such as Egypt, India, Nigeria, and Russia. Germans regard the cultural attractiveness of countries like China, Egypt, Indonesia, Russia, and Turkey higher than that of France, Italy, and the United Kingdom. These results differ significantly from the coefficients calculated with the formula of Kogut and Sigh that show much smaller cultural differences between Germany and the latter than the former countries. Moreover, the results are in contrast to the classifications of cultures discussed in Chapter 5.1 that assign Germany mostly to the same cluster as other Western countries like France, Italy, and the United Kingdom. Thus, it is questionable whether the difference between cultural values and practices is a reasonable measure of Germany's cultural attractiveness.

While the cultural attractiveness concept of Li et al. addresses a major weakness of the Kogut and Singh Index, namely the unrealistic assumption of symmetry, it is faced with similar **shortcomings** with regard to other conceptual and methodological aspects. First, the cultural attractiveness measure *lacks sound theoretical foundation*. For example, the underlying distinction between cultural values and cultural practices has been frequently criticized (Chapter 4.6.3). Since Li et al. relate to this distinction without further explanation, the resulting definition of cultural attractiveness seems to be less theoretically grounded than inspired by the availability of data. A validation of this measure is still missing. Moreover, the calculated cultural attractiveness indices show *little variance* across countries which makes it difficult to derive differentiated implications. While the theoretical minimum of the index is 0 and the theoretical maximum is 18, the actual range is between 13.16 (Brazil's perception of Italy) and 15.72 (South Korea's perception of Thailand). Generally, the cultural attractiveness concept of Li et al. has received little attention in intercultural management literature so far.

5.2.3 Shenkar's Concept of Cultural Frictions

While the concepts of Kogut and Singh and Li et al. are based on the studies of Hofstede and GLOBE and thus on an etic perspective, the concept of cultural frictions by Shenkar follows an *emic approach*. Shenkar, Lu, and Yeheskel (2008, p. 909) criticize that in previous measures of cultural distance, "culture was disconnected from its early roots in anthropology, sociology, history, and political science, with their contextual, process-based, and 'native views', and was set to assume a vastly oversimplified economic role as an 'information cost'." In contrast to positivist and functionalist approaches, the concept of cultural frictions therefore proposes a **social constructionist and postmodern perspective** that shifts the emphasis from abstract differences toward perceptions of specific entities in intercultural encounters.

Particular attention is given to the **historical and political context**. Any perception and interpretation of cultural distance between two countries is shaped by individual and collective experience that can be very different on the two sides. "Where countries have been involved in long and bitter political dispute, and perhaps warfare, then small differences matter; where countries have no conflicting interests, then large differences can be ignored or benignly tolerated" (Chapman et al. 2008, p. 230). Similar cultural distance can therefore be perceived differently depending on the particular historical and political context.

Chapman et al. (2008) explored the perceived cultural distance between Poland and Germany as well as Poland and the United Kingdom. German and British respondents in their study described the distance between their own and the Polish culture in different terms than the Polish respondents did with regard to the respective distance to the German and British culture. With reference to the geographical proximity and historical relations, Germans who share a close and tense relationship with Poland were temperately described as "close neighbors." On the contrary, British who allied with Poland in World War II were more positively valued as "distant friends." German and British respondents further gave diverging descriptions of the Polish culture, showing the effects of other contextual variables, such as wars, occupations, and political and economic dominance on the experience of cultural distance. Such contextual variables may affect the significance of cultural distance: small differences may matter much when the historical context between two cultures is characterized by extremely positive or negative experiences.

Cultural friction is not necessarily disadvantageous, but has similar to its original understanding in physics and mechanical engineering—a **positive and negative potential** (Luo & Shenkar 2011). Too much friction will generate heat and resistance, but too little friction will bring about adverse consequences, for example, slippage, as is the case of a tire interfacing with the road. Viewed from this angle, cultural differences have the potential to either create disruption or synergy. They can cause clashes and animosities, but can also be advantageous for organizations, teams, and individuals. The differences of cultures can, for instance, lead to enrichment or complementarities through increased variety in post-acquisition integration processes, creativity in global teams, or cognitive complexity in individuals (Shenkar 2012).

Shenkar (2012) argues that cultural friction (as independent variable) does not only impact management decisions, but management decisions can also affect the level of cultural friction (as dependent variable). For example, the participation of local partners in a joint venture or the appointment of a local CEO can act like **organizational lubricants** in problematic intercultural encounters, such as Chinese investments in Germany. Conversely, the acquisition of a "national icon" is likely to increase cultural friction (Holtbrügge 2018).

While the metaphor of cultural friction addresses some conceptual shortcomings of previous approaches, the **measurement of friction** remains difficult. While Luo and Shenkar (2011) provide contours for the development of a measurement of friction, their approach requires extensive country-level, industry-level, and firm-level data. Due to this high level of complexity, the measure of cultural friction has—in contrast to the Kogut and Singh Index—received less attention in intercultural management research so far.

5.2.4 Bilateral Trade in Cultural Goods as a Proxy for Cultural Attractiveness

While the previous concepts seek to measure cultural distance based on individual perception, this approach uses objective data on bilateral trade in cultural goods as proxy for cultural attractiveness. It is based on the assumption that the import of cultural goods of country *n* from country *i* reflects the perceived cultural attractiveness of country *i* by country *n*. Conversely, the export of cultural goods from country *n* to country *i* reflects the perceived cultural attractiveness of country *n* by country *i*. Since exports and imports of cultural goods between two countries are likely to differ and to change over time, this measure is asymmetric and time-variant (Disdier et al. 2010).

UNCTAD (2010) classifies cultural goods into two categories, core and optional cultural goods (Table 5.6). Each category has two headings, arts and media within the core category and heritage and

Table 5.6 Categories of goods with cultural content

Core cultural goods	Optional cultural goods
Arts (performing and visual)	*Heritage (arts and crafts)*
Music (CD, tapes), printed music, painting, photography, sculpture, and antiques	Carpets, celebration, paperware, wickerware, yarn, and other
Media (publishing and audio-visual)	*Functional creations (design and new media)*
Books, newspaper, other printed matter, film	Architecture, fashion, interior, glassware, jewelry, toys, recorded media, video games

Source: UNCTAD (2010, p. 112).

functional creation within the optional one. *Core cultural goods* are essentially produced by cultural industries and generally embed a higher cultural content. *Optional cultural goods* are made by creative industries.

One of the most comprehensive studies of bilateral trade in cultural goods was conducted by Fiorini et al. (2017). The study is based on data of 176 countries from the period of 2003–2014 and includes 4,137 country pairs that account for 49.1% of worldwide trade and for 55.8% of trade in cultural goods, respectively. The authors calculate an **index of cultural attractiveness premium** ($\hat{\gamma}$) between two countries that measures, on average over time, how much individuals in (importing) country i consider the culture of (exporting) country n attractive above or below the attractiveness of the average country. Moreover, for each (undirected) pair of different countries, the absolute value of the difference between $\hat{\gamma}_{ni}$ and $\hat{\gamma}_{in}$ is calculated. The result is interpreted as a proxy for the degree of asymmetry in the cultural attractiveness between two countries. Generally, the study provides descriptive evidence of the asymmetry embedded in the bilateral flows of cultural goods.

Table 5.7 reports the two country pairs that show the maximum and minimum values for cultural attractiveness premia and asymmetry. The highest asymmetry is between Paraguay (i) and China (n). In particular, China appears much more attractive for Paraguay relative to the average country ($\hat{\gamma}_{ni}=7.211$). On the contrary, the attractiveness of Paraguay's culture for China is lower than the average country's attractiveness ($\hat{\gamma}_{in}=-3.686$). Thus, individuals in Paraguay tend to put a positive attractiveness premium on Chinese culture while Chinese individuals tend to find Paraguay's culture less attractive than others. Minimum asymmetry is found between Morocco and Singapore ($\hat{\gamma}_{ni}=0.047$; $\hat{\gamma}_{in}=0.046$). In this case there exists an almost symmetric neutrality, with each country awarding the other with a very low attractiveness premium.

Table 5.7 Country pairs with maximum and minimum asymmetry

Country n	Country i	Attractiveness premium of i for n ($\hat{\gamma}_{ni}$)	Attractiveness premium of n for i ($\hat{\gamma}_{in}$)	Asymmetry ($|\hat{\gamma}_{ni} - \hat{\gamma}_{in}|$)
China	Paraguay	7.211	−3.686	10.897
Morocco	Singapore	0.047	0.046	0.001

Source: Fiorini et al. (2017, p. 8).

Fiorini et al. (2017) illustrate the symmetry vs. asymmetry of cultural attractiveness by exploring the case of the United Kingdom, the sixth biggest exporter and the second biggest importer of cultural goods, and its bilateral cultural relationships with other countries. The United Kingdom is regarded as an interesting case because of the legacy of the British Empire and its strong legal, linguistic, and cultural connections to many other countries across the globe as well as its varying degree of integration with the European Union.

A high degree of asymmetry in cultural trade involving the United Kingdom is apparent for countries in the African continent (with few exceptions below the median level of asymmetry including Madagascar and South Africa), countries in the Central Asia region, and few

(Continued)

countries in Latin America. Low asymmetry emerges between the United Kingdom and many European countries (with the notable exception of Ireland), many countries in the South-East Asia region, Russia, North America, and some Latin American countries.

The relatively high asymmetry between the United Kingdom and Ireland (2.700) originates from a very high affinity premium placed on the United Kingdom by Ireland ($\hat{\gamma}$ UK; IRL = 8.677) and only partly reciprocated by the still high affinity premium of the United Kingdom for Ireland ($\hat{\gamma}$ IRL; UK = 5.977). This example shows that not only the asymmetry but also the absolute level of attractiveness premia should be considered when evaluating the cultural attractiveness of countries.

Bilateral trade in cultural goods as a proxy for cultural attractiveness has been frequently used in *international economics research*, for instance, in studies of trade flows and flows of foreign direct investment. Compared to measures more common in intercultural management research, this measure has several **advantages** (Disdier et al. 2010). First, it is based on *objective and quantitative data* provided by official organizations, such as UNCTAD and WTO. This reduces potential distortions caused by sampling bias, coverage bias, social desirability bias, etc. Trade data are available for the entire world, thus allowing for the computation of all existing country pairs. Moreover, data for trade in cultural goods are published annually, while the data needed to calculate the cultural distance indices of Kogut and Singh and Li et al. were collected decades ago. This allows *longitudinal studies* and reflects the likelihood that perceived cultural attractiveness might respond to different events, such as changes of political representation (as in the case of elections), the adoption of new communication technologies capable of better transmitting cultural contents across countries (for instance, the development of machine learning translation algorithms), and the initiatives of governments to promote the visibility of national cultures abroad (e.g., through cultural institutes).

A notable example for the impact of changes in political representation on a country's perceived cultural attractiveness is the election of Donald Trump as President of the United States in 2016. This event is likely to change the way countries around the world perceive the American culture; however, it will not necessarily affect how attractive foreign cultures are to Americans. Consequently, it could be expected that changes in the perceived cultural attractiveness of the United States would materialize in reduced export of cultural goods, while the import of cultural goods by the United States is not likely to be affected.

This assumption is indeed supported by data for the EU-28. While the import of cultural goods from all non-EU countries between 2012 and 2017 increased by 17.9%, imports from the United States decreased by 2.9%. On the contrary, exports of goods to the United States grew significantly faster (58.7%) than average exports to all non-EU countries (23.0%) during that period (Eurostat 2018).

A major **shortcoming** of this measure is that it is *restricted to the level of symbols and artifacts*. Referring to Schein's (2017) iceberg model of culture, cultural goods are the visible and tangible elements on the surface level of culture, while the more fundamental norms and values as well as basic assumptions are not covered by this measure. These nontradable aspects of culture, however, can be an important element of cultural attractiveness. Bilateral trade in cultural goods may therefore rather complement than replace other measures that reflect deeper levels of cultural attractiveness.

Felbermayr and Toubal (2010) propose the voting behavior in the Eurovision Song Contest (ESC) as a measure of cultural attractiveness among European countries. The ESC is an annual pan-European televised show, where every participating country sends an artist to perform a song. The other countries grade those songs on a scale from 0 to 12, either by televoting or (in earlier times) popular juries. Every year, the process gives rise to a matrix of bilateral votes.

The analysis of voting behavior from 1975 to 2003, in which grading rules were stable, shows that some countries systematically award scores above average to each other and behave in a reciprocal way. For example, Cyprus awards to Greece an average of 7.41 points more than Greece receives on average. Greece reciprocates by awarding an excess of 6.26 points beyond the Cypriot mean score. Overgenerous and reciprocal relationships are found for many Scandinavian country pairs and to a lesser extent for Mediterranean countries. However, relationships need not be reciprocal. For example, Finland awards Italy an excess 3.10 points, but gets an average negative excess grade of −0.77 in return. France grades Great Britain 0.86 points below average, while the Brits treat France almost neutrally. With few exceptions, Scandinavian and Mediterranean countries reciprocally award scores below the respective averages. Cyprus and Turkey systematically award each other grades below average. Germany (and Austria) overgrade Turkey without being compensated, which is likely to reflect ethnic ties due to migration. Generally, nonreciprocal behavior is quite frequent. Mutual excess grade correlate with $r = 0.35$ on a $p < 0.01$ level of significance.

5.2.5 Critical Evaluation

The conceptualization and measurement of cultural distance and cultural attractiveness is one of the main topics in intercultural management research. As Zaheer et al. (2012, p. 19) state: "Essentially, international management is management of distance." While this position is widely accepted in the intercultural management literature, there is less consensus about the adequate conceptualization and measurement of cultural distance and attractiveness. The existing concepts differ in their epistemological perspective, theoretical foundation, unit of analysis, underlying data, and temporal concept (Table 5.8).

Research on cultural distance has long been dominated by the index of Kogut and Singh. It has been frequently used either in its original form, extended by Hofstede's later added cultural dimensions long-term orientation and indulgence vs. restraint, or adapted for the cultural dimensions of Schwartz and GLOBE (Beugelsdijk, Ambos & Nell 2018). While the results differ, the calculations all share the fundamental assumption that distance is symmetric. Only in the last years, alternative measures have been developed that are based on the **assumption of asymmetry**, i.e., that the cultural distance between two countries is not necessarily symmetric, but *can have different reasons and implications on the two sides of intercultural encounters.*

Another controversy is the **assumption of linearity**. Like the concept of geographic distance that posits that geographically closer places can usually be reached in shorter time, the concept of cultural

Table 5.8 Synopsis of concepts of cultural distance and cultural attractiveness

	Kogut and Singh index of cultural distance	Cultural attractiveness concept of Li et al.	Shenkar's concept of cultural frictions	Bilateral trade in cultural goods
Epistemological perspective	Etic	Etic	Emic	Etic
Theoretical foundation	Positivism: Hofstede's concept of culture	Positivism: GLOBE study	Constructivism and postmodernism	Positivism: International economics
Unit of analysis	Country level	Country level	Country, industry and firm level	Country level
Underlying data	Subjective	Subjective	Subjective	Objective
Assumed direction of cultural distance/ attractiveness	Symmetry	Asymmetry	Asymmetry	Asymmetry
Temporal concept	Static	Static	Dynamic	Dynamic
Periods of data collection	1968–1972	1990s	Not specified (continuously)	Annually

distance assumes that small cultural distance is less detrimental than larger ones. According to the similarity-attraction theory, cultural commonalities offer greater understanding and ease of interaction. However, diversity research unfolds that difference shall not only be regarded as a disadvantage, but rather as an opportunity for arbitrage, complementarity, or creativity (Stahl & Tung 2015).

Several empirical studies therefore propose a *curvilinear relationship* between cultural distance and various instrumental and outcome variables. For example, expatriate research suggests that adaptation to a foreign culture may be u-shaped (Holtbrügge 2008; Puck, Holtbrügge & Raupp 2017). Adjustment to a relatively similar culture is often as difficult as adjustment to a distant one because differences are not anticipated and similarity can mask small, but important differences. In contrast, greater distance and less similarity may raise awareness of meaningful differences, provide learning opportunities, and inspire adequate measures of diversity management (Zaheer, Schomaker & Nachum 2012).

A vivid example for the challenges of cultural similarity is the ambiguity between variants of English, i.e., British English, American English, Australian English, Indian English, etc. While a common grammar and lexical stock facilitate communication, particularly, homonyms, i.e., words with the same or very similar spelling and pronunciation but different meanings, can lead to interferences and misunderstandings.

While the existing concepts of cultural distance and attractiveness rely on country-level data (complemented by industry- and firm-level data in the case of Shenkar's concept of cultural frictions), Baack et al. (2015) argue that **individual-level perceptions of distance** might diverge from national-level averages. Based on social cognition theory and using an experimental approach, the study showed that individuals are more likely to process information and revise their perceptions of distance when that information confirms their original beliefs. As a result, past experiences and existing beliefs regarding a country can bias individual perceptions of cultural distance. Based on these considerations, cultural distance should not be regarded as objective, but a perceptual concept that should be measured on the individual level.

The perception of cultural difference is likely to be mitigated or amplified by various **moderators of distance** (Zaheer, Schomaker & Nachum 2012). Potential firm-level moderators are the extent of international or regional experience, the home country of the headquarters, and the specific portfolio of international locations. Also, industry-level characteristics can act both as moderators of distance effects and as drivers of perceptions of distance. For example, linguistic distance might play a greater role in industries where communication plays a key role, such as media and the software industry, than it would in highly standardized process manufacturing, such as the chemical, steel, and cement industries.

An important result of existing research is that the choice of adequate measures of cultural distance is **context-dependent** and contingent on the specific management area and research question. For example, differences in individualism vs. collectivism may be more important for expatriates' cultural adjustment, while asymmetries in power distance may be relevant for intercultural leadership and headquarters–subsidiary relations (Drogendijk & Holm 2010). Differences in uncertainty avoidance are potentially the most challenging for intercultural cooperation of firms due to their correlates in terms of differential tolerances toward risk and formalization. Likewise, linguistic distance may be an appropriate measure in the context of intercultural communication and intercultural teamwork (Shenkar 2012).

Finally, postcolonial and constructivist approaches argue that the implications of cultural distance and cultural attractiveness may depend on the **nature of international encounters**. Cultural distance is salient when individuals have little international experience and the period of interaction is short. However, intercultural encounters often involve knowledge and power asymmetries. For example, foreign expatriates as representatives of multinational corporations are regularly in a more powerful position then their local subordinates, while the opposite relation exists between foreign refugees and the local population. In these cases, social differentiation (status, power, income, education, etc.) becomes more relevant than cultural distance. Similarly, cultural distance loses importance when individuals work together over an extended period of time and face the same challenges, such as tight deadlines, demanding tasks, competitive threat, etc. Under these circumstances, differences in values are viewed as less relevant than functional distinction. Individuals are not judged according to their cultural background, but their knowledge and skills (Belhoste & Monin 2013).

5.3 CULTURAL DIVERSITY

Intercultural management research has mostly defined national culture in legal-political terms. According to the legal-political delineation of culture, all citizens of a country are regarded as members of that specific culture. While this delineation may be appropriate in ethnically and linguistically homogeneous countries with little inward and outward migration, such as Japan and Korea, it has limits in countries with large diversity in terms of ethnic background, linguistic affiliation, and intellectual-historical mindset like India, South Africa, United States, etc. In some cases, *intracultural* diversity is even greater than *intercultural* difference (Leung & van de Vijver 2008). In fact, a meta-analysis of 558 studies that used Hofstede's cultural values framework by Taras, Steel, and Kirkman (2016) revealed that approximately 80% of variation in cultural values resides within countries, "confirming that country is often a poor proxy for culture" (p. 455).

Recent research therefore acknowledges that national borders are often arbitrary and seeks for more differentiated operationalizations of culture that take the diversity of ethnicities, languages, religions, etc., into account. With regard to their conceptual foundations, level-based, variance-based, and pattern-based approaches can be distinguished (Figure 5.6).

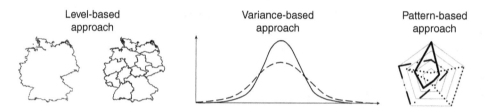

Figure 5.6   Level-based, variance-based, and pattern-based approaches of cultural diversity

5.3.1 Level-Based Concepts of Cultural Diversity

Level-based concepts of cultural diversity are grounded on the observation that cultural values can differ between regions, states, provinces, or districts within a country. **Regional differences within countries** can have *functional reasons* (different climate, geography, economic development, etc.), *institutional reasons* (different language, religion, history, etc.), or be caused by *critical events* (natural disaster, symbolic local political heroes, etc.) (Peterson, Søndergaard & Kara 2018). For the same reasons, neighboring regions that are separated by national borders may share more in terms of values with each other than with other national regions.

In the European Union, cultural similarities between border regions have inspired the establishment of Euroregions. **Euroregions** are trans-border cooperation structures between two or more contiguous territories located in different European countries. They often reflect historical, ethnic, and linguistic communalities.

An example of this concept is the *Euroregion of Tyrol-South Tyrol-Trentino*, consisting of the Tyrol state in Austria and the two Italian Autonomous provinces of South Tyrol and Trentino. The boundaries of the association correspond almost exactly to the former Princely County of Tyrol, a crown land of the Habsburg Monarchy, which for centuries shaped life in the Alpine region until the end of World War I.

The three member states share centuries of cultural, social, and economic ties as well as largely identical geographical conditions. They are also similar in terms of local customs and linguistics. While German is the official language in Tyrol, a majority of the inhabitants of contemporary South Tyrol speak native Austro-Bavarian dialects of the German language. In Trentino, German is the largest minority language. Overall, 62% of the Euroregion are German speakers and 37% Italian speakers (Engl & Zwilling 2007).

While most etic concepts of culture (Hofstede, Schwartz, GLOBE, etc.) only provide data on national averages, several studies applied Hofstede's cultural dimensions and research methodology on the subnational level to assess the relevance of intracultural differences. For example, Huo and Randall (1991) analyzed cultural values in four **Chinese-populated regions**: Taiwan, Beijing, Hong Kong, and Wuhan. After adjusting for age, gender, occupation, and hierarchical level, strong subcultural differences with regard to Hofstede's initial four cultural dimensions were revealed. For instance, respondents in Taiwan score significantly higher on power distance, while those in Wuhan score significantly higher on individualism and masculinity than those in the other three regions. Uncertainty avoidance is particularly strong in Hong Kong.

Fontaine, Richardson, and Foong (2002) studied cultural differences between different ethnic groups in **Malaysia**. They found significant differences between Malay, Chinese, Indian, and students belonging to other ethnic groups. For example, Malays score lower on masculinity and uncertainty avoidance than the Chinese. Chinese and Indians are rather long-term orientated, while Malays and Bumiputera (indigenous peoples) are more short-term orientated.

Thomas and Bendixen (2000) collected data among the six **major ethnic groups in South Africa** (White English, White Afrikaans, Asia, Colored, Xhosa, Zulu, and Sotho) and revealed significant cultural differences, particularly with regard to Hofstede's first five cultural dimensions. For example, they found that power distance is higher among White than Colored and Black South Africans. White English and White Afrikaans show lower levels of uncertainty avoidance than Xhosa, Zulu, and Sotho. Masculinity is significantly higher among Sotho than the other ethnic groups.

Singh and Sharma (2009) conducted a similar study in four **Indian states**. The authors found, among others, a significantly lower degree of power distance in Punjab, a higher degree of uncertainty avoidance in Gujarat, higher degrees of individualism in Punjab and West Bengal, and a higher degree of masculinity in Tamil Nadu compared to the Indian national average.

Hofstede et al. (2010) measured cultural differences within **Brazil** and found that the cultural clustering of states fairly closely follows the administrative division of the country into five regions. In particular, the cultural profiles for these regions show remarkable differences between the Northeast with its Afro-Brazilian roots and the North with its native Indian roots.

The study of Kaasa, Vadi, and Varblane (2014) analyzed subnational differences within a number of **selected European countries**, expressed by mean absolute deviations of Hofstede's initial four cultural dimensions from the respective national averages (Table 5.9). Although within-country differences are relatively small in Bulgaria, Poland, the Netherlands, and Sweden, large differences were found for Ukraine, Spain, and Germany. Figure 5.7 presents a closer look on the 16 German states. It shows, among others, that the East-German states are culturally closer to Poland than to the German average with regard to power distance and individualism.

While most level-based studies of cultural diversity applied Hofstede's cultural dimensions and research methodology, there are also studies that are grounded in other concepts of culture. Based on Schwartz's theory of cultural values, Lenartowicz and Roth (2001) collected data in the four **Brazilian states** of Rio de Janeiro (Cariocas), Rio Grande do Sul (Gauchos), São Paulo (Paulistas), and Minas Gerais (Mineiros). They found that each one of the four subcultures has some cultural characteristic that differentiated it from the others. For example, the modest and reserved Mineiros place less emphasis on achievement than the opportunistic and individualistic Gauchos. The results for restrictive conformity indicated that the Paulistas attach more importance to values such as "being nice to others" and "helpful" as compared to the other

Table 5.9 Mean absolute deviations of Hofstede's cultural dimensions in selected European countries at the NUTS 1 level

Country	Number and type of regions	PDI	UAI	MAS	IND
Belgium	3 regions (Gewesten/Régions)	0.14	0.29	0.10	0.09
Bulgaria	2 regions (Rajoni)	0.09	0.04	0.09	0.07
France	8 Z.E.A.T + DOM	0.14	0.32	0.24	0.24
Germany	16 states (Länder)	0.44	0.52	0.28	0.40
Greece	4 groups of development regions	0.07	0.16	0.22	0.23
Hungary	Statistical large regions	0.12	0.18	0.10	0.28
Netherlands	4 lands (Landsdelen)	0.05	0.13	0.08	0.10
Poland	6 regions (Regiony)	0.18	0.10	0.09	0.12
Romania	4 macroregions (Macroregiuni)	0.28	0.11	0.16	0.33
Russia	7 Federal Districts (Federalnyye okruga)	0.26	0.22	0.19	0.32
Spain	7 groups of autonomous communities	0.25	0.19	0.38	0.40
Sweden	3 lands (Landsdelar)	0.20	0.18	0.12	0.12
UK	12 statistical regions	0.25	0.22	0.22	0.20
Ukraine	5 larger regions	0.23	0.26	0.31	0.22

Note: Larger mean absolute deviations correspond to higher within-country variability.
Source: Kaasa, Vadi & Varblane (2014, p. 840).

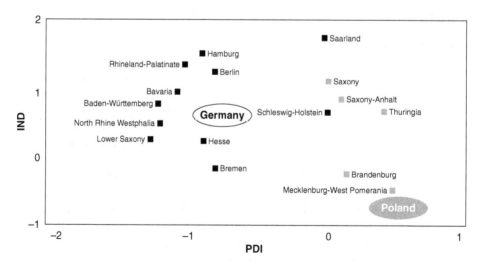

Figure 5.7 Differences in power distance and individualism across German states
Source: Adapted from Kaasa, Vadi & Varblane (2014, p. 844).

three subcultures. For the domain of security, the business-oriented Paulistas place less emphasis on risk taking than the suspicious and reserved Mineiros. Finally, the directed-to-action Paulistas and individualistic and opportunistic Gauchos attach more importance to the self-direction domain than the laid-back Mineiros and fun-oriented Cariocas.

Lenartowicz, Johnson, and White (2003) studied intracountry cultural variations in six locations in **Latin America**: São Paulo and Rio Grande do Sul (Brazil), Montevideo (Uruguay), Bogotá and Cartagena (Colombia), and Caracas (Venezuela). Multiple analysis of variance (MANOVA) showed significant differences across groups on the Rokeach Value Survey data. In particular, the study revealed that the two locations within Brazil and Colombia represent distinct subcultures, and that there is greater cultural similarity across than within national borders.

Dolan et al. (2004) analyzed a sample of business students from two geographically separated regions in **Spain**: North-East (Catalonia) and South-West (Andalusia). The results revealed significant differences in some work/life values shown by Andalusian respondents compared with their Catalonian counterparts. With regard to work values, Andalusia is closer to a collectivist culture, in which aspects of emotional experience and social relations are more important. In contrast, work culture in Catalonia is closer to an individualist culture, in which emotional experience is much more part of one's inner world.

Dheer, Lenartowicz, and Peterson (2015) analyzed intranational cultural differences within eight regions of **India**: North-west (Himachal Pradesh, Punjab, Haryana, Delhi), west (Rajasthan, Gujarat), north-central (Uttar Pradesh, Uttarakhand, Bihar), central (Chhattisgarh, Jharkhand, Orissa, Madhya Pradesh), east (West-Bengal), far-east (Assam, Sikkim, Mizoram, Nagaland, Arunachal Pradesh, Meghalaya, Manipur, Tripura), south-west (Maharashtra, Goa), and south (Karnataka, Telangana, Andhra Pradesh, Kerala, Tamil Nadu). Based on selected items from the World Value Survey, the authors developed measures that specifically reflect Indian values. They found that the north-central region scores higher on institutional noncompliance; a region including far-eastern, western, and south-western India scores higher on male dominance; a region including north-central and western India scores higher on harmony with traditions; a region including north-western and north-central India scores higher on work values; a region including south-western and southern India scores higher on luxury life; a region including north-western, western, and south-western India scores higher on goal orientation; and a region including south-western and southern India scores higher on perception of satisfaction.

In summary, existing research shows that cultural values often differ significantly within countries. This applies not only to ethnically and linguistically diverse countries, such as India and South Africa, but also to seemingly homogeneous countries, such as Germany. Thus, there are reasons to study culture not only on the national level but also on the subnational regional, state, or provincial level.

A major shortcoming of level-based concepts of cultural diversity is the **fragmented state of research**. Numerous studies currently exist in a large number of countries and contain a substantial amount of detailed results. However, despite the significant number of studies in existence, a coherent theoretical framework that systematically explains region-based cultural differences across countries is missing.

Despite ostensible ethnical and linguistic homogeneity, **Germany** is characterized by large subnational cultural differences. After having been mostly autonomous princely states for centuries, German national identity began to develop only in the first half of the nineteenth

(Continued)

century and ultimately led to the proclamation of a nation state of German-speaking populations in 1871. While the country was unified in political and administrative terms, remarkable differences with regard to dialect, religion, customs, and traditions have remained. For example, while the northern and eastern regions are predominantly Protestant, the southern states of Baden-Württemberg and Bavaria have a Catholic majority. Dirndl and lederhosen would look strange on the streets of Berlin, just like the greeting "Grüß Gott." People from Hamburg often have difficulties in understanding the strong Bavarian Austrian dialect, while the Low German dialect spoken in the northern states is difficult to understand for speakers of Standard German. An old joke that used to be told in Hamburg goes like this:

Two Hamburg shipowners meet: "I heard that your daughter has married." "Yes, my son in law is from Munich." "Poor you. Why couldn't he just be from Rio. There you at least understand the people and stop by every now and then."

5.3.2 Variance-Based Concepts of Cultural Diversity

Most etic concepts of cultures, such as those of Hofstede, Trompenaars, and GLOBE, decipher cultures from each other based on their typical members. "We compare what is called central tendencies in the answers from each country" (Hofstede 1991, p. 253). Mathematically, a typical member is represented by the country mean of this particular cultural dimension.

The comparison of typical members, however, may lead to misleading conclusions. As shown in Figure 5.8, although the means of the two exemplary cultures are identical, the variances between the two are different. From a methodological perspective, this phenomenon is referred to as **ecological fallacy**, i.e., the mistaken assumption that individuals belonging to a particular group somehow possess the average characteristics of this group (Chapter 3.3.3). Thus, merely studying the means does not completely reveal the distribution of cultural values within a country (Au 1999).

While the etic studies of Hofstede, Trompenaars, and GLOBE published only country-specific mean values and no data on within-country variations, subsequent research developed measures that take this

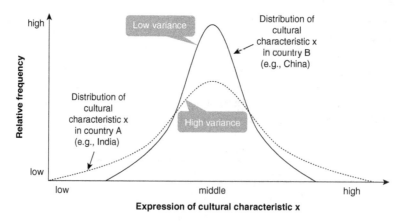

Figure 5.8 Variance of cultural dimensions in two cultures

aspect into account. Among the most influential approaches are Gelfand's concept of cultural tightness and looseness and the concept of ethnolinguistic fractionalization (ELF).

5.3.2.1 Gelfand's Concept of Cultural Tightness and Looseness

Cultural psychologist *Michele Gelfand* proposes that cultures can be differentiated according to the degree to which situational norms are clearly defined and reliably imposed. While the dominating positivist concepts of culture focus on internal values and propose that they are causal for behavior, the concept of tightness vs. looseness emphasizes the **relevance of external influences on behavior**, such as cultural norms and constraints (Gelfand 2018):

- In *tight cultural systems*, there is less variability in the perception of situational norms and greater situational constraint on the behavioral patterns that are appropriate across a wide range of situations. There is a restricted range of behavior that is tolerable within situations, and sanctioning systems are well developed.

- In contrast, in *loose cultural systems*, there is more variability in the perception of situational norms. Values are more heterogeneous and there is a greater range of behaviors that are appropriate across situations. There is a higher tolerance of deviant behavior and sanctioning systems are less well developed.

In order to assess the prevalence of tightness vs. looseness, Gelfand et al. (2011) collected data from 6,823 respondents across 33 nations (Table 5.10). Participants rated the appropriateness of 12 behaviors (i.e., argue, eat, laugh, curse/swear, kiss, cry, sing, talk, flirt, listen to music, read newspaper, bargain) across 15 situations (i.e., bank, doctor's office, job interview, library, funeral, classroom, restaurant, public park, bus, bedroom, city sidewalk, party, elevator, workplace, movies), resulting in a total of 180 behavior situation ratings. For a given situation, the mean appropriateness ratings across behaviors indicate the degree of situational constraint: High values indicate that there are few behaviors considered appropriate in that situation, whereas low values indicate that a wide range of behaviors are considered appropriate in that situation. The 15 situation-specific scores were summed up to a composite tightness score that has a theoretical minimum of 0 (loose cultures) and maximum of 15 (tight cultures).

Table 5.10 Cultural tightness scores of 33 countries according to Gelfand

Nation	Data collection site(s)	Language of survey	Number of participants	Tightness score
Australia	Melbourne	English	230	4.4
Austria	Linz	German	194	6.8
Belgium	Leuven (Flanders region)	Dutch	138	5.6
Brazil	São Paulo	Portuguese	196	3.5
PR China	Beijing	Chinese	235	7.9
Estonia	Tartu	Estonian	188	2.6

(Continued)

Table 5.10 Cultural tightness scores of 33 countries according to Gelfand (Continued)

Nation	Data collection site(s)	Language of survey	Number of participants	Tightness score
France	Paris, Cergy	English	111	6.3
Germany (former East)	Chemnitz	German	201	7.5
Germany (former West)	Rhineland-Palatine/ Frankfurt	German	312	6.5
Greece	Athens	Greek	275	3.9
Hong Kong	Hong Kong	Chinese	197	6.3
Hungary	Budapest, Szeged	Hungarian	256	2.9
Iceland	Reykjavík	Icelandic	144	6.4
India	Ahmedabad, Bhubaneswar, Chandigarh, Coimbatore	Hindi	222	11.0
Israel	Tel-Aviv, Ramat-Gan, Jerusalem, Petach-Tikva	Hebrew	194	3.1
Italy	Padova	Italian	217	6.8
Japan	Tokyo, Osaka	Japanese	246	8.6
Malaysia	Bandar Baru Bangi	Malay	202	11.8
Mexico	Mexico City	Spanish	221	7.2
Netherlands	Groningen	Dutch	207	3.3
New Zeeland	Wellington	English	208	3.9
Norway	Bergen	Norwegian	252	9.5
Pakistan	Hyderabad	Urdu	190	12.3
Poland	Warsaw	Polish	210	6.0
Portugal	Braga	Portuguese	207	7.8
Singapore	Singapore	English	212	10.4
South Korea	Seoul	Korean	196	10.0
Spain	Valencia	Spanish	172	5.4
Turkey	Istanbul	Turkish	195	9.2
Ukraine	Odessa	Ukrainian	184	1.6
UK	Brighton	English	185	6.9
USA	Washington, DC, Maryland, Virginia	English	199	5.1
Venezuela	Caracas	Spanish	227	3.7
Totals/means			**6,823**	**6.5**

Source: Gelfand et al. (2011, p. 1103).

Several **ecological, historical, and institutional antecedents** of cultural tightness vs. looseness were identified (Gelfand et al. 2011). Nations that have encountered ecological and historical threats have much stronger norms and lower tolerance of deviant behavior. Tight nations have higher population density and a higher projected population increase. They have a shortage of natural resources, including a lower percentage of farmland, higher food deprivation, lower food supply and production, lower protein and fat supply, less access to safe water, and lower air quality. Tight nations face more disasters such as floods, tropical cyclones, and droughts and have had more territorial threats from their neighbors. Moreover, historical prevalence of pathogens was higher, as were the number of years of life lost to communicable diseases, the prevalence of tuberculosis, and infant and child mortality rates.

According to Gelfand, Nishii, and Raver (2006), the concept of tightness vs. looseness reflects the **degree of cultural variance at multiple levels in societies**. In societies with strong norms that clearly prescribe appropriate behavior, individuals share many common experiences and are likely to develop higher between-person similarities. By contrast, when norms are comparatively weaker and there is less constraint, people have more varied and idiosyncratic experiences, and individual attributes will be more likely to diverge. Thus, societal tightness-looseness affects variance across individuals in individual attributes (e.g., attitudes, beliefs) as there will generally be more variance across individuals in loose than in tight societies.

Beugelsdijk, Kostova, and Roth (2017) correlated the tightness scores of Gelfand et al. (2011) with the standard deviations of Schwartz's cultural orientations published by Schwartz and Sagie (2000). Countries with tight cultures and strict norms have a higher degree of value consensus reflected in a lower standard deviation. The bivariate correlation between cultural tightness and the standard deviation of Schwartz's cultural value orientations is $r = -0.58$, and the explained variance in a regression analysis controlling for Gelfand's sample characteristics is $r^2 = 0.54$.

5.3.2.2 The Concept of Ethnolinguistic Fractionalization

The concept of ethno-linguistic fractionalization (ELF) aims to capture intracultural diversity with three dimensions: ethnicity, religion, and language. Algebraically, it is based on the **Herfindahl concentration index** and calculated with the following formula:

$$ELF = 1 - \sum_{i=1}^{N} p_i^2$$

where p_i denotes the proportion of the total population of group i, and N denotes the total number of groups in the population. The index assesses the probability that two randomly selected individuals in the population will belong to different groups. The measure scores 0 when in a perfectly homogeneous population and reaches its theoretical maximum value of 1 where an infinite population is divided into infinite groups of one member. Table 5.11 gives some examples of how the measure works.

Alesina et al. (2003) adapted data from various sources to calculate the index for 215 countries:

- The variable *language* is based on data from Encyclopedia Britannica (2001), which reports the shares of languages spoken as mother tongues. It includes 1,055 major linguistic groups for 201 countries or dependencies.

- The variable *religion* is also based on data from the Encyclopedia Britannica (2001). The data cover 294 different religions in 215 countries and dependencies.

Table 5.11 Fractionalization examples

Country	Structure	Ethnolinguistic fractionalization
A	Perfectly homogeneous	0
B	2 groups (0.95, 0.05)	0.10
C	2 groups (0.8, 0.2)	0.32
D	2 groups (0.5., 0.5)	0.50
E	3 groups (0.33, 0.33, 0.33)	0.67
F	3 groups (0.55, 0.30, 0.15)	0.59
G	3 groups (0.75, 0.20, 0.05)	0.40
H	4 groups (0.25, 0.25, 0.25, 0.25)	0.75
I	53 groups (0.48, 0.01, 0.01, ...)	0.76
J	n groups (1/n, 1/n, ...)	1 - (1/n)

Source: Fearon (2003, p. 208).

- The definition of *ethnicity* involves a combination of racial and linguistic characteristics. While for most of Latin America and the Caribbean, ethnicity is based on racial distinctions, the ethnicity data for some European countries (e.g., Belgium, Luxembourg, and Switzerland) and much of sub-Saharan Africa largely reflect languages. The primary source of data in 124 of 190 countries was the Encyclopedia Britannica (2001), completed with data from CIA (2000), Levinson (1998) and Minority Rights Group International (1997). In total, the ethnicity variable covers approximately 650 distinct ethnic groups in 190 countries.

Table 5.12 presents Alesina et al.'s (2003) measures of ethnic, linguistic, and religious fractionalization for 85 selected countries. While some countries like Greece, Iceland, Japan, Norway, and South Korea are very homogeneous in all three dimensions, there are major regions of the world that are highly heterogeneous. The 20 countries with the highest levels of fractionalization are all from Africa, Uganda being the most heterogeneous country with an ELF index of 0.8287. The three dimensions of diversity may vary significantly within a country. For example, Turkey's level of ethnic diversity (0.3200) and linguistic diversity (0.2216) is higher than its level of religious diversity (0.0049). On the contrary, Ecuador shows a high ethnic diversity (0.6550), while the linguistic diversity (0.1308) and religious diversity (0.1417) are low.

Table 5.12 Measures of ethnic, linguistic, and religious fractionalization

Country	Date (Ethnicity data)	Ethnic fractionalization	Linguistic fractionalization	Religious fractionalization
Afghanistan	1995	0.7693	0.6141	0.2717
Argentina	1986	0.2550	0.0618	0.2236
Australia	1986	0.0929	0.3349	0.8211
Bangladesh	1997	0.0454	0.0925	0.2090
Belarus	2001	0.3222	0.4666	0.6116

Table 5.12 Measures of ethnic, linguistic, and religious fractionalization (Continued)

Country	Date (Ethnicity data)	Ethnic fractionalization	Linguistic fractionalization	Religious fractionalization
Belgium	2001	0.5554	0.5409	0.2127
Brazil	1995	0.5408	0.0468	0.6054
Burkina Faso	1983	0.7377	0.7228	0.5798
Cameroon	1983	0.8635	0.8898	0.7338
Canada	1991	0.7124	0.5772	0.6959
Chile	1992	0.1861	0.1871	0.3841
China	1990	0.1538	0.1327	0.6643
Congo	1983	0.8747	0.6871	0.6642
Croatia	1991	0.3690	0.0763	0.4447
Cuba	1994	0.5908	.	0.5059
Czech Republic	1991	0.3222	0.3233	0.6591
Denmark	1996	0.0819	0.1049	0.2333
Ecuador	1989	0.6550	0.1308	0.1417
Ethiopia	1983	0.7235	0.8073	0.6249
Finland	2001	0.1315	0.1412	0.2531
France	1999	0.1032	0.1221	0.4029
Germany	1991	0.1682	0.1642	0.6571
Ghana	1983	0.6733	0.6731	0.7987
Greece	1998	0.1576	0.0300	0.1530
Hong Kong	1994	0.0620	0.2128	0.4191
Hungary	1993	0.1522	0.0297	0.5244
Iceland	1995	0.0798	0.0820	0.1913
India	2000	0.4182	0.8069	0.3260
Indonesia	1990	0.7351	0.7680	0.2340
Iran	1995	0.6684	0.7462	0.1152
Iraq	1983	0.3689	0.3694	0.4844
Ireland	1995	0.1206	0.0312	0.1150
Israel	1995	0.3436	0.5525	0.3469
Italy	1983	0.1145	0.1147	0.3027
Jamaica	1982	0.4129	0.0396	0.6160
Japan	1999	0.0119	0.0178	0.5406
Jordan	1993	0.5926	0.0396	0.0659
Kazakhstan	1999	0.6171	0.6621	0.5898
Kenya	2001	0.8588	0.8860	0.7765

(Continued)

Table 5.12 Measures of ethnic, linguistic, and religious fractionalization (Continued)

Country	Date (Ethnicity data)	Ethnic fractionalization	Linguistic fractionalization	Religious fractionalization
Lebanon	1996	0.1314	0.1312	0.7886
Libya	1995	0.7920	0.0758	0.0570
Liechtenstein	1997	0.5726	0.2246	0.3343
Luxembourg	1996	0.5302	0.6440	0.0911
Malaysia	1996	0.5880	0.5970	0.6657
Mexico	1990	0.5418	0.1511	0.1796
Mongolia	1989	0.3682	0.3734	0.0799
Namibia	1995	0.6329	0.7005	0.6626
Nepal	1991	0.6632	0.7167	0.1417
Netherlands	1995	0.1054	0.5143	0.7222
New Zealand	1996	0.3969	0.1657	0.8110
Nicaragua	1991	0.4844	0.0176	0.4290
Norway	1998	0.0586	0.0673	0.2048
Pakistan	1995	0.7098	0.7190	0.3848
Paraguay	1998	0.1689	0.5972	0.2123
Peru	1981	0.6566	0.3358	0.1988
Philippines	1998	0.2385	0.8360	0.3056
Poland	1998	0.1183	0.0468	0.1712
Portugal	1998	0.0468	0.0198	0.1438
Russia	1997	0.2452	0.2485	0.4398
Rwanda	1996	0.3238	.	0.5066
Saudi Arabia	1995	0.1800	0.0949	0.1270
Singapore	2001	0.3857	0.3835	0.6561
Slovakia	1996	0.2539	0.2551	0.5655
Slovenia	1991	0.2216	0.2201	0.2868
South Africa	1998	0.7517	0.8652	0.8603
South Korea	1990	0.0020	0.0021	0.6604
Spain	1991	0.4165	0.4132	0.4514
Sri Lanka	2001	0.4150	0.4645	0.4853
Sweden	1998	0.0600	0.1968	0.2342
Switzerland	2001	0.5314	0.5441	0.6083
Syria	1993	0.5399	0.1817	0.4310
Taiwan	2001	0.2744	0.5028	0.6845
Tanzania	1995	0.7353	0.8983	0.6334
Thailand	1983	0.6338	0.6344	0.0994

Table 5.12   Measures of ethnic, linguistic, and religious fractionalization (Continued)

Country	Date (Ethnicity data)	Ethnic fractionalization	Linguistic fractionalization	Religious fractionalization
Turkey	2001	0.3200	0.2216	0.0049
Uganda	1983	0.9302	0.9227	0.6332
Ukraine	1998	0.4737	0.4741	0.6157
UAE	1993	0.6252	0.4874	0.3310
UK	1994	0.1211	0.0532	0.6944
USA	2000	0.4901	0.2514	0.8241
Uruguay	1990	0.2504	0.0817	0.3548
Uzbekistan	1995	0.4125	0.4120	0.2133
Vietnam	1995	0.2383	0.2377	0.5080
Zambia	1998	0.7808	0.8734	0.7359
Zimbabwe	1998	0.3874	0.4472	0.7363

Source: Alesina et al. (2003).

A shortcoming of the ELF index is the **problematic definition of ethnicity**. As argued by constructivist approaches of culture, ethnicity is not an objective fact determined by the human gene pool. It is rather a *social construct* that is defined by shared ancestry, origin myth, history, homeland, language or dialect, symbolic systems such as religion, mythology, and ritual, cuisine, style of dress, art, and physical appearance. A single measure of ethnicity for a country therefore misses the social reality that there are multiple dimensions of ethnic identity in all countries.

"Many constructivists (…) would argue that (…) ethnic identities are situational, driven by context, and that it is therefore impossible to divide a population into categories of identity in any time period. A saleswoman in a Kenyan market might present herself as a Luo to a customer speaking that language (as her mother was a Luo-speaker), as a Kikuyu to a customer in an expensive suit (as her father was a Kikuyu), and as a Swahili to her neighbor in the market (as Kiswahili is the lingua franca of East African tradespeople). An American social scientist who asked for her ethnic identity, might get 'Kenyan' as a response. Our trader, when asked for her ethnic identity, might in different contexts answer with Luo, Kikuyu, Swahili, or Kenyan. Constructivists will point out that all of these answers are correct, at one and the same time, and that such complexity undermines any attempt to categorize a population ethnically."

(Laitin & Posner 2001, p. 5)

Measures of ethnic fractionalization therefore largely *depend on the definition and delineation of ethnic groups.* For example, the measures of Alesina et al. (2003) and Fearon (2003) show significant differences for a number of African countries (Posner 2004). The ethnic composition of a country is also likely to *change more dynamically* than other aspects of culture. For example, the study of Campos and Kuzeyev (2007) with fractionalization measures 26 former communist countries covering the period from 1989 to

2002 and shows that transition economies became more ethnically homogeneous during this short period while only small changes were observed for linguistic and religious fractionalization.

A further problem is that ethnic fractionalization indices fail to incorporate potentially relevant information about the *spatial distribution of ethnic groups* around the country. Different ethnic groups are likely to have different effects when they live in mostly separated regions than when they are more evenly dispersed (Posner 2004). Finally, the ELF index contains no information about the *depth or weight of the divisions between different groups* (Luiz 2015). "Of course, it is possible that ethnic diversity matters purely through the multiplicity of interests that it brings to the table (…). But part of the reason that ethnicity diversity strikes researchers (…) as a potentially relevant variable is because they presume that it implies something about the depth of the cleavages between groups and the unbargainability of their demands, not just about the number of interests that need to be reconciled" (Posner 2004, p. 852).

An extreme example of the underestimation of the depth and weight of ethnic differences in indices of fractionalization is **Rwanda**. Both Alesina et al. (2003) and Fearon (2003) ascribe the country a relatively low ethnic diversity of 0.3238 and 0.18, respectively. This index is far below, for example, the one of Switzerland (0.5314 and 0.575, respectively). However, while in Switzerland, the divisions between German-speakers, French-speakers, and Italian-speakers have certainly shaped the country's politics, they have never been a source of intergroup violence. In contrast, the ethnic differences between Hutus and Tutsis in Rwanda caused one of the most horrible genocides in history with millions of people displaced and 800,000 killed (Prunier 1998; Melvern 2004).

5.3.3 Pattern-Based Concepts of Cultural Diversity

Pattern-based concepts of cultural diversity are based on the notion that cultural dimensions are not independent, but appear in combination (Tsui, Nifadkar & Ou 2007; Tung 2007). While the concepts of Hofstede, Trompenaars, GLOBE, etc., usually discuss various cultural dimensions separately, pattern-based concepts focus on **cultural archetypes** as *specific configurations of multiple cultural dimensions*. From this perspective, culture is regarded as an "integrated, complex set of interrelated and potentially interactive patterns characteristic of a group of people" (Lytle et al. 1995, p. 170).

Although Kroeber and Kluckhohn (1952) already stated that "culture comprises *configuration* of values, of normative principles and ideals" (p. 14) and that "the essential part of culture is to be found in the *patterns* embodied in the social traditions of the group" (p. 34), pattern-based approaches of culture have only recently gained attention in the intercultural management literature. One of the most advanced concepts is the **culture archetypes framework of** Venaik & Midgley.

Venaik and Midgley (2015) originally derived cultural archetypes for the four countries Japan, United States, China, and India. In a subsequent study, Midgley, Venaik, and Christopoulos (2019) extended the sample size to 52 countries included in the **Schwartz World Values Survey** (www.worldvaluessurvey.org). In contrast to Hofstede or GLOBE which provide only national-level aggregated data, Schwartz value data are publicly available on the individual level and thus allow for the identification of culture archetypes within and across countries. The concept of Schwartz (1992) includes *10 motivational value types* organized into four categories around a circle (Table 5.13).

Table 5.13 Schwartz's motivational value types

Dimensions	Categories	Values	Definition	Items
Society-oriented values	Self-transcendence	Universalism	Understanding, appreciation, tolerance, and protection for the welfare of all people and for nature	Broadminded, wisdom, social justice, equality, a world at peace, a world of beauty, unity with nature, protecting the environment
		Benevolence	Preservation and enhancement of the welfare of people with whom one is in frequent personal contact	Helpful, honest, forgiving, loyal, responsible
	Conservation	Tradition	Respect, commitment, and acceptance of the customs and ideas that traditional culture or religion provide	Accepting one's portion in life, humble, devout, respect for tradition, moderate
		Conformity	Restraint of actions, inclinations, and impulses likely to upset or harm others and violate social expectations or norms	Self-discipline, obedient, politeness, honoring parents and elders
		Security	Safety, harmony, and stability of society, relationships, and self	Family security, national security, social order, clean, reciprocation of favors
Self-oriented values	Self-enhancement	Power	Social status and prestige, control or dominance over people and resources	Social power, authority, wealth
		Achievement	Personal success through demonstrating competence according to social standards	Successful, capable, ambitious, influential
	Openness to change	Self-direction	Independent thought and action (choosing, creating, exploring)	Creativity, freedom, independent, curious, choosing own goals
		Stimulation	Excitement, novelty, and challenge in life	Daring, a varied life, an exciting life
		Hedonism	Pleasure and sensuous gratification for oneself	Pleasure, enjoying life

Source: Adapted from Schwarz & Sagie (2000, p. 468).

Instead of classifying individuals by averages or grouping them by exogenous factors, such as ethnicity or nationality, Midgley, Venaik, and Christopoulos (2019) draw on topology and matrix algebra to endogenously identify the configurations of values shared by a particular group. Based on this methodology, five **cultural archetypes** were identified (Figure 5.9):

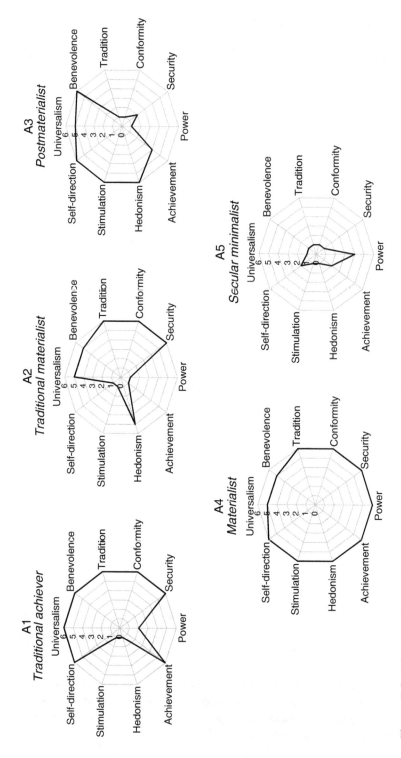

Figure 5.9 Five global archetypes according to Midgley, Venaik, and Christopoulos

Source: Midgley, Venaik & Christopoulos (2019, p. 78).

- Archetype A1 (*traditional achiever*) represents individuals who consider all society-oriented values as well as the two self-oriented values of self-direction and achievement as particularly important.
- Archetype A2 (*traditional materialist*) is similar to A1 individuals in that both regard all society-oriented values as important; the key difference being moderate to high importance for self-oriented value of hedonism in A2 versus high importance for the self-oriented values of self-direction and achievement in A1.
- Archetype A3 (*postmaterialist*) represents individuals who consider all self-oriented values

as important except power and to a lesser extent achievement. These archetypal individuals also give high importance to the society-oriented value of benevolence.

- Archetype A4 (*materialist*) represents individuals who give high importance to both self- and society-oriented values.
- Finally, archetype A5 (*secular minimalist*) is almost a mirror image of A4. It represents individuals who give low importance to all values except to power which they consider to be moderately important.

After the identification of the five culture archetypes, the Euclidian distances between the archetype configurations and the Schwartz values for each individual case were calculated. The resulting proportion of each country sample associated with the respective archetype is presented in Table 5.14.

Table 5.14   Distribution of archetypal cases by country

| | Proportion of each country sample associated with the respective archetype | | | | |
Country	A1 Traditional achiever	A2 Traditional materialist	A3 Postmaterialist	A4 Materialist	A5 Secular minimalist
Andorra	0.12	0.26	0.35	0.25	0.02
Argentina	0.30	0.27	0.18	0.13	0.12
Australia	0.24	0.27	0.24	0.13	0.13
Brazil	0.32	0.38	0.14	0.15	0.02
Bulgaria	0.29	0.27	0.09	0.21	0.14
Burkina Faso	0.39	0.06	0.06	0.44	0.04
Canada	0.32	0.23	0.23	0.18	0.03
Chile	0.19	0.22	0.17	0.37	0.05
China	0.36	0.23	0.08	0.20	0.13
Cyprus	0.43	0.09	0.10	0.35	0.03
Egypt	0.29	0.32	0.01	0.35	0.03
Ethiopia	0.17	0.04	0.09	0.48	0.21
Finland	0.21	0.32	0.25	0.13	0.08
France	0.18	0.32	0.27	0.16	0.07
Georgia	0.44	0.24	0.02	0.29	0.01

(Continued)

Table 5.14 Distribution of archetypal cases by country (Continued)

Country	Proportion of each country sample associated with the respective archetype				
	A1 Traditional achiever	A2 Traditional materialist	A3 Postmaterialist	A4 Materialist	A5 Secular minimalist
Germany	0.21	0.26	0.26	0.14	0.12
Ghana	0.35	0.02	0.01	**0.60**	0.01
Hungary	0.25	0.28	0.08	0.35	0.04
India	0.33	0.08	0.07	0.45	0.07
Indonesia	0.20	0.31	0.07	0.39	0.03
Iran	0.34	0.14	0.04	0.46	0.01
Japan	0.13	0.20	0.16	0.02	0.49
Jordan	0.08	0.05	0.01	**0.85**	0.00
Malaysia	0.24	0.16	0.10	0.36	0.13
Mali	0.28	0.11	0.04	**0.56**	0.01
Mexico	0.31	0.24	0.15	0.25	0.05
Moldova	0.34	0.21	0.09	0.26	0.09
Morocco	0.28	0.10	0.06	**0.51**	0.05
Netherlands	0.08	0.28	0.39	0.12	0.13
Norway	0.21	0.29	0.37	0.08	0.05
Peru	0.40	0.21	0.18	0.13	0.09
Poland	0.41	0.20	0.09	0.27	0.03
Romania	0.32	0.27	0.05	0.28	0.08
Russia	0.22	0.30	0.14	0.23	0.12
Rwanda	0.29	0.14	0.04	0.47	0.07
Serbia and Montenegro	0.18	0.27	0.14	0.22	0.19
Slovenia	0.32	0.20	0.20	0.24	0.04
South Africa	0.18	0.09	0.65	**0.65**	0.02
South Korea	0.09	0.22	0.24	0.23	0.21
Spain	0.21	0.30	0.17	0.27	0.05
Sweden	0.22	0.24	0.39	0.11	0.05
Switzerland	0.20	0.27	0.38	0.11	0.04
Taiwan	0.20	**0.51**	0.11	0.13	0.05
Thailand	0.18	0.18	0.14	0.29	0.21
Trinidad and Tobago	**0.51**	0.14	0.10	0.19	0.06
Turkey	0.35	0.07	0.07	0.47	0.03

Table 5.14 Distribution of archetypal cases by country (Continued)

Country	Proportion of each country sample associated with the respective archetype				
	A1 Traditional achiever	A2 Traditional materialist	A3 Postmaterialist	A4 Materialist	A5 Secular minimalist
UK	0.24	0.30	0.23	0.18	0.06
Ukraine	0.19	0.29	0.12	0.27	0.12
USA	0.23	0.29	0.20	0.16	0.12
Uruguay	0.18	0.36	0.21	0.13	0.12
Vietnam	0.20	0.23	0.07	0.45	0.05
Zambia	0.28	0.06	0.12	0.47	0.08
Mean	*0.26*	*0.22*	*0.15*	*0.29*	*0.08*

Notes: The underlined entries are proportions ≤0.02; the **bold** entries are proportions ≥0.50.
Source: Midgley, Venaik & Christopoulos (2019, pp. 80–81).

Table 5.14 shows that the **distribution of culture archetypes by country** varies widely. There is not a single country in the sample in which all individuals are associated with a single archetype. Instead, all countries have a heterogeneous population of individuals who associate with one archetype or another to a greater or lesser degree. Seven countries have a dominant archetype with more than 50% individuals associated with just one of the five archetypes. The most common dominant archetype is A4 (for five countries), followed by A1 and A2 for one country each. Four of these seven countries are also part of the ten countries that have a negligible proportion of 0.02 or less of their sample individuals associated with one of the five archetypes. The most culturally homogeneous country is Jordan where 85% of the individuals are associated with A4, and conversely, a negligible proportion of the country's sample is associated with archetypes A3 and A5. Six other countries—Ghana, Mali, Morocco, Taiwan, Trinidad and Tobago, South Africa—have 51–65% of their respective samples associated with one of the five archetypes and therefore can be considered to have a dominant, but not a single, archetype.

On the contrary, 45 countries are relatively heterogeneous and require two or more archetypes to represent a cumulative proportion of 51% or more of the country sample. Three countries—Serbia and Montenegro, South Korea, and Thailand—require at least three archetypes to represent 51% or more of the country sample. South Korea is the most culturally heterogeneous country in the sample based on the configurations of the 10 Schwartz values, which is astonishing given the fact that it the most homogeneous country in Alesina et al.'s (2003) measures of ethnic, linguistic, and religious fractionalization. The remaining 42 countries require at least two archetypes to represent 51% or more of the country's sample.

While the studies of Venaik and Midgley (2015) and Midgley, Venaik, and Christopoulos (2019) re-examined existing data from Schwartz, the **cultural archetypes approach of Richter et al.** (2016) applied five of Hofstede's cultural value dimensions (power distance, collectivism, uncertainty avoidance, masculinity, and long-term orientation) and collected data on the individual level with the cultural values scale developed by Yoo, Donthu, and Lenartowicz (2011). Based on data from 10 countries, two cluster analyses to classify individuals into cultural archetypes independent from both the research context and national boundaries were performed. With this procedure, six cultural archetypes were identified (masculine individualists, masculine collectivists, power distant and individualistic risk-takers, low power distant feminines, low power distant short-term-orienteds, and uncertainty avoiding power distants) that show high transnational applicability. While the highest percentage of concentrations of any archetype within a country is around 40–45%, the majority of countries are characterized by a variety of different archetypes.

Pattern-based approaches of intracultural diversity are a **useful way to represent configurations of multiple cultural dimensions** in a comprehensive and parsimonious manner (Midgley, Venaik & Christopoulos 2019). They not only produce a more comprehensive picture of a cultural entity, but also account for the potential reinforcing or countervailing effects of various cultural dimensions. One of the major findings of empirical studies in this context is that cultural archetypes do not necessarily correspond to a country. Instead, various cultural archetypes can be found within a single country as well as across countries. Thus, pattern-based approaches not only contribute to research on intracultural diversity but also on cultural similarities on a supranational level.

5.3.4 Critical Evaluation

Concepts of cultural diversity are based on the observation that national borders are often inadequate to capture the complexity of culture. While this position is widely accepted in the intercultural management literature, there is less consensus about the adequate conceptualization and measurement of cultural diversity (Peterson, Søndergaard & Kara 2018; Tung & Stahl 2018). There are level-based, variance-based, and pattern-based approaches, each with specific assumptions, advantages, and disadvantages (Table 5.15).

Table 5.15 Synopsis of concepts of intracultural diversity

	Level-based concepts	Variance-based concepts	Pattern-based concepts
Key assumption	Cultural values can differ between regions, states, provinces, or districts within a country.	Countries may have equal or very similar cultural means, but large differences in intracultural variation.	Cultural dimensions are not independent, but appear in combination (patterns).
Examples	Studies based on Hofstede's cultural dimensions (Huo & Randall 1991; Fontaine, Richardson & Foong 2002; Thomas & Bendixen 2000; Singh & Sharma 2009; Hofstede et al. 2010; Kaasa, Vadi & Varblane 2014), Schwartz's theory of cultural values (Lenartowicz & Roth 2001; Lenartowicz, Johnson & White 2003), and emic measures (Dolan et al. 2004; Dheer, Lenartowicz & Peterson 2015).	Gelfand's concept of cultural tightness and looseness (Gelfand et al. 2011); concept of ethnolinguistic fractionalization (Fearon 2003; Alesina et al. 2003; Luiz 2015).	Culture archetypes frameworks (Venaik & Midgley 2015; Midgley, Venaik & Christopoulos 2019; Richter et al. 2016).

Table 5.15 Synopsis of concepts of intracultural diversity (Continued)

	Level-based concepts	Variance-based concepts	Pattern-based concepts
Advantages	Level of analysis can be easily adapted to research interests.	Low complexity: measuring diversity as an index number.	Comprehensive picture of cultural entities; account for potential reinforcing and countervailing effects of various cultural dimensions.
Disadvantages	Fragmented state of research: numerous studies in a large number of countries, but lack of coherent theoretical framework.	Dependence on the definition and delineation of ethnic groups; no information about the spatial distribution of ethnic groups around the country and about the depth or weight of the divisions between different groups.	Early state of research: small number of studies and few reviews.

Cultural diversity has several **management implications**. For example, *expatriates* are likely to adapt to a homogeneous culture more easily than a heterogeneous one. This is because contact with a culturally divergent group of individuals may confuse expatriates and prevent them from discerning cultural similarities and differences, forming a scheme for the locals, and thus behaving adequately in different situations (Au 1999). *Intercultural training* for countries with high intracultural diversity should therefore go beyond the transfer of knowledge about its typical members and discuss the reasons, expressions, and consequences of within-country diversity.

According to Dow, Cuypers, and Ertug (2016), within-country cultural diversity (measured in terms of language and religion) can also affect *foreign acquisitions*. Diversity within the host country may be an additional source of behavioral uncertainty and information asymmetry, over and above the effects arising from cross-national differences. At the same time, diversity within the home country may increase the cognitive complexity of the decision-makers, moderating the firm's response to the distance and diversity of the host country. Thus, within-country cultural diversity may not only *impede* but also *facilitate* intercultural relations.

A clear example of *cultural hyperdiversity* is the **United Arab Emirates**. Following the discovery of oil in 1966, the UAE experienced an unprecedented economic boom. However, unlike many other emerging markets, the UAE suffered from an enormous shortage of domestic workers, and massive migrant labor was needed at all skill levels to support the country's growth.

Today, the ratio of nationals to expatriates is the most disproportionate in the world. Local Emiratis represent only about 11% of the entire population of around 9.5 mn. people. Individuals from more than 150 countries live and work in the UAE, with nationals from India,

(Continued)

Pakistan, and Bangladesh representing nearly half of the population. Other large minority groups are from the Philippines, Iran, Egypt, Nepal, Sri Lanka, China, Jordan, Afghanistan, Palestine, the United Kingdom, and South Africa. Dubai, the largest city in the UAE, has a share of 85% foreign-born population, which makes it by far the most culturally heterogeneous city in the world, followed by Toronto with a share of around 45% (Price & Benton-Short 2007).

Studies of culture usually refer to the local population. In the case of the UAE, however, this represents only 11% of all people living in the country. Since Emiratis are mostly employed in the public sector, their share in the business sector is even lower. Thus, while data on cultural values in the UAE presented in intercultural research are formally correct, their practical relevance is low because intercultural interactions between foreigners and Emiratis are much less likely than between foreigners with different cultural backgrounds. Foreign expatriates may therefore find intercultural training with focus on the UAE not only unnecessary but even counterproductive because it is likely to provide a misleading picture of the intercultural challenges in the country (Harrison & Michailova 2012; Holtbrügge 2021).

The effects of within-country cultural diversity on *international encounters* can also be mitigated through across-country cultural similarities. Particularly, pattern-based approaches identify transnational culture archetypes, i.e., groups of individuals who share similar culture values configuration across countries. People characterized by the same or similar culture archetypes are likely to interact more easily even if they have different national backgrounds (Midgley, Venaik & Christopoulos 2019).

SUMMARY

Cultural clusters define supranational similarities between cultures based on diverse criteria, such as intellectual styles, geography, language, and religion.

The cultural distance index by Kogut and Singh aggregates cultural differences along the cultural dimensions of Hofstede. Shenkar's concept of cultural frictions applies a social constructionist perspective and shifts the focus from abstract cultural differences toward the perception of concrete intercultural encounters.

Concepts of cultural diversity are grounded on the observation that cultural values can differ between regions, states, provinces, or districts within a country. Level-based, variance-based, and pattern-based concepts can be distinguished.

 Reflection Questions

1. Do you think that cultural differences are more region-specific or country-specific? Would students from other countries answer this question differently?
2. Pick a country that starts with the same first letter as your first name and categorize it in a cultural cluster according to Galtung, Huntington, Schwartz, and Hofstede. Which categorization do you find most suitable? Why?

3. Samuel Huntington (1993, p. 22) predicted that "nation states will remain the most powerful actors in world affairs, but the principal conflicts of global politics will occur between nations and groups of different civilizations. The clash of civilizations will dominate global politics. The fault lines between civilizations will be the battle lines of the future." How would you assess this prediction?

4. Can you think of any positive implications of cultural distance?

5. Table 5.9 shows the mean absolute deviations of Hofstede's cultural dimensions in selected European countries. While Germany shows very high intracultural variations, these are significantly smaller in geographically much larger Russia. What could be reasons for these differences?

6. Do you agree with the statement that *intracultural* diversity is often greater than *intercultural* diversity? Can you give examples?

7. Compare the concept of cultural archetypes by Venaik and Midgley to a specific variance-based and a level-based concept of intracultural diversity. What are the most important advantages and disadvantages of the archetype framework in comparison to the other concepts?

 End of Chapter Exercise

Global Market Segmentation at Unilever

The British consumer goods company Unilever wants to restructure its worldwide market segmentation strategy. On the one hand, the company seeks to adapt its policies to different customer attitudes and behaviors. On the other hand, Unilever aims to exploit potential advantages of global standardization, such as economies of scale and scope. To balance the opposing advantages of cultural adaptation and global standardization, the company decided to implement a cluster approach.

1. Which concept of cultural clusters would you recommend to Unilever and why?

2. Would your recommended concept differ for the areas of marketing and human resource management?

3. Would you advise Unilever to supplement the selected cluster approach with a concept of intracultural diversity for certain countries?

Further Reading

Different perspectives on cultural clusters can be found in the books by Huntington (1997), Ronen and Shenkar (2017), and Lewis (2018).

A meta-analytical review of different concepts of cultural distance is presented by Beugelsdijk et al. (2018).

The perspective of cultural friction is elaborated upon by Luo & Shenkar (2011).

Different measures of cultural diversity are critically discussed by Dow, Cuypers, and Ertug (2016) and Peterson, Søndergaard, and Kara (2018).

6

INTERCULTURAL COMMUNICATION AND NEGOTIATION

LEARNING OBJECTIVES

By the end of this chapter, you will be able to

- know the intercultural communication process,
- know different styles of intercultural bargaining,
- understand the impact of culture on verbal, para-verbal, non-verbal, and extra-verbal communication,
- explain the interplay between language and cognition,
- comprehend and navigate the challenges of translation in intercultural encounters,
- recommend suitable communication styles for different intercultural settings,
- respond to different tactics of instrumental communication in an intercultural context.

Communication encompasses a large spectrum of areas from advertising and corporate reporting to leadership and merger negotiations. While communication has always been a major challenge of intercultural management, its speed, intensity, and complexity is currently further enhanced through modern information technologies, such as the Internet, social media, mobile devices, etc. This omnipresence of communication in an intercultural context requires a detailed analysis of its elements, forms, and effects.

In the first section, a process model of intercultural communication is developed, and its components are explained. Afterwards, intercultural differences in verbal, para-verbal, non-verbal, and extra-verbal communication are outlined. This is followed by considerations about the relationship between language and cognition. The challenges of translation and translators in intercultural communication are discussed subsequently. Then the specifics of intercultural negotiations are explained. The chapter ends with reflections about the aspect of power and manipulation in intercultural communication.

6.1 PROCESS MODEL OF INTERCULTURAL COMMUNICATION

Communication is defined as the transfer of messages between two or more individuals. It consists of any combination of a sender's speech, writing, gestures, mimic, and other forms of articulation that transmits meaning to one or more receivers. In its most basic sense, communication is covered by the **formula of Lasswell** (1948, p. 37): "Who says what in which channel to whom with what effect?" Since, according to Watzlawick, Bavelas & Jackson (1967), it is impossible not to communicate in interactions with others, this includes both intended and unintended elements and effects.

The **process of communication** is constituted by a sender who encodes a message and transfers it over a channel to a receiver (Figure 6.1). The receiver decodes the transmitted signal back into the message. Both coding and decoding are affected by the context (e.g., time, location) in which sender and receiver are situated. Communication is effective if *coding equivalence* exists, i.e., a message is decoded by the receiver in the same way as it was coded by the sender and vice versa (Shannon & Weaver 1963).

While traditional forms of communication, such as personal conversations, letters, telephone calls, and telegrams, mostly involve one sender and one receiver, mass media allow for a multitude and simultaneity of senders and receivers. For example, TV commercials and internet posts transfer information to a plethora of receivers whose number cannot be limited by the sender. Moreover, social media, such as Facebook, LinkedIn, YouTube, and WhatsApp, dissolve the distinction between senders and receivers and extend the unidirectional process of communication to **complex communication networks**. At the same time, the speed of information transfer as well as the amount of transmitted information is increasing exponentially. Automatic translation programs such as DeepL and Google Translate can even overcome the limits of language and allow communication between individuals who do not share a mutually intelligible language.

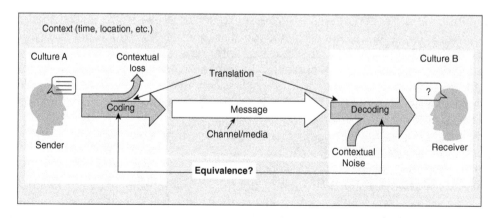

Figure 6.1 Intercultural communication process

Messages consist of a number of **signs**. According to de Saussure (1916), any sign has two elements, the signifier and the signified. The *signifier* relates to the material aspect of a sign, such as a word, image, or object. The *signified* is the meaning that is drawn by the receiver of the sign. From a *technical perspective*, the accurate transfer of the sign from the sender to the receiver is essential. Technical distortions of transmission, such as blurry fonts, dead spots, disconnection, etc. should be avoided. The *cognitive perspective* implies that the perceived signifier is linked with an identical or similar signified. If the receivers are not able to link the signifier to their reservoir of signs, misunderstanding will occur (Figure 6.2).

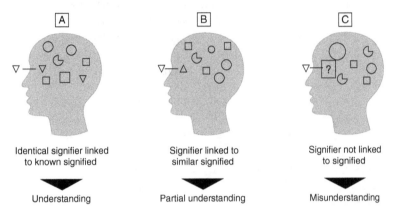

Identical signifier linked to known signified	Signifier linked to similar signified	Signifier not linked to signified
Understanding	Partial understanding	Misunderstanding

Figure 6.2 Allocation of signifier to signified
Source: Adapted from Beamer (1992, p. 288).

The allocation of signifier to signified is affected by various **interferences** which reduce understanding and the effectiveness of communication. Two types of interferences can be distinguished: contextual noise and contextual loss (Krippendorff 1986). *Contextual loss* occurs when the receiver does not perceive all information transmitted by the sender. *Contextual noise* adds unrelated variation to this transmitted quality, yielding the entropy at the receiver.

The likelihood and strength of interferences are increased in an **intercultural context**, i.e., when the individuals involved in the communication process have different cultural backgrounds. For example, the **methods of coding and decoding messages** may differ across cultures. According to Hall (1976), cultures such as Japan and Mexico prefer high-context communication, while a low-context communication style is prevalent in cultures like Germany and Sweden. Senders with a high-context style tend to communicate less explicitly. A considerable part of information is embedded in the context. This may not be adequately perceived by the receiver as part of the message. As a result, substantial *contextual loss* is likely which subtracts from the intended meaning sent and therefore reduces the sender's entropy. On the contrary, receivers from high-context cultures will attribute meaning to the context in which communication takes place. In particular, if the sender is from low-context or different high-context cultures, sender-unintended parts are added to the message. This results in the construction of *contextual noise* on the side of the receiver that alters the sender-intended meaning of the message.

Another source of interference in intercultural communication is the **channel** used by the sender to transmit the message. According to Marshall McLuhan's (1964) statement "The media is the message," the selection of media serves not only a technical function but has also a symbolic meaning and may therefore evoke different interpretations. For example, a telephone call may signal urgency in many Western countries, while it is a medium of convenience in India and many African countries. In Northern Europe, the primary function of telephone calls is the transaction of facts, while in Southern Europe, it has a more personal, social, and phatic component. Thus, the interpretation of communication channels may vary between senders and receivers from different countries.

Interferences in intercultural communication may also occur if the sender's message has to be translated into the language of the receiver. Significant **translation bias** is most likely in the case of large linguistic differences between the involved languages, such as English and Chinese. Moreover, contextual loss may interfere with the translation of specific terminology. For example, a large and differentiated repertoire of accounting terms has been developed in the German language which is difficult to translate into other languages and cultural contexts. Similarly, the meaning of indigenous management concepts, such as *blat* (Russia), *guanxi* (China), and *ringi seido* (Japan) may not be adequately translated into other languages without considerable contextual loss.

A way to reduce the likelihood of interferences in intercultural communication is to incorporate **redundancy**. Contextual loss and noise can be diminished through communicative variance, such as the alternation of communication styles and variations of senders, receivers, media, and contexts. For example, negotiations between two parties may involve diverse teams of participants and take place at different locations and times. Moreover, the combination of different communication channels can increase media richness. For example, oral presentations may be accompanied by pictures and written documents. Redundancy in translation may be ensured through the use of multiple translators. The non-redundant transfer of messages would be the most efficient means of communication, but totally insensitive to transmission errors of any kind. Intercultural communication therefore always has to balance the *trade-off between the economy of information transmission and the avoidance of unintended interferences*.

Communication across cultural and linguistic boundaries is a key subject of **computational linguistics**. *Speech recognition technologies* enable the conversion of spoken messages into text while *speech synthesizers* convert text into speech. Word processors and text editing interfaces for smartphones, tablets and computers increasingly use *spell checkers* to inspect misspellings in written documents. Combined with *auto-correction software*, they can not only reduce spelling mistakes but also improve readability and comprehension of texts. However, they can also lead to humorous or embarrassing false corrections. Thus, advanced linguistic hardware and software technologies can significantly facilitate intercultural communication. At the same time, it creates new interferences and challenges.

6.2 ELEMENTS OF INTERCULTURAL COMMUNICATION

In order to analyze intercultural communication and potential interferences in a systematic way, it is useful to distinguish between verbal, para-verbal, non-verbal, and extra-verbal elements. These are prevalent in both oral and written communication (Table 6.1).

Table 6.1 Elements of oral and written communication

Elements	Oral communication	Written communication
Verbal	Phonology, syntax, semantics, pragmatics	Morphology, syntax, semantics, pragmatics
Para-verbal	Voice set (configuration and interaction of speech organs), voice qualifiers (e.g., volume, pitch, intonation, speed, rhythm, resonance and pauses), vocalizations (vocal characterizers and verbal fillers)	Handwriting style, writing direction, text layout (e.g., punctuation marks, font, font size, line spacing, type area, etc.), ideograms (emoticons and emoji)
Non-verbal	Eye contact (oculesics), touch (haptics), body language (kinesics)	Colors, numbers, symbols, pictures
Extra-verbal	Time, location, clothing, physical appearance	Time (e.g., frequency), space, media (e.g., publisher), paper quality

Oral communication is based on speech and written communication is based on text. While this definition is widely accepted in communication research, the distinction is becoming increasingly blurred. On the one hand, oral communication does not only include speech but also non-verbal elements, such as eye contact and body language. On the other hand, electronic media frequently combine written texts, spoken words, pictures, and films. Therefore, it is more suitable to define oral and written communication according to their physical properties.

Oral communication is fugitive and not restorable (as long as it is not recorded). The message emerges at the moment of speech and is non-reversible. Words once spoken can never be taken back. **Written communication** is pre-arranged. It consists of physical objects that can be stored, copied, and spread. Texts can be edited, modified, and deleted—even after their publication. The different physical properties of oral and written communication require therefore a differentiated analysis of their cultural imprints.

Verbal communication is the use of language to share information with others. Since not only *what* people say is relevant but also *how, when* and *where* something is said, the same message accompanied by different metacommunication can have different meanings. Non-linguistic communication is much more restricted in transfer capacity than the verbal code and can usually not transfer complex meaning. However, it can accentuate, amplify, diminish, or change the effects of verbal messages.

Para-verbal communication refers to the non-lexical properties of speech, i.e., all meaningful sound characteristics that are not phonemes. In oral communication, this includes the voice set (configuration and interaction of speech organs), voice qualifiers (e.g., volume, pitch, intonation, speed, rhythm, resonance, and pauses) and vocalizations (vocal characterizers and verbal fillers). Para-verbal elements of written communication involve elements such as handwriting style, writing direction, text layout (e.g., punctuation marks, font, font size, line spacing, type area, etc.), and ideograms (e.g., emoticons and emoji).

Non-verbal communication is the transfer of meaning without the use of words. In oral communication, it includes the use of visual cues, such as eye contact (oculesics), touch (haptics), and body language (kinesics). Non-verbal elements of written communication are, for example, colors, numbers, symbols, and pictures.

Extra-verbal communication refers to factors which are not directly linked to the act of communication, but inherent to the wider context in which it takes place. In oral communication, it includes mainly time, location, clothing, and physical appearance. Extra-verbal elements of written communication are, for example, the selection of media and the use of time.

The manifestations and relevance of verbal, para-verbal, non-verbal, and extra-verbal elements of communication differ across cultures. According to Hall (1966), low-context cultures, such as Germany, Scandinavia and the United States, prefer verbal communication. The explicit code requires little prior knowledge of the situation. Communication tends to be written rather than oral and is more detailed, yet redundancies lead to slower transmission. In contrast, most Asian and Latin American cultures are characterized by high-context communication. The transfer of information relies heavily on para-verbal, non-verbal, and extra-verbal elements. Communication tends to be oral rather than written and requires extensive prior knowledge of both the sender and the receiver. In the following, the different elements of communication are exemplified and their implications for intercultural encounters are analyzed.

6.2.1 Verbal Communication

Verbal communication is the use of language to share information with others. Linguistics as the scientific study of language distinguishes between five interrelated dimensions of verbal communication, namely phonology, morphology, syntax, semantics, and pragmatics (Table 6.2). In all five dimensions, cultural differences exist that may disturb the effectiveness of intercultural communication.

Table 6.2 Dimensions of verbal communication

Dimension	Definition
Phonology	Study of the sounds (phones) of a language and how they are organized into phonemes.
Morphology	Study of the smallest linguistic entities of a language with grammatical functions (morphemes) and how they are organized into words (lexemes).
Syntax	Study of the structure of language and the rules for combining words into meaningful sentences.
Semantics	Study of the literal, decontextualized, grammatical meaning of words and sentences.
Pragmatics	Study of the relations between the elements of a language and the people who use them.

6.2.1.1 Phonology

Phonology refers to the study of the sounds (phones) of a language and how they are organized into phonemes (Ladd 2008). *Phonetics* studies the sounds of human speech which are similar in all languages. It is concerned with the physical properties of speech in the areas of speech production, transmission, and perception. *Phonemics* deals with sounds that are specific to a particular language and distinguish one word from another in that language.

Idiosyncratic sounds specific to a particular language are often difficult to pronounce for non-native speakers. For instance, for Germans, French, Russians, and speakers of many other languages, the English phone /th/ (voiceless dental fricative /θ/ as in *thing* or voiced dental fricative /ð/ as in *this*) is not a distinct sound. Therefore, they often do not differentiate between /th/ and /z/, or between /th/ and /s/, pronouncing both as /s/. As a result, such words as *thong* and *song* are often pronounced in the same way, thus becoming indistinguishable (Celce-Murcia, Brinton & Goodwin 1996). By contrast, English speakers often have difficulties to pronounce the French /r/ as in *la fourrure* (fur), which is produced further back in the mouth than in English, and to roll the /r/ in Spanish, pronouncing words like *carro* (car) or *perro* (dog) (Martin & Nakayama 2017).

Phonic differences also exist within language areas. One of the most prominent distinctions by which phonic varieties of English can be classified is the pronunciation of the consonant /r/, i.e., whether rhotic or non-rhotic (derived from the Greek letter /ρ/) pronunciations prevail. All varieties of English retain a prevocalic r-sound of some type, but differ in the pronunciation of /r/ after vowels and before consonants and pauses. From the mid-eighteenth century onwards, postvocalic /r/ has been gradually deleted in most parts of England. By the early nineteenth century, the southern British standard was fully transformed into a non-rhotic or "r-less" variety. For example, a rhotic or "r-ful" English speaker pronounces the words *hard* and *butter* as /ˈhɑːrd/ and /ˈbʌtər/, whereas a non-rhotic speaker drops the "r"-sound, pronouncing them as /ˈhɑːd/ and /ˈbʌtə/ (Skandera & Burleigh 2011).

Today, non-rhotic accents are prevalent in most parts of England, New Zealand, Australia, and South Africa. Rhotic accents dominate in Scotland, Ireland, India, Pakistan, and North America. However, in some parts of the United States, such as Boston and New York, non-rhotic accents are common (Bauer 2003a). Historically, native New Yorkers vocalized /r/ in coda positions, following the pattern of the prestige dialects in England. However, over the past century, the prestige norm in the United States, based on Midwestern American English, has favored rhoticity in all positions, gradually displacing traditional New York City pronunciations. The increased use of /r/ is most common in careful speech and among members of the lower middle class who are most likely to be aware of prestige forms, accommodating to upper-middle-class speech (Labov 2006).

Particularly difficult for non-native speakers are languages that have **tonal differences**, such as Chinese, Thai and Vietnamese as well as many Bantu languages (spoken throughout Sub-Saharan Africa) and Kru languages (spoken from the southeast of Liberia to the east of Ivory Coast). For example, the modern Standard Chinese has four different tones but, compared to English, which consists of around 12,000 syllables, it has only 414 syllables (Song 2011). In oral communication, different meanings are therefore expressed in different tones (Duanmu 2007). For example, the syllable 'ma' can have four different meanings that depend on its pronunciation. Most Romanization systems, including pinyin, represent the tones as diacritics on the vowels (Table 6.3).

Unconscious phonic differences or incorrect pronunciations can lead to severe interferences. One approach to avoid them is to increase the redundancy of communication, e.g., by accompanying oral communication with written elements. For example, the meaning of the syllable "ma" is clearly designated by the respective Chinese character, as shown in Table 6.3.

Table 6.3 Example for tonal differences in Standard Chinese

Tone	Example		
	Character	Sound	Translation
First tone (high tone) is a steady high sound, produced as if it were being sung instead of spoken.	妈	mā	mother
Second tone (rising tone) is a sound that rises from middle to high pitch (like in the English "What?!").	麻	má	flax
Third tone (low or dipping tone) descends from mid-low to low; between other tones it may simply be low. Unlike the other tones, the third tone is pronounced with breathiness or murmur.	马	mǎ	horse
Fourth tone (falling or high-falling tone) features a sharp fall from high to low (as in curt commands in English, such as "Stop!").	骂	mà	to curse

6.2.1.2 Morphology

Morphology refers to the study of the smallest linguistic entities of a language with grammatical functions (morphemes) and how they are organized into words (lexemes) (Booij 2012). *Morphemes* consist of two elements: carriers of meanings and grammatical features (e.g., indicators of tense, case, and gender).

In verbal communication, morphemes are visually represented in letters or characters that constitute a writing system. Three major forms of **writing systems** exist (Daniels & Bright 1996; Coulmas 1989):

- Most writing systems use letters that represent different speech sounds (phonemes). *Alphabetic* or *morpho-phonetic writing systems* are based on a standard set of letters that follow a specific order. The most popular is the Latin alphabet consisting of 26 letters (5 vowels and 21 consonants) which many languages modify by adding letters formed using diacritical marks. The longest is the Khmer alphabet (used for Cambodian) with 74 letters.

Misunderstanding and confusion can be caused by neglecting or misusing **letters with diacritic marks** which are often not included in standard computer keyboards, such as "ñ", "ü", and "â". They are not only spelled differently compared to the related letters "n", "u", and "a" but can also change the meaning of words. For example, the Spanish *año nuevo* (new year) is different from *ano nuevo* (new anus), the German *schwül* (humid) is different from *schwul* (gay), and the French *tâche* (task) is different from *tache* (spot, mark).

- In *logographic* or *morpho-syllabic writing systems*, each character represents a semantic unit, such as a word or morpheme. Ancient examples are Egyptian hieroglyphs, Sumerian cuneiforms and Mayan glyphs. The most important existing logographic writing system is that of the Chinese, which characters have been used with various degrees of modification in other languages, such as Japanese, Korean, and ancient Vietnamese.

- *Syllabic systems* consist of a set of written symbols that represent the syllables which make up words. They typically represent an (optional) consonant sound followed by a vowel sound. Examples are Japanese, Cherokee, Yupik, and Vai. The contemporary Japanese language uses two syllabaries, namely *hiragana* and *katakana*, alongside the logographic Chinese characters called *kanji*.

A potential source of misunderstanding in intercultural communication is variations in **morphological processes** (Bauer 2003b). Grammatical information is typically given by *inflectional affixes*. For example, the plural "-s" added to the English word *firm* indicates that more than one firm is concerned, but it does neither change the grammatical category of the word nor does it produce a new lexeme. **Derivational affixes**, in contrast, are capable of creating a new lexeme from a base. They can both change the grammatical category of the word as well as its meaning. For example the derivational suffix "-al" to the noun *government* is used to produce an adjective, while the derivational prefix "non-" changes the meaning of the word without affecting its grammatical category.

In the Russian language, many terms are created through derivational morphology. This means, that added prefixes and suffixes change the meaning of the word rather than just the tense, aspect or number. A vivid example is the word ход (movement, passage) and its many variants, such as вход (entrance), выход (exit), исход (outcome), отход (departure), переход (crossing), подход (approach), приход (arrival), расход (consumption, expense), сход (descent) and уход (escape).

6.2.1.3 Syntax

Syntax involves the study of the structure of language and the rules for combining words into meaningful sentences (Crystal 2011). One basic description of a language's syntax is the **word order**, i.e., the sequence in which the main elements usually appear in a sentence. Most European languages, like English, French, German, Italian, Russian and Spanish, have a *subject–verb–object order*. A *subject–object–verb order* is characteristic, for example, for Hindi and most other Indo-Iranian languages, Japanese, Turkish, nearly all Tibeto-Burman languages, all Dravidian languages and virtually all Caucasian languages. While these two types account for more than 75% of natural languages with a preferred word order, there exist also languages with a *verb-subject-object order* (e.g., Biblical Hebrew, Arabic, Irish, and Filipino) and other variants (Tomlin 1986; Crystal 2010). Differences in word order complicate translation since, because in addition to changing the individual words, the word order must also be changed. This can be especially problematic when translating slogans, bon mots, jokes, puns, fixed expressions, etc.

Word order is particularly critical in languages with low or ambiguous inflection. For example, the German sentence "Das Kind tritt das Pferd" can—depending on the context and pronunciation—mean either "The kid hits the horse" or "The horse hits the kid." In case of intended

(Continued)

ambiguity, an equivalent translation in a language with fixed word order is almost impossible. If the ambiguity is not intended, the ignorance of the context can lead to misleading translation.

Another challenge of translation with regard to syntax is **idiosyncratic grammatical concepts**. While there is a certain set of structural rules innate to humans (universal grammar) (Chomsky 1965), languages often consist of specific grammatical concepts that have no equivalent in other languages. A vivid example is **verbs of motion** found in several Slavic languages. In Russian, for example, all verbs of motion have two aspects, an imperfective aspect and a perfective aspect. The perfective aspect is used for successfully completed actions, while the imperfective aspect signals incomplete, ongoing, interrupted or repeated actions. Many perfective aspects are created with derivational affixes (prefixes or suffixes) and are thus easy to recognize (Table 6.4). However, there is also a large number of unpaired verbs. In these cases, non-native speakers often find it difficult to relate the two aspects to each other, which can lead to misunderstanding. For example, in the sentence "The firm took a quality test last week" (фирма *прошла* тест качества на прошлой неделе), the use of the perfective aspect implies that the test was passed successfully. Using the imperfective aspect (фирма *проходила* тест качества на прошлой неделе) would imply that the result is unknown, or that the firm did not pass the test.

Table 6.4 Examples of paired and unpaired aspects in Russian language

	Imperfective aspect	Perfective aspect	English translation
Paired (with derivational prefixes or suffixes)	делать	сделать	to do
	работать	поработать	to work
	знать	узнать	to know
	замирать	замереть	to freeze
Unpaired	ходить	идти	to go
	проходить	пройти	to undergo
	вести	водить	to lead
	говорить	сказать	to talk, speak, say
	брать	взять	to take, get, obtain
	искать	найти	to find, discover, consider
	садиться	сесть	to sit

6.2.1.4 Semantics

Semantics covers the study of the literal, decontextualized, grammatical meaning of words and sentences. It contains the lexical stock of words and idioms for fundamental concepts and ideas that each language provides (Frawley 1992).

A key direction in intercultural semantics is the study of whether words in one language can be translated into other languages without losing or changing their meaning. Based on the idea of a universal *"alphabet of human thought,"* a concept originally proposed by the German philosopher Gottfried

Table 6.5 Universal semantic primes

Category	Primes
Substantives	I-Me, You, Someone, Something-Thing, People, Body
Relational substantives	Kind, Parts
Determiners	This, The Same, Other~Else
Quantifiers	One, Two, Some, All, Much~Many, Little~Few
Evaluators	Good, Bad
Descriptors	Big, Small
Mental predicates	Know, Think, Want, Don't Want, Feel, See, Hear
Speech	Say, Words, True
Actions, events, movement, contact	Do, Happen, Move, Touch
Location, existence, possession, specification	Be (Somewhere), There Is, Be (Someone)'s, Be (Someone/Something)
Life and death	Live, Die
Time	When~Time, Now, Before, After, A Long Time, A Short Time, For Some Time, Moment
Space	Where~Place, Here, Above, Below, Far, Near, Side, Inside
Logical concepts	Not, Maybe, Can, Because, If
Intensifier, augmentor	Very, More
Similarity	Like~Way~As

Source: Goddard & Wierzbicka (2014, p. 12).

Wilhelm Leibniz in the seventeenth century, Goddard and Wierzbicka (2014) suggest a specifiable set of universal semantic primes that can be literally translated in any language and retain their semantic representation. The current agreed-upon number of fundamental lexico-semantic primes of this **natural semantic meta-language** is 65 (Table 6.5). Semantic primes are innately understood, cannot be expressed in simpler terms and have a universal meaning. All other terms that are not semantic primes may not have exact *synonyms* in other languages. Thus, their translation bears the risk of losing or changing their meaning.

Although English has become a common means of communication for speakers of different languages and a global *lingua franca*, its lexical stock is not neutral and culture-free. Instead, it is deeply shaped by the country's history (Wierzbicka 2006) and carries the culture and language of its speakers (MacKenzie 2013). "There are many varieties of English, including native and non-native varieties (...). I speak English British-ly, Indian-ly, Japanese-ly and so on (...). The question is: How does one speak English interculturally?" (Baxter 1983, p. 306).

Even related languages may have **different lexical stocks** that can lead to interferences and misunderstandings. A vivid example is the English language. Through the worldwide influence of the British Empire, English has been spreading around the world and developed many local variations (Table 6.6):

- *American English* is the most important dialect of English globally. The language was brought to the United States by English immigrants in the sixteenth century. Since then, American English has become a distinct dialect, as reflected in the famous statement of George Bernard Shaw "America and Britain are two countries divided by the same language." The process of coining new lexical items started when English-speaking British-American colonists began borrowing names for unfamiliar flora, fauna, and topography from Native American languages. The languages of other colonizing nations, such as Dutch, French, German, and Spanish, also added to the American vocabulary. Later, particularly technological innovations, business, and sports promoted the development

Table 6.6 Examples of lexical differences between American, British, Australian, and Indian English

British English	American English	Australian English	Indian English
aubergine	eggplant	aubergine	brinjal
autumn	fall	autumn	autumn
barrister, solicitor	lawyer, attorney	barrister, solicitor	lawyer, attorney
bill	check	bill	bill
billion	trillion	billion	1 lakh crore
biscuit	cookie	biscuit, bikkie	bun, biscuit
brackets	parentheses	brackets	brackets
chips	French fries	chips	finger chips
diversion	detour	detour	diversion
electricity	electricity	electricity, current	current
flat	apartment, studio	flat	flat
field	paddock	field	field
lift	elevator	lift	lift
neighbourhood	neighborhood	neighbourhood	colony
note	bill	note	note
pavement	sidewalk	footpath	footpath
roundabout	traffic circle	roundabout	roundabout
share	stock	share	share
stock	inventory	stock	stock
supermarket	grocery store	grocery store, shop	general store, kirana store
toilet	bathroom, restroom	dunny, loo, toilet	toilet
yoghurt, yoghourt	yogurt	yoghurt	curd

of lexical items distinct from British English (Trudgill & Hannah 2017).

- *Australian English* is generally closer to British English, but also includes several loanwords from American English. It arose from the inter-mingling of early settlers coming from different regions of the United Kingdom. It differs considerably from other varieties of English in vocabulary, accent, pronunciation, register, grammar, and spelling (Trudgill & Hannah 2017).

- As a result of the British colonial rule until Indian independence in 1947, British English is an official language of India and by far the most important second language of most educated Indians. *Indian English* has been traditionally very close to British English but contains many loanwords from Hindi and other local languages. In the last few decades, many references to American English have also been incorporated (Sailaja 2009; Sedlatschek 2009).

Particularly challenging in intercultural communication are **homonyms**, i.e., words with the same or very similar spelling and pronunciation, but different meanings. Their correct interpretation largely depends on the context in which they are used. Moreover, senders and receivers of messages must be aware of their existence. Table 6.7 shows examples of "*false friends*," i.e., words that are spelled and pronounced similarly in English and German, but differ significantly in meaning.

Table 6.7 Examples of German-English "false friends"

German term	Translation	'False friend'	Meaning
Bank (Möbel)	bench	bank	bank (financial institution)
Brand	fire	brand	(trade)mark
Chef	boss	chef	cook
Fabrik	factory	fabric	textile
Fasten	fast (not eat)	fasten	attach
Gift	poison	gift	present
Gymnasium	high school	gymnasium (gym)	sports hall
Handy	mobile, cellphone	handy	practical, useful
Konzern	group (of companies)	concern	worry
Kraft	strength, force	craft	handiwork
Meinung	opinion	meaning	sense, significance
Minze	mint	mince	ground meat
Mist	dung, rubbish	mist	fog
Pathetisch	emotional	pathetic	miserable, pitiful
Präservativ	condom	preservative	means of protection
Quote	rate, proportion	quote	citation
Reklamation	complaint, claim	reclamation	recovery
Rock	skirt	rock	cliff (stone)
Stapel	stack	staple	metal paper clip
Tablett	tray	tablet	pill

Sources: Adapted from Dretzke & Nester (2009) and Shellabear (2011).

A vivid example of a homonym in British English and American English is the word "rubber." While this is a pencil eraser in British English, in American English, it is a synonym for condom. The use of this word by individuals who learned British English in the United States can therefore lead to serious misunderstanding.

6.2.1.5 Pragmatics

Pragmatics is the study of the relations between the elements of a language and the people who use them, i.e., their context, preexisting knowledge, inferred intent, and the relationships between senders and receivers. It relates to the actual use of language in different situations and its context-specific intentions and interpretations. The study of pragmatics takes into account that the same term can have different meanings in various situations. For example, formal language and complex sentences may be common and appropriate in certain cultural contexts, and unusual and regarded inadequate in others (Kecskes 2014).

Intercultural differences in pragmatics exist, for example, in the **expression of importance and urgency**. A statement that is understood as binding obligation in high-context cultures may be perceived as stimulating suggestion in low-context cultures. For example, Woodman (2003) analyzed the role of intercultural communication problems in the case of the failed acquisition of British carmaker Rover by BMW and found that German managers often underestimated the relevance of polite statements of their British colleagues, such as "I might tend to disagree" or "I'm not quite with you on that point." As one British manager at Rover mentioned: "I often find that the Germans speak English very well but have more difficulty in understanding the language" (cited in Woodman 2003, p. 74).

A vivid example of context-specific uses and interpretations of words is the **variety of negative replies** in different countries. In particular, many Asian cultures avoid saying "no" in a direct and explicit way, as this would lead to a loss of face and harmony. Whether "'yes' means 'yes,' or 'no,' or 'maybe'" (Brahm 2003) therefore largely depends on the exact wording as well as on the context, i.e., the accompanying non-verbal, para-verbal, and extra-verbal expressions. Table 6.8 summarizes different ways to say "no" in India.

The context-specific use of formal and informal language is reflected in the Japanese dualistic conception of honne (本音) and tatemae (建前). Tatemae ("façade") is the behavior a person displays in public. It refers to societal expectation and is expressed in formal language. Honne ("true sound") reflects a person's true feelings and opinions. It is expressed privately and with more informal language (Doi 1991).

The subtle linguistic differences between honne and tatemae are often difficult to detect by non-native speakers of Japanese. Thus, the uncertainty about whether a statement can be taken at face value or is a "white lie" can lead to serious misunderstandings.

Table 6.8 Different ways to say "no" in India

Ways to say 'no'	Examples
Giving a "no-response" response	Not answering emails
	Ignoring the question
Avoiding the question	Changing the subject
Postponing the response	"Can I get back to you?"
	"Let me ask my team"
Answering with a kind of qualifier	"That might be possible"
	"We'll try our best"
A vague answer	"We are almost nearby"
Repeating the question	"Well, that's an interesting question"
Responding with a question	"Do you think that's possible?"
A very loud silence	"Oh, yes. I remember"

Source: Adapted from Storti (2007, p. 43).

An important aspect of pragmatics is the use of **slang**. Slang is a colloquial variety of language that members of particular cultural subgroups speak to establish group identity. It distinguishes insiders from outsiders, i.e., insiders can understand what is being said, while outsiders cannot. Slang words are mostly used in oral communication and do not stay in the language for a long time (Dalzell & Victor 2014).

In many countries with a high density of migrants, a **hybridization of language** can be observed. A vivid example is *Kiezdeutsch*, an informal dialect spoken in multilingual urban neighborhoods. It emerged in Berlin and other large German cities, in particular among adolescent speakers, and is characterized by a linguistically diverse speech community, encompassing multilingual speakers with a range of different heritage languages (Wiese 2015).

Kiezdeutsch has a simplified grammar and features new constructions, such as the omission of particles and prepositions in certain contexts. It's also sprinkled with Arabic or Turkish words, such as *Yalla* (Arabic for "let's go"), *Ḥabībī* (Arabic for "buddy"), *Wallah* (a compressed form of the Arabic for "by Allah" which is used to mean "really") and *lan* (short for Turkish "ulan" and used to mean "guy" or "dude") (Gregson 2007).

Turkish-born author Feridun Zaimoğlu (2007) denotes this ethnolect as "Kanak Sprak". Kanak is a pejorative term for Turks and other immigrants from Southern Europe, the Middle East or North Africa that expresses their marginalization by mainstream German society. Kanak speech is often used in Hip-hop, films or in common language to emphasize a flamboyant manner, violent tendencies, and an affinity to crime and a status as an outcast from society. While mostly applied in a derogatory sense, Kanak speech has been reappropriated by some immigrants and spoken proudly as a form of self-identification (Gregson 2007).

The growing scope and intensity of intercultural relations favors the **adaptation of terms from other languages**. Borrowings of English terms are particularly common in countries where the United States as the largest English-speaking country has a positive image, such as Germany. English marketing and financial jargon is frequently used in advertisements and corporate communication for concepts like "shareholder value," "due diligence," "performance," "private equity," or "employer branding." While English loanwords are intended to give the speaker a fashionable and prestigious image, the mix of German and English (or pseudo-English) vocabulary (*Denglish*) is sometimes criticized as "linguistic submissiveness" (Elfers 2019). Borrowings of English loanwords are particularly disapproved when they are used in a misleading, distorting or manipulative manner—for example, when the meaning is deliberately left ambiguous.

William Shakespeare's line "What's in a name? A rose by any other name would smell as sweet" said by Juliet in his play "Romeo and Juliet" seems to be no longer true in an intercultural context. Instead, companies and individuals whose names are associated with their country of origin—for example, because they include idiosyncratic letters with diacritic marks such as umlauts (sound alterations)—sometimes change their name or its spelling. A prominent example is the former Siemens CEO Josef Käser. "In the nineties, the US became so much home to him that he even adapted his name. He made Joe Kaeser out of Josef Käser. At that time he was CFO of Siemens Microelectronics based in Silicon Valley. Today he is Siemens boss for the whole world and lives with his wife back in Lower Bavaria. He kept the name from America. He used to be the cheese maker Sepp. First the surname, then the first name, that's how it is in Lower Bavaria. And now, after the long journey from Sepp via Josef to Joe (...), the Bavarian color is still reminiscent of the Sepp of that time in his English" (Pletter 2019).

6.2.2 Para-Verbal Communication

6.2.2.1 Oral Communication

Para-verbal communication refers to the non-lexical properties of speech, i.e., all meaningful sound characteristics that are not phonemes. Since these sound characteristics usually accompany speech, they are also called **paralanguage**. The elements of para-verbal communication can be divided into voice set as background for, and voice qualifiers and vocalizations as accompaniments of, language (Trager 1958; Crystal 1969):

- The *voice set* consists of the configuration and interaction of the speech organs, such as tongue, lips and palate. It depends on a person's genetic and anatomic features (such as sex, age, body build, state of health), psychological features (such as personality and mood), and social features (such as place of origin and social status).

- *Voice qualifiers* are recognizable speech events which include gradable features, such as volume (loud vs. quiet), pitch (high vs. low frequency), intonation (variation in pitch), tempo or speed (fast vs. slow), rhythm (pulse, periodicity), and resonance (timbre, vibrations). Another important voice qualifier is fluency, i.e., the length of pauses between words and sentences as well as between two speakers.

- *Vocalizations* are specifically identifiable sounds which do not belong to the general background of speech. They can be subdivided into vocal characterizers, such as laughing, crying, yelling, whispering, sighing, swallowing, moaning, etc., and vocal segregates (verbal fillers), such as "um", "ah", "uh", etc.

While the study of paralanguage has mostly focused on its physiological and psychological features, research on the social and cultural aspects is scarce. The few existing studies in intercultural management research have particularly looked at cultural differences in vocal qualifiers, such as speech volume and silence.

Hall (1966) was one among the first to analyze cultural differences in **speech volume**. According to his studies, people in the Middle East speak loudly because they associate volume with strength and sincerity. Speaking softly would convey the impression of weakness. Similarly, people in Southern Europe and Latin America are louder in streets and public places than Anglo-Saxons. Germans, too, prefer a high volume when speaking is important. Asians, on the other hand, associate speaking softly with education and good manners. Speaking in a loud voice suggests a person lacks self-control.

Intercultural differences also exist with regard to the use of **silence** as an element of para-verbal communication (Figure 6.3):

- In the United States, speaking is highly valued. Talkativeness and eloquence are considered important leadership traits. On the contrary, silence may be perceived as a sign of hostility or rejection and interpreted as reflecting a lack of knowledge or verbal skills. The uncomfortableness with silence is often filled with comments on the weather (e.g., in the United Kingdom), sports (e.g., Germany) or other small talk (Hasegawa & Gudykunst 1998).

- People in many East Asian countries and–to a lesser degree—Scandinavia see silence as integral and important part of communication. The value of silence as a sign of respect and politeness is exemplified in the ancient proverb "Speech is silver, but silence is golden." Chinese, Japanese, and Koreans would consider a person who speaks without periods of silence as someone who lacks focus and reflection. Instead, the conscious use of silence allows people to reflect other

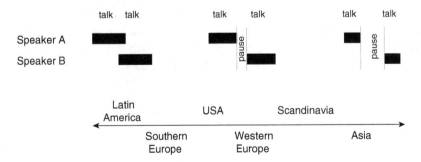

Figure 6.3 Use and value of silence in communication

Source: Based on Hampden-Turner & Trompenaars (2012).

peoples' ideas and to respond in a deliberate way (Nakane 2007).

- The other extreme is Southern Europe and Latin America. People typically speak faster, longer, and frequently interrupt each other. Statements of two individuals often overlap, i.e., a person may start speaking before the other person has fully completed their statement. Interruptions of others are not perceived as rude, but constitute a lively and authentic conversation (Albert & Ha 2004).

Talkativeness is also characteristic to many Indians. "Prolixity is not alien to us in India. We are able to talk at some length. Krishna Menon's record of the longest speech ever delivered at the United Nations (nine hours non-stop), established half a century ago (when Menon was leading the Indian delegation), has not been equaled by anyone from anywhere. Other peaks of loquaciousness have been scaled by other Indians. We do like to speak.

This is not a new habit. The ancient Sanskrit epics, the *Rāmāyaṇa* and the *Mahābhārata*, which are frequently compared with the *Iliad* and the *Odyssey*, are colossally longer than the works that the modest Homer could manage. Indeed, the *Mahābhārata* alone is about seven times as long as the *Iliad* and the *Odyssey* put together" (Sen 2005, p. 3).

6.2.2.2 Written Communication

A major direction of paralinguistics in written communication was traditionally the analysis of **handwriting styles**. *Graphology* aims to identify the writer's personality characteristics and their psychological state at the time of writing. Although the validity of graphology is increasingly called into question, it is still sometimes used as personnel selection method in France and—to a lesser degree—in Switzerland, Italy, Greece, and the Netherlands (Bangerter et al. 2009).

Another field of paralinguistics is the study of the **physiological effects of different writing systems**. While most Western languages are written and read from left to right (e.g., English, German, Russian, Spanish), there are also writing systems that go from right to left (e.g., Arabic, Farsi, Hebrew, Urdu), boustrophedon/bidirectional (e.g., Ancient Greek), vertical downward (e.g., Chinese, Japanese) and vertical upward (e.g., Ogam). A comparative study between Arab and English readers revealed, for example, that Native Arabic readers recognize Arabic words most efficiently when they fixate these words at their very center, while English readers read most efficiently by looking at a location between the beginning and middle of the word. This difference is explained by the fact that Arabic is read from right to left and words are formed from cursive text, i.e., the letters in Arabic naturally join together (even in printed formats), much like hand-written text in English (Jordan et al. 2014).

Differences in writing and reading direction can affect the perception of information in advertisements and on packaging, such as physiological and cognitive *conceptualizations of time*. For example, when individuals in Western countries image an action or sequence of events, they generally conceive of it as occurring from left to right. Native Arabic and Hebrew speakers, however, tend to have a past-right, future-left conceptualization of time. Chae & Hoegg (2013) also found that the congruence of the horizontal position of images in an advertisement with the cultural representation of time corresponds with the individual's attitude toward the advertised product. Moreover, *differences in attention and memory patterns* were observed. According to Hernandez et al. (2017), unidirectional readers (i.e., speakers of only Arab or English) pay less attention to verbal messages on the bottom right corner of a webpage than bidirectional readers (i.e., individuals speaking both Arab and English).

In **printed texts**, paralinguistics involves the physical layout of a page including such elements as punctuation marks, font, font size, line spacing, type area, etc. For example, a full stop "." signals readers to make a short pause and can therefore be interpreted as visual equivalent to a break in oral communication. Similarly, the font and font size of a word can emphasize its relevance and direct the readers' attention into a particular direction (Poyatos 2002).

The **layout of printed texts** differs remarkably between cultures (Bolten et al. 1996). In the United Kingdom and the United States, texts are often printed with disrupted columns and ragged types. Flowing transition between text and illustrations and the use of different stylistic elements should evoke a dynamic effect. In India, the variety of stylistic elements, such as fonts and font sizes, is even larger. For example, opulent ornamentation of texts is common (Rao & Thombre 2015).

In Germany, on the contrary, linear order of columns and block justification are usual. Text and illustrations are clearly separated and paralinguistic elements (e.g., font sizes, fonts, etc.) are used sparsely. This should induce an orderly impression (Bolten et al. 1996). Also in China and Russia, the physical layout of a page is usually less varied and stylistic elements are applied parsimoniously (Zhao 2008; Shubina 2009).

While, in contrast to oral communication, the spectrum of para-verbal elements in written communication is limited, electronic communication offers new opportunities to develop para-linguistic cues in the form of **ideograms**. For example, *semioticized punctuation marks*, such as ":)" (for "happiness") and ":(" (for "sadness"), that could be typed with a standard computer keyboard are frequently used in short messaging services (Tagg 2012). Some word processing programs translate certain strings automatically into *pictograms* or *emoticons*, such as "☺".

In social media applications, **emoji** became popular as equivalents of voice qualifiers in oral communication. Emoji are picture characters of facial expressions, common objects, places, animals, etc. aimed to transfer affective meaning. Originating on Japanese mobile phones in 1997, they were added to several mobile operating systems since the 2010s (Zappavigne 2012). As of September 2021, Unicode 14 provides a full list of 3,633 emoji (https://home.unicode.org/emoji/).

Although emoji are widespread across the world, their use and interpretation is highly *culture-specific*. Based on a data set of 3.88 mn. active users from 212 countries and regions, Lu et al. (2016) found strong relationships of emoji preferences with Hofstede's six cultural dimensions. The most significant correlations were revealed for individualism vs. collectivism and indulgence vs. restraint, with people in individualistic and indulgent societies using more happy emoji, while negative emoji are more common in collectivistic and restraint societies. Miller et al. (2016) found that only 4.5% of emoji symbols examined have consistently low intercultural variance in their sentiment interpretations. In 25% of the cases where participants rated the same rendering, they did not agree on whether the sentiment was positive, neutral, or negative. The results were even less consistent when the impact of platforms is considered, because the same emoji are rendered differently on different devices. Moreover, the level of internet exposure affects the use and interpretation of emoji (Takahashi, Oishi & Shimada 2017).

A survey by Swiftkey (2015) looking at over a billion instances of emoji use identified a number of **cultural differences in the spread of emoji** across the world. "Canadians score highest in emoji categories you might typically think of as 'all-American' (money, raunchy, violent, sports). The French use four times as many heart emoji than other languages, and it's the only language for which a 'smiley' is not number one. Arabic speakers use flowers and plants emoji four times more than average. Russian speakers are the biggest romantics, using three times as much romance-themed emoji than the average. Australia is the land of vices and indulgence according to the emoji data, using double the average amount of alcohol-themed emoji, 65% more drug emoji than average and leading for both junk food and holiday emoji. Judging by their use of emoji, Americans are the most LGBT, using these emoji more than others. Americans also lead for a random assortment of emoji & categories, including skulls, birthday cake, fire, tech, meat and female-oriented emoji."

6.2.3 Non-Verbal Communication

6.2.3.1 Oral Communication

Non-verbal communication is the transfer of meaning without the use of sounds. Since it involves different parts of the body, it is often called **body language**. It can take place consciously or unconsciously and either accompany, reinforce, replace, or occur independently of verbal messages. In oral communication, it includes eye contact (oculesics), touch (haptics) and body movement (kinesics) (Knapp, Hall & Horgan 2014; Burgoon, Guerrero & Floyd 2016; Remland 2016). While the latter is a physical action of one person (that may cause, however, subsequent physical and psychological reactions of others), eye contact and touch involve simultaneous physical activities of at least two persons.

Although the use and understanding of non-verbal communication varies significantly across cultures, there is **little systematic and comprehensive intercultural research**. Empirical studies mostly explore the prevalence of specific gestures and postures in different countries and point to the resulting "do's and don'ts" (Table 6.9). With regard to Schein's (1984) iceberg model of culture, they are thus restricted to the level of observable symbols without systematically analyzing their underlying norms, values and basic assumptions. Moreover, the majority of studies has a comparative methodology (often examining Western and Asian countries), while research on intercultural encounters between individuals with different non-verbal communication styles is scarce (Martin & Nakayama 2017; Jandt 2018; Neuliep 2018).

Eye contact is the most powerful form of non-verbal communication. When two people look at each other's eyes at the same time, an emotional relationship between them is built. Intercultural studies of *oculesics* indicate that the use of eye contact correlates with power distance (Andersen et al. 2003):

- Eye contact is appreciated in many Western countries with low power distance, such as Germany and the United States. It is typically interpreted as engagement, interest, attention, and involvement. Downcast eyes, on the contrary, are interpreted as a lack of confidence or

Table 6.9 Use of various elements of non-verbal communication across the world

Elements	Types		
Oculesics	*Gaze cultures*		*Gaze-avoiding cultures*
	Eye contact is appreciated and signals engagement, interest, attention and involvement. Lack of eye contact is interpreted as a lack of confidence or sign of uncertainty and subordination.		Eye contact with persons in superior roles is avoided. Downcast eyes are a sign of respect, attentiveness and agreement. Direct eye gaze is mostly interpreted as a threat or challenge to the person of higher power.
	Examples: Most Western and Latin American countries		Examples: Most Asian and Arab countries
Haptics	*Contact cultures*	*Moderate-contact cultures*	*Non-contact cultures*
	People touch frequently. Olfactory and tactile stimulation that comes with touching is enjoyed.	Occasional touch of hands and arms (of members of the same sex) is accepted and appreciated.	People avoid touch. Especially, the touch of the head is considered offensive.
	Examples: Latin America, Mediterranean Europe, northern Africa, Middle East	Examples: North America, northern Europe	Examples: China, India, Japan Thailand
Kinesics	*Expressive cultures*		*Temperate cultures*
	People show emotions openly and enthusiastically through gestures and facial expressions.		People avoid public displays of affection and intimacy through gestures and facial expressions.
	Examples: Arab countries, Latin America, Mediterranean Europe		Examples: Northern and western Europe, Asia

Sources: Compiled from Martin & Chaney (2012), Neuliep (2018), and Martin & Nakayama (2017).

sign of uncertainty and subordination. However, people are uncomfortable with unbroken gaze and may interpret this behavior as hostile or aggressive. People in Latin America look into each other's eyes in a more fleeting way. Prolonged eye contact may be interpreted as provocative or challenging.

• In cultures with large power distance, subordinates typically avert direct eye contact with persons in superior roles. For example, people in most Asian and Arab countries lower their eyes when speaking to a superior as a gesture of respect. Downcast eyes can also be a sign of attentiveness and agreement. On the contrary, direct eye gaze is mostly interpreted as a threat or challenge to the person of higher power.

Haptics refers to the use of touch in communication. Tactile communication includes greeting rituals (e.g., handshakes, kissing, hugging) and other gestures used to express the affective relationship between two people (e.g., holding hands, embracing, "high fives," shoulder tap, arm brushing).

Intercultural research of haptics mostly refers to Hall's (1966) concept of proxemics. It indicates that the most potent predictor of differences in touch is *latitude*. Touch is generally more accepted in warmer countries, with more sunlight, and nearer the equator. In cooler climates further from the equator, touch is less appreciated (Andersen 2011).

- *High-contact cultures* encourage touching and engage in it frequently. They enjoy the olfactory and tactile stimulation that comes with touching. Most countries close to the equator in Latin America, Mediterranean Europe, northern Africa and the Middle East are contact cultures.

Cheek kissing is a haptic gesture to indicate friendship, family relationship, perform a greeting, or confer congratulations. In cultures and situations where cheek kissing is the social norm, the failure or refusal to give or accept a kiss is commonly taken as an indicator of antipathy and may require an explanation, such as the person has a contagious disease like a cold.

In France, *faire la bise* is the most common form of greeting between females, males and females, and—particularly in the southern parts of the country—also between males. The French do not actually kiss each other. Instead, they put their cheeks against the other person's cheeks and make kissing noises. The number of kisses the French give varies across the country. While in Paris and most parts of the country, two kisses are common, people kiss three times in the southern parts of France (Auvergne, Rhône-Alpes and some parts of Languedoc-Roussillon). Four kisses are usual in Burgundy, and one kiss in Western Bretagne.

- Most western countries are *moderate-contact cultures*. For example, occasional touch of hands and arms (of members of the same sex) is accepted and appreciated in the United States. Black Americans and those living in the southern states tend to engage in more touch in conversations than white Americans and those living in the northern parts of the country.
- Virtually all Asian countries are *low-contact cultures*. People in China, India, Indonesia, Japan, Thailand, and many neighboring countries avoid public displays of affection and intimacy that involve touch. The touch of the head is in particular considered offensive. The reticence of Asian cultures about the display of public touch can be explained with the Buddhist and Confucian values of decorum and decency which disapprove any uncouth and flamboyant behavior.

Kinesics is related to movements of the body and its various parts (e.g., face, head, arms, hands, fingers, trunk, legs, and feet). Particularly in high-context cultures, body movements can send important non-verbal messages.

Intercultural communication research in the field of kinesics has mostly focused on the analysis of **facial expressions** (Ekman 2003). Based on Charles Darwin (1872), facial expressions have long been understood as universal. Also, the seminal study of Ekman and Friesen (1975) revealed that facial displays of six main emotions (happiness, sadness, anger, fear, disgust, and interest) are similar across cultures. However, cultures may differ in what stimulates an emotion, in rules for controlling the display of emotion, and in behavioral consequences. Moreover, cultural differences in the intensity with which emotions are expressed and perceived exist. The authors reasoned that people judge a foreigner's expressions to be less intense than expressions shown by members of their own culture due to higher uncertainty about the emotional state of a person from an unfamiliar culture.

More recent research questions the universality of facial expressions and suggests that cultural influences, such as individualism vs. collectivism, play a role in the expression of emotion (Andersen et al. 2003). For example, persons in individualistic cultures tend to smile more frequently. This is explained by the belief that individuals are responsible for their relationships and their own happiness. Persons in collectivistic cultures are more likely to suppress their emotional displays because maintaining group harmony is primary. They are also less comfortable expressing negative emotions, such as indignation, annoyance, and distrust, than persons from individualistic cultures.

Jack et al. (2012) showed in a comparative study between members of Western Caucasian and East Asian cultures that the latter show less distinction between emotional categories. Instead, considerable overlaps between surprise, fear, disgust, and anger were found. Moreover, the authors argue that the six basic emotions proposed by Ekman and Friesen (1975) (i.e., happiness, sadness, anger, fear, disgust, and interest) are inadequate to accurately represent the conceptual space of emotions in East Asian culture and likely neglect fundamental emotions such as shame, pride, or guilt (Jack et al. 2012).

With regard to **head movements**, intercultural differences in nodding and shaking the head to indicate agreement and disagreement exist. In most countries, nodding the head up and down expresses "yes" and shaking the head from side to side "no". However, the pattern is reversed in countries like Albania, Bulgaria, Greece, Iran, Sicily, and Turkey where head nodding means "no" (Andonova & Taylor 2012).

A typical gesture in India that is difficult to understand by foreigners is the peculiar head shake or wobble. Looking like a cross between a nod and shake, the head wobble is the non-verbal equivalent of the versatile Hindi word *achha* which can mean anything from "good" to "I understand." It can signal consent, acknowledge someone's presence, or be a gesture of kindness or benevolence. However, giving a vague wobble can also be a way of not making a firm commitment without being offensive. Some people will also give a vague and unenthusiastic wobble if they are feeling undecided or indifferent. The head wobble is more prevalent in south Indian states, such as Kerala and Tamil Nadu, whereas in the mountains of north India, the gesture is less common (Storti 2007).

Arms, hands, and finger movements vary widely across cultures in how they are used and what they mean. Their interpretation is particularly challenging when they are not accompanied by verbal messages, such as in the case of intercultural communication between persons who do not share a common language or deaf people (Mindess 2014).

A notable example is counting methods. It is estimated that across the world there are 27 different ways of counting with fingers (Nishiyama 2013). For example, Germans typically begin counting with the hand closed, i.e., with the "scissors, paper, stone" symbol for "stone." 1 is made with the thumb; 2 with the index finger and the middle finger or the thumb; and three with the index, middle finger, and thumb. Chinese people start with the index finger. 2 is made with the index finger and the middle finger. For 3, the index, middle and ring finger is used. 6 is made by extending the thumb and little finger from the "stone" position. It looks like

(Continued)

the gesture for a telephone. 7 is represented by extending the triple of the thumb, the index finger and the middle finger. 8 is represented by using the thumb and index finger, and opening them to form the Chinese character for 8 (八). 9 is represented by making the shape of the Chinese character for 9 (九), with the index finger. 10 is represented by crossing the index finger and the middle finger. This forms the Chinese character for 10 (十).

The possible consequences of counting the wrong fingers are illustrated in Quentin Tarantino's "Inglourious Basterds." In one scene, a British spy undercover as a German officer, orders another round of whiskey. He tells the bartender "Drei Gläser" ("Three glasses") and holds three fingers up–his index, middle, and ring finger. British typically count with the index finger as the first digit and end with the thumb to represent five. A true German, however, would have ordered "three" with the index, middle finger, and thumb extended (Pika, Nicoladis & Marentette 2009). The British spy realizes he has been outed as an imposter, and the entire bar erupts in a firefight.

"So if you were to hold up an index finger in Western Europe to represent one, they might misunderstand and think you actually meant two. Though you probably wouldn't be murdered like the spy in 'Inglourious Basterds,' you might have to pay for two beers instead of just the one. Moral of the story: The next time you're in Germany, order your drinks the Western European way and avoid a potentially fatal mistake"

(Willet 2014)

A common example of an emblematic finger gesture that may be used independent from speech is *pointing* (Kita 2003). In the United States, pointing with the index finger is common, while Asian cultures typically use their entire hand to point to something. In a number of cultures in the Americas, Africa and Asia, pointing is not made with the hand or fingers, but with movements of the head, lips or nose.

Statements on the meaning of hand gestures in different cultures often suffer from factual errors. A vivid example is the thumbs-up gesture that appears repeatedly in textbook on non-verbal communication and–as shown by Tipton (2008)–became an urban legend through frequent non-validated citations.

Cullen and Parboteeah (2005, p. 498) denote that "the thumbs-up gesture means 'everything is going well' for North Americans and many Europeans, but is a rude gesture in Australia and West Africa." Ball et al. (2006, p. 201) consider it a rude gesture in "southern Italy and Greece" while later mentioning "Italy and Australia" (Ball et al. 2006, p. 213). Hill (2006, p. 112) also says "thumbs up" is rude in Greece. According to Holt and Wigginton (2002, p. 341), the gesture "has an angry and obscene meaning in Latin American societies."

"Generalizations are hazardous, but at least in the case of Australia, the statement is categorically incorrect. The thumbs-up gesture in Australia means exactly what it means in North America, and no misunderstanding will result if a foreigner uses the gesture. Although it is difficult to say exactly, the notion may have migrated from a 1975 book (Condon & Yousef 1975, p. 120), to the quiz originally published in 1987 in Foreign Agriculture, a publication of the U.S.

Department of Agriculture and used by Donald Ball and his colleagues (Ball et al. 2006, p. 213), and then to another book originally published in 1991 (Axtell 1998, chapter 2)."

(Tipton 2008, p. 8).

Cultural differences in emblematic gestures are often related to the historical development of symbolic objects. For example, the crossed fingers for "good luck" were originally a surreptitious "sign of the cross" to signal that the person was a Christian. Later it became the sign of the cross to ward off Satan, and now it just stands for "good luck." While the gesture is common in Christian cultures, this emblem did not occur in non-Christian cultures (Morris et al. 1980).

In a study of gestures in six world regions, Matsumoto and Hwang (2013b) observed **three types of cultural differences** in emblems:

- First, there are *differences in the form of an emblem across cultures in relation to the same verbal message*. For example, gestures related to the verbal message "come" occur in all regions, yet the regions have different forms of the gesture for this verbal message. While in the United States and Western Europe, it is common to make repeated motions with the hand or fingers toward self, in many other regions people typically flutter or curl four fingers toward self.

- Second, the *same gestures may have different meanings*. The "ring," for instance, in which a circle is made with the thumb and index finger and the other three fingers are open, can mean "ok" in the United States and "no money" in Latin American countries. Also, bringing both hands together in the front and bowing has multiple meanings across cultures, such as "thank you," "hello," and "goodbye."

Misunderstandings that may result from different interpretations of gestures across cultures are illustrated in the following fictional encounter between a cowboy and an Indian: "A cowboy and an Indian meet on the prairie. The Indian points at the cowboy with his forefinger. In response, he raises his forefinger and middle finger, spread apart. The Indian folds his hands in front of his face. Then the cowboy shakes his right hand loosely. They both ride away.

The cowboy arrives home and tells his wife, "Just imagine, I met a redskin today. With his forefinger, he threatened to shoot me. At this, I signified with my hand that I would shoot him twice. And as he promptly pled for mercy, I indicated to him that he should clear off."

In a wigwam some miles to the west, the Indian tells his squaw, "Just imagine, I met a paleface today. I asked him, 'What's your name?' To this he replied, 'Goat'. Then I asked him, 'Mountain goat?' 'No, river goat.' he answered" (Koch, Krefeld & Oesterreicher 1997, p. 57).

- A third type of difference is *culturally unique emblems*. For example, 'flicking a finger on the neck' is a gesture only used in Russia. According to the legend, an unknown Russian craftsman offered some sound engineering advice during the building of the Peter and Paul fortress in Petersburg. As a result, Peter the Great offered the man any reward he desired, so the craftsman asked to be branded with a sign on his neck that allowed him to drink for free in any Russian tavern—the craftsman would just come in, point to his scar, and get drunk free of charge (Manaev 2018).

Trunk movements are often used as gestures of greeting or respect. While many trunk-related gestures, such as curtsy and kowtow, have mainly historic relevance or are used only in specific situations (e.g., in front of royalty or religious contexts), others are still common in some cultures. An example is *bowing*, i.e., lowering the torso and head in direction to another person or symbol. Several degrees of the lowness of the bow are regarded as appropriate for different circumstances and social encounters. Bowing is most prominent in Asian countries, such as Cambodia, China, India, Japan, Korea, Laos, Nepal, Thailand, and Vietnam.

The significance of bowing as a sign of apology in Japan is illustrated in the case of the Swiss elevator manufacturer Schindler. After a 16-year-old boy died in an elevator accident in Tokyo in 2006, the company was harshly criticized for its businesslike communication and insensitivity toward the victim's family. Only after Schindler's president Roland Hess flew into Tokyo and offered a Japanese-style bow during a live-broadcasted news conference, the Japanese public accepted the company's apology (Kalbermatten 2011).

Finally, **legs and feet movements** are used and interpreted differently across cultures. For example, in the United States, men often cross their legs by placing the ankle on the knee to signal a relaxed attitude. Europeans, Asians, and Middle Easterners view the crossing of the legs mostly as inappropriate. Particularly, people in India and Arab countries avoid sitting with the sole of their foot pointing at another person because this is—like the left hand—considered unclean. Instead, people prefer standing or sitting with their legs in a parallel position with their body weight equally placed on both feet.

Gestures can send strong political messages across cultures. One of the most iconic gestures of a politician in the twentieth century was the genuflection of the former German chancellor Willy Brandt in Warsaw on December 7, 1970. After laying down a wreath at the monument to the Nazi-era Warsaw Ghetto Uprising, Brandt, very surprisingly, and to all appearances spontaneously, knelt. With his head bowed low, he remained silently in that position for twenty seconds. "I have been often asked what the gesture was all about. Was it planned? No, it wasn't. As I stood on the edge of the Germany's historical abyss, feeling the burden of millions of murders, I did what people do when words fail" (Brandt 1989, p. 214).

6.2.3.2 Written Communication

In written communication, non-verbal elements can accompany or replace textual messages. They include, for example, colors, numbers, symbols, and pictures (Czinkota & Ronkainen 2012; Ghauri & Cateora 2014; de Mooij 2019; Alon et al. 2020).

The meaning of **colors** differs significantly across cultures—with large context-specific variations (Evans 2017). For example, white is mostly associated with weddings, angels, doctors, peace and purity in Europe and North America, while it symbolizes unhappiness, death and funerals in China, India, and Japan. Accordingly, widows wear white clothes in India while they are typically dressed in black in Western countries. Red is the symbol of luck in China, while it symbolizes both danger and love in Western countries. In Germany, brown is associated with Nazism (Table 6.10).

Table 6.10 Interpretations of colors across the world

Color	Asia	Europe	Africa	Americas
Black	Wealth, health (Far East), evil, ward off evil (India), bad luck (Thailand)	Death, funerals, anarchism, fear, anger, despondency	Funerals, death, evil (Middle East), jihadism, wisdom (Africa)	Mourning, religion, respect, fear, anger, envy, jealousy (Mexico)
Blue	Mourning (Iran, Korea), immortality (China), Krishna, sport (India)	Depression, tradition, authority, calm, peace, hope, liberalism	Protection (Middle East), mourning, spirituality (Iran)	Trouble (Cherokee), mourning (Mexico), Democratic Party (USA)
Brown	Land (Aboriginals), mourning (India)	Dependable, wholesome, Nazism (Germany)	Earth	Disapproval (Nicaragua)
Green	Adultery (China), hope (India), new life, fertility (China, Far East), eternal life (Japan)	Irish, spring, Christmas, good luck, jealousy, environmentalism	Corruption, drugs (North Africa), hope (Egypt), strength, fertility (Middle East), prestige (Saudi Arabia), Islam	Death (South America), money (USA)
Orange	Buddhism, Hinduism, sacred (Hindi), happiness	Religion (Ireland), Halloween, Royals (Netherlands), post-communist democratic revolutions (Eastern Europe)		Halloween
Red	Good luck, bride, long life (China), purity, fertility, power (India), earth (Aboriginals), life (Japan), sacrifice (Hebrew)	Danger, love, Christmas, socialism, communism	Mourning (South Africa), chiefs (Nigeria)	Success triumph (Cherokee), Republican Party (USA)
Purple	Mourning, misfortune (China, Korea, Thailand), wealth (Japan), sorrow (India)	Royalty, mourning, feminism	Mourning (Middle East)	Mourning (Brazil), feminism
White	Death (China, Japan), funerals, unhappiness (India), Parseism	Weddings, angels, doctors, peace, purity	Victory, purity	Light, cool, purity
Yellow	Nourishing, royalty (China), courage (Japan), wisdom (Buddhism), sacred, mourning (Burma), Lamaism	Happiness, hope, warmth, cowardice, hazards (with black)	Mourning (Egypt), prosperity (Middle East), highest ranked people (Africa)	Sunny, hope, cowardice

Sources: Compiled from Peterson & Cullen (2000), Aslam (2006), and Brown (2016).

Colors may be linked to a particular nationality, such as green to Ireland, orange to the Netherlands, and bleu, blanc, rouge (*tricolore*) to France. Also, references to religions are common, such as green to Islam, orange to Buddhism and Hinduism, yellow to Lamaism, and white to Parseism. In Christianity, colors reflect different periods in the liturgical year.

Colors are frequently used to describe political parties. In Germany, for example, "black" stands for the Christian Democratic Party/Christian Social Union, "red" for the Social Democratic Party, "green" for the Green Party, "yellow" for the Free Democratic Party, "dark red" for the Left Party, and "blue" for the Alternative for Germany. Also, the various coalitions that emerge in German elections on the national, state, and municipal level are often described with colors, traffic lights and even foreign flags. "Black-red" stands for a grand coalition of the Christian Democrats with the Social Democrats, and "red-green" for a coalition between the Social Democrats and the Greens. "Traffic light" or "Senegal" describes a coalition between the Social Democrats, the Liberals and the Greens, and "Kiwi" a coalition between the Christian Democrats and the Greens. The term "Jamaica Coalition" refers to the coincidence that the symbolic colors of the conservative Christian Democratic Party, the liberal Free Democratic Party and the Green Party are also the colors of the flag of Jamaica. It also alludes to the perception (from a German point of view) of such an alliance as an "exotic" constellation. Similarly, "Kenya Coalition" stands for the coalition between the Christian Democratic Party, the Social Democratic Party and the Green Party. A "Zimbabwe Coalition" would also involve the Free Democratic Party, while a "Bahamas Coalition" consists of the Christian Democratic Party, the Free Democratic Party and the Alternative for Germany.

Differences in color associations and preferences are particularly relevant for **marketing communication**. For example, Madden, Hewett, and Roth (2000) explored the extent to which consumers in different countries like various colors and the meanings they associate with them. They found that the colors blue, green, and white are all well liked across countries and share similar meanings. In contrast, black and red also received high liking ratings, yet in many cases their meanings are considerably different. They also reported that East Asians tend to make greater distinctions among colors in terms of their affective meaning compared to North and Latin Americans.

Intercultural differences in non-verbal communication also exist with regard to **numbers**. Various cultures consider certain numbers superstitious. For example, 13 is regarded as unlucky number in Germany and the United States. Many buildings in these countries therefore omit floor 13. Similarly, row 13 is usually missing in planes. In China, the pronunciation of the word for the number 4 "sì" (四) is similar to the word for death "sǐ" (死). 8 "bā" (八) is a lucky number as it is pronounced similar to the word "fā" (发), which means "wealth," "fortune," and "prosper." It is common to consider this numerology when planning major events, such as weddings. For example, the opening ceremony in the Beijing Summer Olympics began on 8/8/08 at 8:08 pm.

Symbols are marks or signs that are understood as representing an idea, object, or relationship. While many symbols have a universal meaning and are used across the globe (e.g., white pigeon or Aesculapian staff), others are specific to certain contexts and cultures. For example, the meaning of religious symbols is often understood by their particular devotees, only. Particularly challenging in intercultural communication are symbols that have different meanings in different cultures. An example is the swastika which is regarded as symbolic expression of Nazism in Germany, while it symbolizes peace and harmony in Buddhism, Jainism, and Hinduism (Nakagaki 2018).

Probably the largest intercultural differences in extra-verbal communication can be observed in the use and interpretation of **pictures**. With regard to their composition, Kitayama et al. (2003) revealed significant perceptual differences between individualistic and collectivistic cultures. People in collectivistic cultures, such as Japan, are better at incorporating contextual information during perception of a focal object, while people in individualistic cultures, such as the United States, put less emphasis on contextual information when perceiving a focal object.

Berning and Holtbrügge (2016) analyzed the interpretation of pictures published in the German media about Chinese acquisitions of German firms. They found that the Chinese respondents usually started with a statement about the background. The entire setting of the picture was important for understanding and interpreting. Persons and foreground objects were always mentioned at the end of the description. All Chinese participants had difficulties to understand and comment pictures with artificial, non-realistic backgrounds. In contrast, the German participants paid more attention to the focal objects and perceived the pictures analytically. When a picture contained a person, they focused on him/her and his/her features. In cases where a focal object could not be identified, the German participants were confused and unable to give a well-grounded interpretation.

The use of non-verbal elements of communication is particularly relevant in the design and perception of **websites**. Comparative studies in this context mostly analyzed the impact of context orientation with regard to Hall (1976). For example, Würtz (2005) showed that websites of companies in high-context cultures use animation more frequently, especially in connection with images of moving people. In low-context cultures, animation is mainly reserved for highlighting effects, e.g., of text. Low-context cultures are also more consistent in the use of colors. Usunier and Roulin (2010) found that websites from companies in low-context countries are easier to find, use colors and graphics more purposefully, and make navigation more user-friendly than websites from high-context communication countries. In many studies, however, the results are not consistent and effect sizes are relatively small. Moreover, the impact of national culture on the use of non-verbal elements in websites is moderated by a number of other factors, such as corporate culture, industry culture, firm size, etc. (Usunier, Roulin & Ivens 2009).

6.2.4 Extra-verbal Communication

6.2.4.1 Oral Communication

Extra-verbal communication refers to factors which are not directly linked to the act of communication, but inherent to the wider context in which it takes place. In oral communication it includes mainly time, location, clothing, and physical appearance (visible, tactile and odoriferous aspects).

The **use of time** in communication correlates highly with power distance (Levine 1997). In cultures with high power distance, letting others wait is a common extra-verbal indicator of power asymmetries. Lateness is often used by people in higher social ranks to signal their status and relevance. In cultures with low power distance, appointments, and meetings typically start on time. Those present will usually not wait for latecomers. Punctuality communicates equality, reliability, and the supremacy of abstract rules over personal relations.

"Russian President Vladimir Putin did not invent being late, but he may have perfected it as a power play and means of communication (...). Putin kept Trump waiting in a guest house for nearly one hour past his planned departure time (...). Putin once made German Chancellor Angela Merkel wait for four hours, and he usually keeps the president or prime minister of Ukraine waiting for three hours." However, as Jonathan Eyal, a Russia expert at the Royal United Services Institute, mentions, "Putin seems to have a very healthy respect for monarchs (...). The British queen, he was only late for her for 14 minutes. The king of Spain he only kept waiting for 20 minutes (...). On the whole, it's a sort of graduated thing that indicates more or less how seriously he takes you or how pleased he is with you" (Lockie 2018).

The **choice of location** is another important element of extra-verbal communication. Meetings in Western countries often take place in locations that can be conveniently reached by all participants, such as meeting rooms in hotels or at airports. Augé (1992) calls these locations *non-places* because they look similar across the world, are highly anonymous and lack authenticity. In Asia, locations with symbolic value (e.g., historic sites) are often selected. The significance of the place signals the relevance of the meeting or attendees.

The choice of location can also affect the impression of reading. "When we prepare to read, for instance, a novel, we find ourselves in a concrete place whose characteristics can consciously or unconsciously affect our reception of it, that is, the recreation of that narrative: a public library, a park bench, the presence of nature that might seem to blend with the fictional world or strike certain chords in the reader, a noisy cafeteria (where nevertheless we can attain that typical 'public privacy'), a night flight, a train or bus that takes us to, or brings us back from, a desired or undesired place; after a satisfying meal, or while savoring (even though for only a few minutes) a cup of coffee, by a fireplace (perhaps with a storm raging outside), or cozily in bed (our own or at an hotel where we brought our book); or in the cold, or with poor lighting" (Poyatos 2002, p. 26).

A specific aspect of location choice on the microlevel is the **seating arrangement**. In many Asian countries, the seating arrangement reflects the hierarchical order between the attendees. According to Chinese cosmology, the south represents the symbol of supreme authority, power and position, that from the architecture of the Forbidden City in Beijing to daily banquets, the most honorable seat is facing south, while the seat facing north is comparatively less important (Chen 2018). Therefore, the most honorable person (in most cases the principal guest) is usually seated facing the south or door. The principal host will be sitting alongside. The second-ranking guest and second-ranking host will be placed at the other side of the table (Figure 6.4). This seating arrangement often irritates Westerners who mostly prefer sitting alongside their team members with the other team sitting at the opposite side of the table. This allows for informal and confidential conversations among the team members during negotiations. Moreover, Westerners are more comfortable to talk to people in front of them, while Asians avoid direct confrontation.

Clothing and physical appearance include the visible, tactile and odoriferous signals people send in encounters with others. In several countries, proverbs about the communicative function of clothes exist, such as "Clothes make people" ("Kleider machen Leute"), "Dress for Success," and "Good clothes open all doors"

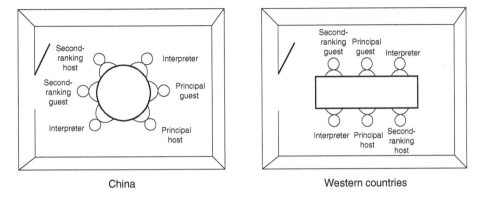

Figure 6.4 Typical seating arrangements in Asia and Western countries

("Приличная одежда открывает все двери"). Consequently, there are many guidebooks about proper dress code and etiquette which make stereotypical advices like "Men should wear dark suits," "Women should wear costumes or skirts that are at least knee length" and "Make sure you always have neat professional hairstyle, light make-up, moderate amount of perfume, manicured nails and fresh breath" (http://etiquette-tips.com/office-etiquette/want-to-know-about-business-professional-dress-code). These are often accompanied with tips about avoiding clothing *faux pas*, such as "If you're unsure about what to wear, your safest bet is to dress conservatively" and "The best way to decide what to wear is to dress similarly to your coworkers in the country" (https://www.mindtools.com/pages/article/avoiding-cross-cultural-faux-pas-clothing.htm).

Such recommendations about dress code are not only *unsubstantiated* and *contradictory* but also *confound empirical observations of locals with normative requirements for foreigners*. With regard to Schein's (1984) iceberg model of culture, they are restricted to the level of observable symbols without systematically analyzing their underlying norms, values and basic assumptions. Moreover, guidebooks mostly describe the prevalence of clothing styles in different countries, while research about intercultural encounters between individuals with different clothing styles and the consequences of not assimilating to local dress codes is scarce.

Comparative studies show that egalitarian cultures with low power distance (e.g., the United States) typically emphasize more on comfort than on style, which in turn is more emphasized in hierarchical cultures (such as, for example, Russia). Moreover, clothing styles of people with different social and organizational status are more similar in cultures with low power distance, while distinctive clothing is an important signifier of social roles and economic wealth in cultures with large power distance. In masculine cultures (e.g., Italy, Japan, Mexico), the clothing styles of men and women differ more significantly than in feminine cultures (e.g., Scandinavia) where clothes are more androgynous and less gender-specific (Solomon & Rabolt 2008).

The **dress code for women in Islamic countries** is particularly strict. According to the traditional Islamic law (*Shari'a*), women must cover everything except their hands and faces. As stated in the *Qur'ān* (chapter 24, verse 31): "And say to the believing women that they should lower their gaze and guard their modesty; that they should not display their beauty

(Continued)

and ornaments except what (must ordinarily) appear thereof; that they should draw their veils over their bosoms and not display their beauty."

In secular Muslim countries like Egypt, Tunisia, and Turkey, women often wear a *hijab*–a veil that covers the head and chest and may be worn in a tightly- or loosely-fitting form. In Saudi Arabia, the *niqab* is most common. It also covers a woman's face, except for her eyes. The *chador*, a full cloak that covers the entire body and the hair, is worn by many women in Islamic Orthodox countries, such as Iran and Pakistan. Women in Afghanistan and regions under the rule of the Islamic State are often forced to wear a *burka* that covers the entire head and has translucent veil which hides the eyes.

While veiling is a legal and social norm in many Islamic countries, there are also Muslim women who decide to wear a veil by their own will. "The veil became (...) a mode of resisting West-ernization and the commodification of the native Muslim woman for the white male gaze. In other words, the voluntary return to and adoption of the veil becomes a liberatory move where the Muslim woman rejected the excessively Western and consumer culture in favor of her own traditions (...). Postcolonial feminism explicitly situates the *woman's right to choose the veil* as a marker of her identity (...). True, the women here *might choose to belong to a patriarchal, cultural nationalist framework that is not congenial to the woman's freedom, but it still remain a 'free will' of a kind*. Does the autonomy of the individual–to choose the *burqa* or the beauty parlor (...)–contradict, contest or endorse the patriarchal space of culture?" (Nayar 2010, p. 157).

While research about dress code is mostly based on comparative methodologies, few studies analyze intercultural perceptions of foreigners with different clothing styles. They often focus on Muslim women's clothing in non-Muslim countries and show that wearing culturally specific clothes may have negative **stereotyping effects**. For example, Choi, Poertner, and Sambanis (2019) revealed in an empirical study in Germany that immigrant women wearing a *hijab* receive significantly less assistance during everyday social interactions relative to immigrants without a *hijab* or those wearing a cross. Muslim women wearing a *hijab* are perceived as less intelligent (Mahmud & Swami 2010) and a source of scrutiny and suspicion in countries with Muslim minorities (Sayed & Pio 2010). Moreover, they are faced with significant discrimi-nation on the labor market and obstacles to reach senior management positions (Arar & Shapira 2016).

From a **postcolonial perspective**, it is often criticized that the standard Western business attire is seen as global norm and all other forms of clothing (e.g., kaftan, kurta, kippah, sari, turban, etc.) as exotic deviations (Maynard 2004). Members of cultural minorities are therefore expected to assimilate to the putative universal style. Particularly in the work context, individuals are often advised to hide their cultural and religious differences and to confirm with the clothing style of the majority. Although anti-discrimination laws forbid discrimination based on appearance in many countries, the symbolic persuasion to fit dominant modes of clothing is often substantial.

For a long time, elegant business attire was common in Germany. Executives usually wore dark suits and ties. Recently, however, this is changing and more and more CEOs are appearing in smart casual.

"Clemens Graf von Hoyos, Chairman of the German Knigge Society and therefore the country's supreme guardian of good manners, is observing a 'new casualness' (...). The fact that business is moving in this direction has a lot to do with demographic change. The number of young people continues to fall, and good university graduates have long been able to pick and choose their employers (…). Members of the freedom-loving Millennial Generation find it less attractive to join a traditional business corporation with all its departmental, divisional and sectoral managers and their associated reporting channels. By appearing in public in their shirt-sleeves, bosses are signaling: we may look old, but inside we are young and dynamic (…). For women, however, this only applies to a limited degree (…). Female executives in Germany usually stay with their trouser suits. There's not much room for experimentation when you want to be taken seriously."

(https://www.deutschland.de/en/topic/business/careers-work/take-it-easy)

6.2.4.2 Written Communication

Like in oral communication, extra-verbal elements in written communication refer to the wider context in which it takes place. This includes, for example, the selection of media and the use of time.

As demonstrated by McLuhan (1964), the **selection of media** serves not only a technical function, but has also a *symbolic meaning* that may differ across cultures. Comparative research particularly analyzed the impact of content orientation and power distance on media selection. Richardson and Smith (2007) argue that members of high-context cultures see greater benefit in using a medium that is able to carry more non-verbal cues (e.g., eye gaze, facial expression, etc.) and extra-verbal cues (e.g., room settings, clothes, etc.), such as face-to-face communication and video conferences compared to telephone calls, emails, and letters. In their study of American and Japanese students' media choice, however, they found only weak support for their argumentation.

Huang et al. (2003) revealed that power distance has a significant effect on whether emails are an acceptable medium of communication. Emails do not have the ability to embed symbols and cues that can display status and respect. Therefore, they are less accepted in cultures with high power distance. In low power-distance cultures, on the contrary, the relationship aspect of communication is less relevant than the content aspect (Trevino, Lengel & Daft 1987). Therefore, the lack of symbols and cues is not considered problematic (Leonard, Scotter & Pakdil 2009).

The **use of time** in written communication refers mainly to the frequency and response time of messages. Holtbrügge, Weldon, and Rogers (2013) revelad that monochronic cultures value *promptness* in email communication while emphasizing *preciseness* at the same time. Answers are usually expected to be received within a short period of time of 24–48 hours. Although emails typically arrive unexpectedly, they—in contrast to people entering the room or telephone calls—do not require immediate response, but can be answered at a convenient time. Thus, they may not be perceived as major distraction in linear-segmented schedules and agendas. On the contrary, polychronic cultures view promptness more fluidly. Individuals accept longer response time when messages are regarded as less relevant. Moreover, the need for preciseness is lower.

A current example of the relevance of timing as element of para-verbal communication is the media industry. Traditionally, TV series have been broadcasted in a linear way, for example

(Continued)

one episode a week on the same day and at the same time. This linear business model has been disrupted by video streaming services, such as Amazon Prime and Netflix, which offer entire seasons of TV series as box sets on-demand. Thus, viewers do no longer depend on media corporations' schedules, but can decide autonomously and watch, for example, several episodes of a single TV series in one sitting (*binge watching*). This shift from external to internal locus of control is particularly relevant for people in individualistic and low power-distance cultures, such as the United States where binge watching is most common (Jenner 2017).

6.3 LANGUAGE AND COGNITION

Language is not an objective means to *describe* reality but also *constructs* reality. Particularly the interpretative concept of culture posits that language and cognition are interrelated. Already Wittgenstein (1922, 5.6) noted: "The limits of my language mean the limits of my world." In a similar vein, Sapir (1929, p. 209) postulated. "The 'real world' is to a large extent unconsciously built up on the language habits of the group. No two languages are ever sufficiently similar to be considered as representing the same social reality. The worlds in which different societies live are distinct worlds, not merely the same world with different labels attached."

According to the **Sapir-Whorf Hypothesis**, the language people speak affects and reflects their perception of reality. People have a more differentiated perception of their world if their language is more complex. In turn, the environment in which people live shapes the development of their language. The lexical stock of a language is usually more differentiated in areas that are particularly relevant in the respective language area. For example, it was found that the Eskimo languages have considerably more words for "snow" and use them in a more differentiated way than English native speakers (Krupnik & Müller-Wille 2010). Similarly, Arabic is rich in terms to describe camels and camel-riding equipment, which have no equivalent in the English language (Kashgary 2011). Thus, people who live in an environment in which certain phenomena or objects play an important role are more aware of their different characteristics and appearances and able to describe them in more detail than people in other environments.

An example of the **differentiated lexical stocks of languages** is given by Lewis (2018, p. 8) who found that Zulu—a Bantu language spoken in South Africa—has 39 words for "green": "In the days before automatic transport and national highways, the Zulu people would often make long treks across their savannah grasslands. There were no signposts or maps and lengthy journeys had to be described by those who had traveled the route before. The language adapted itself to the requirements of its speakers. English copes with concepts such as contract deadlines and stock futures, but (the) tongue is seen as poverty stricken and inadequately descriptive by Africans and Native Americans, whose languages abound in finely wrought, beautiful logical descriptions of nature, causation, repetition, duration and result."

Several empirical studies of the **influence of the natural conditions on the development of language** exist. Regier, Carstensen, and Kemp (2016) found that the complexity of the lexicon in several semantic domains correlates with societal complexity, and societal complexity tends to be lower in regions near the equator. Thus, languages spoken in warm regions might tend to have fewer and broader semantic categories than languages spoken in countries closer to the poles. For example, the latter tend to have different words for "snow" and "ice," while languages spoken in warmer climates often have only one word. This association appears to be mediated by the communicative need to talk about snow and ice. Thus, variations in semantic categories across languages are traceable in part to local communicative needs.

Winawer et al. (2007) conducted a color matching experiment with English and Russian speakers that relates to the concept of **categorical perception**. It is based on the observation that several continua, such as colors, musical tones and facial expressions, are perceived as a discontinuous set of discrete categories. The number and organization of these categories vary considerably between languages. For example, Russian makes an obligatory distinction between "синий" (siniy—dark blue) and "голубой" (goluboy—light blue). There is no single generic word for "blue" in Russian that includes the entire spectrum of shades which English speakers usually associate with this color. In order to analyze whether these differences in the native languages impact categorical perception, the participants were simultaneously shown three color squares and asked to say which of the two color squares shown at the bottom of the screen was perceptually identical to the square shown on top. When asked to select which of two colors matched a "siniy" target, participants were faster if the distractor was "goluboy" than if it was a different shade of "siniy" and vice versa. English speakers, who would call all the stimuli "blue," did not show the same cross-category advantage. The authors explained this categorical advantage of Russian speakers in this experiment with the fact that they—unlike English speakers—*cannot avoid distinguishing* between light and dark blues. Thus, language forces people to attend to certain aspects of their experience by making them linguistically obligatory. "Languages differ in what they *must* convey and not in what they *can* convey" (Jakobson 1959, p. 236).

The circular relationship between language and cognition is extensively discussed in the debate about **political correctness** (Hughes 2010). Their advocates argue that language reflects the values of dominant social groups and therefore often offends and marginalizes persons of other genders, ethnicities, religions, sexual orientations, abilities, or social classes. To avoid this verbal discrimination, the use of neutral or inclusive terms is suggested that minimize assumptions about the background of people. For example, in English, the third-person pronoun "he" may be avoided by using gender-neutral alternatives, such as singular "they" or "he or she." Critics regard political correctness as a form of censorship and confusing language. Moreover, they argue that the avoidance of discriminatory speech will not end discriminatory mindsets and practices (Maass, Suitner & Merkel 2014).

The strive for politically correct language is particularly strong in the United States. The focus is on avoiding offensive, derogative and exclusive terms with regard to ethnicity, age and people with disabilities. In contrast, the discourse about gender plays a less important role than, for example, in Germany and France. These intercultural differences can be explained by differences in grammar and lexical stocks. While the genus disappeared almost completely in English grammar, French and German language often use male generic terms. In Germany, the Act on General Equal Treatment therefore requires gender-neutral

(Continued)

descriptions of professions and job tasks (Wiemann 2010). On the contrary, France has banned the use of inclusive language in official documents in 2017 for reasons of linguistic clarity and simplicity (Muguet 2017).

Chen (2013) tested whether languages with strong **time reference** (e.g., English, Hindi, and Spanish) foster *future-oriented behavior*. The study revealed that speakers of languages that grammatically associate the future and the present save more, retire with more wealth, smoke less, practice safer sex, and are less obese. This holds both across and within countries when comparing demographically similar native households.

Huang and Kim (2020) found that firms located in countries whose languages do not require future events to be grammatically marked (e.g., German, Japanese, and Mandarin) are more prone to *cost stickiness*, i.e., asymmetric sensitivity of costs to activity changes. In countries with weak time reference language, costs decrease to a lesser extent when sales decline than costs increase when sales rise by the same magnitude. This relationship between time reference in languages and asymmetric cost behavior is robust to various country-level formal institutions and alternative measures of costs.

The Sapir-Whorf-Hypothesis of linguistic relativity has been extensively discussed in the context of **multilingualism**. Bi- or multilinguals are individuals who use two or more languages or dialects in their everyday lives, be it simultaneously (e.g., in bilingual families or firms) or sequentially (e.g., in the context of immigration or expatriation). Similar to biculturals, it can be distinguished between *native bilinguals* who learn two native languages simultaneously and during infancy, and *successive bilinguals* who learn two different languages at different times of their lives. Both types of bilinguals together represent more than half of the world's population (Pavlenko 2014).

In one of the earliest studies, Ervin (1964) showed French adults who lived in the United States and were fluent in both French and English a series of illustrations and asked them to make up a three-minute story to accompany each scene. She found that the stories more often featured female achievement, physical aggression, verbal aggression toward parents, and attempts to escape blame when the participants spoke English, while the French stories were more likely to include domination by elders, guilt, and verbal aggression toward peers.

One of the largest studies of the code-switching capabilities of bilinguals was conducted by Pavlenko (2006). The author found that nearly two-thirds of the bilingual participants stated that they feel like a different person sometimes when they use their different languages. The participants did not only show changes in verbal but also in non-verbal behaviors when switching languages. "Languages may create different, and sometimes incommensurable, worlds for their speakers who feel that their selves change with the shift in the language (…). For bilinguals, and in particular for immigrants and expatriates, the two languages may be linked to different linguistic repertoires, cultural scripts, frames of expectation, autobiographic memories, and levels of proficiency and emotionality" (Pavlenko 2006, p. 27).

While code-switching and code-mixing of bilinguals are now usually perceived as valuable cognitive capabilities, bilingualism has long been regarded as dysfunctional, diseased or even "linguistic schizophrenia." Nazi scholars in the 1930s equated bilingualism with Jews and other ethnic minorities, such as East Prussians and Silesians. They argued that bilinguals experience a pathological inner split and suffer intellectual and moral deterioration in their struggle to become one. They also referred to the "bilinguality of feelings" and the "mercenary relativism" of bilinguals who switch principles and values as they switch languages (Pavlenko 2014).

6.4 LANGUAGE AND TRANSLATION

One of the key characteristics of intercultural communication is the **involvement of speakers with different native languages**. "Language is the first and foremost means and source through which the 'connecting' of different socio-cultural, institutional and individual worlds occurs" (Piekkari & Tietze 2011, p. 267). It is estimated that around 7,000 languages exist in the world. Figure 6.5 displays the distribution of major languages in the world and Figure 6.6 the number of native and non-native speakers of the 15 most-spoken languages. While English is by far the most common language, only a minority of people in the world are English native speakers. Nearly 50% have a "small" language as their native language that is spoken by less than 1 mn. people.

When speakers of different native languages are involved in an intercultural conversation, a decision about the most adequate **language policy** has to be made. Depending on the language proficiency of the participants, the following alternatives exist (Figure 6.7):

- In the case of two interlocutors with different mother tongues who are fluent in the mother tongue of the other person at least passively, a *polyglot dialogue* can take place where each person communicates in his/her mother tongue. For example, a German speaks his/her native language German and a French speaks his/her native language French. If the participants are not fluent in the native language of the other person, an interpreter is needed to translate between the two involved languages.

- *Lingua franca communication* requires that the interlocutors are fluent in a common third language. Both persons communicate in this third language and not in their respective mother tongue. The most common third language is English as global business language. However, in certain regions and disciplines, other widely spoken languages may be appropriate. For example, Arabic is spoken as a trade language across the Sahara as far as the Sahel, and Russian is still common in Eastern Europe and Post-Soviet countries. French was the language of diplomacy from the seventeenth century until the mid-twentieth century, and is still the *lingua franca* of the International Olympic Committee, Fédération Internationale de Football Association and Fédération Internationale de l'Automobile.

- *Mother tongue asymmetry* is characterized by one person communicating in his/her mother tongue while the other person communicates in the mother tongue of his/her interlocutor. For example, a French person speaks in his/her native language French and his/her German interlocutor uses French as foreign language. This asymmetric language policy is usually applied when the foreign language proficiency of the person who does not speak in his/her native language is very high or when no interpreter is available.

Figure 6.5 Distribution of major languages in the world

Source: https://en.wikipedia.org/wiki/Template:Distribution_of_languages_in_the_world.

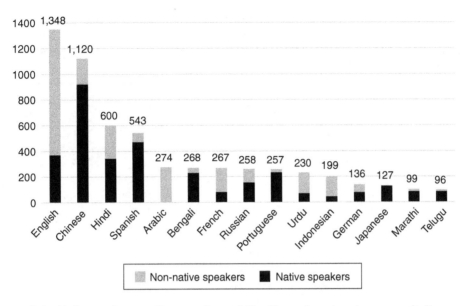

Figure 6.6 Native and non-native speakers of the 15 most-spoken languages in the world
Source: Adapted from Eberhard, Simons & Fennig (2021).

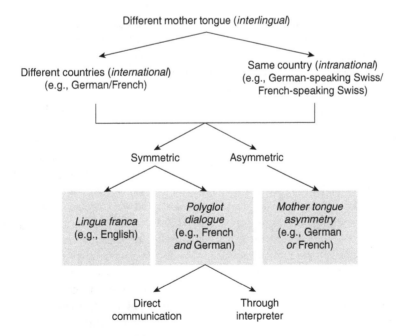

Figure 6.7 Language choices between speakers of different native languages
Source: Adapted and extended from Ammon (2003, p. 232).

The choice of an adequate language policy depends mostly on the **foreign language proficiency** of the participants which differs considerably across the globe. Generally, foreign language skills correlate negatively with the size of the country and positively with the quality of the education system.

According to the Education First (2018) *English Proficiency Index*, English skills are the strongest in Europe, with Sweden, the Netherlands, Norway, Denmark, Luxembourg, Finland, Slovenia, Germany, Belgium, and Austria occupying 10 out of the top 12 positions in the "Very High Proficiency" band. The two other countries in the top category are Singapore and South Africa. The Middle East has the weakest English proficiency. While most countries in the region experienced an improvement in the last years, they still belong to the "Very Low Proficiency" band. In Asian countries (e.g., China and Japan), English proficiency did not improve despite high investments in English. Latin America even experienced a slight decline in English proficiency, while African countries showed strong gains.

A study of Eurostat (2019) shows that 35% of the working-age adults in the EU-28 know at least one foreign language, 21.0% two or more, and 8.4% three or more foreign languages. The percentage is the highest in Luxembourg (51.2%), followed by Belgium (26.9%) and Denmark (24.6%). It is the lowest in Bosnia and Herzegovina (0.7%), Romania (0.9%), Greece (2.7%) and Hungary (2.7%). There is a clear generation gap favoring younger people in relation to self-reported foreign language skills. Moreover, foreign language skills are stronger among people who had completed a tertiary level of education.

The **use of a foreign language** in intercultural communication has different effects. Neeley, Hinds, and Cramton (2012) observed that many non-native speakers feel that their restricted capacity in the foreign language reduces their communication effectiveness and their general competencies. They might even distrust native speakers who they suspect abuse their superior linguistic agility to take advantage of them. This can result in avoiding contact with native speakers, clustering with people from a shared language background, and switching to the use of native languages. The authors observed that these negative interaction patterns are not only primarily caused by cultural differences but rather by the perceived differences in language abilities.

Neuro-imaging studies revealed that the use of a foreign language significantly increases neural activity in frontal brain regions implicated in controlled processing and working memory functions (Abutalebi 2008). Volk, Köhler, and Pudelko (2014) argue that this increased working memory load leaves fewer processing capacities for other cognitive tasks, thus hindering individual decision making and self-regulation. On the contrary, Hadjichristidis, Geipel and Surian (2017) highlighted that foreign language use can also improve decision-making and self-regulation. For example, foreign language use involves an increase of memory load in the early phases of information processing, thus reducing the capture of attention by tempting stimuli. Moreover, experiences and their associated emotions are coded in the language in which they occur and thus more accessible when the same language is used at retrieval. Therefore, certain mental constructs, such as stereotypes, which have been shaped by years of cultural learning in a native language context may exert less influence when processing a foreign language.

When speakers of two or more native languages in intercultural communication are not able or do not want to communicate in a foreign language, some form of translation is required. This can be achieved by the interlocutors themselves or through an external interpreter. In order to establish **equivalence of**

meaning between the message in the source and the target language, linguistic differences in their phonology, morphology, syntax, semantics and pragmatics must be considered.

Translation between **languages with different writing systems** is particularly difficult. An example is Chinese. While the Chart of Generally Utilized Characters of Modern Chinese lists 7,000 characters (with literate individuals know and use between 3,000 and 4,000 characters), the Latin alphabet consists of only 26 letters. On the contrary, English has around 12,000 syllables, while Chinese has only 414 (Song 2011). The translation of English terms into Chinese is therefore confronted with the challenge of highly asymmetric morphemic and phonemic structures of the two languages. Alternative approaches to translation are presented in Table 6.11.

Translations are also challenging in the case of **significant differences of lexical stocks**, for example, as a result of different histories, ideologies, political, and economic systems. An example is the translation of Western management terms into Russian since Russia's transition from a socialist to a market economy starting in the late 1990s. "The end of communism marked a new linguistic beginning in that the language that described Soviet economic practices and procedures became instantly redundant" (Holden, Kuznetsova & Fink 2008, p. 115). In order to fill these lexical and conceptual voids, massive borrowing of Western business and management terminology took place.

Three **alternative approaches to translation** can be distinguished:

- *Literal translation* is often impeded by ignorance or misunderstanding of the underlying concept. A vivid example is the term "power distance" for which a number of different translations can be found that capture the specific meaning of Hofstede's concept only partially: "дистанция власти" ("distance of power"), "властная дистанция" ("domineering distance"), "дистанция от власти" ("distance from power") and "дистанция до власти" ("distance to power"). According to Pshenichnikova (2003, p. 35), "these variants (..) demonstrate attempts to transform and adapt this foreign methodological concept to native Russian cultural assumptions and attitudes toward power by linguistic spatial means."

- *Corresponding translation* is often used when a close lexical equivalent of the original term does not exist. A common example is the translation of "management" as "управление" ("upravlenie"). In the Soviet period, however, this term denoted the implementation of decisions made by state authorities rather than autonomous decision-making of managers. Hence a frequent English translation of this word is "administration" (Holden, Kuznetsova & Fink 2008). Corresponding translation is particularly complex—and often misleading—when the translated term has been historically used in a different context and is therefore enriched with different meaning. An example is the translation of "challenge" in management textbooks as "испытание" ("ispytanie") or "вызов" ("vyzov"). While the first term has a religious connotation in the sense of "temptation," the latter was used in nineteenth century Russian in the context of duels (Pshenichnikova 2003).

- In the absence of adequate lexical equivalents—and often with the attempt to make a cosmopolitan impression—the *absorption of foreign terms* is used. Common examples are "маркетинг" (often pronounced on the second syllable) for "marketing" and "менеджмент" for "management." While the composition of these words corresponds with Russian phonemics and morphology, other loanwords, such as "хедхантер" ("headhunter"), "рекрутер" ("recruiter") and "тимбилдинг" ("team building"), lead to unreasonable usages or even "barbarisms" (Pshenichnikova 2003, p. 30).

Table 6.11 Alternative approaches of adapting western brand names into Chinese

	Example	Characters	Sound	Meaning
No adaptation	The name has no resemblance to the original in sound or in meaning	Heineken	喜力	Xǐ lì	"Happy power"
		KFC	肯德基	Kěn dé jī	(no meaning)
		Pizza Hut	必胜客	Bì shèng kè	"Guarantee wins guests"
Sound adaptation	The name sounds like the original but is semantically unrelated	Audi	奥迪	Aò dí	(no meaning)
		Bosch	博世	Bó shì	'Big world'
		McDonald's	麦当劳	Mài dāng láo	(no meaning)
Meaning adaptation	The name is semantically related to the original but sounds different	General Electric	通用电气	Tōng yòng qì chē	'General Electric'
		General Motors	通用汽车	Tōng yòng diàn qì	'General Motors'
		Volkswagen	大众汽车	Dà zhòng qì chē	'Car for the masses'
Dual adaptation	The name is semantically related to the original and sounds similar	Coca-Cola	可口可乐	Kě kǒu kě lè	"Can be tasty, can be happy"
		Nike	耐克	Nài kè	"Endurance conquer"
		Porsche	保时捷	Bǎo shí jié	"Fast and time-saving"

Sources: Adapted from Holtbrügge & Puck (2008) and Fetscherin et al. (2012).

The equivalence of translation is particularly relevant in contexts where the exact meaning of terms has far-reaching legal consequences, such as **international contracts and trials**. For example, international joint venture contracts are often formulated in two languages. Dual-language contracts can suffer from imprecise translation or semantic ambiguity. This is more likely, the greater the lexical and conceptual differences between the two languages. For example, for the case of English and Chinese legal language, three types of translation challenges can be distinguished (Cao 2002):

- *Legal usage vs. ordinary meaning.* Legal language consists of several terms that have a technical legal as well as an ordinary meaning. Translators of legal texts therefore need to identify the legal meaning of a term and distinguish it from the ordinary meaning to render the legal term appropriately into the target language. One example is the concept of *ejusdem generis*. Legal contracts usually need to set out the precise scope of the parties' rights and obligations. These will often be expressed as a list of items that closes with a general item at the end of the enumeration. According to the principle of *ejusdem generis*, the general term at the end will be interpreted narrowly to fall within the class created by the preceding specific terms in the enumeration. However, neither the Chinese language nor Chinese law has a class presumption. Therefore, the interpretation of an enumeration In an English and a Chinese text will be different (Torbert 2007).

- *Lack of lexical equivalence.* As a result of the separate legal traditions, there are many common law concepts in English unknown to the Chinese law that was influenced to a certain extent by the civil law system. An example is the translation of terms related to the concept of 'equity' in the common law, as in "the law of equity." As China had no equivalence for this term either linguistically or in its legal system, the Chinese term 衡平法 ("héngpíng fǎ") was coined for "law of equity" ("héng" literally means "weighing" or "measuring," "píng'" means "fair" or "equal," and "fǎ" is for "law"). This new lexical item, however, does not have any substantive meaning in the Chinese law (Cao 2002).

- *Polysemy.* Certain words in legal English do not have unambiguous equivalents in Chinese and verse visa. Instead, various options are available that require a careful selection. An example is the term 'legal person' which in English normally refers to a body with individual legal powers, privileges, rights, duties, or liabilities. This could be a natural person (e.g., a human being) or an artificial person (e.g., a corporation). In Chinese law and legal documents, the term 法人 ("fǎ rén") is widely used in this context ("fǎ" means "law" and "rén" means "person"). In contemporary usage in Chinese law, however, "fǎ rén" can have different legal meanings, such as for-profit or not-for-profit legal persons as well as incorporated or unincorporated legal persons. Thus, when translating the term into another language, it is essential to take into account the immediate context in which it is used to determine what kind of legal person it refers to (Cao 2002).

Dual-language contracts may not only be affected by objective lexical and conceptual differences, but also by **intentional dichotomies**. These may occur if one party takes advantage of asymmetric language proficiency and seeks undue commercial advantage by writing alternate meanings into translated documents. This risk of cheating is higher, the less fluent one party is in the native language of the other party.

Foreign companies in China often face difficulties with dual language contracts. As one British lawyer observed:

"Of the hundreds of dual language contracts proposed by Chinese companies and reviewed by one of my firm's China attorneys, we've never seen a single one where the Chinese portion was less favorable to the Chinese company than the English portion. But we've seen plenty where the Chinese portion is better or much better for the Chinese company than the English portion. Chinese companies love using a contract with an English portion that is more favorable to the foreign company than the Chinese portion and then relying on the English speaking company to assume that the English language portion will control (...). No matter what the English language portion of your contract says, it behooves you to know exactly what the Chinese language portion says as well."

(Harris 2018)

The intercultural challenges of translation are multiplied in the case of interpreting. **Interpreting** is a form of translation in which an interpreter produces an immediate and final translation based on a one-time exposure to an expression in a source language (Spencer-Oatey & Xing 2008). It can either be consecutive, with the interpreter speaking only during the breaks provided by the original speaker, or simultaneous, with the interpreter speaking at the same time as the original speaker. Simultaneous interpretation is regarded one of the most complex cognitive activities of the human brain (Setton 1999).

In order to manage its high complexity and establish translation equivalence, different **standards for intercultural interpreters** exist. According to the California Healthcare Interpreters Association (2002, p. 30), "interpreters demonstrate accuracy and completeness by acting to

- convey verbal and non-verbal messages and speaker's tone of voice without changing the meaning of the message,
- clarify the meaning of non-verbal expressions and gestures that have a specific or unique meaning within the cultural context of the speaker,
- maintain the tone and the message of the speaker even when it includes rudeness and obscenities,

- reveal and to correct interpreting errors as soon as recognized,
- clarify meaning and to verify understanding, particularly when there are differences in accent, dialect, register and culture,
- maintain the same level of formal/informal language (register) used by the speaker, or to request permission to adjust this level in order to facilitate understanding when necessary to prevent potential communication breakdown."

The standards to intercultural interpreters emphasize that interlingual communication does not only involve verbal messages but also para-verbal, non-verbal, and extra-verbal elements. Given the variety of intercultural differences with regard to accents, dialects, kinesics, haptics, timing, etc., the **unbiased reproduction of non-linguistic communication** is an important prerequisite of translation equivalence. This refers particularly to expressions of members of high-context cultures.

One of the first occasions where simultaneous interpretation was applied were the **Nuremberg Trials** against leading Nazi war criminals from November 1945 to August 1946. Every seat in the courtroom was equipped with headphones, earphones and switch dials that allowed the judges, defendants, defenders, prosecutors, and press-correspondents to select which language they wished to listen to: English, French, German, and Russian.

There were 36 interpreters working in three shifts with 12 interpreters in the room at any time. They were divided into four desks, according to the language into which they translated. The Russian desk, for example, was made up of the German-into-Russian, the French-into-Russian and the English-into-Russian interpreter. The interpreters received the original speech through their earphones and translated into microphones into the language to which they were assigned. This *one-direction translation policy* considered that interpreters are often better to translate from a particular language than into that language. Moreover, two-direction interpretation would have put twice as much pressure on the interpreters.

The Nuremberg Trials also did feature a *non-relay system*. In a relay system, an interpreter first translates the original speech into only one language, for example, English. Afterwards, the other interpreters translate from this language into the other languages. While this mode requires half the interpreting personnel compared to a non-relay system, it bears the risk of losing accuracy because of the double translation involved. Moreover, there is a considerable delay between the original and the interpreted versions. This would have been a major disadvantage at the trial, where the defense and the prosecution have to hear what was said quickly enough to raise objections in time (Gaiba 1998).

6.5 INTERCULTURAL NEGOTIATION

Intercultural communication often takes place in the form of negotiation. It is characterized by the following **features** (Gelfand & Dyer 2000; Lewicki, Barry & Saunders 2020):

- Two or more *parties* have or perceive to have a *conflict or misalignment of interest* over one or more different issues.
- The parties are willing to communicate about the division and exchange of one or more *scarce resources*. These can be either tangible (e.g., money, goods) or intangible (e.g., information, rights, privileges).
- The parties believe in a *possible negotiation gain*, i.e., outcomes that are superior to a unilateral decision.
- The parties make provisional *offers and counteroffers* to each other.
- The parties believe that they are *interdependent* and that their *outcomes are determined jointly*.

Negotiations are conducted frequently in various areas, such as diplomacy, company takeovers and joint ventures, project tenders, sales contracts, industrial relations, and conflict settlements. In an intercultural context, the parties engaged in a negotiation are from two or more different cultures. Cultural differences affect both negotiation tactics and negotiation outcomes. Moreover, these relations are likely to be influenced by the context in which the negotiation takes place (Figure 6.8).

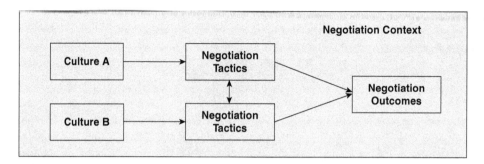

Figure 6.8 Impact of culture on negotiation tactics and outcomes

The vast majority of studies of the **impact of culture on negotiation tactics and outcomes** have been conducted in Western contexts (notably the United States), while studies about other cultures are scarce. Moreover, the literature has a predominantly comparative focus with few studies applying an intercultural methodology, i.e., analyzing negotiations between parties from different cultural backgrounds (Gelfand & Dyer 2000; Brett 2014; Usunier 2018; Ghauri, Ott & Rammal 2020). Table 6.12 displays key characteristics of negotiation with regard to the dimensions of culture developed by Hall and Hofstede.

Based on Hofstede's cultural dimensions, Coene and Jacobs (2017) developed a typology of seven **mindsets of negotiation** that differ between cultures. Their main characteristics and exemplary countries are summarized in Table 6.13. While, for example, *competitors* regard negotiation as a contest and see the price as the main decision criterion, *organizers* focus more on expertise and technical details. For *reciprocators*, trust and personal relationships are essential, and *diplomats* seek out for grand principles and philosophy rather than best practices.

The influence of culture on negotiation can be illustrated using the example of **bargaining processes** analyzed from the perspective of game theory (Figure 6.9). In a price negotiation, a buyer usually faces a seller who have both reservation prices in mind, i.e., a price above/below they are not willing to buy/sell. Naturally, this reservation price is not revealed to the other party. The first offer of the buyer (FO_B) will be under his/her reservation price (RP_B) and the first offer of the seller (FO_S) above his/her reservation price (RP_S). The range between buyer's and seller's reservation prices defines the zone of possible agreement (ZOPA). Outside of this zone, it is rational for the parties to walk away and look for the best alternative to a negotiated agreement (BATNA).

In feminine cultures like Norway, the first offer of the seller is typically close to the final negotiation price (FO_{S2}). Accordingly, the bargaining ranges of both parties become relatively small. The negotiation will usually focus on contract details, such as payment conditions, delivery dates, etc. On the contrary, the first offer is more extreme and sometimes even beyond the reservation price of the buyer in more masculine cultures, such as the Middle East (FO_{S1}). The counteroffer of the buyer (FO_B) may be alike. To avoid that the other party walks away, the second offer is usually more moderate and inside its suspected bargaining range. Since the bargaining ranges of both parties are relatively large, several subsequent offers and counteroffers are likely. The provisional offers and counteroffers of the two parties will finally lead to a negotiated price at some point within the ZOPA.

Table 6.12 Impact of culture on negotiation tactics and outcomes

	Impact of culture	
Preparation of negotiation	*Low uncertainty avoidance*	*High uncertainty avoidance*
	Less detailed preparation; lower awareness of reservation points and BATNA	Detailed preparation; higher awareness of reservation points and BATNA
Negotiation style	*Contact cultures*	*Non-contact cultures*
	Focus on soft factors; emotional	Focus on hard factors; rational
Negotiation tactics	*Individualism*	*Collectivism*
	Focus on problem solving; rules and principles are important	Focus on social relationship; personal characteristics and relationships are important
Negotiation process	*Monochronic time orientation*	*Polychronic time orientation*
	Linear processing (item by item); agendas are important	Cyclic processing (back and forth); loose agendas
First offer	*Feminine cultures*	*Masculine cultures*
	Moderate	Extreme
Distribution of negotiation gains	*High power distance*	*Low power distance*
	Higher tolerance for asymmetric negotiation gains	Lower tolerance for asymmetric negotiation gains
Attempted outcomes	*Short-term orientation*	*Long-term orientation*
	Deal-making	Relationship-building
Form and relevance of agreements	*High context communication*	*Low context communication*
	Focus on oral agreements; contracts regarded as provisional and subject to change	Focus on written documents; contracts regarded as final and legally binding

Sources: Compiled from Graham, Mintu & Rodgers (1994), Natlandsmyr & Rognes (1995), Leung (1997), and Hofstede & Usunier (2003).

Individualistic and short-term oriented cultures, such as the United States, will usually attempt to reach a higher negotiation gain ("deal-making"), while in collectivistic and long-term oriented cultures, such as China, a balance between seller's and buyer's negotiation gain ('relationship building') is strived for. However, the latter applies only to repeated and intracultural negotiations. In one-off encounters with parties from other cultures, negotiators from collectivist cultures, such as China, distinguish clearly between in-groups and out-groups and show a more aggressive negotiation style toward the latter (Fang 2006). Negotiators from individualistic cultures, such as the United States, would not make such distinctions (Gelfand & Dyer 2000).

Table 6.13 Mindsets of negotiation

	Competitor	Organizer	Connected	Diplomat	Reciprocator	Marathonian	Craftsman
Cultural dimensions							
Power Distance	Low	Low	Low	Low	High	High	Medium
Individualism	High	High	High	High	Low	Low to medium	Medium
Masculinity	High	Medium to high	Very low	Medium	Medium	Medium to high	High
Uncertainty avoidance	Low to medium	High	Medium	High	High	Low	High
Long-term orientation	Low to medium	High	Low to medium	High	N/A	Medium to high	High
Indulgence	High	Low to medium	Medium to high	Low to medium	N/A	Low to medium	Medium
Characteristics	• Negotiation as contest • "Winner takes it all" mentality • Little emotional attachment • Price is absolutely vital • Negotiation can be left with a significant amount of uncertainty	• Important role of experts in decision-making • Focus on expertise and technical details • Importance of procedures, transparency and reliability • Open discussion of strengths and weaknesses	• Focus on creativity and innovative solutions • Negotiation as team process • Importance of trust and personal relationships	• Grand principles and philosophy rather than best practices • Relevance of eloquence and emotional words • Solutions should be elegant • Rules are omnipresent	• Importance of trust and personal relationships • Respect for hierarchy • Importance of rituals and customs • Negotiation as exchange of favors	• Never ending loops of negotiation and renegotiation	• Quest for perfection • Relationship first-task second • Consensus orientation • Learn how to 'read the air'
Exemplary countries	Australia, Canada, Ireland, New Zealand, South Africa (white), United Kingdom, United States	Austria, Czechia, Germany, Hungary, Israel, Luxembourg, Switzerland (German)	Denmark, Estonia, Finland, Iceland, Latvia, Lithuania, Netherlands, Norway, Sweden	Belgium, France, Italy (North), Malta, Poland, Switzerland (French & Italian), Spain	East Africa, West Africa, Middle East, Latin America, Korea, Pakistan, Russia, Taiwan, Thailand	China, Hong Kong, India, Indonesia, Jamaica, Malaysia, The Philippines, Singapore, Vietnam	Japan

Source: Adapted from Coene & Jacobs (2017).

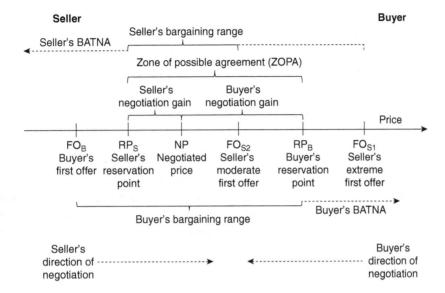

Figure 6.9 Elements of the bargaining process

Sources: Adapted from Fisher, Ury & Patton (1992) and Raiffa, Richardson & Metcalfe (2002).

The role of culture in bargaining can be illustrated by using the example of the **Brexit negotiations** between the United Kingdom and the EU. After 52% of the British electorate had voted in favor of leaving the EU on 23 June 2016, the British Government served the withdrawal notice under Article 50 of the Treaty on European Union on 29 March 2017. This officially gave the country until 29 March 2019 to negotiate the divorce or rupture conditions. On 14 November 2018, the British Government negotiated a draft Withdrawal Agreement with the EU that was, however, not approved by the British Parliament in several votes. Upon request of the British Prime Minister, the exit date was extended to 12 April 2019 and later to 31 October 2019, before the United Kingdom finally left the EU on 31 January 2020.

The British negotiation stance showed all the hallmarks of an archetypal hard-bargaining strategy from the very beginning. This included aggressive portrayals of the EU, unwillingness to compromise, unrealistic expectations, frequent resort to threats, the depiction of the negotiations in zero-sum terms, not offering justification or evidence-based argumentation to make a case for its position, and a notable reluctance to communicate its position to the public or its negotiating partner.

(Martill & Staiger 2018, p. 2)

Martill and Staiger (2018) argue that British hard bargaining is a consequence of three ideational factors particular to the UK case: the dominance of a conservative ideology of statecraft, a majoritarian institutional culture, and weak socialization into European structures. In the context of the Brexit negotiations, however, the UK's bargaining power was

(Continued)

perceived considerably lower than that of their negotiation partners. For example, the trade relationships with the EU are significantly more important for the United Kingdom than for the EU. The consequences of a "no-deal Brexit" (BATNA) would therefore have been more negative for the United Kingdom than for the EU (Ott & Ghauri 2019). The bargaining position of the United Kingdom was further weakened by the fact that both, the extension of Brexit talks and the terms of future EU-UK free trade agreements required a unanimous vote and ratification of all EU governments.

The tactics and outcomes of intercultural negotiations are not only influenced by the cultural attributes of the involved parties but also by the **negotiation context**. While several contextual factors, such as the number of parties (bilateral vs. multilateral), type of conflict (distributive vs. integrative), negotiation frequency (one-off vs. repeated), negotiators' roles (e.g., buyer vs. seller) and relationship between the parties (anonymous vs. personal), are relevant for any negotiation, two factors are particularly salient in an international context.

- Similar to a home team advantage in sports, the *location of negotiation* is likely to affect both negotiation tactics and outcomes. Brown and Baer (2011) found that residents of an office space outperform the visiting party in a distributive negotiation. People are more familiar with their own surroundings and tend to be more comfortable and confident in them. In addition, negotiating on one's home field allows for easier access to information and control of the negotiation environment. A specific tactic that is associated with home location advantage is the exercise of time pressure on the other party. Notably Chinese negotiators often use this tactic against foreign negotiators that have a previously fixed return date and are thus more ready to make compromises toward the end of their stay in China to avoid returning without an agreement (Graham & Lam 2003).

- Moreover, the *intercultural competence* of the two parties is an important context factor. Imai and Gelfand (2010) found that negotiators with higher cultural intelligence tend to have higher cooperative motives and epistemic motivation. These psychological characteristics enable them to overcome hurdles endemic to intercultural negotiation by adopting more integrative negotiation tactics and investing more cognitive effort into accurately understanding their culturally different counterparts. Dyads consisting of negotiators with higher cultural intelligence engage in complementary sequences of integrative information behaviors, which in turn predict joint profit. Notably, this effect was present even when controlling for cognitive ability, emotional intelligence, openness, extraversion, and international experience.

A specific means of intercultural negotiation on the country-level is **cultural diplomacy**, i.e., the promotion of the culture, language, ideology, etc. of a country to foreigners. Cultural diplomacy is a form of *soft power* aimed "to affect others to obtain the outcomes one wants through attraction rather than coercion or payment" (Nye 2008, p. 94). It seeks to harness the elements of culture to induce foreign publics, opinion makers and leaders to have a positive view of the country's people, culture and policies as well as to prevent, manage and mitigate conflict with the target country (Lenczowski 2008). Common instruments of cultural diplomacy are exhibitions, educational programs (such as universities and language programs abroad), scientific and cultural exchanges, etc. Several countries have institutionalized their cultural diplomacy activities in *foreign cultural institutes,* such as Alliance Française (France), British Council (United Kingdom), Confucius Institute (China), Goethe-Institut (Germany) and Instituto Cervantes (Spain).

One of the most controversial initiatives of cultural diplomacy is the Chinese **Confucius Institute Program** (Liu 2020). Operating under the Ministry of Education, its aim is to promote Chinese language and culture, support local Chinese teaching internationally, and facilitate cultural exchanges. Beyond educational aims, the Confucius Institutes are regarded "an important part of China's overseas propaganda set-up", as admitted by the former head of Chinese propaganda and media relations Li Changchun (cited in The Economist, 24.10.2009). The Confucius Institutes are often criticized to undermine academic freedom at host universities, engage in industrial and military espionage, observe Chinese students abroad and advance the Chinese government's political agendas on controversial issues, such as Taiwan, Tibet, and human rights (Hubbert 2019). In a more subtle way, teaching with the simplified Chinese characters rather than the traditional Chinese characters used in Taiwan "would help to advance Beijing's goal of marginalizing Taiwan in the battle for global influence" (Ding & Saunders 2006, p. 21).

6.6 INSTRUMENTAL FORMS OF INTERCULTURAL COMMUNICATION

An implicit assumption of communication is that it is intended to achieve understanding and consensus. However, communication can have different purposes, such as establishing or reinforcing power asymmetries between individuals or purposefully misleading others. According to Habermas (1984), two main **forms of communication** can be distinguished:

- *Argumentative communication* is characterized through the absence of coercive force, the mutual search for understanding, and the compelling power of the better argument. Four validity claims exist: That what people say makes linguistic sense (comprehensibility), accords in some way with objective reality (truth), accords with the normative values of the listeners and is socially acceptable (conduct or rightness), and expresses what they truly believe and is proved by the subsequent actions to be sincere (sincerity or authenticity). As argumentative communication is based on the notion of reason, separated from force and avoids coercion, it provides the foundation of legitimate power.

- Communication that violates these criteria is called *instrumental communication.* It is characterized through factors of manipulation and dominance that can be internal (e.g., misleading information, discriminatory language, etc.) or external to the actual speech act (e.g., who determines the ordering of the discussion, who can participate, in what way, etc.). Instrumental communication "colonizes the lifeworld" and in doing so not just mediates our experience of the world but becomes also "a medium of domination and social power" (Habermas, cited in Outhwaite 2009, p. 25). As instrumental communication is based on ideology, force and coercion, it provides the foundation of illegitimate power.

While the considerations about intercultural communication in the previous sections are based on the assumption of argumentative reason, communication in an intercultural context can also take an instrumental form. In the following, different tactics of instrumental communication are outlined. Finally, potential reactions to instrumental communication that violates the principles of argumentative rationality are discussed.

6.6.1 Tactics of Instrumental Communication

6.6.1.1 Fake News

Fake news consists of deliberate disinformation. They have little or no basis in fact, but are presented as being factually accurate. In contrast to satire and parody which use humor or exaggeration in a transparent and entertaining way, fake news are spread usually with the intent to mislead receivers to damage others (Young 2017). Table 6.14 presents a classification of different **types of fake news**.

Table 6.14 Spectrum of fake news

Type	Definition
False connection	Use of headlines, visuals or captions that don't support the content. Often intended to generate attention and bias audience.
Misleading content	Misleading use of information to frame an issue or an individual. For example, important details are omitted that would suggest different interpretations.
False context	Genuine content is shared with false contextual information. For example, false location and time specifications are made.
Imposter content	Genuine sources are impersonated with false, made-up sources. Examples are made-up or distorted citations.
Manipulated content	Genuine information or imagery is manipulated to deceive and sufficiently change the narrative, as with a 'photoshoped' image. Often based on facts, but include embellishments that have no factual basis.
Fabricated content	Content is 100% false, designed to deceive and do harm. Published in the style of reputable media to create legitimacy. Unlike parody, there is no implicit understanding between the sender and the receiver that the item is false. Vulnerability to fabricated news is higher if they rely on preexisting political, social, or cultural tension.

Sources: Based on Wardle & Derakhshan (2017) and Tandoc, Lim & Ling (2018).

Tandoc, Lim, and Ling (2018) proposed classifying the various types of fake news along two dimensions: facticity and intention:

- **Facticity** refers to the degree to which fake news are based on verifiable facts. For example, satire relies on facts but presents it in a diverting format. Parodies and false connections take a broad social context upon which they fashion fictitious accounts, while manipulations use one-sided facts.

Fabrications have no factual basis, but usually draw on preexisting memes or partialities that are weaved into a narrative, often with a political bias, that the reader accepts as legitimate.

- The author's immediate **intention** refers to the degree to which the creator of fake news intends to mislead. Satire and parody use some level of mutually understood suspension of reality to work. They assume an open disclaimer that they are not real news. In the case of the other types of fake news, no disclaimer is made. The ultimate goal of mis-informing and deceiving people is reached through the immediate intention that the fake news they see is real. The role of the audi-ence, however, is not only sharing and believing in fake news, but in legitimizing it to qualify as fake news. "While news is con-structed by (authors), it seems that fake news is coconstructed by the audience, for its fakeness depends a lot on whether the audi-ence perceives the fake as real. Without this complete process of deception, fake news remains a work of fiction. It is when audiences mistake it as real news that fake news is able to play with (author's) legitimacy" (Tandoc, Lim & Ling 2018, p. 148).

The relevance of fake news has increased in *post-truth politics*, i.e., the relegation of facts and expert opinions to be of secondary importance relative to appeal to emotion (McIntyre 2018). Their aim is to promote particular ideologies or people, often by discrediting others (Allcott & Gentzkow 2017). *Media outlets* use fake news to attract viewers to generate advertising revenue. Publishing outrageous stories with false content that go viral benefits advertisers and improves ratings. *Confirmation bias* and *social media algorithms*, like those used on Facebook and Twitter, further advance the spread of fake news (Braun & Eklund 2019).

In intercultural communication, fake news is particularly common in the context of foreign politics, military conflicts, and migration. They often *address existing cultural stereotypes and prejudices*. Fake news related to other cultures is usually difficult to detect as they often refer to information that is hard to falsify, such as anonymous informants or sources published in foreign languages. Moreover, *lack of personal experience* complicates independent verification and opinion formation.

Individuals and organizations may not only be senders but also **receivers and targets of fake news**. Online platforms and social media allow everyone to post information, photos, videos and narratives about newsworthy events and to reach a mass audience. Unlike journalists, influencers don't attempt to provide independent, reliable, accurate, and comprehensive information, but to persuade their followers to think and behave based on their recommendations. As sensationalist posts usually receive more likes, shares and comments, there is a strong motivation to choose and shape facts selectively, suppressing those that are likely to receive less attention or disagreement (Tandoc, Lim & Ling 2018). As a consequence, indi-viduals and organizations can easily become the target of online firestorms that have little or no factual evidence (Pfeffer, Zorbach & Carley 2014). The development of *news bots*, i.e., automated accounts that disseminate news and information on social networks, automates and accelerates this *echo chamber cycle*, adding what unwary readers of the news might interpret as legitimacy of the item (Lokot & Diakopoulos 2016).

Foreign companies are a frequent target of **online firestorms** and instrumental social media campaigns. A vivid example is China, the country with the largest number of internet users and one of the strictest internet regulations in the world.

In the last years, the Chinese government has sparked several public debates in social media about foreign companies that have ostensibly hurt Chinese values and interests, such

(Continued)

as referring to Taiwan as an independent state in their corporate communication. The governmental control of the internet usually not allows foreign companies to address their Chinese stakeholders and the public and explain their policies. Instead, they feel forced to apologize and change their communication policy to reduce the risk of being boycotted by clients or hindered in their daily work.

One example is the German carmaker Daimler which used a statement of the Dalai Lama "Look at situations from all angles, and you will become more open" in an advertisement posted on its worldwide Instagram channel on February 5, 2018 (Lohse-Friedrich 2019). Although Instagram is blocked in China, the post immediately received harsh critique in the Chinese media. It can be no longer reconstructed whether the entry was first noticed by private users or government officials and then disseminated.

Daimler immediately deleted the Instagram post and published a statement on China's state-controlled social media network Weibo: "We will promptly take steps to deepen our understanding of Chinese culture and values, our international staff included, to help standardize our actions to ensure this sort of issue doesn't happen again." The Chinese newspaper *People's Daily* described the German automaker in a commentary as "enemy of the people" and criticized Mercedes-Benz China for apologizing, even though the mistake was made in Germany: "The apology lacks sincerity and reflects the German carmaker's lack of understanding of Chinese culture and values." This was accompanied by numerous posts on Weibo. In response, the then Daimler CEO Dieter Zetsche and Greater China CEO Hubertus Troska wrote a letter to the Chinese Ambassador in German, stating: "Daimler deeply regrets the hurt and grief that its negligent and insensitive mistake has caused to the Chinese people. Daimler fully and unreservedly recognizes the seriousness of the situation, which the company has caused and sincerely apologizes for." Finally, the Chinese government stopped the firestorm with a comment entitled "Daimler's misguided quote should be a reminder to foreign companies." It says: "The failure of Daimler is just another example (…) of a foreign company that used distorted facts for promotion which seriously intervene in Chinese sovereignty rights". After this statement of the Chinese government, the firestorm in the Chinese social media stopped immediately. However, Daimler received numerous negative posts on its worldwide social media accounts that criticized its "Kowtow to the Chinese government."

Like many other firestorms, the example of Daimler in China followed a typical course. The initial public criticism is usually related to verifiable facts. Posts of influential social media users (such as in the case of China the Chinese government) are shared and further disseminated by a large number of followers in a short time. The subsequent posts contain less and less content, but are fueled with rumors and offensive statements: "The essential feature is that the messages in a firestorm are predominantly opinion, not fact, thus having a high affective nature" (Pfeffer, Zorbach & Carley 2014, p. 118).

The technologically most advanced form of fake news is **deep fakes**. Deepfake technology leverages artificial intelligence to insert faces and voices into video and audio recordings of actual people. The use of a machine learning technique known as generative adversarial network enables the creation of realistic-looking videos or audios which appear as if someone said or did something they never said or did (Fletcher 2018). As the production of deep fakes is getting progressively easier, the capacity to make such media is growing continuously. Already today deepfake technology is so advanced that it often can no longer be distinguished whether content is genuine or manipulated. This leads to a "'liar's dividend'—the advantage gained by deceivers from a climate of 'truthiness', 'post-truth', and general distrust of the media (…). The mantra 'fake news' has thereby become an instantly recognized shorthand for a host of propositions about the supposed corruption and bias of a wide array of journalists, and a useful substitute for argument when confronted with damaging factual assertions" (Chesney & Citron 2019, p. 1785).

6.6.1.2 Doublespeak

Doublespeak is the deliberate use of words to disguise, obscure, or change meaning. The term originates in *George Orwell's* (1949) dystopic novel *Nineteen Eighty-Four* where it is applied to describe the manipulative communication strategy of a totalitarian regime. "Doublespeak is language which makes the bad seem good, the negative seem positive, the unpleasant seem unattractive, or at least tolerable" (Lutz 1996, p. 1). It is "the ability to lie, whether knowingly or unconsciously, and to get away with it" (Hermann 1992, p. 3).

From a linguistic perspective, doublespeak is a **rhetoric strategy at the intersection of pragmatics, semantics, and syntax** with the intent to manipulate others. It seeks to establish or reinforce power asymmetries between sender and receiver through the deliberate use of ambivalence, euphemisms, jargon, simplifications and personifications (Figure 6.10).

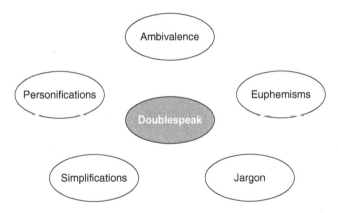

Figure 6.10 Features of doublespeak

The strategy of **deliberate ambivalence** includes the purposeful use of words that are open to more than one interpretation (Hua 2018). For example, the speaker disguises whether terms are used in a literal or figurative sense, broad or specific sense, carefully or thoughtlessly, etc. It is often applied by far right-wing politicians, racists and fascists to allow for multiple readings and denial of intended discriminatory messages (Bull & Simon-Vandenbergen 2014; Feldman & Jackson 2014). While the members of the addressed speech community are likely to understand the message in the intended way, the used terms are sufficiently equivocal to distance oneself from interpretations that could lead to prosecution (Engel & Wodak 2013). "In short: fascists frequently do not say what they mean, or mean what they say, and knowledge of the complex intertextual, interdiscursive, socio-legal and organizational histories of fascism are required in order to fully make sense of fascist discourse" (Richardson 2017, p. 450).

In intercultural communication, the term **"diversity"** is often used in a deliberately ambivalent way. Based on the belief that the term awakens positive associations, several countries and organizations have introduced diversity programs, value diversity of their members and postulate diversity as important success factor. "Diversity" is regarded to be the opposite of genuine negative terms, such as "simple-mindedness," "uniformity," and "monotony," and expected to promote fairness, innovation, and success.

The concrete meaning of "diversity," however, often remains blurred. For example, it is unclear whether diversity is defined in terms of separation, variety or disparity, and—as a consequence—whether measures of Euclidean distance, entropy or variance are used (Harrison & Klein 2007). In many cases, the dimensions of diversity remain vague and it is not specified whether "diversity" applies to general characteristics and attitudes, such as skin color, gender, sexual orientation, and religious affiliation, or also to work-related features, like mindset, working method, leadership style, form of communication, dress and make-up, etc. Likewise, the limits of "diversity" are often not clarified, i.e., whether any deviation from the norm is accepted or this is limited by the paramount unity of the organization. For example, does "diversity" have to occur within the boundaries of immutable societal values or—to put it in an extreme way—include tolerance for "cultures built around extreme xenophobia, genital mutilation, cannibalism, slavery, or human sacrifice?" (Yates 1998). Without specifying the delineation, dimensions and measurement of "diversity," the term remains ambiguous and its meaning largely depends on the interpretation of the audience.

Euphemisms are inoffensive or dull terms used in place of more blunt synonyms. They are an instrumental way "not to say what you mean" (Holder 2007). Euphemisms may be used to amuse, mark profanity or refer to taboo topics in a polite way. They become doublespeak when a less emotive word or expression is used to mislead or deceive the audience about unpleasant realities, e.g., referring to genocide as "ethnic cleansing" or to deportations as "operations" or "sending back" (Schrover & Schinkel 2013, p. 1128).

A vivid example of euphemism in intercultural communication is the term "multiculturalism." In education, it is often used for classes with a high degree of foreign students with low fluency in the local language and low degree of cultural integration. The term "multicultural neighborhood" is frequently used euphemistically by real estate agents to describe areas with a high degree of migrants, social inequality, and high crime rates. "Multicultural workforce" often stands for low-skilled and low-paid labor migrants with low legal protection. While being a genuine inclusive term, "multicultural" can also exclude members of the dominant culture. "On college campuses, some students are upset that white students are using multicultural spaces. Apparently 'multicultural' (in this context) is Newspeak for 'no whites allowed'" (Black 2019).

Doublespeak **jargon** has the effect of making the simple seem complex, the trivial seem profound, or the insignificant seem important. The semantic strategy of using *sophisticated technical terms* (often Latin or Greek loanwords) is frequently practiced by politicians, bureaucrats, lawyers and scientists to show competence, control, and legitimacy. This is often accompanied by *formal and complex syntax*. For example, long sentences and embedded clauses are preferred. *Unfounded but seemingly precise estimates* (e.g., "53.61%" instead of "many") shall further suggest factuality of the representation and hence credibility of the speaker (Schrover & Schinkel 2013). "The inflated style itself is a kind of euphemism. A mass of Latin words fall upon the facts like soft snow, blurring the outline and covering all the details. The great enemy of clear language is insincerity" (Orwell 1946).

Jargon is a powerful tool as it gives an air of prestige, profundity or authority to one's speech (Schrover & Schinkel 2013). It is aimed to receive credibility through language and not through the message. Laymen, less-educated people and non-native speakers often refrain from questions and objections as they fear to be exposed as unqualified and implausible.

Opposite to jargon, **simplifications** aim to make the complex seem simple, the disputed seem obvious, or the specific seem general. Simplifications can relate to semantics, syntax, and phonetics. For example, *everyday language* and *slang* are perceived as indication of straight talking and clear words. *Simplified grammar* and *short sentences* are used to give the impression of busyness and action orientation. Moreover, *local dialect* can signal authenticity and speaking the "voice of the people."

Simplifications often aim to establish putative consensus between sender and receiver (and the "common sense") about in fact controversial issues. This consensus strategy can be boosted through *assuring expressions*, such as "As everyone knows…," "The truth is…," "It has been shown that…," "Experts agree that…," or "There is no doubt that…" (Carroll 2001). Simplifications often go along with *hidden interpretations* and the presentation of personal opinions as facts. One rhetoric tactic is to accompany descriptions with evaluating adverbs or adjectives that lead the perception of the audience into a particular direction. For example the phrase "the company assessed the cultural conditions in the country" describes a verifiable fact, while "the company accurately assessed the cultural conditions in the country" includes an evaluation of the sender under the guise of a factual report.

Jargon and simplification are often used in a *mutually reinforcing* way through intentional variations of the *levels of description* (general versus specific) and the *relative completeness of descriptions* (many or few details mentioned). "Rhetorical and semantic contrasts function within the overall strategy of positive self-presentation and negative other-presentation. 'Our' good actions are described at a low, specific level, with many details, whereas 'our' controversial actions are either ignored or described at a fairly abstract level (and in euphemistic terms) and with few details" (Schrover & Schinkel 2013, p. 1130).

Personifications focus on the sender and/or receiver instead of the message. Three different forms can be distinguished: personal attack, association, and the construction of the sender as single collective actor.

- *Personal attacks* are directed toward the speaker instead of addressing the speaker's argument. They are a form of *logical fallacy*, because the truth of a statement does not depend on the person who makes it (Bull & Simon-Vandenbergen 2014). The credibility of the speaker is often impeached by referring to unchangeable personal traits, such as place of birth or parentage, for which the person cannot be made responsible. Examples are terms such as "bastard" or "Nazi grandchild."

- *Associations* connect the individual with esteemed or ill-reputed others. They aim to transfer the positive or negative image of the named person to the sender, receiver, or subject of a message. For example, an association like "I agree with Mahatma Gandhi (Nelson Mandela, Dalai Lama, Anne Frank, etc.) that …" makes the following statement appear important. The statement is charged with meaning, even if the content may be banal.

A well-known example of a negative image transfer was the association of the former Soviet leader Mikhail S. Gorbachev with the Nazi propagandist Joseph Goebbels by the former German chancellor Helmut Kohl. In an interview with the magazine Newsweek he said in October 1986: "I don't consider him to be a liberal. He is a modern communist leader who understands public relations. Goebbels, who was one of those responsible for the crimes of the Hitler Era, was an expert in public relations, too." After Kohl's statement received harsh critique, Herbert Schmülling, a government spokesman, said that Kohl "neither compared the two persons nor intended to make such a comparison. (Instead Kohl sought to) make it clear that the impact of public relations efforts does not necessarily say anything about the quality of the politics in question" (cited in McCartney 1986).

While Helmut Kohl's statement does not make a comparison in a strictly syntactic sense, mentioning the two persons in the same breath clearly links them in the eyes of the audience. Even if the sender might not have intended to make such an association, the interpretation of the statement by the audience is steered into a certain direction.

- An extreme form of personification is the *construction of the sender as a single collective actor*. Populists often use the rhetoric tactic of personalizing "the people" as a unified subject. "Right-wing versions define 'the people' as 'ordinary folk', 'the nation', and 'patriots' against the dominant elites represented by liberalism, leftist parties, the media, universities, and national and international organizations that champion globalism, cosmopolitanism, foreign interests, and 'others' groups (from racial minorities to immigrants). In contrast, left-wing populism generally understands 'the people' as workers, peasants, and immigrants against 'the elites' represented by economic/financial powers, the oligarchy, the media, and international capital" (Waisbord 2018, p. 26).

6.6.1.3 Non-Linguistic Tactics of Instrumental Communication

While fake news and doublespeak are verbal tactics of instrumental communication, there exist also a number of non-linguistic instruments that can be used to mislead, discriminate or dominate others. In line with the classification developed in Chapter 6.2, para-verbal, non-verbal and extra-verbal tactics can be distinguished.

Para-verbal characteristics of **ethnocentric speech** are, for example, talking loudly and slowly, and exaggerated pronunciation (Lukens 1978). While these speech patterns are supposedly used to help persons who are not fluent in the language of conversation to follow it, they impose a hierarchy between the sender and receiver. Ethnocentric speech promotes the speaker into a dominant position and marginalizes the culturally different audience to recipients of orders.

Cultural and racial bias can also be expressed through *non-verbal* behaviors, such as facial expressions and body movements. For example, antipathy and avoidance are signaled through interpersonal "coldness" including fewer smiles, more physical distance, less eye contact and more frequent blinking (Dovidio, Kawakami & Gaertner 2002). These and other non-verbal **expressions of racial bias** affect not only the senders and receivers, but also passive, naïve observers. As the experiments of Willard, Isaac & Carney (2015) reveal, individuals can get infected by racial bias by merely observing subtle non-verbal cues of others.

An important *extra-verbal* element of instrumental communication that is external to the current speech act is **agenda setting**. This involves decisions about who determines the ordering of the discussion, who can participate, in what way, etc. Gatekeepers may deliberately apply rules of conversation that favor some cultures and discriminate others. Moreover, the choice of language can be used to include or exclude speakers of certain languages from the discourse. While argumentative reason would imply to select a language that is shared by the largest number of participants in a multilingual conversation, the instrumental selection of language is motivated by political reasons. For example, individuals may switch to a language that is not understood by some participants in a conversation to make potential objections less likely. As one middle manager of a German MNC in the study of Schuster, Holtbrügge, and Engelhard (2019) remarked: "Although our official corporate language is English, we often switch to German when we talk about technical details—or when we want that foreign colleagues do not understand everything."

The use of a particular **language as a matter of inclusion and exclusion** is satirically illustrated in Amélie Nothomb's (1999) autobiographic novel *Fear and Trembling*. The protagonist Amélie is the daughter of Belgium diplomats who spent the first five years of her life in Japan and speaks Japanese fluently. After graduating from university in Brussels, she returned to Tokyo and started to work as an interpreter in a large Japanese company.

She was immediately in charge of serving tea (*ôchakumi*) for a group of twenty guests. Very proud to have used the most refined Japanese formulas and traditional manners, she was brutally reprimanded by her boss Mr. Saito: "You created an extremely bad atmosphere in this morning's meeting: how could our partners feel at ease, with a white woman who understood their language. From now on, you will not speak Japanese." Forbidden to speak or claim to understand Japanese, she was not able to observe the rule of total silence and submissiveness: "That is impossible. Nobody can obey such an order", she exclaimed. "There always is a way to obey. This is what Western brains should understand."

Vance (2010, p. 4) comments this scene in her intercultural analysis of the novel as follows: "The worst is to be a foreigner who understands, who speaks Japanese and claims to be able to figure out the Nipponese mentality."

6.6.2 Responses to Instrumental Communication

A main challenge of intercultural communication is arguing with people who violate the assumptions of argumentative rationality. The search for adequate responses to instrumental communication has become particularly relevant in the discourse with ethnocentrists, xenophobes, and racists. Depending on the form and degree of instrumental communication, the spectrum of responses reaches from disputing about facts over impeaching the person's credibility and irony to ending the conversation.

6.6.2.1 Disputing about Facts

Because fake news, doublespeak and other tactics of instrumental communication have the potential to substantially undermine the credibility of individuals and organizations, detecting fakes and other manipulative forms of communication becomes crucial. In this context, **linguistic analytics** provides various technical tools:

- *Algorithms for fake news detection* usually analyze news content and social context features of electronic media communication (Shu et al. 2017). For example, techniques of forensic psychology, such as deep syntax and rhetoric structure approaches, are used to capture the differences between deceptive and truthful sentences. Moreover, various stance-based and propagation-based models of social context analysis exist.

- *Deepfake video detection tools* are based on digital media forensics. Particularly, recurring neural network technologies are used to detect intraframe inconsistencies and temporal inconsistencies between frames (Güera & Delp 2018). These technologies analyze, for example, multiple camera views, differences in lightning conditions and the use of different video codecs.

Holtbrügge and Conrad (2020) analyzed the CSR reports of international carmakers to detect discrepancies between announced and realized CSR strategies. Based on a **linguistic content analysis**, they found that CSR reports of decouplers and implementors differ in terms of morphology, syntax, semantics, and pragmatics. For example, decouplers use more articles, more words per sentences, a more negative emotional tone and fewer words connected to risks and anxiety. Only weak intercultural differences between the analyzed firms were revealed.

Beyond technical tools aimed to analyze the truth of messages, instrumental communication in an intercultural context involves several **cognitive aspects** that are often difficult to handle. According to the constructivist concept of culture (Geertz 1973), the very idea of argumentative rationality and its key features, such as reason, logic, truth, etc., is culture-bound and relative to specific language, culture, and socio-historical conditions. Different **forms of cultural relativism** exist that affect the intercultural discourse on argumentative rationality (Baghramian & Carter 2018):

- *Relativism about truth* (*alethic relativism*) indicates that what is true for one culture may not be true for another. In the absence of absolute facts, any discourse about truth is affected by culture-specific frameworks and assumptions. For example, incommensurable terminologies and indigenous concepts (such as *blat, guanxi, jugaad*, etc.) lead to differences in perception and thus different understandings of truth. "Truth hollows its way into the real thanks to the dimension of speech. There is neither true nor false prior to speech" (Lacan 1988, p. 228).

- *Epistemic relativism* denotes that cognitive norms which determine what counts as knowledge vary with and are dependent on the underlying cultural and conceptual framework (Seidel 2014). For example, while the tradition of Enlightenment in Western cultures regards scientific knowledge as fundamental to rational discourse, many African and South-East Asian cultures accept also religious belief systems as legitimate foundations of knowledge. Argumentative communication may therefore not necessarily be based on the independent use of reason, but on spirituality, mysticism, superstition, etc. (Rorty 1979).

- *Relativism about logic*: Different cultures may have incompatible, but internally coherent systems of logic because validity and rules of inference are defined by and relative to the practices of a given community. A vivid example is the way how different cultures deal with logical contradictions. While the *law of non-contradiction* is fundamental to Western thought, many Asian cultures are more willing to accept that conflicting views may be compatible (such as the principles of "ying" and "yang") and therefore are less disposed to recognize or condemn contradictions (Nisbett 2003).

- *Relativism about science* is based on the doctrine that all observations are theory-laden. Different assumptions, classifications and measurements could lead to equally acceptable, but fundamentally different statements. A vivid example is the duality of emic and etic approaches of culture. "Theories can be at odds with each other and yet compatible with all possible data even in the broadest possible sense. In a word, they can be logically incompatible and empirically equivalent" (Kuhn 1970, p. 179).

Like all cultural norms, values, and behaviors, different understandings of truth, knowledge, reason, etc. are not simply "out there" and manifested as objective facts. In contrast, they can be used in intercultural communication in a manipulative way to gain advantages in negotiations. For example, the reference to the concept of face prevalent in many Asian countries may be used strategically to reduce the spectrum of negotiation strategies Western negotiators would apply. Based on the (false) assumption that it is inappropriate to let their Asian counterparts lose face in public, they would refrain from confrontational bargaining tactics as a misunderstood form of cultural adjustment. Thus, the dispute about facts is not only affected by intercultural differences in communication patterns but also by **differences in interests and power asymmetries**.

6.6.2.2 Redirecting the Discourse

While disputing about facts may be the preferred response strategy of rational communicators, it is often difficult or even counterproductive when arguing with extremists. Their worldview is usually not based on empirically testable—and thus principally falsifiable—theories, but selective interpretations of facts which only serve to confirm their worldview. When communicators violate the conditions of argumentative rationality, such as comprehensiveness, truth, rightness, and sincerity, ignoring their message and redirecting the discourse can be an adequate response strategy. As Habermas (2016, p. 38) argues with reference to right-wing populism in Germany: "The mistake (…) lies in acknowledging the battlefront that right-wing populism is defining: 'Us' against the system (…). Only by ignoring their interventions, one can pull the ground from under the feet of the right-wing populists" (Habermas 2016, p. 38). In more profane words, this is expressed by the popular metaphorical adage: "Never wrestle with a pig, you'll both get dirty and the pig will enjoy it."

As the Slovenian philosopher Slavoj Žižek (2003) argues, disputing with extremists about facts bears the **risk of implicitly accepting manipulative discourse categories**. "Knowledge does not necessarily involve truth (…). For example we know Lacan's statement that (…) the

(Continued)

factual truth can be combined with untruth. Let me give you a (…) dramatic example, which makes the same point clearly. Let's take what Nazis claimed about the Jews (…). Even if some of what they claimed was true–nonetheless, anti-Semitism was totally a lie. The moment you even think about endorsing, accepting a discussion of this level, (you'll get lost). For example, let us say, I am a Nazi and you are an honest liberal. I say 'Jews seduce our young girls', 'Jews exploit us'. In response, you say 'No, this is a lie'. Then comes a naïve university neutral idiot and says 'Oh it's difficult, let's take an objective look at it'. You sell your soul to the devil if you do this, because let us be clear, the result will be unambiguous. Yes, the Nazis exaggerated it but not quite. Many Jews were also rich in Germany, and they definitely exploited Germans (…). Some Jews definitely were seducing German girls. Why not? Why is this false? Even if the Nazi were to be true, they lied in the disguise of truth. Because the true question is not 'Is it true what they are claiming about the Jews?' The true question is 'Why, in order to sustain their politics, did they need this fantasy of the Jews?' 'Why did they need this phantasmatic figure of the Jews?'"

6.6.2.3 Impeaching the Person's Credibility

The impeachment of a person's credibility can be regarded as **response to the instrumental communication tactics of personification**. In contrast to disputing about facts, it is not directed toward the content of a message but its sender. Two forms can be distinguished:

- *Providing factual evidence*: The communicator can be confronted with previous statements that contradict his or her current message. Another technique is to doubt the person's competence or experience in the matter in question, for example by referring to his or her inadequate qualification. A risk of this technique is that post-truth politics just regards the lack of formal education as sign of credibility (McIntyre 2018).

- *Entrapment*: In this case, the communicator is brought to reveal their lack of credibility themselves. For example, the person can be confronted with information that he or she should be aware of but is not. Moreover, the person can be tempted to make unreasonable or inconsistent statements that undermine his or her credibility in the eyes of the audience.

A neo-Nazi mayoral candidate whose party protests against the German government's proimmigration policies was questioned about his policies in a public debate ahead of the municipal elections in Völklingen (State of Saarland). Uwe Faust, representing the satirical 'Die Partei', appeared to set a trap for the ultra-right candidate when he asked him a joke question over a supposed regulation. "According to the building code, paragraph 126, each owner is obliged to label his property with the number given by the municipality. I find it alarming that in Völklingen many house numbers are displayed in Arabic numerals. How would you like to take action against this creeping foreigner infiltration?" The neo-Nazi candidate replied: "You just wait until I am mayor. I will change that. Then there will be normal numbers." As he appeared to answer the question seriously, around 600 audience members began howling with laughter. He appeared to brush off the raucous crowd, adding: "Wait a moment, Mr. Faust, until I'm Lord Mayor, and I'll change that" (cited in Farrell 2017).

6.6.2.4 Irony

The use of irony aims at ridiculing and unmasking a person or argument throuh ignorance. According to Socrates, it is a strategy of dissimulation of ignorance as a means of confuting to adversary (Leibowitz 2010). Other means of irony are exaggerations and taking metaphorical statements literally in the disguise of sincerity (Hutcheon 1995). In contrast to serious discourse about arguments, irony seeks to deconstruct doublespeak and discriminatory language through deliberate misunderstanding (Ortmanns 2015).

Irony is a **frequently used rhetoric strategy of artists and comedians**. In November 2017, the artist collective Center for Political Beauty built a replica of the Memorial to the Murdered Jews of Europe on the doorstep of Björn Höcke, the leader of the right-wing Alternative for Germany party in the state of Thuringia. The group erected the guerrilla artwork with 24 cement stelae of varying sizes on a private property neighboring Björn Höcke's house. Höcke gained media attention after giving a controversial speech in Dresden in January 2017 in which he called for a 180-degree shift in the way that the history of World War II is considered, and referred to the Berlin memorial as a "Monument of shame."

The Center for Political Beauty has responded by setting up what they call a "civil society defense of the constitution" group in Thuringia, aimed at the "long-term tracking of right-wing extremists in Germany." As the artists explained, "Because Höcke is a 'secret admirer' of the memorial, we are building one for him directly on his doorstep."

Members of the group of activists said they have been anonymously living as neighbors, "sharing a fence with the right's 'poster boy'" and would only remove the art, which is planned to remain through 2019, once the politician agreed to a deal: If Höcke were to fall to his knees in front of the Holocaust Memorial to beg forgiveness for Germany's actions during World War II, as former chancellor Willy Brandt had once infamously done, the collective said they would stop their action (cited in Bennold 2017).

A major challenge of irony as a response to instrumental communication is that it is sensitive to the particular cultural context. It is often based on word games, bon mots, jokes, puns, fixed expressions, etc. that are difficult to translate into other languages (Lievois & Schoentjes 2010). Moreover, irony often includes subtle allusions to current events, locations, customs or persons of interests. It may therefore not be understood or misunderstood in other cultural contexts.

6.6.2.5 Ending the Conversation

When communicators violate the conditions of argumentative rationality in an extreme way and cate-gorically refuse to mutually search for understanding, individuals may consider to end the conversation, silence the dialogue and walk away. Speech ought not to be tolerated if it seriously threatens to "destroy the collective bonds that normally hold society together" (Bollinger 1986, p. 191).

From an **economic perspective**, potential gains and losses of breaking-off the conversation are compared similar to the calculation of the best alternative to a negotiated agreement (BATNA) in intercultural negotiations. If the disadvantages prevail, ending the conversation would be the most reasonable strategy.

From an **ethical perspective**, ending the conversation is usually based on the motive to give extremists no voice. In line with the "paradox of tolerance" (Popper 1966, p. 265), providing extremists a platform could ruthlessly suppress the speech of those who they discriminate. Moreover, arguing with them could lead to contagion or repulsion effects. Others might perceive this as act of legitimacy and either leave the ground of argumentative rationality themselves or turn away as this contradicts their personal, organizational or cultural values.

The risk of this response strategy is to silence voices with which one disagrees. Extremists often use this in a welcomed way to accuse others of opinion dictatorship and violating the principle of free speech. As Rosenfeld (1987, p. 1482) concludes: "Even if one agrees that the intolerant have no moral right to be tolerated, and that no one has any ethical obligation to tolerate them, powerful political or psychological reasons may still justify tolerating the intolerant."

SUMMARY

Communication is effective if a message is decoded by the receiver in the same way as it was coded by the sender and vice versa. The risk of misunderstandings significantly increases in an intercultural context, as the strength and likelihood of interferences is high.

Successful intercultural communication is contingent on individuals' understanding of culturally diverse forms of verbal, para-verbal, non-verbal, and extra-verbal communication.

The language people speak influences and reflects their perception of reality.

Cultural values determine individuals' negotiation style, tactics, as well as process and influence what kind of outcomes negotiators strive for, how negotiation gains will be distributed, and how agreements will look like.

 Reflection Questions

1. Explain the intercultural communication process in your own words. Which elements do you regard most critical?
2. Think of a popular phrase or saying from your culture. How would you express its meaning to someone from a different culture?
3. Have you ever experienced a situation of intercultural communication failure? If so, what was the situation like and why do you think it occurred? When and how did you discover that something was misunderstood? How did you resolve the misunderstanding?
4. Intercultural guidebooks often recommend that, when working in another country, you should dress similarly to your coworkers in that country. How would this recommendation be interpreted from a postcolonial perspective of intercultural management?
5. Have you ever tried to use irony in an intercultural encounter but failed? How would you describe this situation and what happened afterwards?
6. Which characteristics of BATNA are rather universal and which are rather culture-specific?

7. How can differences in gestures and body language complicate intercultural negotiations and impede the conclusion of a deal?
8. Have you ever experienced instrumental communication in interactions with people of other cultural backgrounds, such as fake news, doublespeak, or non-linguistic tactics? If yes, how did you react?

 End of Chapter Exercise

Supplier Negotiations in China

Imagine you are the head of the global sourcing department of a large German electronics company. In the next week, you will fly to China to negotiate a large contract with a new Chinese supplier. Your key criteria for closing this deal are price, quality, and delivery reliability. You assume that the last two criteria are particularly difficult for the Chinese supplier.

1. How is the negotiation process likely to proceed?
2. What is your strategy to receive a commitment to quality and delivery reliability that you can depend on?
3. Which forms of verbal, para-verbal, non-verbal, and extra-verbal communication do you expect on the side of the Chinese team? How would you respond?
4. During the negotiation, the Chinese team provides you with information about the company that you find doubtful. What would you do to assess the validity of this information?

 Further Reading

The books by Martin and Nakayama (2017), Hua (2018), Jandt (2018), Neuliep (2018), and Klyukanov (2020) are comprehensive introductions to intercultural communication.

An interdisciplinary overview is provided in the handbooks of Kotthoff and Spencer-Oatey (2008), Jackson (2012), Kim (2017), and Rings and Rasinger (2020).

The intercultural aspects of business negotiations are discussed by Usunier (2018), Ghauri, Ott, and Rammal (2020), and in the handbook of Khan and Ebner (2019).

7

INTERCULTURAL MANAGEMENT OF INDIVIDUALS, TEAMS, AND ORGANIZATIONS

LEARNING OBJECTIVES

By the end of this chapter, you will be able to

- know the impact of culture on career patterns, motivation, and leadership,
- understand the effects of cultural diversity on teamwork,
- comprehend the effects of culture on organizational design and inter-organizational collaboration,
- critically evaluate the methodologies and results of intercultural management studies.

Cultural differences often result in different management practices and outcomes. Evidence for the strong impact of culture on management exists on all levels. On the individual level, cultural differences affect, for example, career patterns, work motivation, and leadership styles. These implications are discussed in the next section.

Afterwards, the impact of culture on the team level is elaborated. Research in this context is particularly focused on multicultural teams and their effectiveness in different contexts.

On the corporate level, cultural differences often lead to preferences for different organizational structures and processes. This topic is addressed in the final section.

7.1 INDIVIDUAL LEVEL: CAREER PATTERNS, MOTIVATION, AND LEADERSHIP IN DIFFERENT CULTURES

7.1.1 Culture and Career Patterns

Numerous studies show that career expectations and career patterns differ across cultures. More specifically, effects of culture on recruitment and selection, training and development, and promotion can be distinguished.

7.1.1.1 Recruitment and Selection

Research has revealed significant cultural differences in terms of *recruitment and selection criteria* (Figure 7.1). In cultures that are high on performance orientation or universalism, such as the United States, "hard criteria" (i.e., education, job-related knowledge and competencies, technical and cognitive skills) are more relevant than provenance or outer appearance (Aycan 2005). Cultures that are high on femininity, low on performance orientation, oriented toward ascribed status, or particularistic rely more on "soft criteria" (e.g., social and interpersonal skills, social class, age). A vivid example is China, where ascribed status and sociopolitical connections (*guanxi*) have long been more important than applicants' merit and credentials (Cheung & Gui 2006; Huang 2008). In India, belonging to the same "in-group" as the manager (e.g., the same family, homeland or caste) is a key selection criterion (Holtbrügge, Friedmann & Puck 2010).

Important determinants of *recruitment channels* are uncertainty avoidance and collectivism. Countries that score high on these two cultural dimensions prefer internal recruitment. The promotion of current employees to higher positions in the organization ensures and rewards loyalty to the firm and strengthens in-group ties (Holtbrügge, Friedmann & Puck 2010). Moreover, internal recruitment confirms the existing status in the organization and thus reduces uncertainty (Prince & Kabst 2019).

Recruitment sources and methods in cultures that are characterized by universalism or performance orientation are predominantly formal, structured, and widespread. Moreover, the focus is on job-related criteria. On the contrary, cultures that are high on uncertainty avoidance, oriented toward ascribed status or collectivistic, prefer informal and network-based recruitment sources. For example, employee referrals are one of the most widely used recruitment sources in countries like India (Holtbrügge, Friedmann & Puck 2010), China (Wang & Seifert 2017) and the Middle East (Al-Jahwari & Budhwar 2016), while they are regarded as a form of nepotism in universalistic and individualistic cultures, such as Germany and the United States (Schlachter & Pieper 2019).

According to the India Recruiting Trends 2016 study of LinkedIn, at least 65% of recruiters in India use **employee referral programs** (Chaturvedi 2015). They are most common in IT-companies. **Infosys** uses a mobile application "ConnectInfy", where employees can refer their friends for Infosys job opportunities, search and share open positions across multiple social networking platforms, get real-time status updates for referred profiles, and earn rewards. **Tata Consultancy Services** has a referral program called "Rapid Hire," which provides 24×7 referral help desk to encourage employee referrals. The resumes are collected and provided on the spot screening, followed by a preliminary evaluation and instant feedback. **Wipro** uses a similar fully automated employee referral program called "Wiplinks" (Behera & Pathy 2013).

Employee referrals have a positive effect on prehire recruitment outcomes, such as the quantity and quality of the applicant pool and lower recruitment costs, and on posthire outcomes, such as job satisfaction, job performance, and turnover. "The employees making referrals understand the workplace culture and ethics better. They know what kind of candidates their organization is looking for. Moreover, since their reputation is under the scanner, they will recommend only those candidates who can match the organization's expectations & culture, and are capable of doing a great job. This enables hiring managers to sift through lesser resumes and get a head start on promising leads" (SHRM India Content Team 2017).

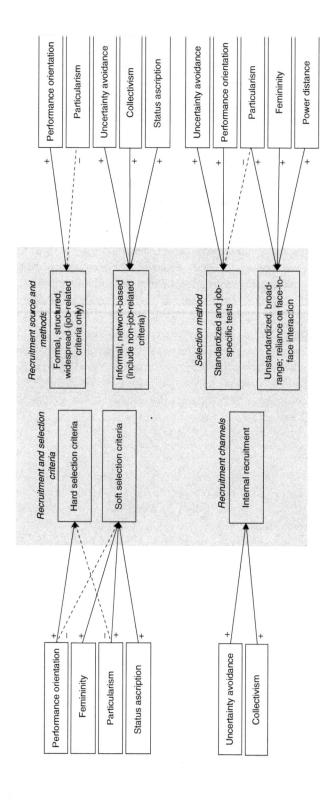

Figure 7.1 Cultural influences on recruitment and selection

Source: Based on Aycan (2005).

Regarding *selection methods*, standardized tools (e.g., cognitive ability tests, personality inventories, psychometric tests, assessment centers) are common in cultures that are high on performance orientation or universalism. Moreover, uncertainty avoidance increases the use of standardized tests (Prince & Kabst 2019). On the other hand, selection methods tend to be less standardized, broad-ranged, and rely on face-to-face interactions in cultures that are high on particularism, femininity, or power distance.

7.1.1.2 Training and Development

Cultural differences can also be observed with regard to the ways in which employees are trained and developed (Figure 7.2). Extant research shows that *training needs* in performance-oriented or universalistic cultures are mostly determined based on performance outcomes (Aycan 2005). In low performance–oriented and particularistic cultures, such as India, employees who maintain good relations with higher managers are often selected for attractive training programs (i.e., training overseas or in resorts) as a reward for their loyalty (Holtbrügge, Friedmann & Puck 2010). Moreover, in-group favoritism based on kinship or tribal ties is common. In collectivistic and high power distance cultures, such as the Middle East, training needs of the work group are determined by the pater-nalistic manager who is assumed to know what is best for the employees (Wilkins 2001). In low power distance cultures, training needs are usually determined jointly by the employee and his/her superior.

Regarding *training contents and methods*, group-focused training with greater attention on the collective self and enhancement of in-group capability is more effective in collectivistic cultures. On the contrary, individual-focused training that emphasizes personal capability and private self is more effective for participants from individualistic cultures (Earley 1994). Research also found that individuals in high uncertainty avoidance and high power distance cultures are more receptive to one-way lecturing rather than participative discussions. The instructor is perceived as an individual of (superior) authority and is expected to provide definitive answers and guidelines. On the contrary, individuals in cultures characterized by low uncertainty avoidance and low power dis-tance prefer interactive teaching methods and are more open to discuss training contents critically (Aycan 2005).

Training design is also affected by intercultural variation in *learning style*. By linking Kolb's (1984) model of learning style preferences to the cultural values of learners, Holtbrügge and Mohr (2010) found a statistically significant positive effect of individualism on the preference for a "convergence" learning style, i.e., the combination of active experimentation with abstract conceptualization. Moreover, the degree of masculinity increases the likelihood of preferring an "assimilator" learning style, characterized by the combination of abstract conceptualization and reflective observation.

7.1.1.3 Promotion

A third important aspect of career patterns that differs across cultures is the *criteria of promotion decisions* (Figure 7.2). In collectivistic, low performance–oriented or high power distance cultures, in-group favoritism in promotion decisions is common (Aycan 2005). In such cultural contexts, promotion criteria include seniority, loyalty, and good interpersonal relationships with superiors. For example, seniority plays an important role in Asian countries like Japan, Korea, Malaysia, Thailand,

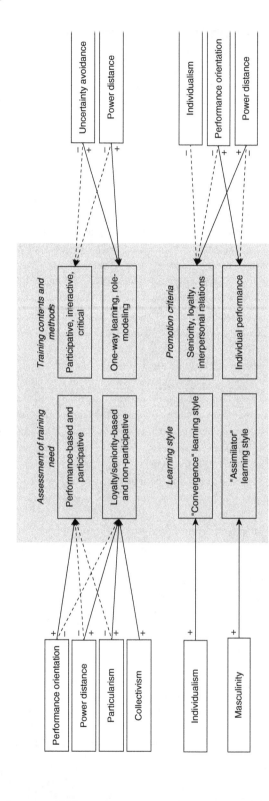

Figure 7.2 Cultural influences on training, development, and promotion

Sources: Based on Earley (1994), Aycan (2005), and Holtbrügge & Mohr (2010).

and Vietnam, where respect for age is a key cultural value (Zhu, Warner & Rowley 2007). In the Middle East, promotion is often based on family ties or close friendships (Budhwar et al. 2019), while in Russia, good relationships and personal loyalty to superiors are key (Gurkov & Zelenova 2011–12).

An extreme example for the **relevance of personal relationships and loyalty for promotion decisions in Russia** is the *Saint Petersburg Connection* of Russian President Vladimir Putin. A large number of senior politicians and managers of state-owned enterprises were—like Putin—born in the city of Leningrad (renamed to Saint Petersburg in 1991), studied together with him or worked with Putin since his appointment as advisor and later member of the Government of Saint Petersburg in the early 1990s. Prominent examples include the following (Pribylovskij 2016):

- German Gref (former Minister of Economics and Trade, CEO of Sberbank)
- Boris Gryzlov (former Interior Minister and Speaker of the State Duma)
- Viktor Ivanov (Chairman of the Board of Directors of Aeroflot)
- Sergei Ivanov (former Minister of Defense, Deputy Prime Minister and Chief of Staff of the Presidential Executive Office)
- Dmitrij Kosak (former Deputy Prime Minister)
- Aleksej Kudrin (former Minister of Finance)
- Valentina Matviyenko (former Governor of Saint Petersburg, Chairwoman of the Federation Council)
- Alexej Miller (CEO of Gazprom)
- Sergey Mironov (former Chairman of the Federation Council)
- Vitaly Mutko (former Deputy Prime Minister and Minister of Sport)
- Sergey Naryshkin (former Chairman of the State Duma and Kremlin Chief of Staff, Director of the Foreign Intelligence Service)
- Leonid Rejman (former Minister of Communications and Information Technologies)
- Igor Sechin (former Deputy Prime Minister, CEO of Rosneft)
- Viktor Zubkov (former Prime Minister and Deputy Prime Minister)

In high performance-oriented or low power distance cultures, promotion decisions are primarily based on merit. In countries like Germany and the United States, individual performance and significant contributions to the organization are more important than interpersonal relationships. However, nepotism, i.e., the preferential treatment of family members within an employment context by giving them positions based on kinship ties rather than merit or abilities, is quite prevalent in American and European family firms (Jaskiewicz et al. 2013; Firfiray et al. 2018). This example shows that national cultures shape career patterns and expectations; however, their impact on the values and behaviors of individuals—as in many other areas of management—may be amplified, mitigated, or modified by other manifestations of culture, such as corporate cultures, industry cultures, professional cultures, etc. (Chapter 2.2).

7.1.1.4 Typology of Career Models by Evans, Lank and Farquhar

While several studies have analyzed the impact of various cultural dimensions on individual aspects of careers, Evans, Lank, and Farquhar (1989) proposed a **typology of career models** that combines the recruitment channels (internally or externally), the stage at which those with high potential are identified (entry or later on), the type of work experiences acquired within or outside the company or industry (specialist vs. generalist), and the criteria for selection and promotion (Figure 7.3):

- In the *Japanese model* (*elite cohort approach*), potential managers are recruited from the best university graduates and regularly trained and assessed during an intensive potential identification phase lasting up to eight years. During this phase, junior managers rotate through various areas (which may include working at the assembly line). Whether an employee rises to a management level or has to leave the company (*up or out*), depends on numerous internal assessments. Career steps are small but frequent.
- In contrast to the Japanese model, in which potential managers are initially deployed at lower hierarchical levels, the entry into the *Latin model* (*elite political approach*) takes place at a medium to high hierarchical level. For example, in France the potential identification takes place after the recruitment at elite universities (*grandes écoles*) directly during the entry phase. In addition to performance, the career advancement depends in particular on the successful use of the relationships that were usually established at the university. Self-promotion and alliance-building are key, and frequent transitions between the corporate, political, and educational sectors are common.

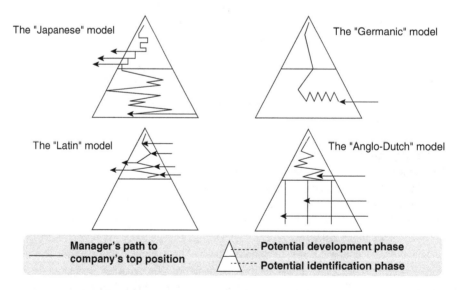

Figure 7.3 Career models in different cultures
Source: Adapted from Evans, Lank & Farquhar (1989, p. 126).

The exceptional role of elite universities for professional careers in France can be illustrated by using the example of the **École nationale d'administration (ENA)** in Strasbourg. The ENA selects and undertakes initial training of senior French officials and is one of the main pathways to high positions in the public and private sectors. Four of the last six French presidents (Valéry Giscard d'Estaing, Jacques Chirac, François Hollande, and Emmanuel Macron) have been ENA graduates. Moreover, several heads of government and ministers, presidents of international organizations and industry leaders, such as Guillaume Pepy (CEO of SNCF), Michel Bon (former CEO of Carrefour and France Telecom), Louis Gallois (former CEO of EADS), Henri de Castries (former CEO of Axa) and Pierre-André de Chalendar (CEO of Saint-Gobain), are ENA alumni.

Although the extremely difficult entrance exam is open to everyone and supposedly meritocratic, ENA students are mostly children of wealthy families, often those with past connections to the school. Critics have, therefore, accused the ENA of educating a narrow ruling class who are prone to groupthink and averse to alternative perspectives (Guilbaud 2018). In the wake of populist protests, such as the *gilets jaunes* (yellow vests), against the tight network of ENA graduates as an elite governing class out of touch with civilians, French President Macron announced the closure of the institution in 2021. Public institutions should offer "chances to all of our young people on the basis of merit and not their social or family origins (…). If we want to build a society of equal opportunity and national excellence, we must reset the rules for recruitment, careers, and access to the upper echelons of the civil service (…). That's why we will change the system of training, selection, and career development by getting rid of the ENA and several other institutions" (cited in Cuddy 2019).

- In the *Germanic model* (*functional approach*), the potential identification mostly takes place during a one- or two-year apprenticeship trial. While cross-functional rotation is typical for this phase, advancement to the top management levels is primarily based on the development of expert knowledge in a narrowly defined functional area, often referred to as "chimney careers." A high number of managers have earned a doctoral degree in engineering or business administration. Careers from the cradle to the grave in a single company are not uncommon.

- The *Anglo-Dutch model* (*managed development approach*) is characterized by a generalist perspective in personnel recruitment and development. Without concentrating on special elites, junior managers are selected for particular functions; however, their cross-functional applicability is assessed in internal assessment centers. Career advancement, which begins after a systematic test and development phase of around six years, is then associated with frequent cross-functional job changes. In contrast to functional specialization in the Germanic model, the focus here is on general management skills.

The validity of the typology of Evans, Lank, and Farquhar (1989) was confirmed in several empirical studies (Bauer & Bertin-Mourot 1996; Davoine & Ravasi 2013). Although the internationalization of firms and careers has led to the cross-cultural convergence of some career patterns, cultural influences remain strong. Research, however, is restricted to older top managers at the end of their professional careers, while young professionals ("generations X and Y") may have different career expectations (Dries, Pepermans, & De Kerpel 2008). Moreover, the typology is limited to Western industrialized countries and does not consider divergent career patterns in emerging markets, such as China, India, and Russia (Khapova & Korotov 2007; Chawla, Dokadia & Rai 2017).

7.1.2 Culture and Work Motivation

The question whether work motivation is universal or culture-bound has been frequently discussed in intercultural management literature. Although the concept of motivation is generally relevant across the globe, important cultural differences exist. As Adler and Gundersen (2008, p. 186) note: "Human needs may well include fundamental or universal aspects, but their importance and the ways in which they express themselves differ across cultures."

A vivid example for **neglecting cultural differences in work motivation** is the failed operations of **Wal-Mart** in Germany. When the American retailer entered the German market in 1997, it tried to transfer most of its management practices. For example, the check-in and check-out desk cashiers were ordered to always smile at customers. The German employees, however, felt uncomfortable with this practice of emotional labor, as showing emotions in public is uncommon in a country characterized by a low score on Hofstede's indulgence vs. restraint dimension. Another intercultural difference between the United States and Germany relates to power distance. While American employees are accustomed to strict guidelines (e.g., about prohibiting inter-office romances and reporting inappropriate behavior of colleagues), German employees were reluctant to accept rules that restrict their personal space. On the contrary, they expected to be consulted by their superiors about important work-related issues. Also, extreme salary differences between mostly American managers and German blue-collar workers caused discontent. Finally, Wal-Mart refused to adopt German collective agreements and to consult with elected works councils. While trade unions and workers representatives are disregarded in the individualistic US-culture, they are an important and respected part of the more collectivistic and communitarian German culture. As a result of these intercultural conflicts in work motivation, Wal-Mart Germany was faced with frequent resignations of managers and high employee turnover rates. Along with other reasons, this led to the company's withdrawal from the German market in 2006 (Christopherson 2007; Hamza & Nizam 2016; Tsui-Auch & Chow 2019).

Existing research has identified significant and consistent effects of culture on various aspects of work motivation (Chiang 2005; Chiang & Birtch 2005). Referring to **Hofstede's cultural dimensions**, the following relationships were found (Table 7.1):

- High *power distance* cultures value structured and closely supervised tasks. Incentives based on organizational status are common. Moreover, large salary differences between hierarchical levels exist. An exception is the United States where power distance is small,

Table 7.1   Relation between Hofstede's cultural dimensions and work motivation

Cultural dimension	Impact on work motivation
Power distance	Structured supervised tasks, large salary differences
Uncertainty avoidance	Job security, fixed rewards, formalized job descriptions
Individualism vs. collectivism	Group membership, social needs
Masculinity vs. femininity	Performance-oriented rewards, status symbols
Long-term orientation	Life-long employment, personal development
Indulgence vs. restraint	Work-life balance, emotional relations

but salary differences are among the highest in the world. On the contrary, tasks in cultures with low power distance are less regulated and occupations are equipped with larger discretionary space.

- In cultures characterized by strong *uncertainty avoidance*, job guarantees, stress-reducing work in teams, and fixed rewards resulting in predictable work outcomes and wages are highly advocated. Moreover, formalized job descriptions and written rules are preferred. In contrast, individuals in low uncertainty avoidance cultures are more tolerant of alternative behavior and consider creative and innovative tasks intrinsically enjoyable.

- In *collectivistic* countries, affiliation and appreciation needs are generally more important than those of self-fulfillment. Accordingly, working in teams and group-oriented assessment criteria are of high value. Work is not viewed as an independent entity but rather embedded in the relationship context. In *individualistic* cultures, on the contrary, career advancement opportunities and individual performance criteria are preferred. People in these cultures see organizations less as a social system and more as a set of functions, tasks, people, and resources in which individuals compete.

- The degree of *masculinity* prevailing in a culture mainly affects the preferred form of incentives. In masculine cultures, performance-oriented rewards, monetary incentives, and status symbols (company cars, office size, expense accounts, etc.) are of high value. *Feminine* cultures prefer social benefits, flexible working hours, and purposeful work content. Solidarity with others is more important than competition and individual power.

- In cultures with a *long-term orientation*, life-long employment, personnel development, and a remuneration policy based on long-term criteria are valued, while short-term and highly flexible performance incentives have little effect. In cultures with a *short-term orientation*, frequent job changes are common. Employees prefer short deadlines and quick feedback.

- In *indulgent* cultures, work-life balance is of great importance. Employees are more likely to leave their employer when they are not satisfied with their job. *Restraint* cultures, on the other hand, place a high value on control and professionalism. With regards to the workplace and work content, technical features (quality, functionality, precision, etc.) are more important than emotional aspects (design, aesthetics, image, etc.).

The interaction of various cultural dimensions and their impact on motivation can be illustrated by using the example of the Japanese carmaker **Toyota**. Job descriptions usually only express the rank in the organizational layers, without specifying the tasks, responsibilities, and required skills. In line with Japan's *collectivist orientation*, employees mostly work together in teams, where jobs overlap and connect to enhance team spirit and team performance. This, however, makes it difficult to accurately measure individual outcomes. Therefore, incentives are paid as team bonuses and do not take individual performance into account. Individual bonuses are only given based on seniority, tenure, and family situation, reflecting *long-term orientation*. In accordance with the pronounced *masculinity* of the Japanese culture, this system of work motivation applies exclusively to Toyota's male core employees (Kiyoshi 2006; Saruta 2006).

7.1.3 Culture and Leadership

The relationship between culture and leadership is a key topic in comparative management research that has been addressed in numerous studies (e.g., Ardichvili & Kuchinke 2002; Byrne & Bradley 2007; Jogulu 2010; Gutierrez, Spencer & Zhu 2012). One of the most comprehensive approaches to compare leadership styles in different countries is the GLOBE study (House et al. 2014). From a large pool of leadership items derived from extant research, a factor analysis identified six **global leadership dimensions** (Dorfman, Hanges & Brodbeck 2004):

- *Charismatic/value-based leadership* reflects the ability to inspire, motivate, and expect high performance outcomes from others based on firmly held core values. It largely corresponds to the transformational leadership approach (Bass & Riggio 2006) and includes six primary leadership dimensions: visionary, inspirational, self-sacrifice, integrity, decisive, and performance oriented.
- *Team-oriented leadership* emphasizes effective team building and the implementation of a common purpose or goal among team members. This global leadership dimension includes five primary leadership dimensions: collaborative team orientation, team integrator, diplomatic, malevolent (reverse scored), and administratively competent.
- *Participative leadership* denotes the degree to which managers involve others in making and implementing decisions. The opposite of this leadership dimension is autocratic leadership style. It includes two primary leadership dimensions labeled nonparticipative and autocratic (both reverse scored).
- *Humane-oriented leadership* reflects supportive and considerate leadership, including compassion and generosity as well. It includes two primary leadership dimensions labeled modesty and humane orientation.
- *Autonomous leadership* refers to independent and individualistic leadership attributes. This dimension is measured by a single primary leadership dimension labeled autonomous leadership, consisting of individualistic, independence, autonomous, and unique attributes.
- *Self-protective leadership* focuses on ensuring the safety and security of the individual and the group through status enhancement and face saving. It includes five primary leadership dimensions labeled self-centered, status conscious, conflict inducer, face saver, and procedural.

A major question addressed by GLOBE concerns the extent to which specific leader attributes and behaviors are universally endorsed as contributing to effective leadership (*culture-free*), and the extent to which attributes and behaviors are linked to cultural characteristics (*culture-bound*). In order to answer this question, over 1,000 chief executive officers and more than 5,000 members of the top management teams in over 1,000 corporations in 24 countries were studied (House et al. 2014).

The leadership style that is most strongly endorsed in all societal clusters is the *charismatic/value-based leadership style*. On a 7-point Likert-scale, it shows a high mean value of 5.82 (minimum = 5.35, maximum = 6.05) across all societal clusters (Table 7.2). Regardless of the stage of economic development of a country and its cultural characteristics, employees prefer leaders who emphasize a charismatic and transformational leadership style. However, there is also a "dark side" of charisma, evidenced by narcissistic, totalitarian, exploitative, and self-aggrandizing charismatics (Den Hartog et al. 1999).

A second leadership dimension showing a high degree of universal acceptance is the *team-oriented leadership style* (mean = 5.73, minimum = 5.47, maximum = 5.96). Although generally endorsed, it is found to be particularly critical for effective leadership in the Southern Asian, Confucian Asian, and Latin American clusters.

The leadership styles found to be more dependent on the cultural contexts are the participative, humane, autonomous, and self-protective leadership styles. The Germanic, Anglo, and Nordic clusters were particularly supportive of *participative leadership*.

Leaders who show a *humane leadership orientation*, as perceived by their followers, are especially valued in the Asian, sub-Saharan Africa, and Anglo clusters. On the contrary, humane leaders are less endorsed in Latin America and Nordic Europe.

The assessment of the *autonomous leadership* dimension shows the largest variance across countries. Compared to the other clusters, it is most strongly endorsed in Eastern European countries. Many business leaders in these countries emphasize their uniqueness and their autonomous performance.

While *self-protective leadership* is generally viewed as neutral or negative, this varies significantly by culture. For example, self-protective leader attributes are seen as extremely inhibiting to effective leadership in Nordic and Germanic European cultures; however far less so in Asian cultures.

From a comparative perspective, distinctive country patterns can be observed (House et al. 2014). The United States, for example, scores high on the dimensions of charismatic/value-based, team-oriented, participative, and humane-oriented leadership. On the contrary, the scores for the dimensions of autonomous and self-protective leadership are low. Germany scores low on team-oriented, humane-oriented, and self-protective leadership, and high on participative and autonomous leadership. Russia has the highest score for autonomous and the lowest scores for participative and humane-oriented leadership. And with the exception of the charismatic/value-based dimension, China and Japan show moderate scores for most leadership styles.

When **correlating the predominant leadership styles with the nine cultural dimensions of the GLOBE project,** performance orientation and humane orientation show the strongest impacts (Table 7.3). Performance orientation has a negative relationship with self-protective leadership style and strong to very strong positive relationships with all other leadership styles. Similarly, strong to very strong positive relationships between humane orientation and the charismatic/value-based, team-oriented, participative, and humane-oriented leadership styles are revealed, while the relationship with the autonomous leadership style is strongly negative. The other seven GLOBE cultural dimensions show partial correlations with the six leadership dimensions, without any indication of systematic patterns.

Table 7.2 Leadership scores for GLOBE societal clusters

	Charismatic/ value-based	Team-oriented	Participative	Humane-oriented	Autonomous	Self-protective
Eastern Europe	5.74	5.88	5.08	4.76	4.20	3.67
Latin America	5.99	5.96	5.42	4.85	3.51	3.62
Latin Europe	5.78	5.73	5.37	4.45	3.66	3.19
Confucian Asia	5.63	5.61	4.99	5.04	4.04	3.72
Nordic Europe	5.93	5.77	5.75	4.42	3.94	2.72
Anglo	6.05	5.74	5.73	5.08	3.82	3.08
Sub-Saharan Africa	5.79	5.70	5.31	5.16	3.63	3.55
Southern Asia	5.97	5.86	5.06	5.38	3.99	3.83
Germanic Europe	5.93	5.62	5.86	4.71	4.16	3.03
Middle East	5.35	5.47	4.97	4.80	3.68	3.79
Mean	5.82	5.73	5.35	4.87	3.86	3.42
Min	5.35	5.47	4.97	4.42	3.51	2.72
Max	6.05	5.96	5.86	5.38	4.20	3.83
SD	0.21	0.14	0.33	0.31	0.24	0.38

Source: Dorfman, Hanges & Brodbeck (2004, p. 680); own calculations.

Table 7.3 Cultural values as predictors of GLOBE leadership dimensions

Societal culture dimensions (values)	GLOBE leadership dimensions					
	Charismatic/ value-based	Team-oriented	Participative	Humane-oriented	Autonomous	Self-protective
Uncertainty avoidance		+ +	− −	+ +		+ +
Power distance	− −		− −			+ +
Institutional collectivism					− −	
In-Group collectivism	+ +	+ +				
Gender egalitarianism	+ +		+ +			
Assertiveness			− −	+ +		− −
Future orientation	+	+		+		
Performance orientation	+ +	+	+ +	+	+ +	−
Humane orientation	+	+	+ +	+ +	− −	

Notes: "+" indicates a positive relationship between the culture dimension and the leadership dimension; "+ +" indicates strong positive relationship between the culture dimension and the leadership dimension; "−" indicates a negative relationship between the culture dimension and the leadership dimension; "− −" indicates a strong negative relationship between the culture dimension and the leadership dimension.

Source: Dorfman et al. (2012, p. 507).

The former German general manager of a large German company in India described the **complexity of leadership in a foreign country** in a personal conversation as follows: "Before I went to India, I participated in an intercultural training and read many books about Indian culture. I was very aware of the Indian caste system and the fact that Indians prefer authoritarian leaders. So when I arrived here, I tried to adapt to the Indian culture and manage the company accordingly.

After a while I recognized that some of our best employees had left the company. I was very astonished because I seemed to have done everything right. When I asked one of my Indian colleagues for advice, he explained: 'You are right that the average Indian would prefer authoritarian leaders. But our employees are different. They applied because they expected a more participative style that our company is known for. And then they were disappointed that we are just like any other Indian company and quit.'

When I heard this, I put everything aside that I learnt about leadership in India and begun to manage the company in the way I would manage a company in Germany: participative. And this turned out to be the most successful way."

A specific and important aspect of leadership is **ethical leadership**. Based on GLOBE data, Resick et al. (2006) analyzed the degree to which four aspects of ethical leadership—character/integrity, altruism, collective motivation, and encouragement—contribute to effective leadership across cultures. The authors found that the endorsement of the *character/integrity* dimension (referring to patterns of intentions, inclinations, and virtues that provide the moral foundation for behavior) is the highest for societies included in the Nordic European cluster and the lowest for the Middle Eastern cluster. Regarding the *altruism* dimension (which involves engaging in behaviors intended to help others without expecting any external rewards), the mean endorsement is the lowest in the Nordic European and Latin European clusters and the highest in Southeast Asian societies. *Collective motivation* (referring to increasing followers' awareness of ethical behavior) is valued most by societies in the Anglo, Latin American, and Nordic clusters than in societies in the Middle Eastern cluster. Finally, Middle Eastern societies tend to endorse *encouragement* (defined as leaders' identification with and respect for their followers) to a lesser degree than societies comprising the remaining ten culture clusters.

Also based on the GLOBE study, Parboteeah, Bronson, and Cullen (2005) analyzed whether national culture affects the willingness to justify ethically suspect behaviors. The authors found that *performance orientation* and *assertiveness* are positively related to the willingness to justify ethically suspect behaviors. The emphasis on competition, achievement, and individual outcomes may direct one's focus on merely fulfilling an objective, ultimately overlooking the means by which one fulfills it. On the contrary, *institutional collectivism* and *humane orientation* have negative effects. In collectivist and humane-oriented societies, the role of the group and solidarity with others is emphasized. Any ethically suspect behavior would disturb these fundamental values and is, therefore, rejected.

While the GLOBE study compared leadership styles between different countries, more recent research shows that **leadership is also contingent on intracultural diversity**. Aktas, Gelfand, and Hanges (2016) combined data from the GLOBE project with data on cultural tightness vs. looseness from Gelfand et al. (2011). Analyses of data across 29 countries show that *cultural tightness* is positively related to the endorsement of autonomous leadership and negatively related to the endorsement of charismatic and team leadership, even when controlling for in-group collectivism, power distance, and future orientation at the societal and organizational level of analysis. People from culturally tight societies believe that autonomous, individualistic, and independent leaders who do not seek collaboration from colleagues are more effective than those from loose cultures. This result is explained by the high need for closure in tight cultures, allowing for quick decisions by autonomous leaders and does not require extensive consultations with others. Consequently, people from culturally tight societies view leaders who are team-oriented as less effective than do loose cultures. The study also shows a negative relationship between tightness and the perceived effectiveness of charismatic leadership. This means that the status quo and prevention orientation of tight cultures renders visionary and inspirational leadership attributes to be seen as less effective as compared with loose cultures that focus more on innovation (Chua, Roth & Lemoine 2015).

In a similar study, Youssef and Christodoulou (2018) found a strong **negative relationship between intracultural variation and managerial discretion**. The authors argue that executives in heterogeneous societies—in terms of individualism, uncertainty tolerance, and power distance—are faced with a greater number of stakeholder groups and, thus, constrained in the number of actions they can take. In such situations, participative leadership would likely be perceived as the most effective style, as this reflects the degree to which executives take into consideration the needs of others and involve stakeholders in their decision-making processes. By doing so, executives would be able to reduce the number of constraints placed on their actions. Conversely, in homogeneous cultures in which executives enjoy more managerial discretion, autonomous leaders who work independently, without collaboration or feedback from others, would be more effective.

7.1.4 Critical Evaluation

Several *comparative management studies* have analyzed the impact of culture on leadership and—to a lesser degree—careers and motivation in different countries. Particularly, the GLOBE study provides a comprehensive overview of culturally endorsed leadership styles and preferences across the world. However, few studies have taken a *cross-cultural perspective* and analyzed the **transferability of motivational practices and leadership styles** from one country to another. The few existing studies in this context mostly take a North-American perspective and either implicitly assume universality or apply models and measures developed in this region, while the transferability of concepts developed in other parts of the world has rarely been analyzed (Dickson et al. 2012; Mayrhofer et al. 2016). As House (1995, p. 443) states, most leadership theories and measures have originated in the United States and have embedded dominant American cultural assumptions and values: "stressing individualism rather than collectivism; emphasizing rationality rather than asceticism, spirituality, religion, or superstition; stated in terms of individual rather than group incentives; stressing follower responsibilities rather than rights; assuming hedonistic rather than altruistic motivation; and assuming centrality of work and democratic value orientation."

The lack of cross-cultural research becomes particularly apparent in the context of executives and employees who work outside of their home country. Little is known, for example, about the implications of mismatch between the promotion, motivation, and leadership practices of foreign expatriates and the respective preferences and expectations of local employees. Moreover, the management of multicultural teams consisting of members with diverse cultural backgrounds has hardly been addressed. **Practical implications often remain vague**, as the conclusions of the authors of the GLOBE study illustrate: "A CEO needs to match the society's expectations with regard to an idealized level of leadership. CEOs that fall below this expectation most often results in negative outcomes either in the form of poor TMT (top-management team) attitudes or firm performance. The good news is that CEOs who exceed the society's expectations can expect to find superior TMT outcomes and firm performance" (Dorfman et al. 2012, p. 512).

Another shortcoming of comparative management studies on careers, motivation, and leadership in different cultures is that they—with few exceptions (e.g., Aktas, Gelfand & Hanges 2016; Youssef & Christodoulou 2018)—report **national averages**. Country means, however, do not adequately reflect the distribution of leadership preferences within a country. Countries may have equal or very similar cultural means, but large differences in intracultural variation. This applies particularly to culturally diverse countries, such as India, South Africa, and the United States (Chapter 5.3.2). Moreover, there is a growing number of managers with a *bi- or even multicultural background*. Their leadership style is presumably not only influenced by their country of origin, but also by their country of education, country of first work experience, country of first leadership position, etc. This diversity of cultural influences, however, cannot be adequately captured by country means.

There is a large number of managers who were born in one country, educated in another, and have led firms in a third country. A notable example is *Anshu Jain*. He is a British Indian manager, born in India, who served as the Co-CEO of Deutsche Bank from 2012 until July 2015. Jain studied economics at the University of Delhi, India, and holds an MBA in Finance from the University of Massachusetts Amherst, Unites States (Jain 2014).

Indra Nooyi is an Indian-American business executive and former chairman and CEO of PepsiCo (2006-2016). She was born in Madras (now Chennai), India, and completed her schooling in the Indian state of Tamil Nadu. Nooyi received bachelor degrees in physics, chemistry, and mathematics from the University of Madras in 1974, and a postgraduate diploma from the Indian Institute of Management Calcutta in 1976. In 1980, Nooyi earned a master's degree in Public and Private Management at the Yale School of Management, United States (Zweigenhaft & Domhoff 2011).

Indian-American *Satya Nadella* is CEO of Microsoft since 2014. He was born in Hyderabad, India, in a Telugu Hindu family. Nadella attended the Hyderabad Public School before receiving a bachelor's in electrical engineering from the Manipal Institute of Technology in Karnataka in 1988. In 1990, he received a master's in computer science at the University of Wisconsin-Milwaukee and in 1996, an MBA from the University of Chicago Booth School of Business, United States (Nadella 2017).

Moreover, while national cultures shape the management style of individuals, their effect may be amplified, mitigated, or modified by **other manifestations of culture**, such as corporate cultures, industry cultures, professional cultures, department cultures, generation cultures, class cultures, and gender cultures (Chapter 2.2). For example, Peretz & Rosenblatt (2011) combined data from GLOBE and CRANET in 21 countries and found that cultural values (namely, power distance, future orientation, and uncertainty avoidance) affect the investment of firms in employee training, while the strength of these effects is significantly amplified by organizational characteristics, such as firm size and technology level. An important finding of the GLOBE study is that organizational culture is at least as strong as national culture in predicting perceptions of leadership preferences. "Contrary to the conventional wisdom, our analysis of the correlation between the nine cultural values and nine global leadership dimensions of CEO behavior shows that, with a few exceptions, national culture values do not directly predict CEO leadership behavior. Instead, we demonstrate that national culture values are antecedent factors which influence leadership expectations" (Dorfman et al. 2012, p. 510).

Extant research is also criticized from an **epistemological perspective**. Most studies on career patterns, motivation, and leadership in an intercultural context are based on a positivist research methodology and compare them on basis of ex-ante defined terms and concepts, such as the cultural dimensions developed by Hofstede and the GLOBE study. According to the *constructivist concept of culture*, culture is not an objectively given and preexisting reification; rather, it is constructed through the process of social interaction (Chapter 4.8). Individuals negotiate the norms which guide their actions and behaviors, as well as the individual roles and places they assume within that society. For example, language is not a neutral device to studying motivation and leadership across countries. Instead, its role as a transmitter of meaning is idiosyncratic to specific social groups and individuals (Jepson 2009). Moreover, it is unclear whether etic approaches are capable of fully grasping relevant culture-specific emics inherent to indigenous management concepts, such as *codetermination* (Germany), *ubuntu* (South Africa), *ringi seido* (Japan), or *guanxi* (China) (Schaffer & Riordan 2003).

Finally, positivist approaches analyze different career management styles from a functional perspective and, thus, **neglect their inherent political aspects**. Like few other management functions, career patterns, motivation, and leadership impose and reflect power relations in organizations that are likely to differ across cultures. These are even amplified in a cross-cultural context when mostly Western managers lead non-Western subordinates. In particular, *postcolonial management research*, therefore, seeks to understand their underlying social processes, analyze intercultural interactions regarding power asymmetries, and deconstruct their mythical and symbolical aspects (Nkomo 2011; Jackson 2012).

7.2 GROUP LEVEL: MULTICULTURAL TEAMS

7.2.1 Cultural Diversity and Multicultural Team Performance

On the group level, intercultural management research is mainly interested in the study of multicultural teams. In many organizations, the institutionalized interaction of individuals from different cultural backgrounds has received great practical relevance (Marquard & Horvath 2001; Earley & Gibson 2002; Halverson & Tirmizi 2008). Examples of areas where they are most common are project management (Puck, Mohr & Rygl 2008), research and development (Gassmann 2001), and top management (Kilduff, Angelmar & Mehra 2000).

One **reason for the introduction of multicultural teams** is the growing internationalization of customers that is reflected through the internalization of cultural diversity within organizations. For example, customers in the international tourism and hospitality industry have increasingly diverse religious, linguistic, and dietary backgrounds, which is taken into account by the cultural diversity of the service staff (Holtbrügge, Wilson & Berg 2006). In decision-making processes, a wider range of perspectives should lead to better problem definitions and problem solutions. Moreover, the institutionalized communication of employees with different national and cultural backgrounds should promote creativity and the adaptation of innovations. This is particularly relevant in research and development departments, knowledge-intensive firms, and technology start-ups. In multinational corporations, they are also often used to improve the worldwide coordination of value activities conducted in different countries (Berg & Holtbrügge 2010).

However, multicultural teams are also faced with several **challenges**. As their members come from different cultures, they are inevitably shaped by different, often conflicting views of management practices. According to similarity attraction theory, interactions with people who are culturally different tend to be less satisfying (McPherson, Smith-Lovin & Cook 2001). Cultural differences in values and behavior are also likely to affect team outcomes negatively, since value conflicts normally imply that there is no common ground on which to collaborate and communicate (Stahl et al. 2010). Additionally, different native languages can lead to communication problems and misunderstandings (Chen, Geluykens & Choi 2006). Language barriers may lead to negative cognitive and emotional reactions and, thus, reduce team members' perceived trustworthiness (Tenzer, Pudelko & Harzing 2014).

The **relationship between cultural diversity and team performance** has been analyzed in a multitude of empirical studies. While Cox, Lobel & McLeod (1991) and Gibson (1999) revealed a positive relationship, Thomas, Ravlin & Wallace (1996) and Maderer, Holtbrügge & Schuster (2014) found a negative effect. Kilduff, Angelmar, and Mehra (2000) could not verify any significant influence. Summarizing the main results of these studies, an *inverted u-shaped relationship* between cultural diversity and multicultural team performance can be assumed (Figure 7.4). While too little cultural diversity means that the benefits of multicultural teams, such as increased creativity and satisfaction, cannot be exploited, too much cultural diversity can increase communication problems, decrease trust and social integration, and amplify the clash between different working styles.

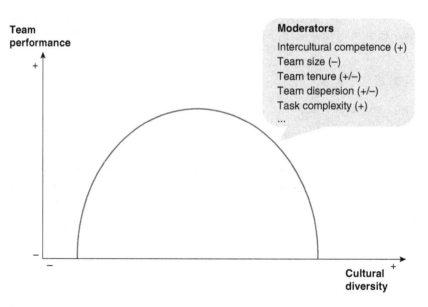

Figure 7.4 Relationship between team diversity and team performance

An example of the frequent use of multicultural teams is the German IT company **SAP**. Multicultural teams at SAP are intended to combine the focus on precision and quality typical of Germans, the speed and achievement orientation prevalent in the United States, and the creativity and flexibility found in many Asian countries. However, the company also experienced that high cultural diversity of teams may also delay projects and lead to employee frustration. Therefore, one of the lessons learned is: "Do not involve more than two continents, three native languages, and six nationalities" (Schuster, Holtbrügge & Heidenreich 2009).

7.2.2 Moderators of Multicultural Team Performance

The relationship between cultural diversity and team performance is moderated by several personal, structural, and contextual factors. An important moderator on the personal level is the **international experience and intercultural competence** of the team members. Internationally experienced and interculturally competent team members possess more cultural knowledge, cultural open-mindedness, as well as intercultural communication and collaboration skills, which facilitate the integration of diverse mentalities and mindsets (Matveev & Milter 2004).

Cultural boundary-spanning capabilities are especially pronounced in **bicultural team members**. The study of Engelhard and Holtbrügge (2017) shows a significant positive association between biculturalism and team facilitating activities. This effect is stronger than those of foreign language skills and international experience. The study also reveals a mediating effect of internal group processes and group cohesion on the relationship between team facilitation and team performance. The aptitude of biculturals as multicultural team facilitators can be ascribed to their *cultural frame switching capability*, which can be either developed through being born into a bicultural family or having lived in two (or more) different countries for a longer period of time during the early stages of their socialization (Hong 2010; Fitzsimmons 2013). Biculturals are valuable in multicultural teams because they have knowledge about and identify with norms and value systems from two different cultures. Hereby, they often do not merge the two cultures that they have internalized but react depending on situational cues (Brannen & Thomas 2010). This phenomenon of cultural frame switching refers to the ability to alternate between multiple cultural interpretive frames (Benet-Martínez et al. 2002; Cheng, Lee & Benet-Martínez 2006). Thus, biculturals are able to bridge cultures and successfully interact with people from different cultural backgrounds, regardless of the concrete cultures involved (Jang 2017; Backmann et al. 2020).

An important structural moderator of the relationship between cultural diversity and multicultural team performance is **team size**. As teams grow in size, reduced communication effectiveness and satisfaction diminish the positive effects of cultural diversity. With regard to the moderation effects of **team tenure**, existing studies show inconsistent results. While Thomas, Ravlin, and Wallace (1996) and Earley and Mosakowski (2000) consider the length of teamwork to amplify the performance effects of cultural heterogeneity, the meta-analysis of Stahl et al. (2010) reveals a negative effect. The latter can be explained by decreased creativity of teams that have spent more time together compared with teams with less tenure. Similarly, the effects of **team dispersion** are ambiguous. On the one hand, collaboration is more difficult in multicultural virtual teams, as the lack of face-to-face contact reduces communication effectiveness and impedes trust building. In particular, the transfer of para-verbal, non-verbal, and extra-verbal elements of communication is more difficult if communication channels with low media richness (e.g., letters, telephone calls, emails, etc.) are used (Jarvenpaa & Leidner 1999). On the other hand, the lack of face-to-face contact in geographically dispersed teams limits the cues that team members tend to rely on for determining similarity and for social categorization. Communication contributions, therefore, tend to be more evenly balanced in dispersed teams (Gibson & Gibbs 2006).

Finally, the relationship between cultural diversity and multicultural team performance is moderated by contextual factors. Gibson (1999), Salk and Brannen (2000), and Maznevski and Chudoba (2000) provide evidence that **task complexity** amplifies the performance of multicultural teams. Since complex tasks are characterized by ambiguity, difficulty, and a lack of structure, they require a higher degree of communication and interaction among team members to be completed successfully (Man & Lam 2003). Thus, they offer greater opportunities for process gains through divergence, such as enhanced creativity (Stahl et al. 2010). On the contrary, routine tasks require quick decisions and coordinated behavior of team members, which is less likely to occur in culturally diverse than homogeneous teams.

The negative effect of low task complexity is illustrated, for example, in the study of Maderer, Holtbrügge, and Schuster (2014) in European **football teams**. The study reveals that culturally heterogeneous teams are less successful than teams that consist of players with a more homogeneous background. This result is robust for different measures of cultural diversity. The authors conclude that cultural diversity is detrimental for tasks with low complexity and greater time constraints, and that the task of football teams is obviously not complex enough to exploit the advantages of cultural diversity, as illustrated by the famous statement of the former German national coach Sepp Herberger: "Das Runde muss ins Eckige" ("The round thing must go in the rectangular thing").

7.2.3 Critical Evaluation

The great practical relevance of multicultural teams has prompted a multitude of theoretical and empirical studies. Existing research, however, reveals inconclusive results. One reason for this is the **inconsistent definition and measurement of cultural diversity**. For instance, Kilduff, Angelmar, and Mehra (2000) measure a team member's cultural background with nationality, whereas other studies take on a more complex conceptualization. Earley and Mosakowski (2000) use self-assessments, while Cox, Lobel, and McLeod (1991) and Gibson (1999) refer to data from Hofstede (1980). They discriminate between homogeneous and heterogeneous teams, however, on account of a single dimension only—namely, that of individualism vs. collectivism. In contrast, Thomas, Ravlin & Wallace (1996) and Maderer, Holtbrügge, and Schuster (2014) refer to Hofstede's original four dimensions (i.e., power distance, individualism, masculinity, and uncertainty avoidance), and develop an index of global team heterogeneity based on Euclidean distances (Chapter 5.2.1).

Another methodological shortcoming of existing research is **sample bias**. The majority of studies were conducted in North America (sometimes with members of the same nationality but different ethnic background), while respondents from Asia, Africa, Europe, and Latin America are significantly underrepresented. Most studies were conducted in experimental settings and based on student samples (e.g., Cox, Lobel & McLeod 1991; Thomas, Ravlin & Wallace 1996; Gibson 1999). Moreover, the researched multicultural teams were predominantly composed ad hoc for the reason of the study, while there are few field studies of teams that had already been working together for a longer period of time (e.g., Earley & Mosakowski 2000; Maderer, Holtbrügge & Schuster 2014).

Finally, previous research is mostly focused on structural aspects of multicultural teams (e.g., team composition, team tenure, etc.), while **team processes** have hardly been studied. Thus, knowledge about affective, cognitive, and behavioral dynamics of multicultural teamwork is scarce (Burke et al. 2007; Hajro, Gibson & Pudelko 2017).

7.3 CORPORATE LEVEL: ORGANIZATION IN DIFFERENT CULTURES

7.3.1 Culture and Organizational Design

On the corporate level, intercultural management research is mostly interested in the design of organizational structures and processes across cultures. According to Hofstede (2001), **organizational structures** differ with the degree of power distance and uncertainty avoidance in a country. Organizations in countries with high *power distance* tend to have more levels of hierarchy, a higher proportion of supervisory personnel, and more centralized decision-making. In high *uncertainty avoidance* cultures, organizations are likely to be more formalized and have more written rules and procedures. The degree of specialization is usually higher and technical competence is highly valued. Stability and predictability are more important than innovation and risk-taking.

When combining the two cultural dimensions of power distance and uncertainty avoidance, four **generic models of organizational structures** representing different cultures can be identified (Figure 7.5):

- In Northern Europe, the United Kingdom, and the United States, organizations are structured in the form of *village markets*. Managers have a more generalist view of the company and often a strong entrepreneurial orientation. A key requirement is the ability to identify market opportunities and to convince others to pursue them. Therefore, informal, personal communication is emphasized. A high degree of flexibility allows managers to adapt the structure according to the people working in it. Jobs and responsibilities are frequently changed to attract, retain, and develop talent. The "bottom line" is the key criterion of output control.

- German firms are often referred to as *well-oiled machines*. They are likely to be highly decentralized, specialized, and formalized. German firms tend to be compartmentalized by function (sometimes referred to as "chimney" organization). Coordination is achieved through routines, rules, and procedures, and throughput control is prevalent. Since the focus is on efficiency rather than flexibility, recruitment and promotion decisions are mostly based on technical expertise. As a consequence, most top executives of large German firms have an engineering background (Heidrick & Struggles 2020).

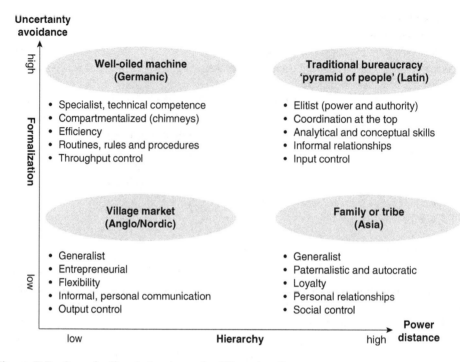

Figure 7.5 Organizational structures in different cultures

Sources: Adapted from Hofstede (2001, p. 376) and Schneider & Barsoux (2003, p. 93).

An extreme example of **German engineering culture**—and of its potentially harmful effects—is the carmaker **Volkswagen (VW)**. Since the transformation of the company into a joint-stock company in 1960, seven out of 10 CEOs received an education in engineering. As a result, VW's top management has been primarily focused on technical aspects and less on effective corporate governance. For example, the former CEO Martin Winterkorn is said to have cared about even the most arcane design details of every car, such as the clearance between door frame and door leaf. This technology-obsessive culture is argued to be one of the major causes of the "Dieselgate" emissions scandal, the largest corporate scandal in German corporate history. VW intentionally programmed diesel engines to activate their emissions controls only during laboratory emissions testing to meet high emission standards (Holtbrügge & Conrad 2020).

- Companies in France and other Latin countries represent *traditional bureaucracies*. They are usually highly centralized and formalized with a focus on power and authority. The role of the CEO is to provide coordination at the top and to make key decisions. This requires a high level of analytical and conceptual skills that need not to be industry- or company-specific. These skills are developed in the *grandes écoles* of engineering and administration where life-long networks with the future corporate and political elite are established. The recruitment of graduates from the most prestigious institutions is an important form of input control.

- Companies in Asia typically follow the *family or tribe model*. They are often organized around a powerful founder and, thus, tend to be paternalistic and autocratic. Like in the Anglo/Nordic model, managers are generalists rather than specialists. Loyalty and personal relationships are more important than formal structures and rules. Consequently, the focus is on social control and less on quantitative performance criteria.

Cultural differences also affect **organizational processes**. This can be illustrated by comparing **decision-making processes** across Europe. In Western and Northern European countries with a *monochronic time orientation*, such as Germany, collective decision-making is usually characterized by a long planning phase. Planning is a structured process with clearly defined steps that are completed in sequential order. The involvement of various stakeholders (work councils, supervisory board, administration, etc.) is highly regulated. Once a decision is made, it is finalized and implemented without any changes (Armbrüster 2005).

In Mediterranean countries with a *polychronic time orientation*, such as France, the planning phase is shorter and more incremental (Hall & Hall 1990). While greater emphasis is placed on efficiency in Germany, the balance of power relationships is essential in polychronic-oriented countries. This involves a large number of informal meetings and personal encounters. Usually, a general decision will be made earlier than in Germany; however this can be adapted to changing circumstances (Barsoux & Lawrence 2013).

In Eastern Europe, polychronic time orientation is accompanied by high degrees of uncertainty avoidance, power distance, and collectivism (Hofstede 2001). A strong desire for harmony, hierarchy, and risk aversion, as well as a lack of adequate regulation lead to long and complex decision-making processes. Information-sharing and open discussions in groups are avoided to maintain harmony and save face. Decisions are delegated to supervisors who, in turn, often need to consult with their superiors. As a result, the implementation of decisions is likely to take place under time pressure and requires a high degree of improvisation (Fink & Meierewert 2004).

A vivid example of the differences between decision-making styles in France and Germany is the binational TV and media company **ARTE**. German managers describe the French style of decision-making as very informal. Professional problem-solving often does not take place in offices and meeting rooms, but during coffee breaks and lunch times. Moreover, German employees find it difficult to adapt to the French practice of leaders behaving as "enlightened despots." French managers, on the other hand, often struggle with German directness and attention to detail.

After almost 30 years of collaboration, the decision-making styles at ARTE have converged. For example, informal communication is common in daily business, while formal agendas and systematic minute-taking are used for complex projects. The combination of divergent management styles often leads to intensive discussions between French and German employees, ultimately, increasing creativity and diversity of perspectives (Barmeyer, Davoine & Stokes 2019).

Another example for the impact of cultural differences on organizational processes is **project management**. In the *waterfall model* (typical for monochronic cultures, such as Germany), the focus is on quality and transparency. The synoptic process starts with the analysis of requirements, followed by the design and development of various prototypes. The final product will be launched only after extensive tests. In all steps, comprehensive documentation is essential. In contrast, the *agility model* (typical for polychronic cultures, such as India) is more incremental and collaborative. Here, the phases of the development process are interwoven and different versions of the product can be launched at any time. The focus is on speed and flexibility. Multiple adjustments to customer preferences are possible at any time (Estler et al. 2014).

7.3.2 Culture and Interorganizational Collaboration

Cultural differences in organizational structures and processes become particularly challenging in institutionalized international cooperation, such as international joint ventures and mergers and acquisitions. While extant research demonstrated that the success of international cooperation is affected by the **cultural distance** between the collaborating firms, empirical evidence on the role of cultural differences on postacquisition performance is inconclusive. One stream of studies pointed to a *negative effect* of cultural distance on postacquisition performance. This is explained by increased costs of integration (Stahl & Voigt 2008), cultural collisions during the postacquisition period (Buono, Bowditch & Lewis 1985), and reduced knowledge transfer (Björkman, Stahl & Vaara 2007). National cultural differences are, thus, a potential obstacle to achieving synergy realization, employee satisfaction, and shareholder value (Rottig 2017). However, cultural distance can also have *positive effects*, such as diversified resources and increased learning opportunities. For example, culturally distant mergers can spur innovation and learning by helping break rigidities (Sarala & Vaara 2010). Moreover, partners who perceive large cultural distance between each other are more sensitive and predisposed to working toward managing these cultural differences, since they pay attention to national cultural factors (Goulet & Schweiger 2006; Chakrabarti, Gupta-Mukherjee & Jayaraman 2009).

Slangen (2006) proposes a reconciliation of the two conflicting literature streams and argues that it is not the cultural distance between the collaborating firms *per se*, but the form and effectiveness of acculturation that affects collaboration success. If the collaborating firms are aware of their cultural differences, they can choose the most appropriate strategy for postacquisition acculturation (Morosini & Singh 1994).

Acculturation comprises all "changes induced in (two cultural) systems as a result of the diffusion of cultural elements in both directions" (Berry 1980, p. 215). The concept of acculturation was originally developed to explain how individuals (e.g., migrants, refugees, expatriates, international students, etc.) adapt to foreign countries and has subsequently been extended to organizational phenomena (Berry 2006). An important difference between individual and organizational acculturation is that individuals often have the option to acculturate or to leave the organization or country. On the other hand, the institutionalized cooperation between organizations is usually more difficult to terminate, as there tend to be few alternatives and high dissolving costs.

Based on Berry (1980), Nahavandi and Malekzadeh (1988) developed a typology that distinguishes between four **modes of acculturation** in international collaborations (Figure 7.6):

- *Assimilation* is a unilateral process in which one partner adopts the cultural norms of the other partner. This form of acculturation may occur in acquisitions of less successful firms

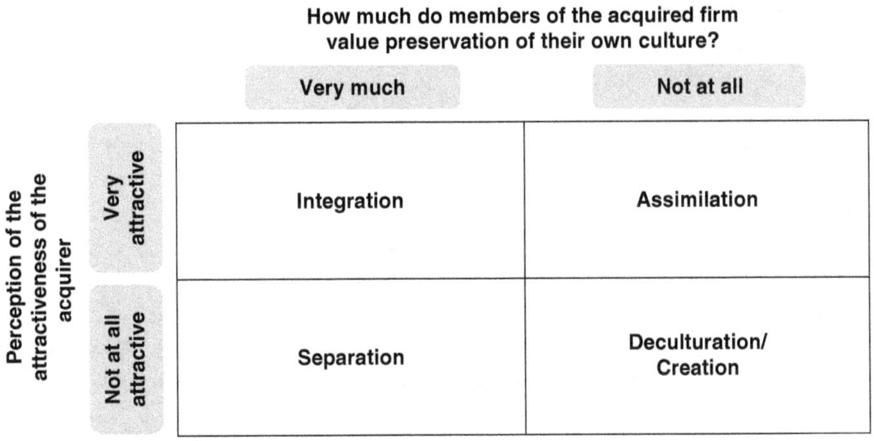

**How much do members of the acquired firm
value preservation of their own culture?**

		Very much	Not at all
Perception of the attractiveness of the acquirer	**Very attractive**	Integration	Assimilation
	Not at all attractive	Separation	Deculturation/ Creation

Figure 7.6 Modes of acculturation

Sources: Modified from Berry (1983) and Nahavandi & Malekzadeh (1988, p. 83).

or when the cultural values and behaviors of one partner are perceived to aggravate future performance. Moreover, it is often found in hostile takeovers and collaborations of firms with significant differences in size. An example is the acquisition of the German telecommunications company D2 by British Vodafone. After the acquisition, all elements of the D2 brand (brand name, colors, signs, etc.) were gradually removed and D2 became an integral part of Vodafone (Halsall 2008).

- *Separation* occurs when both partners preserve their culture of origin by remaining independent from each other. This form of acculturation is typical for diversified cooperation that is primarily motivated by financial reasons. Moreover, legal restrictions may impede intense cultural exchange between the partners. An example is Star Alliance. While the partners of this airline alliance integrated many physical assets (e.g., computer systems, check-in counters, city offices, airport lounges, etc.), their corporate cultures remain unaffected (Holtbrügge 2004).

- In the case of *integration*, the partners contribute equally to the collaboration. Neither partner tries to dominate the other; instead, they combine the "best of both worlds." Integration leads to some degree of change in all partners' cultures and the exchange of cultural elements is balanced. An example is Airbus, where the corporate culture is strongly influenced by the norms, values, and behaviors of the home countries of both major partners, France and Germany (Barmeyer & Mayrhofer 2008).

- *Deculturation* or *creation* means that both cultures are rejected and a new cultural identity is established. This may occur when the involved organizations do not value their own cultures (e.g., when they are perceived to impede further internationalization). Collaborations of firms with equally strong but incommensurable cultures often prefer this form of acculturation. An example is Aventis. After the merger of the German chemical and pharmaceutical company Hoechst with the French company Rhône-Poulenc, all cultural associations of both partners were removed.

For example, English became the new corporate language instead of French or German, and their headquarters were removed from Paris and Frankfurt to the French-German border town of Strasbourg (Müller-Stewens & Alscher 2011).

Although the typology of Nahavandi and Malekzadeh (1988) has received large attention in intercultural management literature, it has rarely been tested in empirical studies. Moreover, it has been criticized for its underlying positivist and functionalist epistemology (Ward 2008). Subsequent studies, therefore, emphasized the relevance of a **constructivist perspective** (Gertsen, Søderberg & Torp 1998). This accentuates the dynamic nature of acculturation and argues that intercultural collaboration typically cannot implement "a single mode of acculturation that will be shared by all organization members. It may be more accurate to describe these blended organizations as experiencing an ongoing acculturative process that results in many different cultural groups, each a unique outcome of the acculturation process" (Elsass & Veiga 1994, p. 438).

An example for the **dynamics of acculturation modes** is the **activities of Chinese firms in Germany**. When the first Chinese firms entered the German market in the early 2000s, they initially preferred an assimilation or integration strategy. However, the attempts to impose elements of the Chinese culture on the acquired German companies caused strong tension and resistance among the German managers and employees. Chinese values and management styles were not only perceived as alien, but—given the negative country-of-origin image of China in Germany—as inferior and hostile (Holtbrügge & Kreppel 2015). Subsequent Chinese investors learned from this experience and opted mostly for a separation and light-touch assimilation mode. Most of the later market entrants kept the existing management of the German company after the acquisition, conserved the original name and brands of the acquired company, and maintained the "Made in Germany" label. This mode of acculturation allows the acquired firm to exploit the large potentials of the Chinese market and to simultaneously leverage Germany's positive country-of-origin effects in the eyes of consumers and employees (Liu & Woywode 2013).

7.3.3 Cross-Cultural Transfer of Organizational Practices

Decisions about the **appropriate balance between local adaptation and global standardization** are not only relevant for interorganizational cooperation, but for international companies as well. *Local adaptation* is based on the notion that operating in another cultural environment requires firms to adjust their structures and processes accordingly. The concept of cultural adjustment proposes that foreign firms should follow the customs and conventions of the host culture ("When in Rome, do as the Romans do") in order to meet the expectations of local stakeholders and gain their legitimacy. While local adaptation may be adequate from a culturalist perspective, the universalist approach states the advantages of *global standardization*, such as the opportunity to achieve worldwide economies of scale and positive image transfers across countries. Moreover, global standardization may be appropriate when dealing with global customers and other stakeholders.

The decision between local adaptation and global standardization often requires **ethical judgment** (Donaldson 1989). Ethical standards as to what is regarded as right and wrong, or good and evil, show high variance across cultures. For example, homosexuality, premarital sex, and extramarital affairs are viewed as sin and severely punishable transgressions in most Arab countries; while morally tolerated as a form of sexual self-determination in Western countries. In intercultural encounters, incommensurable ethical standards may lead to moral dilemmas (Robertson & Crittenden 2003). When certain values and practices (e.g., treatment of women, minority rights, individual liberty, bribery, insider trading, etc.) are deemed unacceptable, local adaptation would be considered as morale arbitrage and *ethical relativism*. On the other hand, global standardization may neglect the specific conditions of the local context and seen as *ethical imperialism* (Logsdon & Wood 2005).

In the intercultural management context, moral dilemmas may be caused by indigenous management concepts, such as the concept of *blat* in Russia. Originating in the former Soviet Union, *blat* refers to the use of informal agreements and connections to achieve results or get ahead (Ledeneva 1998; Michailova & Worm 2003; Puffer et al. 2010). Although the nature of blat has changed after the collapse of the former Soviet Union, the phenomenon is still relevant when doing business in Russia (Ledeneva 2009). From a Western perspective, this is often associated with undermining formal rules and laws, the misuse of public office for private advantage, or even corruption. In Russia, however, *blat* is often seen as a legitimate circumvention of inefficient and rigid formal rules and procedures. Accordingly, Ledeneva (2009, p. 258) describes *blat* as a way of "corrupting the corrupt regime."

The example of *blat* illustrates that the evaluation of local management practices depends essentially on the perspective of the observer. What may seem ineffective, irresponsible, or even illegal from a Western perspective may be regarded as efficient, suitable, and tolerable from a local standpoint. Thus, intercultural management must reflect the diversity and multiplicity of perspectives and avoid both ethical imperialism and ethical relativism.

An example of **ethical relativism** is the cultural adaptation of **IKEA** in international markets. The 2012 catalogue published in Sweden shows a photo of a man and a woman in a colorfully decorated room. Another photo shows parents with their two children in the bathroom brushing their teeth. In the UK catalogue, a couple is shown lying side by side in bed. In the catalogue published in Saudi Arabia, the women are airbrushed in all three pictures. Although it is still very common for Islamic women in Saudi Arabia to require permission from their husbands to work, study, or even drive a car, the appearance of women in advertisements is not legally prohibited. After international protests, IKEA released a statement on its worldwide website that 'excluding women from the Saudi Arabian version of the catalogue is in conflict with the Ikea Group values' (Paterson 2012).

In Russia, IKEA set up a competition inviting people to be photographed in their Russian stores, with the images to be voted on online. The winning image was to be featured on the cover of the 2017 IKEA catalogue. The prize was supposed to go to two men posing intimately together. Their entry received thousands more votes than the nearest rival, spurred on by a campaign from the "Straight Alliance for LGBT Equality" page on VK—the Russian

(Continued)

equivalent of Facebook. However, instead of publishing the photo in the catalogue, a message in Russian was placed: "The photo is removed from competition at the request of the participants." While it is unclear why participants requested the removal, the potential win may have been problematic for IKEA, as Russia prohibits "homosexual pro-paganda" and messages which support equality between homosexual and heterosexual relations (England 2016).

7.3.4 Critical Evaluation

As on the individual and group level, management decisions and outcomes on the corporate level are affected by culture. The impact of culture on organizational structures and processes is particularly challenging in international activities of firms. In this context, the consideration of cultural differences is not only a matter of performance and efficiency, but involves ethical judgment about different and sometimes incommensurable moral values and practices.

While extant research has proposed a number of concepts about how companies may cope with these challenges, **empirical evidence is scarce**. For example, few studies have analyzed the determinants and implications of different acculturation modes. Existing case studies provide valuable insights (e.g., Elsass & Veiga 1994; Larsson & Lubatkin 2001), however, they are hardly transferable to other contexts. Similarly, the processes and consequences of ethical judgment in intercultural encounters need further attention.

Like in other areas of intercultural management, there is also a **lack of multilevel studies**. While national cultures are relevant, their impact is likely to be moderated by other manifestations of culture, such as organizational and industry cultures. These may amplify the impact of cultural differences on the societal level (e.g., when the organizational culture is an extreme representation of the respective societal culture) or diminish their effect (e.g., when the industry culture has a strong converging effect).

Finally, compared to etic concepts of culture, such as those developed by Hall, Hofstede, and GLOBE, culture-specific emics have received little attention. These include, among others, national stereotypes and xenophobia, historical conflicts, as well as inferiority-superiority relations between countries (e.g., between former colonial powers and colonized nations). While **constructivist and postcolonial approaches** have occasionally addressed these aspects, they receive little attention in intercultural management research.

SUMMARY

The consideration of cultural differences is relevant on the individual, team, and corporate level. On the individual level, culture affects preferred leadership styles, motivation, and career patterns.

On the team level, performance depends on a number of moderators, including team members' international experience and intercultural competence, team size, tenure, dispersion, and task complexity.

On the organizational level, cultural differences are mostly reflected in the design of organizational structures and processes. In interorganizational collaborations, the selection of an adequate acculturation mode is essential.

Reflection Questions

1. Do you think recruitment and promotion in your country is more based on merit or personal connections? What would you recommend to foreign investors from countries with opposite recruitment and promotion policies?
2. Name two different types of leadership and explain which one you would prefer and why. To what extent is your explanation based on culture and how much is it a personal preference?
3. Assume that you work as a general manager in the subsidiary of a Dutch company in China. What would be your biggest intercultural leadership challenges?
4. According to your experience: How do cultural differences impact team work? What can be done to minimize potential negative effects of cultural diversity?
5. Would you prefer working in a multicultural team or in a team composed of individuals only from your culture? Would your answer depend on the type of task (administrative work vs. creative work)?
6. Is it ethnocentric to transfer ethical standards across countries?
7. Imagine you are an intercultural management consultant in the field of M&As. A major Norwegian firm in the oil and gas industry recently acquired a financially struggling Polish firm. The CEO of the Norwegian firm asks you for advice on how to manage the Polish subsidiary effectively. Which form of acculturation would you suggest?

End of Chapter Exercise

Multicultural Teamwork

It is more and more common for individuals to work in multicultural teams. Examples are project teams in multinational corporations, study groups in education, and sport teams.

1. Which challenges do multicultural teams face in different areas?
2. What role does the duration of collaboration play in the performance of multicultural teams?
3. Imagine you are appointed as the leader of a multicultural project team. Which leadership challenges are you likely to face? How would you try to cope with them?

Further Reading

Aycan (2005) summarizes the results of studies of work motivation in different cultures.

Leadership behavior and effectiveness across cultures are analyzed by House et al. (2014) and Gupta and Van Wart (2016).

The determinants and outcomes of multicultural teams are discussed by Earley and Gibson (2002) and in the edited volume of Halverson and Tirmizi (2008). A meta-analysis of research on multicultural work groups is provided by Stahl et al. (2010).

The books by Schneider and Barsoux (2003), Bhagat, Triandis, and McDevitt (2012), Aycan, Kanungo, and Mendonca (2014), and Steers and Osland (2020) include longer sections about motivation, leadership, and organization from a comparative management perspective.

Meta-analyses of the impact of culture on interorganizational collaboration are provided by Stahl and Voigt (2008) and Rottig (2017).

8

INTERCULTURAL COMPETENCE

LEARNING OBJECTIVES

By the end of this chapter, you will be able to

- distinguish the affective, cognitive, and behavioral dimensions of intercultural competence,
- know the antecedents and outcomes of intercultural competence,
- comprehend and apply the intercultural learning cycle,
- measure intercultural competence with self-reported, informant-based, and observer-based evaluations.

Intercultural competence is an important prerequisite to manage intercultural relations in an effective and efficient way. It is relevant for both individuals and organizations with frequent intercultural encounters.

In the following, the relevance of intercultural competence is explained and a definition of intercultural competence is provided. Afterwards, the affective, cognitive and behavioral dimensions of intercultural competence are outlined. This is followed by a dynamic view of intercultural competence as a stage model and learning cycle. The next sections discuss the antecedents and outcomes of intercultural competence. Afterwards, various measurement concepts are presented. The chapter closes with a critical outlook and future directions.

8.1 RELEVANCE AND DEFINITION

The ability to manage intercultural encounters in an effective way has become a **major competence of internationally operating companies and individuals**. Intercultural competence is particularly relevant for expatriates who live and work outside their home country (Chen et al. 2011; Lee & Sukoco 2010; Wang et al. 2014), but also for other employees of multinational corporations who frequently interact with foreign colleagues, customers, and other stakeholders (Johnson et al. 2006; Matveev 2017). It is regarded as an important prerequisite of global leadership effectiveness (Caligiuri & Tarique 2012) and global career success (Bird et al. 2010). Moreover, intercultural competence was found to affect the performance of multicultural teams (Matveev & Milter 2004; Matveev & Nelson 2004) and the success of intercultural negotiations (Groves et al. 2015). It has a salient effect on strategic change and firm performance (Le & Kroll 2017), and contributes to the success of international mergers and acquisitions (Barmeyer & Mayrhofer 2008). Knight and Kim (2009) found intercultural competence to be particularly relevant for small- and medium-sized firms as it compensates for their lower financial and tangible resources as compared to large multinational corporations. Consequently, it is mentioned frequently as key recruitment criterion (Gerhards et al. 2017) and has become an integral part of education programs in business schools and beyond (Eisenberg et al. 2013; Holtbrügge & Engelhard 2016).

While the relevance of intercultural competence for companies and individuals is undisputed, there is less consensus about the **essence and definition** of this concept. For example, terms such as multi-cultural competence, cross-cultural adaptation, intercultural sensitivity, global mindset, or cultural intelligence are sometimes used in an equivalent and sometimes in a divergent sense (Deardorff 2006; Spitzberg & Changnon 2009). One of the earliest studies of Gertsen (1990, p. 341) defines intercultural competence as the "ability to function effectively in another culture." Similarly, Hammer et al. (2003, p. 422) denote it as "the ability to think and act in interculturally appropriate ways." While these two definitions focus on the outcomes of intercultural competence, Johnson et al. (2006, p. 530) also point to the capabilities of culturally competent individuals and define it as "an individual's effectiveness in drawing upon a set of knowledge, skills, and personal attributes in order to work successfully with people from different national cultural backgrounds at home or abroad."

8.2 DIMENSIONS OF INTERCULTURAL COMPETENCE

The various definitions of intercultural competence all refer to the existence of at least two individuals, namely the self and the culturally distinct other, and the relationship between the two. Based on this consideration, Thomas (1993) developed a **dyadic model of intercultural encounters** that consists of three dimensions of intercultural competence: cultural self-awareness, cultural empathy, and intercultural behavioral competence.

- *Cultural self-awareness* implies to know how one's own perception, thinking, feeling, and behavior are influenced by one's own cultural standards (Chen and Starosta 1998). Self-awareness refers to the degree to which people are aware of their strengths and weaknesses in interpersonal skills, their own philosophies and values, how past experiences have helped shape them into who they are as a person, and the impact their values and behavior have on relationships with others (Bird et al. 2010). High cultural self-awareness provides a foundation for strategically acquiring new competencies and skills, whereas low

self-awareness promotes self-deception and arrogance.

- *Cultural empathy (cultural sensitivity)* allows individuals to take the others' viewpoint and understand how others' perception, thinking, feeling, and behavior is influenced by their cultural standards. While culture as "software of the mind" (Hofstede 1991) guides individuals to think and act in a way that is accepted and expected in their social context, human behavior is also influenced by universal needs (such as sleep, hunger, thirst, safety, etc.) as well as an individual's personality (such as age, personality traits, etc.). Therefore, cultural empathy includes the ability to distinguish between behavior that is culture-bound and behavior that has universal or individual motives (Storti 2001).

- *Intercultural behavioral competence* refers to the ability to act appropriately in intercultural encounters. It does not only require the willingness to interact effectively but also the actual capability to do so (Thomas et al. 2008). An important prerequisite of this ability is intercultural communication competence (Arasaratnam & Doerfel 2005; Chen 2017). This includes fluency in other languages as well as the adaptation to differentiate communication styles.

While the concept of Thomas focuses on the relationship between two culturally distinct individuals in intercultural encounters, **individual-centric models of intercultural competence** relate to the abilities and capabilities of culturally competent persons (for an overview, see Spitzberg and Changnon 2009). Based on Gertsen (1990), affective, cognitive, and behavioral (conative or communication-related) competencies can be distinguished (Figure 8.1).

The **affective dimension** refers to a positive attitude towards foreign cultures, realistic expectations and acceptance, as well as respect for cultural differences. Existing research has identified several parameters with two partially overlapping factors being particularly relevant:

- A fundamental affective component is *cultural open-mindedness*. Open-minded persons are "prepared to entertain doubts about their views" (Adler 2004, p. 1) and "to revise or reject the position they hold if sound objections are brought against it" (Hare 1979, p. 9). Individuals with a high degree of cultural open-mindedness expect cultural differences to be present in intercultural encounters and are open to learning from dissimilar others (Fujimoto et al. 2000). Cultural close-mindedness, on the contrary, results from taking one's own assumptions to be correct, obvious, and universal (Riggs 2010). Mentalities remain persistent and divergent worldviews are ignored and not recognized.
- Another important affective component is a low degree of *ethnocentrism* (Bennett 1993).

Ethnocentrism is an individual's nationalistic self-centeredness. It is based on the belief that persons from other cultures are inferior (Bizumic & Duckitt 2012). Ethnocentric individuals interpret and evaluate others' behavior using their own standards and make little effort to modify their own behavior to suit their values (Young, Haffejee & Corsun 2017). Ethnocentric tendencies inhibit the individual in coping effectively with new social norms and values. Ethnorelative individuals, on the contrary, emphasize the complexity and contradictions of different cultures. They have a high degree of tolerance of cultural ambiguity, and sophisticated, rather than simplistic, constructs of cultural differences and similarities.

While ethnocentrism is predominantly treated as an adverse attribute in intercultural management literature (Michailova et al. 2017), anthropology and psychology regard it first of all as an essentially descriptive and natural outcome of enculturation. In any culture, people learn that certain social values and behaviors are accepted and expected

(Continued)

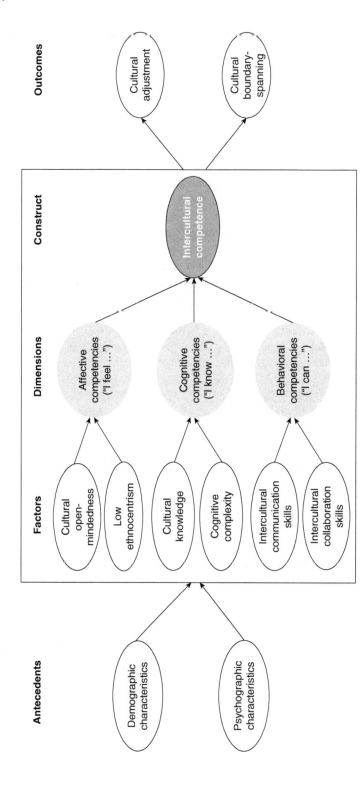

Figure 8.1 Model of intercultural competence

and others are not. In this sense, ethnocentrism has a positive effect as it directs and coordinates the behavior of the members of a culture and forms their identity. This also means that observations and judgments of other cultures are necessarily biased in favor of one's own cultural background. Ethnocentrism becomes dysfunctional if individuals neglect the fact that cultural norms and behaviors are grounded and valuable only in a particular historic, geographic, and social context. If people regard their own cultural values and behavior as universal and generally superior to others, pathological forms of ethnocentrism evolve that may result in prejudice, discrimination, and even ethnic cleansing (Neuliep & McCroskey 1997).

The **cognitive dimension** relates to the acquisition, processing, and application of knowledge about other cultures. It includes the knowledge and awareness of cultural differences as well as the ability to understand how a person's thinking, acting, and behavior depend on the individual cultural background.

- *Cultural knowledge* includes both culture-general as well as culture-specific components. Culture-general knowledge comprises meta-knowledge of cultural differences. This means knowing what culture is and how cultures vary (content knowledge). Moreover, it comprises an understanding of how culture affects behavior and of which behaviors may be more culture-bound than others (process knowledge) (Johnson et al. 2006; Thomas 2006). Culture-specific knowledge, as the second component, contains factual, conceptual, and attributional elements (Bird et al. 1993). Factual knowledge relates to a country's history, geography, economy, politics, law, customs, food, etc. Conceptual knowledge includes an understanding of a culture's distinct value system and how it affects human behavior. It is largely reflected by cultural standards and cultural dimensions (e.g., Hall 1959; Hofstede 2001; House et al. 2004). While these two types of culture-specific knowledge are explicit, attributional knowledge is tacit, informal, and personal. It reflects a heightened awareness of appropriate behavior, building upon factual and conceptual knowledge to correctly attribute the behavior of individuals in a culture.

- *Cognitive complexity* refers to the way that individuals absorb and process cultural knowledge. More cognitively complex individuals are able to organize their perceptions into differentiated categories and have a more developed set of categories for making discriminations among cultures. They can observe subtle cultural nuances in human behavior or communication style, while a naïve traveler may only notice differences in the money, the food, or the toilets (Bennett 1986). As categories for cultural difference become more complex and sophisticated, perception becomes more interculturally sensitive. Thus, cognitive complexity enhances the information-processing capability of an individual and reduces simplistic stereotyping (Lloyd & Härtel 2010).

Numerous studies analyzed whether cognitive complexity is related to **political attitudes** and particularly attitudes toward foreigners. One of the earliest accounts of Adorno et al. (1950) on the authoritarian personality indicates that individuals on the right edge of the political spectrum are mostly characterized by cognitive simplicity. Later studies found that this is also

(Continued)

typical for supporters of left-wing political positions and ideologies (Rokeach 1960). Thus, a *curvilinear relationship* can be expected, with cognitive simplicity dominating at the extreme right and the extreme left, and cognitive complexity prevalent among individuals with moderate political positions (Weinberg 2012).

By applying the concept of cognitive complexity as an instrument to measure *deliberative quality*, Kesting, Reiberg, and Hocks (2018) analyzed the discourse quality in the German Bundestag in debates on immigration policies. They found that the cognitive complexity of all parties underwent major drops in 2016. The discourse on immigration policy at that point in time was mainly covering the events in Cologne on New Year's Eve when a high number of incidents of sexual harassments by immigrants occurred. This event led to a shift in media coverage, more negative reports of populists and ultimately a decline of discourse quality in the German parliament. Moreover, the authors found significant differences in discourse quality between the parties, with opposition parties having a lower discourse quality in their statements than governing parties.

Being interculturally competent is not limited to possessing a positive attitude toward and knowledge of foreign cultures; individuals must also be able to express these characteristics. The correct coding and decoding of messages across cultures and the application of adequate verbal and non-verbal communication styles is reflected in the **behavioral dimension**:

- An important component of this is *intercultural communication skills*. These allow a person to interact directly with members of other cultures without mediating interpreters. Fluency in foreign languages includes not only terminological and syntactic aspects but also semantic and pragmatic elements, i.e., the meaning and use of different terms in different cultural settings (Arasaratnam & Doerfel 2005; Chen 2017). Moreover, intercultural communication is facilitated through the awareness of and adaptability to different non-verbal communication styles.

- Finally, *intercultural collaboration skills* involve a person's consideration of different ways of thinking, learning, and acting (Leung & Cheng 2014). For example, individuals from different cultures may have colliding time orientations, decision-making styles, and leadership expectations. The ability to integrate diverse mentalities and mindsets is particularly relevant for multicultural teamwork and cross-border cooperation (Lloyd & Härtel 2010).

8.3 STAGE MODEL OF INTERCULTURAL COMPETENCE

It is widely accepted in intercultural management literature that intercultural competence is not a binary construct (individuals are interculturally competent or not), but that various degrees of intercultural competence exist. According to Bennett (1986), three ethnocentric and three ethnorelative stages can be distinguished and positioned along a continuum (Figure 8.2). This six-stages model has been confirmed in subsequent empirical studies (Paige et al. 2003; Hammer 2011).

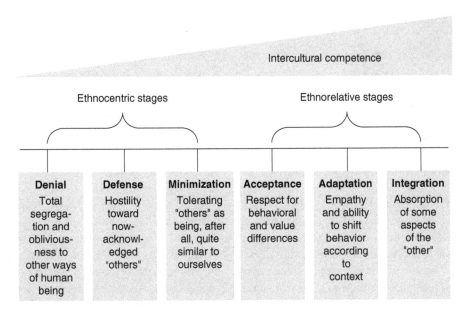

Figure 8.2 Bennett's stage model of intercultural competence
Source: Adapted from Bennett (1986).

8.3.1 Ethnocentric Stages

- At the first stage of *denial*, individuals either neglect, ignore, or do not care about cultural differences. Persons at the denial stage have generally been raised in culturally homogenous environments. The isolation from other cultural groups can either be unintentional, due to certain life circumstances, or represent an intentional and ongoing separation.

- At the *defense* stage, persons feel threatened by difference and thus try to protect their personal view of the world. The defense stage is characterized by feelings of superiority regarding the individual's own culture. At the same time, other cultures are devalued and negative stereotypes are applied to them. If individuals experience a foreign culture over a long period of time, such as during expatriation, the defense behavior can also take the opposite form. Long-term sojourners then perceive the host culture as superior while denigrating their own original culture.

- At the subsequent stage of *minimization*, people recognize superficial cultural differences, but believe that similarities prevail and that basically all human beings are the same. The belief in general similarity is either based on physical or transcendent universalism. While physical universalism refers to universal human needs, transcendent universalism is based on spiritual, political, religious, or other overarching similarities (Schwartz 1994).

8.3.2 Ethnorelative Stages

- At the *acceptance* stage, cultural differences are not only recognized but also appreciated. Differences are analyzed within their own cultural context and diverse cultures are no longer believed to have different value. There are two substages of acceptance. In behavioral relativism, persons accept that specific behavioral patterns are shared by cultural groups and are thus dependent on the respective cultural context. Value relativism, by contrast, means accepting that beliefs and value orientations are contingent on cultural communities and hence differ across cultural groups.

- At the subsequent *adaptation* stage, persons try to understand the way of thinking of other cultures. Adaptation can take the form of empathy and pluralism. Empathy refers to the capability of shifting one's own frame of reference and thus understanding different views of the world. Pluralism means that individuals have fully internalized various worldviews (Adams & van de Vijver 2015).

- *Integration* represents the final stage of intercultural competence. Persons at this stage understand themselves as facilitators of cultural transition since they have internalized various cultural worldviews and are able to transcend the cultures they belong to. The integration stage comprises two substages. The first is contextual evaluation which refers to an individual's ability to interpret situations by applying appropriate cultural frames of reference. In contrast to that, constructive marginality means that identity is not solely based on one culture. Individuals in this substage are likely to belong to a marginal reference group which makes them capable of mediating between various cultures (Hanek, Lee & Brannen 2014).

Integration is different from assimilation, as illustrated by London Mayor Sadiq Khan during a visit in Chicago in 2016. Practicing Muslim Khan, whose parents migrated from Pakistan to London two years before his birth, argues that new immigrants should not have to assimilate, but that the government should instead do more to help them to integrate. "One of the lessons from around the world is that a laissez faire or hands-off approach to social integration doesn't work (...). We shouldn't be embarrassed to say that immigrants should learn our way of life—for example, people employed in public-sector jobs in London should speak English (...). We need rules, institutions and support to enable people to integrate into cohesive communities and for the avoidance of doubt, I don't mean assimilation, I mean integration, and there's a difference. People shouldn't have to drop their cultures and traditions when they arrive in our cities and countries. We play straight into the hands of those who seek to divide us, of extremists and terrorists around the world, when we imply that it's not possible to hold Western values dear and to be a Muslim" (Khan 2016).

8.4 DEVELOPING INTERCULTURAL COMPETENCE AS LEARNING CYCLE

While the dimensions and stages of intercultural competence have been frequently studied, it is less clear how intercultural competence is developed over time. Existing research in this context argues that the affective, cognitive, and behavioral dimensions of intercultural competence are not independent, but that some dimensions can be regarded as antecedents of others (Leung et al. 2014). In this vein, a sequence between the various dimensions and factors can be proposed and the development of intercultural competence can be conceptualized as an **intercultural learning cycle** (Figure 8.3).

The learning cycle starts with the *observation of others' behavior*. Observation of human behavior is not objective, but biased through perception filters. In intercultural encounters, selective perception is mainly caused by cultural lenses which direct attention to some aspects of behavior while others are blinded out. For example, studies found individuals from Western cultures pay attention primarily to the focal subject and the categories to which it belongs, whereas East Asians attend more to the entire field and the relationship between the subject and their environment (Nisbett & Miyamoto 2005). This perception bias is lower when individuals possess high self-awareness and open-mindedness, as well as knowledge of verbal and non-verbal communication styles. "You can't very well expect to recognize when the locals are behaving like locals if you have no knowledge of how the locals typically behave" (Storti 2001, p. 78). These affective and cognitive skills enable individuals to distinguish between observation and interpretation, and to *suspend judgment* about the observed behavior (Storti 1999). The *description of others' behavior in neutral terms* is supported by culture-general knowledge, which allows individuals to picture the behavior of people from other cultures along abstract dimensions, such as those developed by Hall, Hofstede, or

Figure 8.3 Intercultural learning cycle

House et al. Low ethnocentrism and culture-specific knowledge improve then the ability to make isomorphic attributions, i.e., to *understand others' behavior from the host culture's perspective* and to avoid fundamental attribution errors (Wiseman et al. 1989).

According to Decartes, suspending judgment is an important prerequisite of gaining knowledge (Broughton 2002). *Cartesian doubt* is a systematic metacognitive process of recognizing a person's own basic assumptions and values and eliminating preconceptions and prejudgments. Suspending judgment does not mean withholding judgment, but holding judgment back until all relevant information is available.

In an intercultural context, suspending judgment prevents individuals from *cultural attribution error*. When people make quick judgements, they often unconsciously and thoughtlessly interpret the behavior of others on the background of their own cultural values and basic assumptions. This neglects that the reasons and meaning of behavior in other cultures may be fundamentally different. The habit to suspend judgment until enough information about the cultural context of others' behavior is available is therefore one of the most important attributes in achieving intercultural competence (Triandis 2006).

Interculturally competent individuals are further able to *predict how others view one's own behavior*. Culture-specific knowledge and a high degree of cognitive complexity allow individuals to put themselves in others' shoes and to perceive the situation from their perspective (Storti 2001). *Culturally adequate behavior* as the next step of the intercultural learning cycle involves especially intercultural communication and collaboration skills. It does not necessarily require the adaptation of one's behavior to the host culture. Particularly, if this seems to be ethically inappropriate or economically not feasible, the *explanation of one's own behavior* ('comply or explain') is useful. This allows the individual to demonstrate intercultural competence, but at the same time to avoid having to engage in undesired behavior (Storti 2001). Moreover, it helps the individual to better *predict the reaction of others*. The realistic projection of others' behavior improves then the individuals' intercultural sensitivity and perception skills and initiates the learning cycle again.

8.5 ANTECEDENTS OF INTERCULTURAL COMPETENCE

There is consensus in intercultural management literature that the development of intercultural competence is favored by distinct individual characteristics. The identification of these antecedents of intercultural competence is particularly relevant for the recruitment and selection of individuals who are frequently engaged in intercultural encounters. With regard to personal antecedents, psychographic and demographic factors can be distinguished.

8.5.1 Psychographic Factors

Psychographic factors relate to individual traits which favor the development of intercultural competence. In contrast to the abilities of culturally competent persons discussed earlier, these personal traits are not features but antecedents of intercultural competence (Ang et al. 2007).

Previous research in the area of personality psychology suggests that most individual differences in personality can be understood in terms of five basic dimensions (Costa & McCrae 1992): openness to experience, extroversion, neuroticism vs. emotional stability, agreeableness, and conscientiousness. These **big five factors of personality** have been repeatedly confirmed through factor analyses across time, contexts, and cultures (John & Srivastava 1999). The taxonomy has therefore gained large attention in intercultural competence research (Caligiuri 2000; Ward et al. 2004; Ang et al. 2006; Caligiuri & Tarique 2012; Wilson et al. 2013; van der Zee & van Oudenhoven 2014):

- *Openness to experience* describes the extent to which individuals are original, innovative, curious, and willing to take risks. Individuals with a higher degree of openness are more likely to engage in international encounters and to accept cultural differences. This makes them less likely to adopt racial stereotypes and ethnocentric attitudes (Oolders et al. 2008; Li, Mobley & Kelly 2016). Likewise, the motivation to acquire cultural knowledge should be higher as these individuals are more curious to learn about different cultures (Major et al. 2006).
- *Extroversion* is the degree to which individuals are sociable, talkative, and seek social activities. Extroverts are more likely to establish fruitful intercultural relationships, which enable them to comprehend other cultures more easily (Caligiuri 2000; Mol et al. 2005). They are more likely to try new things and expose themselves to new situations. Their expressive, spontaneous, and less inhibited nature should allow them to vary their behavior more effectively than those who are more self-conscious and introverted (Ang et al. 2006).
- *Emotional stability* is an individual's tolerance for ambiguity and ability to manage potential stressful conditions. Emotionally stable persons are likely to be more calm, self-confident, and collected. Moreover, they are more likely to cope well with living and working in new cultural environments. Emotional stability makes individuals more resilient (Ward & Fischer 2008) and can thus be regarded as a stress-buffering trait which protects individuals from negative responses to diversity (van der Zee & van Oudenhoven 2014).
- Individuals who score high on *agreeableness* are perceived as friendly, kind, sympathetic, cooperative, warm, and considerate. Agreeable individuals find it easier to adjust to unfamiliar cultural settings and are more likely to deal with problems collaboratively (Caligiuri 2000; Mol et al. 2005). They should also be better able to avoid or deescalate social conflicts and their broad behavioral repertoire should allow them to adjust their communication to different cultural contexts more easily (Ang et al. 2006).
- Among the big five factors of personality, *conscientiousness* has shown the weakest correlation with intercultural competence. Individuals who score high on this factor show higher cultural awareness during interactions with people from other cultures (Mol et al. 2005). Moreover, they tend to consider social norms and preferences before and during intercultural encounters (Ang et al. 2006). However, conscientious individuals also seek to avoid ambiguous situations, such as interacting with people from different cultures. Thus, they will have lower tolerance of cultural differences than less conscientious individuals.

Apart from stable personality traits, also more dynamic and state-like characteristics, such as the **self-efficacy** of individuals, influence their capability of dealing with intercultural situations. Self-efficacy is defined as the degree to which an individual is confident about successfully executing specific behaviors and accomplishing required tasks (Bandura 1997). Self-efficacy strongly predicts the development of intercultural competence (MacNab & Worthley 2012). Individuals with a high degree of self-efficacy believe in their ability to successfully perform in foreign cultures and are thus motivated to engage in intercultural encounters. Increased intercultural interaction can result in feedback from foreign interaction partners which facilitates the acquisition of cultural knowledge. Self-efficacy also increases the individuals' confidence in their own performance and helps them to persist in adjusting to challenging tasks and unknown working habits (Ang et al. 2006).

8.5.2 Demographic Factors

While the impact of psychographic factors on the development of intercultural competence is obvious, their identification is often difficult. Personality traits and self-efficacy are latent constructs which cannot be directly observed (John & Benet-Martínez 2000). Intercultural management research has therefore also analyzed demographic antecedents of intercultural competence which are easier to measure and to include in recruiting and selection procedures (Alon et al. 2018). Particularly, the analysis of **bi- and multiculturalism** has gained large attention in recent research.

Multiculturals are "people who have internalized more than one cultural profile" (Brannen & Thomas 2010, p. 6). Multiculturalism can either result *from birth* or *through extensive intercultural experience in multiple countries* (Fitzsimmons 2013; Friedman et al. 2012; Hanek, Lee & Brannen 2014). Individuals who identify with two or more distinct cultures because of having internalized more than one set of cultural schemas are often ascribed a high competence to act as facilitators in intercultural encounters (Thomas et al. 2008; Hong 2010). They often do not merge the internalized cultures, but react depending on situational cues (Hong et al. 2000). This *cultural frame-switching capability* allows them to subconsciously change between different cultural schemas that reside within the individual (Hong et al. 2000; Benet-Martínez et al. 2006; Fitzsimmons 2013).

Biculturals are capable as mediators and facilitators of the relationships between culturally diverse group members (Hong et al. 2000; Hong 2010; Dau 2016). They exceed monocultural team members in taking over internal and external boundary-spanning activities and absorbing uncertainty on the part of other team members (Engelhard & Holtbrügge 2017). "Those who speak more than one language and own more than one culture are (…) more likely to build bridges than barricades and boundaries" (Baker & Jones 1998, p. 299). Chao and Moon (2005) also propose that team members who share cultural fragments with members of other groups are more likely to bridge structural holes between these groups. According to Lakshman (2013), biculturals show higher cognitive and emotional competencies which allow them to take over leadership roles in multicultural teams. Brannen and Thomas (2010) attribute biculturals with higher cultural complexity or metacognition. This involves the ability to transfer cultural knowledge gained from a specific experience to broader principles that can be used during interactions in other cultural settings.

Carlos Ghosn, the former Chairman and CEO of Renault-Nissan, has often been regarded as the quintessential prototype of a multicultural (Stahl & Brannen 2013). He was born in Brazil, moved to Lebanon when he was six with his Lebanese parents, went to university in Paris, and had assignments with Michelin in France, Germany, South America, and the United States. In 2001, he became the CEO of Nissan in Japan and, in 2005, of Renault in France. He had successfully led the Renault-Nissan Alliance until he was arrested in Japan in 2017 on allegations of under-reporting his earnings and misuse of company assets.

In an interview in 2005, he mentioned as one of the key reasons for his success the fact that he grew up in a multicultural environment: "Being in a multicultural environment in childhood is going to give you intuition, reflexes and instincts. You may acquire basic responsiveness later on, but it's never going to be as spontaneous as when you have been bathing in this environment during childhood (…). When I arrived in Japan, a country I did not know at all, a culture I didn't know at all, a country which I didn't visit practically at all, I saw that I was able to connect with people in a culture which is known as being very strong. I had just to admit the fact that I was able to connect more easily with people than some of my colleagues; this is when I started to say to myself, well this is an asset for a turnaround situation" (cited in Fitzsimmons, Miska & Stahl 2011, p. 200).

8.6 OUTCOMES OF INTERCULTURAL COMPETENCE

It is often argued that job performance is the ultimate measure of intercultural effectiveness and that psychological and behavioral outcomes are of interest only to the extent that they mediate the effects of intercultural competence on intercultural effectiveness (Mol, Born & van der Molen 2005). While job performance can be regarded as a key objective, the understanding of this construct is culture-bound and "no universally accepted definition of performance exists in the cross-cultural literature" (Black & Mendenhall 1990, p. 131). Moreover, the functional chain between intercultural competence and job performance is complex and not well researched. Thus, we regard psychological and behavioral effects as primary outcomes of intercultural competence and focus on cultural adjustment and cultural boundary-spanning as the two most commonly addressed concepts in this context.

8.6.1 Cultural Adjustment

Since Black, Mendenhall, and Oddou (1991) published their seminal work on international assignments, cultural adjustment has become a key concept in intercultural management and expatriate research. Cultural adjustment refers to the degree of psychological comfort and the ease of stress that expatriates have with various dimensions of their host culture. Black et al. (1991) regard it as a multifaceted concept that consists of three major dimensions, namely adjustment to the general environment, to the work situation, and to interacting with host nationals. The *adjustment to the general environment* delineates the psychological comfort with regard to the host culture environment, including weather, food, and living conditions. The second dimension of adjustment relates to the *work situation,* that is the psychological ease with respect to dissimilar values, expectations, and standards at the foreign location of employment. The third dimension depicts the *adjustment to encounters with host-country nationals* including conversations at work and interactions in private life. Empirical studies and meta-analyses (Hechanova; Beehr & Christiansen 2003b; Bhaskar-Shrinivas et al. 2005; Holtbrügge 2008; Puck, Holtbrügge & Raupp 2017) reveal that—among other individual, work-related, and environmental factors—intercultural competence is a key antecedent of cultural adjustment.

While adjustment has often been stressed as necessary behavior of expatriates, there is evidence that this concept no longer adequately reflects the challenges of globalization (Williams 2002). One limitation of this concept is the unidirectional approach regarding the direction of the adjustment process. Cultural adjustment assumes that only expatriates have to adjust to the other culture and adapt their behavior by imitating the behavior of members of the host culture. However, expatriates are often regarded as home-country representatives and delegated with the aim to transfer knowledge and corporate values to the host country. Perfect adjustment would therefore make the idea of expatriation obsolete, and locals instead of expatriates would be recruited because of lower labor and expatriation costs. Moreover, cultural over-adaptation is inefficient in countries with low performance standards and impedes the implementation of a global corporate culture and human resource policy (Mol, Born & van der Molen 2005; Puck, Holtbrügge & Raupp 2017). Thus, cultural adjustment is not always a useful indicator of intercultural competence.

Cultural adjustment is particularly inappropriate in countries with insufficient human and labor rights standards. Individuals who find certain cultural values and practices (e.g., treatment of women, minority rights, individual liberty, bribery, insider trading, etc.) unacceptable may be unwilling to adjust to these values. In this situation, the "When in Rome, do as the Romans do" account of adaptation may lead to severe ethical dilemmas (Miska, Stahl & Mendenhall 2013). Instead, ethical decision-making and acting on a person's moral intentions may be more appropriate than adjustment (Hamilton & Knouse 2001).

An **extreme form of cultural adjustment** is described by the renowned French poet Michel Houellebecq in his controversial novel *Submission* (2015). The dystopic novel imagines a situation in which the fictional Muslim Brotherhood Party upholding Islamist and patriarchal values wins the 2022 presidential election in France. The newly elected Muslim president ends gender equality, allows polygamy, and forces all women to wear the hijab. Mandatory education ends with junior school, around age twelve. Unemployment is solved by women being forced from the workforce.

The entire changes in the French society are seen through the eyes of François, a middle-aged literature professor at the Sorbonne who believes in nothing and who consequently is bound by nothing other than himself and his own needs. After initial skepticism, François finally followed the example of several of his colleagues and converted to Islam. He regained his former well-paid job and looked at the prospect of making arranged marriages with attractive young wives. This submission is described as pragmatic, superficial, and the result of complete indifference.

Research on **host-country individuals' evaluations of foreigners' cultural adjustment** has yielded inconsistent results. While Pornpitakpan (1999) found that host-country members gave positive evaluations of both moderate and high acculturation levels, the respondents in the studies of Francis (1991) and Thomas and Toyne (1995) gave more positive evaluations regarding moderate, and less so regarding high cultural adaptation levels of foreigners. Cho, Morris, and Dow (2018) argue that these divergent findings can be explained by different **diversity ideologies** (Thomas, Plaut & Tran 2014), i.e., background beliefs people hold about cultural differences. *Multiculturalism* emphasizes that cultures are unique, separate legacies and implies a notion of cultural authenticity rooted in fidelity to traditional ways. *Polyculturalism* emphasizes that cultures are interacting systems which contribute to each other, and implies notion of authenticity based on hybridity and historical uniqueness. While multicultural individuals are concerned about high accommodators who drop the mannerisms of their heritage completely, polycultural individuals appreciate the ability and flexibility of foreigners to learn and adjust to another culture.

Cultural adjustment may also be criticized as a form of **cultural appropriation**. Cultural appropriation is the adoption of an element or elements of one culture by members of another culture. This can include the use of another culture's religious and cultural traditions, symbols, artifacts, language, or other aspects of observable or non-observable culture (Rogers 2006). When cultural elements are copied from a minority culture by members of a dominant culture, this practice is often perceived negatively and regarded as a form of postcolonialism. In particular, it is criticized if cultural elements are trivialized, decontextualized, and used without deeper understanding and respect (Young & Brink 2012).

In the management context, Cho, Morris & Dow (2018) studied how local people perceive the cultural adjustment of foreigners and their attempt to "do as the Romans do." They found that the local's evaluation of a visitor's cultural adjustment depends on their diversity ideologies. Individuals with a *multicultural ideology*, who emphasize the need to preserve minority traditions and the notion of cultural authenticity perceive high degrees of cultural adjustment more critically than individuals with a *polycultural ideology*, who emphasize that cultures are interacting systems that contribute to each other.

After the recital of Amanda Gorman's poem *The Hill We Climb* at Joe Biden's presidential inauguration on January 20, 2021 received worldwide attention, its translation into other languages became a matter of controversy. Several intended translators were accused of *cultural appropriation* if they were not—like Amanda Gorman-black, young, and female. For example, Catalan translator Victor Orbiols was removed from the job by his employers, who claimed he did not have the right "profile." "But if I cannot translate a poet because she is a woman, young, Black, an American of the twenty-first century, neither can I translate Homer because I am not a Greek of the eighth century BC. Or could not have translated Shakespeare because I am not a sixteenth century Englishman" (cited in Hucal 2021).

8.6.2 Cultural Boundary Spanning

Echoing this growing criticism of the cultural adjustment concept, recent studies propose to consider cultural boundary spanning as a more appropriate outcome variable of intercultural competence (Engelhard & Holtbrügge 2018). Cultural boundary spanning is different from adjustment as it does not produce consistent behavior with one foreign culture but rather involves **bridging and linking processes** such as information gathering, interacting with other assignees, and connecting previously unconnected people in diverse cultural environments (Au & Fukuda 2002; Barner-Rasmussen et al. 2014; Reiche 2011).

Boundary spanners can act as cultural brokers (Trevillion 1991) and bidirectional interpreters (Vora, Kostova & Roth 2007). For example, Di Marco et al. (2010) found that cultural boundary spanners communicate more frequently and have a positive effect on initial performance and adaption performance in multicultural project networks. Moreover, as cultural boundary spanning involves active information seeking and the ability to explain subjects to colleagues with other cultural backgrounds, it also has a positive effect on knowledge transfer. Accordingly, studies found that boundary spanning is positively related to the individual efforts of inpatriates (i.e., managers transferred from a foreign subsidiary to the headquarters) to transfer knowledge and their perceptions of the headquarters staff's efforts to acquire subsidiary-specific knowledge (Reiche 2011; Schuster, Holtbrügge & Engelhard 2019). However, while the usefulness of cultural boundary spanning as an outcome measure of intercultural competence is obvious, empirical studies in this context are still missing.

8.7 MEASURING INTERCULTURAL COMPETENCE

To identify, select and match interculturally competent individuals, an assessment of their competences is vital. In particular, a decision about the evaluator(s) and the measurement instrument has to be made (Deardorff 2006; Liao & Thomas 2020). With regard to the locus of judgment, three broad measurement approaches of intercultural competence can be distinguished: self-reported, informant-based, and observer-based evaluations (Table 8.1).

Table 8.1 Advantages and disadvantages of different measurement concepts

Locus of judgement	Advantages	Disadvantages
Self	<ul><li>High predictive power</li><li>Detailed and genuine knowledge of self</li><li>Convenient and least complex method</li></ul>	<ul><li>Self-serving bias (classical attribution error)</li><li>Social desirability bias</li></ul>
Informant (peer, supervisor, subordinate)	<ul><li>No self-serving bias</li><li>Perspective of interaction partners considered</li></ul>	<ul><li>Actor-observer bias</li><li>Perception bias (for example, halo effect, similarity-attraction effect, etc.)</li></ul>
Observer, researcher	<ul><li>Objective observation</li></ul>	<ul><li>Participatory observation difficult</li><li>Reactivity of measurement</li><li>Ethical concerns</li></ul>

Source: Adapted from Müller & Gelbrich (2001, p. 263).

8.7.1 Self-Reported Evaluations

In self-reported measures, focal individuals report about their own intercultural competence. The most common form is standardized scales, but also behavior description interviews can be used, in which interviewees describe their own experiences and past behaviors.

An example of a self-evaluation instrument which has been frequently used in practice is the **Intercultural Competence Profiler (ICP)** developed by Trompenaars and Hampden-Turner (https://www3.thtconsulting.com/tools/intercultural-competence-profiler-icp/). It consists of 58 statements that have to be evaluated on a 5-point scale which relate to four dimensions with three subcategories:

- *Recognition* (worldly consciousness, diverse ideas and practices, global dynamics): How competent is a person to recognize cultural difference around him or her?
- *Respect* (acceptance, self-determination, human dignity): How respectful is a person regarding these differences?
- *Reconciliation* (human relationships, time, and nature): How competent is a person to reconcile cultural differences?
- *Realization* (controlling tasks, managing individuals, facilitation team): How competent is a person is to realize the necessary actions to implement the reconciliation of cultural differences?

The ICP can be conducted online and respondents get immediate feedback about their intercultural competence profile. The ICP database contains approximately 100,000 records from over 100 countries. It is argued to be free of cultural bias, but no formal test of intercultural validity of the ICP is reported (Hampden-Turner & Trompenaars 2012).

A widespread self-reported measure of intercultural competence in the academic context is the **Cultural Intelligence Scale (CQS)** introduced by Earley and Ang (2003). CQ is a multidimensional construct composed of a motivational, cognitive, metacognitive, and behavioral dimension. Thus, it is largely consistent with the differentiation into affective, cognitive, and behavioral competences developed above (Ott & Michailova 2018; Rockstuhl & van Dyne 2018):

- *Motivational CQ* describes an individual's capability to direct attention and energy toward cultural differences. Moreover, it contains the willingness to adjust to other cultures and the drive to seek cross-cultural interactions.
- *Cognitive CQ* refers to culture-specific knowledge as well as general cognitive skills used to form ideas about living and working in foreign environments.
- *Metacognitive CQ* reflects an individual's cultural consciousness and awareness during interactions with people from other cultures. Moreover, it includes the capability of processing and storing cultural knowledge and information.
- *Behavioral CQ* refers to an individual's capability to exhibit appropriate verbal and non-verbal behavior during intercultural interactions.

Previous research show that self-reports of cultural competence is generally not only the most convenient and least complex assessment method but also predict performance better than alternative measures (Rockstuhl et al. 2011). This can be ascribed to the fact that the respondent has the most detailed and genuine knowledge of him- or herself. In particular, self-reports reflect a person's cultural self-efficacy as they measure perceived capabilities as important antecedents of intercultural competence (Leung et al. 2014).

A disadvantage of self-reported measures is the self-serving bias. This classical attribution error relates to the tendency of individuals who perceive themselves as less interculturally competent to ascribe this to external reasons and less to their own personality. Moreover, self-reported measures of intercultural competence have been shown to be associated with social desirability, i.e., the tendency of individuals to answer questions in a manner that will be viewed favorably by their superiors and peers (Worthington et al. 2000; Taras 2020). The influence of social desirability may be of particular concern when self-reported measures are used in high-stakes selection contexts. One solution to reduce the risk of faking personality is to ask the respondents to additionally provide supporting information to justify their responses (Levashina, Morgeson & Campion 2012).

8.7.2 Informant-Based Evaluations

In informant-based measures, informants (e.g., supervisors, peers, and subordinates) report about a focal person's intercultural competence. One example is the CQS, which was originally developed for self-assessments of intercultural competence, but is also available as informant-based instrument (Earley & Ang 2003). A major advantage of this method is that it considers the perspective of the interaction partners in intercultural encounters. This allows particularly for a valid assessment of behavioral competences. Moreover, self-serving bias of respondents is avoided. Informant-based evaluations are therefore particularly useful to assess a person's intercultural reputation among their peers.

Critical issues include the possibility that informants may differ in their opportunities to observe a focal person's behavior and in the training they receive as observers (Leung et al. 2014). Potential reasons of perception bias are halo effects (specific positive traits influence the overall evaluation of a person) and similarity-attraction effects (informants may evaluate focal individuals more positively who are similar to themselves in important respects). One approach to deal with these potentially biasing influences is the use of multisource ratings which ask multiple informants to provide ratings based on recall (Ang et al. 2015).

8.7.3 Observer-Based Evaluations

Observer-based evaluations through non-involved observers or researchers decrease the risk of subjective bias and allow for the most objective assessment of intercultural competence. However, while observers are the most objective and independent evaluators, they are also the least familiar with the focal individual. Thus, participatory observation requires an intensive involvement in intercultural encounters over an extended period of time, which is often difficult to ensure. Moreover, reactivity of measurement may still be present as the focal individual is aware of their observation. Covert observation where the focal individual is not informed involves lower observation effects, but bears severe ethical concerns. For example, it may infringe the right to privacy and lack informed consent from the people being observed (Alder & Alder 2000). Therefore, empirical studies that rely on observer-based evaluations of intercultural competence are rare (Kim & Van Dyne 2012).

In a **review of available intercultural competence tests**, Matsumoto and Hwang (2013a) show that important validity criteria are only partially fulfilled. Many intercultural competence tests lack valid criterion variables of intercultural adjustment or boundary-spanning, have limited breadth of cross-cultural samples, and rely on single research methodologies (Yari et al. 2020). A notable exception is the CQS, which has been frequently applied in empirical studies using a variety of measurement methods and shows high construct validity across a broad range of cultures and respondent groups (Ang et al. 2007; Chen, Lin & Sawangpattanakul 2011; Johnson & Buko 2013; Rockstuhl et al. 2011). Many scholars therefore call for greater methodological diversity in the measurement of intercultural competence and propose that intercultural competence assessments should include a "mix of quantitative and qualitative methods (…) including interviews, observation, and judgment by self and others" (Deardorff 2006, p. 241). Moreover, more emphasis should be given to the construct equivalence, measurement equivalence, and data collection equivalence in intercultural studies (Hult et al. 2008).

A measure that addresses these issues is the **business cultural intelligence quotient (BCIQ)**. The BCIQ uses a combination of quasi-direct observations and objective direct measurements. It contains 20 true/false knowledge questions and 40 self-reported questions that measure frequency of behavior, ideas, and actions, representing four dimensions of intercultural competence: global knowledge, motivation, learning and communicative adaption, and cognitive preparation and learning behavior. The BCIQ has been specifically designed to measure intercultural competence in a business context and applied, among others, in studies of expatriation and global virtual teams (Alon et al. 2016).

8.8 CRITICAL OUTLOOK AND FUTURE DIRECTIONS

While intercultural competence is proclaimed as increasingly relevant, there is still confusion about the various terms used in decades of research. Thus, a **precise conception and definition** of intercultural competence is necessary (Deardorff 2016). If researchers do not state what intercultural competence is and what it is not, the essence of the concept is left to the imagination of the reader.

An important question in this context is whether the concept of intercultural competence itself is **universal or culture-bound** (Ott & Michailova 2018; Fang, Schei & Selart 2018). The current literature in this field is dominated by Western authors who—at least implicitly—assume universality. However, there is evidence that the conceptualization of intercultural competence varies in an African, Asian, or Arab context (Manian & Naidu 2009; Nwosu 2009; Zaharna 2009). Therefore, it may be necessary to adapt conceptual frameworks and research methodologies to different cultural contexts (Holtbrügge 2013).

There is also a need for more **contextualization**. For example, it is likely that different perspectives exist in business firms, education, health care, space missions, peacekeeping forces, and diplomacy (Anand & Lahiri 2009; Deardorff; Arasaratnam-Smith 2017; Euwema & Van Emmerik 2007; Kealey 2004). Also, different perspectives are likely to be prevalent at different hierarchical levels and functional specializations. Top managers who negotiate international mergers may require other intercultural competences than blue-collar workers who are forced to collaborate with colleagues from other cultures after a merger.

Another avenue for future research is the need for **multilevel frameworks**. These would allow researchers to illustrate mutual effects of intercultural competence across various levels of analysis, such as the individual, team, and company-level. Combining micro and macro perspectives would help to gain a better understanding of how interculturally competent employees contribute to improved organizational outcomes (Leung et al. 2014). An interesting question in this context is, for example, how the outcomes of teamwork and negotiation processes are influenced by individuals with different levels of intercultural competence (Chua et al. 2012; Imai & Gelfand 2010). Moreover, it would be interesting to learn more about the relationship between an interculturally competent workforce and the international competitiveness of firms (Bird et al. 2010).

Research on the outcomes of intercultural competence shall also consider **potential negative effects**. While existing literature has almost entirely focused on the positive impacts of intercultural competence, recent studies advocate for a more balanced treatment (Rockstuhl & van Dyne 2018). For example, Fang, Schei, and Selart (2018) found that individuals with high intercultural competence try to benefit themselves, thus, likely reducing the total benefit to the group and the entire organization. Lorenz et al. (2020) revealed that individuals high in cognitive and metacognitive CQ are more likely to utilize their cultural knowledge to behave opportunistically. Moreover, they tend to perceive ethics to be relativistic, judge their own behaviors based on contextual factors rather than on moral absolutes and justify their seemingly culturally competent behaviors under the disguise of cultural adjustment. Thus, future research should explore the conditions under which intercultural competence leads to desired or undesired consequences.

Advances in **neuroscience** may allow more insights into the cognitive processes of interculturally competent individuals. For example, brainwaves, skin resistance, and facial expressions may be measured in intercultural experiments (Rahnuma et al. 2011; Shaules 2015; Chang 2017). Future research should also consider the growing impact of **digitalization**. Intercultural collaboration makes more and more use of electronic media, such as email, video conferencing, and virtual collaboration platforms. The impact of these computer-mediated communication technologies, however, is not yet well understood (Holtbrügge et al. 2012).

More research is also needed about the **dynamic aspects** of intercultural competence and its performance effects over time (Leung et al. 2014). Existing research is mostly static and compares the antecedents and outcomes of interculturally competent and less competent individuals under different conditions, whereas less is known about how individuals develop intercultural competence over time. This includes analyzing whether intercultural competence evolves through frequent intercultural encounters or whether it can be purposefully developed through systematic intercultural training (Landio, Bennett & Bennett 2003).

Finally, there is a lack of research about the **political aspects** of intercultural competence. Intercultural encounters often involve asymmetric power relations. Emotions, cognitions, and behaviors are therefore not only influenced by different cultural values, but also by different interests, and economic as well as political power. For example, asylum seekers and political refugees have a much weaker position in intercultural encounters than representatives of multinational corporations and may feel forced to assimilate rather than motivated to integrate into the host country (Vertovec 2010; Dutta & Dutta 2013). This important aspect of power asymmetries, however, has been mostly neglected in intercultural competence literature so far.

SUMMARY

Intercultural competence describes individuals' ability to effectively manage intercultural encounters. It is becoming increasingly important for global career success and leadership effectiveness.

Intercultural competence comprises of three main dimensions: an affective dimension that refers to individuals' cultural open-mindedness and low ethnocentrism; a cognitive dimension which includes cultural knowledge and cognitive complexity; and a behavioral dimension related to intercultural communication and collaboration skills.

Bennett's stage model of intercultural competence and the intercultural learning cycle are two models that describe the diverse stages or phases in the development of individuals' intercultural competencies.

Certain personality traits, such as openness to experience, extroversion, self-efficacy, and bi- or multiculturalism are positively related to intercultural competence.

Two of the main outcomes of intercultural competence are cultural adjustment and cultural boundary-spanning.

Reflection Questions

1. Which phases of the intercultural learning cycle do you consider most important? Which phases do you regard most challenging?
2. How would you describe your own 'journey' towards intercultural competence? Were there situations or events that helped you improve your cultural awareness and intercultural skills?
3. Have you ever experienced an intercultural situation in which you would have wished for a higher intercultural competence on the side of your counterpart? What was the situation like and how did you feel?
4. How would you asses your own intercultural competence? Do you think that your assessment is reliable?
5. Use the Cultural Intelligence Scale to evaluate the intercultural competence of one of your fellow students and let him/her evaluate your intercultural competence on the same scale. Do the results surprise you? Would a self-assessment of your intercultural competence lead to different results?
6. In which situations do you regard cultural adjustment and when cultural boundary-spanning as reasonable output measures of intercultural competence?
7. Is it always advisable to act according to the motto: 'When in Rome, do as the Romans do'?

 End of Chapter Exercise

Assessing Intercultural Competence

Imagine you are a human resource manager in a multinational corporation who is conducting a job interview.

1. Which questions would you ask in the job interview in order to gauge the candidate's intercultural competence?
2. According to your opinion: Can all the dimensions of intercultural competence be assessed in the same way?
3. Which additional information would you collect to assess the intercultural competence of the applicant?

Further Reading

The antecedents and outcomes of intercultural competence are elaborated upon by Earley and Ang (2003) and Matveev (2017).

The handbooks by Ang and van Dyne (2008) and Deardorff (2009) give an interdisciplinary overview of the wide spectrum of intercultural competence research.

The concept of cultural adjustment is elaborated by Black, Mendenhall, and Oddou (1991). A current review of empirical studies that investigated the cultural adjustment of managers is provided by Puck, Holtbrügge, and Raupp (2017).

The concept of cultural boundary-spanning is exemplified by Barner-Rasmussen et al. (2014).

Ontological, epistemological, causal, and functional explanations as to why and when counter-cultural business practices might be preferred are provided by Caprar et al. (2022).

9

INTERCULTURAL TRAINING

LEARNING OBJECTIVES

By the end of this chapter, you will be able to

- understand the relevance of intercultural training,
- compare the most common culture-specific and culture-general trainings,
- assess the determinants of intercultural training effectiveness,
- explain the opportunities of intercultural training in an online context,
- propose suitable training methods for different contexts.

A key topic of intercultural management research and practice is the question how intercultural competence of individuals can be increased. Originally developed to prepare military personnel on international missions, methods of intercultural training have been gradually adapted by firms and non-profit organizations with international activities. While intellectual methods seek to improve the cognitive understanding of other cultures, experiential methods also address the affective and behavioral dimensions of intercultural competence.

   In the following, the relevance of intercultural training is explained and a definition of intercultural training is provided. Afterwards, a typology of intercultural trainings methods is developed, before important methods of culture-specific and culture-general training are described. This is followed by a discussion of training effectiveness. The chapter closes with a critical outlook and future directions.

9.1 RELEVANCE AND DEFINITION

The growing need for intercultural competence has inspired institutions and organizations in different areas to design and implement various methods of intercultural training. Unlike more formal forms of vocational training with codified curricula and recognized degrees, intercultural training consists of a broad variety of different aims, contents, and methods. Based on previous **definitions** (e.g., Gudykunst & Hammer 1983; Earley 1987; Brislin & Yoshida 1994), we define intercultural training as formal efforts to increase the intercultural competence of a person. It aims to improve the affective, cognitive, and behavioral dimensions of intercultural competence to help participants feel, think, and behave more effectively in intercultural encounters. Intercultural training goes beyond business etiquette and illustrations of "dos and don'ts." Instead, it intends to enhance the awareness of differences and similarities between cultures and to enable individuals to cope with these more effectively.

Methods of intercultural training were originally developed to prepare military personnel on international missions (Pusch 2004; Glazer 2020). An early example is Ruth Benedict's (1946) book, *The Chrysanthemum and the Sword. Patterns of Japanese Culture*, which was written at the invitation of the US Office of War Information. It aimed to understand and predict the behavior of the Japanese after World War II and became influential in training American soldiers and politicians about Japanese culture during the occupation of Japan.

Since the 1960s and 1970s, intercultural training has been gradually introduced in multinational corporations to train their expatriates for international assignments. With growing international activities of firms, the **relevance of intercultural training** has grown as well. While one of the first empirical studies conducted by Tung (1981) showed that around 30% of American expatriates received intercultural training in the 1980s, this figure increased to 65% in 2015 (KPMG 2015).

Intercultural training can be provided in house or through specialized trainers and training firms. A status report of the **intercultural training profession** by Salzbrenner, Schulze, and Franz (2014) among 405 intercultural trainers from over 40 countries found that around one quarter are affiliated with academic institutions, one quarter are self-employed, and another quarter are employed in private companies. Around 10% work in non-profit organizations. More than 3,000 intercultural professionals are organized in the Society for Intercultural Education, Training, and Research (SIETAR) (https://www.sietareu.org/).

9.2 TYPOLOGY OF INTERCULTURAL TRAINING METHODS

In intercultural management literature, several methods of intercultural training are described (for an overview, see Fowler & Mumford 1995; Seelye 1996; Cushner & Brislin 1997; Landis, Bennett & Bennett 2004; Holtbrügge 2019/2020; Landis & Bhawuk 2020). Most of them can be classified according to the typology of Gudykunst & Hammer (1983) which differentiates between two dimensions: the **geographic scope** of the training (culture-general vs. culture-specific) and the **didactic approach** through which training is delivered (intellectual vs. experiential).

Culture-specific training aims at preparing individuals for a concrete national or regional culture. It refers to "information about a given culture and guidelines for interaction with members of that culture" (Brislin & Pedersen 1976, p. 6). The classical example is a future expatriate who is about to begin an assignment in another country. In contrast, **culture-general training** seeks to increase cultural self-awareness and to reach a sensitization of the individual for cultural differences in general. Its aim is to expose "the trainee to a variety of cultural habits, norms, roles, values, and circumstances to provide the trainee with a 'sample of experiences' which reflect the variations that exist anywhere on earth" (Triandis 1977, p. 21). Culture-general training is offered, for example, to members of multicultural teams or supranational organizations consisting of people from a large number of different cultural backgrounds.

With regard to the didactic approach, **intellectual training** seeks to impart knowledge by mostly passive methods of instruction. It is based on the supposition that a cognitive understanding of a culture is necessary to interact effectively in intercultural encounters. While intellectual training primarily focuses on transferring knowledge (cognitive dimension), the aim of **experiential training** is to change attitudes and behaviors (affective and behavioral dimension). It assumes that people learn best from their experiences and involves structured activities, such as role-plays and simulations, which are designed to confront the trainee with typical situations that may be encountered in interactions with members of a foreign culture. The exposure is typically followed by a cognitive debriefing where the trainers discuss the reactions of the trainees and draw conclusions from their experiences.

Combining these two dimensions, four **categories of intercultural training** can be distinguished: intellectual culture-general, intellectual culture-specific, experiential culture-general, and experiential culture-specific training (Figure 9.1). While some methods can be clearly assigned to one category, others may involve certain aspects of other categories as well:

- *Intellectual culture-specific training* contains information about a specific culture. For example, country facts and historical backgrounds are imparted through mainly cognitive approaches, such as books, lectures, discussions, videos, online platforms, etc. Moreover, language courses and culture assimilator training may be provided where trainees analyze a series of problematic intercultural encounters (Fiedler, Mitchell & Triandis 1971).

- *Intellectual culture-general training* offers generic information about culture and its influence on management practices and interpersonal behavior. For example, different concepts of culture, such as those developed by Hofstede (2001), Hampden-Turner and Trompenaars

Figure 9.1 Typology of intercultural training methods

(2012), and House et al. (2004), may be explained. Moreover, cultural self-awareness training aims to improve the trainees' awareness of their own cultural background and how it influences their feeling, thinking, and behavior, and how it may be perceived by members of other cultures.

- The aim of *experiential culture-general training* is to let participants experience situations which might occur in real-life intercultural encounters. For this reason, several simulations with artificial or synthetic cultures, such as BaFá BaFá, Barnga, or Ecotonos, have been

developed (Hofstede, Pedersen & Hofstede 2002; Fowler & Pusch 2010). Another method is on-the-job training in multicultural teams.

- *Experiential culture-specific training* through case studies and role-plays is aimed to let trainees experience the norms, values, and symbols of a specific culture. In contrast-culture training, life-like interactions between the trainees and trained actors (often members of the target culture) are simulated. The main difference to intellectual training is that not only cognitive but also affective and behavioral competences are imparted.

Each of the four training types has its **advantages and disadvantages** (Landis et al. 2004). Intellectual culture-general training is often cheaper and faster than other approaches and provides a general understanding of cultural issues. However, trainees often criticize the abstract level of knowledge imparted and the lack of emotional components. Intellectual culture-specific training enhances the cognitive knowledge about culture-specific issues, but has only limited direct impact on the behavior of individuals in interactions with persons from a particular culture. Experiential culture-specific training provides semi-authentic experiences, but is difficult to conduct for larger groups and may contribute to stereotypes of other cultures. Experiential culture-general training allows for a holistic learning approach, but may be judged as "fun and games" and not be taken seriously (Brislin & Pedersen 1976; Triandis 1977; Fowler & Blohm 2004).

In the following section, the most important methods of intercultural training are described and evaluated in detail.

9.3 CULTURE-SPECIFIC TRAINING

9.3.1 Intellectual Culture-Specific Training

Culture briefings provide factual knowledge of the history, politics, laws, economy, and arts of a specific country. This may be provided through traditional media, such as books, lectures, and videos, or online resources. Written materials may be preferred if precision of information is required, while lectures are useful for introducing new topics and presenting abstract concepts. They may be provided by either professional trainers, country specialists, or returned expatriates. Videos have a higher media richness by integrating audio and visual elements and can bring real-life situations into the training. Beyond videos specifically produced for this purpose, popular movies may be used as a tool for intercultural training (Roell 2010; Pandey & Ardichvili 2015). While all three media are unidirectional and position the trainee in a passive position, this may be preferred by restrained individuals who do not feel threatened by having to do something (Fowler & Blohm 2004).

Online resources incorporate texts, sound, pictures, and videos and often combine unidirectional media with online interactions. Comprehensive platforms are, for example, Cultural Detective (https://www.culturaldetective.com), Culture Wizard (https://www.rw-3.com/), and Globiana (http://globiana.com/). While these websites primarily address employees of business firms, special platforms exist for preparing members of the Foreign Service for international assignments (Fowler & Pusch 2010). Web-based inter-cultural training has worldwide reach and can connect people irrespective of location and time. Unlimited connectivity unwinds the traditional hierarchy between trainers and trainees and allows for learning from peers and instructors. A disadvantage of interactive online resources is that the providers have little control over their contents. If a large number of persons contribute to the platform, false or misleading information may be posted. Moreover, development of online resources of high quality is costly and time-consuming. Therefore, web-based training is particularly useful if a large number of individuals require training.

More time-consuming are **language courses**, which may be conducted either in classes or through self-study. From an intercultural perspective, these should not only include teaching the vocabulary and grammar of a foreign language but also the ability to use the language in a culturally appropriate way. Thus, language teaching with an intercultural dimension particularly aims to raise the participants' awareness of and adaptability to different verbal and non-verbal communication styles (Arasaratnam & Doerfel 2005).

For this reason, language courses may be combined with **languages games** (Fowler & Pusch 2010). One example is *Redundancia* developed by Dianne Saphiere (1995a). It aims to increase the awareness of the changes that occur in the behavior and reactions to the behavior of others when communicating in a foreign language. Participants experience speaking a language non-fluently, how it affects their ability to stay focused and connected with the listeners, and how it influences perceptions of competence and confidence. This experience should help individuals to build empathy for non-fluent speakers and improve communicative competence across language barriers.

Culture assimilator training is based on the interactionist concept of culture (Thomas 1993). It pri-marily aims to improve the *understanding of behavior* in intercultural encounters. As a first step, the trainees are presented a series of problematic intercultural encounters between the members of two different cultures which are often classified according to central cultural standards, i.e., emic dimensions of the particular culture. These critical incidents or "well-meaning clashes" (Brislin 2000) are typically derived from interviews with experts who have frequent interactions with members of the target culture. After-wards, a number of alternative explanations or attributions are given, of which the trainees have to select the one that is most appropriate. Then the suggested explanations are evaluated and information about the underlying cultural standards is provided. Each critical incident finishes with an explanation of the relevant historical background and recommendations of adequate behavior in similar situations (Fiedler, Mitchell & Triandis 1971).

Most early culture assimilators were developed with the USA as either the reference culture or the target culture (Bhawuk 2001). For example, the culture assimilator for Japanese visiting the USA of Ito & Triandis (1989) consists of 57 incidents which are classified into five categories: behaviors in a hierarchy, face-saving behaviors, harmony or emotional control of behaviors, group goal-related behaviors, and norm-related behaviors. Müller and Thomas (1995) developed a culture assimilator for German exchange students in the USA. It consists of 40 critical incidents which refer to nine cultural standards: patriotism, egalitarianism, calmness (easy-going), action orientation, achievement orientation, individualism, social acceptance, interpersonal distance, and relation between sexes. *Turning bricks into jade* deals with interactions among North Americans and Chinese (Wang et al. 2000). It includes 41 incidents based on actual events related to individualism vs. collectivism, guanxi, hierarchies, gender relations in the work-place, regulations, deference to authority, work incentives, and ownership.

For Germany as the reference culture, Alexander Thomas published a series of booklets (in German) with culture assimilator exercises for around 50 American, Asian, African, and Oceanian countries as target cultures (e.g., Juskowicz, Stilljanow & Thomas 2007; Mayr & Thomas 2008; Mitterer, Mimler & Thomas 2013; Thomas & Schenk 2015). Part of this comprehensive project is the culture assimilator for foreigners visiting Germany developed by Schroll-Machl (2016). The critical incidents are classified into seven categories: objectivism (task-focus), appreciation for rules, regulations and structures, rule-orientation, time planning, separation of personality and living spheres, low-context communication, and individualism.

Example: Mr. Müller in Russia

Critical incident

Mr. Müller has been sent to Russia and wants to visit the factory he manages in order to familiarize himself with the working conditions and to identify possible problems. Immediately during the first tour, he discovered that employees put the empty boxes that are no longer needed next to the assembly line. The boxes are piled up so high that there is the possibility of an accident if they were to fall onto the assembly line, putting the production in jeopardy. He suggests to his deputy to pile up the boxes somewhere else, and asks him to bring up the issue at the next meeting with the responsible production manager. After some time, he makes another visit to the factory and notices that the empty boxes are still piled up in the same spot. He is surprised that his suggestion has been ignored.

Why was no action taken based on Mr. Müller's suggestion?

Interpretations of the situation

1. The deputy and the production manager found Mr. Müller's suggestion unimportant and engaged themselves with something more important to them.
2. It was Mr. Müller's mistake to make a suggestion instead of giving an instruction. An instruction would have been put into action.
3. Mr. Müller spoke to the wrong hierarchical ranking. In the Russian hierarchy, his deputy's position is beneath the position of the production manager.
4. *Mr. Müller should have made his suggestion, to pile up the boxes somewhere else, directly to the employees.*

Cultural-historical explanation of the culture standard "hierarchy"

At the operational level, a central element of the socialist economy was the one-man management principle. This means that the general director was responsible for all the activities of the company (even under criminal law). It was general practice that the general director alone was responsible for noticing defects at all levels of the business. Subsequently the general director would direct lower ranked employees to remedy the defects without involving hierarchy. There was almost no communication between different hierarchical levels.

However, since the introduction of western management styles to Russia, many of the older qualified employees are still used to the principle of the socialist economy. Instructions from managers with a lower hierarchical position are often ignored by the employees because they are convinced that there is no coordination with the higher management.

Culture assimilator training is easily administered and portable. It is particularly useful for individuals with little intercultural experience who would like to prepare for first encounters with members of related cultures (Triandis 1995b). Trainees develop more accurate expectations of intercultural behavior and improve knowledge of intercultural communication styles (Albert 1995). The learning outcomes mainly depend on how realistic the critical incidents are and how difficult it is to find the most appropriate explanation. "The ideal incident must describe (1) common occurrence in which a (trainee) and a (person from a another culture) interact, (2) a situation which the (trainee) finds conflicting, puzzling, or which is likely to misinterpret, and (3) a situation which can be interpreted in a fairly unequivocal manner, given sufficient knowledge about the culture" (Fiedler, Mitchell & Triandis 1971, p. 101).

One of the main disadvantages is that there is not always a right answer to intercultural problems. Participants may complain that they receive too little information to make a well-grounded judgment. Moreover, culture assimilators do not work well for people who prefer a more active learning style. As the training procedure is widely standardized, individuals may also become easily saturated (Fowler & Blohm 2004). Most importantly, it remains unclear whether culture assimilators provide metacognitive benefits, i.e. whether the knowledge gained in a particular critical incident can be transferred to theoretically similar circumstances with dissimilar surface features (Earley & Peterson 2004).

Some of the disadvantages of culture assimilator training may be overcome through the use of **intercultural case studies** (e.g., Holtbrügge & Haussmann 2017). They are more comprehensive and include more information than short critical incidents. They may be accompanied by supporting documents and the trainees can be asked to search for additional information online. When intercultural case studies are conducted as group exercises, the training is more interactive and the trainees may learn from other group members. This often improves their analytical and decision-making skills. Moreover, the trainees learn that intercultural cases can be evaluated differently and experience the need to suspend judgement, which is an important element of the *intercultural learning cycle*. Like with culture assimilator training, it is important to adapt the case studies to the professional and educational background of the participants.

9.3.2 Experiential Culture-Specific Training

Like several other methods, **contrast-culture training** was developed in the late 1960s in the military sector. It uses an instructed actor as a foreign counterpart in a role-playing situation to experience cultural differences and promote cultural self-awareness. A trainee usually volunteers to be Mr. or Ms. Smith, who interacts with an actor named Mr. Khan, who is trained to provide a culture contrast and to engage in a controlled dialogue that elicits the assumptions of the target culture. The context of this dialogue can be adapted to the specific professional and educational backgrounds of the participants (DeMello 1995).

An example of a more complex contrast-culture role play is *NDaba* (Zulu: for "business" or "matter"), developed by students from the Department of International Management at the University of Erlangen-Nürnberg. The trainees are instructed to play the members of a recruitment and selection committee of a fictional multinational corporation's subsidiary in South Africa. The five members of this committee represent foreign expatriates, different South African ethnic groups, and different corporate functions. They receive individual role

(Continued)

instructions that range from rational decision-making to indigenous management styles. Their task is to select the most suitable candidates for two middle-management positions out of a pool of six applicants for each position with very diverse professional, educational, family, and ethnic backgrounds. The participants are provided with the job description and the candidates' curriculum vitae. These correspond to the common South African style.

During the role-play, conflicts between different cultural norms, values, and behaviors occur. For example, while the two foreign expatriates typically focus on previous job experience and merit, the Xhosa committee member stresses the relevance of social harmony and consensual decision-making. The white South African member with Boer descent represents a pronounced ethnocentric and xenophobic position, while the Zulu member strongly believes in the healing and fortune telling powers of the *Isangoma*, South African healers.

The main aim of the role-play is to increase the participants' awareness of cultural differences and the impact of ethnocentrism. Moreover, they should experience how large cultural differences may affect communication and decision-making processes.

Contrast-culture training allows the trainees to experience and understand how their culture is perceived by members of the target culture. This experience, however, is not genuine, but mediated through trained actors. Thus, the training effectiveness largely depends on their theatrical ability. Moreover, members of collectivist cultures particularly may find it inappropriate to be singled-out of the group and therefore be reluctant to participate in the role-play (Fowler & Blohm 2004). Moreover, participants may find interactions with trained actors, who merely simulate typical behaviors of another culture, artificial. More authentic **intercultural simulations and role-plays** are therefore conducted with members of the involved cultures.

An example is the intercultural negotiation training *Interact* developed by *Jürgen Bolten* (2002). It aims to simulate joint venture talks between companies from different countries. The participants are divided into two to four groups. Each group is comprised of three to five participants, with at least two of the participants being members of one of the following corresponding cultures for which training materials written in the country's native language are available: Australia, China, Chile, Germany, France, Great Britain, Italy, the Netherlands, Russia, Spain, and the United States. The remaining group members should already be familiar with that culture. Negotiation-level knowledge of the reference country's language or *lingua franca* will be assumed.

The groups are provided with a case study of a sports clothing company that operates in either Western Europe, Eastern Europe, Asia, or the USA, and are requested to make several marketing and production decisions for their region. After two periods, it becomes obvious that further expansion is only possible outside the respective home region, which requires cooperation with another company. The groups therefore gradually engage in joint venture-negotiations with the other groups. The task is to convince the other groups of their business concept and to find the most appropriate partner. During these negotiations, the groups are confronted with different culture-specific negotiation styles and negotiation languages. At the end of the sixth period, it becomes clear which joint venture is the most successful. An important part of the training is the videotaping of the negotiation process which allows the participants to reflect on their intercultural behavior after the end of the simulation.

Study stays abroad can be regarded as either exposure to another culture which requires pre-departure intercultural training, or as intercultural training itself that prepares individuals for future international assignments (Behrnd & Porzelt 2012). Many study programs include compulsory or obligatory stays abroad of one or two semesters. Some universities also offer double degrees and multicountry programs where the intercultural experience is even more intense. In Europe, such programs are often supported by the Erasmus+ program, a 14.7 bn. € framework program that provides grants for students to undertake exchange semesters and work placements abroad. In 2016, the Erasmus+ program spent 2.27 bn. € to support 725,000 Europeans with mobility grants to study, train, teach, and work as volunteers abroad (ec.europa.eu/programmes/erasmus-plus). National institutions, such as the German Academic Exchange Service (DAAD), provide scholarships for exchange semesters as well.

For many students, study abroad stays are their first intensive and extensive intercultural experiences. Thus, they have a major impact on their intercultural socialization. Study abroad stays, however, do not improve intercultural competence per se. Instead, the motivation to study abroad is a main antecedent. For example, Holtbrügge and Engelhard (2016) found that intrinsic motivation and cultural curiosity increase the students' intercultural competence. On the contrary, the motivation to extend their CV had no effect. Study abroad programs should therefore be accompanied by intercultural preparation, multicultural team assignments, and extracurricular activities that support intercultural interactions.

A vivid example of a study program that combines international content, intercultural preparation, multicultural team assignments, and study stays abroad is the Master in International Business Studies (MIBS) at the University of Erlangen-Nürnberg. Each year's student group consists of approximately 60 students from more than 30 countries around the globe. Beyond courses in international management, marketing, finance, and economics taught by an international faculty in four different languages, the students develop essential communication and intercultural skills. They have the opportunity to earn credits at more than 140 partner universities worldwide, including various double degree options. The wide variety of language courses completes the intercultural focus of the program (https://www.wiso.rw.fau.eu/study/study-options/masters/international-business-studies/).

International field trips (study tours) offer a shorter intercultural experience. They may include visits of foreign companies and institutions, lectures at foreign universities, and intercultural workshops (Anderson et al. 2006; Wood & St. Peters 2014). Like study abroad programs, international field trips do not necessarily improve intercultural competence. Field trips may even increase the participants' ethnocentrism if the exposure to the other culture is too short to overcome the culture shock that may be experienced particularly in culturally distant countries. Moreover, the vacation-like experience of international field trips may lead to surface-level perceptions of differences, like food, clothing, etc. and unrealistic expectations of the foreign culture and thus decrease the participant's awareness of cultural differences.

9.4 CULTURE-GENERAL TRAINING

9.4.1 Intellectual Culture-General Training

The purpose of intellectual culture-general training is to provide generic information about cultural differences (content knowledge) and their influence on management practices and interpersonal behavior (process knowledge). The most basic form is **cultural dimensions training**, where the trainees learn about different concepts of culture, such as those developed by Hofstede (2001), Trompenaars and Hampden-Turner (2012), and House et al. (2004). Besides several books on these concepts, videos with their main proponents, such as Geert Hofstede and Fons Trompenaars, are available, in which important aspects of these concepts are explained. Also, smartphone applications explaining these concepts exist. More sophisticated are exercises and dialogues (Dolan & Kawamura 2015), video sequences (Klinge, Rohmann & Piontkowski 2009), and the minicases developed by Hofstede, Pedersen, and Hofstede (2002), where trainees have to analyze intercultural encounters according to Hofstede's six cultural dimensions.

Culture-general assimilators are very similar to culture-specific assimilators, as they also feature critical incidents, and are conducted in a similar manner. The difference is that they focus on themes that can be applied to interactions with people from any culture. Rather than focusing on a particular target country, their emphasis is on etic cultural dimensions that can be applied across countries, such as individualism vs. collectivism, concepts of the self, or motivation for behaviors (Bhawuk 2001). For example, the culture-general assimilator of Brislin (1986) consists of 100 critical incidents that cover categories like anxiety and related emotional states, prejudice and ethnocentrism, time and space, roles, categorization, and values that have been identified in the literature as important for intercultural encounters. Since culture-general assimilators are based on the same procedure as culture-specific assimilators, their advantages and disadvantages are very similar.

The main purpose of **cultural self-awareness training** is to improve the trainees' awareness of their own cultural background and how it influences their feeling, thinking, and behavior. Individuals with little intercultural exposure often take their world view for granted and universal. The aim of cultural self-awareness training is therefore to help trainees move outside their own cultural frame and to become aware of their cultural biases. It encourages trainees to engage in cultural self-assessment through, for example, introspection, self-questioning, and self-reflexive orientation in interactions with culturally distinct individuals (Bhawuk & Brislin 2000).

An example is the exercise *Culture Circles* developed by Gary Coombs and Yolanda Sarason (1998). Trainees begin discussing their own cultural background as a source of identity and pride. They are asked to describe some of the customs, rituals, and ceremonies associated with their culture and those aspects they are most proud of. The intention is to help the participants to explore aspects of their cultural background they may not have thought about. Afterwards, they are requested to imagine themselves with any different cultural identity and to reflect how this would change their feeling, thinking, and behavior. In the debriefing, they shall justify their preference and decide whether they would take the opportunity for change or remain the same.

9.4.2 Experiential Culture-General Training

Simulations with artificial cultures aim to experience the impact of intercultural differences on behavior. Since the 1970s, several methods with different contents and procedures have been developed and gradually introduced in intercultural training programs in governmental organizations and private firms (Salzmann 2020). For example, BaFá BaFá, and Barnga have been regularly used in the predeparture training for State Department employees and family since the 1980s (Fowler & Pusch 2010).

Most intercultural simulations provide preconstructed cultures with rules and reward systems, styles of interacting, and sometimes artificial language. They often refer to important etic dimensions of culture, such as individualism vs. collectivism, time and space orientations, and different communication styles. The ascription of universal cultural dimensions to artificial cultures intends to prevent participants from deferring to unknown stereotypes specific to a particular culture (Wiggins 2012). The procedure of simulations with artificial cultures is often similar (Table 9.1). First, the participants are divided into groups with different cultural rules which first have to be learned and practiced. Afterwards, visits of "observers" and/or intercultural encounters take place. These visits typically result in misperception, misinterpretation, and emotions that simulate culture shock. The simulations end with a debriefing session where the participants share their experiences and discuss them with the trainer (Hofstede, Pedersen & Hofstede 2002):

- Probably the most well-known simulation is *BaFá BaFá* created by R. Garry Shirts in 1977 under contract with the US Navy (www.stsintl.com/business/bafa.html). It works best with approximately 20–30 participants divided into two groups named Alpha culture and Beta culture. The two groups have widely different sets of artificial cultural rules. The Alpha culture is masculine, hierarchical, relationship-oriented, collectivist, communicative, and non-competitive. The Beta culture is egalitarian, highly competitive, values negotiation, meritocratic, and uses an artificial trading language. Both cultures have a practice of exchanging cards, but the meaning of this practice is entirely different in the two cultures. A foreign visitor will therefore miss this point because of surface familiarity with the card-exchange practice (Shirts 1995).

- *Barnga* was developed by Sivasailam Thjagarajan and Barbara Steinwachs (1995). The trainees play a card game tournament called "Five Tricks" with different rules for each group without being aware of it. Players sit around tables in a non-limited number of small groups and each player tries to win as many rounds of play as possible. Once the players have learned the rules, they are not allowed to speak anymore. After some minutes, the winner and loser (taker of the most and fewest tricks) change tables. Without being aware of it, players soon find themselves at a table with other players whose rules are minimally different. Even when players recognize that

Table 9.1 Comparison of BaFá BaFá, Barnga, and Ecotonos

	BaFá BaFá	Barnga	Ecotonos
Optimum number of participants	20–30 (may be more depending on the number of instructors)	20–40	15–20
Required number of instructors	2	1	3
Required number of rooms	2	1	1
Number of interactions	One	One	Not restricted

One of the most interesting outcomes of BaFá BaFá is how quickly the trainees often identify with "their" given culture while participating in the training. One question in the debriefing is typically about which culture the participant would prefer to belong to. Interestingly, the vast majority of both the Alpha and the Beta cultures report that they would prefer "their" culture. This experience illustrates how quickly a distinction between "us and them" is made, given the fact that the trainees learned the rules of "their" artificial culture only a few minutes before.

newcomers to a table are not playing the exact same game, they tend to cling to their own rules, convinced the others are in error and cheating.

- *Ecotonos* was created by Nipporica Associates and Dianne Saphiere (1995b). Participants are divided into three fictitious cultural groups: Aqulla, Delphinus, and Zante. There are ten types of rule cards for each of ten characteristics, such as leadership, teamwork, gestures, listening styles, and problem solving. Each type of card has three variations representing a position with regard to one of these characteristics. For example, variations in decision-making preferences include consensus, democratic, and autocratic. All teams get one of the variations for three to four cultural characteristics so that each team has a different cultural script. After some time to discuss its cultural rules and to create a myth about its origins, all groups get the same task or case study to work on. This could be a physical or an intellectual task, a business-oriented or a committee-oriented case, depending on the objectives of the session. When the participants are well into working on their task, groups are recombined in such a way that each team consists of players from all three cultures. These newly formed teams then continue to work on the same problem, but now bringing to the task three different sets of cultural characteristics. Ecotonos has the merit of being very flexible in the choice of culture scripts and tasks. Compared to BaFá BaFá, real workplace situations are simulated more closely and it can be used more than once with the same group.

Simulations with artificial cultures aim to experience how lost one can feel in a foreign country whose cultural standards are unknown. The trainees become aware that other cultures are often interpreted from the perspective of one's own culture and mostly described in negative terms. This experience, however, can lead to *mixed results*. For example, the study of Bücker and Korzilius (2015) showed that the use of Ecotonos supports the development of the metacognitive, motivational, and behavioral dimensions of the CQS of Ang et al. (2007). Moreover, it enhances the confidence in cross-cultural encounters, while no effect on communication effectiveness was revealed. On the contrary, Bruschke, Gartner, and Seiter (1993) found in a study with US university students that BaFá BaFá increased their dogmatism and ethnocentrism. Particularly if the experience conflicts with strong opinions and convictions held by participants, they may refuse to invest in it or learn from it (Noesjirwan & Bruin 1989).

In order to reduce these potentially negative outcomes, an extensive *debriefing* is essential for allowing the participants to make sense of the experience. Hofstede and Pedersen (1999) recommend trainers to let the participants first briefly present their results in terms of the game's content matter. If there is a win/lose aspect to the game, the trainers should comment on it and emphasize that one set of rules is not intrinsically better than another. This makes it easier for the participants to take the distance needed for reflection. The final discussion may than reflect upon experienced intercultural misunderstandings and the game's relevancy for real life.

An international simulation that combines elements of synthetic and authentic cultures is *Oasistan* (de Jong & Warmeling 2017). Developed in 1999 at the Delft University of Technology in the Netherlands, it evolves from an oil exploration and production project in the Caspian Sea. It includes four main types of teams: representatives of (1) the fictional country of Oasistan (members of the Royal family and its entourage, business people from the energy sector, and people from traditional agricultural industries), (2) 'The West' (representatives of various European institutions, the World Trade Organization and Royal Dutch Shell), (3) Emerging Markets institutions and firms (representatives of the Russian government, Gazprom, Petrobras, and Sinopec), and (4) one local and one global NGO. All teams receive individual role instructions that are structured along important cultural dimensions derived from Hofstede (2001), Trompenaars and Hamden-Turner (2012), and Schwartz (1994), and represent typical value patterns of the countries and regions involved (i.e., Europe, North America, Middle East, Russia, China, and Brazil). The aim of the simulation is to experience the difficulty and awkwardness of being confronted with cultural differences and to recognize and understand these differences through cultural dimensions. One advantage compared to simulations with purely artificial cultures is that Oasistan involves some realistic elements which typically increase the trainee's motivation to participate in the role-play.

X-Culture, developed and administered by Vas Taras, is a large-scale multicultural team simulation where students work in multicultural virtual teams to collectively complete a course project (https://x-culture.org/). Every semester, thousands of students and professionals from over 40 countries take part in the X-Culture competition. For several months, they work together in teams of up to six students from different countries on real-life business projects submitted by corporate partners. The students' intercultural competence is evaluated before and after their participation in the project by using the motivation subscale of the cultural intelligence scale (CQS) of Ang et al. (2007). According to the study of Taras et al. (2013), participation in the project leads to a statistically significant drop in perceived intercultural differences across all samples and measures. The change in perceived differences does not depend on the countries represented on the respondents' teams. Thus, the training is able to lower perceived intercultural differences in general and independently from the specific cultures with which the students have direct contact in their teams.

Finally, **on-the-job training in multicultural teams** encourages interculturally experienced persons to share their expertise and experience with interculturally less competent team members. On-the-job training can be adapted to the specific work context so that the acquired intercultural skills can be more easily applied in practice. It focuses on real-life situations and on real teams instead of artificial exercises and trainees who interact with each other only for the purpose of the training. However, on-the-job training is often less structured and the effects largely depend on the intercultural knowledge-sharing efforts of the team members. Moreover, interculturally less competent persons may be more willing to learn from professional external trainers than from other team members with whom they regularly interact in their work context. Intercultural training on-the-job is therefore most common in expatriate preparation where the incoming expatriate is sent to the foreign country prior to the departure of the incumbent expatriate. During the time frame in which both persons are working in the foreign subsidiary, the experienced expatriate introduces the new expatriate to key personnel and the new work environment and facilitates his or her cultural adjustment (Brewster 1995).

9.5 EFFECTIVENESS OF INTERCULTURAL TRAINING

The effectiveness of intercultural training has been studied mainly with student and expatriate samples (Bhawuk 2017). According to a systematic review of empirical studies in **tertiary education** of Sit, Mak, and Neill (2017), group discussions, lectures, individual or group exercises, and role-plays are the most frequently used training methods. Culture assimilators, case studies, field trips, and language preparations belong to the lesser used methods. Intercultural training programs with behavioral components have the most consistent evidence of effectiveness. Programs that combine cognitive and behavioral components are more effective than those that consist of cognitive methods alone.

In the context of **expatriate assignments**, the reviews of Black and Mendenhall (1990), Deshpande and Viswesvaran (1992), and Littrell et al. (2006) reveal a positive relationship between predeparture intercultural training and expatriate adjustment. This is supported by the meta-analysis of Morris and Robie (2001), however the positive effect of intercultural training on cultural adjustment was generally weak. In a meta-analysis of 28 studies of intercultural training effectiveness published between 1988 and 2000, Mendenhall et al. (2004) found that lectures, presentations, culture assimilators, and class discussions are the most common methods. Given the predominantly intellectual nature of these methods, intercultural training is most effective in enhancing knowledge and trainee satisfaction, but less effective in changing behavior and attitudes, and in improving performance and cultural adjustment. While existing research mainly reveals positive effects of intercultural training, there are also studies which observed no influence or even a negative impact of intercultural training on cultural adjustment (Black & Gregersen 1991; Gregersen & Black 1992; Kealey & Protheroe 1996; Puck, Kittler & Wright 2008).

Intercultural training—if not carefully designed and implemented—can not only be ineffective but even dysfunctional and harmful. According to the constructivist concept of culture, cultural values, norms, and behaviors are not preexisting and objective facts, but social constructs. Teaching supposed characteristics of other cultures can therefore lead the participants' attention to intercultural differences that would otherwise not exist, not be perceived, or not be relevant.

Intercultural training which aims primarily at the explanation of the "do's and don'ts" may also distract participants from deeper-level aspects of other cultures. The trainees may mistakenly assume that it is all about avoiding the don'ts, and not focusing their attention on the more relevant but less visible differences in values and norms. However, the knowledge of other cultures' eating and greeting habits does not guarantee successful business relations.

Moreover, the focus on national culture might underestimate other reasons of human behaviors. Culture is rarely the only or even the dominant reason for misunderstandings and management failures. Instead, cultural influences often amplify or mitigate other factors, such as personality, incentive structures, and power asymmetries. Intercultural training that neglects these factors and the complexity of interaction effects bears the risk of misleading the trainees instead of improving their orientation.

One reason for the inconsistent findings may be that existing studies are predominantly focused on the **length** of predeparture intercultural training, but rarely account for training content and methods. Indeed, Fowler and Yamaguchi (2020) provide a detailed analysis of the *expected* outcomes of various **methods** of intercultural training, but few studies examined their *actual* effects. For example, Morris and Robie (2001) could not test the effectiveness of different training methods because of the small sample of studies available. An exception is the study of Earley (1987) which distinguished between documentary and interpersonal training methods and showed that both have added benefits in preparing managers for intercultural work assignments. According to Waxin and Panaccio (2005), intercultural training generally facilitates all three facets of expatriates' adjustment, with experiential culture-specific training being the most effective type. Similarly, Okpara and Kabongo (2011) found that experiential culture-specific training has a stronger impact on the cultural adjustment of expatriates than intellectual and culture-general training.

Beyond length and methods, the **timing** of intercultural training is particularly relevant for the preparation of expatriates (Bennett, Aston & Colquhoun 2000). Predeparture training allows the employee and family members to enter the assignment already equipped with basic knowledge and realistic expectations of the host culture. This may help reduce the intensity of culture shock. However, if the training is offered too far before the start of the foreign assignment, the learning readiness may not be acute, and much of the learning is at risk of being forgotten by the time of the departure. Postarrival training, on the other hand, is valued because the assignees have already made some real-life intercultural encounters which they can bring to the training (Selmer 2001). Then, the expatriates' learning readiness is often at its peak because they have already made authentic intercultural experiences (Wurtz 2014). Shortly after the beginning of a foreign assignment, however, the expatriates may be pressured by their new job and less willing to spend considerable time for intercultural training.

Another important element of intercultural training design is the **trainer**. The trainer must often fulfill a complex set of expectations and serves as coach, educator, facilitator, counselor, moderator, and cultural role model (Paige 1996; Bennett, Aston & Colquhoun 2000). Beyond broad cultural knowledge, extensive intercultural experience and the knowledge of foreign languages are instrumental. Further requirements are cultural empathy and the ability to adapt to different learning styles of the participants. Despite the key role of the trainer, empirical studies of the proposed trainer competencies are still lacking.

While the methods, length, timing, and trainer constitute important elements of training design, the effectiveness of intercultural training is also contingent on various external and internal factors. According to the literature review of Kempf and Holtbrügge (2020), the **moderators** identified in previous studies can be assigned either to the environment in which the intercultural learning process takes place or to personal attributes of the trainees (Figure 9.2). An important environmental factor of intercultural training for expatriates is the *cultural distance* between the home and the host culture, which is likely to moderate the relationship between the training design and its outcomes in the form of an inverted u-curve. When the cultural distance is low, the trainees may not perceive any need for intercultural training. This increases with cultural distance and the lack of familiarity with the foreign culture (Lee & Croker 2006). The effectiveness of intercultural training decreases again once the cultural differences become too large and make it difficult for the participants to grasp and reproduce the training content. Important organizational moderators are the *type of the assignment* (e.g., long-term delegation vs. virtual assignment) and the *ownership structure* (e.g., national firm vs. joint-venture).

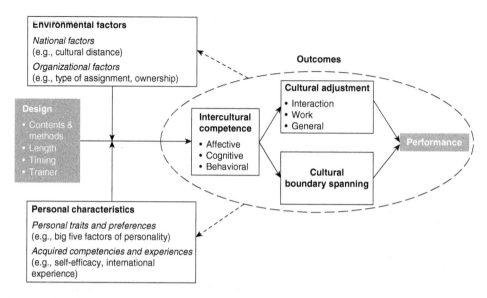

Figure 9.2 Moderators and mediators of intercultural training effectiveness
Source: Adapted from Kempf & Holtbrügge (2020, p. 314).

While intercultural training mostly focuses—at least implicitly—on expatriates, there is a large number of managers and specialists who stay in their home country, but extensively interact with individuals in other countries. These may be customers, suppliers, or coworkers in foreign subsidiaries. Holtbrügge and Schillo (2008) developed a training concept for such virtual delegates that differs from concepts for traditional expatriates in terms of training content and training methods.

With reference to training content, two differences are particularly important, namely the lack of personal experiences in the foreign country and of face-to-face communication. Virtual delegates remain in their home country most of the time. Because of this spatial separation of private and business life, no adjustment to living conditions in the foreign country is necessary. Only adjustment to the work-context is required. For example, virtual delegates do not have to learn how to use chopsticks, to greet people, or to dress in a culturally appropriate way. In contrast to traditional expatriates, virtual assignees will not experience hot summers in India, power cuts in China, or crowded subways in Japan. Intercultural training for virtual delegates should therefore concentrate on work-related aspects, such as different perceptions of deadlines, decision-making processes, or attitudes to work in an intercultural context.

With reference to the lack of face-to-face communication, training for virtual delegates should include information about new technologies, such as videoconferences, chat rooms, or blogs and their compatibility across national and organizational borders. In contrast, knowledge of important elements of face-to-face communication, such as olfactory and tactile stimulation or dress code is less relevant. In addition to learning new technologies, virtual delegates must be able to select the appropriate communication media according to the given task and cultural context they work in ("netiquette"). Particularly useful is information on different communication styles and communication training which takes into account the characteristics of electronic media.

Regarding different training methods, cognitive elements, such as information about work-related aspects of other cultures and the culture-specific use of electronic media, is indispensable. This can be imparted most efficiently by intellectual methods such as lectures, presentations, or fact sheets, while experiential methods are less useful. In virtual assignments, in which tasks are managed from a distance, communication takes place mainly via electronic media. This offers the opportunity to reflect longer on possible answers and the use of expressions. Acting spontaneously in a culturally-adequate way is less important.

Among the personal characteristics, the trainees' *self-efficacy* is particularly beneficial (Osman-Gani & Rockstuhl 2009; Fan & Lai 2014). Trainees with a high degree of self-efficacy are more confident and psychologically capable of transferring the acquired skills to actual intercultural challenges. Moreover, *openness to experience* and a high *propensity to change stereotypes* facilitate the training success (Alexandra 2018; Oolders, Chernyshenko & Stark 2008).

Existing research suggests that intercultural training does not directly improve cultural adjustment (Kempf & Holtbrügge 2020). Instead, this relationship is **mediated** by increased *intercultural competence*. Depending on the prevalent methods of intercultural training, this consists of cognitive and behavioral components. Cognitive and behavioral competencies are interconnected and amplify each other in the intercultural learning process (Osman-Gani & Rockstuhl 2009). An increased intercultural competence then facilitates the *cultural adjustment* of expatriates (Moon, Choi & Jung 2012), i.e., adjustment to interactions with host country nationals, adjustment to work, and general adjustment (Black, Mendenhall & Oddou 1991). Beyond adjustment, *cultural boundary spanning* is an important mediator of intercultural training. Cultural boundary spanning is different from adjustment as it does not only produce consistent behavior with one foreign culture but rather involves bridging and linking processes, such as information gathering, interacting with other assignees, and connecting previously unconnected people in diverse cultural environments (Engelhard & Holtbrügge 2018). Thus, boundary spanning is not only relevant for expatriates but also for all employees with frequent intercultural encounters.

The ultimate outcome of intercultural training is increased *performance*, which at the same time can be the starting point of a new **intercultural learning cycle**. Self-confident trainees are likely to achieve higher performance, which in turn increases their self-efficacy. The training outcomes can also affect trainees' competencies and experiences as well as the perception of environmental factors. For example, enhanced intercultural competence motivates trainees to discover and comprehend foreign countries, which leads to an increased international experience if the trainees actually follow this desire (Moon, Choi & Jung 2012). Furthermore, intercultural competence, cultural adjustment, and cultural boundary spanning reduce the perceived cultural distance (Selmer 2005), which in turn facilitates intercultural learning.

9.6 CRITICAL OUTLOOK AND FUTURE DIRECTIONS

Although the effectiveness of intercultural training has been frequently examined, existing research is limited by several **methodological shortcomings**. As mentioned above, empirical studies in this context are mostly based on student samples and experimental designs. While this allows for drawing conclusions about the effectiveness of intercultural training in tertiary education, it is doubtful whether the results can be transferred to other fields. In the expatriate context, previous studies predominantly test the effect of intercultural training on trainees' cultural adjustment, while other outcomes, such as cultural boundary spanning, are hardly considered. Moreover, few studies take potential moderators and mediators of intercultural training effectiveness into account (Kempf & Holtbrügge 2020). The outcomes of intercultural training are mostly measured based on trainees' self-perceptions and with control group designs. Longitudinal studies which measure the increase of intercultural competence, cultural adjustment, and cultural boundary spanning based on evaluations of superiors, peers, or subordinates are still missing. Finally, there is a lack of comprehensive theoretical explanations of training success (Lenartowicz, Johnson & Konopaske 2014).

In order to increase the acceptance and effectiveness of intercultural training, educators should invest in the **development of innovative training methods**. Several established methods have their origin in the 1960s and 1970s, and were developed for military purposes. Today, *globalization* is significantly increasing the need for intercultural training, while at the same time, *digitalization* considerably broadens the spectrum of training methods (Kirste & Holtbrügge 2019). Moreover, novel measurement technologies, such as functional magnetic resonance imaging (fMRI) and electroencephalogram (EEG) developed in *cultural neuroscience*, may help to better understand the cognitive effects of intercultural training and improve its effectiveness (Chang 2017; Han & Mäkelä 2020).

A promising tool may be the application of **social media** (Wankel 2016). This allows for the connection of an unlimited number of individuals across the globe. Trainees and trainers from a variety of cultural backgrounds can interact virtually and in an asynchronous way, thus adapting the training to their job schedule and personal preferences. Another major advantage is the opportunity to outsource intercultural training materials. All participants can provide pictures, videos, podcasts, blogs, etc. with real-life examples. The incorporation of automatic translation utilities even allows the participants to get access to materials in languages which they do not speak. Like with online platforms, careful monitoring is inevitable for correcting factual errors and misleading information.

Another requirement of effective intercultural training is its **adaptation to individual learning styles**. For example, US Americans prefer a detached communication style ("just the facts, please"), whereas Latin Americans are more comfortable with an attached and emotionally expressive style, with issues being dissembled with verve and emotion (Fowler & Blohm 2004). More fundamentally, the study of Holtbrügge & Mohr (2010) found learning style preferences according to Kolb (1984) varying with individuals' cultural values. For example, there is a positive influence of individualism on the preference for active experimentation and abstract conceptualization, while masculinity is associated with a preference for abstract conceptualization and reflective observation. Thus, a one-size-fits-all model might be unlikely to help trainees achieve the required learning outcomes. One response to the growing cultural diversity of the participants in intercultural training programs who differ with regard to their preferred learning styles may be the increased use of multimedia platforms that allow the trainees to select from a wide range of intellectual and experiential training methods their most preferred ones.

Similarly, the **adaptation to the trainees' intercultural experience and competence** is required. For example, introverted technical specialists with little international exposure may require culture-general and experiential training, while a manager with several years of international experience may prefer short culture briefings as preparation for a new international assignment (Littrell et al. 2006). More generally, intercultural training should be regarded as an integrated part of personnel development instead of a short-term, ad-hoc-measure that is offered to future expatriates in the context of foreign assignments. This would also allow for improvement of the affective and behavioral competencies that are difficult to address in short preparation trainings.

Intercultural training should be adapted for **applications outside the student and expatriate context**. One area of application is *team sport players*. In many team sports, such as football, basketball, handball, and hockey, the increasing cultural diversity requires players with high intercultural competence (Maderer, Holtbrügge & Schuster 2014). However, professional team sport players are often lacking in their academic background and are reluctant toward abstract conceptualization, while their perceptual skills are superior (Williams et al. 2011). Thus, training programs need to consider their specific training requirements and cognitive competencies. Another field of application is *teachers* who are faced with an increasingly diverse body of pupils. Teachers in multicultural classrooms require knowledge about a variety of countries, cultures, and religions. Moreover, they often have to cope with pupils' limited language skills, mistrust, and their own lack of authority. Thus, intercultural training programs should focus particularly on intercultural trust-building and communication competencies (Cushner, McClelland & Safford 2015).

Migrants and refugees constitute maybe the greatest challenge for intercultural training programs. In contrast to other groups, their residence in a foreign country is mostly involuntary. They escaped civil wars, natural disasters, physical violence, and death, and often had to leave behind all insignia that made up their previous identity. Often traumatized by terrible experiences in their home country, they are regularly faced with discrimination and xenophobia in their new host country which is mostly alien to them. While migrants and refugees typically lack local language skills, they are often adept in mobile technologies and social media. Online pedagogies can therefore be useful for bridging cultural and educational gaps (O'Mara & Harris 2016). Moreover, image-based approaches of intercultural training can be efficient (Arizpe et al. 2014). Generally, intercultural training should take into consideration that migrants and refugees often live in highly culturally diverse neighborhoods and are confronted with a magnitude of different and often contradictory cultural stimuli. Therefore, a broader concept of intercultural training is required, which takes phenomena, such as bi-, multi-, and polyculturalism, identity construction, and cultural third places into consideration (Kim 2015; van de Vijver et al., 2015).

Finally, more emphasis should be put on the **ethical aspects** of intercultural training. Most intercultural training programs are based on a functionalist and positivist approach. They relate to seemingly neutral concepts of culture, such as those of Hofstede and GLOBE, and regard increased performance as their ultimate goal (Joy & Poonamallee 2013). While the participants are predominantly trained in tools and techniques of culturally contingent profit-making, less attention is dedicated to the moral standards and consequences of different decisions and behaviors in intercultural encounters. Thus, the prevailing instrumental and performance-oriented perspective should be accompanied by a patient deconstruction of evolving interactions and negotiations of meaning and hidden value assumptions (Szkudlarek 2009).

SUMMARY

Intercultural training includes all formal efforts to increase an individual's intercultural competence.

Intercultural training methods can be classified in terms of the geographic scope of the training (culture-general vs. culture-specific) and the applied didactic approach (intellectual vs. experiential).

The effectiveness of intercultural training is dependent on training characteristics, including training length, timing, and the responsible trainer. Moreover, internal and external moderators, such as personality traits and the cultural distance between home and host country, are relevant.

Intercultural training can be improved, for instance, through the application of innovative training methods (such as online trainings), the consideration of trainees' competences and intercultural experiences, and the adaptation to trainees' learning style.

Reflection Questions

1. Imagine a Danish expatriate is being sent to a Mexican subsidiary together with her husband and children on a three-year contract. Do you believe that it is important to include the manager's family in the intercultural training? If yes, what type of training would you suggest for the manager and her family members?
2. From your perspective, which role does the trainer play in the effectiveness of intercultural training?
3. Have you ever participated in an intercultural training? What was your experience like and did you notice any changes in your attitudes and your ability to manage intercultural encounters?
4. What type of intercultural training would you recommend to a German manager about to transfer to a South Korean subsidiary as the new chief financial officer?
5. Name each step of the intercultural learning cycle. What kind of activities and exercises can be used for each step?
6. Intercultural training is increasingly conducted in a digital format. Which aims of intercultural training can be realized more effectively and which less effectively in a digital format?
7. How would you implement an intercultural training on a social media platform of your choice? Would it be experiential or intellectual? Culture-general or culture-specific?
8. How would you measure the effectiveness of intercultural training?

 End of Chapter Exercise

Designing an Intercultural Training Program

Tech Corp. is a large European-based multinational corporation with activities spanning across the globe. Around 200 employees are sent to foreign subsidiaries as managers and technical experts annually. They predominantly work as long-term expatriates, but there are also short-term, frequent flyer, and virtual assignments. While in the past the focus of preparation was on technical skills, the company now wants to improve the intercultural competence of its expatriates.

1. Develop an intercultural training program for Tech Corp. that reflects the different assignment types and host countries in which the company operates.
2. Previous experience has shown that technical specialists often do not pay much attention to intercultural aspects. How would you incentivize their participation in the intercultural training?
3. In a second step, Tech Corp. wants to extend the intercultural training to expatriates who are already on their foreign assignment. Due to travel restrictions, some expatriates are not able to physically attend training activities in other countries. How would you address these restrictions in a digital training format?

Further Reading

Key reference books on intercultural training are the handbooks by Landis, Bennett, and Bennett (2003) and Landis and Bhawuk (2020).

The books by Hofstede, Pedersen, and Hofstede (2002) and Dolan and Kawamura (2015) are excellent field guides and manuals for intercultural training offering a large selection of instructor resources.

The moderators and mediators of intercultural training effectiveness are discussed by Kempf and Holtbrügge (2020).

The cultural determinants of learning style preferences are analyzed by Holtbrügge and Mohr (2010). Kirste and Holtbrügge (2019) discuss the challenges and opportunities of intercultural training in an online context.

REFERENCES

Abutalebi, J. (2008). Neural aspects of second language representation and language control. *Acta Psychologica*, 128(3), 466–478.

Adams, B.G. & van de Vijver, F.J.R. (2015). The many faces of expatriate identity. *International Journal of Intercultural Relations*, 49, 322–331.

Adler, J. (2004). Reconciling open-mindedness and belief. *Theory and Research in Education*, 2(2), 127–142.

Adler, N.J. & Gundersen, A. (2008). *International Dimensions of Organizational Behavior*. 5th ed., Mason, OH: Thomson.

Adorno, T.W., Frenkel-Brunswik, E., Levinson, D. & Sanford, N. (1950). *The Authoritarian Personality*. New York, NY: Harper & Brothers.

Agadjanian, V. & Zotova, N. (2012). Sampling and surveying hard-to-reach populations for demographic research: A study of female labor migrants in Moscow, Russia. *Demographic Research*, 26(5), 131–150.

Ager, A. & Strang, A. (2008). Understanding integration: A conceptual framework. *Journal of Refugee Studies*, 21(2), 166–191.

Ailon, G. (2008). Mirror, mirror on the wall: 'Culture's consequences' in a value test of its own design. *Academy of Management Review*, 33(4), 885–904.

Aktas, M., Gelfand, M. & Hanges, P. (2016). Cultural tightness–looseness and perceptions of effective leadership. *Journal of Cross-Cultural Psychology*, 47(2), 294–309.

Al-Jahwari, M. & Budhwar, P.S. (2016). Human resource management in Oman. In: Budhwar, P.S. & Mellahi, K. (eds.), *Handbook of Human Resource Management in the Middle East*. Cheltenham-Northampton: Edward Elgar, 87–122.

Albert, C. (1999). *Francophonie et identités culturelles*. Paris: Karthala.

Albert, R.D. (1995). The intercultural sensitizer/culture assimilator as a cross-cultural training method. In: Fowler, S.M. & Mumford, M.G. (eds.), *Intercultural Sourcebook: Cross-Cultural Training Methods*. Vol. 1, Yarmouth, ME: Intercultural Press, 157–168.

Albert, R.D. & Ha, I.A. (2004). Latino/Anglo-American differences in attributions to situations involving touch and silence. *International Journal of Intercultural Relations*, 28(3–4), 253–280.

Allcott, H. & Gentzkow, M. (2017). Social media and fake news in the 2016 election. *Journal of Economic Perspectives*, 31(2), 211–236.

Alder, P.A. & Alder, P. (2000). Observational techniques. In: Denzin, N.K. & Lincoln, Y.S. (eds.), *Handbook of Qualitative Research*. Thousand Oaks, CA: SAGE, 377–392.

Alesina, A., Devleeschauwer, A., Easterly, W., Kurlat, S. & Wacziarg, R. (2003). Fractionalization. *Journal of Economic Growth*, 8(2), 155–194.

Alexandra, V. (2018). Predicting CQ development in the context of experiential cross-cultural training: The role of social dominance orientation and the propensity to change stereotypes. *Academy of Management Learning & Education*, 17(1), 62–78.

Alon, I., Boulanger, M., Elston, J.A., Galanaki, E., Martínez de Ibarreta, C., Meyers, J., Muñiz-Ferrer, M. & Vélez-Calle, A. (2018). Business cultural intelligence quotient: A five-country study. *Thunderbird International Business Review*, 60(3), 237–250.

Alon, I., Boulanger, M., Meyers, J. & Taras, V. (2016). The development and validation of the business cultural intelligence quotient. *Cross Cultural & Strategic Management*, 23(1), 78–100.

Alon, I., Jaffe, E., Prange, C. & Vianolli, D. (2020). *Global Marketing. Strategy, Practice, and Cases*. New York-London: Routledge.

Altbach, P.G. & Knight, J. (2007). The internationalization of higher education: Motivations and realities. *Journal of Studies in International Education*, 11(3/4), 290–305.

Alvesson, M. & Sveningsson, S. (2015). *Changing Organizational Culture: Cultural Change Work in Progress*. 2nd ed., London-New York: Routledge.

Ali, A.J. & Al-Owaihan, A. (2008). Islamic work ethic: A critical review. *Cross-Cultural Management*, 15(1), 5–19.

Ammon, U. (2003). The International standing of the German language. In: Maurais, J. & Morris, M.A. (eds.), *Languages in a Globalising World*. Cambridge: Cambridge University Press, 231–249.

Anand, R. & Lahiri, I. (2009). Intercultural competence in health care: Developing skills for interculturally competent care. In: Deardorff, K. (ed.), *Sage Handbook of Intercultural Competence*. Thousand Oaks, CA: SAGE, 387–401.

Anderson, B. (2006). *Imagined Communities: Reflections on the Origin and Spread of Nationalism*. Revised ed., London-New York: Verso.

Andersen, P.A. (2011). Tactile traditions: Cultural differences and similarities in haptic communication. In: Hertenstein, M.J. & Weiss, S.J. (eds.), *The Handbook of Touch: Neuroscience, Behavioral, and Health Perspectives*. New York, NY: Springer, 351–369.

Andersen, P.A., Hecht, M.L., Hoobler, G.D. & Smallwood, M. (2003). Nonverbal communication across cultures. In: Gudykunst, W.B. (ed.), *Cross-Cultural and Intercultural Communication*. Thousand Oaks, CA: SAGE, 73–90.

Anderson, P.H., Lawton, L., Rexeisen, R.J. & Hubbard, A.C. (2006). Short-term study abroad and intercultural sensitivity: A pilot study. *International Journal of Intercultural Relations*, 30(4), 457–469.

Andonova, E. & Taylor, H.A. (2012). Nodding in dis/agreement: A tale of two cultures. *Cognitive Processsing*, 13(Supplement 1), 79–82.

Ang, S., van Dyne, L. & Koh, C. (2006). Personality correlates of the four-factor model of cultural intelligence. *Group & Organization Management*, 31(1), 100–123.

Ang, S. & van Dyne, L. (eds.) (2008), *Handbook of Cultural Intelligence*. London-New York: Routledge.

Ang, S., van Dyne, L., Koh, C., Ng, K.Y., Templer, K.J., Tay, C. & Chandrasekar, N.A. (2007). Cultural intelligence: Its measurement and effects on cultural judgment and decision making, cultural adaptation and task performance. *Management and Organization Review*, 3(3), 335–371.

Ang, S., van Dyne, L. & Rockstuhl, T. (2015). Intercultural intelligence. Origins, conceptualization, evolution, and methodological diversity. In: Gelfand, M., Chiu, C.-y. & Hong, Y.-y. (eds.), *Handbook of Advances in Culture and Psychology*, Vol. 5. Oxford: Oxford University Press, 273–323.

Appiah, K.A. (2018). *The Lies That Bind: Creed, Country, Colour, Class, Culture*. London: Profile Books.

Arar, K. & Shapira, T. (2016). Veiling and management: Muslim women managers in Israel. *International Journal of Cross Cultural Management*, 16(3), 367–384.

Arasaratnam, L.A. & Doerfel, M.L. (2005). Intercultural communication competence: Identifying key components from multicultural perspectives. *International Journal of Intercultural Relations*, 29(2), 137–163.

Ardichvili, A. & Kuchinke, K.P. (2002). Leadership styles and cultural values among managers and subordinates. A comparative study of four Countries of the former Soviet Union, Germany, and the US. *Human Resource Development International*, 5(1), 99–117.

d'Argens, J.-P. (1738). *Lettres juives*. The Hague.

Arizpe, E., Bagelman, C., Devlin, A.M., Farrell, M. & McAdam, J.E. (2014).Visualizing intercultural literacy: Engaging critically with diversity and migration in the classroom through an image-based approach. *Language and Intercultural Communication*, 14(3), 304–321.

Arkes, H.R. & Tetlock, P.E. (2004). Attributions of implicit prejudice, or "Would Jesse Jackson 'fail' the implicit association test?". *Psychological Inquiry*, 15(4), 257–278.

Armbrüster, T. (2005). *Management and Organization in Germany*. New York, NY: Routledge.

Arreola, D. (ed.) (2004). *Hispanic Spaces, Latino Places: Community and Cultural Diversity in Contemporary America*. Austin, TX: University of Texas Press.

Askegaard, S., Arnould, E.J. & Kjeldgaard, D. (2005). Postassimilationist ethnic consumer research: Qualifications and extensions. *Journal of Consumer Research*, 32(1), 160–170.

Aslam, M.M. (2006). Are you selling the right colour? A cross-cultural review of colour as a marketing cue. *Journal of Marketing Communications*, 12(1), 15–30.

Au, K.Y. (1999). Intra-cultural variation: Evidence and implications for international business. *Journal of International Business Studies*, 30(4), 799–812.

Au, K.Y. & Fukuda, J. (2002). Boundary spanning behaviors of expatriates. *Journal of World Business*, 37(4), 285–296.

Augé, M. (1992). *Non-lieux. Introduction à une anthropologie de la surmodernité*. Paris: Seuil.

Avanzi, M. & Mettra, M. (2017). *La francophonie ou le français hors de France*. Paris: Garnier.

Axtell, R.E. (1998). *Gestures: The Do's and Taboos of Body Language Around the World*. New York, NY: John Wiley & Sons.

Aycan, Z. (2005). The interplay between cultural and institutional/structural contingencies in human resource management practices. *International Journal of Human Resource Management*, 16(7), 1083–1119.

Aycan, Z., Kanungo, R.N. & Mendonca, M. (2014). *Organizations and Management in Cross-Cultural Context*. Los Angeles, CA: SAGE.

Aycan, Z., Kanungo, R., Mendonca, M., Yu, K., Deller, J., Stahl, G. & Kurshid, A. (2000). Impact of culture on human resource management practices: A 10-country comparison. *Applied Psychology*, 49(1), 192–221.

Baack, D.W., Dow, D., Parente, R. & Bacon, D.R. (2015). Confirmation bias in individual-level perceptions of psychic distance. An experimental investigation. *Journal of International Business Studies*, 45, 938–959.

Backmann, J., Kanitz, R., Tian, A.W., Hoffmann, P. & Hoegl, M. (2020). Cultural gap bridging in multinational teams. *Journal of International Business Studies*, 51, 1283–1311.

Baghramian, M. & Carter, J.A. (2018). Relativism. In: Zalta, E.N. (ed.), *The Stanford Encyclopedia of Philosophy*. Winter 2018 Edition, https://plato.stanford.edu/archives/win2018/entries/relativism/.

Bajaj, V. (2011). For wealthy Indian family, Palatial House is not a Home. *New York Times*, 18.10.2011. https://www.nytimes.com/2011/10/19/business/global/this-luxurious-house-is-not-a-home.html.

Baker, C. & Jones, S.P. (1998). *Encyclopedia of Bilingualism and Bilingual Education*. Clevedon: Multilingual Matters.

Ball, D.A., McCulloch, W.H., Frantz, P.L., Geringer, J.M. & Minor, M.S. (2004). *International Business: The Challenge of Global Competition*. 9th ed., Boston, MA: McGraw Hill/Irwin.

Ball, D.A., McCulloch, W.H., Frantz, P.L., Geringer, J.M. & Minor, M.S. (2006). *International Business: The Challenge of Global Competition*. 10th ed., Boston, MA: McGraw Hill/Irwin.

Bandura, A. (1997). *Self-Efficacy: The Exercise of Control*. New York, NY: Freeman.

Banerjee, S.B. & Prasad, A. (2008). Introduction to the special issue on critical reflections on management and organizations. A postcolonial perspective". *Critical Perspectives on International Business*, 4(2/3), 90–98.

Bangerter, A., König, C.J., Blatti, S. & Salvisberg, A. (2009). How widespread is graphology in personnel selection practice? A case study of a job market myth. *International Journal of Selection and Assessment*, 17(2), 219–230.

Banton, M. (2007). Weber on ethnic communities: A critique. *Nations and Nationalism*, 13(1), 19–35.

Barabantseva, E. (2011). *Overseas Chinese, Ethnic Minorities and Nationalism: De-Centering China*. New York, NY: Routledge.

Barkema, H.G., Bell, J.H.J. & Pennings, J.M. (1996). Foreign entry, cultural barriers, and learning. *Strategic Management Journal*, 17(2), 151–166.

Barker, C. & Jane, E.A. (2016). *Cultural Studies: Theory and Practice*. 5th ed., London: SAGE.

Barmeyer, C., Bausch, M. & Mayrhofer, U. (2021). *Constructive Intercultural Management. Integrating Cultural Differences Successfully*. Cheltenham-Northampton: Edward Elgar.

Barmeyer, C., Davoine, E. & Stokes, P. (2019). When the 'well-oiled machine' meets the 'pyramid of people': Role perceptions and hybrid working practices of middle managers in a binational organization – ARTE. *International Journal of Cross Cultural Management*, 19(3), 251–272.

Barmeyer, C. & Mayrhofer, U. (2008). The contribution of intercultural management to the success of international mergers and acquisitions: An analysis of the EADS group. *International Business Review*, 17(1), 28–38.

Barmeyer, C. & Mayrhofer, U. (2009). Management interculturel et processus d'intégration: une analyse de l'alliance Renault-Nissan. *Management & Avenir*, 22(2), 109–131.

Barner-Rasmussen, W., Ehrnrooth, M., Koveshnikov, A. & Mäkelä, K. (2014). Cultural and language skills as resources for boundary spanning within the MNC. *Journal of International Business Studies*, 45(7), 886–905.

Barney, J.B. (1986). Organizational culture: Can it be a source of sustained competitive advantage? *Academy of Management Review*, 11(3), 656–665.

Barsoux, J.L. & Lawrence, P. (2013). *French Management: Elitism in Action*. Abingdon: Routledge.

Baskerville, R.F. (2003). Hofstede never studied culture. *Accounting, Organizations and Society*, 28(1), 1–14.

Bass, B.M. & Riggio, R.E. (2006). *Transformational Leadership*. 2nd ed. Mahwah, NJ: Lawrence Erlbaum.

Batt, J. & Wolczuk, K. (2002). *Region, State and Identity in Central and Eastern Europe*. London: Routledge.

Bauer, L. (2003a). *An Introduction to International Varieties of English*. Hong Kong: Hong Kong University Press.

Bauer, L. (2003b). *Introducing Linguistic Morphology*. 2nd ed., Edinburg, TX: Edinburgh University Press.

Bauer, M. & Bertin-Mourot, B. (1996). *Vers un modèle européen de dirigeants? Trois modèles contrastés de production de l'autorité légitime au sommet des grandes entreprises. Comparaison Allemagne, France, Grande-Bretagne*. Paris: Abacus Edition.

Baugh, A.C. & Cable, T. (2012). *A History of the English Language*. 6th ed., London-New York: Routledge.

Baumgartner, H. & Steenkamp, J.-B.E.M. (2001). Response styles in marketing research: A cross-national investigation. *Journal of Marketing Research*, 38(2), 143–156.

Baxter, J. (1983). English for intercultural competence. An approach to intercultural communication training. In: D. Landis & Brislin, R.W. (eds.), *Handbook of Intercultural Training*. Vol. II: *Issues in Training Methodology*. New York, NY: Pergamon Press, 290–324.

Bayart, J.-F. (2005). *The Illusion of Cultural Identity*. London: Hurst & Company.

Beamer, L. (1992). Learning intercultural communication competence. *Journal of Business Communication*, 29(3), 285–303.

Behera, B. & Pathy, M. (2013). Employee referrals. The best leveraged talent acquisition strategy amid recession. *IOSR Journal of Business and Management*, 14(1), 1–10.

Behrnd, V. & Porzelt, S. (2012). Intercultural competence and training outcomes of students with experiences abroad. *International Journal of Intercultural Relations*, 36(2), 213–223.

Belhoste, N. & Monin, P. (2013). Constructing differences in a cross-cultural context: National distance, social differentiation or functional distinction. *Human Relations*, 66(12), 1529–1561.

Benedict, R. (1934). *Patterns of Culture*. Boston, MA: Houghton Mifflin.

Benedict, R. (1946). *The Chrysanthemum and the Sword. Patterns of Japanese Culture.* Boston, MA: Mariner.

Benedikter, T. (2009). *Language Policy and Linguistic Minorities in India: An Appraisal of the Linguistic Rights of Minorities in India.* Münster: LIT Verlag.

Benet-Martínez, V., Lee, F. & Leu, J. (2006). Biculturalism and cognitive complexity expertise in cultural representations. *Journal of Cross-Cultural Psychology,* 37(4), 386–407.

Benet-Martínez, V., Leu, J., Lee, F. & Morris, M.W. (2002). Negotiating biculturalism. Cultural frame switching in biculturals with oppositional versus compatible cultural identities. *Journal of Cross-Cultural Psychology,* 33(5), 492–516.

Benhabib, S. (2002). *The Claims of Culture. Equality and Diversity in the Global Era.* Princeton-Oxford: Princeton University Press.

Bennett, M.J. (1986). A developmental approach to training for intercultural sensitivity. *International Journal of Intercultural Relations,* 10(2), 179–196.

Bennett, M.J. (1993). Towards ethnorelativism. A developmental model of intercultural sensitivity. In: Paige, R.M. (ed.), *Education for the Intercultural Experience,* 2nd ed., Yarmouth, ME: Intercultural Press, 21–71.

Bennett, R. Aston, A. & Colquhoun, T. (2000). Cross-cultural training: A critical step in ensuring the success of international assignments. *Human Resource Management,* 39 (2/3), 239–250.

Bennold, K. (2017). For one far-right politician, forgetting Germany's past just got harder. *New York Times,* 25.12.2017. https://www.nytimes.com/2017/12/25/world/europe/germany-bjorn-hocke-bornhagen.html?rref=collection%2Fbyline%2Fkatrin-bennhold&action=click&contentCollection=undefined&region=stream&module=inline&version=latest&contentPlacement=74&pgtype=collection.

Berg, N. & Holtbrügge, D. (2010). Global teams: A network analysis. *Team Performance Management,* 16(3/4), 187–211.

Berger, P.L. & Luckmann, T. (1966). *The Social Construction of Reality. A Treatise in the Sociology of Knowledge.* New York, NY: Doubleday.

Berman, P. (2003). *Terror and Liberalism.* New York-London: Norton & Company.

Bernardi, R.A. (2006). Associations between Hofstede's cultural constructs and social desirability response bias. *Journal of Business Ethics,* 65(I), 43–53.

Berning, S.C. & Holtbrügge, D. (2016). Pictures as means of intercultural communication. The case of Chinese firms in Germany. In: Tirpitz, A. & Schleus, R.R. (eds.), *Yearbook of Market Entry Advisory 2015. Communication in International Business.* Berlin: epub, 175–205.

Bernstein, E. (2004). *Culture and Customs of Germany.* Westport-London: Greenwood Press.

Berry, H., Guillén, M.F. & Zhou, N. (2010). An institutional approach to cross-national distance. *Journal of International Business Studies,* 41(9), 1460–1480.

Berry, J.W. (1969). On cross-cultural comparability. *International Journal of Psychology,* 4(2), 119–128.

Berry, J.W. (1976). *Human Ecology and Cognitive Style. Comparative Studies in Cultural and Psychological Adaptation.* Beverly Hills, CA: SAGE.

Berry, J.W. (1980). Social and cultural change. In: Triandis, H.C. & Brislin, R.W. (eds.), *Handbook of Cross-Cultural Psychology,* Vol. 5, Boston, MA: Allyn & Bacon, 211–279.

Berry, J.W. (1983). Acculturation: A comparative analysis of alternative forms. In: Samuda, R.J. & Woods, S.L. (eds.), *Perspectives in Immigrant and Minority Education.* Lanham, MD: University Press of America, 66–77.

Berry, J.W. (2006). Contexts of acculturation. In: Sam, D.L. & Berry, J.W. (eds.), *Cambridge Handbook of Acculturation Psychology.* Cambridge: Cambridge University Press, 27–42.

Berry, J.W., Poortinga, Y.H., Breugelmans, S.M. Chasiotis, A. & Sam, D.L. (2011). *Cross-Cultural Psychology: Research and Applications.* 3rd ed. Cambridge: Cambridge University Press.

Bethencourt, F. (2013). *Racism. From the Crusades to the Twentieth Century.* Princeton-Oxford: Princeton University Press.

Beugelsdijk, S., Ambos, B. & Nell, P.C. (2018). Conceptualizing and measuring distance in international business research: Recurring questions and best practice guidelines. *Journal of International Business Studies,* 49(9), 1113–1137.

Beugelsdijk, S., Kostova, T., Kunst, V.E., Spadafora, E. & van Essen, M. (2018). Cultural distance and firm internationalization: A meta-analytical review and theoretical implications. *Journal of Management,* 44(1), 89–130.

Beugelsdijk, S., Kostova, T. & Roth, K. (2017). An overview of Hofstede-inspired country-level culture research in international business since 2006. *Journal of International Business Studies,* 48(1), 30–47.

Beugelsdijk, S., Maseland, R. & van Hoorn, A. (2015). Are scores on Hofstede's dimensions of national culture stable over time? A cohort analysis. *Global Strategy Journal,* 5(3), 223–240.

Beugelsdijk, S., Maseland, R., Onrust, M., van Hoorn, A. & Slangen, A. (2015). Cultural distance in international business and management: From mean-based to variance-based measures. *International Journal of Human Resource Management,* 26(2), 165–191.

Bhabha, H.K. (1994). *The Location of Culture.* New York, NY: Routledge.

Bhagat, R.S. & Prien, K.O. (1996). Cross-cultural training in organizational contexts. In: Landis, D. & Bhagat, R.S. (eds). *Handbook of Intercultural Training,* Vol. 2, Thousand Oaks, CA: SAGE, 216–230.

Bhagat, R.S., Triandis, H.C. & McDevitt, A.S. (2012). *Managing Global Organizations.* Cheltenham-Northampton: Edward Elgar.

Bhaskar-Shrinivas, P., Harrison, D.A., Shaffer, M.A. & Luk, D.M. (2005). Input-based and time-based models of international adjustment: Meta-analytic evidence and theoretical extensions. *Academy of Management Journal,* 48(2), 257–281.

Bhatia, S. (2002). Acculturation, dialogical voices and the construction of the diasporic self. *Theory & Psychology,* 12(1), 55–77.

Bhawuk, D.P.S. (2001). Evolution of culture assimilators. Toward theory-based assimilators. *International Journal of Intercultural Relations,* 25, 141–163.

Bhawuk, D.P.S. (2017). Intercultural training effectiveness, assessment of. In: Kim, Y.Y. (ed.), *International Encyclopedia of Intercultural Communication.* Hoboken, NJ: Wiley.

Bhawuk, D.P.S. & Brislin, R.W. (2000). Cross-cultural training: A review. *Applied Psychology,* 49(1), 162–191.

Bing, J.W. (2004). Hofstede's consequences: The impact of his work on consulting and business practices. *Academy of Management Perspectives,* 18(1), 80–87.

Bird, A., Heinbuch, S., Dunbar, R. & McNulty, M. (1993). A conceptual model of the effects of area studies training programs and a preliminary investigation of the model's hypothesized relationships. *International Journal of Intercultural Relations,* 17(4), 415–435.

Bird, A., Mendenhall, M., Stevens, M.J. & Oddou, G. (2010). Defining the content domain of intercultural competence for global leaders. *Journal of Managerial Psychology,* 25(8), 810–828.

Bizumic, B. & Duckitt, J. (2012). What is and is not ethnocentrism? A conceptual analysis and political implications. *Political Psychology,* 33(6), 887–909.

Björkman, I., Stahl, G. & Vaara, E. (2007). Cultural differences and capability transfer in cross-border acquisitions: The mediating roles of capability complementarity, absorptive capacity, and social integration. *Journal of International Business Studies,* 38(4), 658–672.

Black, J.S. & Gregersen, H.B. (1991). Antecedents to cross-cultural adjustment for expatriates in pacific rim assignments. *Human Relations,* 44(5), 497–515.

Black, J.S. & Mendenhall, M. (1990). Cross-cultural training effectiveness: A review and a theoretical framework for future research. *Academy of Management Review,* 15(1), 113–136.

Black, J.S., Mendenhall, M. & Oddou, G. (1991). Toward a comprehensive model of international adjustment: An integration of multiple theoretical perspectives. *Academy of Management Review*, 16(2), 291–317.

Black, S. (2019). How 1984 turned into an instruction manual. *Sovereign Man*, 18.2.2019. https://www.sovereignman.com/trends/how-1984-turned-into-an-instruction-manual-24609/.

Blunt, P. (1986). Techno- and ethnocentrism in organizational studies: Comment and speculation prompted by Ronen and Shenkar. *Academy of Management Review*, 11(4), 857–859.

Boas, F. (1901). The mind of primitive man. *Science*, 13, 281–289.

Boje, D. (2008). *Storytelling Organizations*. London-Thousand Oaks-New Delhi: SAGE.

Bollinger, L.C. (1986). *The Tolerant Society: Freedom of Speech and Extremist Speech in America*. New York, NY: Oxford University Press.

Bolten, J. (2002). *Interact 2.0: Intercultural Negotiation Training*. Berlin: Wissenschaft & Praxis.

Bolten, J., Dathe, M., Kirchmeyer, S., Roennau, M., Witchalls, P. & Ziebell-Drabo, S. (1996). Interkulturalität, Interlingualität und Standardisierung bei der Öffentlichkeitsarbeit von Unternehmen. Gezeigt an amerikanischen, britischen, deutschen, französischen und russischen Geschäftsberichten. In: Kalverkämper, H. & Baumann, K.-D. (eds.), *Fachliche Textsorten: Komponenten, Relationen, Strategien*. Tübingen: Narr, 389–425.

Bond, M.H. (1991). *Beyond the Chinese Face. Insights From Psychology*. Oxford: Oxford University.

Booij, G. (2012). *The Grammar of Words. An Introduction to Linguistic Morphology*. Oxford: Oxford University Press.

Børretsen, P. (2003). *How to Understand and Use a Norwegian. A User's Manual and Troubleshooter's Guide*. Oslo: Capellen.

Bourdieu, P. (1973). *Cultural Reproduction and Social Reproduction*. London: Tavistock.

Brannen, M.Y. & Thomas, D.C. (2010). Bicultural individuals in cross cultural management. Implications and opportunity. *International Journal of Cross Cultural Management*, 10(1), 5–16.

Braun, J.A. & Eklund, J.L. (2019). Fake news, real money: Ad tech platforms, profit-driven Hoaxes, and the business of journalism. *Digital Journalism*, 7(1), 1–21.

Brett, J.M. (2014). *Negotiating Globally. How to Negotiate Deals, Resolve Disputes, and Make Decisions Across Cultural Boundaries*. 3rd ed., San Francisco, CA: Wiley.

Broughton, J. (2002). *Descartes's Method of Doubt*. Princeton-Oxford: Princeton University Press.

Brouthers, K.D. & Brouthers, L.E. (2001). Explaining the national cultural distance paradox. *Journal of International Business Studies*, 32(1), 177–189.

Browaeys, M.-J. & Price, R. (2019). *Understanding Cross-Cultural Management*. 4th ed., Harlow: Pearson.

Brown, G. & Baer, M. (2011). Location in negotiation: Is there a home field advantage? *Organizational Behavior and Human Decision Processes*, 114, 190–200.

Brown, L.N. (2016). Exploit color psychology in marketing for international reach. *Inspiratti*, 2.7.2016. https://www.inspiratti.com/color-psychology-international-marketing/1073/.

Buschmann, R., Hujer, M. & Pfeil, G. (2018). "Kanaken" und "Kartoffeln". Als die deutsche Nationalelf in Grüppchen zerfiel. *Der Spiegel*, 24.08.2018.

Boussebaa, M. Sinha, S. & Gabriel, Y. (2014). Englishization in offshore call centers. A postcolonial perspective. *Journal of International Business Studies*, 45(9), 1152–1169.

Bowker, J. (2006). *World Religions. The Great Faiths Explored & Explained*. London: Dorling Kindersley.

Boyacigiller, N. & Adler, N.J. (1991). The Parochial Dinosaur. Organizational science in a global context. *Academy of Management Review*, 16(2), 262–290.

Boyett, J. (2006). *12 Major World Religions*. Berkeley, CA: Zephyros Press.

Brahm, L.J. (2003). *When Yes Means No! (Or Yes or Maybe): How to Negotiate a Deal in China: How to Negotiate Deals in China*. Singapore: Tuttle Publishing.

Brandt, W. (1989). *Erinnerungen*. Munich: Propyläen.

Brannen, M.Y., Garcia, D. & Thomas, D.C. (2009). Biculturals as national bridges for intercultural communication and collaboration. *Proceedings of the 3rd ACM International Workshop on Intercultural Collaboration*, 207–210.

Brannen, M.Y. & Thomas, D.C. (2010). Bicultural individuals in organizations. Implications and opportunity. *International Journal of Cross Cultural Management*, 10(1), 5–16.

Braun, M. (2003). Errors in comparative survey research. An overview. In: Harkness, J.A., van de Vijver, F.J.R. & Mohler, P.P. (eds.), *Cross-Cultural Survey Methods*. Hoboken: Wiley, 137–142.

Braun, W. & Warner, M. (2002). The 'culture-free' vs. 'culture-specific' management debate. In: Joynt, P. & Warner, M. (eds.), *Managing Across Cultures: Issues and Perspectives*. 2nd ed. London: Thompson, 13–25.

Bray, D. (2005). *Social Space and Governance in Urban China: The Danwei System From Origins to Reform*. Stanford, CA: Stanford University Press.

Brewer, P. & Venaik, S. (2014). The ecological fallacy in national culture research. *Organization Studies*, 35(7), 1063–1086.

Brewster, C. (1995). Effective expatriate training. In: Selmer, J. (ed.), *Expatriate Management: New Ideas for International Business*. Westport, CT: Quorem, 57–71.

Briggs, J. (2005). The use of indigenous knowledge in development: Problems and challenges. *Progress in Development Studies*, 5(2), 99–114.

Brislin, R.W. (1986). A culture general assimilator: Preparation for various types of sojourns. *International Journal of Intercultural Relations*, 10(2), 215–234.

Brislin, R.W. (2000). *Understanding Culture's Influence on Behavior*. 2nd ed., Fort Worth, TX: Harcourt.

Brislin, R.W. (1970). Back-translation for cross-cultural research. *Journal of Cross-Cultural Psychology*, 1(3), 185–216.

Brislin, R.W. & Kim, E.S. (2003). Cultural diversity in people's understanding and uses of time. *Applied Psychology*, 52(3), 363–382.

Brislin, R.W. & Pedersen, P. (1976). *Cross-Cultural Orientation Programs*. New York, NY: Gardner.

Brislin, R.W. & Yoshida, T. (1994). The content of cross-cultural training. An introduction. In: Brislin, R.W. & Yoshida, T. (eds.), *Improving Intercultural Interactions: Models for Cross-Cultural Training Programs*. Thousand Oaks, CA: SAGE, 1–14.

Brouthers, K.D. (2002). Institutional, cultural and transaction cost influences on entry mode choice and performance. *Journal of International Business Studies*, 33(2), 203–221.

Bruschke, J.C., Gartner, C. & Seiter, J.S. (1993). Student ethnocentrism, dogmatism, and motivation: A study of BAFA BAFA. *Simulation and Gaming*, 21(1), 9–20.

Buckley, P.J., Chapman, M., Clegg, J. & Gajewska-De Mattos, H. (2014). A linguistic and philosophical analysis of emic and etic and their use in international business research. *Management International Review*, 54(3), 307–324.

Budhwar, P., Pereira, V., Mellahi, K. & Singh, S.K. (2019). The state of HRM in the middle east: Challenges and future research agenda. *Asia Pacific Journal of Management*, 36, 905–933.

Bücker, J.J.L.E. & Korzilius, H. (2015). Developing cultural intelligence: Assessing the effect of the Ecotonos cultural simulation game for international business students. *International Journal of Human Resource Management*, 26(15), 1995–2014.

Bull, P. & Simon-Vandenbergen, A.-M. (2014). Equivocation and doublespeak in far right-wing discourse: An analysis of nick Griffin's performance on BBC's question time. *Text & Talk*, 34(1), 1–22.

Buono, A.F., Bowditch, J.L. & Lewis, J. (1985). When cultures collide: The anatomy of a merger. *Human Relations*, 38(5), 477–500.

Burgoon, J.K., Guerrero, L.K. & Floyd, K. (2016). *Introduction to Nonverbal Communication*. New York, NY: Routledge.

Burke, C.S., Priest, H.A., Upshaw, C.L., Salas, E. & Pierce, L. (2007). A sensemaking approach to understanding multicultural teams: An initial framework. In: Stone, D.L. & Stone-Romero, E.F. (eds.), *The Influence of Culture on Human Resource Management Processes and Practices*. New York, NY: Psychology Press, 269–306.

Burleigh, M. & Wippermann, W. (1991). *The Racial State: Germany 1933–1945*. Cambridge-New York: Cambridge University Press.

Byrne, G.J. & Bradley, F. (2007). Culture's influence on leadership efficiency: How personal and national cultures affect leadership style. *Journal of Business Research*, 60(2), 168–175.

California Healthcare Interpreters Association (2002). California Standards for Healthcare Interpreters. Ethical Principles, Protocols, and Guidance on Roles & Intervention. http://www.chiaonline.org/resources/Pictures/CHIA_standards_manual_%20March%202017.pdf.

Caligiuri, P.M. (2000). The big five personality characteristics as predictors of expatriate's desire to terminate the assignment and supervisor-rated performance. *Personnel Psychology*, 53(1), 67–88.

Caligiuri, P. & Tarique, I. (2012). Dynamic cross-cultural competencies and global leadership effectiveness. *Journal of World Business*, 47(4), 612–622.

Campos, N.F. & Kuzeyev, V.S. (2007). On the dynamics of ethnic fractionalization. *American Journal of Political Science*, 51(3), 620–639.

Cao, D. (2002). Finding the elusive equivalents in Chinese/English legal translation. *Babel*, 48(4), 330–341.

Caprar, D.V., Kim, S., Walker, B.W. & Caligiuri, P. (2022). Beyond "Doing as the Romans Do": A review of research on countercultural business practices. *Journal of International Business Studies*, https://doi.org/10.1057/s41267-021-00479-2.

Cappelli, P., Singh, H., Singh, J. & Useem, M. (2010). The India way: Lessons for the U.S. *Academy of Management Perspectives*, 24(2), 6–24.

Cardon, P.W. (2008). A critique of hall's contexting model. A meta-analysis of literature on intercultural business and technical communication. *Journal of Business and Technical Communication*, 22(4), 399–428.

Carens, J. (2000). *Culture, Citizenship and Community. A Contextual Exploration of Justice as Evenhandedness*. New York, NY: Oxford University Press.

Carroll, R.T. (2001). *Becoming a Critical Thinker. A Guide for the New Millennium*. London: Pearson.

Carvel, J. (2004). Tebbit's cricket loyalty test hit for six. *The Guardian*, 8.1.2004. https://www.theguardian.com/uk/2004/jan/08/britishidentity.race.

Cattell, R.B. (1950). The principal culture patterns discoverable in the syntal dimensions of existing nations. *Journal of Social Psychology*, 32(2), 215–253.

Cavusgil, S.T. & Das, A. (1997). Methodological issues in empirical cross-cultural research: a survey of the management literature and a framework. *Management International Review*, 37(1), 71–96.

Cazenave, N.A. (2016). *Conceptualizing Racism. Breaking the Chains of Racially Accommodative Language*. Lanham, MD: Rowman & Littlefield.

Celce-Murcia, M., Brinton, D.M. & Goodwin, J.M. (1996). *Teaching Pronunciation. A Referece for Teachers of English to Speakers of Other Languages*. Cambridge: Cambridge University Press.

Chae, B. & Hoegg, J. (2013). The future looks 'right': Effects of the horizontal location of advertising images on product attitude. *Journal of Consumer Research*, 40(2), 223–238.

Chakrabarti, R., Gupta-Mukherjee, S. & Jayaraman, N. (2009). Mars-Venus marriages: Culture and cross-border M&A. *Journal of International Business Studies*, 40, 216–236.

Chakrabarti, V. (1998). *Indian Architectural Theory: Contemporary Uses of Vastu Vidya*. London: Routledge.

Chan, A.K.-L. (2002). *Mencius. Contexts and Interpretations*. Honolulu, HI: University of Hawaii Press.

Chang, W.-W. (2017). Approaches for developing intercultural competence: An extended learning model with implications from cultural neuroscience. *Human Resource Development Review*, 16(2), 158–175.

Chao, G.T. & Moon, H. (2005). The cultural mosaic: A metatheory for understanding the complexity of culture. *Journal of Applied Psychology*, 90(6), 1128–1140.

Chao, M.M. & Chiu, C.-Y. (2011). Epistemic functions of culture. In: Leung, A.K.-y., Chiu, C.-y., Hong, Y.-y. (eds.), *Cultural Processes: A Social Psychological Perspective*. Cambridge: Cambridge University Press, 81–95.

Chapman, M., Gajewska-De Mattos, H., Clegg, J. & Buckley, P.J. (2008). Close neighbours and distant friends. Perceptions of cultural distance. *International Business Review*, 17(3), 217–234.

Chatterjee, S.R. (2009). Managerial ethos of the Indian tradition: Relevance of a wisdom model. *Journal of Indian Business Research*, 1(2/3), 136–162.

Chaturvedi, A. (2015). At least 65% recruiters in India use employee referral programmes to get quality talent. *The Economic Times*, 20.10.2015. https://economictimes.indiatimes.com/jobs/at-least-65-recruiters-in-india-use-employee-referral-programmes-to-get-quality-talent-survey/articleshow/49460019.cms?utm_source=contentofinterest&utm_medium=text&utm_campaign=cppst.

Chawla, D., Dokadia, A. & Rai, S. (2017). Multigenerational differences in career preferences, reward preferences and work engagement among Indian employees. *Global Business Review*, 18(1), 181–197.

Chen, A.S.-y., Lin, Y.-c. & Sawangpattanakul, A. (2011). The relationship between cultural intelligence and performance with the mediating effect of culture shock: A case from Philippine laborers in Taiwan. *International Journal of Intercultural Relations*, 35, 246–258.

Chen, C. & Moyzis, R.L. (2018). Cultural genomics: Promises and challenges. *Journal of Cross-Cultural Psychology*, 49(5), 764–788.

Chen, G., Kirkman, B.L., Kim, K., Farh, C.I.C. & Tangirala, S. (2011). When does cross-cultural motivation enhance expatriate effectiveness? A multilevel investigation of the moderating roles of subsidiary support and cultural distance. *Academy of Management Journal*, 53(5), 1110–1130.

Chen, G.-M. (2017). Issues in the conceptualization of intercultural communication competence. In: Chen, L. (ed.), *Intercultural Communication*. Boston-Berlin: de Gruyter, 349–368.

Chen, G.M. & Starosta, W.J. (1998). A review of the concept of intercultural awareness. *Human Communication*, 2(1), 27–54.

Chen, M.K. (2013). The effect of language on economic behavior: Evidence from savings rates, health behaviors, and retirement assets. *American Economic Review*, 103(2), 690–731.

Chen, S., Geluykens, R. & Choi, C.J. (2006). The importance of language in global teams: A linguistic perspective. *Management International Review*, 46(6), 679–696.

Chen, X. (2018). Multidimensional study of hospitality and the host-guest paradigm in China. *International Journal of Contemporary Hospitality Management*, 30(1), 495–513.

Cheng, C.-Y., Lee, F. & Benet-Martínez, V. (2006). Assimilation and contrast effects in cultural frame switching: Bicultural identity integration and valence of cultural cues. *Journal of Cross-Cultural Psychology*, 37(6), 742–760.

Chesney, R. & Citron, D.K. (2019). Deep fakes: A looming challenge for privacy, democracy, and national security. *California Law Review*, 107, 1753–1819.

Cheung, C.-k., & Gui, Y. (2006). Job referral in China: The advantages of strong ties. *Human Relations*, 59(6), 847–872.

Chhodkar, J.S., Brodbeck, F.C. & House, R.J. (eds.) (2007). Culture and leadership across the World. *The GLOBE Book of In-depth Studies of 25 Societies*. New York, NY: Taylor & Francis.

Chiang, F. (2005). A critical examination of Hofstede's thesis and its implication to international reward management. *International Journal of Human Resource Management*, 16(9), 1545–1563.

Chiang, F. & Birtch, T.A. (2005). A taxonomy of reward preference: Examining country differences. *Journal of International Management*, 11, 357–375.

Chiao, J.Y. (2009). Cultural neuroscience: A once and future discipline. *Progress in Brain Research*, 178, 287–304.

Chiao, J.Y. & Blizinsky, K.D. (2010). Culture–gene coevolution of individualism–collectivism and the serotonin transporter gene. *Proceedings of The Royal Society B*, 277, 529–537.

Chiao, J.Y. & Li, S.-C., Seligman, R. & Turner, R. (eds.) (2016). *The Oxford Handbook of Cultural Neuroscience*. Oxford: Oxford University Press.

Child, J. (1981). Culture, contingency and capitalism in the cross-national study of organizations. *Research in Organizational Behaviour*, 3, 303–356.

Chilisa, B. (2011). *Indigenous Research Methodologies*. London-New Delhi-Thousand Oaks: SAGE.

Chinni, D. & Gimpel, J. (2011). *Our Patchwork Nation: The Surprising Truth About the 'Real' America*. New York, NY: Gotham Books.

Cho, H., Rivera-Sánchez, M. & Sun, S. (2009). A multinational study on online privacy: Global concerns and local responses. *New Media & Society*, 11(3), 395–416.

Cho, J., Morris, M.W. & Dow, B. (2018). How do the Romans feel when visitors 'Do as the Romans Do'? Diversity ideologies and trust in evaluations of cultural accommodation. *Academy of Management Discoveries*, 4(1), 11–31.

Choi, D.D., Poertner, M. & Sambanis, N. (2019). Parochialism, social norms, and discrimination against immigrants. *Proceedings of the National Academy of Sciences of the United States of America*, 116(33), 16274–16279.

Chomsky, N. (1965). *Aspects of the Theory of Syntax*. Boston, MA: MIT Press.

Christensen, C.M. (1997). *The Innovator's Dilemma. When New Technologies Cause Great Firms to Fail*. Boston, MA: Harvard Business School Press.

Christopherson, S. (2007). Barriers to "US style" lean retailing: The case of Wal-Mart's failure in Germany. *Journal of Economic Geography*, 7, 451–469.

Chua, R.Y.J., Roth, Y. & Lemoine, J.-F. (2015). The impact of culture on creativity: How cultural tightness and cultural distance affect global innovation crowdsourcing work. *Administrative Science Quarterly*, 60(2), 189–227.

Chua, R.Y.J., Morris, M.W. & Mor, S. (2012). Collaborating across cultures: Cultural metacognition and affect-based trust in creative collaboration. *Organizational Behavior and Human Decision Processes*, 118, 116–131.

CIA (2000). *The World Factbook*. Washington, DC: CIA.

Cline, M.G. (1984). *Language and Society in the German-Speaking Countries*. Cambridge: Cambridge University Press.

Clooney, G. (2019). Boycott Sultan of Brunei's hotels over cruel anti-gay laws. *Deadline*, 28.3.2019. https://deadline.com/2019/03/george-clooney-sultain-of-brunei-hotels-boycott-beverly-hills-hotel-anti-gay-laws-brunei-1202584579/.

Coene, J.-P. & Jacobs, M. (2017). *Negotiate Like a Local. 7 Mindsets to Increase Your Business Success Rate in International Business*. Helsinki: Hofstede Insights.

Cohen, R. (2008). *Global Diasporas. An introduction*. 2nd ed., London-New York: Routledge.

Coombs, G. & Sarason, Y. (1998). Culture circles: A cultural self-awareness exercise. *Journal of Management Education*, 22(2), 218–226.

Condon, J. & Yousef, F. (1975). *Introduction to Intercultural Communication*. Indianapolis, IN: Bobbs-Merrill.

Costa, P.T. & McCrae, R.R. (1992). Normal personality assessment in clinical practice. The NEO personality inventory. *Psychological Assessment*, 4(1), 5–13.

Coulmas, F. (1989). *The Writing Systems of the World*. London: Blackwell.

Cox, T.H., Lobel, S.A. & McLeod, P.L. (1991). Effects of ethnic group cultural differences on cooperative and competitive behavior on a group task. *Academy of Management Journal*, 34(4), 827–847.

Crystal, D. (1969). *Prosodic Systems and Intonation in English*. Cambridge: Cambridge University Press.

Crystal, D. (2010). *The Cambridge Encyclopedia of Language*. 3rd ed., Cambridge: Cambridge University Press.

Crystal, D. (2011). *Dictionary of Linguistics and Phonetics*. 6th ed., Malden, MA: Blackwell.

Cuddy, A. (2019). ENA: The elite French school that trains presidents. *BBC News*, 20.4.2019. https://www.bbc.com/news/world-europe-47991257.

Cuervo-Cazurra, A., Andersson, U., Brannen, M.Y., Nielsen, B.B. & Reuber, A.R. (2016). From the editors: Can I trust your findings? Ruling out alternative explanations in international business research. *Journal of International Business Studies*, 47(8), 881–897.

Cullen, J.B. & Parboteeah, K.P. (2005). *Multinational Management: A Strategic Approach*. 3rd ed., Mason, OH: Thomson Southwestern.

Cushner, K. & Brislin, R.W. (1997). Key concepts in the field of cross-cultural training. An introduction. In Cushner, K. & Brislin, R. (eds.), *Improving Intercultural Interactions: Modules for Cross-Cultural Training Programs*. Vol. 2, Thousand Oaks, CA: SAGE, 1–17.

Cushner, K., McClelland, A. & Safford, P. (2015). *Human Diversity in Education: An Intercultural Approach*. 8th ed., Boston, MA: McGraw-Hill.

Cuypers, I.R.P., Ertug, G., Heugens, P.P.M.A.R., Kogut, B. & Zou, T. (2018). The making of a construct: Lessons from 30 years of the Kogut and Singh cultural distance index. *Journal of International Business Studies*, 49(9), 1138–1153.

Czinkota, M.R. & Ronkainen, I.A. (2012). *International Marketing*. 10th ed., Mason, OH: South Western, Cengage Learning.

DAAD & DZHW (2018). Wissenschaft weltoffen. Facts and Figures on the International Nature of Studies and Research in Germany. Bonn-Hannover. http://www.wissenschaftweltoffen.de/publikation/wiwe_2018int_verlinkt.pdf.

Dalzell, T. & Victor, T. (eds.) (2014). *The Concise New Partridge Dictionary of Slang and Unconventional English*. 2nd ed., London-New York: Routledge.

Daniels, J., Radebaugh, L. & Sullivan, D. (2004). *International Business. Environments and Operations*. 10th ed., Upper Saddle River, NJ: Person-Prentice Hall.

Daniels, P.T. & Bright, W. (1996). *The World's Writing Systems*. Oxford: Oxford University Press.

Darton, W. (1790). Inhabitants of the World. Unknown.

Darwin, C. (1859). *On the Origin of Species by Means of Natural Selection, or the Preservation of Favoured Races in the Struggle for Life*. London: John Murray.

Darwin, C. (1872). *The Expression of the Emotions in Man and Animals*. London: John Murray.

Das, G. (2010). *The Difficulty of Being Good: On the Subtle Art of Dharma*. Oxford: Oxford University Press.

Dau, L.A. (2016). Biculturalism, team performance, and cultural-faultline bridges. *Journal of International Management*, 22(1), 48–62.

David-Fox, M. (2015). *Crossing Borders: Modernity, Ideology, and Culture in Russia and the Soviet Union*. Pittsburg, PA: The University of Pittsburg Press.

Davoine, E. & Ravasi, C. (2013). The relative stability of national career patterns in European top management careers in the age of globalisation: A comparative study in France/Germany/Great Britain and Switzerland. *European Management Journal*, 31(2), 152–163.

Deal, T. & Kennedy, A.E. (1982). *Corporate Cultures*. Reading, PA: Addison-Wesley.

Deardorff, D.K. (2006). Identification and assessment of intercultural competence as a student outcome of internationalization. *Journal of Studies in International Education*, 10(3), 241–266.

Deardorff, D.K. (ed.) (2009). *The Sage Handbook of Intercultural Competence*. Thousand Oaks, CA: SAGE.

Deardorff, D.K. (2016). How to assess intercultural competence. In: Hua, Z. (ed.), *Research Methods in Intercultural Communication. A Practical Guide*. Chichester: Wiley, 120–134.

Deardorff, D.K. & Arasaratnam-Smith, L.A. (eds.) (2017). *Intercultural Competence in Higher Education: International Approaches, Assessment and Application*. London: Routledge.

Deardorff, D.K., de Wit, H., Heyl, J.D. & Adams, T. (2012). *The SAGE Handbook of International Higher Education*. Thousand Oaks, CA: SAGE.

DeMello, C. (1995). Acting the culture contrast. In: Fowler, S.M. & Mumford, M.G. (eds.), *Intercultural Sourcebook: Cross-Cultural Training Methods*. Vol. 1, Yarmouth, ME: Intercultural Press, 59–68.

Denzin, N.K., Lincoln, Y.S. & Smith, L.T. (eds.) (2008). *Handbook of Critical and Indigenous Methodologies*. Los Angeles, CA: SAGE.

Deresky, H. (2006). *International Management. Managing Across Borders and Cultures*. 5th ed., Upper Saddle River, NJ: Person-Prentice Hall.

Derrida, J. (1976). *Of Grammatology*. Baltimore-London: Johns Hopkins University Press.

Deshpande, S.P. & Viswesvaran, C. (1992). Is cross-cultural training of expatriate managers effective? A meta-analysis. *International Journal of Intercultural Relations*, 16: 295–310.

Deutscher, G. (2010). *Through the Language Glass. Why the World Looks Different in Other Languages*. London: Arrow Books.

Dheer, R.J.S., Egri, C. & Treviño, L.J. (2021). A cross-cultural exploratory analysis of pandemic growth. The case of COVID-19. *Journal of International Business Studies*, 52, 1871–1892.

Dheer, R.J.S., Lenartowicz, T. & Peterson, M.F. (2015). Mapping India's regional subcultures: Implications for international management. *Journal of International Business Studies*, 46(4), 443–467.

Dickson, M.W., Castaño, N., Magomaeva, A. & Den Hartog, D.N. (2012). Conceptualizing leadership across cultures. *Journal of World Business*, 47(4), 483–492.

Dikötter, F. (2015). *The Discourse of Race in Modern China*. 2nd ed. Oxford: Oxford University Press.

Ding, S. & Saunders, R.A. (2006). Talking up China: An analysis of China's rising cultural power and global promotion of the Chinese language. *East Asia*, 23(2), 3–33.

Disdier, A.-C., Tai, S.H.T., Fontagné, L. & Mayer, T. (2010). Bilateral trade of cultural goods. *Review of World Economics*, 145(4), 575–595.

Doi, T. (1991). Formal appearance and inner feeling: Tatemae and honne. In: Finkelstein, B, Imamura, A.E. & Tobin, J.J. (eds.), *Transcending Stereotypes: Discovering Japanese Culture and Education*. Yarmouth, ME: Intercultural Press, 12–16.

Dolan, S.L., Díez-Piñol, M., Fernández-Alles, M., Martín-Prius, A. & Martínez-Fierro, S. (2004). Exploratory study of within-country differences in work and life values: The case of Spanish business students. *International Journal of Cross Cultural Management*, 4(2), 157–180.

Dolan, S.L. & Kawamura, K.M. (2015). *Cross Cultural Competence. A Field Guide for Developing Global Leaders and Managers*. Bingley: Emerald.

Donaldson, T. (1989). *The Ethics of International Business*. Oxford: Oxford University Press.

Dorfman, P.W., Hanges, P.J. & Brodbeck, F.C. (2004). Leadership and cultural variation. In: House, R.J., Hanges, P.J., Javidan, M., Dorfman, P.W. & Gupta, V. (eds.), *Culture, Leadership, and Organizations. The GLOBE Study of 62 Societies*. Thousand Oaks, CA: SAGE, 669–719.

Dorfman, P., Javidan, M., Hanges, P., Dastmalchian, A. & House, R. (2012). GLOBE: A twenty year journey into the intriguing world of culture and leadership. *Journal of World Business*, 7, 504–518.

Douglas, S.P. & Craig, C.S. (2007). Collaborative and iterative translation: An alternative approach to back translation. *Journal of International Marketing*, 15(1), 30–43.

Dovidio, J.F., Hewstone, M., Glick, P. & Esses, V.M. (2010). Prejudice, stereotyping and discrimination: Theoretical and empirical overview. In: Dovidio, J.F., Hewstone, M., Glick, P. & Esses, V.M. (eds.), *The Sage Handbook of Prejudice, Stereotyping and Discrimination*. Thousand Oaks, CA: SAGE, 3–28.

Dovidio, J.F., Kawakami, K. & Gaertner, S.L. (2002). Implicit and explicit prejudice and interracial interaction. *Journal of Personality and Social Psychology*, 82(1), 62–68.

Dow, D., Cuypers, I.R. & Ertug, G. (2016). The effects of within-country linguistic and religious diversity on foreign acquisitions. *Journal of International Business Studies*, 47(3), 319–346.

Dretzke, B. & Nester, M. (2009). *False Friends: A Short Dictionary*. Stuttgart: Reclam.

Dries, N., Pepermans, R. & De Kerpel, E. (2008). Exploring four generations' beliefs about career: Is 'satisfied' the new 'successful'? *Journal of Managerial Psychology*, 23(8), 907–928.

Drogendijk, R. & Holm, U. (2010). The role of national culture on the headquarters subsidiary relationship in the multinational corporation: The effect of power distance. In: Andersson, U. & Holm, U. (eds.), *Managing the Contemporary Multinational*. Cheltenham: Edward Elgar, 403–439.

Drogendijk, R. & Slangen, S. (2006). Hofstede, Schwartz, or managerial perceptions? The effects of different cultural distance measures on establishment mode choices by multinational enterprises. *International Business Review*, 15(4), 361380.

Duanmu, S. (2007). *The Phonology of Standard Chinese*. 2nd ed., Oxford: Oxford University Press.

Dülfer, E. & Joestingmeier, B. (2011): *International Management in Diverse Cultural Areas*. 2nd ed., Munich-Vienna: Oldenbourg.

Dunlop, C.T. (2015). *Cartophilia. Maps and the Search for Identity in the French-German Borderland*. Chicago-London: University of Chicago Press.

Dutta, M.J. & Dutta, D. (2013). Multinational going cultural: A postcolonial deconstruction of cultural intelligence. *Journal of International and Intercultural Communication*, 6(3), 241–258.

van Dyne, L., Ang, S. & Koh, C. (2008). Development and validation of the CQS. In: Ang, S. & van Dyne, L. (eds.), *Handbook of Cultural Intelligence*. London-New York: Routledge, 16–38.

Eagleton, T. (2000). *The Idea of Culture*. Malden, MA: Blackwell.

Earley, P.C. (1987). Intercultural training for managers: A comparison of documentary and interpersonal methods. *Academy of Management Journal*, 30: 685–698.

Earley, P.C. (1994). Self or group? Cultural effects of training on self-efficacy and performance. *Administrative Science Quarterly*, 39(1): 89–117.

Earley, P.C. & Ang, S. (2003). *Cultural Intelligence. Individual Interactions Across Cultures*. Stanford, CA: Stanford University Press.

Earley, P.C. & Gibson, C.B. (2002). *Multinational Work Teams. A New Perspective*. New York, NY: Routledge.

Earley, P.C. & Mosakowski, E. (2000). Creating hybrid team cultures: An empirical test of transnational team functioning. *Academy of Management Journal*, 43(1), 26–49.

Earley, P.C. & Peterson, R.S. (2004). The elusive cultural chameleon: Cultural intelligence as a new approach to intercultural training for the global manager. *Academy of Management Learning & Education*, 3(1), 100–115.

Eberhard, D.M., Simons, G.F., & Fennig, C.D. (eds.) (2021). *Ethnologue: Languages of the World*. 24th ed., Dallas: SIL International.

Education First (2018). English Proficiency Index. Lucerne 2018. https://www.ef.com/__/~/media/centralefcom/epi/downloads/full-reports/v8/ef-epi-2018-english.pdf.

Edwards, T., Sánchez-Mangas, R., Jalette, P., Lavelle, J. & Minbaeva, D. (2016). Global standardization or national differentiation of HRM practices in multinational companies? A comparison of multinationals in five countries. *Journal of International Business Studies*, 47(8), 997–1021.

Egloff, B. & Schmukle, S.C. (2002). Predictive validity of an implicit association test for assessing anxiety. *Journal of Personality and Social Psychology*, 83(6), 1441–1455.

Eisenberg, J., Lee, H.-J., Brück, F., Brenner, B., Claes, M.-T., Mironski, J. & Bell, R. (2013). Can business schools make students culturally competent? Effects of cross-cultural management courses on cultural intelligence. *Academy of Management Learning & Education*, 12(4), 603–621.

Ekman, P. (2003). *Emotions Revealed. Recognizing Faces and Feelings to Improve Communication and Emotional Life*. New York, NY: Times Books.

Ekman, P. & Friesen, W.V. (1975). *Unmasking the Face: A Guide to Recognizing Emotions from Facial Expressions*. New York, NY: Prentice Hall.

Elfers, A. (Hrsg.) (2019). *Der Anglizismen-Index 2019: Deutsch Statt Denglisch*. Paderborn: IFB Verlag Deutsche Sprache.

Elsass, P.M. & Veiga, J.F. (1994). Acculturation in acquired organizations: A force-field perspective. *Human Relations*, 47(4), 431–453.

Ely, R.J. (1995). The power in demography: Women's social constructions of gender identity at work. *Academy of Management Journal*, 38(3), 589–634.

Ely, R.J. & Thomas, D.A. (2001). Cultural diversity at work: The effects of diversity perspectives on work group processes and outcomes. *Administrative Science Quarterly*, 46(2), 229–273.

Encyclopedia Britannica (2001). https://www.britannica.com/.

Engel, J. & Wodak, R. (2013). Calculated ambivalence and holocaust denial in Austria. In Wodak, R. & Richardson, J.E. (eds.), *Analysing Fascist Discourse: European Fascism in Talk and Text*. New York, NY: Routledge, 73–96.

Engelhard, F. & Holtbrügge, D. (2017). Biculturals, team facilitation and multicultural team performance. An information-processing perspective. *European Journal of Cross-Cultural Competence and Management*, 4(3/4), 236–262.

Engelhard, F. & Holtbrügge, D. (2018). Beyond adjustment: Cultural boundary spanning. In: Munoz, J.M. (ed.), *Global Business Intelligence*. London: Routledge, 23–35.

Engl, A. & Zwilling, C. (2007). Cross-border Cooperation between historical legacies and New Horizons. In: Woelk J., Palermo, F. & Marko, J. (eds.), *Tolerance Through Law. Self-Governance and Minority Rights in South Tyrol*. Leiden-Boston: Martinus Nijhoff Publishers, 161–176.

England, C. (2016). Gay Russian couple who were set to win competition to be faces of Ikea catalogue have entry removed. Organisers claim the photograph they entered was taken down at the men's request. *The Independent*, 6.10.2016. https://www.independent.co.uk/news/world/europe/russia-ikea-gay-couple-contest-competition-catalogue-cover-entry-removed-deleted-a7348611.html.

Ervin, S. (1964). Language and TAT content in Bilinguals. *Journal of Abnormal and Social Psychology*, 68(5), 500–507.

Esmer, Y. (2002). Is there an Islamic civilization? *Comparative Sociology*, 1, 265–298.

Estler, H., Nordio, M., Furia, C.A., Meyer, B. & Schneider, J. (2014). Agile vs. structured distributed software development: A case study. *Empirical Software Engineering*, 19, 1197–1224.

Eurostat (2015). *People in the EU – Who Are We and How Do We Live?* Luxembourg: Publications Office of the European Union.

Eurostat (2015). *Culture Statistics*. Luxembourg: Publications Office of the European Union.

Eurostat (2018). *The EU in the World 2018. A Statistical Portrait*. Luxembourg: Statistical Office of the European Union.

Eurostat (2019). Foreign Language Skills Statistics. https://ec.europa.eu/eurostat/statistics-explained/index.php/Foreign_language_skills_statistics#Number_of_foreign_languages_known.

Euwema, M.C. & van Emmerik, I.J.H. (2007). Intercultural competencies and conglomerated conflict behaviors in intercultural conflicts. *International Journal of Intercultural Relations*, 31, 427–441.

Evans, G. (2017). *The Story of Colour: An Exploration of the Hidden Messages of the Spectrum*. London: Michael O'Mara Books.

Evans, P., Lank, E. & Farquhar, A. (1989): Managing human resources in the international firm: Lessons from practice. In: Evans, P., Doz, Y. & Laurent, A. (eds.), *Human Resource Management in the International Firm. Change, Globalization, Innovation*. London, Springer, 113–143.

Fain, N. & Wagner, B. (2014). R&D-marketing integration in innovation—does culture matter? *European Business Review*, 26(2), 169–187.

Faist, T. & Kivisto, P. (eds.) (2007). *Dual Citizenship in Global Perspective: From Unitary to Multiple Citizenship*. New York, NY: Palgrave Macmillan.

Fan, Y. (2002). Questioning guanxi: Definition, classification and implications. *International Business Review*, 11(5), 543–561.

Fan, J. & Lai, L. (2014). Pre-training perceived social self-efficacy accentuates the effects of a cross-cultural coping orientation program: Evidence from a longitudinal field experiment. *Journal of Organizational Behavior*, 35(6), 831–850.

Fang, F., Schei, V. & Selart, M. (2018). Hype or hope? A new look at the research on cultural intelligence. *International Journal of Intercultural Relations*, 65, 148–171.

Fang, T. (2003). A critique of Hofstede's fifth national culture dimension. *International Journal of Cross Cultural Management*, 3(3), 347–368.

Fang, T. (2006). Negotiation. The Chinese style. *Journal of Business & Industrial Marketing*, 21(1), 50–60.

Farh, J.-L., Cannella, A.A. & Lee, C. (2006). Approaches to scale development in Chinese management research. *Management and Organization Review*, 2(3), 301–318.

Farrell, J. (2017). German neo-Nazi mayoral candidate laughed at when he called to ban Arabic house numbers. Otfried Best appears to take a satirical question seriously. *The Independent*, 4.9.2017. https://www.independent.co.uk/news/world/europe/german-neo-nazi-mayor-candidate-arabic-house-numbers-ban-western-digits-otfried-best-volklingen-a7928726.html.

Faulkner, S.L., Baldwin, J.R., Lindsley, S.L. & Hecht, M.L. (2006). Layers of meaning: An analysis of definitions of culture. In: Baldwin, J.R., Faulkner, S.L., Hecht, M.L. & Lindsley, S.L. (eds.), *Redefining Culture. Perspectives Across the Disciplines*. Mahwah, NJ: Lawrence Erlbaum, 27–52.

Faust, M. (2018). Theorizing German and Chinese culture standards. An emic approach to explain cultural differences from a Yin Yang perspective. *China Media Research*, 14(4), 24–36.

Fearon, J.D. (2003). Ethnic and cultural diversity by country. *Journal of Economic Growth*, 8(2), 195–222.

Fei, X. (2015). *Globalization and Cultural Self-Awareness*. Berlin: Springer.

Felbermayr, G.J. & Toubal, F. (2010). Cultural proximity and trade. *European Economic Review*, 54(2), 279–293.

Feldman, D. & Jackson, P. (eds.) (2014). *Doublespeak: The Rhetoric of the Far Right Since 1945*. Stuttgart: ibidem.

Ferguson, N. (2003). *Empire: How Britain Made the Modern World*. London: Allen Lane.

Fetscherin, M., Alon, I., Little, R. & Chan, A. (2012). In China? Pick your brand name carefully. *Harvard Business Review*, 90(9), 26.

Feuchtwang, S. (2016). Chinese religions. In: Woodhead, L., Kawanami, H. & Partridge, C.H. (eds.), *Religions in the Modern World: Traditions and Transformations*. 3rd ed., London: Routledge, 143–172.

Fidrmuc, J. & Ginsburgh, V. (2007). Languages in the European Union: The quest for equality and its cost. *European Economic Review*, 51(6), 1351–1369.

Fiedler, F.E., Mitchell, T. & Triandis, H.C. (1971). The culture assimilator: An approach to cross-cultural training. *Journal of Applied Psychology*, 55(2), 95–102.

Field, J.G., Bosco, F.A., Kraichy, D., Uggerslev, K.L. & Geiger, M.K. (2021). More alike than different? A comparison of variance explained by cross-cultural models. *Journal of International Business Studies*, 52, 1798–1817.

Figes, O. (2010). *The Crimean War*. New York, NY: Metropolitan.

Fink, G. & Meierewert, S. (2004). Issues of time in international, intercultural management: East and Central Europe from the perspective of Austrian managers. *Journal for East European Management Studies*, 9(1), 61–84.

Fink, G., Neyer, A.-K. & Kölling, M. (2006). Understanding cross-cultural management interaction: Research into cultural standards to complement cultural value dimensions and personality traits. *International Studies of Management & Organization*, 36(4), 38–60.

Fiorini, M., Giovannetti, G., Lanati, M. & Santi, F. (2017). *Asymmetric Cultural Proximity and Greenfield FDI*. European University Institute, Robert Schuman Centre for Advanced Studies, Global Governance Programme, Fiesole: EUI Working Paper RSCAS2017/56.

Firfiray, S., Cruz, C., Neacsu, I. & Gomez-Mejia, L.R. (2018). Is nepotism so bad for family firms? A socioemotional wealth approach. *Human Resource Management Review*, 28(1), 83–97.

Fischer, M.S., Hoßfeld, U., Krause, J. & Richter, S. (2019). The concept of race is the result of racism, not its prerequisite. *Jana Declaration*. https://www.uni-jena.de/unijenamedia/universit%C3%A4t/ abteilung+hochschulkommunikation/presse/jenaer+erkl%C3%A4rung/jenaer_erklaerung_en.pdf.

Fisher, R., Ury, W. & Patton, B. (1992). *Getting to Yes: Negotiating Agreement Without Giving In*. 2nd ed., Boston-New York: Houghton Mifflin Harcourt.

Fiske, S.T. (1998). Stereotyping, prejudice, and discrimination. In: Gilbert, D.T., Fiske, S.T. & Lindzey, G. (eds.), *The Handbook of Social Psychology*. 4th ed., Vol. 2, New York, NY: McGraw-Hill, 357–411.

Fitzsimmons, S. (2013). Multicultural employees. A framework for understanding how they contribute to organizations. *Academy of Management Review*, 38(4), 525–549.

Fitzsimmons, S.R., Miska, C. & Stahl, G.K. (2011). Multicultural employees: Global business' untapped resource. *Organizational Dynamics*, 40, 199–206.

Fletcher, J. (2018). Deepfakes, artificial intelligence, and some kind of dystopia: The new faces of online post-fact performance. *Theatre Journal*, 70(4), 455–471.

Flores, R., Aguilera, R., Mahdian, A. & Vaaler, P. (2013). How well do supranational regional grouping schemes fit international business research models? *Journal of International Business Studies*, 44, 451–474.

Fontaine, R., Richardson, S. & Foong, P.Y. (2002). The tropical fish problem revisited. A Malaysian perspective. *Cross Cultural Management: An International Journal*, 9(4), 60–70.

Foucault, M. (1977). *Discipline and Punish. The Birth of the Prison*. London: Penguin.

Fougère, M. & Moulettes, A. (2007). The construction of the modern west and the backward rest: Studying the discourse of Hofstede's *culture's consequences. Journal of Multicultural Discourses*, 2(1), 1–19.

Fougère, M. & Moulettes, A. (2011). Disclaimers, dichotomies and disappearances in international business textbooks. A postcolonial deconstruction. *Management Learning*, 43(1), 5–24.

Fowler, S.M. & Blohm, J.M. (2004). An analysis of methods for intercultural training. In: Landis, D., Bennett, J.M. & Bennett, M.J. (eds.), *Handbook of Intercultural Training*. 3rd ed., Thousand Oaks, CA: SAGE, 37–84.

Fowler, S.M. & Mumford, M.G. (eds.). (1995). *Intercultural Sourcebook: Cross-Cultural Training Methods*, Vol. 1., Yarmouth, ME: Intercultural Press.

Fowler, S.M. & Pusch, M.D. (2010). Intercultural simulation games. A review (of the United States and beyond). *Simulation & Gaming*, 41(1), 94–115.

Fowler, S.M. & Yamaguchi, M. (2020). An analysis of methods for intercultural training. In: Landis, D. & Bhawuk, D.P.S. (eds.), *The Cambridge Handbook of Intercultural Training*. 4th ed., Cambridge: Cambridge University Press, 192–257.

Fraga, L. & Garcia, J.A. (2010). *Latino Lives in America: Making It Home*. Philadelphia, PA: Temple University Press.

Francis, J.N. (1991). When in Rome? The effects of cultural adaptation on intercultural business negotiations. *Journal of International Business Studies*, 22(3), 403–428.

Frawley, W. (1992). *Linguistic Semantics*. Hillsdale, NJ: Lawrence Erlbaum Associates.

Frenkel, M. (2008). The multinational corporation as a third space: Rethinking international management discourse on knowledge transfer through Homi Bhabha. *Academy of Management Review*, 33(4), 924–942.

Frenkel, M. & Shenhav, Y. (2006). From binarism back to hybridity. A postcolonial reading of management and organization studies. *Organization Studies*, 27(6), 855–876.

Friedman, R., Liu, W., Chi, S.C.S., Hong, Y.Y. & Sung, L.-K. (2012). Cross-cultural management and bicultural identity integration: When does experience abroad lead to appropriate cultural switching? *International Journal of Intercultural Relations*, 36(1), 130–139.

Fujimoto, Y., Härtel, C.E.J., Härtel, G.F. & Baker, N.J. (2000). Openness to dissimilarity moderates the consequences of diversity in well-established groups. *Asia Pacific Journal of Human Resources*, 38(3), 46–61.

Fuller-Love, N. (2008). Culture clash: A case study of Rover and BMW. *International Business Research*, 1(1), 93–100.

Furrer, O., Liu, B.S.-C. & Sudharshan, D. (2000).The relationships between culture and service quality perceptions. Basis for cross-cultural market segmentation and resource allocation. *Journal of Service Research*, 2(4), 355–371.

Fukuyama, F. (2018). *Identity. The Demand for Dignity and the Politics of Resentment*. London: Profile Books.

Gaiba, F. (1998). *The Origins of Simultaneous Interpretation: The Nuremberg Trial*. Ottawa, ON: University of Ottawa Press.

Gabriel, Y. (2000). *Storytelling in Organizations: Facts, Fictions, and Fantasies*. Oxford: Oxford University Press.

Galor, O. & Özak (2016). The agricultural origins of time preference. *American Economic Review*, 106(10), 3064–3103.

Galtung, J. (1981). Structure, culture, and intellectual style: An essay comparing saxonic, teutonic, gallic and nipponic approaches. *Social Science Information*, 20, 817–856.

Gambrel, P.A. & Cianci, R. (2003). Maslow's hierarchy of needs: Does it apply in a collectivist culture. *Journal of Applied Management and Entrepreneurship*, 8(2), 143–161.

Garg, R. & Berning, S.C. (2017). Indigenous Chinese management philosophies: Key concepts and relevance for modern Chinese firms. In: Christiansen, B. & Koc, G. (eds.), *Transcontinental Strategies for Industrial Development and Economic Growth*. Hershey, PA: IGI Global, 43–57.

Gassmann, O. (2001). Multicultural teams: Increasing creativity and innovation by diversity. *Creativity and Innovation Management*, 10(2), 88–95.

Geertz, C. (1965). *The Social History of an Indonesian Town*. Cambridge, MA: MIT Press.

Geertz, C. (1973). *The Interpretation of Cultures*. New York, NY: Basic Books.

Geertz, C. (1983). *Local Knowledge. Further Essays in Interpretative Anthropology*. New York, NY: Basic Books.

Gelfand, M.J. (2018). *Rule Makers Rule Breakers: How Tight and Loose Cultures Wire Our World*. New York, NY: Scribner.

Gelfand, M.J. & Dyer, N. (2000). A cultural perspective on negotiation: Progress, pitfalls, and prospects. *Applied Psychology*, 49(1), 62–99.

Gelfand, M.J., Erez, M. & Aycan, Z. (2007). Cross-cultural organizational behavior. *Annual Review of Psychology*, 58, 479–514.

Gelfand, M.J., Nishii, L.H., & Raver, J.L. (2006). On the nature and importance of cultural tightness-looseness. *Journal of Applied Psychology*, 91(6), 1225–1244.

Gelfand, M.J., Raver, J.L., Nishii, L., Leslie, L.M., Lun, J., Lim, B.C., Duan, L., Almaliach, A., Ang, S., Arnadottir, J., Aycan, Z., Boehnke, K., Boski, P., Cabecinhas, R., Chan, D., Chhokar, J., D'Amato, A., Ferrer, M.,

Fischlmayr, I.C., Fischer, R., Fülöp, M., Georgas, J., Kashima, E.S., Kashima, Y., Kim, K. Lempereur, A., Marquez, P., Othman, R., Overlaet, B., Panagiotopoulou, P., Peltzer, K., Perez-Florizno, L.R., Ponomarenko, L. Realo, A., Schei, V., Schmitt, M., Smith, P.B., Soomro, N., Szabo, E., Taveesin, N., Toyama, M., van de Vliert, E., Vohra, N., Ward, C. & Yamaguchi, S. (2011). Differences between tight and loose cultures: A 33-nation study. *Science*, 332, 1100–1104.

Gellner, E. (1983). *Nations and Nationalism*. Oxford: Blackwell.

Gerhards, J., Hans, S., Carlson, S. & Drewski, D. (2017). The globalisation of labour markets: A content analysis of the demand for transnational human capital in job advertisements. *Soziale Welt*, 68, 25–44.

Gertsen, M.C. (1990). Intercultural competence and expatriates. *International Journal of Human Resource Management*, 1(3), 341–362.

Gertsen, M.C., Søderberg, A.-M. & Torp, J.E. (eds.) (1998). *Cultural Dimensions of International Mergers and Acquisitions*. Berlin-New York: de Gruyter.

Ghauri, P.N. & Cateora, P.R. (2014). *International Marketing*. 4th ed., London: McGraw-Hill.

Ghauri, P.N., Grønhaug, K. & Strange, R. (2020). *Research Methods in Business Studies*. 5th ed., Cambridge: Cambridge University Press.

Ghauri, P.N., Ott, U.F. & Rammal, H.G. (2020). *International Business Negotiations. Theory and Practice*. Cheltenham-Northampton: Edward Elgar.

Ghauri, P.N. & Usunier, J.-C. (eds.) (2003). *International Business Negotiations*. 2nd ed., Oxford: Pergamon-Emerald.

von Ghyczy, T., von Oetinger, B. & Bassford, C (eds.) (2001). *Clausewitz on Strategy. Inspiration and Insight From a Master Strategist*. New York, NY: John Wiley.

Gibson, C. (1999). Do they do what they believe they can? Group efficacy and group effectiveness across tasks and cultures. *Academy of Management Journal*, 42(2), 138–152.

Gibson, C.B. & Gibbs, J.L. (2006). Unpacking the concept of virtuality: The effects of geographic dispersion, electronic dependence, dynamic structure, and national diversity on team innovation. *Administrative Science Quarterly*, 51(3), 451–495.

Gibson, J.W., Greenwood, R.A. & Murphy, E.F. (2009). Generational differences in the workplace: Personal values, behaviors, and popular beliefs. *Journal of Diversity Management*, 4(3), 1–7.

Glazer, S. (2020). Training for cross-cultural competence in the United States Military. In: Landis, D. & Bhawuk, D.P.S. (eds.), *The Cambridge Handbook of Intercultural Training*. 4th ed., Cambridge: Cambridge University Press, 440–474.

Goddard, C. & Wierzbicka, A. (2014). *Words and Meanings. Lexical Semantics Across Domains, Languages, and Cultures*. Oxford: Oxford University Press.

Gokmen, Y., Baskici, C. & Ercil, Y. (2021). The impact of national culture on the increase of COVID-19: A cross-country analysis of European countries. *International Journal of Intercultural Relations*, 81, 1–8.

Gould, S.J. (1995). The Buddhist perspective on business ethics: Experiential exercises for exploration and practice. *Journal of Business Ethics*, 14(1), 63–70.

Goulet, P.K. & Schweiger, D.M. (2006). Managing culture and human resources in mergers and acquisitions. In: Stahl, G.K. & Björkman, I. (eds.), *Handbook of Research in International Human Resource Management*. Cheltenham: Edward Elgar, 405–429.

Graham, J. (1985). The influence of culture on the negotiation process. *Journal of International Business Studies*, 16(1), 81–96.

Graham, J. & Lam, N.M. (2003). The Chinese negotiation. *Harvard Business Review*, 81(10), 82–91.

Graham, J.L., Mintu, A.T. & Rodgers, W. (1994). Explorations of negotiation behaviors in ten foreign cultures using a model developed in the United States. *Management Science*, 40(1), 72–95.

Granet, M. (1936). *La pensée chinoise*. Paris: Editions Albin Michel, 1968.

Groene, J.P. (1976). *All Men Are Created Equal. Some Reflections on the Character of the American Revolution.* Oxford: Oxford University Press.

Greenwald, A.G., McGhee, D.E. & Schwartz, J.L.K. (1998). Measuring individual differences in implicit cognition: The implicit association test. *Journal of Personality and Social Psychology*, 74(6), 1464–1480.

Greenwald, A.G., Poehlman, T.A., Uhlmann, E.L. & Banaji, M.R. (2009). Understanding and using the implicit association test: III. Meta-analysis of predictive validity. *Journal of Personality and Social Psychology*, 97(1), 17–41.

Greenwood, R., Suddaby, R. & Hinings, C.R. (2002). Theorizing change: The role of professional associations in the transformation of institutionalized fields. *Academy of Management Journal*, 45(1), 58–80.

Gregersen, H.B. & Black, J.S. (1992). Antecedents to commitment to a parent company and a Foreign operation. *Academy of Management Journal*, 35(1), 65–90.

Gregson, J. (2007). Immigrants Help Create New Type of German Language. *dw.com*, 8.12.2007. https://www.dw.com/en/immigrants-help-create-new-type-of-german-language/a-2989308.

Groves, K.S., Feyerherm, A. & Gu, M. (2015). Examining cultural intelligence and cross-cultural negotiation effectiveness. *Journal of Management Education*, 39(2), 209–243.

Gudykunst, W. & Hammer, M. (1983). Basic training design. Approaches to intercultural training. In: Landis, D. & Brislin, R.W. (eds.), *Handbook of Intercultural Training*. Vol. 1: *Issues in Theory and Design*. New York, NY: Pergamon Press, 118–154.

Gudykunst, W.B. & Nishida, T. (2001). Anxiety, uncertainty, and perceived effectiveness of communication across relationships and cultures. *International Journal of Intercultural Relations*, 25(1), 55–71.

Güera, D. & Delp, E.J. (2018). Deepfake video detection using recurrent neural networks. *Proceedings oft he 15th IEEE International Conference on Advanced Video and Signal Based Surveillance (AVSS). Auckland*, 1–6.

Guilbaud, D. (2018). *L'illusion méritocratique*. Paris: Odile Jacob.

Gupta, V., Van Wart, M. & Suino, P. (2016). *Leadership Across the Globe*. New York-London: Routledge.

Gupta, V., Hanges, P.J. & Dorfman, P. (2002). Cultural clusters: Methodology and findings. *Journal of World Business*, 37, 11–15.

Gupta, V. & Hanges, P.J. (2004). Regional and climate clustering of societal cultures. In: House, R.J., Hanges, P.J., Javidan, M., Dorfman, P.W. & Gupta, V. (eds.), *Culture, Leadership, and Organizations. The GLOBE Study of 62 Societies*. Thousand Oaks, CA: SAGE, 178–218.

Gurkov, I. & Zelenova, O. (2011-12). Human resource management in Russian companies. *International Studies of Management & Organization*, 41(4), 65–78.

Gutierrez, B., Spencer, S.M. & Zhu, G. (2012), Thinking globally, leading locally: Chinese, Indian, and Western leadership. *Cross Cultural Management: An International Journal*, 19(1), 67–89.

Gutiérrez, K.D., Baquedano-López, P. & Tejeda, C. (1999). Rethinking diversity: Hybridity and hybrid language practices in the third space. *Mind, Culture, and Activity*, 6(4), 286–303.

Guttormsen, D.S.A., Lauring, J. & Chapman, M. (eds.) (2021). *Field Guide to Intercultural Research*. Cheltenham-Northampton: Edward Elgar.

Haarmann, H. (2002): *Geschichte der Schrift*. München: Beck.

Habermas, J. (1984). *The Theory of Communicative Action*. Boston, MA: Beacon Press.

Habermas, J. (2016). Für eine demokratische Polarisierung. *Blätter für deutsche und internationale Politik*, 11, 35–42. https://www.eurozine.com/for-a-democratic-polarization-an-interview-with-jurgen-habermas/?pdf.

Hadjichristidis, C., Geipel, J. & Surian, L. (2017). How Foreign language affects decisions: Rethinking the brain drain model. *Journal of International Business Studies*, 48(5), 645–651.

Haffner, S. (1998). *The Rise and Fall of Prussia*. London: Weidenfeld and Nicolson.

Haire, M., Ghiselli, E.E. & Porter, L.W. (1966). *Managerial Thinking: An International Study*. New York, NY: John Wiley & Sons.

Hajro, A., Gibson, C.B. & Pudelko, M. (2017). Knowledge exchange processes in multicultural teams: Linking organizational diversity climates to teams' effectiveness. *Academy of Management Journal*, 60(1), 345–372.

Håkanson, L. & Ambos, B. (2010). The antecedents of psychic distance. *Journal of International Management*, 16(3), 195–210.

Hall, E.T. (1959). *The Silent Language*. New York, NY: Doubleday.

Hall, E.T. (1966). *The Hidden Dimension*. New York, NY: Doubleday.

Hall, E.T. (1976). *Beyond Culture*. New York, NY: Doubleday.

Hall, E.T. (1983). *The Dance of Life. The Other Dimension of Time*. New York, NY: Doubleday.

Hall, E.T. & Hall, M.R. (1990). *Understanding Cultural Differences: Germans, French and Americans*. Boston-London: Intercultural Press.

Halsall, R. (2008). Intercultural mergers and acquisitions as 'legitimacy crises' of models of capitalism: A UK-German case study. *Organization*, 15(6), 787–809.

Halverson, C.B. & Tirmizi, S.A. (eds.) (2008). *Effective Multicultural Teams: Theory and Practice*. Berlin: Springer.

Hamilton, J. & Knouse, S. (2001). Multinational enterprise decision principles for dealing with cross cultural ethical conflicts. *Journal of Business Ethics*, 31, 77–94.

Hammer, M.R. (2011). Additional intercultural validity testing of the intercultural development inventory. *International Journal of Intercultural Relations*, 35, 474–487.

Hammer, M.R., Bennett, M.J. & Wiseman, R. (2003). Measuring intercultural sensitivity. The intercultural development inventory. *International Journal of Intercultural Relations*, 27(4), 421–443.

Hammelehle, S. (2018). Who Are We? Examining the State of German Identity. *Spiegel*, 29.8.2018. http://www.spiegel.de/international/germany/who-are-we-examining-the-state-of-german-identity-a-1225133.html.

Hammerich, K. & Lewis, R.D. (2013). *Fish Can't See Water: How National Culture Can Make or Break Your Corporate Strategy*. New York, NY: Wiley.

Hampden-Turner, C. & Trompenaars, F. (1997). Response to geert hofstede. *International Journal of Intercultural Relations*, 21(1), 149–159.

Hampden-Turner, C. & Trompenaars, F. (2000). *Building Cross-Cultural Competence. How to Create Wealth From Conflicting Values*. New Haven-London: Yale University Press.

Hampden-Turner, C. & Trompenaars, F. (2012). *Riding the Waves of Culture. Understanding Diversity in Global Business*. 3rd ed., London-Boston: Nicholas Brealey International.

Hamza, S. & Nizam, I. (2016). Why Walmart fails in Germany? An analysis in the perspective of organizational behaviour. *International Journal of Accounting & Business Management*, 4(2), 206–215.

Han, S. & Mäkelä, I.E. (2020). Cultural neuroscience basis of intercultural training and education. In: Landis, D. & Bhawuk, D.P.S. (eds.), *The Cambridge Handbook of Intercultural Training*. 4th ed., Cambridge: Cambridge University Press, 601–616.

Handball Time (2013). Zwischen 28,57 und 61,36 Prozent—Der Anteil der Bundesliga-Legionäre im Positionsvergleich. *Handball World*. https://www.handball-world.news/o.red.r/news-1-1-1-51570.html.

Hanek, K., Lee, F. & Brannen, M.Y. (2014). Individual differences among global/multicultural individuals: Cultural experiences, identity, and adaptation. *International Studies of Management and Organization*, 44(2), 5–89.

Hanges, P.J., Dickson, M.W. & Sipe, M.T. (2004). Rationale for GLOBE statistical analysis. Societal rankings and test of hypotheses. In: House, R.J., Hanges, P.J., Javidan, M., Dorfman, P.W. & Gupta, V. (eds.),

(2004). *Culture, Leadership, and Organizations. The GLOBE Study of 62 Societies*. Thousand Oaks, CA: SAGE, 219–233.

Harbison, F. & Myers, C.A. (1959). *Management in the Industrial World. An International Analysis*. New York-Toronto-London: McGraw-Hill.

Hare, W. (1979). *Open-Mindedness and Education*. Montreal, QC: McGill-Queen University Press.

Harkness, J. (2003). Questionnaire translation. In: Harkness, J.A., van de Vijver, F.J.R. & Mohler, P.P. (eds.), *Cross-Cultural Survey Methods*. Hoboken, NJ: Wiley, 35–56.

Harris, D. (2018). Dual Language China Contracts: Don't Get Fooled! *harrisbricken.com*, 4.4.2018. https://harrisbricken.com/chinalawblog/dual-language-china-contracts-dont-get-fooled/.

Harrison, D.A. & Klein, K.J. (2007). What's the difference? Diversity constructs as separation, variety, or disparity in organizations. *Academy of Management Review*, 32(4), 1199–1228.

Harrison, E.C. & Michailova, S. (2012). Working in the Middle East: Western female expatriates' experiences in the United Arab Emirates. *International Journal of Human Resource Management*, 23(4), 625–644.

Den Hartog, D.N., House, R.J., Hanges, P.J., Ruiz-Quintanilla, S.A. & Dorfman, P.W. (1999). Culture specific and cross-culturally generalizable implicit leadership theories: Are attributes of charismatic/transformational leadership universally endorsed? *Leadership Quarterly*, 10(2), 219–256.

Harvey, P. (2000). *An Introduction to Buddhist Ethics: Foundations, Values and Issues*. Cambridge: Cambridge University Press.

Harzing, A.-W. (2000). Cross-national industrial mail surveys. Why do response rates differ between countries? *Industrial Marketing Management*, 29(3), 243–254.

Harzing, A.-W. (2005). Does the use of English-language questionnaires in cross-national research obscure national differences? *International Journal of Cross Cultural Management*, 5(2), 213–224.

Harzing, A.-W. (2006). Response styles in cross-national survey research. A 26-country Study. *International Journal of Cross Cultural Management*, 6(2), 243–266.

Harzing, A.-W. et al. (2009). Rating versus ranking: What is the best way to reduce response and language bias in cross-national research? *International Business Review*, 18(4), 417–432.

Hasegawa, T. & Gudykunst, W.B. (1998). Silence in Japan and the United States. *Journal of Cross-Cultural Psychology*, 29(5), 668–684.

Hayek, F.A. (1949). *Individualism and Economic Order*. London: Routledge & Kegan Paul.

Hechanova, R., Beehr, T.A. & Christiansen, N.D. (2003). Antecedents and consequences of employees' adjustment to overseas assignment: A meta-analytic review. *Applied Psychology*, 52(2), 213–236.

Heider, F. (1958). *The Psychology of Interpersonal Relations*. New York, NY: Wiley.

Heidrick & Struggles (2020). Route to the Top 2019. https://www.heidrick.com/Knowledge-Center/Publication/Route_to_the_Top_2019.

Henderson, E. (2005). Not letting evidence get in the way of assumptions: Testing the clash of civilizations thesis with more recent data. *International Politics*, 42, 458–469.

Henderson, E.A. & Tucker, R. (2001). Clear and present strangers: The clash of civilizations and international conflict. *International Studies Quarterly*, 45, 317–338.

Hennersdorf, A. (2019). Todesstrafe für Homosexuelle. Thyssenkrupp macht weiter Geschäfte mit Brunei. *Wirtschaftswoche*, 3.4.2019. https://www.wiwo.de/angela-hennersdorf/4625392.html.

Hermann, E.S. (1992). *Beyond Hypocrisy: Decoding the News in an Age of Propaganda Including the Doublespeak Dictionary*. Boston, MA: South End Press.

Hermans, H.J.M. (2001). The dialogical self: Toward a theory of personal and cultural positioning. *Culture & Psychology*, 7(3), 243–281.

Hermans, H.J.M. & Hermans-Konopka, A. (eds.) (2010). *Dialogical Self Theory: Positioning and Counter-Positioning in a Globalizing Society*. Cambridge: Cambridge University Press.

Hernandez, M.D., Wang, Y., Sheng, H., Kalliny, M. & Minor, M. (2017). Escaping the corner of death? An eye-tracking study of reading direction influence on attention and memory. *Journal of Consumer Marketing*, 34(1), 1–10.

Hickson, D.J., Hinings, C.R., McMillan, C.J. & Schwitter, J.P. (1974). The culture-free context of organization structure: A trinational comparison. *Sociology*, 8, 59–80.

Hill, C.W.L. (1997). *International Business. Competing in the Global Market Place*. Chicago, IL: Irwin.

Hill, C.W.L. (2006). *Global Business Today*. 4th ed., Boston, MA: McGraw-Hill/Irwin.

Hobsbawm, E. (1992). *Nations and Nationalism Since 1780*. 2nd ed., Cambridge: Cambridge University Press.

Hofstede, G. (1980). *Culture's Consequences*. Beverly Hills, CA: SAGE.

Hofstede, G. (1984). National cultures and corporate cultures. In: Samovar, L.A. & Porter, R.E. (eds.), *Communication Between Cultures*. Belmont, CA: Wadsworth, 51–63.

Hofstede, G. (1991). *Cultures and Organizations. Software of the Mind*. Maidenhead: McGraw-Hill.

Hofstede, G. (1996). Riding the waves of commerce. A test of trompenaars' 'model' of national culture differences. *International Journal of Intercultural Relations*, 220(2), 189–198.

Hofstede, G. (2001). *Culture's Consequences. Comparing Values, Behaviors, Institutions and Organizations Across Nations*. 2nd ed., Thousand Oaks-London-New Delhi: SAGE.

Hofstede, G. (2002). Dimensions do not exist: A reply to Brendan McSweeney. *Human Relations*, 55(11), 1–8.

Hofstede, G. (2006). What did GLOBE really measure? Researchers' minds versus respondents' minds. *Journal of International Business Studies*, 37(6), 882–896.

Hofstede, G. (2010). The GLOBE debate. Back to relevance. *Journal of International Business Studies*, 41(8), 1339–1346.

Hofstede, G. (2013). Values Survey Module 2013 Questionnaire. *English Language Version*. https://geerthofstede.com/wp-content/uploads/2016/07/VSM-2013-English-2013-08-25.pdf.

Hofstede, G. & Bond, M.H. (1988). The confucius connection. From cultural roots to economic growth. *Organizational Dynamics*, 16(4), 5–21.

Hofstede, G., Garibaldi de Hilal, A.V., Malvezzi, S., Tanure, B. & Vinken, H. (2010). Comparing regional cultures within a country. Lessons from Brazil. *Journal of Cross-Cultural Psychology*, 41(3), 336–352.

Hofstede, G. & Hofstede, G.J. (2005). *Cultures and Organizations. Software of the Mind*. 2nd ed., London-New York: McGrawHill.

Hofstede, G., Hofstede, G.J. & Minkov, M. (2010). *Cultures and Organizations. Software of the Mind*. 3rd ed., London-New York: McGrawHill.

Hofstede, G., Neuijen, B., Ohayv, D.D. & Sanders, G. (1990). Measuring organizational cultures: A qualitative and quantitative study across twenty cases. *Administrative Science Quarterly*, 35(2), 286–316.

Hofstede, G. & Usunier, J.-C. (2003). Hofstede's dimensions of culture and their influence on international business negotiations. In: Ghauri, P.N. & Usunier, J.C. (eds.), *International Business Negotiations*. 2nd ed., Oxford: Pergamon-Emerald, 137–153.

Hofstede, G.J. & Pedersen, P.B. (1999). Synthetic cultures: Intercultural learning through simulation games. *Simulation & Gaming*, 30(4), 415–440.

Hofstede, G.J., Pedersen, P.B. & Hofstede, G. (2002). *Exploring Culture. Exercises, Stories and Synthetic Cultures*. Boston-London: Intercultural Press.

Holden, N.J. (2002). *Cross-Cultural Management: A Knowledge Management Perspective*. Harlow: Pearson.

Holden, N., Kuznetsova, O. & Fink, G. (2008). Russia's long struggle with western terms of management and the concepts behind them. In: Tietze, S. (ed.), *International Management and Language*. London: Routledge, 114–127.

Holden, N., Michailova, S. & Tietze, S. (eds.) (2015). *Routledge Companion to Cross-Cultural Management.* New York, NY: Routledge.

Holder, R.W. (2007). *How Not to Say What You Mean. A Dictionary of Euphemisms.* 4th ed., Oxford: Oxford University Press.

Holmes, P. (2015). Intercultural encounters as socially constructed experiences: Which concepts? Which pedagogies? In Holden, N., Michailova, S. & Tietze, S. (eds.), *Routledge Companion to Cross-Cultural Management.* New York, NY: Routledge, 237–247.

Holt, D.H. & Wigginton, K.W. (2002). *International Management.* Mason, OH: Thomson Southwestern.

Holtbrügge, D. (2002). *Weißrussland. Land zwischen Polen und Rußland.* 2nd ed., München: Beck.

Holtbrügge, D. (2004). Management of international strategic cooperation: Situational conditions, performance criteria and success factors. *Thunderbird International Business Review*, 46(3), 255–274.

Holtbrügge, D. (ed.) (2008). *Cultural adjustment of expatriates: Theoretical concepts and empirical studies.* Mering-München: Rainer Hampp.

Holtbrügge, D. (2013). Indigenous management research. *Management International Review*, 53(1), 1–11.

Holtbrügge, D. (2018). Political strategies of Chinese firms in Germany. An institutionalist perspective. *International Journal of Emerging Markets*, 13(6), 1438–1456.

Holtbrügge, D. (2019/2020). Preparation for Foreign assignments. *Personalführung*, 12(1), 22–27.

Holtbrügge, D. (2021). Expatriates at the base-of-the-pyramid. Precarious employment or fortune in a foreign land? *Journal of Global Mobility*, 9(1), 44–64.

Holtbrügge, D. & Conrad, M. (2020). Decoupling in CSR reports. A linguistic content analysis of the Volkswagen Dieselgate scandal. *International Studies of Management & Organisation*, 50(3), 253–270.

Holtbrügge, D. & Engelhard, F. (2016). Study abroad programs: Individual motivations, cultural intelligence, and the mediating role of cultural boundary spanning. *Academy of Management Learning & Education*, 15(3), 435–455.

Holtbrügge, D., Friedmann, C.B. & Puck, J.F. (2010). Recruitment and retention in foreign firms in India: A resource-based view. *Human Resource Management*, 49(3), 439–455.

Holtbrügge, D. & Garg, R. (2016). Indigenous Indian management philosophies. Key concepts and relevance for modern Indian firms. In: Malik, A. & Pereira, V. (eds.), *Indian Culture and Work Organisations in Transition.* London-New York: Routledge, 59–75.

Holtbrügge, D. & Haussmann, H. (eds.) (2017). *The Internationalization of Firms. Case Studies From the Nürnberg Metropolitan Region.* 2nd ed., Augsburg-München: Hampp.

Holtbrügge, D. & Kittler, M. (2007). Understanding misunderstanding in intra- and intercultural communication. Findings of a Sino-German experiment. In: Oesterle, M.-J. (ed.), *Internationales Management im Umbruch. Globalisierungsbedingte Einwirkungen auf Theorie und Praxis Internationaler Unternehmensführung.* Wiesbaden: Gabler, 341–370.

Holtbrügge, D. & Kreppel, H. (2015). Employer attractiveness of Chinese, Indian and Russian firms in Germany: Signaling effects of HR practices. *Corporate Reputation Review*, 18, 223–242.

Holtbrügge, D. & Mohr, A.T. (2010). Cultural determinants of learning style preferences. *Academy of Management Learning & Education*, 9(4), 622–637.

Holtbrügge, D. & Oberhauser, M. (2019). CSR orientation of future top managers in India. *Journal of Indian Business Research*, 11(2), 162–178.

Holtbrügge, D. & Puck, J.F. (2008). *Geschäftserfolg in China. Strategien für den größten Markt der Welt.* Berlin: Springer.

Holtbrügge, D. & Schillo, K. (2008). Intercultural training requirements for virtual assignments: Results of an explorative empirical study. *Human Resource Development International*, 11(3), 271–286.

Holtbrügge, D., Weldon, A. & Rogers, H. (2013). Cultural determinants of email communication styles. *International Journal of Cross Cultural Management*, 13(1), 89–110.

Holtbrügge, D., Wilson, S. & Berg, N. (2006). Human resource management at star alliance: Pressures for standardization and differentiation. *Journal of Air Transport Management*, 12(6), 306–312.

Holzmüller, H. & Stöttinger, B. (2001). International marketing managers' cultural sensitivity: Relevance, training requirements and a pragmatic training concept. *International Business Review*, 10(6), 597–614.

Homburg, C., Alavi, S., Rajab, T. & Wieseke, J. (2017). The contingent roles of R&D–sales versus R&D–marketing cooperation in new-product development of business-to-business firms. *International Journal of Research in Marketing*, 34(1), 212–230.

Hong, H-J. (2010). Bicultural competence and its impact on team effectiveness. *International Journal of Cross Cultural Management*, 10(1), 93–120.

Hong, Y., Morris, M.W., Chiu, C. & Benet-Martínez, V. (2000). Multicultural minds. A dynamic constructivist approach to culture and cognition. *American Psychologist*, 55(7), 709–720.

Hood, J. (2003). The relationship of leadership style and CEO values to ethical practices in organizations. *Journal of Business Ethics*, 43, 263–273.

Hood, R.W., Hill, P.C. & Spilka, B. (2018). *The Psychology of Religion: An Empirical Approach*. 5th ed., New York-London: Guilford Press.

van Hoorn, A. (2015). Differences in work values. Understanding the role of intra- versus inter-country variation. *International Journal of Human Resource Management*, 26(7), 1002–1020.

van Hoorn, A. & Maseland, R. (2010). Cultural differences between East and West Germany after 1991: Communist values vs. economic performance? *Journal of Economic Behavior and Organization*, 76(3), 791–804.

Houellebecq, M. (2015). *Soumission*. Paris: Flammarion.

House, R.J. (1995). Leadership in the twenty-first century: A speculative inquiry. In A. Howard (ed.), *The Changing Nature of Work*. San Francisco, CA: Jossey-Bass, 411–450.

House, R.J. (2004). Preface. In: House, R.J., Hanges, P.J., Javidan, M., Dorfman, P.W. & Gupta, V. (eds.), *Culture, Leadership, and Organizations. The GLOBE Study of 62 Societies*. Thousand Oaks, CA: SAGE, XXI–XXVII.

House, R.J., Dorfman, P.W., Javidan, M., Hanges, P.J. & Sully do Luque, M.F. (2014). *Strategic Leadership Across Cultures: GLOBE Study of CEO Leadership Behavior and Effectiveness in 24 Countries*. Los Angeles, CA: SAGE.

House, R.J., Hanges, P.J., Javidan, M., Dorfman, P.W. & Gupta, V. (eds.) (2004). *Culture, Leadership, and Organizations: The GLOBE Study of 62 Societies*. Thousand Oaks, CA: SAGE.

House, R.J. & Javidan, M. (2004). Overview of GLOBE. In: House, R.J., Hanges, P.J., Javidan, M., Dorfman, P.W. & Gupta, V. (eds.) (2004). *Culture, Leadership, and Organizations. The GLOBE Study of 62 Societies*. Thousand Oaks, CA: SAGE, 9–28.

Howe, N. & Strauss, W. (2000). *Millennials Rising: The Next Great Generation*. New York, NY: Vintage Books.

Hsu, F.L.K. (1963). *Clan, Caste, and Club. A Comparative Study of Chinese, Hindu, and American Ways of Life*. Princeton, NJ: Van Nostrand.

Hua, Z. (2018). *Exploring Intercultural Communication: Language in Action*. 2nd ed., London-New York: Routledge.

Huang, L., Lu, M. & Wong, B.K. (2003). The impact of power distance on email acceptance: Evidence from the PRC. *Journal of Computer Information Systems*, 44, 93–101.

Huang, W. & Kim, J. (2020). Linguistically induced time perception and asymmetric cost behavior. *Management International Review*, 60, 755–785.

Huang, X. (2008). Guanxi networks and job searches in China's emerging labour market: A qualitative investigation. *Work, Employment & Society*, 22(3), 467–484.

Huoal, G. (2021). Amanda Gorman's Inauguration Poem Appears in German. *Deutsche Welle*, 30.03.2021. https://www.dw.com/en/amanda-gormans-inauguration-poem-appears-in-german/a-56754197.

Huddy, L. & Khatib, N. (2007). American patriotism, national identity, and political involvement. *American Journal of Political Science*, 51(1), 63–77.

Huo, Y.P. & Randall, D.M. (1991). Exploring subcultural differences in Hofstede's value survey: The case of the Chinese. *Asia Pacific Journal of Management*, 8, 159–173.

Hubbert, J. (2019). *China in the World: An Anthropology of Confucius Institutes, Soft Power, and Globalization*. Honolulu, HI: University of Hawai'i Press.

Hughes, G. (2010). *Political Correctness. A History of Semantics and Culture*. New York, NY: John Wiley & Sons.

Hult, G.T.M., Ketchen, D.J., Griffith, D.A., Finnegan, C.A., Gonzalez-Padron, T., Harmancioglu, N., Huang, Y., Talay, M.B. & Cavusgil, S.T. (2008). Data equivalence in cross-cultural international business research. Assessment and guidelines. *Journal of International Business Studies*, 39(6), 1027–1044.

Hunt, V., Prince, S., Dixon-Fyle, S. & Yee, L. (2018). *Delivering Through Diversity*. McKinsey & Company.

Huntington, S.P. (1993). The clash of civilizations? *Foreign Affairs*, 72(3), 22–49.

Huntington, S.P. (1996). *The Clash of Civilizations and the Remaking of World Order*. London: Penguin Books.

Hutcheon, L. (1995). *Irony's Edge. The Theory and Politics of Irony*. London-New York: Routledge.

Huynh, T.L.D. (2020). Does culture matter social distancing under the COVID-19 pandemic? *Safety Science*, 130, 104872.

Hwang, K.-k. (1987). Face and favor. The Chinese power game. *American Journal of Sociology*, 92(4), 944–974.

Iastrebov, G. (2013). The stratification of Russian society in a comparative context. From 'Lofty' theories to sad reality. *Sociological Research*, 52(2), 62–86.

Imai, L. & Gelfand, M.J. (2010). The culturally intelligent negotiator: The impact of cultural intelligence (CQ) on negotiation sequences and outcomes. *Organizational Behavior and Human Decision Processes*, 112, 83–98.

Inglehart, R. (1997). *Modernization and Postmodernization: Cultural, Economic, and Political Change in 43 Societies*. Princeton, NJ: Princeton University Press.

Inglehart, R. (2018). *Cultural Evolution. People's Motivations Are Changing, and Reshaping the World*. Cambridge: Cambridge University Press.

Inglehart, R. & Baker, W.E. (2000). Modernization, cultural change, and the persistence of traditional values. *American Sociological Review*, 65(1), 19–51.

Inkeles, A. (1997). *National Character. A Psycho-Social Perspective*. London-New York: Taylor & Francis.

Institute of International Education (2017). *A Quick Look at Global Mobility Trends*. Washington, DC: IIE.

Ioffe, G. (2003). Understanding Belarus: Belarussian identity. *Europe-Asia Studies*, 55(8), 1241–1272.

D'Iribarne, P., Chevrier, S., Henry, A., Segal, J.-P. & Tréguer-Felten, G. (2020). *Cross-Cultural Management Revisited: A Qualitative Approach*. Oxford: Oxford University Press.

Ito, K. & Triandis, H.C. (1989). *Culture Assimilator for Japanese Visiting the United States*. Department of Psychology, Chicago, IL: University of Illinois.

Jack, G. & Westwood, R. (2010). *International and Cross-Cultural Management Studies. A Postcolonial Reading*. New York, NY: Palgrave Macmillan.

Jack, R.E., Garrod, O.G.B., Yu, H., Caldara, R. & Schyns, P.G. (2012). Facial expressions of emotion are not culturally universal. *Proceedings of the National Academy of Sciences of the United States of America*, 109(19), 7241–7244.

Jackson, J. (ed.) (2012). *The Routledge Handbook of Language and Intercultural Communication*. London: Routledge.

Jackson, T. (2011). *International Management Ethics: A Critical, Cross-cultural Perspective*. Cambridge: Cambridge University Press.

Jackson, T. (2012). Postcolonialism and organizational knowledge in the wake of China's presence in Africa: Interrogating South-South relations. *Organization*, 19(2), 181–204.

Jackson, T. (2013). Reconstructing the Indigenous in African management research. Implications for international management studies in a globalized world. *Management International Review*, 53(1), 13–38.

Jackson, T., Amaeshi, K. & Yavuz, S. (2008). Untangling African Indigenous management: Multiple influences on the success of SMEs in Kenya. *Journal of World Business*, 43(4), 400–416.

Jain, A. (2014). An Indian with a British passport who works for a German bank. *Deccan Herald*, 27.4.2014. https://www.deccanherald.com/content/388741/anshu-jain-indian-british-passport.html.

Jakobson, R. (1959). On linguistic aspects of translation. In: Brower, R.A. (ed.), *On Translation*. Cambridge: Harvard University Press, 232–239.

Jandt, F.E. (2018). *An Introduction to Intercultural Communication: Identities in a Global Community*. 9th ed., Los Angeles, CA: SAGE.

Jang, S. (2017). Cultural brokerage and creative performance in multicultural teams. *Organization Science*, 28(6), 993–1009.

Jarvenpaa, S.L. & Leidner, D.E. (1999). Communication and trust in global virtual teams. *Organization Science*, 10(6), 791–815.

Jaskiewicz, P., Uhlenbruck, K., Balkin, D.B. & Reay, T. (2013). Is nepotism good or bad? Types of nepotism and implications for knowledge management. *Family Business Review*, 26, 121–139.

Javidan, M., House, R.J., Dorfman, P.W., Hanges, P.J. & Sully de Luque, M. (2006). Conceptualizing and measuring cultures and their consequences: A comparative review of GLOBE's and Hofstede's approaches. *Journal of International Business Studies*, 37(6), 897–914.

Jenner, M. (2017). Binge-watching: Video-on-demand, quality TV and mainstreaming fandom. *International Journal of Cultural Studies*, 20(3), 304–320.

Jepson, D. (2009). Studying leadership at cross-country level: A critical analysis. *Leadership*, 5(1), 61–80.

Jogulu, U.D. (2010). Culturally linked leadership style. *Leadership and Organizational Development Journal*, 31(8), 705–719.

John, O.P. & Benet-Martínez, V (2000). Measurement: Reliability, construct validation, and scale construction. In: Reis, H.T. & Judd, C.M. (eds.), *Handbook of Research Methods in Social and Personality Psychology*. New York, NY: Cambridge University Press, 339–369.

John, O.P. & Srivastava, S. (1999). The Big Five trait taxonomy: History, measurement, and theoretical perspectives. In: Pervin, L.A. & John, O.P. (eds.), *Handbook of Personality. Theory and Research*. 2nd ed., New York-London: Guilford Press, 102–138.

Johnson, B. & Buko, S. (2013). Cultural Intelligence Scale (CQS). Testing cross-cultural transferability of CQS in Ukraine. *Studies of Changing Societies*, 4(10), 51–67.

Johnson, J.P., Lenartowicz, T. & Apud, S. (2006). Cross-cultural competence in international business: Toward a definition and a model. *Journal of International Business Studies*, 37(4), 525–543.

Johnson, T.P. & van de Vijver, F.J.R. (2003). Social desirability in cross-cultural research. In: Harness, J., van de Vijver, F.J.R. & Mohler, P. (eds.), *Cross-Cultural Survey Methods*. New York, NY: Wiley, 193–202.

de Jong, M. & Warmeling, H. (2017). OASISTAN: An intercultural role-playing simulation game to recognize cultural dimensions. *Simulation & Gaming*, 48(2), 178–198.

Jordan, T.R., Almabruk, A.A., Gadalla, E.A., McGowan, V.A., White, S.J., Abedipour, L. & Paterson, K.B. (2014). Reading direction and the central perceptual span: Evidence from Arabic and English. *Psychonomic Bulletin & Review*, 21(2), 505–511.

Joshi, A., Neely, B., Emrich, C., Griffiths, D. & George, G. (2015). Gender research in AMJ: An overview of five decades of empirical research and calls to action. *Academy of Management Journal*, 58(5), 1450–1475.

Joskowloz, L., Stilijanow, U. & Thomas, A. (2007). *Beruflich in Australien. Trainingsprogramm für Manager, Fach- und Führungskräfte*. Göttingen: Vandenhoeck & Ruprecht.

Joy, S. & Poonamallee, L. (2013). Cross-cultural teaching in globalized management classrooms: Time to move from functionalist to postcolonial approaches? *Academy of Management Learning & Education*, 12(3), 396–413.

Jubany, O. (2017). *Screening Asylum in a Culture of Disbelief. Truths, Denials and Skeptical Borders*. New York, NY: Palgrave Macmillan.

Juderías, J. (1914). *La Leyenda negra y la verdad histórica*. Madrid: Tipografía de la Revista de Archivos, Bibliotecas y Museos, 1914.

Jullien, F. (2016). *Il n'y a pas d'identité culturelle*. Paris: Herne.

Jung, C.G. (1961). *Memories, Dreams and Reflections*. New York, NY: Vintage Books.

Kaasa, A., Vadi, M. & Varblane, U. (2014). Regional cultural differences within European countries: Evidence from multi-country surveys. *Management International Review*, 54(6), 825–852.

Kalbermatten, P. (2011). Schindler elevators and the challenges of the Japanese market. In: Haghirian, P. & Gagnon, P. (eds.), *Case Studies in Japanese Management*. Hackensack, NJ: World Scientific, 203–229.

Kane, R.B. (2002). *Disobedience and Conspiracy in the German Army, 1918–1945*. Jefferson, PA: McFarland.

Kant, I. (1788). *Critic der practischen Vernunft*. Riga: Hartknoch.

Kappeler, A. (2014). *The Russian Empire. A Multi-Ethnic History*. London: Routledge.

Kara, A. & Peterson, M.P. (2012). The dynamic societal cultural milieu of organizations; origins, maintenance and change. In: Tihanyi, L. et al. (eds.), *Institutional Theory in International Business and Management. Advances in International Management*, Vol. 25. Bingley: Emerald, 341–371.

Karsten, L. & Illa, H. (2005). Ubuntu as a key African management concept. Contextual background and practical insights for knowledge application. *Journal of Managerial Psychology*, 20(7), 607–620.

Kashgary, A.D. (2011). The paradox of translating the untranslatable: Equivalence vs. non-equivalence in translating from Arabic into English. *Journal of King Saud University—Languages and Translation*, 23, 47–57.

Kashima, Y. (2000). Conceptions of culture and person for psychology. *Journal of Cross-Cultural Psychology*, 31(1), 14–32.

Katan, D. (2004). *Translating Cultures: An Introduction for Translators, Interpreters and Mediators*. 2nd ed., London: Routledge.

Kealey, D.J. (2004). Research on intercultural effectiveness and its relevance to multicultural crews in space. *Aviation, Space, and Environmental Medicine*, 75(Supplement 1), C58–C64.

Kealey, D.J. & Protheroe, D.R. (1996). The effectiveness of cross-cultural training for expatriates: An assessment of the literature on the issue. *International Journal of Intercultural Relations*, 20, 141–165.

Kecskes, I. (2014). *Intercultural Pragmatics*. Oxford: Oxford University Press.

von Keller, E. (1982). *Management in fremden Kulturen. Ziele, Ergebnisse und methodische Probleme der kulturvergleichenden Managementforschung*. Bern-Stuttgart: Haupt.

Kempf, C. & Holtbrügge, D. (2020). Moderators and mediators of cross-cultural training effectiveness. Literature review and development of a theoretical model. *European Journal of International Management*, 14(2), 293–326.

Kennedy, P. (1987). *The Rise and Fall of the Great Powers. Economic Change and Military Conflict From 1500 to 2000: Economic Change and Military Control From 1500–2000*. New York, NY: Random House.

Kennedy, R.F., Roy, C.S. & Goldman, M.L. (2013). *Race and Ethnicity in the Classical World. Ann Anthology of Primary Sources in Translation*. Indianapolis-Cambridge: Hackett.

Kesting, N., Reiberg, A. & Hocks, P. (2018). Discourse quality in times of populism: An analysis of German parliamentary debates on immigration policy. *Communication & Society*, 31(3), 77–90.

Khan, A., Lindridge, A. & Pusaksrikit, T. (2018). Why some South Asian Muslims celebrate Christmas: Introducing "acculturation trade-offs". *Journal of Business Research*, 82(1), 290–299.

Khan, S. (2016). Time to let go of segregation – globally. *Chicago Tribune*, 14.09.2016. https://www.chicagotribune.com%2Fnews%2Fopinion%2Fcommentary%2Fct-sadiq-khan-mayor-london-integration-perspec-0915-md-20160914-story.html&usg=AOvVaw0qi_6KDTyubicB8qTjzbkb.

Khan, M.A. & Ebner, N. (eds.) (2019). *The Palgrave Handbook of Cross-Cultural Business Negotiation*. Cham: Palgrave Macmillan.

Khapova, S.N. & Korotov, K. (2007). Dynamics of Western career attributes in the Russian context. *Career Development International*, 12(1), 68–85.

Khilnani, S. (1999). *The Idea of India*. New York, NY: Farrar Straus Giroux.

Kieser, A. (1989). Organizational, institutional, and societal evolution: Medieval craft guilds and the genesis of formal organizations. *Administrative Science Quarterly*, 34(4), 540–564.

Kilduff, M., Angelmar, R. & Mehra, A. (2000). Top management-team diversity and firm performance. Examining the role of cognitions. *Organization Science*, 11(2), 21–34.

Kim, H.S. & Sasaki, J.Y. (2014). Cultural neuroscience: Biology of the mind in cultural contexts. *Annual Review of Psychology*, 65, 487–514.

Kim, U. (1994). Significance of paternalism and communalism in the occupational welfare system of Korean firms. A national survey. In: Kim, U., Triandis, H.C., Kagitcibasi, C., Choi, S.-C. & Yoon, G. (eds.), *Individualism and Collectivism. Theory, Method, and Applications*. London: SAGE, 251–266.

Kim, Y.J. & van Dyne, L. (2012). Cultural intelligence and international leadership potential: The importance of contact for members of the majority. *Applied Psychology*, 61(2), 272–294.

Kim, Y.Y. (2015). Finding a "home" beyond culture: The emergence of intercultural personhood in the globalizing world. *International Journal of Intercultural Relations*, 46, 3–12.

Kim, Y.Y. (ed.) (2017). *International Encyclopedia of Intercultural Communication*. Hoboken, NJ: Wiley.

Kirkman, B.L., Lowe, K.B. & Gibson, C.B. (2006). A quarter century of culture's consequences. A review of empirical research incorporating Hofstede's cultural values framework. *Journal of International Business Studies*, 37(3), 285–320.

Kirste, L. & Holtbrügge, D. (2019). Experiential learning in the digital context: An experimental study of online cultural intelligence training. *Journal of Teaching in International Business*, 30(2), 147–174.

Kita, S. (ed.) (2003). *Pointing. Where Language, Culture, and Cognition Meet*. London: Taylor & Francis.

Kitayama, S., Duffy, S., Kawamura, T. & Larsen, J.T. (2003). Perceiving an object and its context in different cultures: A cultural look at new look. *Psychological Science*, 14(3), 201–206.

Kittler, M.G., Rygl, D. & Mackinnon, A. (2011). Beyond culture or beyond control? Reviewing the use of Hall's high-/low-context concept. *International Journal of Cross Cultural Management*, 11(1), 63–82.

Kiyoshi, T. (2006). Effects of wage and promotion incentives on the motivation levels of Japanese employees. *Career Development International*, 11(3), 193–203.

Klinge, K., Rohmann, A. & Piontkowski, U (2009). Intercultural sensitization with synthetic cultures: Evaluation of a computer-based multimedia learning tool. *International Journal of Intercultural Relations*, 33(6), 507–515.

Kluckhohn, C. & Murray, H.A. (1965). Personality formation. The determinants. In: Kluckhohn, C. & Murray, H.A. & (eds.), *Personality in Nature, Society, and Culture*. 2nd ed., New York, NY: Alfred A. Knopf, 53–67.

Kluckhohn, F.R. & Strodtbeck, F.L. (1961). *Variations in Value Orientations*. Evanston, IL: Row, Peterson.

Klyukanov, I. (2020). *Principles of Intercultural Communication*. 2nd ed., New York, NY: Routledge.

Knapp, M.L., Hall, J.A. & Horgan, T.G. (2014). *Nonverbal Communication in Human Interaction*. 8th ed., Boston, MA: Wadsworth.

Knight, G.A. & Kim, D. (2009). International business competence and the contemporary firm. *Journal of International Business Studies*, 40(2), 255–273.

Koch, P., Krefeld, T. & Oesterreicher, W. (1997). *Neues aus Sankt Eiermarkt. Das kleine Buch der Sprachwitze*. München: Beck.

Kogut, B. & Singh, H. (1988). The effect of national culture on the choice of entry mode. *Journal of International Business Studies*, 19(3), 411–432.

Kolb, D.A. (1984). *Experiential Learning. Experience as a Source of Learning and Development*. Englewood Cliffs, NJ: Prentice Hall.

Kolstø, P. & Blakkisrud, H. (eds.) (2004). *Nation-Building and Common Values in Russia*. Lanham, MD: Rowman & Littlefield.

Konara, P. & Mohr, A. (2019). Why we should stop using the Kogut and Singh index. *Management International Review*, 59(3), 335–354.

Kotthoff, H. & Spencer-Oatey, H. (eds.) (2008). *Handbook of Intercultural Communication*. Berlin-New York: Mouton de Gruyter.

KPMG (2015). Global Assignment Policies and Practices: Survey 2015. https://assets.kpmg.com/content/dam/kpmg/pdf/2015/04/gapp-survey-2015.pdf (accessed January 15, 2017).

Kra, P. (2002). The concept of national character in 18th century France. *Cromohs*, 7, 1–6. http://www.cromohs.unifi.it/7_2002/kra.html.

Kraidy, M. (2006). *Hybridity, or the Cultural Logic of Globalization*. Philadelphia, PA: Temple University Press.

Krippendorff, K. (1986). *Information Theory. Structural Models for Qualitative Data*. Newbury Park, CA: SAGE.

Kroeber, A.L. & Kluckhohn, C. (1952). Culture: A critical review of concepts and definitions. *Papers of the Peabody Museum of American Archaeology and Ethnology*, 47, 1–223. Cambridge, MA: Harvard University Press.

Kruglanski, A.W., Pierro, A., Mannetti, L. & De Grada, E. (2006). Groups as epistemic providers: Need for closure and the unfolding of group-centrism. *Psychological Review*, 113(1), 84–100.

Krupnik, I. & Müller-Wille, L. (2010). Franz Boas and Inuktitut Terminology for ice and snow: From the emergence of the field to the "Great Eskimo Vocabulary Hoax". In: Krupnik, I., Aporta, C., Gearheard, S., Laidler, G.J. & Holm, L.K. (eds.), *SIKU. Knowing Our Ice: Documenting Inuit Sea-Ice Knowledge and Use*. New York, NY: Springer, 385–410.

Kucera, T. (2012). Can "citizen in uniform" survive? German civil-military culture responding to a war. *German Politics*, 21(1), 53–72.

Kuhn, T.S. (1970). *The Structure of Scientific Revolutions*. Chicago, IL: University of Chicago Press.

de Laborde, E. (1743). *Essais sur le génie et le caractère des nations*. Brussels: Frederic Leonard.

Labov, W. (2006). *The Social Stratification of English in New York City*. Cambridge: Cambridge University Press.

Lacan, J. (1988). *The Seminar. Book I. Freud's Papers on Technique, 1953–54*. Cambridge: Cambridge University Press.

Ladd, D.R. (2008). *Intonational Phonology*. 2nd ed., Cambridge: Cambridge University Press.

Laitin, D. & Posner, D. (2001). The implications of constructivism for constructing ethnic fractionalization indices. *APSA-CP: The Comparative Politics Newsletter*, 12, 1–7.

Lall, M.-C. (2001). *India's Missed Opportunity: India's Relationship With the Non-resident Indians*. Farnham: Ashgate.

Lam, K.-C.J. (2003). Confucian business ethics and the economy. *Journal of Business Ethics*, 43(1/2), 153–162.

Landis, D., Bennett, J. & Bennett, M. (eds.) (2004). *Handbook of Intercultural Training*. 3rd ed., Thousand Oaks, CA: SAGE.

Landis, D. & Bhawuk, D.P.S. (eds.) (2020). *The Cambridge Handbook of Intercultural Training*. 4th ed., Cambridge: Cambridge University Press.

Larsson, R. & Lubatkin, M. (2001). Achieving acculturation in mergers and acquisitions: An international case survey. *Human Relations*, 54(12), 1573–1607.

Lasswell, H.D. (1948). The structure and function of communication in society. In: Bryson, L. (ed.), *The Communication of Ideas. A Series of Addresses*. New York, NY: Harper & Brothers, 32–51.

Lawson, S. (2006). *Culture and Context in World Politics*. Houndmills: Palgrave MacMillan.

Lakshman, C. (2013). Biculturalism and attributional complexity: Cross-cultural leadership effectiveness. *Journal of International Business Studies*, 44(9), 922–940.

Le, S. & Kroll, M. (2017). CEO international experience: Effects on strategic change and firm performance. *Journal of International Business Studies*, 48(5), 573–595.

Ledeneva, A.V. (1998). *Russia's Economy of Favours: Blat, Networking and Informal Exchange*. Cambridge: Cambridge University Press.

Ledeneva, A. (2009). From Russia with blat: Can informal networks help modernize Russia? *Social Research*, 76(1), 257–288.

Lee, J., Soutar, G.N. & Louviere, J.J. (2005). An alternative approach to measuring Schwartz's values: The best-worst scaling approach. *Journal of Personality Assessment*, 90(4), 335–347.

Lee, L.-Y. & Croker, R. (2006). A contingency model to promote the effectiveness of expatriate training. *Industrial Management & Data Systems*, 106(8), 1187–1205.

Lee, L.Y. & Sukoco, B.M. (2010). The effects of cultural intelligence on expatriate performance: The moderating effects of international experience. *International Journal of Human Resource Management*, 21(7), 963–981.

Lee, W.E. (2011). *Warfare and Culture in World History*. New York, NY: NYU Press.

Leerssen, J. (2000). The rhetoric of national character. A programmatic survey. *Poetics Today*, 21(2), 267–292.

Leibowitz, D.M. (2010). *The Ironic Defense of Socrates: Plato's Apology*. Cambridge: Cambridge University Press.

Lenartowicz, T., Johnson, J.P. & Konopaske, R. (2014). The application of learning theories to improve cross-cultural training programs in MNCs. *International Journal of Human Resource Management*, 25(12), 1697–1719.

Lenartowicz, T, Johnson, J. & White, C. (2003), The neglect of intra-cultural variation in international management research: An Iberoamerican perspective. *Journal of Business Research*, 56, 999–1008.

Lenartowicz, T. & Roth, K. (2001). Does subculture within a country matter? A cross-cultural study of motivational domains and business performance in Brazil. *Journal of International Business Studies*, 32(2), 305–325.

Lenczowski, J. (2008). Cultural diplomacy, political influence and integrated strategy. In: Waller, J.M. (ed.), *Strategic Influence: Public Diplomacy, Counterpropaganda and Political Warfare*. Washington, DC: The Institute of World Politics Press, 74–99.

Leonard, K.M., Van Scotter, J.R. & Pakdil, F. (2009). Culture and communication: Cultural variations and media effectiveness. *Administration & Society*, 41(7), 850–877.

Leonard, K.M., Scotter, J.R., Pakdil, F., Chamseddine, N.J., Esatoglu, E., Gumus, M. & Koyuncu, M., Wu, L.L., Mockaitis, A.I., Salciuviene, L., Oktem, M.K., Surkiene, Tsai, F.-S. (2011). Examining media effectiveness across cultures and national borders: A review and multilevel framework. *International Journal of Cross Cultural Management*, 11(1), 83–103.

Leung, K. (1997). Negotiation and reward allocations across cultures. In: Early, P.C. & Erez, M. (eds.), *New Perspectives on International Industrial/Organisational Psychology*. San Francisco, CA: Jossey-Bass, 640–675.

Leung, K. (2012). Indigenous Chinese management research: Like it or not, we need it. *Management and Organization Review*, 8(1), 1–5.

Leung, K., Ang, S. & Tan, M.L. (2014). Intercultural competence. *Annual Review of Organizational Psychology*, 1(1), 489–519.

Leung, K. & Cheng, G. (2014). Intercultural interaction in the work context: A cultural tuning perspective. In: Chan, D. (ed.), *Individual Adaptability to Changes at Work. New Directions in Research*. New York, NY: Routledge/Taylor & Francis, 156–174.

Leung, K. & van de Vijver, F. (2008). Strategies for strengthening causal interferences in cross cultural research. The consilience approach. *International Journal of Cross Cultural Management*, 8(2), 145–169.

Levashina, J. Morgeson, F.P. & Campion, M.A. (2012). Tell me some more: Exploring how verbal ability and item verifiability influence responses to Biodata questions in a high-stakes selection context. *Personnel Psychology*, 65(2), 359–383.

Lévi-Strauss, C. (1958). *Anthropologie Structurale*. Paris: Libraire Plon.

Levine, R. (1997). *A Geography of Time. Temporal Misadventures of a Social Psychologist, or How Every Culture Keeps Time Just a Little Bit Differently*. New York, NY: Basic Books 1997.

Levinson, D. (1998). *Ethnic Groups Worldwide. A Ready Reference Handbook*. Phoenix, AZ: Oryx Press.

Levy, O., Beechler, S., Taylor, S. & Boyacigiller, N.A. (2007). What we talk about when we talk about 'global mindset': Managerial cognition in multinational corporations. *Journal of International Business Studies*, 38(2), 231–258.

Lewicki, R., Barry, B. & Saunders, D. (2020). *Negotiation*. 8th ed., New York-London: McGraw-Hill.

Lewin, K. (1936). *Principles of Topological Psychology*. New York-London: McGraw-Hill.

Lewis, A. (2003). *Theory of Economic Growth*. London: Routledge.

Lewis, R.D. (2012). *When Teams Collide: Managing the International Team Successfully*. London-Boston: Nicholas Brealey.

Lewis, R.D. (2018). *When Cultures Collide: Leading Across Cultures*. 4th ed., Boston-London: Nicholas Brealey.

Li, C., Brodbeck, F.C., Shenkar, O., Ponzi, L.J. & Fisch, J.-H. (2017). Embracing the Foreign: Cultural attractiveness and international strategy. *Strategic Management Journal*, 38(4), 950–971.

Li, D. (2016). *On Chinese Culture*. Singapore: Springer.

Li, M., Mobley, W.H. & Kelly, A. (2016). Linking personality to cultural intelligence: An interactive effect of openness and agreeableness. *Personality and Individual Differences*, 89, 105–110.

Li, X. & Shan, P.F. (2015). *Ethnic China: Identity, Assimilation, and Resistance*. Lanham, MD: Lexington Books.

Liao, Y. & Thomas, D.C. (2020). *Cultural Intelligence in the World of Work. Past, Present, Future*. Cham: Springer.

Lievois, K. & Schoentjes, P. (eds.) (2010). *Translating Irony. Linguistica Antverpiensia, Themes in Translation Studies*. Department of Translators & Interpreters, Artesis University College: Antwerp.

Lilla, M. (2018). *The Once and Future Liberal: After Identity Politics*. New York, NY: Harper.

Lindeman, M. & Verkasalo, M. (2005). Measuring values with the short Schwartz's value survey. *Journal of Personality Assessment*, 85(2), 170–178.

Linton, R. (1936). *The Study of Man: An Introduction*. New York, NY: Appleton-Century-Crofts.

Lippi-Green, R. (2012). *English With an Accent. Language, Ideology, and Discrimination in the United States*. 2nd ed., London-New York: Routledge.

Littrell, L.N., Salas, E., Hess, K.P., Paley, M. & Riedel, S. (2006). Expatriate preparation: A critical analysis of 25 years of cross-cultural training research. *Human Resource Development Review*, 5(3), 355–388.

Liu, H. (2015). *The Chinese Strategic Mind*. Cheltenham-Northampton: Edward Elgar.

Liu, X. (2020). *China's Cultural Diplomacy. A Great Leap Outward?* Abington-New York: Routledge.

Liu, Y. & Woywode, M. (2013). Light-touch integration of Chinese cross-border M&A: The influences of culture and absorptive capacity. *Thunderbird International Business Review*, 55(4), 469–483.

Livingston, G. & Brown, A. (2017). Intermarriage in the U.S. 50 Years After Loving v. Virginia. One-in-six newlyweds are married to someone of a different race or ethnicity. *Pew Research Center*, 18.5.2017. https://www.pewsocialtrends.org/wp-content/uploads/sites/3/2017/05/Intermarriage-May-2017-Full-Report.pdf.

Lloyd, S. & Härtel, C. (2010). Intercultural competencies for culturally diverse work teams. *Journal of Managerial Psychology*, 25(8), 845–875.

Lockie, A. (2018). Putin made Trump wait an hour before their summit in a move that's both a power play and a backhanded compliment. *Business Insider*, 16.7.2018. https://www.businessinsider.de/putin-made-trump-wait-before-summit-power-play-compliment-2018-7?r=US&IR=T.

Logsdon, J.M. & Wood, D.J. (2005). Global business citizenship and voluntary codes of ethical conduct. *Journal of Business Ethics*, 59, 55–67.

Lohse-Friedrich, K. (2019). *Chinas Public Diplomacy. Wachsendes Reputationsrisiko für internationale Unternehmen*. Mercator Institute for China Studies China Monitor, June. https://www.merics.org/sites/default/files/2019-06/SCREEN_Merics_China-Monitor_PublicDiplomacy_deutsch_0.pdf.

Lokot, T. & Diakopoulos, N. (2016). News bots: Automating news and information dissemination on Twitter. *Digital Journalism*, 4(6), 682–699.

Lokshin, P. (2014). Deutsche Pseudomarken in Russland Liebesgrüße aus Düsseldorf. *Der Spiegel*, 24.12.2014. http://www.spiegel.de/wirtschaft/unternehmen/made-in-germany-deutsche-pseudomarken-in-russland-a-1007512.html.

Lorenz, M.P., Ramsey, J.R., Andzulis, J. & Franke, G.R. (2020). The dark side of cultural intelligence: Exploring its impact on opportunism, ethical relativism, and customer relationship performance. *Business Ethics Quarterly*, 30(4), 552–590.

Lovett, S., Simmons, L. & Kali, R. (1999). Guanxi versus the market: Ethics and efficiency. *Journal of International Business Studies*, 30, 231–247.

Lu, J.G., Jin, P. & English, A.S. (2021). Collectivism predicts mask use during COVID-19. *Proceedings of the National Academy of Sciences of the United States*, 118(23), 1–8.

Lu, X., Ai, W., Liu, X., Li, Q., Wang, N., Huang, G. & Mei, Q. (2016). Learning from the Ubiquitous language. An empirical analysis of emoji usage of smartphone users. *Proceedings of the 2016 ACM International Joint Conference on Pervasive and Ubiquitous Computing, Heidelberg, September 12–16, 2016*, 770–780.

Luiz, M.J. (2015). The impact of ethno-linguistic fractionalization on cultural measures: Dynamics, endogeneity and modernization. *Journal of International Business Studies*, 46, 1080–1098.

Lukens, J. (1978). Ethnocentric speech. *Ethnic Groups*, 2, 35–53.

Luo, Y. (1997). Guanxi: Principles, philosophies, and implications. *Human Systems Management*, 16(1), 43–51.

Luo, Y. & Shenkar, O. (2011). Toward a perspective of cultural friction in international business. *Journal of International Management*, 17(1), 1–14.

Lutz, W. (1996). *The New Doublespeak: Why No One Knows What Anyone's Saying Anymore*. New York, NY: HarperCollins.

Lyotard, J.-F. (1984). *La Condition Postmoderne: Rapport Sur le Savoir*. Paris: Minuit.

Lytle, A.L., Brett, J.M., Barsness, Z.J., Tinsley, C.H. & Janssens, M. (1995). A paradigm for confirmatory cross-cultural research in organizational behavior. *Research in Organizational Behavior*, 17, 167–214.

Ma, L. & Tsui, A.S. (2015). Traditional Chinese philosophies and contemporary leadership. *Leadership Quarterly*, 26(1), 13–24.

Maass, A., Suitner, C. & Merkel, E. (2014). Does political correctness make (social) sense. In: Forgas, J.P., Vincze, O. & László, J. (eds.), *Social Cognition and Communication*. New York, NY: Pschology Press, 331–346.

MacKenzie, I. (2013). *English as a Lingua Franca: Theorizing and Teaching English*. London: Routledge.

MacCoun, R.J. (1998). Biases in the interpretation and use of research results. *Annual Review of Psychology*, 49, 259–287.

MacNab, B.R. & Worthley, R. (2012). Individual characteristics as predictors of cultural intelligence development. The relevance of self-efficacy. *International Journal of Intercultural Relations*, 36(1), 62–71.

Maderer, D., Holtbrügge, D. & Schuster, T. (2014). Professional football squads as multicultural teams: Cultural diversity, intercultural experience, and team performance. *International Journal of Cross Cultural Management*, 14(2), 215–238.

Madden, T.J., Hewett, K. & Roth, M.S. (2000). Managing images in different cultures: A cross-national study of color meanings and preferences. *Journal of International Marketing*, 8(4), 90–107.

Mahmud, Y. & Swami, V. (2010). The influence of the hijab (Islamic head-cover) on perceptions of women's attractiveness and intelligence. *Body Image*, 7(1), 90–93.

Major, D.A., Turner, J.E. & Fletcher, T.D. (2006). Linking proactive personality and the Big Five to motivation to lean and development activity. *Journal of Applied Psychology*, 91, 927–935.

Malešević, S. (2006). *Identity as Ideology: Understanding Ethnicity and Nationalism*. Houndsmith: Palgrave McMillan.

Malinowski, B. (1948). *Magic, Science and Religion and Other Essays*. Boston, MA: The Free Press.

Man, D.C. & Lam, S.S.K. (2003). The effects of job complexity and autonomy on cohesiveness in collectivistic and individualistic work groups: A cross-cultural analysis. *Journal of Organizational Behavior*, 24, 979–1001.

Manaev, G. (2018). 5 gestures only Russians understand. *Russia Beyond*, 23.11.2018. https://www.rbth.com/lifestyle/329565-5-gestures-only-russians-understand.

Mandis, S.G. (2016). *The Real Madrid Way: How Values Created the Most Successful Sports Team on the Planet*. Dallas, TX: Benbella Books.

Manian, R. & Naidu, S. (2009). India. A cross-cultural overview of intercultural competence. In: Deardorff, D.K. (ed.), *The Sage Handbook of Intercultural Competence*. Thousand Oaks, CA: SAGE, 233–248.

Mann, M. (2005). *The Dark Side of Democracy. Explaining Ethnic Cleansing*. Cambridge: Cambridge University Press.

Mar-Molinero, C. (2000). *The Politics of Language in the Spanish-Speaking World: From Colonization to Globalisation*. London-New York: Routledge.

Markowsky, R. & Thomas, A. (1995). *Studienhalber in Deutschland: Interkulturelles Orientierungstraining für amerikanische Studenten, Schüler und Praktikanten*. Heidelberg: Asanger.

Markus, H.R. & Kitayama, S. (1998). The cultural psychology of personality. *Journal of Cross-Cultural Psychology*, 29(1), 63–87.

Marquard, M. & Horvath, L. (2001). *Global Teams. How Top Multinationals Span Boundaries and Cultures With High-speed Teamwork*. Palo Alto, CA: Davies-Black Publishing.

Marsden, D. (1991). Indigenous management. *International Journal of Human Resource Management*, 2(1), 21–38.

de Maria, B. (2008). Neo-colonialism through measurement. A critique of the corruption perception index. *Critical Perspectives on International Business*, 4(2/3), 184–202.

Di Marco, M.K., Taylor, J.E. & Alin, P. (2010). Emergence and role of cultural boundary spanners in global engineering project networks. *Journal of Management in Engineering*, 26(3), 123–132.

Martill, B. & Staiger, U. (2018). Cultures of negotiation: Explaining Britain's hard bargaining in the Brexit negotiations. *Dahrendorf Forum IV, Working Paper No. 4, Berlin-London*.

Martin, J.N. & Nakayama, T.K. (2017). *Intercultural Communication in Contexts*. 7th ed., New York, NY: McGraw-Hill.

Martin, J.S. & Chaney, L.H. (2012). *Global Business Etiquette. A Guide to International Communication and Customs*. 2nd ed., Santa Barbara, CA: Praeger.

Marx, K. (1867). *Capital*. Vol. 1: *The Process of Production of Capital*. Chicago, IL: Kerr.

Maseland, R., Dow, D. & Steel, P. (2018). The Kogut and Singh national cultural distance index: Time to start using it as a springboard rather than a crutch. *Journal of International Business Studies*, 49(9), 1154–1166.

Maseland, R. & van Hoorn, A. (2009). Explaining the negative correlation between values and practices: A note on the Hofstede–Globe debate. *Journal of International Business Studies*, 40(3), 527–532.

Maslow, A. (1954). *Motivation and Personality*. New York, NY: Harper.

Mateo, M.M., Cabanis, M., de Echeverría Loebell, N.C. & Krach, S. (2012). Concerns about cultural neurosciences: A critical analysis. *Neuroscience and Biobehavioral Reviews*, 36, 152–161.

Matsumoto, D. & Hwang, H.C. (2013a). Assessing cross-cultural competence: A review of available tests. *Journal of Cross-Cultural Psychology*, 44(6), 849–873.

Matsumoto, D. & Hwang, H.C. (2013b). Cultural similarities and differences in emblematic gestures. *Journal of Nonverbal Behavior*, 37(1), 1–27.

Matveev, A. (2017). *Intercultural Competence in Organizations: A Guide for Leaders, Educators and Team Players*. Berlin: Springer.

Matveev, A.V. & Milter, R.G. (2004). The value of intercultural competence for performance of multicultural teams. *Team Performance Management*, 10(5/6), 104–111.

Matveev, A.V. & Nelson, P.E. (2004). Cross cultural communication competence and multicultural team performance. Perceptions of American and Russian managers. *International Journal of Cross-Cultural Management*, 4(2), 253–270.

Maurice, M., Sorge, A. & Warner, M. (1980). Societal differences in organizing manufacturing units: A comparison of France, West Germany and Great Britain. *Organization Studies*, 1(1), 59–86.

Mayer, C.-H., Boness, C. & Thomas, A. (2004). *Beruflich in Südafrika. Trainingsprogramm für Manager, Fach- und Führungskräfte*. Göttingen: Vandenhoeck & Ruprecht.

Maynard, M. (2004). *Dress and Globalisation*. Manchester: Manchester University Press.

Mayr, S. & Thomas, A. (2008). *Beruflich in Frankreich. Trainingsprogramm für Manager, Fach- und Führungskräfte*. Göttingen: Vandenhoeck & Ruprecht.

Mayrhofer, W., Briscoe, J.P., Hall, D.T., Dickmann, M., Dries, N., Dysvik, A., Kaše, R., Parry, E. & Unite, J. (2016). Career success across the globe. Insights from the 5C project. *Organizational Dynamics*, 45(3), 197–205.

Maznevski, M. & Chudoba, K. (2000). Bridging space over time: Global virtual team dynamics and effectiveness. *Organization Science*, 11(5), 473–492.

Maznevski, M.L., DiStefano, J.J., Gomez, C.B., Noorderhaven, N.G. & Wu, P.-C. (2002). Cultural dimensions at the individual level of analysis. The cultural orientations framework. *International Journal of Cross Cultural Management*, 2(3), 275–295.

Mbigi, L. (2005). *Ubuntu: The Spirit of African Transformation Management*. Randburg: Knowres.

McCartney, R.J. (1986). Apparently Compares Gorbachev and Goebbels. Kohl Embarrassed by Public Relations Gaffe. *Los Angeles Times*, 25.10.1986. https://www.latimes.com/archives/la-xpm-1986-10-25-mn-7408-story.html.

McClelland, D.C. (1961). *The Achieving Society*. Princeton, NJ: Van Nostrand.

McGregor, D. (1964). *The Human Side of Enterprise*. New York, NY: McGraw-Hill.

McIntyre, L. (2018). *Post-Truth*. Cambridge, MA: MIT Press.

McLuhan, M. (1964). *Understanding Media: The Extensions of Man*. London: Routledge.

McPherson, M., Smith-Lovin, L. & Cook, J.M. (2001). Birds of a feather: Homophily in social networks. *Annual Review of Sociology*, 27(1), 415–444.

McSweeney, B. (2002). Hofstede's model of national cultural differences and their consequences: A Triumph of faith—a failure of analysis. *Human Relations*, 55(1), 89–118.

McSweeney, B. (2009). Dynamic diversity: Variety and variation within countries. *Organization Studies*, 30(9), 933–957.

McSweeney, B. (2013). Fashion founded on a flaw. The ecological mono-deterministic fallacy of Hofstede, GLOBE, and followers. *International Marketing Review*, 30(5), 483–504.

Melvern, L. (2004). *Conspiracy to Murder: The Rwandan Genocide*. London-New York: Verso.

Mendenhall, M.E., Stahl, G.K., Ehnert, I., Oddou, G., Osland, J.S. & Kühlmann, T.M. (2004). Evaluation studies of cross-cultural training programs. A review of the literature from 1988 to 2000. In: Landis, D., Bennett, J. & Bennett, M. (eds.), *Handbook of Intercultural Training*. 3rd ed., Thousand Oaks, CA: SAGE, 129–143.

Mesoudi, A. (2011). *Cultural Evolution. How Darwinian Theory Can Explain Human Culture and Synthesize the Social Sciences*. Chicago-London: University of Chicago Press.

Meyer, J.W. & Scott, W.R. (1983). *Organizational Environments: Ritual and Rationality*. Beverly Hills, CA: SAGE.

Michailova, S., Piekkari, R., Storgaard, M. & Tienari, J. (2017). Rethinking ethnocentrism in international business research. *Global Strategy Journal*, 7(4), 335–353.

Michailova, S. & Worm, V. (2003). Personal networking in Russia and China: Blat and guanxi. *European Management Journal*, 21(4), 509–519.

Midgley, D.F., Venaik, S. & Christopoulos, D. (2019). Culture as a configuration of values: An archetypal perspective. In: Gunnthorsdottir, A. & Norton, D.A. (eds.), *Experimental Economics and Culture*. Bingley: Emerald, 63–88.

Mikkelson, D. (1999). Did the Chevrolet Nova Fail to Sell in Spanish-Speaking Countries?, *snoopes.com*, 3.4.1999. https://www.snopes.com/fact-check/chevrolet-nova-name-spanish/.

Miller, G.A. (1987). Meta-analysis and the culture-free hypothesis. *Organization Studies*, 8(4), 309–325.

Miller, H., Thebault-Spieker, J., Chang, S., Johnson, I., Terveen, L. & Hecht, B. (2016). "Blissfully happy" or "ready to fight": Varying interpretations of emoji. *Proceedings of the International Conference on Weblogs and Social Media*. https://grouplens.org/site-content/uploads/Emoji_Interpretation.pdf.

Mindess, A. (2014). *Reading Between the Signs. Intercultural Communication for Sign Language Interpreters*. Boston-London: Intercultural Press.

Minkov, M. (2011). *Cultural Differences in a Globalizing World*. Bingley: Emerald.

Minkov, M. (2013). *Cross-cultural Analysis. The Science and Art of Comparting the World's Modern Societies and Their Cultures*. Los Angeles, CA: SAGE.

Minkov, M., Blagoev, V. & Bond, M.H. (2015). Improving research in the emerging field of cross-cultural sociogenetics: The case of serotonin. *Journal of Cross-Cultural Psychology*, 46(3), 336–354.

Minkov, M. & Hofstede, G. (2011). The evolution of Hofstede's doctrine. *Cross Cultural Management: An International Journal*, 13, 10–20.

Minkov, M. & Hofstede, G. (2014). Nations versus religions: Which has a stronger effect on societal values? *Management International Review*, 54(6), 801–824.

Minority Rights Group International (1997). *World Directory of Minorities*. London: Minority Rights Group International.

Miska, C., Stahl, G.K. & Mendenhall, M.E. (2013). Intercultural competencies as antecedents of responsible global leadership. *European Journal of International Management*, 7(5), 550–569.

Mitterer, K., Mimler, R. & Thomas, A. (2013). *Beruflich in Indien. Trainingsprogramm für Manager, Fach- und Führungskräfte*. 2nd ed., Göttingen: Vandenhoeck & Ruprecht.

Mol, S.T., Born, M.P. & van der Molen, H.T. (2005). Developing criteria for expatriate effectiveness: Time to jump off the adjustment bandwagon. *International Journal of Intercultural Relations*, 29(3), 339–353.

Mol, S.T., Born, M.P., Willemsen, M.E. & van der Molen, H.T. (2005). Predicting expatriate job performance for selection purposes. *Journal of Cross-Cultural Psychology*, 36(5), 590–620.

de Mooij, M. (2019) *Global Marketing and Advertising. Understanding Cultural Paradoxes.* 5th ed., London: SAGE.

Moon, K.H., Choi, K.B. & Jung, S.J. (2012). Previous international experience, cross-cultural training, and expatriates' cross-cultural adjustment: Effects of cultural intelligence and goal orientation. *Human Resource Development Quarterly*, 23(3), 285–330.

Morosini, P., Shane, S. & Singh, H. (1998). National cultural distance and cross-border acquisition performance. *Journal of International Business Studies*, 29(1), 137–156.

Morosini, P. & Singh, H. (1994). Post-cross-border acquisitions: Implementing 'national culture-compatible' strategies to improve performance. *European Management Journal*, 12(4), 390–400.

Morris, D., Collett, P., Marsh, P. & O'Shaughnessy, M. (1980). *Gestures: Their Origins and Distribution.* New York, NY: Scarborough.

Morris, M.A. & Robie, C. (2001). A meta-analysis of the effects of cross-cultural training on expatriate performance and adjustment. *International Journal of Training & Development*, 5(2), 112–125.

Morris, M.W., Leung, K., Ames, D. & Lickel, B. (1999). Views from inside and outside: Integrating emic and etic insights about culture and justice judgment. *Academy of Management Review*, 24(4), 781–796.

Müller, A. & Thomas, A. (1995). *Studienhalber in den USA. Interkulturelles Orientierungstraining für deutsche Studenten, Schüler und Praktikanten.* Heidelberg: Asanger.

Müller, S. & Gelbrich, K. (2001). Interkulturelle Kompetenz als neuartige Anforderung an Entsandte: Status quo und Perspektiven der Forschung. *Schmalenbachs Zeitschrift für betriebswirtschaftliche Forschung*, 53(3), 246–272.

Müller, S. & Gelbrich, K. (2004). *Interkulturelles Marketing.* München: Vahlen.

Müller-Stewens, G. & Alscher, A. (2011). The acquisition of Aventis by Sanofi: Attack as defense – play 2: The closing and integration of Sanofi-Aventis. In: Zentes, J., Swoboda, B. & Morschett, D. (eds.), *Fallstudien zum Internationalen Management. Grundlagen-Praxiserfahrungen-Perspektiven.* 4th ed., Wiesbaden: Gabler, 681–697.

Muguet, J. (2017). Edouard Philippe décide de bannir l'écriture inclusive des textes officiels. *Le Monde*, 21.11.2017.

Muratbekova-Touron, M. (2011). Mutual perception of Russian and French managers. *International Journal of Human Resource Management*, 22(8), 1723–1740.

Murdoch, J.D., Speed, W.C., Pakstis, A.J., Heffelfinger, C.E. & Kidd, K.K. (2013). Worldwide population variation and haplotype analysis at the serotonin transporter gene SLC6A4 and implications for association studies. *Biological Psychiatry*, 74, 879–889.

Murphy, J. & Zhu, J. (2012). Neo-colonialism in the academy? Anglo-American domination in management journals. *Organization*, 19(6), 915–927.

Moulettes, A. (2007). The absence of women's voices in Hofstede's *cultural consequences* a postcolonial reading. *Women in Management Review*, 22(6), 443–455.

Mullen, M.R. (1995). Diagnosing measurement equivalence in cross-national research. *Journal of International Business Studies*, 26(3), 573–596.

Mushaben, J.M. (2008). *The Changing Faces of Citizenship: Integration and Mobilization Among Ethnic Minorities in Germany.* New York-Oxford: Berghahn Books.

Nadella, S. (2017). *Hit Refresh: The Quest to Rediscover Microsoft's Soul and Imagine a Better Future for Everyone.* New York, NY: HarperCollins.

Nahavandi, A. & Malekzadeh, A.R. (1988). Acculturation in mergers and acquisitions. *Academy of Management Review*, 13(1), 79–90.

Najmark, N.M. (2002). *Fires of Hatred: Ethnic Cleansing in Twentieth-Century Europe.* Cambridge, MA: Harvard University Press.

Nakagaki, T.K. (2018). *The Buddhist Swastika and Hitler's Cross: Rescuing a Symbol of Peace From the Forces of Hate*. Berkeley: Stone Bridge Press.

Nakane, I. (2007). *Silence in Intercultural Communication: Perceptions and Performance*. Amsterdam: John Benjamins.

Nakata, C. (ed.) (2009). *Beyond Hofstede. Culture Frameworks for Global Marketing and Management*. London: Palgrave Macmillan.

Nasif, E.G., Al-Daeaj, H., Ebrahimi, B. & Thibodeaux, M.S. (1991). Methodological problems in cross-cultural research: An updated review. *Management International Review*, 31(1), 79–91.

Natlandsmyr, J.H. & Rognes, J. (1995). Culture, behavior, and negotiation outcomes: A comparison and cross-cultural study of Mexican and Norwegian negotiators. *International Journal of Conflict Management*, 6, 5–29.

Nayar, P.K. (2010). *Postcolonialism: A Guide for the Perplexed*. New York, NY: Continuum.

Negandhi, A. (1974). Cross-cultural management studies: Too many conclusions, not enough conceptualization. *Management International Review*, 14(6), 59–67.

Neiburg, F. & Goldman, M (1998). Anthropology and politics in studies of national character. *Cultural Anthropology*, 13(1), 56–81.

Neeley, T.B., Hinds, P.J. & Cramton, C.D. (2012). The (un)hidden turmoil of language in global collaboration. *Organizational Dynamics*, 41(3), 236–244.

Nees, G. (2000). *Germany. Unraveling an Enigma*. Yarmouth-London: Intercultural Press.

Neuliep, J.W. & McCroskey, J.C. (1997). The development of a U.S. and generalized ethnocentrism scale. *Communication Research Reports*, 14(4), 385–398.

Neuliep, J.W. (2018). *Intercultural Communication: A Contextual Approach*. 7th ed., Los Angeles, CA: SAGE.

Ng, S.I., Lee, J.A. & Soutar, G.N. (2007). Are Hofstede's and Schwartz's value frameworks congruent? *International Marketing Review*, 24(2), 164–180.

Nguyen-Phuong-Mai, M. (2017). *Intercultural Communication. An Interdisciplinary Approach: When Neurons, Genes, and Evolution Joined the Discourse*. Amsterdam: Amsterdam University Press.

Nguyen-Phuong-Mai, M. (2020). *Cross-Cultural Management. With Insights From Brain Science*. New York-London: Routledge.

Niebuhr, R. (1941). *The Nature and Destiny of Man. A Christian Interpretation*. Vol. 1: *Human Nature*. New York, NY: Charles Sribner's Sons.

Nicolson, P. (2015). *Gender, Power and Organization: A Psychological Perspective on Life at Work*. London-New York: Routledge.

Nisbett, R.E. (2003). *The Geography of Thought: How Asians and Westerners Think Differently and Why*. New York, NY: Free Press.

Nisbett, R.E. & Miyamoto, Y. (2005). The influence of culture: Holistic versus analytic perception. *Trends in Cognitive Sciences*, 9(10), 467–473.

Nishiyama, Y. (2013). Counting with the fingers. *International Journal of Pure and Applied Mathematics*, 85(5), 859–868.

Nkomo, S.T. (2011). A postcolonial and anti-colonial reading of 'African' leadership and management in organization studies: Tensions, contradictions and possibilities. *Organization*, 18(3), 365–386.

Noesjirwan, J. & Bruin, K. (1989). Culture, prejudice and simulation/gaming in theory and practice. In Crookall, D. & Saunders, D. (eds.), *Communication and Simulation*. Clevedon: Multilingual Matter, 155–168.

Nothomb, A. (1999). *Stupeur et Tremblements*. Paris: Albin Michel.

Nwosu, P.O. (2009). Understanding Africans' conceptualization of intercultural competence. In: Deardorff, D.K. (ed.), *The Sage Handbook of Intercultural Competence*. Thousand Oaks, CA: SAGE, 158–178.

Nydell, M.K. (2012). *Understanding Arabs. A Guide for Modern Times*. 5th ed., Boston-London: Nicholas Brealey.

Nye, J.S. (2008). Public diplomacy and soft power. *The ANNALS of the American Academy of Political and Social Science*, 616(1), 94–109.

Özkazanç-Pan, B. (2008). International management research meets 'The Rest of the World'. *Academy of Management Review*, 33(4), 964–974.

Özil, M. (2018). *My Life. Gunning for Greatness*. London: Hodder & Stoughton.

Okamura, J.Y. (1981). Situational ethnicity. *Ethnic and Racial Studies*, 4(4), 452–465.

Okpara, J.O. & Kabongo, J.D. (2011). Cross-cultural training and expatriate adjustment: A study of western expatriates in Nigeria. *Journal of World Business*, 46, 22–30.

O'Leary, M. & Chia, R. (2007). Epistemes and structures of sensemaking in organizational life. *Journal of Management Inquiry*, 16(4), 392–406.

O'Mara, B. & Harris, A. (2016). Intercultural crossings in a digital age: ICT pathways with migrant and refugee-background youth. *Race, Ethnicity and Education*, 19(3), 639–658.

Oolders, T., Chernyshenko, O.S. & Stark, S. (2008). Cultural intelligence as a mediator of relationships between openness to experience and adaptive performance. In: Ang, S. & van Dyne, L. (eds.), *Handbook of Cultural Intelligence. Theory, Measurement and Applications*. Armonk-London: Sharpe, 145–158.

Ortmanns, C. (2015). Irony's potential as subversive strategy. A case study of anti-racist stand-up comedy. *Maastricht Journal of Liberal Arts*, 6, 49–63.

Orwell, G. (1946). *Politics and the English Language*. London: Horizon. https://www.orwell.ru/library/essays/politics/english/e_polit.

Orwell, G. (1949). *Nineteen Eighty-Four*. London: Secker & Warburg.

Osgood, C.E. (1951). Culture: Its empirical and non-empirical character. *Southwestern Journal of Anthropology*, 7(2), 202–214.

Osland, J.S., Bird, A., Mendenhall, M. & Osland, A. (2012). Developing global leadership capabilities and global mindset: A review. In: Stahl, G.K., Mendenhall, M. & Oddou, G.R. (eds.), *Readings and Cases in International Human Resource Management and Organizational Behavior*. New York-London: Routledge, 107–130.

Osman-Gani, A.M. & Rockstuhl, T. (2009). Cross-cultural training, expatriate self-efficacy, and adjustments to overseas assignments: An empirical investigation of managers in Asia. *International Journal of Intercultural Relations*, 33(4), 277–290.

Oswald, F.L., Mitchell, G., Blanton, H., Jaccard, J. & Tetlock, P.E. (2013). Predicting ethnic and racial discrimination: A meta-analysis of IAT criterion studies. *Journal of Personality and Social Psychology*, 105(2), 171–192.

Othwaite, W. (2009). *Habermas: A Critical Introduction*. 2nd ed., Cambridge: Polity.

Ott, U.F. & Ghauri, P.N. (2019). Brexit negotiations: From negotiation space to agreement zones. *Journal of International Business Studies*, 50(1), 137–149.

Ott, D.L. & Michailova, S. (2018). Cultural intelligence: A review and new research avenues. *International Journal of Management Reviews*, 20(1), 99–119.

Paige, R.M. (1996). Trainer competencies: The missing conceptual link in orientation. *International Journal of Intercultural Relations*, 10(2), 135–158.

Paige, R.M (2004). Instrumentation in intercultural training. In: Landis, D., Bennett, J. & Bennett, M. (eds.), *Handbook of Intercultural Training*. 3rd ed., Thousand Oaks, CA: SAGE, 85–125.

Paige, R.M., Jacobs-Cassuto, M., Yershova, Y.A. & DeJaeghere, J. (2003). Assessing intercultural sensitivity: An empirical analysis of the Hammer and Bennett intercultural development inventory. *International Journal of Intercultural Relations*, 27(4), 467–486.

Pan, Y., Rowney, J.A. & Peterson, M.F. (2011). The structure of Chinese cultural traditions: An empirical study of business employees in China. *Management and Organization Review*, 8(1), 77–95.

Pandey, S. & Ardichvili, A. (2015). Using films in teaching intercultural concepts: An action research project at two universities in India and the United States. *New Horizons in Adult Education & Human Resource Development*, 27(4), 36–50.

Parboteeah, K.P., Bronson, J.W. & Cullen, J.B. (2005). Does national culture affect willingness to justify ethically suspect behaviors? A focus on the GLOBE national culture scheme. *International Journal of Cross Cultural Management*, 5(2), 123–137.

Park, S.H. & Luo, Y. (2001). Guanxi and organizational dynamics: Organizational networking in Chinese firms. *Strategic Management Journal*, 22(5), 455–477.

Parsons, T. & Shils, E.A. (1951). *Toward a General Theory of Action*. Cambridge: Harvard University Press.

Paterson, T. (2012). Ikea airbrushes women from its Saudi catalogue. Swedish furniture giant criticised for removing images in bid not to upset Arab customers. *The Independent*, 2.10.2012. https://www.independent.co.uk/news/world/middle-east/ikea-airbrushes-women-from-its-saudi-catalogue-8193204.html.

Patsiurko, N., Campbell, J.L. & Hall, J.A. (2012). Measuring cultural diversity: Ethnic, linguistic and religious fractionalization in the OECD. *Ethnic and Racial Studies*, 35(2), 195–217.

Pavlenko, A. (2006). Bilingual selves. In Pavlenko, A. (ed.): *Bilingual Minds. Emotional Experience, Expression, and Representation*. Clevedon: Multilingual Matters, 1–33.

Pavlenko, A. (2014). *The Bilingual Mind: And What It Tells Us about Language And Thought*. Cambridge: Cambridge University Press.

Payandeh, M. (2010). The limits of freedom of expression in the Wunsiedel decision of the German federal constitutional court. *German Law Review*, 11(8), 929–942.

Peltonen, T. (2020). The role of religion in cross-cultural management: Three perspectives. In: Szkudlarek, B., Romani, L., Caprar, D.V. & Osland, J.S. (eds.), *The SAGE Handbook of Contemporary Cross-Cultural Management*. Los Angeles, CA: SAGE, 240–254.

Perrett, R.W. (2016). *An Introduction to Indian Philosophy*. Cambridge: Cambridge University Press.

Peretz, H. & Rosenblatt, Z. (2011). The role of societal cultural practices in organizational investment in training: A comparative study in 21 countries. *Journal of Cross-Cultural Psychology*, 42(5) 817–831.

Persaud, R. & Sajed, A. (eds.) (2018). *Race, Gender, and Culture in International Relations: Postcolonial Perspectives*. London: Routledge.

Peters, T.J. & Waterman, R.H. (1982). *In Search of Excellence*. New York, NY: Harper and Row.

Peterson, L.K. & Cullen, C.D. (2000). *Global Graphics Color: Designing With Color for an International Market: A Guide Around the World*. Beverly, CA: Rockport Publishers

Peterson, M.F. (2003). Review of the book "Culture's consequences: Comparing values, behaviors, institutions, and organizations across nations, 2nd ed., by Geert Hofstede". *Administrative Science Quarterly*, 48(1), 127–131.

Peterson, M.F. & Søndergaard, M. (2014). Countries, within-country regions, and multiple-country regions in international management: A functional, institutional, and critical event (FICE) perspective. *Management International Review*, 54(6), 781–800.

Peterson, M.F., Søndergaard, M. & Kara, A. (2018). Traversing cultural boundaries in IB: The complex relationships between explicit country and implicit cultural group boundaries at multiple levels. *Journal of International Business Studies*, 49, 1081–1099.

Pfeffer, J., Zorbach, T. & Carley, K.M. (2014). Understanding online firestorms: Negative word-of-mouth dynamics in social media networks. *Journal of Marketing Communications*, 20(1–2), 117–128

Phillipson, R. (2015). Linguistic imperialism of and in the European Union. In: Behr, H. & Stivachtis, H.Y. (eds.), *Revisiting the European Union as Empire*. New York, NY: Routledge, 134–163.

Piekkari, R. & Tietze, S. (2011). A world of languages: Implications for international management research and practice. *Journal of World Business*, 46, 267–269.

Pieterse, J.N. (2015). *Globalization and Culture: Global Mélange*. 3rd ed., Lanham, MD: Rowman & Littlefield.

Pink, S. (2007). *Doing Visual Ethnography*. 2nd ed., London-New Delhi-Thousand Oaks: SAGE.

Pika, S., Nicoladis, E. & Marentette, P. (2009). How to order a beer: Cultural differences in the use of conventional gestures for numbers. *Journal of Cross-Cultural Psychology*, 40(1), 70–80.

Pike, K.L. (1954). *Language in Relation to a Unified Theory of the Structure of Human Behavior*. Glendale, CA: Summer Institute of Linguistics.

Pletter, R. (2019). Joe Kaeser: Der Industriekanzler. *Die Zeit*, 2.5.2019. https://www.zeit.de/2019/19/joe-kaeser-siemens-ag-finanzvorstand-grosskonzern-management.

Pornpitakpan, C. (1999). The effects of cultural adaptation on business relationships: Americans selling to Japanese and Thais. *Journal of International Business Studies*, 30(2), 317–337.

Popper, K. (1966). *The Open Society and Its Enemies*. 5th ed., London: Routledge & Kegan Paul.

Pörksen, B. (2018). Schaut genau hin! *Die Zeit*, 13.09.2018. https://www.zeit.de/2018/38/debatten-kultur-pauschalismus-bernhard-poerksen/komplettansicht.

Porter, M.E. (1980). *Competitive Strategy. Techniques for Analyzing Industries and Competitors*. New York, NY: Free Press.

Posner, D.N. (2004). Measuring ethnic fractionalization in Africa. *American Journal of Political Science*, 48(4), 849–863.

Poyatos, F. (2002). *Nonverbal Communication Across Disciplines. Vol. III: Narrative Literature, Theater, Cinema, Translation*. Amsterdam-Philadelphia: John Benjamins.

Prasad, A. (2003). The Gaze of the other. Postcolonial theory and organizational analysis. In: Prasad, A. (ed.), *Postcolonial Theory and Organizational Analysis. A Critical Engagement*. New York, NY: Palgrave, 3–43.

Prasad, A. (2009). Contesting hegemony through genealogy. Foucault and cross cultural management research. *International Journal of Cross Cultural Management*, 9(3), 359–369.

Price, M. & Benon-Short, L. (2007). Immigrants and world cities: From the hyper-diverse to the bypassed. *GeoJournal*, 68(2–3), 103–117.

Pribylovskij, V. (2016). *Vokrug Putina. Biograficheskij spravochnik*. Moscow: Panorama.

Prince, N.R. & Kabst, R. (2019). Impact of national culture on organizations' use of selection practices. *Employee Relations*, 41(6), 1145–1161.

Prunier, G. (1998). *The Rwanda Crisis, 1959-1994: History of a Genocide*. 2nd ed., London: C. Hurst & Co. Publishers.

Pshenichnikova, I. (2003). The challenges of socialization in business education. The case of the school of management, St. Petersburg State University. *Anthropology of East Europe Review*, 21(2), 29–36.

Puck, J.F., Kittler, M.G. & Wright, C. (2008). Does it really work? Re-assessing the impact of pre-departure cross-cultural training on expatriate adjustment. *International Journal of Human Resource Management*, 19(12), 2182–2197.

Puck, J.F., Holtbrügge, D. & Raupp, J. (2017). Expatriate adjustment. A review of concepts, drivers, and consequences. In: Bader, B., Schuster, T. & Bader, A.K. (eds.), *Expatriate Management: Transatlantic Dialogues*. London: Palgrave, 297–336.

Puck, J.F., Mohr, A.T. & Rygl, D. (2008). An empirical analysis of managers' adjustment to working in multi-national project teams in the pipeline and plant construction sector. *International Journal of Human Resource Management*, 19(12), 2252–2267.

Puffer, S.M., McCarthy, D.J. & Boisot, M. (2010). Entrepreneurship in Russia and China: The impact of formal institutional voids. *Entrepreneurship Theory and Practice*, 34(3), 441–467.

Pugh, D.S. & Hickson, D.J. (1976). *Organization Structure in Its Context: The Aston Programme 1.* Farnborough, Hants: Saxon House/Lexington Books.

Pusch, M.D. (2004). Intercultural training in historical perspective. In: Landis, D., Bennett, J. & Bennett, M. (eds.), *Handbook of Intercultural Training.* 3rd ed., Thousand Oaks, CA: SAGE, 13–36.

Rahnuma, K.S., Wahab, A., Majid, H.A. & Crüts, B. (2011). Analyzing brain activity in understanding cultural and language interaction for depression and anxiety. *Procedia—Social and Behavioral Sciences,* 27, 299–305.

Raiffa, H., Richardson, J. & Metcalfe, D. (2002). *Negotiation Analysis. The Science and Art of Collaborative Decision Making.* Cambridge, MA: Harvard University Press.

Ralston, D.A. (2008). The crossvergence perspective. Reflections and projections. *Journal of International Business Studies,* 39(1), 27–40.

Rao, R.N. & Thombre, A. (2015). *Intercultural Communication: The Indian Context.* New Delhi: SAGE.

Rash, F. (1998). *The German Language in Switzerland: Multilingualism, Diglossia and Variation.* Bern: Lang.

Raudenbush, S.W., Bryk, A.S., Cheong, Y.F., Congdon, R. & du Toit, M. (2011). *HLM7 Hierarchical Linear and Nonlinear Modeling User Manual: User Guide for Scientific Software International's (S.S.I.) Program.* Skokie, IL: Scientific Software International.

Redding, S.G. (1994). Comparative management theory: Jungle, Zoo or Fossil Bed? *Organization Studies,* 15(3), 323–359.

Reed, P.J., Spiro, E.S. & Butts, C.T. (2016). Thumbs up for privacy? Differences in online self-disclosure behavior across national cultures. *Social Science Research,* 59(9), 155–170.

Reeves, J. (2004). *Culture and International Relations: Narratives, Natives and Tourists.* London: Routledge.

Regier, T., Carstensen, A. & Kemp, C. (2016). Languages support efficient communication about the environment: Words for snow revisited. *PLoS ONE,* 11(4), 1–17.

Reiche, B.S. (2011). Knowledge transfer in multinationals: The role of inpatriates' boundary spanning. *Human Resource Management,* 50(3), 365–389.

Reisigl, M. & Wodak, R. (2001). *Discourse and Discrimination: Rhetorics of Racism and Antisemitism.* London-New York: Routledge.

Remland, M.S. (2016). *Nonverbal Communication in Everyday Life.* 4th ed., Los Angeles, CA: SAGE.

Resick, C.J., Hanges, P.J., Dickson, M.W. & Mitchelson, J.K. (2006). A cross-cultural examination of the endorsement of ethical leadership. *Journal of Business Ethics,* 63, 345–359.

Reus, T.H. & Lamont, B.T. (2009). The double-edged sword of cultural distance in international acquisitions. *Journal of International Business Studies,* 40(8), 1298–1316.

Richardson, J.E. (2017). Fascist discourse. In: Floderew, J. & Richardson, J.E. (eds.), *The Routledge Handbook of Critical Discourse Studies.* London-New York: Routledge, 447–462.

Richardson, R.M. & Smith, S.W. (2007). The influence of high/low-context culture and power distance on choice of communication media: Students' media choice to communicate with professors in Japan and America. *International Journal of Intercultural Relations,* 31, 479–501.

Richerson, P.J. & Boyd, R. (2005). *Not by Genes Alone. How Culture Transformed Human Evolution.* Chicago, IL: University of Chicago Press.

Richter, N.F., Hauff, S., Schlaegel, C., Gudergan, S., Ringle, C.M. & Gunkel, M. (2016). Using cultural archetypes in cross-cultural management studies. *Journal of International Management,* 22(1), 63–83.

Ricks, D.A. (2006). *Blunders in International Business.* 4th ed., Malden, MA: Blackwell.

Riggs, W. (2010). Open-mindedness. *Metaphilosophy,* 41(1/2), 172–188.

Rings, G. & Rasinger, S. (eds.) (2020). *The Cambridge Handbook of Intercultural Communication.* Cambridge: Cambridge University Press.

Rippin, A. (2008). *The Islamic World.* London-New York: Routledge.

Roberson, D. (2005). Color categories are culturally diverse in cognition as well as in language. *Cross-Cultural Research*, 39(1), 56–71.

Robertson, C.J. & Crittenden, W.F. (2003). Mapping moral philosophies: Strategic implications for multinational firms. *Strategic Management Journal*, 24(4), 385–392.

Rockstuhl, T. & van Dyne, L. (2018). A bi-factor theory of the four-factor model of cultural intelligence: Meta-analysis and theoretical extensions. *Organizational Behavior and Human Decision Processes*, 148, 124–144.

Rockstuhl, T., Seiler, S., Ang, S., van Dyne, L. & Annen, H. (2011). Beyond General Intelligence (IQ) and Emotional Intelligence (EQ): The Role of Cultural Intelligence (CQ) on cross-border leadership effectiveness in a globalized world. *Journal of Social Issues*, 67(4), 825–840.

Roell, C. (2010). Intercultural training with films. *English Teacher Forum*, 2, 1–15.

Rösch, M. & Segler, K.G. (1987). Communication with Japanese. *Management International Review*, 27(4), 56–67.

Rogers, R.A. (2006). From cultural exchange to transculturation: A review and reconceptualization of cultural appropriation. *Communication Theory*, 16(4), 474–503.

Rokeach, M. (1960). *The Open and Closed Mind*. New York, NY: Basic Books.

Romani, L., Barmeyer, C., Primecz, H. & Pilhofer, K. (2018). Cross-cultural management studies: State of the field in the four research paradigms. *International Studies of Management & Organization*, 48(3), 247–263.

Romani, L., Primecz, H. & Topçu, K. (2010). Paradigm interplay for theory development: A methodological example with the Kulturstandard method. *Organizational Research Methods*, 14(3) 432–455.

Ronen, S. & Shenkar, O. (1985). Clustering countries on attitudinal dimensions: A review and synthesis. *Academy of Management Review*, 10(3), 435–545.

Ronen, S. & Shenkar, O. (2013). Mapping world cultures: Cluster formation, sources and implications. *Journal of International Business Studies*, 44(9), 867–897.

Ronen, S. & Shenkar, O. (2017). *Navigating Global Business. A Cultural Compass*. Cambridge: Cambridge University Press.

Rorty, R. (1979). *Philosophy and the Mirror of Nature*. Princeton, NJ: Princeton University Press.

Rosenfeld, M. (1987). Review: Extremist speech and the paradox of tolerance. *Harvard Law Review*, 100(6), 1457–1481.

Rottig, D. (2017). Meta-analyses of culture's consequences for acquisition performance: An examination of statistical artifacts, methodological moderators and the context of emerging markets. *International Journal of Emerging Markets*, 12(1), 8–37.

Rubenstein, R.E. & Crocker, J. (1994). Challenging Huntington. *Foreign Policy*, 96(3), 113–128.

Sackmann, S. (ed.) (1997).*Cultural Complexity in Organisations*. London: SAGE.

Saee, J. (2005). *Managing Organizations in a Global Economy: An Intercultural Perspective*. Mason, OH: Thomson Southwestern.

Said, E.W. (1978). *Orientalism*. London: Routledge.

Said, E.W. (1993). *Culture and Imperialism*. London: Random House.

Said, E.W. (2001). The clash of ignorance. Labels like "Islam" and "the West" serve only to confuse us about a disorderly reality. *The Nation*, 2.10.2001. https://www.thenation.com/article/clash-ignorance/.

Sailaja, P. (2009). *Indian English*. Edinburgh: Edinburgh University Press.

Salk, J.E. & Brannen, M.Y. (2000). National culture, networks, and individual influence in a multinational management team. *Academy of Management Journal*, 43(2), 191–202.

Salzbrenner, S., Schulze, T. & Franz, A. (2014). *A Status Report of the Intercultural Profession 2014*. 2nd ed.,. http://hwcdn.libsyn.com/p/a/1/8/a18530fd276b9b2e/Status_Report_Intercultural_Profession_2014_

2nd_edition.pdf?c_id=8332779&expiration=1521032293&hwt=6bfb2655844477c5c300cece3e 72cc62.

Salzmann, M.B. (2020). Intercultural simulation. In: Landis, D. & Bhawuk, D.P.S. (eds.), *The Cambridge Handbook of Intercultural Training*. 4th ed., Cambridge: Cambridge University Press, 258–280.

Saphiere, D.H. (1995a). *Redundancía: A Foreign Language Simulation*. Conifer, CO: Nipporica Associates.

Saphiere, D.H. (1995b). Ecotonos. A multicultural problem-solving simulation. In: Fowler, S.M. & Mumford, M.G. (eds.), *Intercultural Sourcebook: Cross-Cultural Training Methods*. Vol. 1, Yarmouth, ME: Intercultural Press, 117–126.

Sapir, E. (1929). The status of linguistics as a science. *Language*, 5(4), 207–214.

Sarala, R.M. & Vaara, E. (2010). Cultural differences, convergence, and crossvergence as explanations of knowledge transfer in international acquisitions. *Journal of International Business Studies*, 41, 1365–1390.

Saroglou, V. & Cohen, A.B. (2013). Cultural and cross-cultural psychology of religion. In: Paloutzian, R.F. & Park, C.L. (eds.), *Handbook of the Psychology of Religion and Spirituality*, 2nd ed., New York, NY: Guilford Press, 330–354.

Saruta, M. (2006). Toyota production systems: The 'Toyota Way' and labour-management relations. *Asian Business and Management*, 5, 487–506.

Saunders, P. (1990). *Social Class and Stratification*. London: Routledge.

de Saussure, F. (1916). *Cours de linguistique générale*. Lausanne-Paris: Payot.

Sayed, J. & Pio, E. (2010). Veiled diversity? Workplace experiences of Muslim women in Australia. *Asia Pacific Journal of Management*, 27(1), 115–137.

Skandera, P. & Burleigh, P. (2011). *A Manual of English Phonetics and Phonology*. 2nd ed., Tübingen: Narr.

Schaffer, B.S. & Riordan, C.M. (2003). A review of cross-cultural methodologies for organizational research: A best-practices approach. *Organizational Research Methods*, 6(2), 169–215.

Schmid, S. & Kotulla, T. (2011). 50 years of research on international standardization and adaptation. From a systematic literature analysis to a theoretical framework. *International Business Review*, 20(5), 491–507.

Schein, E.H. (1984). Coming to a new awareness of organizational culture. *Sloan Management Review*, 25(2), 3–16.

Schein, E.H. & Schein, P. (2017). *Organizational Culture and Leadership*. 5th ed., Hoboken, NJ: Wiley.

Scherer, A.G. & Patzer, M. (2011). Beyond universalism and relativism: Habermas's contribution to discourse ethics and its implications for intercultural ethics and organization theory. In Tsoukas, H. & Chia, R. (eds.), *Philosophy and Organization Theory*. Bingley: Emerald, 155–180.

Schlachter, S.D. & Pieper, J.R. (2019). Employee referral hiring In organizations: An integrative conceptual review, model, and agenda for future research. *Journal of Applied Psychology*, 104(11), 1325–1346.

Schmitz, L. & Weber, W. (2014). Are Hofstede's dimensions valid? A test for measurement invariance of uncertainty avoidance. *Interculture Journal*, 13(22), 11–26.

Schneider, D.J. (2004). *The Psychology of Stereotyping*. New York, NY: Guilford Press.

Schneider, S.C. & Barsoux, J.-L. (2003). *Managing Across Cultures*. 2nd ed., Harlow: Prentice Hall.

Schollhammer, H. (1969). The comparative management theory jungle. *Academy of Management Journal*, 12(1), 81–97.

Schroll-Machl, S. (2016). *Doing Business With Germans. Their Perception, Our Perception*. 6th ed., Göttingen: Vandenhoeck & Ruprecht.

Schrover, M. & Schinkel, W. (2013) Introduction. The language of inclusion and exclusion in the context of immigration and integration. *Ethnic and Racial Studies*, 36(7), 1123–1141.

Schubert, G. (ed.) (2016). *Routledge Handbook of Contemporary Taiwan*. London: Routledge.

Schuster, T., Holtbrügge, D. & Engelhard, F. (2019). Knowledge sharing of inpatriates: Empirical evidence from an ability-motivation-opportunity perspective. *Employee Relations*, 41(5), 971–996.

Schuster, T., Holtbrügge, D. & Heidenreich, S. (2009). Konfiguration und Koordination von Unternehmungen in der Softwarebranche. Das Beispiel SAP. In: Holtbrügge, D., Holzmüller, F. & von Wangenheim, F. (eds.), *Internationalisierung von Dienstleistungen mit 3K. Konfiguration-Koordination-Kundenintegration*. Wiesbaden: Gabler, 173–202.

Schwartz, N. (2003). Culture-sensitive context effects. A challenge for cross-cultural surveys. In: Harkness, J.A., van de Vijver, F.J.R. & Mohler, P.P. (eds.), *Cross-Cultural Survey Methods*. Hoboken, NJ: Wiley, 93–100.

Schwartz, S.H. (1992). Universals in the content and structure of values: Theoretical advances and empirical tests in 20 countries. *Advances in Experimental Social Psychology*, 25, 1–65.

Schwartz, S.H. (1994). Are there universal aspects in the structure and contents of human values? *Journal of Social Issues*, 50(4), 19–45.

Schwartz, S.H. (1999). A theory of cultural values and some implications for work. *Applied Psychology. An International Review*, 48(1), 23–47.

Schwartz, S.H. (2006). A theory of cultural value orientations: Explication and applications. *Comparative Sociology*, 5(2/3), 137–182.

Schwartz, S.H. (2014). Rethinking the concept and measurement of societal culture in light of empirical findings. *Journal of Cross-Cultural Psychology*, 45(1), 5–13.

Schwartz, S.H. & Bilsky, W. (1987). Toward a universal psychological structure of human values. *Journal of Personality and Social Psychology*, 53(3), 550–562.

Schwartz, S.H. & Ros, M. (1995). Value priorities in West European nations: A cross-cultural perspective. In: Ben-Shakhar, G. & Lieblich, A. (eds.), *Studies in Psychology in Honor of Solomon Kugelmass*. Jerusalem: Magnes Press, 322–347.

Schwartz, S.H. & Sagie, G. (2000). Value consensus and importance: A cross-national study. *Journal of Cross-Cultural Psychology*, 31(4), 465–497.

Schwartz, S.H., Verkasalo, M., Antonovsky, A. & Sagiv, L. (1997). Value priorities and social desirability: Much substance, some style. *British Journal of Social Psychology*, 36(1), 3–18.

Sedlatschek, A. (2009). *Contemporary Indian English. Variation and Change*. Amsterdam-Philadelphia: John Benjamins.

Seelye, N. (ed.), (1996). *Experiential Activities for Intercultural Learning*. Yarmouth, ME: Intercultural Press.

Seidel, M. (2014). *Epistemic Relativism: A Constructive Critique*. Basingstoke: Palgrave Macmillan.

Selmer, J. (2001). The preference for predeparture or postarrival cross-cultural training—An exploratory approach. *Journal of Managerial Psychology*, 16(1), 50–58.

Selmer, J. (2005). Cross-cultural training and expatriate adjustment in China: Western joint venture managers. *Personnel Review*, 34: 68–84.

Selmer, J., Chiu, R.K. & Shenkar, O. (2007). Cultural distance asymmetry in expatriate adjustment. *Cross Cultural Management: An International Journal*, 14(2), 150–160.

Sen, A. (2005). *The Argumentative Indian. Writings on Indian Culture, History and Identity*. London: Penguin Books.

Sen, A. (2006). *Identity and Violence. The Illusion of Destiny*. London: Penguin Books.

Senge, P.M. (1991). *The Fifth Discipline. The Art and Practice of the Learning Organization*. New York, NY: Wiley.

Senghaas, D. (2002). *The Clash within Civilisations: Coming to Terms With Cultural Conflicts*. London-New York: Routledge.

Seremani, T.W. & Clegg, S. (2016). Postcolonialism, organization, and management theory: The role of "epistemological third spaces." *Journal of Management Inquiry*, 25(2) 171–183.

Setton, R. (1999). *Simultaneous Interpretation: A Cognitive-Pragmatic Analysis*. Amsterdam: John Benjamins.

Shaules, J. (2015). *The Intercultural Mind: Connecting Culture, Cognition, and Global Living*. Boston-London: Intercultural Press.

Shannon, C.E. & Weaver, W. (1963). *Mathematical Theory of Communication*. Chicago, IL: University of Illinois Press.

Shellabear , S. (2011). *False Friends in Business English*. Freiburg: Haufe.

Shenkar, O. (2001). Cultural distance revisited: Towards a more rigorous conceptualization and measurement of cultural differences. *Journal of International Business Studies*, 32(3), 519–535.

Shenkar, O. (2012). Beyond cultural distance: Switching to a friction lens in the study of cultural differences. *Journal of International Business Studies*, 43(1), 12–17.

Shenkar, O., Luo, Y. & Yeheskel, O. (2008). From "distance" to "friction": Substituting metaphors and redirecting intercultural research. *Academy of Management Review*, 33(4), 905–923.

Shimoni, B. with Bergmann, H. (2006). *Managing in a Changing World: From Multiculturalism to Hybridization–The Production of Hybrid Management Cultures in Israel, Thailand, and Mexico*. Academy of Management Perspectives, 20(3), 78–89.

Shirts, G.R. (1995). Beyond ethnocentrism: Promoting cross-cultural understanding with BaFa' BaFa'. In: Fowler, S.M. & Mumford, M.G. (eds.), *Intercultural Sourcebook: Cross-Cultural Training Methods*: Vol. 1, Yarmouth, ME: Intercultural Press, 93–100.

SHRM India Content Team (2017). Referral System: Reshaping the Talent Acquisition Scenario. *shrm.org*, 13.6.2017. https://www.shrm.org/shrm-india/pages/india-referral-system-reshaping-the-talent-acquisition-scenario.aspx.

Shu, K., Sliva, A., Wand, S., Tang, J. & Liu, H. (2017). Fake news detection on social media: A data mining perspective. *ACM SIGKDD Explorations Newsletter*, 19(1), 22–36.

Shubina, N.L. (2009). Neverbalnaya semiotika pechatnogo teksta kak oblast lingvisticheskogo znaniya. Izvestiya Rossijskogo gosudarstvennogo pedagogicheskogo universiteta im. *A.I. Gercena*, 184–192.

Shweder, R.A. & Good, B. (eds.) (2005). *Clifford Geertz by His Colleagues*. Chicago, IL: University of Chicago Press.

Singh, A. (2011). My manager told me to choose between fasting or playing—I chose to fast. How Muslim footballers including Mesut Ozil and Amr Zaki approach Ramadan. *Goal.com*, 27.8.2011. http://www.goal.com/en-gb/news/2871/special/2011/08/27/2637353/my-manager-told-me-to-choose-between-fasting-or-playing-i.

Singh, D.P. & Sharma, M.K. (2009). Unfolding the Indian cultural mosaic: A cross-cultural study of four regional cultures. *International Journal of Indian Culture and Business Management*, 2(3), 247–267.

Singh, J.G. (1996). *Colonial Narratives/Cultural Dialogues. 'Discoveries' of India in the Language of Colonialism*. London-New York: Routlegde.

Sircova, A., van de Vijver, F.J.R., Osin, E., Milfont, T.L., Fieulaine, N., Kislali-Erginbilgic, A., Zimbardo, P.G. & 54 members of the International Time Perspective Research Project (2015). Time perspective profiles of cultures. In: Stolarski, M. et al. (eds.), *Time Perspective Theory; Review, Research and Application: Essays in Honor of Philip G. Zimbardo*. Berlin: Springer, 169–187.

Sit, A., Mak, A.S. & Neill, J.T. (2017). Does cross-cultural training in tertiary education enhance cross-cultural adjustment? A systematic review. *International Journal of Intercultural Relations*, 57(1), 1–18.

Sivakumar, K. & Nakata, C. (2001). The stampede toward Hofstede's framework: Avoiding the sample design pit in cross-cultural research. *Journal of International Business Studies*, 32(3), 555–574.

Slangen, A.H.L. (2006). National cultural distance and initial foreign acquisition performance: The moderating effect of integration. *Journal of World Business*, 41(2), 161–170.

Smircich, L. (1983). Concepts of culture and organizational analysis. *Administrative Science Quarterly*, 28(3), 339–358.

Smith, A. (2010). Mesut Özil: National treasure. *sport.scotsman.com*, 27.6.2010. http://sport.scotsman.com/sport/Mesut-zil-National-Treasure.6386348.jp.

Smith, A.D. (1986). *The Ethnic Origins of Nations*. Oxford: Blackwell.

Smith, A.D. (1991). *National Identity*. Reno, NV: University of Nevada Press.

Smith, C. (2018). World Cup 2018: The black and white and brown faces of Les Bleus. *The New Yorker*, 22.6.2018. https://www.newyorker.com/sports/replay/world-cup-2018-the-black-and-white-and-brown-faces-of-les-bleus.

Smith, H. (2009).*The World's Religions*. San Francisco, CA: HarperOne.

Smith, L.T. (2012). *Decolonizing Methodologies: Research and Indigenous Peoples*. 2nd ed., London-New York: Zed Books.

Smith, P.B. (2006): When elephants fight, the grass gets trampled: The GLOBE and Hofstede projects: Commentary. *Journal of International Business Studies*, 37(6), 915–921.

Smith, P.B., Dugan, S. & Trompenaars, F. (1996). National culture and the values of organizational employees. A dimensional analysis across 43 nations. *Journal of Cross-Cultural Psychology*, 27(2), 231–264.

Smith, P.B., Peterson, M.F. & Schwartz, S.H. (2002). Cultural values, sources of guidance, and their relevance to managerial behavior: A 47-nation study. *Journal of Cross-Cultural Psychology*, 33(2), 188–208.

Snyder, T. (2004). *Reconstruction of Nations: Poland, Ukraine, Lithuania, Belarus, 1569–1999*. Yale, CT: Yale University Press.

Soares, A.M., Farhangmehr, M. & Shoham, A. (2007). Hofstede's dimensions of culture in international marketing studies. *Journal of Business Research*, 60(3), 277–284.

Solomon, M.R. & Rabolt, N.J. (2008). *Consumer Behavior in Fashion*. 2nd ed., London: Pearson.

Søndergaard, M. (1994). Research note: Hofstede's consequences. A study of reviews, citations and replications. *Organization Studies*, 15(3), 447–456.

Song, J.J. (ed.) (2011). *The Oxford Handbook of Linguistic Typology*. Oxford: Oxford University Press.

Song, M. & Thieme, R.J. (2006). A cross-national investigation of the R&D–marketing interface in the product innovation process. *Industrial Marketing Management*, 35(3), 308–322.

Sorge, A., Noorderhaven, N. & Koen, C. (2015). *Comparative International Management*. 2nd ed., London-New York: Routledge.

Sorokowska, A. et al. (2017). Preferred interpersonal distances: A global comparison. *Journal of Cross-Cultural Psychology*, 48(4), 577–592.

Spencer-Oatey, H. & Xing, J. (2008). The impact of culture on interpreter behavior. In: Kotthoff, H. & Spencer-Oatey, H. (eds.), *Handbook of Intercultural Communication*. Berlin-New York: Mouton de Gruyter, 219–236.

Spitzberg, B. & Changnon, G. (2009). Conceptualizing intercultural competence. In: Deardorff, D.K. (ed.), *The SAGE Handbook of Intercultural Competence*. Thousand Oaks, CA: SAGE, 2–52.

Spruyt, H. (2002). The origins, development, and possible decline of the modern state. *Annual Review of Political Science*, 5, 127–149.

Stahl, G.K. & Brannen, M.Y. (2013). Building cross-cultural leadership competence: An interview with Carlos Ghosn. *Academy of Management Learning and Education*, 12(3), 494–502.

Stahl, G.K., Maznevski, M.L., Voigt, A., Jonsen, K. (2010). Unraveling the effects of cultural diversity in teams: A meta-analysis of research on multicultural work groups. *Journal of International Business Studies*, 41(4), 690–709.

Stahl, G.K. & Tung, R.L. (2015). Towards a more balanced treatment of culture in international business studies: The need for positive cross-cultural scholarship. *Journal of International Business Studies*, 46(4), 391–414.

Stahl, G.K. & Voigt, A. (2008). Do cultural differences matter in mergers and acquisitions? A tentative model. *Organization Science*, 19(1), 160–176.

Stanczak, G.C. (ed.) (2007). *Visual Research Methods: Image, Society, and Representation*. London-Thousand Oaks-New Delhi: SAGE.

Stayman, D.M. & Deshpande, R. (1989). Situational ethnicity and consumer behavior. *Journal of Consumer Research*, 16(3), 361–371.

Steenkamp, J.B.E.M. (2001). The role of national culture in international marketing research. *International Marketing Review*, 18(1), 30–44.

Steinwachs, B. (1995). A game for all seasons. In: Fowler, S.M. & Mumford, M.G. (eds.), *Intercultural Sourcebook: Cross-Cultural Training Methods*: Vol. 1, Yarmouth, ME: Intercultural Press, 101–108.

Steers, R.M. & Osland, J.S. (2020). *Management Across Cultures. Challenges, Strategies, and Skills*. 4th ed., Cambridge: Cambridge University Press.

Stoop, I., Billiet, J., Koch, A. & Fitzgerald, R. (2010). *Improving Survey Response. Lessons learned from the European Social Survey*. Chichester: Wiley.

Storti, C. (1999). *Figuring Foreigners Out: A Practical Guide*. Boston-London: Nicholas Brealey Publishing.

Storti, C. (2001). *The Art of Crossing Cultures*. 2nd ed. Boston-London: Intercultural Press.

Storti, C. (2007). *Speaking of India. Bridging the Communication Gap When Working With Indians*. Boston, MA: Intercultural Press.

Stouffer, S.A. & Toby, J. (1951). Role conflict and personality. *American Journal of Sociology*, 56(5), 395–406.

Swiftkey (2015). Swiftkey Emoji Report. https://de.scribd.com/doc/262594751/SwiftKey-Emoji-Report.

Szkudlarek, B. (2009). Through western eyes: Insights into the intercultural training field. *Organization Studies*, 30(9), 975–986.

Szkudlarek, B., Romani, L., Caprar, D.V. & Osland, J.S. (eds.) (2020). *The SAGE Handbook of Contemporary Cross-Cultural Management*. Los Angeles, CA: SAGE.

Tagg, C. (2012). *The Discourse of Text Messaging*. London: Continuum.

Talhelm, T., Zhang, X., Oishi, S., Shimin, C., Duan, D., Lan, X. & Kitayama, S. (2014). Large-scale psychological differences within China explained by rice versus wheat agriculture. *Science*, 344, 603–608.

Tajfel, H. (1981). *Human Groups and Social Categories: Studies in Social Psychology*. Cambridge: Cambridge University Press.

Tajfel, H. (ed.) (1982). *Social Identity and Intergroup Relations*. Cambridge: Cambridge University Press.

Takahashi, K., Oishi, T. & Shimada, M. (2017). Is ☺ smiling? Cross-cultural study on recognition of emoticon's emotion. *Journal of Cross-Cultural Psychology*, 48(10), 1578–1586.

Tandoc, E.C., Lim, Z.W. & Ling, R. (2018) Defining "fake news". A typology of scholarly definitions. *Digital Journalism*, 6(2), 137–153.

Taras, V. (2020). Conceptualising and measuring cultural intelligence: Important unanswered questions. *European Journal of International Management*, 14(2), 273–292.

Taras, V., Caprar, D., Rottig, D., Sarala, R., Zakaria, N., Zhao, F., Jimenez, A., Lei, W.S., Minor, M., Bryla, P., Ordenana, X., Bode, A., Schuster, A., Vaiginiene, E., Froese, F., Bathula, H., Yajnik, N., Baldegger, R. & Huang, V., (2013). A global classroom? A multi-method evaluation of effectiveness of international collaboration exercises in international management education. *Academy of Management Learning & Education*, 12(3), 414–435.

Taras, V., Kirkman, B.L. & Steel, P. (2010). Examining the impact of *culture's consequences*. A three-decade, multilevel, meta-analytic review of Hofstede's cultural value dimensions. *Journal of Applied Psychology*, 95(3), 405–439.

Taras, V., Steel, P. & Kirkman, B. (2012). Improving national cultural indices using a meta-analysis of Hofstede's dimensions. *Journal of World Business*, 47(3), 329–341.

Taras, V., Steel, P. & Kirkman, B.L. (2016). Does country equate with culture? Beyond geography in the search for cultural boundaries. *Management International Review*, 56(4), 455–487.

Tenzer, H., Pudelko, M. & Harzing, A.-W. (2014). The impact of language barriers on trust formation in multinational teams. *Journal of International Business Studies*, 45, 508–535.

Teper, Y. (2016). Official Russian identity discourse in light of the annexation of Crimea: National or imperial? *Post-Soviet Affairs*, 32(4), 378–396.

Tharoor, S. (1997). *India. From Midnight to the Millennium*. Delhi: Viking.

Tharoor, S. (2018). *Inglorious Empire: What the British Did to India*. London: Hurst & Company.

Thomas, A. (1993). Psychologie interkulturellen Lernens und Handelns. In: Thomas, A. (ed.), *Kulturvergleichende Psychologie. Eine Einführung*. Göttingen: Hogrefe, 377–424.

Thomas, A. (2010). Culture and cultural standards. In: Thomas, A., Kinast, E.-A. & Schroll-Machl, S. (eds.), *Handbook of Intercultural Communication and Cooperation. Basics and Areas of Application*. 2nd ed., Göttingen: Vandenhoeck & Ruprecht, 17–27.

Thomas, A., Kinast, E.-A. & Schroll-Machl, S. (eds.) (2010): *Handbook of Intercultural Communication and Cooperation. Basics and Areas of Application*. 2nd ed., Göttingen: Vandenhoeck & Ruprecht.

Thomas, A. & Schenk, E. (2015). *Beruflich in China. Trainingsprogramm für Manager, Fach- und Führungskräfte*. 5th ed., Göttingen: Vandenhoeck & Ruprecht.

Thomas, A. & Bendixen, M. (2000). The management implications of ethnicity in South Africa. *Journal of International Business Studies*, 31(3), 507–519.

Thomas, D.C. (2006). Domain and development of cultural intelligence. The importance of mindfulness. *Group & Organization Management*, 31(1), 78–99.

Thomas, D.C., Cuervo-Cazurra, A. & Brannen, M.Y. (2011). From the editors: Explaining theoretical relationships in international business research: Focusing on the arrows, NOT the boxes. *Journal of International Business Studies*, 42(9), 1073–1078.

Thomas, D.C., Elron, E., Stahl, G., Ekelund, B.Z., Ravlin, E.C., Cerdin, J.-L., Poelmans, S. et al. (2008). Cultural intelligence: Domain and assessment. *International Journal of Cross Cultural Management*, 8(2), 123–143.

Thomas, D.C. & Peterson, M.F. (2018). *Cross-Cultural Management: Essential Concepts*. 4th ed., Los Angeles, CA: SAGE.

Thomas, D.C., Ravlin, E. & Wallace, A. (1996). Effects of cultural diversity in work groups. *Research in the Sociology of Organizations*, 14, 1–33.

Thomas, D.C. & Toyne, B. (1995). Subordinates' responses to cultural adaptation by Japanese expatriate managers. *Journal of Business Research*, 32(1), 1–10.

Thomas, K.M., Plaut, V.C. & Tran, N.M. (eds.) (2014). *Diversity Ideologies in Organizations*. London: Routledge.

Tihanyi, L., Griffith, D.A. & Russell, C.J. (2005). The effect of cultural distance on entry mode choice, international diversification, and MNE performance: A meta-analysis. *Journal of International Business Studies*, 36(3), 270–283.

Tipton, F.B. (2008). 'Thumbs-up is a rude gesture in Australia': The presentation of culture in international business textbooks. *Critical Perspectives on International Business*, 4(1), 7–24.

Tomlin, R.S. (1986). *Basic Word Order: Functional Principles*. London: Croom Helm.

Torbert, P.M. (2007). Globalizing legal drafting: What the Chinese can teach us about Ejusdem generis and all that. *Scribes Journal of Legal Writing*, 11, 41–50.

Toynbee, A.J. (1946). *A Study of History*. Oxford: Oxford University Press.

Trager, G.L. (1958). Paralanguage. A first approximation. *Studies in Linguistics*, 13, 1–12.

Trevillion, S. (1991). *Caring in the Community*. London: Longman.

Trevino, L.K., Lengel, R.H. & Daft, R.L. (1987). Media symbolism, media richness, and media choice in organizations: A symbolic interactionist perspective. *Communication Research*, 14(5), 553–574.

Triandis, H.C. (1980). *Handbook of Cross-Cultural Psychology.* Vol. 1-6. Boston, MA: Allyn and Bacon.

Triandis, H.C. (1995a). *Individualism & Collectivism.* London-New York: Routledge.

Triandis, H.C. (1995b). Culture specific assimilators. In: Fowler, S.M. & Mumford, M.G. (eds.), *Intercultural Sourcebook: Cross-Cultural Training Methods*: Vol. 1, Yarmouth, ME: Intercultural Press, 179–186.

Triandis, H.C. (1977). Theoretical framework for evaluation of cross-cultural training effectiveness. *International Journal of Intercultural Relations*, 1, 19–45.

Triandis, H.C. (2006). Cultural intelligence in organizations. *Group & Organization Management*, 31(1), 20–26.

Triandis, H.C., McCusker, C., Betancourt, H., Iwao, S., Leung, K., Salazar, J.M., Setiadi, B., Sinha, J.B.P., Touzard, H. & Zaleski, Z. (1993). An etic-emic analysis of individualism and collectivism. *Journal of Cross-Cultural Psychology*, 24(3), 366–383.

Triandafyllidou, A. (ed.) (2016). *Routledge Handbook of Immigration and Refugee Studies.* New York, NY: Routledge.

Trompenaars, F. (1994). *Riding the Waves of Culture. Understanding Cultural Diversity in Business.* Chicago, IL: Irwin.

Trompenaars, F. & Woolliams, P. (2003). *Business Across Cultures.* Chichester: Capstone.

Trudgill, P. & Hannah, J. (2017). *International English: A Guide to the Varieties of Standard English.* 6th ed. New York, NY: Routledge.

Tung, R.L. (1981). Selection and training of personnel for overseas assignments. *Columbia Journal of World Business*, 16(1), 68–78.

Tung, R.L. (2007). The cross-cultural research imperative: The need to balance cross-national and intra-national diversity. *Journal of International Business Studies*, 39(1), 41–46.

Tung, R.L. & Stahl, G.K. (2018). The tortuous evolution of the role of culture in IB research: What we know, what we don't know, and where we are headed. *Journal of International Business Studies*, 49(9), 1167–1189.

Tung, R.L. & Verbeke, A. (2010). Beyond Hofstede and GLOBE: Improving the quality of cross-cultural research. *Journal of International Business Studies*, 41(8), 1259–1274.

Turner, J.H. (1985). *Sociology. The Science of Human Organization.* Chicago, IL: Nelson Hall.

Tsui, A.S. (2004). Contributing to global management knowledge: A case for high quality indigenous research. *Asia Pacific Journal of Management*, 21(4), 491–513.

Tsui, A.S., Nifadkar, S.S. & Ou, A.Y. (2007). Cross-national, cross-cultural organizational behavior research: Advances, gaps and recommendations. *Journal of Management*, 33(3), 426–478.

Tsui-Auch, L.S. & Chow, D. (2019). MNEs' agency within institutional contexts: A study of Walmart's post-acquisition practices in Mexico, Germany, and Japan. *Journal of International Management*, 25(2), 100655.

Tulgan, B. & Martin, C.A. (2001). *Managing Generation Y: Global Citizens Born in the Late Seventies and Early Eighties.* Amherst, MA: HRD Press.

UEFA (2015). The European Club Footballing Landscape. Club Licensing Benchmarking Report. Financial Year 2015. https://www.uefa.com/MultimediaFiles/Download/OfficialDocument/uefaorg/Finance/02/42/27/91/2422791_DOWNLOAD.pdf.

UN (2019). Monthly Summary of Military and Police Contribution to United Nations Operations. https://peacekeeping.un.org/sites/default/files/msrs_february_2019.pdf.

UNCTAD (2010). *Creative Economy Report.* Geneva: UNCTAD Publications. http://unctad.org/en/Docs/ditctab20103_en.pdf.

UNDESA (2017). *Trends in International Migrant Stock. The 2017 Revision.* New York, NY: United Nations Publications.

UNESCO (2001). Universal declaration of cultural diversity. Adopted by the 31st Session of the General Conference of UNESCO. Paris, 02.11.2001.

UNESCO (2009). *Investing in Cultural Diversity and Intercultural Dialogue*. Paris: UNESCO Publishing.

Urry, J. (2002). Mobility and proximity. *Sociology*, 36(2), 255–274.

Usunier, J.-C. (2011). Language as a resource to assess cross-cultural equivalence in quantitative management research. *Journal of World Business*, 46(3), 314–319.

Usunier, J.-J. (2018). *Intercultural Business Negotiations: Deal-Making or Relationship Building*. London-New York: Routledge.

Usunier, J.-C., van Herk, H. & Lee, J.A. (2017). *International & Cross-Cultural Business Research*. Los Angeles, CA: SAGE.

Usunier, J.-C. & Roulin, N. (2010). The influence of high- and low-context communication styles on the design, content, and language of business-to-business web sites. *Journal of Business Communication*, 47(2), 189–227.

Usunier, J.-C., Roulin, N. & Ivens, B.S. (2009). Cultural, national, and industry-level differences in B2B web site design and content. *International Journal of Electronic Commerce*, 14(2), 41–88.

Vance, C. (2010). Culture shock in a Japanese firm: Amélie Nothomb's Stupeur et tremblements. *Global Business Languages*, 6(7), http://docs.lib.purdue.edu/gbl/vol6/iss1/7.

Venaik, S. & Brewer, P. (2013). Critical issues in the Hofstede and GLOBE national culture models. *International Marketing Review*, 30(5), 469–482.

Venaik, S. & Midgley, D.F. (2015). Mindscapes across landscapes: Archetypes of transnational and subnational culture. *Journal of International Business Studies*, 46(9), 1051–1079.

Vertovec, S. (2010). Towards post-multiculturalism? Changing communities, conditions and contexts of diversity. *International Social Science Journal*, 61(199), 83–95.

van de Vijver, F.J.R., Blommaert, J., Gkoumasi, G. & Stogianni, M. (2015). On the need to broaden the concept of ethnic identity. *International Journal of Intercultural Relations*, 46, 36–46.

van de Vijver, F.J.R. & Leung, K. (1997). *Methods and Data Analysis for Cross-Cultural Research*. Thousand Oaks, CA: SAGE.

Vlasik, B. & Stertz, B.A. (2000). *Taken for a Ride. How Daimler-Benz Drove Off With Chrysler*. New York, NY: Wiley.

van de Vliert, E. (2009). *Climate, Affluence, and Culture*. Cambridge: Cambridge University Press.

van de Vliert, E., Kluwer, E.S. & Lynn, R. (2000). Citizens of warmer countries are more competitive and poorer: Culture or chance? *Journal of Economic Psychology*, 21(2), 143–165.

van de Vliert, E., Schwartz, S.H., Huismans, S.E., Hofstede, G. & Daan, S. (1999). Temperature, cultural masculinity, and domestic political violence. A cross-national study. *Journal of Cross-Cultural Psychology*, 30(3), 291–314.

Volk, S., Köhler, T. & Pudelko, M. (2014). Brain drain: The cognitive neuroscience of foreign language processing in multinational corporations. *Journal of International Business Studies*, 45(7), 862–885.

Vora, D., Kostova, T. & Roth, K. (2007). Roles of subsidiary managers in multinational corporations: The effect of dual organizational identification. *Management International Review*, 47(4), 595–620.

Wagener, A. (2012). Deconstructing culture. Towards an interactional triad. *Journal of Intercultural Communication*, 29, https://immi.se/intercultural/nr29/wagener.html.

Waisbord, S. (2018). Why populism is troubling for democratic communication. *Communication, Culture and Critique*, 11(1), 21–34.

Wang, D., Feng, T., Freeman, S., Fan, D. & Zhu, C.J. (2014). Unpacking the "skill–cross-cultural competence" mechanisms. Empirical evidence from Chinese expatriate managers. *International Business Review*, 23, 530–541.

Wang, M., Brislin, R.W., Wang, W. Z., Williams, D. & Chao, J. (2000). *Turning Bricks Into Jade: Critical Incidents for Mutual Inderstanding Among Chinese and Americans.* Yarmouth, ME: Intercultural Press.

Wang, W. & Seifert, R. (2017). Employee referrals: A study of 'close ties' and career benefits in China. *European Management Journal*, 35(4), 514–522.

Wankel, C. (2016). Developing cross-cultural managerial skills through social media. *Journal of Organizational Change Management*, 29(1), 116–124.

Ward, C. (2008). Thinking outside the Berry boxes: New perspectives on identity, acculturation and intercultural relations. *International Journal of Intercultural Relations*, 32(2), 105–114.

Ward, C., Leong, C.-H. & Low, M. (2004). Personality and sojourner adjustment. An exploration of the big five and the cultural fit proposition. *Journal of Cross-Cultural Psychology*, 35(2), 137–151.

Ward, C. & Fischer, R. (2008). Personality, cultural intelligence, and cross-cultural adaptation. A test of the mediation hypothesis. In: Ang, S. & van Dyne, L. (eds.), *Handbook of Cultural Intelligence. Theory, Measurement and Applications.* Armonk, London: Sharpe, 159–173.

Ward, K. (1998). *Religion and Human Nature.* Oxford: Oxford University Press.

Wardle, C. & Derakhshan, H. (2017). *Information Disorder. Toward an Interdisciplinary Framework for Research and Policymaking.* Council of Europe Report, DGI 2017, 09, Strasbourg, https://rm.coe.int/information-disorder-report-version-august-2018/16808c9c77.

Warnick, J.F. & Landis, D. (eds.) (2015). *Neuroscience in Intercultural Contexts.* New York, NY: Springer.

Waxin, M.-F. & Panaccio, A. (2005). Cross-cultural training to facilitate expatriate adjustment: It works! *Personnel Review*, 34, 51–67.

Watzlawick, P., Bavelas, J.B. & Jackson, D.D. (1967). *Pragmatics of Human Communication: A Study of Interactional Patterns, Pathologies and Paradoxes.* Ney York, NY: Norton.

Way, B.M. & Lieberman, M.D. (2010). Is there a genetic contribution to cultural differences? Collectivism, individualism and genetic markers of social sensitivity. *Social Cognitive and Affective Neuroscience*, 5, 203–211.

Weber, M. (1930). *The Protestant's Ethic and the Spirit of Capitalism.* New York, NY: Scribner's.

Weick, K.E. (1995). *Sensemaking in Organizations.* Thousand Oaks, CA: SAGE.

Weick, K.E., Sutcliffe, K.M. & Obstfeld, D. (2005). Organizing and the process of sensemaking. *Organization Science*, 16(4), 409–421.

Weiner, M. (ed.) (2004). *Race, Ethnicity and Migration in Modern Japan.* London-New York: RoutledgeCurzon.

Weinberg, A. (ed.) (2012). *The Psychology of Politicians.* Cambridge: Cambridge University Press.

Weiss, S.E. (1994): Negotiating with "Romans". Part 1. *Sloan Management Review*, 35, 51–62.

Welge, M.K. & Holtbrügge, D. (1999). International management under postmodern conditions. *Management International Review*, 39(4), 305–322.

Wells, P.S. (1999). *The Barbarians Speak: How the Conquered Peoples Shaped Roman Europe.* Princeton-Oxford: Princeton University Press.

Welsch, W. (2008). *Unsere Postmoderne Moderne.* 7th ed., Berlin: Akademie Verlag.

Westwood, R. (2006). International business and management studies as an orientalist discourse: A postcolonial critique. *Critical Perspectives on International Business*, 2(2), 91–113.

Westwood, R.I. & Jack, G. (2007). Manifesto for a post-colonial international business and management studies. A provocation. *Critical Perspectives on International Business*, 3(3), 246–265.

White, M. (2009). *A Short Course in International Marketing Blunders. Mistakes by Companies That Should Have Known Better.* 3rd ed., Petaluma, CA: World Trade Press.

Whorf, B.L. (1956). *Language, Thought, and Reality: Selected Writings of Benjamin Lee Whorf.* New York-London: John Wiley.

Wiemann, J. (2010). Obligation to contract and the German general act on equal treatment (Allgemeines Gleichbehandlungsgesetz). *German Law Journal*, 11(10), 1131–1146.

Wierzbicka, A. (2006). *English. Meaning and Culture*. Oxford: Oxford University Press.

Wiese, H. (2015). "This migrants' babble is not a German dialect!": The interaction of standard language ideology and "us"/"them" dichotomies in the public discourse on a multiethnolect. *Language in Society*, 44(3), 241–368.

Wiggins, B.E. (2012). Toward a model for intercultural communication in simulations. *Simulation & Gaming*, 43(4), 1–23.

Wildt, M. (2012). *Hitler's Volksgemeinschaft and the Dynamics of Racial Exclusion: Violence Against Jews in Provincial Germany, 1919–1939*. Oxford-New York: Berghahn Books.

Wilkins, S. (2001). Training and development in the United Arab Emirates. *International Journal of Training and Development*, 5(2), 153–165.

Willard, G., Isaac, K.J. & Carney, D.R. (2015). Some evidence for the nonverbal contagion of racial bias. *Organizational Behavior and Human Decision Processes*, 128(5), 96–107.

Willet, M. (2014). How to Order A Beer Like A True German. *Business Insider*, 31.3.2014. https://www.businessinsider.com/order-a-beer-like-a-german-2014-3?r=DE&IR=T.

Williams, A.M., Ford, P.R., Eccles, D.W. & Ward, P. (2011). Perceptual-cognitive expertise in sport and its acquisition: Implications for applied cognitive psychology. *Applied Cognitive Psychology*, 25(3), 432–442.

Williams, P. (2002). The competent boundary spanner. *Public Administration*, 80(1), 103–124.

Wilson, A. (2021). *Belarus: The Last European Dictatorship*. New Haven-London: Yale University Press.

Wilson, J., Ward, C. & Fischer, R. (2013). Beyond culture learning theory. What can personality tell us about cultural competence? *Journal of Cross-Cultural Psychology*, 44(6), 900–927.

Wilton, D. (2004). *Word Myths: Debunking Linguistic Urban Legends*. Oxford: Oxford University Press.

Winawer, J., Witthoft, N., Frank, M.C., Wu, L., Wade, A.R. & Boroditsky, L. (2007). Russian blues reveal effects of language on color discrimination. *Proceedings of the National Academy of Sciences of the United States of America*, 104(19), 7780–7785.

Wiseman, R.L., Hammer, M.R. & Nishida, N. (1989). Predictors of intercultural communication competence. *International Journal of Intercultural Relations*, 13, 349–370.

Wittgenstein, L. (1922). *Tractatus Logico-Philosophicus*. London: Kegan Paul, Trench, Trubner & Co.

Woldu, H., Budhwar, P.S. & Parkes, C. (2006). A cross-national comparison of cultural value orientations of Indian, Polish, Russian and American employees. *International Journal of Human Resource Management*, 17(6), 1076–1094.

Wong-MingJi, D. & Mir, A.H. (1997). How international is international management. Provincialism, parochialism, and the problematic of global diversity. In: Prasad, P., Mills, A.J., Elmes, M.B. & Prasad, A. (eds.), *Managing the Organizational Melting Pot: Dilemmas of Workplace Diversity*. Thousand Oaks, CA: SAGE, 340–364.

Woodman, G. (2003). *Intercultural Communication Online. Designing a Training Concept for German-British Interactions*. Munich: Langenscheidt-Longman.

The World Bank (2019). Exports of goods and services (% of GDP). https://data.worldbank.org/indicator/NE.EXP.GNFS.ZS?year_high_desc=true.

Worthington, R.L., Mobley, M., Franks, R.P. & Tan, J.A. (2000). Multicultural counseling competencies: Verbal content, counselor attributions, and social desirability. *Journal of Counseling Psychology*, 47(4), 460–468.

Wright, S.C. & Taylor, D.M. (2007). The social psychology of cultural diversity. Social stereotyping, prejudice, and discrimination. In: Hogg, M.A. & Cooper, J. (eds.), *The Sage Handbook of Social Psychology*. Thousand Oaks, CA: SAGE, 361–387.

Wood, E.D. & St. Peters, H.Y.Z. (2014). Short-term cross-cultural study tours: Impact on cultural intelligence. *International Journal of Human Resource Management*, 25(4), 558–570.

Würtz, E. (2005). Intercultural communication on web sites: A cross-cultural analysis of web sites from high-context cultures and low-context cultures. *Journal of Computer-Mediated Communication*, 11(1), 274–299.

Wurtz, O. (2014). An empirical investigation of the effectiveness of pre-departure and in-country cross-cultural training. *International Journal of Human Resource Management*, 25(14), 2088–2101.

Xu, J., Shim, S., Lotz, S. & Almeida, D. (2004). Ethnic identity, socialization factors, and culture-specific consumption behavior. *Psychology & Marketing*, 21(2), 93–112.

Xu, S. & Yang, R. (2009). Indigenous characteristics of Chinese corporate social responsibility conceptual paradigm. *Journal of Business Ethics*, 93(2), 321–333.

Yari, N., Lankut, E., Alon, I. & Richter, N.F. (2020). Cultural intelligence, global mindset, and cross-cultural competencies: A systematic review using bibliometric methods. *European Journal of International Management*, 14(2), 210–250.

Yates, S. (1998). Multiculturalism relies on a level of doublespeak that would have shocked even Orwell. *fee.org*, 1.1.1998. https://fee.org/articles/the-menace-of-multiculturalism-by-alvin-j-schmidt/.

Yeganeh, H. (2014). A weighted, mahalanobian, and asymmetrical approach to calculating national cultural distance. *Journal of International Management*, 20(4), 436–463.

Yeh, R.-S. (1988). On Hofstede's treatment of Chinese and Japanese values. *Asia Pacific Journal of Management*, 6(1), 149–160.

Yeh, Q.-J. & Xu, X. (2010). The effect of confucian work ethics on learning about science and technology knowledge and morality. *Journal of Business Ethics*, 95(1), 111–128.

Yildiz, H.E. & Fey, C. (2016). Are the extent and effect of psychic distance perceptions symmetrical in cross-border M&As? Evidence from a two-country study. *Journal of International Business Studies*, 47(7), 830–857.

Yoo, B., Donthu, N. & Lenartowicz, T. (2011). Measuring Hofstede's five dimensions of cultural values at the individual level: Development and validation of CVSCALE. *Journal of International Consumer Marketing*, 23(3–4), 193–210.

Young, C.A., Haffejee, B. & Corsun, D.L. (2017). The relationship between ethnocentrism and cultural intelligence. *International Journal of Intercultural Relations*, 58(2), 31–41.

Young, J.O. & Brunk, C.G. (2012). *The Ethics of Cultural Appropriation*. Malden, MA: Wiley-Blackwell.

Young, K. (2017). *Bunk: The Rise of Hoaxes, Humbug, Plagiarists, Phonies, Post-Facts, and Fake News*. Minneapolis, MN: Graywolf Press.

Young, R.J.C. (2003). *Postcolonialism. A Very Short Introduction*. Oxford: Oxford University Press.

Yousef, D.A. (2000). Organizational commitment as a mediator of the relationship between Islamic work ethic and attitudes toward organizational change. *Human Relations*, 53(4), 513–537.

Youssef, M.S.H. & Christodoulou, I. (2018). Exploring cultural heterogeneity. The effect of intra-cultural variation on executives' latitude of actions in 18 countries. *International Journal of Cross Cultural Management*, 18(2), 241–263.

Yu, V. (2018). Why do millions of Chinese people want to be "spiritually Finnish"? *The Guardian*, 5.8.2018. https://www.theguardian.com/world/shortcuts/2018/aug/05/why-do-millions-of-chinese-people-want-to-be-spiritually-finnish.

Yum, J.O. (1988). The impact of confucianism on interpersonal relationships and communication patterns in East Asia. *Communications Monographs*, 55(4), 374–388.

Zaharna, R.S. (2009). An associative approach to intercultural communication competence in the Arab World. In: Deardorff, D.K. (ed.), *The Sage Handbook of Intercultural Competence*. Thousand Oaks, CA: SAGE, 179–195.

Zaheer, S., Schomaker, M. & Nachum, L. (2012). Distance without direction: Restoring credibility to a much-loved construct. *Journal of International Business Studies*, 43, 18–27.

Zaidman, N. (2001). Cultural codes and language strategies in business communication. Interactions between Israeli and Indian businesspeople. *Management Communication Quarterly*, 14, 408–441.

Zaimoğlu, F. (2007). *Kanak Sprak. 24 Mißtöne vom Rande der Gesellschaft*. Berlin: Rotbuch.

Zappavigne, M. (2012). *Discourse of Twitter and Social Media*. London: Bloomsbury.

van der Zee, K. & van Oudenhoven, J.P. (2014). Culture shock or challenge? The role of personality as a determinant of intercultural competence. *Journal of Cross-Cultural Psychology*, 44(6), 928–940.

Zhao, J. (2008). *Interkulturalität von Textsortenkonventionen: Vergleich deutscher und chinesischer Kulturstile: Imagebroschüren*. Berlin: Frank & Timme.

Zhu, Y., Warner, M. & Rowley, C. (2007). Human resource management with "Asian" characteristics: A hybrid people-management system in East Asia. *International Journal of Human Resource Management*, 18(5), 745–768.

Zimbardo, P.G. & Boyd, J.N. (1999). Putting time in perspective: A valid, reliable individual-differences metric. *Journal of Personality and Social Psychology*, 77, 1271–1288.

Zimmerman, W. (2014). *Ruling Russia. Authoritarianism From the Revolution to Putin*. Princeton, NJ: Princeton University Press.

Zinoviev, A. (1986). *Homo Sovieticus*. New York, NY: Grove Atlantic.

Žižek, S. (2003). Arguing with racists and fascists. Lecture at the European Graduate School, Saas Fee. https://www.youtube.com/watch?v=SkSV4xyKkds.

Zúquete, J.P. (2018). *The Identitarians: The Movement Against Globalism and Islam in Europe*. Notre Dame: University of Notre Dame Press.

Zweigenhaft, R.L. & Domhoff, G.W. (2011). *The New CEOs: Women, African American, Latino, and Asian American Leaders of Fortune 500 Companies*. Lanham, MD: Rowman & Littlefield Publishers.

INDEX

A

Acculturation
  assimilation, 278–279
  concept, 278
  deculturation/creation, 279
  dynamics of, 280
  modes of, 278–279, 279 (figure)
  separation, 279
Achieved status, 102
Activity orientation, 74–75
Adler, N.J., 262
Adorno, T.W., 289–290
Affective autonomy, 106
Affirmation bias, 66
Alesina, A., 173, 174, 177, 178, 183
Alon, I., 296, 302–303
Ang, S., 301, 318, 319
Angelmar, R., 272, 274
Anglo-Dutch model, 261
Antecedents of intercultural competence
  agreeableness, 295
  bi- and multiculturalism, 296
  conscientiousness, 295
  cultural knowledge, 296
  demographic factors, 296–297
  emotional stability, 295
  extroversion, 295
  openness, 295
  psychographic factors, 294–296
  self-efficacy, 295
Ardichvili, A., 30
Argumentative communication, 239
Ascribed status, 102
Autonomous leadership, 264, 265
Autonomy cultures, 106

B

Baack, D.W., 165
Back translation, 60
Baer, M., 238
BaFá BaFá, 317, 317 (table)
Baker, W.E., 32
Ball, D.A., 212
Bargaining process, 234, 237 (figure)
Barnga, 317–318, 317 (table)
Barsoux, J.-L., 81

Bavelas, J.B., 190
BCIQ. See Business cultural intelligence quotient (BCIQ)
Behavioral CQ, 301
Being orientation, 74
Belarusian ethnicity, 137
Bendixen, M., 167
Benedict, R., 45, 308
Bennett, M.J., 290, 291 (figure), 304
Berg, N., 3, 271–272
Berger, P.L., 124
Berman, P., 140
Berning, S.C., 217
Berry, J.W., 278
Beugelsdijk, S., 156, 173
Bhabha, H.K., 54
Biden, J., 299
Binarism concept, 54
Black, J.S., 297, 320
Blizinsky, K.D., 36
Blunt, P., 148
Body language, 208
Bolten, J., 314
Bond, M.H., 122
Boness, C., 122
Boyd, J.N., 76
Brannen, M.Y., 126, 274, 296
Braun, W., 49
Brexit negotiations, 237
Briggs, J., 57
Brislin, R.W., 316
Brodbeck, F.C., 109
Bronson, J.W., 268
Brown, G., 238
Bruschke, J.C., 318
Bücker, J.J.L.E., 318
Buckley, P.J., 48
Buddhist civilization, 138 (table), 139, 139 (figure)
Buddhist concept, 72
Buddhist work ethics, 32
Business context, 3
Business cultural intelligence quotient (BCIQ), 302–303

C

Caesar, J., 43
Calibration equivalence, 59

Campos, N.F., 177–178
Career patterns, 254
    Anglo-Dutch model, 261
    career models, typology, 260, 260 (figure)
    Germanic model, 261
    Japanese model, 260
    Latin model, 260
    promotion, 257, 258 (figure), 259
    recruitment and selection, 254–255, 256 (figure),
        257
    training and development, 257
Carney, D.R., 246
Carstensen, A., 223
Cattell, R.B., 140–141, 141 (table)
Causal inference errors, 65
Causality, economic development, 31
Center-periphery scheme, 136–137, 136 (figure)
Chae, B., 206–207
Chao, G.T., 296
Chapman, M., 159
Charismatic/value-based leadership, 264, 265
Chen, M.K., 96, 224
Chhodkar, J.S., 109
Chiao, J.Y., 36
Chinese Confucius Institute Program, 239
Chiu, R.K., 158
Cho, J., 298, 299
Choi, D.D., 220
Christensen, C.M., 50
Christodoulou, I., 269
Christopoulos, D., 178, 179, 180 (figure)
Chudoba, K., 274
Class culture, 19
Clegg, S., 55
Clothing and physical appearance, 218–219
Cluster adjacency, 150
Cluster cohesiveness, 150
Coconut cultures, 81–82
Coene, J.-P., 234
Cognitive CQ, 301
Collectivistic cultures, 59, 91–93, 92 (table)
Collectivistic orientation, 74
Colors, context-specific variations, 214, 215 (table),
    216
Communitarian cultures, 101
Comparative management research
    contingency theory, 49
    dominant paradigm, 49–50
    moderators, 49
Comprehensive intercultural research, 208
Conceptualization, research projects, 56 (table), 57
Confucian civilization, 138 (table), 139, 139 (figure)
Confucian work ethics, 32
Conrad, M., 248

Conservativism, 30
Construct bias, 57
Constructivist concept
    biculturals typology, 126, 127 (figure)
    central tendencies, 130
    cricket test, 125
    critical evaluation, 129–130
    deconstruction, 129
    emic epistemology, 124
    hyphenated identities, 126
    immigrants, 125
    intercultural contact zones, 130
    intercultural management research, 129
    intercultural psychology, 126
    interpretative ontology, 130
    postcolonial studies, 126–127
    postmodern management research, 129
    power asymmetries, 127
    reputation asymmetries, 127
    social construction of reality, 124
Context orientation, 77–79, 77 (table), 78
    (figure)
Context-sensitive research methods, 57
Contingency theory, 49
Coombs, G., 316
Co-plot multidimensional scaling technique, 143, 144
    (figure)
Corporate culture, 17–18
Corporate level management
    constructivist and postcolonial approach, 282
    critical evaluation, 282
    interorganizational collaboration, 278–280, 279
        (figure)
    organizational design, 275–278, 276 (figure)
    organizational practices, cross-cultural transfer,
        280–282
Corporate participative leaders, 63
Corporate social responsibility (CSR), 52
Corresponding translation, 229
Corruption Perception Index, 54
Coverage bias, 59
Cox, T.H., 272, 274
Cramton, C.D., 228
Crocker, J., 21
Cross-cultural management research, 62–63
    cultural distance, 51
    differentiation approach, 50
    informal communication style, 51
    intercultural communication, 51
    moderators, 50
    standardization approach, 50
    transferability, 50, 51
CSR. See Corporate social responsibility (CSR)
Cullen, J.B., 212, 268

Cultural attractiveness, 164 (table)
    bilateral trade, cultural goods, 160–163, 160 (table), 161 (table)
    GLOBE study, 157, 158
    scores, 158
    shortcomings, 159
Cultural attractiveness index, 117
Cultural attribution bias, 13
Cultural attribution error, 12–13, 39, 66, 294
Cultural clusters
    Buddhist civilization, 138 (table), 139, 139 (figure)
    center-periphery scheme, 136–137, 136 (figure)
    cleft countries, 140
    cluster adjacency, 150
    cluster cohesiveness, 150
    cluster formation, 147–148
    Confucian civilization, 138 (table), 139, 139 (figure)
    Confucian-influenced region, 145
    co-plot multidimensional scaling technique, 143, 144 (figure)
    critical evaluation, 150, 151 (table), 152–153
    critique, 140
    cultural identity, 138
    differences, 150, 151 (table), 152
    East European cultures, 145
    emic approach, 135
    English-speaking region, 144–145
    GLOBE study, 145–147, 146 (figure)
    Hindu civilization, 138 (table), 139, 139 (figure)
    intellectual styles, 136
    Japan, 138 (table), 139, 139 (figure)
    Latin America civilization, 138 (table), 139, 139 (figure)
    Latin American region, 145
    multivariate data analysis, limitations, 141
    Muslim Middle East cultural group, 145
    Muslim world, 138 (table), 139, 139 (figure)
    national syntality, 140
    nesting procedure, 148
    North Africa cultural group, 145
    Orthodox world, 138 (table), 139, 139 (figure)
    regional, 141–143, 142 (table)–143 (table)
    shortcomings, 148
    similarities, 151 (table), 152
    South Asian region, 145
    sub-Saharan Africa civilization, 138 (table), 139, 139 (figure)
    sub-Saharan cultural group, 145
    supranational cultural groupings, 144
    theoretical foundations, 152–153
    torn countries, 140
    two-dimensional spatial representation, 143
    Western civilization, 138, 138 (table), 139 (figure), 140
    West European region, 144

Cultural collectivism, 36
Cultural concepta, 15
Cultural crossvergence, 99
Cultural differences, 233
    organizational structures, 275–278, 276 (figure)
    types, 213
Cultural distance, 135, 164 (table)
    assumption of symmetry, 157
    context-dependent, 165
    Euclidean distances, 153, 156
    indices, 153, 154 (table)–155 (table)
    international encounters, 165
    Mahalanobis method, 156
    mathematical misspecification, 156
    oversimplification, 156
    postcolonial and constructivist approach, 165
Cultural diversity
    benefits, 3
    challenges and opportunities, 1, 2, 2 (figure)
    communication styles, 2
    critical evaluation, 184, 184 (table)–185 (table)
    intercultural difference, 166
    intracultural diversity, 166
    level-based concepts, 166–170, 166 (figure), 168 (figure), 168 (table)
    management implications, 185
    management problems, 1
    multicultural team performance, 271–273, 272 (figure)
    pattern-based concepts (See Pattern-based concepts, cultural diversity)
    physical boundaries, 2–3
    UNESCO Universal Declaration of Cultural Diversity, 2
    variance-based concepts (See Variance-based concepts, cultural diversity)
Cultural empathy, 286–287
Cultural frictions, 159–160
Cultural goods, bilateral trade
    advantages, 162
    assumption of asymmetry, 163
    assumption of linearity, 163–164
    core and optional, 160–161
    critical evaluation, 163–165, 164 (table)
    cultural attractiveness premium, 161
    curvilinear relationship, 164
    distance, individual-level perceptions, 165
    Eurovision Song Contest (ESC), 163
    international economics research, 162
    machine learning, 162
    maximum and minimum asymmetry, 161, 161 (table)
    moderators of distance, 165
    proxy, 160
    shortcomings, 162

Cultural identity, 46
Cultural Intelligence Scale (CQS), 301
Cultural neurogenetics, 36
Cultural neuroscience, 36
Cultural orientations
    activity orientation, 74–75
    human–nature orientation, 71–73, 71 (table)
    man–nature orientation, 73
    relational orientation, 73–74
    time orientation, 75
Cultural pentagon model, 26–28,
    27 (figure)
Cultural percepta, 14
Cultural perception bias, 57
Cultural perception error, 17
Cultural self-awareness, 286
Culture
    actor's perspective, 14
    ancient times, 42
    attributes, 13–14, 13 (figure)
    biology, 12, 35–37
    career patterns, 254–262
    class, 19
    classification, 130, 130 (figure)
    colonization, 43
    complexity reduction, 38
    coordination function, 39
    corporate, 17–18
    cultural attribution bias, 13
    cultural attribution error, 12–13, 39
    cultural change inertia, 31
    cultural concepta, 15
    cultural percepta, 14
    cultural perception error, 17
    definition, 12, 12 (figure), 88
    democratic vs. authoritarian systems, 30
    department, 18–19
    dimensions, 77–83, 89–96, 100–103, 106–107, 109
        (table), 116–117
    discrimination, 38–39, 38 (figure)
    ecological fallacy, 131
    economic development level, 30
    economy, 31–32
    epistemological categories, 14, 15 (figure)
    Fall of the Iron Curtain, 45
    favoritism, 38, 38 (figure)
    gender, 19
    generation, 19
    Homo Sovieticus, 31
    identity establishment, 37
    industry, 18
    interorganizational collaboration, 278–280, 279
        (figure)
    intracultural diversity, 131
    layers implications, 17
    leadership, 264–269
    legal–political system, 30–31
    limitations, 131
    management, 46
    methodological and theoretical foundations, 45
    multitude of perspectives, 12
    national, 17 (See also National culture)
    neo-institutional theory, 28, 28 (figure)
    nomadic, 29
    observer's perspective, 14
    organizational design, 275–278, 276 (figure)
    orientation function, 37
    physical environment, 29–30
    physiological and psychological properties, 12
    polyculturalism, 131
    prejudices, 38, 38 (figure)
    professional, 18
    religion, 32, 33 (table)–34 (table), 35
    risk, 132
    role of climate, 29
    Schein's iceberg model, 15–16, 16 (figure), 40
    sensemaking system, 37–38
    social control function, 39
    social identity theory, 37
    stereotypes, 38, 38 (figure)
    theory of environmental adaptation, 28, 28
        (figure)
    theory of social construction, 28 (figure), 29
    unit of analysis, 12
    universal dimensions, 84, 84 (table)
    work motivation, 262–264
Culture-bound approach, 49
Culture conceptualization, 62
Culture-free approach, 49
Culture-general training, 308–310
    artificial cultures, 316–318
    assimilators, 316
    cultural dimensions training, 316
    cultural self-awareness training, 316
    experiential, 316–320, 317 (table)
    intellectual, 316
    on-the-job training, 319–320
Culture-specific training, 308–310
    contrast-culture training, 313–315
    culture assimilator training, 311, 313
    culture briefings, 310
    experiential, 313–315
    intellectual, 310–313
    intercultural simulations, 314
    International field trips, 315
    language courses, 311
    languages games, 311
Cuypers, I.R.P., 156, 185

D

Daniels, J., 65
d'Argens, J.-P., 43
Darton, W., 43, 43 (figure)
Darwin, C., 35, 210
Das, G., 52
Data analysis
    cross-cultural management, 62–63
    culture conceptualization, 62
    culture effects, 63
    ecological fallacy, 63, 64 (figure)
    hierarchical linear modeling (HLM), 63–64,
        65 (figure)
    levels, 63
Data collection, 56 (table)
    calibration equivalence, 59
    collectivistic cultures, 59, 62
    coverage bias, 59
    inconsistent scoring, 60
    individualistic cultures, 62
    intracultural and cross-cultural representativeness, 58
    marginalized population segments, 59
    measurement equivalence, 59
    methods, 59
    metric equivalence, 59–60
    noncontact bias, 59
    nonprobability sampling, 58
    nonresponse bias, 59
    nonverbal methods, 62
    observation, 62
    participants inclusion, 66
    probability sampling, 58
    replica studies, 66
    scalar inequivalence, 60
    selection bias, 58
    social desirability bias, 61
    storytelling, 62
    study population, 58
    translation equivalence, 60
Data sets, 66
Deal, T., 18
Deardorff, D.K., 302
Deepfake video detection tools, 248
de Laborde, E., 43
de Maria, B., 54
Demographic imperative culture, 7, 8 (table)
Department culture, 18–19
Derivational affixes, 197
de Saussure, F., 191
Deshpande, R., 125
Deshpande, S.P., 320
Dheer, R.J.S., 169
Diffusive cultures, 102
Di Marco, M. K., 299

Discretionary interpretations, 64, 65
Doing orientation, cultures, 74
Dolan, S.L., 169
Donthu, N., 183
Dorfman, P., 146
Doublespeak, 243–246, 243 (figure)
    associations, 245
    deliberate ambivalence, 243
    diversity, 244
    euphemisms, 244
    features, 243, 243 (figure)
    jargon, 244–245
    liberalism, 246
    multiculturalism, 244
    personal attacks, 245
    personifications, 245
    rhetoric strategy, 243
    simplifications, 245
Dow, B., 298, 299
Dow, D., 185
Drucker, P., 1
Dual-language contracts, 231–232

E

Earley, P.C., 273, 274, 301, 321
East European cultures, 145
Ecological fallacy, 63, 64 (figure), 131
Economic imperative culture, 7, 8 (table)
Economic systems theory, 49
Ecotonos, 317 (table), 318
Education, multilateral peace missions, 6
Egalitarian cultures, 106
Ekman, P., 210, 211
Electronic communication, 82
Embeddedness, 106
Emic approach, 47–48, 47 (table)
Emic epistemology, 124
Emoji
    cultural differences, 208
    social media, 207
Emotional cultures, 101
Employee referral programs, 255
Engelhard, F., 247, 273, 315
English, A.S., 97
Epistemic relativism, 248–249
Epistemological perspectives, 47
    research streams, 48, 48 (figure)
Ertug, G., 185
Ervin, S., 224
Esmer, Y., 32
Ethical imperative culture, 8, 8 (table)
Ethical imperialism, 281
Ethical leadership, 268
Ethical relativism, 281

Ethnic delineation, 20 (table), 22–23
Ethnocentric bias, 57, 103
Ethnocentric speech, 246
Ethnocentrism, 30, 57, 287
Ethno-linguistic fractionalization (ELF), 173, 174 (table)
   Encyclopedia Britannica, 173–174
   ethnicity, 177
   Herfindahl concentration index, 173
   measures of, 174, 174 (table)–177 (table)
Etic approach, 47–48, 47 (table)
Euphemisms, 244
Evans, P., 260, 261
Extra-verbal communication, 194
   agenda setting, 247
   oral, 217–221, 219 (figure)
   written, 221–222
Eye contact, 208–209

F

Facial expressions, 210–211
Factual errors, 64, 65
Fake news, 240–243, 240 (table)
   confirmation bias, 241
   deep fakes, 242
   detection, 248
   facticity, 240
   intention, 240–241
   online firestorms, 241–242
   post-truth politics, 241, 243
   receivers and targets, 241
   social media algorithms, 241
   truthiness, 243
   types, 240, 240 (table)
Fang, F., 303
Farquhar, A., 260, 261
Fascist regimes, 44
Faust, M., 124
Fearon, J.D., 23, 177, 178
Felbermayr, G.J., 163
Feminine cultures, 93–94, 94 (table)
Field, J.G., 92
Fink, G., 229
Fiorini, M., 161
Fontaine, R., 167
Foong, P.Y., 167
Foreign language proficiency, 228
Foucault, M., 55
Fowler, S.M., 321
Francis, J.N., 298
Francophonie, 24
Friesen, W.V., 210, 211
Future orientation, cultures, 75

G

Gallic approach, 79
Galor, O., 95–96
Galtung, J., 136–138, 136 (figure)
Game theory, 234
Garcia, D., 126
Garg, R., 52
Gartner, C., 318
Geertz, C., 69, 124, 125, 131
Geipel, J., 228
Gelbrich, K., 142
Gelfand, M.J., 171, 171 (table)–172 (table), 173, 238, 268
Gender culture, 19
Gene-culture coevolution, 37
Generation culture, 19
Genetic disposition, 36
Geographic delineation, 20 (table), 21–22
Germanic model, 261
Gertsen, M.C., 286, 287
Ghauri, P.N., 56, 214, 237–238
Ghosn, C., 296
Gibson, C.B., 97, 272, 274
Global Leadership and Organizational Behavior
   Effectiveness (GLOBE) study, 49, 63, 66, 69, 97,
   145–147, 146 (figure), 159, 170
   complexity, 118
   country scores conceptualization, 117
   critical evaluation, 117–118
   criticism, 118
   cultural attractiveness index, 117
   cultural practices, 116, 117
   cultural values, 116, 117
   deprivation hypothesis, 117
   of Germany, 116, 116 (figure)
   intercultural management literature, 118
   marginal utility, 117
   multiphase, multimethod, and multisample research
      project, 108
   scores, 109, 110 (table)–115 (table)
   societal culture dimensions, 108, 109 (table)
Goddard, C., 199
Goebbels, J., 246
Gorbachev, M.S., 246
Gorman, A., 299
Graphology, 206
Group level management
   critical evaluation, 274–275
   multicultural team performance, 271–274,
      272 (figure)
Gudykunst, W., 308
Gundersen, A., 262
Gupta, V., 146

H

Habermas, J., 239
Hadjichristidis, C., 228
Hall, E.T., 46–47, 69, 131, 191, 194, 205, 210, 217, 293–294
  communication, 76
  context orientation, 77–79, 77 (table), 78 (figure)
  critical evaluation, 83
  culture dimensions, 76, 77 (table)
  space orientation, 81–83, 82 (figure)
  time orientation, 79–81, 80 (table)
Hammer, M., 308
Hampden-Turner, C., 49, 104, 300–301, 309–310, 316, 319
  achieved status, 102
  ascribed status, 102
  communitarian cultures, 101
  content validity, 103
  critical evaluation, 103–104
  criticism, 103
  cultural dimensions, 99, 100 (figure)
  cultural diversity, 99
  diffusive cultures, 102
  emotional cultures, 101
  ethnocentric bias, 103
  individualist cultures, 101
  innerdirected cultures, 102
  neutral cultures, 101
  outerdirected perspective, 102–103
  particularism, 100–101
  sequential time orientation, 103
  seven-dimensional model, 104
  specific cultures, 102
  synchronous time orientation, 103
  universalism, 100–101
Handwriting styles, 206
Hanges, P.J., 146
Haptics, 209
Harmony cultures, 107
Harmony orientation, 73
Harzing, A.-W., 60, 61
Head movements, 211
Heider, F., 12
Herfindahl concentration index, 173
Hernandez, M.D., 207
Hewett, K., 216
Hierarchical linear modeling (HLM), 63–64, 65 (figure)
  Venn diagram, 64, 65 (figure)
Hierarchical orientation, 74
Hierarchy cultures, 106–107
Hierarchy indication, polychronic cultures, 81
High-context cultures, 77 (table), 78
Hinds, P.J., 228
Hinduist caste system, 72
Hinduization, 45–46
Hispanophone, 24

HLM. See Hierarchical linear modeling (HLM)
Hocks, P., 290
Hoegg, J., 206–207
Hofstede, G., 1, 29, 32, 36, 47, 49, 60, 63, 66, 69, 84–99, 101, 104, 107, 108, 117, 118, 119, 122–125, 129–131, 141–143, 142 (table)–143 (table), 153, 159, 166, 167, 168 (table), 170, 178, 183, 234, 274, 275, 293–294, 309–310, 316, 319
  advantages, 107
  age of study, 98–99
  analytical clarity, 98
  collectivism, 91–93, 92 (table)
  consequences, 97
  construction and labeling, 97
  COVID-19, societies' responses, 97
  critical evaluation, 97–99
  criticism, 97
  cultural crossvergence, 99
  cultural dimensions, 262–264, 263 (table)
  cultural values, 84, 85 (table)–88 (table)
  femininity, 93–94, 94 (table)
  generalizability, 98
  individualism, 91–92, 92 (table)
  indulgence, 96, 96 (table)
  items validity, 98
  long-term-orientation, 94, 95 (table)
  masculinity, 93, 94 (table)
  power distance, 89–90, 90 (table)
  replica studies, 99
  restraint, 96, 96 (table)
  short-term-orientation, 95, 95 (table)
  uncertainty avoidance, 90, 91 (table)
  unit of analysis, 99
  universal dimensions, culture, 84, 84 (table)
  Values Survey Module, 84
  work-related values, 98
Holden, N.J., 229
Holt, D.H., 212
Holtbrügge, D., 52, 82, 83, 217, 221, 247, 248, 272, 273, 274, 315, 321, 322, 324
Houellebecq, M., 298
House, R.J., 108–109, 118, 293–294, 310, 316
Hsu, F.L.K., 92
Huang, L., 221
Huang, W., 224
Humane-oriented leadership, 264, 265
Human–nature orientation
  Buddhist concept, 72
  Chinese morale philosophy, 72
  dynamic aspect, 72
  management context, 72
  optimistic image of man, 71, 72
  pessimistic image of man, 71, 72
  static and dynamic perspective, 71, 71 (table)
Human resource management, 3

Huntington, S.P., 32, 138–140, 138 (table), 139 (figure)
Huynh, T.L.D., 97
Hwang, H.C., 213, 302
Hybridization concept, 54

I

Identitarian Movement, 46
Ideograms, 207
Idiosyncratic grammatical concepts, 198
Imai, L., 238
Indigenous management research
  ancient indian philosophies, 52, 52 (table)
  corporate social responsibility (CSR), 52
  global management knowledge, 51, 53
  in non-Western countries, 51, 53
  research methods, 53
Individualistic cultures, 62, 91–92, 92 (table), 101
Individualistic orientation, 73
Individual level management
  critical evaluation, 269–271
  culture and career patterns, 254–262
  culture and leadership, 264–269
  culture and work motivation, 262–264
  epistemological perspective, 271
  national averages, 270
Indulgent cultures, 96, 96 (table)
Industrial and service societies, 31
Industry culture, 18
Inflectional affixes, 197
Inglehart, R., 31, 32
Innerdirected cultures, 102
Institutionalist theory, 49
Instrumental communication
  argumentative, 239
  cognitive aspects, 248
  cultural relativism, 248–249
  deepfake video detection tools, 248
  discourse categories, 249–250
  doublespeak, 243–246, 243 (figure)
  economic perspective, 252
  entrapment, 250
  ethical perspective, 252
  factual evidence, 250
  fake news, 240–243, 240 (table), 248
  forms of, 239
  irony, 251
  linguistic analytics, 247–248
  non-linguistic tactics, 246–247
  personification, 250
  power asymmetries, 249
  response strategy, 249
Instrument translation, 60–61
Intellectual autonomy, 106

Intellectual–historical delineation, 20 (table), 25
Intercultural behavioral competence, 287
Intercultural collaboration skills, 290
Intercultural communication, 51
  channel, 191
  coding and decoding messages, 191
  complex communication networks, 190
  computational linguistics, 192
  contextual loss and noise, 191
  elements of, 192, 193 (table)
  extra-verbal, 194 (See also Extra-verbal communication)
  instrumental forms (See Instrumental communication)
  intercultural context, 191
  interferences, 191
  language, 189 (See also Language)
  Lasswell formula, 190
  non-verbal (See Non-verbal communication)
  para-verbal, 193 (See also Para-verbal communication)
  process, 190, 190 (figure)
  redundancy, 192
  signs, 191, 191 (figure)
  skills, 290
  translation bias, 192
  verbal, 193 (See also Verbal communication)
Intercultural competence
  advantages and disadvantages, 300, 300 (table)
  affective dimension, 287
  antecedents, 294–297
  behavioral dimension, 290
  cognitive complexity, 289
  cognitive dimension, 289
  companies and individuals, 285
  contextualization, 303
  cross-cultural literature, 297
  cultural adjustment, 297–299
  cultural appropriation, 299
  cultural boundary spanning, 299–300
  cultural empathy, 286–287
  cultural knowledge, 289
  cultural open-mindedness, 287
  cultural self-awareness, 286
  digitalization, 304
  dyadic model, 286
  dynamic aspects, 304
  ethnocentric stages, 291
  ethnocentrism, 287
  ethnorelative stages, 292
  individual-centric models, 287
  informant-based evaluations, 302
  Intercultural behavioral competence, 287
  intercultural collaboration skills, 290

intercultural communication skills, 290
learning cycle, 292–294, 293 (figure)
model, 287, 288 (figure)
multilevel frameworks, 303
negative effects, 303
neuroscience, 304
observer-based evaluations, 302–303
political aspects, 304
psychological and behavioral effects, 297
self-reported evaluations, 300–301
stage model, 290, 291 (figure)
universal/culture-bound, 303
Intercultural Competence Profiler (ICP), 300–301
Intercultural diversity, 6
Intercultural learning cycle, 313
Intercultural marketing blunders, 4–5, 4 (table)
Intercultural negotiation
  bargaining process, 234, 237 (figure)
  Brexit negotiations, 237
  Chinese Confucius Institute Program, 239
  collectivistic and long-term oriented cultures, 235
  context, 238
  cultural differences, 233
  cultural diplomacy, 238
  features, 233
  game theory, 234
  individualistic and short-term oriented cultures, 235
  intercultural competence, 238
  location, 238
  mindsets of, 234, 236 (table)
  tactics and outcomes, 234, 234 (figure), 235 (table)
Intercultural training
  advantages and disadvantages, 310
  constructivist cultural concept, 320
  cultural adjustment, 323
  culture-general training (See Culture-general training)
  culture-specific training (See Culture-specific training)
  didactic approach, 308
  effectiveness, 320–323, 322 (figure)
  ethical aspects, 325
  expatriate assignments, 320
  expatriate context, 325
  experiential training, 309
  geographic scope, 308
  individual learning styles, 324
  innovative training methods, 324
  intellectual training, 309
  learning cycle, 323
  methodological shortcomings, 323–324
  methods, 321
  migrants and refugees, 325
  moderators, 321, 322 (figure)
  predeparture length, 321

social media, 324
tertiary education, 320
timing, 321
trainees' intercultural experience and competence, 324
trainer, 321
typology of, 309, 309 (figure)
vocational training, 307
International cooperation, 3
Interorganizational collaboration
  acculturation, 278–279, 279 (figure)
  constructivist perspective, 280
  cultural distance, 278
Intracultural diversity, 131
Isaac, K.J., 246
Islamic countries, women dress code, 219–220
Ito, K., 311

J

Jack, R.E., 211
Jackson, D.D., 190
Jackson, T., 52
Jacobs, M., 234
Jain, A., 270
Japanese model, 260
Jin, P., 97
Johnson, J., 169
Johnson, J.P., 286
Jullien, F., 46
Jung, C.G., 8

K

Kaasa, A., 30, 167
Kabongo, J.D., 321
Kaeser, J., 204
Kant, I., 121
Kempf, C., 223, 321
Kennedy, A.E., 18
Kesting, N., 290
Kilduff, M., 272, 274
Kim, D., 286
Kim, J., 224
Kim, U., 93
Kinesics, 210
Kirkman, B.L., 97, 98–99, 166
Kirste, L., 324
Kitayama, S., 217
Kittler, M.G., 83
Kluckhohn, C., 12, 45, 70, 178
Kluckhohn, F.R., 46, 69, 72, 75, 91–92, 94, 99, 101–103, 107, 119, 122, 131
  critical evaluation, 75–76
  cultural dimensions, 76
  cultural orientations, 70, 70 (table)–71 (table)
  human behavior, 70

Knight, G.A., 286
Kogut, B., 153, 154 (table)–155 (table), 156–159, 162
Kohl, H., 246
Köhler, T., 228
Kolb, D. A., 257, 324
Konara, P., 156
Korzilius, H., 318
Kostova, T., 173
Kroeber, A.L., 12, 178
Kuchinke, K.P., 30
Kuzeyev, V.S., 177–178

L

Lakshman, C., 296
Landis, D., 308, 310
Language
    categorical perception, 223
    choices, 225, 227 (figure)
    and cognition, 189, 222–225
    corresponding translation, 229
    cosmopolitan impression, 229
    distribution, 225, 226 (figure)
    equivalence of meaning, 228–229
    foreign language proficiency, 228
    inclusion and exclusion matter, 247
    intentional dichotomies, 231
    intercultural interpreters, standards of, 232
    international contracts and trials, 231
    interpretation, 232
    legal usage vs. ordinary, 231
    lexical equivalence, 231
    lexical stocks, 222, 229
    lingua franca communication, 225
    literal translation, 229
    mother tongue asymmetry, 225
    multilingualism, 224
    native and non-native speakers, 225, 227 (figure)
    natural conditions, 223
    non-linguistic communication, 232
    Nuremberg Trials, 233
    policy, 225
    political correctness, 223
    polyglot dialogue, 225
    polysemy, 231
    Sapir-Whorf hypothesis, 222, 224
    time reference, 224
    and translation, 225–233
    western brand names, 229, 230 (table)
    writing systems, 229
Lank, E., 260, 261
Lasswell formula, 190
Latin model, 260
Leadership
    altruism, 268

dimensions, 264
    ethical, 268
    GLOBE study, 264, 265, 268
    intracultural diversity, 268
    intracultural variation and managerial discretion, 269
    predictors, 265, 267 (table)
    preferences, 4
    scores, 265, 266 (table)
    styles, 4, 265, 269
Ledeneva, A.V., 52, 281
Legal-political delineation, 20–21
Legal-political system, 30–31
Leibniz, G.W., 198–199
Lenartowicz, T., 167, 169, 183
Level-based concepts, cultural diversity, 166 (figure)
    Brazil, 167
    Brazilian states, 167
    Chinese-populated regions, 167
    European countries, 167
    functional reasons, 166
    India, 167, 169
    institutional reasons, 166
    Latin America, 169
    Malaysia, 167
    mean absolute deviations, 168 (table)
    power distance and individualism, 168 (figure)
    South Africa, 167
    Spain, 169
Lévi-Strauss, C., 45
Levine, R., 80
Levinson, D., 174
Lewin, K., 81
Li, C., 117, 157, 159, 162
Lim, Z.W., 240
Ling, R., 240
Linguistic delineation, 20 (table), 23–24
Literal translation, 229
Littrell, L.N., 320
Lobel, S.A., 272, 274
Long-term-oriented cultures, 94, 95 (table)
Lorenz, M.P., 303
Low-context cultures, 77–78, 77 (table)
Lowe, K.B., 97
Lu, J.G., 97
Lu, X., 207
Luckmann, T., 124
Luo, Y., 159, 160

M

Mackinnon, A., 83
Madden, T.J., 216
Maderer, D., 272, 274
Mahalanobis method, 156
Mak, A.S., 320

Malekzadeh, A.R., 278, 280
Malinowski, B., 45
Man–nature orientation, 73
Marketing communication, 4, 216
Markowski, R., 121
Martill, B., 237
Marx, K., 19
Masculine cultures, 93, 94 (table)
Maseland, R., 117
Maslow, A., 3, 73
Mastery cultures, 107
Mastery orientation, 73
Matsumoto, D., 213, 302
Mayer, C.-H., 122
Maznevski, M., 75, 76, 274
McGregor, D., 72
McLeod, P.L., 272, 274
McLuhan, M., 191, 221
McSweeney, B., 129
Measurement equivalence, 59
Media selection, 221
Mehra, A., 272, 274
Mendenhall, M.E., 297, 320
Mental culture, 15
Metacognitive CQ, 301
Methodological shortcomings, 83
Metric equivalence, 59–60
Midgley, D.F., 178, 179, 180 (figure), 183
Military, multilateral peace missions, 6
Miller, H., 207
Minkov, M., 31, 32, 84
Mir, A.H., 57
Mohr, A.T., 156, 324
Monochronic time orientation, 79, 80 (table)
Moon, H., 296
Morphemes, 196
Morphological processes, 197
Morris, M.A., 321
Morris, M.W., 298, 299
Mosakowski, E., 273, 274
Motivational CQ, 301
Müller, A., 120, 311
Müller, S., 142
Multiculturalism, 298
Multicultural societies, 45
Multicultural team performance, 4
    bicultural team members, 273
    cultural diversity, 271–272
    international experience and intercultural
        competence, 273
    moderators of, 273–274
    task complexity, 274
    team dispersion, 273–274
    team diversity, 272, 272 (figure)
    team size, 273
    team tenure, 273
Multivariate data analysis, limitations, 141
Murray, H.A., 12
Muslim Middle East cultural group, 145

N
Nachum, L., 156
Nadella, S., 270
Nahavandi, A., 278, 280
National characters, typologies, 43, 43 (figure)
National culture, 40
    advantages and disadvantages, delineations, 20,
        20 (table)
    change of national borders, 21–22
    cultural pentagon model, 26–28, 27 (figure)
    degree of ethnic diversity, 27
    delineations evaluation, 26
    emergence of nation states, 43
    ethnic delineation, 20 (table), 22–23
    ethnic fractionalization, 23, 24 (figure)
    geographic delineation, 20 (table), 21–22
    intellectual–historical delineation, 20 (table), 25
    legal–political delineation, 20–21
    linguistic delineation, 20 (table), 23–24
    passport approach, 20
National participative systems, 63
National wealth, 31
Natural selection concept, 35
Neeley, T.B., 228
Neill, J.T., 320
Neo-institutional theory, 28, 28 (figure)
Neutral cultures, 101
Nipponic approach, 79
Nishii, L.H., 173
Nomadic culture, 29
Noncontact bias, 59
Nonprobability sampling, 58
Nonresponse bias, 59
Non-verbal communication
    elements, 208, 209 (table)
    oral, 208–214
    racial bias expressions, 246
    written, 214, 215 (table), 216–217
Nonverbal methods, 62
Nooyi, I., 270
North Africa cultural group, 145
Nothomb, A., 247
Numbers, intercultural differences, 216

O
Oddou, G., 297
Okpara, J.O., 321
Online privacy, 82
Oral communication, 193
    extra-verbal, 217–221, 219 (figure)

non-verbal, 208–214, 209 (table)
para-verbal, 204–206, 205 (figure)
Ordinary least square (OLS) regression-based analysis, 63–64
Organizational lubricants, 160
Organizational practices, cross-cultural transfer
  ethical judgment, 281
  global standardization, 280
  local adaptation, 280
Organizational structures
  decision-making process, 277
  generic models, 275–277, 276 (figure)
  organizational process, 277
  power distance, 275
  project management, 278
Orthodox world, 138 (table), 139, 139 (figure)
Orwell, G., 74, 243
Özak, 95–96

P
Pan, Y., 123
Panaccio, A., 321
Paralanguage, 204
Paralinguistics, 206–207
Para-verbal communication
  ethnocentric speech, 246
  oral, 193, 204–206, 205 (figure)
  written, 193, 206–208
Parboteeah, K.P., 212, 268
Parsons, T., 99
Participative leadership, 264, 265
Particularism, 100–101
Past orientation, cultures, 75
Pattern-based concepts, cultural diversity
  cultural archetypes, 178, 179, 180 (figure), 181
  distribution, 181, 181 (table)–183 (table), 183
  Euclidian distances, 181
  multiple cultural dimensions, 184
  Schwartz World Values Survey, 178
Pavlenko, A., 224
Peace imperative culture, 8 (table), 9
Peach cultures, 82
Pedersen, P.B., 316, 318
Personification, 250
Peters, T.J., 18
Peterson, M.F., 169
Phonemics, 47
Phonetics, 47
Phonology
  idiosyncratic sounds, 194–195
  non-rhotic accents, 195
  rhotic accents, 195
  tonal differences, 195, 196 (table)
Pictures, intercultural communication, 217

Pike, K.L., 47
Poertner, M., 220
Politics, intercultural interactions, 5
Polo, M., 3
Polychronic time orientation, 80, 80 (table)
Polyculturalism, 131, 298–299
Pornpitakpan, C., 298
Porter, M.E., 50
Postcolonial management research
  Asia, underrepresentation, 55
  binarism concept, 54
  hybridization concept, 54
  intense debates and extraordinary heterogeneity, 55
  knowledge domination, 53
  political and ideological hegemony, 53
  postcolonialism, 54
  Ubuntu, 55
Postmodern approach, 45
Poststructuralist approach, 45
Power distance, 89–90, 90 (table)
Pragmatics
  adaptation of languages, 204
  Asian cultures, 202
  cultural contexts, 202
  formal language and complex sentences, 202
  importance and urgency expression, 202
  language hybridization, 203
  linguistic submissiveness, 204
  say "no," India, 202, 203 (table)
  slang, 203
Present orientation, 75
Printed texts, 207
Probability sampling, 58
Professional culture, 18
Protestant Ethics, 32, 72
Puck, J.F., 164, 230, 255, 257, 271, 298
Pudelko, M., 228
Puffer, S.M., 52
Punctuality, cultures, 80, 81
Putin, V., 89, 218, 259

Q
Queuille, H., 75

R
Races, census categories, 22–23
Racist regimes, 35
Radebaugh, L., 65
Raver, J.L., 173
Ravlin, E., 272, 274
Regier, T., 223
Reiberg, A., 290
Re-Islamization, 46
Relational orientation, 73–74

Religiousness, 35
Resick, C.J., 268
Restrained cultures, 96, 96 (table)
Richardson, R.M., 83, 221
Richardson, S., 167
Richter, N.F., 183
Robie, C., 321
Rogers, H., 82, 221
Ronen, S., 147–148, 149 (figure), 150, 153
Ros, M., 107
Rosenfeld, M., 252
Roth, K., 167, 173
Roth, M.S., 216
Roulin, N., 217
Rubenstein, R.E., 21
Russianization, 46
Rygl, D., 83

S
Sagie, G., 173
Said, E.W., 43, 54, 140
Salk, J.E., 274
Sambanis, N., 220
Saphiere, D.H., 311
Sapir, E., 222
Sapir-Whorf hypothesis, 222, 224
Sarason, Y., 316
Saxonic style, 79
Scalar inequivalence, 60
SCCT. See Structure of Chinese cultural traditions
    model (SCCT)
Schaeffler, G., 19
Schei, V., 303
Schein, E.H., 129, 162, 208, 219
Schein's iceberg model, 15–16, 16 (figure), 40, 98
Schenk, E., 123, 124
Schillo, K., 322
Schneider, S.C., 81
Schomaker, M., 156
Schroll-Machl, S., 120, 312
Schuster, T., 247, 272, 274
Schwartz, S.H., 32, 49, 69, 97, 104–108, 131, 143–145,
    144 (figure), 163, 173, 178, 319
    affective autonomy, 106
    autonomy cultures, 106
    circular model, 105, 105 (figure)
    complexity, 107–108
    critical evaluation, 107–108
    cultural value orientations, 104, 104 (table)
    culture dimensions, 106–107
    data collection, 107
    egalitarian cultures, 106
    embeddedness, 106
    harmony cultures, 107
        hierarchy cultures, 106–107
        intellectual autonomy, 106
        mastery cultures, 107
        motivational value types, 178, 179 (table)
        sample compositions, 107
        Schwartz Value Survey (SVS), 105
        sub-national regions, 105
Schwartz Value Survey (SVS), 105, 123, 178
Seating arrangement, 218, 219 (figure)
Seiter, J. S., 318
Selart, M., 303
Selection bias, 58
Self-awareness imperative culture, 8, 8 (table)
Self-protective leadership, 264, 265
Self-serving bias, 301
Selmer, J., 158, 159–160
Semantics
    false friends, 201, 201 (table)
    homonyms, 201
    lexical stocks, 200–201, 200 (table)
    natural semantic meta-language, 199
    primes, 198–199, 199 (table)
Sen, A., 67, 132, 206
Senge, P.M., 50
Sequential time orientation, 103
Seremani, T.W., 55
Shakespeare, W., 204
Sharma, M. K., 167
Shenkar, O., 147–148, 149 (figure), 150, 153, 158, 159,
    160
Shils, E.A., 99
Shirts, G.R., 317
Short-term-oriented cultures, 95, 95 (table)
Silence, in communication, 205, 205 (figure)
Singh, D.P., 167
Singh, H., 153, 154 (table)–155 (table), 156–159, 162
Sircova, A., 76
Sit, A., 320
Slangen, A.H.L., 278
Smith, P.B., 108, 118
Smith, S.W., 83, 221
Social cognition theory, 165
Social construct, 22, 29, 35, 36
Social control function, 39
Social desirability bias, 61
Social identity theory, 37
Society, intercultural challenge, 5
Søndergaard, M., 21, 97, 166, 184
Sorokowska, A., 81
Space orientation, 82 (figure)
    coconut cultures, 81–82
    electronic communication, 82
    figurative sense, 81
    literal sense, 81

online privacy, 82
    peach cultures, 82
    private and public spheres, 83
Speech volume, 205
Stahl, G.K., 1, 131, 164, 272, 273, 274, 278, 296–297
Staiger, U., 237
Star Alliance, 3
Stayman, D.M., 125
Steel, P., 98–99, 166
Steinwachs, B., 317
Stereotyping effects, 220
Storti, C., 37, 80, 203 (figure), 211, 293, 210
Strodtbeck, F.L., 46, 69, 72, 75, 91–92, 94, 99,
    101–103, 107, 119, 122, 131
    critical evaluation, 75–76
    cultural dimensions, 76
    cultural orientations, 70, 70 (table)–71 (table)
    human behavior, 70
Structure of Chinese cultural traditions model
    (SCCT), 123
Subjugation orientation, 73
Sub-Saharan Africa civilization, 138 (table), 139, 139
    (figure)
Sub-Saharan cultural group, 145
Sullivan, D., 65
Sun Tzu, 43
Surian, L., 228
SVS. See Schwartz Value Survey (SVS)
Symbols
    and artifacts, religious institutions, 32
    intercultural communication, 216–217
Synchronous time orientation, 103
Syntax, 197–198, 198 (table)
Systematic intercultural research, 208

T

Talkativeness, 205, 206
Tandoc, E.C., 240
Taras, V., 98–99, 166, 319
Team-oriented leadership, 264, 265
Team sports, 6
Technological imperative culture, 8, 8 (table)
Teutonic approach, 79
Tharoor, S., 25
Theory of environmental adaptation, 28, 28 (figure)
Theory of social construction, 28 (figure), 29
Thjagarajan, S., 317
Thomas, A., 120, 121, 122, 131, 167, 286, 311
    critical evaluation, 123–124
    cultural dimensions, 120
    cultural standards, 119, 120 (figure), 121 (table), 122,
        122 (table)
    emic approach, 119, 123
    etic conceptualization, 123

    interpretations, 121
    research methodology, 119
    structure of Chinese cultural traditions model
        (SCCT), 123
    unconditional obedience, 122
Thomas, D.C., 126, 272–274, 296, 298
Time orientation, 75, 79–81, 80 (table)
Tipton, F.B., 65, 212
Toubal, F., 163
Toyne, B., 298
Translation equivalence, 60
Triandis, H.C., 91–92, 311
Trompenaars, F., 49, 66, 69, 97, 104, 125, 129–131, 170,
    178, 300–301, 309–310, 316, 319
    achieved status, 102
    ascribed status, 102
    communitarian cultures, 101
    content validity, 103
    critical evaluation, 103–104
    criticism, 103
    cultural dimensions, 99, 100 (figure)
    cultural diversity, 99
    diffusive cultures, 102
    emotional cultures, 101
    ethnocentric bias, 103
    individualist cultures, 101
    innerdirected cultures, 102
    neutral cultures, 101
    outerdirected perspective, 102–103
    particularism, 100–101
    sequential time orientation, 103
    seven-dimensional model, 104
    specific cultures, 102
    synchronous time orientation, 103
    universalism, 100–101
Tung, R.L., 308

U

Uncertainty avoidance, 90–91, 91 (table), 98
UNESCO Universal Declaration of Cultural Diversity, 2
Universalism, 100–101
Usunier, J.-C., 50, 56, 60, 61, 217, 235

V

Vadi, M., 30, 167
Vance, C., 247
van de Vliert, E., 29
van Hoorn, A., 117
Varblane, U., 30, 167
Variance-based concepts, cultural diversity
    cultural dimensions, 170, 170 (figure)
    cultural variance, 173
    ecological antecedent, 173
    ecological fallacy, 170

ethno-linguistic fractionalization (ELF), 171, 173–178, 174 (table)–177 (table)
historical antecedent, 173
institutional antecedent, 173
loose cultural systems, 171, 171 (table)–172 (table)
tight cultural systems, 171, 171 (table)–172 (table)
Venaik, S., 178, 179, 180 (figure), 183
Verbal communication
dimensions, 194, 194 (table)
morphology, 196–197
phonology, 194–195, 196 (table)
pragmatics, 202–204, 203 (table)
semantics, 198–202, 199 (table), 200 (table), 201 (table)
syntax, 197–198, 198 (table)
Verbs of motion, 198
Visual ethnography, 62
Visweswaran, C., 320
Vocalizations, 205
Vocational training, 307
Voice qualifiers, 204–205, 207
Voice set, 204
Volk, S., 228
von Clausewitz, C., 43
Vora, D., 299

W
Wallace, A., 272, 274
Warner, M., 49
Waterman, R.H., 18
Watzlawick, P., 190
Waxin, M.-F., 321
Weber, M., 22, 32, 72, 121
Websites, 217
Weldon, A., 82, 221
Western civilization, 138, 138 (table), 139 (figure), 140
White, C., 169
Wierzbicka, A., 199
Wigginton, K.W., 212

Willard, G., 246
Winawer, J., 223
Wittgenstein, L., 222
Woldu, H., 75–76
Wong-MingJi, D., 57
Woodman, G., 202
Word order, 197
Work motivation
cultural differences, 262
cultural dimensions, 262–264, 263 (table)
Wal-Mart operation, 262
Work vs. private life, cultural difference, 4
Writing systems
alphabetic/morpho-phonetic, 196
diacritic marks, 196
logographic/morpho-syllabic, 196–197
physiological effects, 206
syllabic systems, 197
Written communication, 193
extra-verbal, 221–222
non verbal, 214, 215 (table), 216–217
para-verbal, 206–208
Wulff, Christian, 5–6
Würtz, E., 217

X
Xu, S., 51–52

Y
Yamaguchi, M., 321
Yang, R., 51–52
Yeh, R.-S., 98
Yeheskel, O., 159
Yoo, B., 183
Youssef, M.S.H., 269

Z
Zaheer, S., 156, 163
Zimbardo, P.G., 76

CPSIA information can be obtained
at www.ICGtesting.com
Printed in the USA
JSHW042205230522
26107JS00003B/55